Philippines

North Luzon p113

Manila p48

Around Manila p95

Southeast Luzon p165

Mindoro p192

Cebu & Eastern Visayas p277

Boracay & Western Visayas p211

Palawan p377

Mindanao p342

Paul Harding, Greg Bloom, Celeste Brash,
Michael Grosberg, Iain Stewart

PLAN YOUR TRIP

ON THE ROAD

PHILIPPINE EAGLE P368

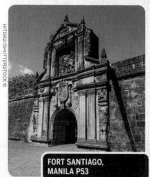

FORT SANTIAGO,
MANILA P53

Contents

BATAD P152

ON THE ROAD

CHOCOLATE HILLS,
BOHOL P319

GOODOLGA/GETTY IMAGES ©

Contents

COVID-19

We have re-checked every business in this book before publication to ensure that it is still open after the COVID-19 outbreak. However, the economic and social impacts of COVID-19 will continue to be felt long after the outbreak has been contained, and many businesses, services and events referenced in this guide may experience ongoing restrictions. Some businesses may be temporarily closed, have changed their opening hours and services, or require bookings; some unfortunately could have closed permanently. We suggest you check with venues before visiting for the latest information.

Right:
Dinagyang
Festival (p235)

FROLOVA_ELENA/SHUTTERSTOCK ©

WELCOME TO
the
Philippines

As much as I like perfect beaches, it's for the subtler things that I love the Philippines. It's those long rooftop jeepney rides through the mountains of North Luzon, followed by a round of gin shots with indigenous elders in the da-pay (meeting area). It's that fresh-fish lunch on an interminable bangka journey through Palawan. It's a frosty San Miguel at sundown. It's friends with names like Bing and Bong, and phrases like 'comfort room'. It's – dare I say it – karaoke. Now that's love.

By Greg Bloom, Writer

🐦 @AsiaBloom 📷 goryogoesaround

For more about our writers, see p472

The Philippines

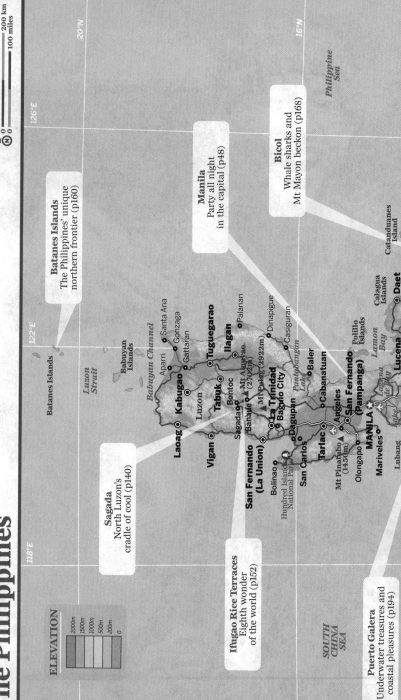

ELEVATION
- 2000m
- 1500m
- 1000m
- 500m
- 200m
- 0

Batanes Islands
The Philippines' unique northern frontier (p160)

Sagada
North Luzon's cradle of cool (p140)

Ifugao Rice Terraces
Eighth wonder of the world (p152)

Manila
Party all night in the capital (p48)

Bicol
Whale sharks and Mt Mayon beckon (p168)

Puerto Galera
Underwater treasures and coastal pleasures (p194)

200 km
100 miles

Luzon Strait

Babuyan Channel

Batanes Islands

Babuyan Islands

Aparri
Santa Ana
Gonzaga
Gattaran
Palanan

Laoag
Kabugao
Tabuk
Bontoc
Tuguegarao
Ilagan
Dinapigue

Vigan
Sagada
Banaue
Mt Amuyao (2702m)
Mt Pulag (2922m)
Casiguran
Pantabangan Lake

San Fernando (La Union)
La Trinidad
Baguio City
Dagupan
Baler

Bolinao
Hundred Islands National Park
San Carlos
Tarlac
Cabanatuan

Tarlac
Angeles
San Fernando (Pampanga)
Mt Pinatubo (1454m)
Olongapo
MANILA
Polillo Islands
Lamon Bay

Mariveles
Laguna de Bay
Lucena

Lubang Island

Calagua Islands
Daet

Catanduanes Island

SOUTH CHINA SEA

Philippine Sea

Luzon

20°N

16°N

118°E

122°E

126°E

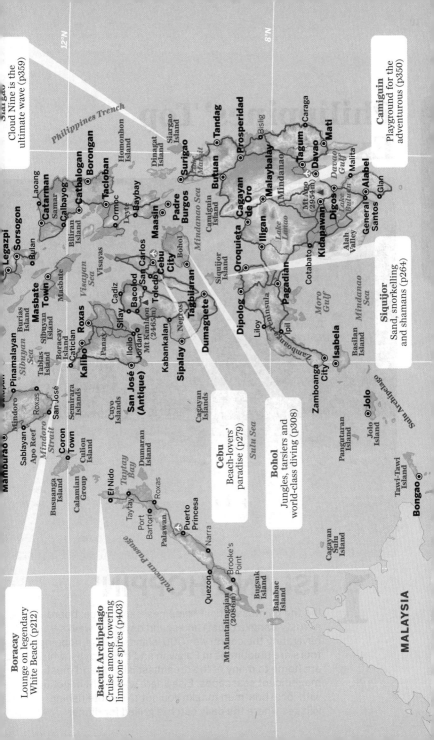

Siargao
Cloud Nine is the
ultimate wave (p359)

Camiguin
Playground for the
adventurous (p350)

Siquijor
Sand, snorkelling
and shamans (p264)

Cebu
Beach-lovers'
paradise (p279)

Bohol
Jungles, tarsiers and
world-class diving (p308)

Boracay
Lounge on legendary
White Beach (p212)

Bacuit Archipelago
Cruise among towering
limestone spires (p403)

12°N
8°N

Philippines Trench

MALAYSIA

Caraga
Bislig
Tandag
Prosperidad
Siargao
Island
Dinagat Island
Siargao
Surigao
Tagum
Davao
Mati
Butuan
Malaybalay
Mindanao
Davao
Gulf
Homonhon
Island
Laoang
Catarman
Calbayog
Borongan
Samar
Catbalogan
Tacloban
Baybay
Ormoc
Leyte
Biliran
Island
Maasin
Padre
Burgos
Cagayan
de Oro
Mt Apo
(2954m)
Malita
Alabel
General
Santos
Glan
Digos
Kidapawan
Lake
Buluan
Alah
Valley
Cotabato
Oroquieta
Iligan
Lake
Lanao
Camiguin
Island
Mindanao Sea
Siquijor
Island
Dipolog
Pagadian
Zamboanga
Peninsula
Ipil
Liloy
Moro
Gulf
Mindanao
Sea
Isabela
Basilan
Island
Zamboanga
City
Jolo
Jolo
Island
Pangutaran
Island
Sulu Archipelago
Cagayan
Sulu
Island
Tawi-Tawi
Bongao
Legazpi
Sorsogon
Bulan
Masbate
Town
Masbate
Burias
Island
Sibuyan
Island
Sibuyan
Sea
Tablas
Island
Roxas
Panay
Kalibo
Caticlan
Boracay
Island
Iloilo
Jordan
Silay
Cadiz
Bacolod
San Carlos
Toledo
Cebu
City
Negros
Mt Kanlaon
(2465m)
Kabankalan
Sipalay
Dumaguete
Tagbilaran
Bohol
Visayas
Visayan
Sea
San José
(Antique)
Semirara
Islands
Cuyo
Islands
Cagayan
Islands
Sulu Sea
Mindoro
Roxas
San José
Sablayan
Apo Reef
Mindoro
Strait
Coron
Town
Culion
Island
Busuanga
Island
Calamian
Group
Dumaran
Island
El Nido
Taytay
Port
Barton
Roxas
Palawan
Puerto
Princesa
Narra
Quezon
Brooke's
Point
Bugsuk
Island
Balabac
Island
Mt Mantalingajan
(2086m)
Taytay
Bay
Palawan
Passage
Pinamalayan
Mamburao
Mindoro

Philippines' Top Experiences

1 ISLAND HOPPIN'

It's the quintessential Philippines' experience: board a trusty bangka (boat) and spend days – or weeks – navigating the country's 7000 islands. Island-hopping tours are ubiquitous in Palawan and the Visayas, which are home to many of the dreamiest islands and most magnificent seascapes. Elsewhere you might negotiate with local boatmen to take you out to remote fishing villages where the daily catch is grilled for dinner.

Bacuit Archipelago

Cruising through Palawan's labyrinthine Bacuit Archipelago off El Nido is an experience not to be missed. These islands present a beguiling mixture of imposing limestone escarpments, palm-tree-lined beaches, paradisiacal lagoons and aquatic and terrestrial wildlife. p403

Left: Cadlao Island (p403)
Right: Kayaking (p396), El Nido

Calamian Islands

Isolated fishing villages, magnificent coral reefs and mysterious inland lakes abound in this archipelago in the far north of Palawan Province. Use the main island of Busuanga as a base for bangka or sea-kayaking expeditions to countless small islands where lonely beaches await. p405

Above: Views of Coron Town from Mt Tapyas (p405)

Puerto Galera

This former galleon port-of-call boasts sensationally scenic bays and teeming marine life in the surrounding Verde Island Passage. Bangka, yacht and liveaboard trips, with a scuba-dive option, have gained steam since the pandemic due to Puerto Galera's proximity to Manila. p194

Above: Clownfish, Puerto Galera

2 WALKS ON THE WILD SIDE

It's not all about coastal pleasures in the Philippines. The major islands boast mountainous interiors carpeted by forests and pock-marked by caves, making them ideal for trekking and spelunking. North Luzon is the epicentre, with waterfalls cascading off jagged peaks, and rice terraces that soar so high they are known as the eighth wonder of the world.

Ifugao Rice Terraces

Hewn out of the hillsides by the Ifugao people centuries ago, the rice terraces around Banaue and Batad in North Luzon are truly spectacular. Take extra days to hike around lesser-known villages like Cambulo and Hapao. p152

Above: Ifugao's Rice Terraces, Batad

Camiguin Island

Made for do-it-yourself adventurers, the peaks and valleys of volcanic Camiguin Island offer streams and canyons for scrambling, mountains for scaling, and pools at the base of thundering water-falls in which to wash off the day's exertions. p350

Above top: Katibawasan Falls (p351)

Sagada

A mellow mountain retreat deep in the heart of the wild Cordillera mountains of North Luzon, Sagada has all the elements of a backpacker Shangri-La: awesome hikes, eerie caves, hanging coffins, strong coffee, earthy bak-eries, and cosy and cheap accommodation. p140

Above: Sumaging Cave (p141)

3 BEACH LIFE

Those looking for the perfect beach may finally find it in the Philippines: there is one made-to-order on each of the country's 7000-plus islands. Whether you want to be far away from everybody, dancing to techno beats in the sand, kite-surfing the day away, or watching the sun drop with a fruity cocktail in your hand, you have come to the right place.

ZSTOCKPHOTOS/GETTY IMAGES ©

SOFT_LIGHT/SHUTTERSTOCK ©

Siargao

For decades a well-guarded secret, Siargao has blossomed into the darling of Philippine tourism, offering crescent-shaped beaches, design-led boutique resorts and its signature tasty waves. p359

Top left: Cloud Nine (p362)

Siquijor

The magic of Siquijor lies in its ring road – 72km of nearly traffic-free coastal bliss. Bike past waterfalls and centuries-old churches in pursuit of radiant white sand beaches that you'll have to yourself. p264

Above left: Siquijor

Boracay

Famously placed in 'rehab' in 2018, the diminutive party island reopened just in time for the pandemic to hit. With sublime White Beach looking better than ever, Boracay is poised for a major rebound. p212

Above: Boracay

4 INTO THE DEEP

Plunge into nature's washing machine: the Philippine Sea, world-renowned for its diverse marine life. The archipelago occupies the heart of the so-called Coral Triangle, and its reefs explode with colour and kooky-looking critters – a delight for seasoned scuba divers and casual snorkellers alike. If you're in the right place at the right time you might spy whale sharks, dugong (sea cows) or sea turtles passing by.

Cebu

Coral walls ring nearly the entirety of this long central Visayan island, attracting divers to places such as Moalboal, where schooling sardines present an unmissable spectacle, and Malapascua, where thresher shark encounters await. p279

Left: Whale shark (p304), Cebu

Southern Negros

From the agreeable city of Dumaguete you are well-positioned to take in world-class diving at Apo Island, Dauin or Sipalay, or go dolphin- and whale-watching at Bais. p243

Anilao

The birthplace of scuba diving in the Philippines is back. The pandemic has Manila denizens rediscovering Anilao's excellent dive sites and striking coastline, with fabulous dive resorts mushrooming to accommodate them. p103

Bottom left: Feather star crinoid, Anilao

5 GOING GREEN

As one of the most biodiverse places on the planet, the Philippines has plenty to protect. There are several laudable ecotourism initiatives and places where green tourism thrives. But you'll need to do your homework to find them. Start by travelling independently, as many domestic tour operators don't give a hoot about conservation, although there are notable exceptions.

Bohol

Cetacean watching with re-formed poachers, river-kayak and SUP trips, a sanctuary for tarsiers, and responsible scuba diving at Balicasag Island are among the many highlights of Bohol, a wildlife mini-Mecca in the Visayas. p308

Below: Tarsier, Bohol

Batanes Islands

Traditional customs endure in the northern Batanes chain. Basic homestays and cycling sum up the environmental ethos. p160

Above: Sabtang Island (p163)

Bicol

Smouldering Mt Mayon commands the countryside of Bicol, a beacon for eco-conscious travellers drawn to the region's national parks and marine life. Donsol is the place for eco-friendly whale shark interactions. p168

Right: Mt Mayon (p179)

6 CULTURE CLUB

AKARAT PHASURA/SHUTTERSTOCK ©

The Philippines isn't just about beaches and adventure. There are centuries-old stone churches, wooden houses that combine native and European elements, and heritage mansions that have been turned into lovely hotels. WWII buffs can visit sombre memorials across the archipelago that commemorate battles, landings and death marches. Those who prefer more contemporary culture can get their fill of the arts in cities like Manila and Cebu.

Manila

The megacity is Asia's rising star in contemporary art and design circles, and even the long-maligned culinary scene is making a splash, as cutting-edge restaurants open alongside earthy cafes and craft-beer bars. p48

Vigan

Traditional *kalesa* (horse-drawn carriages) clank along cobbles in the remarkably well-preserved Old Town of Vigan, where Mexican, Chinese, Filipino and Spanish architectural styles mingle. p121

Above: BarTech (p125)

Ati-Atihan

The Philippines just isn't the Philippines without the colourful fiestas (festivals) that every township hosts annually. The January Ati-Atihan Festival, a week-long Mardi Gras in Kalibo, near Boracay, is the grand-daddy of them all. p227

Need to Know

For more information, see Survival Guide (p435)

Currency
Philippine peso (P)

Language
Tagalog (Filipino), English

Visas
Tourists of most nationalities receive a free 30-day visa on arrival. You can extend your visa for a fee, but be sure to check the current rules and fees before you travel.

Money
ATMs are widely available. Take some cash if travelling in remote areas; otherwise, credit cards are accepted at hotels, restaurants and some shops.

Mobile Phones
Local SIM cards are widely available, and data and phone credit is cheap. Roaming is possible but expensive.

Time
Asean common time (GMT plus eight hours)

When to Go

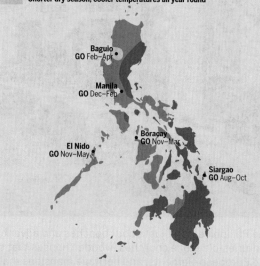

Tropical climate, rain all year round
Tropical climate, wet and dry season
Shorter dry season, cooler temperatures all year round

Baguio
GO Feb–Apr

Manila
GO Dec–Feb

Boracay
GO Nov–Mar

El Nido
GO Nov–May

Siargao
GO Aug–Oct

High Season
(Dec–Apr)

➡ High season is dry season for most of the country; December to February are the coolest, most pleasant months.

➡ Many resorts triple rates around New Year and before Easter.

Shoulder
(May & Nov)

➡ Rising May temperatures herald the onset of the wet season around Manila and elsewhere.

➡ November sees high-season rates kick in.

Low Season
(Jun–Sep)

➡ Accommodation prices drop 30% in resort areas.

➡ Passing typhoons can cause days of torrential rain.

➡ Eastern seaboard is usually dry, if susceptible to typhoons.

Useful Websites

Philippine Newslink (www.philnews.com) Thorough pile of news, views, links.

ClickTheCity.com (www.clickthecity.com) A great listings site for happenings in Manila and around the country.

Lonely Planet (www.lonelyplanet.com/philippines) Destination information, hotel reviews, traveller forum and more.

Experience Philippines (www.experiencephilippines.org) Tourism authority site; good for planning.

National Commission for Culture & the Arts (ncca.gov.ph) Arts listings and articles on all things Filipino.

Important Numbers

Dial ☑0 before area codes when calling from a mobile phone or a landline outside that region.

Country code	☑63
Emergency	☑117
International dialling code	☑00
International operator	☑108
PLDT directory assistance	☑101171

Exchange Rates

Australia	A$1	P37
Canada	C$1	P40
Euro zone	€1	P58
Japan	¥100	P44
New Zealand	NZ$1	P34
Thailand	10B	P15
UK	£1	P68
USA	US$1	P49

For current exchange rates see www.xe.com

Daily Costs

Budget: Less than P1750 (US$35)

➡ Dorm bed or single room: P400–800

➡ Local meals and three beers: P600

➡ Medium-range bangka or jeepney ride: P80

➡ Tricycle ride: P10

Midrange: P1750–5000 (US$35–100)

➡ Air-conditioned double room: P800–3000

➡ Restaurant meal with drinks: P700

➡ Group van or bangka tour: P1000

➡ Daily motorbike rental: P500

Top end: More than P5000 (US$100)

➡ Boutique resort: P3500–10,000

➡ Meal and drinks at a resort restaurant: P1500

➡ One-way domestic plane ticket: P2000

➡ Private island-hopping trip: P3000-6000

Opening Hours

Offices and banks are closed on public holidays, although shops and malls stay open.

Banks 9am to 4.30pm Monday to Friday (most ATMs operate 24 hours)

Post Offices 8am to 5pm Monday to Friday, to 1pm Saturday

Restaurants 7am or 8am to 10pm or 11pm

Arriving in the Philippines

Public transport from both the Manila and Cebu international airports requires changing jeepneys several times and isn't advisable given that taxis are so cheap.

Ninoy Aquino International Airport (NAIA; Manila) Yellow metered taxis are the best option for getting into town. They are cheap (P300 average to most hotels) and usually plentiful at all four NAIA terminals. Uber is another option, with fares averaging P350 to P450. Check carefully which terminal you arrive at (and, especially, depart from) – you'll need up to an hour to switch terminals (p443).

Mactan-Cebu International Airport (CEB; Cebu) You'll find a taxi rank of regular metered taxis (P40 flag fall) on the right as you exit. Uber is also an option. Either costs about P300 to the city centre.

Getting Around

Air Several discount carriers link a vast range of destinations.

Boat Bangkas, 'fastcraft', car ferries and large passenger ships with bunk beds and private cabins link the islands.

Van Often the quickest overland option and generally shadows the same routes as buses.

Bus Comfort and reliability runs the gamut from hobbling skeletons way past their expiration date to long-haul, modern vehicles with air-con and wi-fi.

Tricycle These sidecars bolted to motorcycles are everywhere and will transport you several blocks or kilometres. Being replaced with quieter e-trikes in some places.

Jeepney Workhorse of the Philippines, both within cities and towns, as well as between more far-flung destinations.

For much more on **getting around**, see p444

First Time Philippines

For more information, see Survival Guide (p435)

Checklist

➡ Print out your onward ticket – airlines won't allow you to board a Philippines-bound flight without it.

➡ Make sure your passport is valid for six months past your arrival date.

➡ Check airline baggage restrictions.

➡ Inform your debit-/credit-card company.

➡ Arrange for appropriate travel insurance.

What to Pack

➡ Sunglasses and sunscreen

➡ Earplugs – roosters and karaoke operate at full volume

➡ Headlamp – brownouts, blackouts and no electricity are common

➡ Cash is king so bring a waist-belt to keep it secure

➡ Sarong or pullover for those ridiculously cold air-con buses and ferries

➡ Dry bag

➡ Mask, snorkel, rash guard and reef booties for snorkelling

➡ Water bottle

Top Tips for Your Trip

➡ If you're comfortable on a motorbike, it's a great way both to overcome unreliable bus schedules and to experience the sights and sounds of ordinary rural life.

➡ Stay flexible so you can reroute if a typhoon is approaching your projected path. Advance transport and hotel bookings usually aren't a necessity outside of 'superpeak' periods.

➡ Keep track of weather-related disturbances through www.typhoon2000.ph and www1.pagasa.dost.gov.ph.

➡ Bring a water bottle and fill it up for P5 (or for free) at ubiquitous water-refilling stations.

➡ Basketball players rejoice: nearly every village, no matter how small and remote, has a court. Call 'next' and be ready to compete.

➡ Schedule at least half a day for connecting flights back to Manila or Cebu, to account for possible delays.

What to Wear

Because of the tropical climate, the Philippines by necessity is a casual place. That being said, despite the heat most Filipinos look fairly unfazed – of course, they're used to it – and tend to wear trousers in urban areas (offices of course) and for trips to the mall.

In beach towns, flip-flops or sandals, shorts, T-shirts or tank tops, and a bathing suit (bikinis are fine) are all you'll need. Outside of beach settings, lightweight and comfortable is the way to go. In rural areas and villages, locals tend to avoid overly revealing clothing – although again, shorts and flip-flops are the norm for both sexes.

In Muslim areas of Mindanao, locals dress more conservatively. Women, especially, avoid wearing revealing clothing.

Sleeping

During the high season, reservations are recommended at popular tourist areas such as Boracay or El Nido. At other times, you should do fine walking in.

Resorts These range from ultraluxurious, the rival of any in Southeast Asia, to basic, fan-cooled bungalows.

Hotels Many cater to the domestic market, which means generic concrete construction and air-con. Five-star hotels in Manila are truly sumptuous affairs.

Pensionnes Sort of a catch-all term referring to less expensive, independently owned hotels.

Hostels Those that target foreign travellers tend to be more comfortable and stylish, but also more expensive, than ones for primarily young Filipinos.

Etiquette

Anger management Don't lose your temper – Filipinos will think you're *loco-loco* (crazy).

Food Abstain from grabbing that last morsel on the communal food platter – your hosts might think you're a pauper.

Transport For transport frustrations, smile and adopt the Filipino maxim – *bahala na* (whatever will be will be).

Karaoke When engaged in karaoke (and trust us, you will be), don't insult the person who sounds like a chicken getting strangled, lest it be taken the wrong way.

Jeepneys Don't complain about neighbours getting cosy with you on jeepneys – space is meant to be shared.

Restaurants Filipinos hiss to gain someone's attention, often in restaurants to signal the waiter. It's not considered rude.

Language

English is widely spoken in urban centres and areas frequented by tourists. Even in the most rural areas, a few basic expressions might be understood. Along with English, the other official language is Tagalog (Filipino). The country's unique colonial history means Spanish speakers will recognise many words. While Filipino is the lingua franca, there are 165 other languages spoken throughout the archipelago – Cebuano (Visayan) and Ilocano are two of the most widespread.

Bargaining

Modest haggling is expected at many outdoor markets, particularly if those markets cater to tourists. Note, though, that prices for food and drink are usually set.

Bargaining is the rule when renting motorbikes or hiring tricycles, bangkas or taxis for the day. It is also possible to negotiate with hotels if you don't have a booking, especially in resort areas in the low season.

Tipping

Restaurants 10% service charge added to bill in cities, tourist hotspots. Otherwise leave 5% to 10%.

Taxis Round up taxi fares, but consider tipping more (P50 to P70) for honest taxi drivers who turn on the meter.

Hotels Not expected, but slide P50 to porters or leave a few hundred pesos in the staff tip box at resorts.

Guides Always tip your guides; they can really use it.

STEPHANE BIDOUZE/SHUTTERSTOCK ©

Basketball game in a village in El Nido (p395)

Month by Month

January

New Year is a 'superpeak' period, and hotel rates can quadruple in resort areas. Away from the eastern seaboard, the weather is usually pretty good – relatively cool and dry, although rain can linger into January.

🎎 Ati-Atihan Festival

The Philippines' most famous and riotous festival is this weeklong mardi gras in Kalibo, Panay, which peaks in the third week of January. Other towns in the region, such as Cadiz and Iloilo, hold similar festivals on the weekend nearest 26 January. (p227)

🎎 Procession of the Black Nazarene

A life-size and highly revered black image of Christ in Quiapo Church (Manila) is paraded through the streets in massive processions on 9 January and again during the week before Easter (Holy Week). (p65)

🎎 Sinulog Festival

The granddaddy of Cebu's fiestas sees celebrants engaged in *sinulog* dancing, a unique two-steps-forward, one-step-back shuffle meant to imitate the rhythm of the river. (p283)

February

It's peak season for foreign travellers, so book ahead. The Christmas winds continue to howl, thrilling kite-surfers, while surf season continues in San Fernando (La Union) and *butanding* (whale shark) activity picks up in Donsol.

🎎 Chinese New Year

The lunar new year in late January or early February is popular even among non-Chinese Filipinos. Dragon dances, street parties and huge fireworks displays take place in Manila.

🎎 Panagbenga Flower Festival

During the last week in February, the streets in the northern mountain city of Baguio (p131) come alive with song, dance and a grand floral parade with spectacular floats.

March

Temperatures begin to rise in March but it's still dry throughout the country. Holy Week sometimes falls at the end of the month.

April

Everything shuts down during Holy Week, which leads up to Easter, when *sinakulo* (passion plays) and *pasyon* (a recitation of the Passion of Christ) are staged throughout the country. Resort prices again hit 'superpeak' levels.

🎎 Crucifixion Ceremonies

The Easter crucifixion ceremony in San Fernando (p107), north of Manila, presents a macabre tableau, with devotees literally being nailed to wooden crosses. Similar

re-enactments of Christ's suffering occur in several towns.

★☆ Lang-Ay Festival

In Bontoc (p145), deep in the heart of the Cordillera of North Luzon, surrounding communities come together for parades, decked out in traditional tribal dress.

★☆ Lenten Festival of Herbal Preparation

On the 'spooky' island of Siquijor, faith healers and witch doctors gather around a big pot on Black Saturday, chanting and preparing a medicinal concoction some say cures all that ails you. (p267)

★☆ Moriones Festival

Marinduque's colourful Moriones Festival is a week-long *sinakulo* during which the streets are overrun by masked locals engaging in mock sword fights and playing pranks on bystanders. (p190)

May

Scorching heat, beaches packed with vacationing locals and light winds can make this an uncomfortable time to travel, although flat seas ease boat travel. Consider cooler highland destinations such as the Cordillera of North Luzon.

★☆ Magayon Festival

A street party lasting the entire month of May in Legazpi, Bicol region, with nightly street markets, pop-up bars, music stages, dance performances, chilli-eating contests and more. (p175)

Top: MassKara Festival (p244), Bacolod

Bottom: Ati Atihan Festival (p227), Kalibo

✺ Pahiyas

This famous fiesta takes place around 15 May in the town of Lucban, south of Manila, where houses are decked out with colourful *kiping* (leaf-shaped rice wafers) decorations, which are later eaten. (p105)

✺ Rodeo Masbateño

Cowboy up for Masbate's rodeo in late April or early May, with bull-riding, lasso contests and other events that will have you clicking your spurs. (p187)

June

The onset of the wet season brings welcome respite from the heat. June also marks the start of typhoon season, so check the radar and reroute if necessary.

✺ Baragatan Festival

In the third week of June, residents of Puerto Princesa, Palawan, flood the grounds of the Provincial Capitol Building in a massive display of merry-making. (p380)

✺ Hugyaw Silay Kansilay Festival

This weeklong festival in Silay, Negros, celebrates the founding of the city, culminating in gaudily dressed dancers parading down the main street and a 'dance competition'. (p251)

✺ Pintados-Kasadyaan

This 'painted festival' in Tacloban on 29 June celebrates pre-Spanish traditional tattooing practices, albeit using water-based paints for the festival's body decorations. (p324)

August

It's the rainiest month (except for on the eastern seaboard, where it's the driest), so you'll get fabulous discounts on accommodation.

✺ Kadayawan sa Dabaw Festival

Davao's big festival showcases its Muslim, Chinese and tribal influences with parades, performances, and fruit and flower displays. It's held in the third week of August. (p368)

October

Things start to dry out after the heavy rains of August and September, but typhoons are still common. High-season prices start to kick in.

✺ Lanzones Festival

The northern Mindanao island of Camiguin goes crazy for this small yellow fruit, with parades, dance contests and of course a pageant. (p352)

✺ MassKara Festival

Mischievous masked men stir the masses into a dancing frenzy on the streets of Bacolod, capital of Negros Occidental, during the weekend closest to 19 October. (p244)

✺ Todos los Santos

Families laden with food gather at the local cemetery to spend All Saints Day (1 November) remembering their departed loved ones.

December

The northeast Christmas winds ramp up, launching kitesurfing season in Boracay and surf season in northwest Luzon.

✺ Shariff Kabungsuan Festival

This festival in Cotabato on Mindanao from 15 to 19 December celebrates the arrival of Islam in the region and includes river parades of decorated boats.

WHAT THE FIESTA IS GOING ON?

Nearly every barangay (village or neighbourhood) has one. And there's one nearly every day. Fiestas, an integral part of Filipino life and identity, are generally associated with celebrations during the feast of the patron saint. However, like other facets of the culture, some are best understood as the result of syncretism; older rituals and beliefs related to bountiful harvests and abundant seas have been blended into a Catholic architecture, often at the behest of missionaries centuries ago. There are still festivities strictly concerned with planting and indigenous, pre-Hispanic traditions. Regardless of the origins, they're jubilant affairs, with entire towns spruced up for loved ones' homecomings.

Itineraries

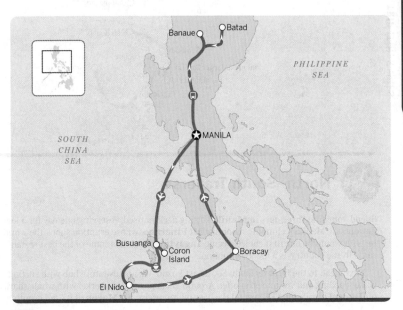

Greatest Hits

Fly into **Manila**, worth a one-day stopover to tour historic Intramuros and its nearby museums.

On day two fly to **Busuanga** in Palawan's Calamian Islands. Visit majestic **Coron Island**, dive the WWII wrecks, do a kayak tour and camp overnight on an idyllic offshore island such as Calumbuyan, Pass or North Cay.

Next, take a ferry to Palawan's other crown jewel, **El Nido**, home to some of the world's prettiest beaches and jumping-off point for island-hopping trips in the spectacular Bacuit Archipelago. Enjoy El Nido's burgeoning drinking and dining scene, then hit **Boracay**, where the party never stops.

Fly back to Manila and take an overnight bus to **Banaue**, jumping-off point for the rice terraces of Ifugao. Enjoy the Zen-like peace and quiet of **Batad** for a day before taking a bus back to Manila to catch your flight home.

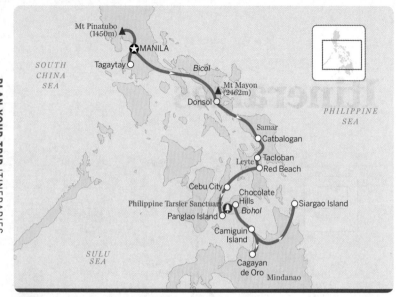

North–South Traverse

1 MONTH

Spend your first three days in **Manila** getting acclimatised, reserving one day for a journey outside Manila – climbing moonlike **Mt Pinatubo**, whose eruption shook the world in 1991, would be our first choice. Scenic **Tagaytay**, which has some of the best restaurants in the country, is a mellower option.

Next, head to the Bicol region in Southeast Luzon. It's an adventure hub with surfing, wakeboarding and volcanoes on offer. Around Legazpi you can snorkel with whale sharks off **Donsol** or ride an ATV around the base of impressive **Mt Mayon** (if it's not erupting).

Proceeding south, cross the San Bernardino Strait to the rugged islands of Samar and Leyte in the eastern Visayas. Along the way, have the spelunking adventure of a lifetime in **Catbalogan**. Stop off in **Tacloban**, Imelda Marcos' home town. It was devastated by Typhoon Haiyan (known locally as Typhoon Yolanda) but has reinvented itself as a hip provincial centre. Head to nearby **Red Beach** for a dose of WWII history. Then take a ferry to the Visayas' gritty capital, **Cebu City**, for modern comforts and nightlife.

You'll be approaching week three of your trip by now, and possibly ready for some serious beach time. Take the fast ferry to Tagbilaran, the capital of Bohol and gateway to the beach resorts of **Panglao Island**. From Panglao you are well positioned to enjoy all Bohol has to offer: go diving, snorkelling and dolphin-spotting offshore, then head inland to stand-up paddle the Loboc River, view the **Chocolate Hills**, kayak with fireflies on the Abatan River and spot palm-sized primates at the **Philippine Tarsier Sanctuary**.

Next, move north from Panglao and catch a classic back-door ferry: 3½ hours from Jagna, Bohol, to **Camiguin Island**. Camiguin can keep both adventurous travellers and beach bums satisfied for days. Spend at least several here, then make the short hop over to mainland Mindanao by ferry. For your last few days, choose between **Cagayan de Oro**, a buzzy university town with white-water rafting, and **Siargao**, the Philippines' top surf spot as well as an idyllic island with lagoons and mangroves galore.

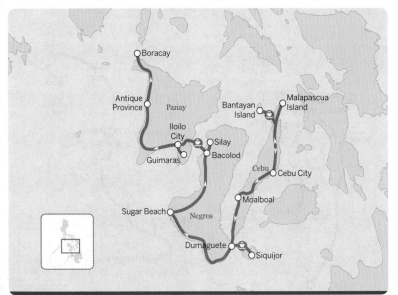

4 WEEKS Voyage to the Visayas

Beach-lovers and dive buffs need look no further than this central group of idyllic islands.

Kick things off in **Cebu City**, soaking up some history during the day before partying it up at night. Then it's time to hit the islands: divers will want to head straight to **Malapascua Island**, where you'll have a good chance of encountering thresher sharks; while sun worshippers should check in on laid-back **Bantayan Island**. Double back to Cebu City and continue south to adventure mecca **Moalboal**, where waterfalls abound and you can go freediving with schooling sardines.

Continue to Cebu's southern tip and cross the narrow Tañon Strait to Negros and **Dumaguete**, which is all about promenading on the scenic boulevard, great seafood, rowdy nightlife and superb diving at Apo Island. Next, take a detour to the mellow island of **Siquijor**, just 1¼ hours away by ferry. Spend a day or three here and be sure to visit one of its famed folk healers.

Retreat to Dumaguete and take the long bus ride around the southern horn of Negros to delightfully laid-back **Sugar Beach** on the west coast. It's a divine sweep of fine golden sand in range of quality diving and mangrove kayaking. From here another long bus journey north takes you to **Bacolod**, where you can revel in great food and bar-hopping, and take a side trip to **Silay** for a fascinating journey through haciendas and sugar-cane plantations.

From Bacolod it's an easy fast-ferry trip over to **Iloilo City** on the island of Panay. Check out the colonial architecture of the Jaro District and have a night out in Small-ville. A short boat ride away is **Guimaras**, a gem of an island with low-key resorts, mountain-biking and famous mangoes. Return to Iloilo and meander north via **Antique Province**, where hidden beaches await, before alighting on **Boracay** to whoop it up on White Beach.

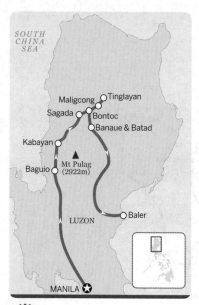

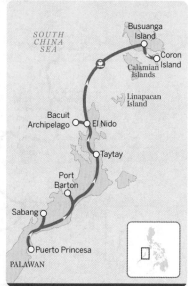

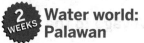

3 WEEKS North Luzon

Not a beach person? The mountains of the Philippines' main island delight with rice terraces, trekking and hill tribes.

Head north from **Manila** to **Baguio**. Visit some of the city's fascinating ethnographic museums.

From Baguio, take a bus to **Kabayan**, centre of Ibaloi culture and base for hikes in Mt Pulag National Park. Next, **Sagada** beckons. This tranquil backpacker village is tough to leave.

Take a jeepney to **Bontoc** and explore the amphitheatre-like rice terraces of **Maligcong** on a day trip. Continue north to **Tinglayan**, a base for treks into indigenous Kalinga villages where the contemporary world feels far away.

Head back to Bontoc, then continue to **Banaue** and **Batad**, site of Luzon's most famous rice terraces. Stunning hikes will keep you busy for days. Try to spend at least a night or two in a homestay.

With a little R&R in mind, catch a bus south to San Jose (you might have to overnight here) to connect to another bus to the surfing town of **Baler**.

2 WEEKS Water world: Palawan

The Philippines' star attraction lends itself to easy south–north exploration.

Spend an evening in **Puerto Princesa** checking out the city's culinary scene and a day exploring the surrounding countryside. From Puerto, organise a ride to **Sabang**, a laid-back beachfront village and the base for trips through the famous Underground River.

From Sabang, hightail it further north to **Port Barton**, a beautiful and relaxing retreat with chilled-out beach bars. Heading north again, reserve at least a day for undiscovered **Taytay** before rejoining the tourist masses in **El Nido**, sandwiched between limestone cliffs and the fantastically picturesque **Bacuit Archipelago**.

From El Nido, take a boat to **Busuanga Island**. If you have time, the trip to Busuanga can be done as a five-day islandhopping expedition through the heavenly Linapacan and Calamian archipelagos. From Busuanga, venture out to the striking lakes of **Coron Island** and some of the best wreck diving in the world. Flights and ferries are available to usher you back to Manila and reality.

Plan Your Trip

Diving in the Philippines

Whether you're more comfortable diving on a shallow coral garden or are looking for deep technical dives, the Philippines is one of the world's best diving destinations. Its varied underwater landscape includes remote reefs, extinct volcanoes, magnificent walls, caves and shipwrecks, while its marine biodiversity is second to none.

Planning Your Dive

When to Go

Many parts of the country boast year-round diving, but the Philippines is affected by the annual cycles of the northeast (*amihan*) and southwest (*habagat*) monsoon winds that create a dry season (November to May, with some regional variations) and a wet season (June to October), as well as by typhoons periodically from June to December.

Dry Season

The *amihan* winds that affect the country from November until April dispel much of the remaining rain. The sea can be choppy and turbid from December to March; many dive centres have alternative sites to visit if weather disturbances are affecting specific areas. Mid-November is regarded as the start of the 'tourist season' and during Christmas and New Year dive centres and resorts are overflowing with divers, so reservations are recommended. The *amihan* dies down in late March and the sea becomes flat and calm, with incredible visibility that peaks during April and May.

Wet Season

The height of the rainy season for most of the country (June to October) corresponds

Best Dives

Best Reef Diving

Tubbataha Reefs and Apo Reef are in another league, but don't overlook Padre Burgos, Apo Island and Camiguin (Mantigue Island and Jigdup Reef).

Best Wall Diving

Verde Island (Puerto Galera), Moalboal (Pescador Island or White Beach) and Samal Island's Mushroom Rock.

Best for Sharks

Tubbataha Reefs (white-tips, grey reef sharks, leopard sharks and hammerheads) are again in another league, followed by Apo Reef and Malapascua (thresher sharks).

Best Beginner Diving

Boracay, Alona Beach and El Nido.

Best Macro

Anilao and Siquijor.

Best Snorkelling

Snorkelling with Donsol's whale sharks is hard to beat, though Coral Gardens at Puerto Galera is a fantastic place to see reef fish.

with the height of the typhoon season; this results in major tropical downpours. While heavy rain can cause lower visibility, many of the diving areas have sheltered spots in the lee of the prevailing winds that afford reasonable diving and adequate visibility. Still, remote live-aboard and safari diving are rarely offered from July through to October, and many dive operators close during this period.

What You'll See

The Philippines' amazing diversity of marine life is mostly of the small- to medium-sized variety. Divers who have travelled the world recognise the Philippines as one of the world's best macro (small marine life) diving locations. Outside of Tubbataha, Apo Reef and a handful of other locations, you rarely get the big pelagic (open-sea marine life) action that characterises neighbours such as Palau in the south Pacific. However, the sheer range of marine life and the diversity of coral here is among the world's best.

Sadly, that coral remains under constant threat, as destructive fishing methods such as cyanide and dynamite fishing are still widely practised and pollution also takes its toll. The best Philippines dive sites have been given marine-protected status and have thus been spared such ravages.

What to Bring

Dive centres are typically well stocked with a wide variety of well-maintained and reasonably new hire equipment. Technical divers will find what they need at dive centres offering technical diving, including reels and accessories, mixed gas and, in many cases, rebreathers. Many operators also sell equipment, and most internationally recognised brands can be bought and serviced throughout the islands.

Choosing a Dive Operator

The diving environment can often be deceptive in the Philippines. Clear water and great visibility can lead to disorientation and going below the planned depth. Currents can be a major factor on many dives, and the sea conditions and weather can change in a matter of minutes at certain times of the year.

Thus it is strongly advised that you dive with a highly professional dive operator. A PADI affiliation can be a good indication of a dive operation's commitment to safety and customer service. In addition, check out operators' safety procedures and emergency plans. Do they have oxygen, is it brought along on dive boats, and are there personnel trained to administer it on board? Take a look at the hire equipment: is it relatively new and well maintained? Finally, find an instructor or divemaster that speaks a language you are comfortable with.

Certification

All dive centres in the Philippines require that a diver be certified by a recognised international training agency and should ask to see your card (many of them take your word for it if you forget your card).

RESPONSIBLE DIVING

Following these guidelines will help ensure a safe and enjoyable experience.

➡ Be aware of local laws, regulations and etiquette about marine life and the environment, and don't feed fish.

➡ Practise proper buoyancy and avoid touching or standing on living marine organisms or dragging equipment across the reef.

➡ Be conscious of your fins. Even without contact, the surge from fin strokes near the reef can damage delicate organisms.

➡ Resist the temptation to collect or buy corals or shells or to loot marine archaeological sites (ie shipwrecks).

➡ Ensure that you take your rubbish – and any other litter you may find – away from dive sites. Plastics, in particular, are a serious threat to marine life.

➡ Minimise your disturbance of marine animals. Never touch whale sharks or ride on the backs of turtles. Avoid hand-fed whale-shark interaction programs.

A green sea turtle in Moalboal (p300), Cebu

Operators rarely ask to see a log book to assess a diver's experience. Most live-aboard trips require at least an advanced certification, but the good news is that all levels of certification training, from basic open-water to instructor, are widely available and great value throughout the country.

Technical Diving

Technical diving is big throughout the Philippines, and there is no shortage of deeper sites for technical training. The wrecks at the bottom of Coron Bay and Subic Bay make for outstanding technical diving, as do Coron Caves and caves near El Nido.

Qualified technical-dive training outfits include Tech Asia (p195), the technical-diving arm of Asia Divers in Puerto Galera; **Tech Divers** (www.tech-divers.com), also based in Puerto Galera; Cebu-based **Kontiki Divers** (www.kontikidivers.com); and **PhilTech** (www.philtech.net), based in Makati.

Some live-aboards also offer technical diving, mixed gas and rebreather equipment and training to qualified divers on request.

Costs

Dive prices vary significantly from region to region. Provided you have a few people along with you, you can expect to pay as little as US$22 up to US$35 per dive with a divemaster, including all equipment and a relatively short boat trip. Prices go down a bit if you have your own equipment, and two- or three-tank dives usually cost less than single-tank dives. PADI open-water certification courses vary widely from resort to resort and can cost anywhere from US$350 to US$500.

Of course, safety is more important than price when choosing a dive operator. Often (but certainly not always) more expensive dive outfits have better equipment and service and/or more experienced guides.

➡ Budget destinations include Dumaguete, Moalboal, Puerto Galera and Padre Burgos in Leyte.

➡ Midrange destinations include Alona Beach (Panglao Island), Malapascua, Camiguin Island, Coron and Siquijor.

➡ Top-end destinations include Anilao, Mactan Island, Dauin (Negros) and Boracay.

Dive Sites

Luzon

Anilao (p103) Home to the nation's unofficial scuba-diving capital, where many Manila-based divers make their first training dives. Anilao is busy most weekends with city-dwelling enthusiasts, as it is a convenient 2½-hour drive from Manila. The most famous dive site in Anilao is Cathedral Rock, a marine sanctuary just offshore. Nearby Sombrero Island presents a cavalcade of crevices and coral- and gorgonian-covered boulders which attract pelagic species such as rainbow runners and yellowtails. At Mainit Point you have a chance of seeing white-tip, black-tip and grey reef sharks, as well as schools of tuna and jacks.

Subic Bay (p109) The former US Naval Base and current Freeport Zone has several wrecks to dive including the impressive USS *New York*.

Batanes (p160) Way up north, this region is only just opening up to divers. The Kural Marine Sanctuary consists of coral-covered underwater pinnacles, while Blue Hole is for advanced divers only.

Donsol (p180) In southeast Luzon, Donsol is popular for snorkelling with whale sharks. The season usually lasts from early December to late May or early June.

Ticao Island (p188) The Manta Bowl is an outstanding dive site for spotting manta rays; dive outfits in Donsol or Ticao Island will get you there.

Mindoro

Puerto Galera (p194) A major training centre with more than 20 dive operations along the two main beaches of Sabang and Small La Laguna. The isthmus that contains these beaches juts out into the Verde Island Passage, and consequently some of the sites, especially those off Escarceo (Lighthouse) Point, can experience unpredictable sea conditions and strong currents, so diving with an experienced local guide is an absolute necessity. But there are also plenty of less challenging sites, perfect for intermediate divers and the many divers who take their basic certification course here.

Apo Reef (p210) Two hours off Mindoro's west coast, this is the Philippines' best dive site outside of Tubbataha. Here you'll likely spot more sharks than other divers. Some live-aboard trips head 20km west of Apo Reef to Hunter's Rock, an underwater pinnacle known for sea snakes.

LIVE-ABOARDS

Live-aboards (boats that divers sleep on during dive trips) are a popular way to visit the Philippines' more remote dive sites, or to visit several sites in a week. They range from custom dive boats and yachts to converted fishing vessels and modified bangka boats.

Live-aboard dive safaris depart from and/or are organised by dive operators in Puerto Galera, Boracay, northern Palawan and throughout the Visayas. Live-aboards are the only way to visit the Philippines' marquee dive site, the Tubbataha Reefs (p380) in the Sulu Sea. The window for diving Tubbataha is mid-March to mid-June.

Choosing a live-aboard boat should be as much or more a function of assessing the safety, seaworthiness and professionalism of an operation rather than the price. The following recommended operators all run Tubbataha trips from March to June, and focus on other areas the rest of the year.

P/Y Atlantis Azores (www.atlantishotel.com/py-atlantis-azores) Luxury motorised live-aboard yacht with bases in Dauin and Puerto Galera.

M/Y Discovery Palawan (www.discoveryfleet.com; 7-day/6-night trip US$2000-3750) Large live-aboard cruise ship plies the El Nido–Coron–Apo Reef–Batangas route.

Philippine Siren (http://sirenfleet.com) A luxury live-aboard schooner that patrols the Central Visayas when it's not in Tubbataha.

M/Y Palau Sport (www.palausport.com; 6-day/7-night trip US$2400) Focus is on Tubbataha and Palau, but does central Visayan trips from June to July.

Diving in the Philippines

0 — 200 km
0 — 100 miles

0 — 50 km
0 — 25 miles

Negros
Cebu
Cebu City — Mactan Island
Moalboal — Cabilao Island
Panglao & Balicasag Islands — Bohol
Lilo-an — *Bohol Sea*
Dumaguete — Siquijor Island
Apo Island

Batanes Islands

Babuyan Islands

Babuyan Channel

SOUTH CHINA SEA

LUZON

Baguio City

PHILIPPINE SEA

Polillo Islands

Olongapo — **MANILA**

Lamon Bay

Calagua Islands

Subic Bay — *Laguna de Bay*

Lubang Island — **Lucena**

Catanduanes Island

Anilao — *Verde Island*

Puerto Galera — Marinduque

Mindoro — *Sibuyan Sea*

Apo Reef — San José

Donsol

Manta Bowl

Busuanga Island — *Mindoro Strait*

Tablas Island — Romblon

Burias Island

Calamian Group — Coron Bay — Maniguin Island

Boracay Island — Masbate

Samar

Bacuit Archipelago — Taytay Bay

Visayan Sea

Biliran Island

San José (Antique) — Malapascua — Leyte — **Tacloban**

Panay — Visayas

Port Barton — Cuyo Islands

Iloilo — Cebu

Homonhon Island

Palawan — Dumaran Island — *Cagayan Islands*

Bacolod — **Cebu City**

Siargao Island

Honda Bay — *Sulu Sea*

Negros — Bohol

Padre Burgos

Quezon

Negros

Camiguin

Dumaguete — See Enlargement

Butuan

Tubbataha Reefs

Cagayan de Oro

Bugsuk Island

MINDANAO

Balabac Island

Samal & Talikud Islands

Cagayan Sulu Island

Zamboanga City

Moro Gulf

Davao

Davao Gulf

Turtle Islands

Pangutaran Island — Jolo Island

Basilan Island

Alah Valley

General Santos

Jolo

Mindanao Sea

Sarangani Bay

MALAYSIA

Tawi-Tawi Island

Sulu Archipelago

Bongao

Celebes Sea

Visayas

The Visayas comprises numerous islands, large and small, encompassing some of the country's most exciting diving. The list of dive sites around Bohol, a, Siquijor and Southern Negros is practically infinite.

Cebu Island (p279) Old-school dive mecca Moalboal (p301) has a spectacular wall that starts just offshore, plus turtle-laden Pescador island and a famous school of sardines. Malapascua (p295) offers close encounters of the thresher-shark kind on Monad Shoal, while Mactan Island (p292), home to Cebu City's international airport, caters to weekend divers flying in from Manila and North Asia.

Bohol (p308) The waters around Cabilao Island (p317) and Panglao Island (p313) are rich with marine life, and Balicasag Island (p316) is consistently rated among the best recreational dive sites in the country.

Dauin (p256) In Southern Negros, Dauin, along with nearby Apo Island (p255) and Siquijor (p264), are hugely popular dive areas. The sites are more spread out in these parts than at Alona Beach or Moalboal.

Boracay (p212) This is a popular training spot with a few good dives of its own.

Padre Burgos (p329) On Sogod Bay in Southern Leyte is reef diving on par with anything else in the Visayas, with possibility of spotting whale sharks from February to June.

More obscure, harder-to-reach sites include **Maniguin Island** off Panay, famous for its hammerhead-shark population; and **Blue Hole** off Romblon, an advanced diver favourite inside an extinct volcano.

Mindanao & Sulu

Check the latest travel advisories for central Mindanao when planning your trip.

Samal Island (p374) The area around Davao, particularly Samal Island, has been a popular dive destination for decades. Ligid Caves is the most famous site around Samal.

General Santos (p371) Home to a couple of dive centres and an extremely impressive drop-off that stretches for over 10km along the coastline. Sarangani Bay features Gutsy's Reef, a deep reef dive where you can spot white-tip sharks, giant trevally and schools of surgeon fish.

Camiguin (p350) Off the central north coast of Mindanao, Camiguin bears reminders of its volcanic origins and more recent tectonic events at dive sites such as Jigdup Reef, a sea mount that rises from the deep sea floor to the surface. Mantigue Island (p350) offers stunning visibility and turtles galore on its vibrant reef.

Siargao (p359) It's better known for surfing but Blue Cathedral is a good dive site, while Shark Point attracts large pelagic life.

Palawan

The long finger of Palawan points to some great diving, whichever way you look at it.

Coron Bay (p406) Off Busuanga Island in the north, with its sunken Japanese WWII fleet, this bay is a must-see for wreck-diving enthusiasts. Aside from wreck diving, Busuanga has some outstanding coral reefs that often get overlooked in all the excitement, as well as a unique dive in an inland lake on Coron Island.

Bacuit Archipelago (p403) Known more for what's above water than what's below, although there are a smattering of good dive sites around El Nido (p397).

Port Barton (p390) Decent reef, wall and wreck diving, island-hopping and a couple of operators.

Puerto Princesa (p379) & **Tubbataha Reefs Natural Park** (p380) Puerto Princesa has a few dive sites in Honda Bay, but is chiefly known as the jumping-off point for live-aboards visiting the remote Tubbataha Reefs.

Other Resources

➡ *Coral Reef Fishes: Indo-Pacific and Caribbean* (Ewald Lieske and Robert Myers) – a useful guide to Philippines' reef fish

➡ www.divephil.com – all things Philippines-dive-related

➡ www.coronwrecks.com – Coron wreck dives

➡ www.divescover.com – dive operators and dive site descriptions

➡ www.scubaboard.com – global scuba forum

➡ www.tubbatahareef.org – the Philippines' remotest dive site

➡ Green Fins (www.greenfins.net) – a conservation initiative

Plan Your Trip

Outdoor Activities

The Philippines isn't just about finding an isolated beach and getting catatonic. From taming volcanoes and catching barrels on Cloud Nine to navigating cave systems in Samar, the Philippines can capably raise any adrenalin junkie's pulse.

Mountain Climbing

Forming part of the Pacific Ring of Fire, the Philippines has scores of mountains over 2000m, many of them active or extinct volcanoes. Some of these volcanoes are more active than others (a thrilling prospect for many visitors), most notably the smoking Mt Mayon, so get in touch with local authorities before setting out. You'll need to register and obtain permits for the most popular climbs. See the wonderful website www.pinoymountaineer. com for comprehensive profiles of dozens of climbs across the country.

Where to Go

Mt Mayon The country's most iconic and picture-postcard-perfect volcano, the conical-shaped Mt Mayon (p179; 2462m) is one of the Philippines' most active, and had been continuously erupting for several weeks when this edition went to press. If trails are open it's possible to climb part way up, either as a day trip or overnight hike.

Mt Pinatubo The serene, ice-blue crater lake of Mt Pinatubo (p112; 1450m) is the country's ultimate view. Reaching it involves a thrilling 4WD ride through a bizarre moonscape formed by one of the 20th century's most cataclysmic volcanic eruptions, followed by an easy 45-minute hike.

Mt Pulag Luzon's highest peak (p140; 2922m) is one of the country's most popular climbs, with several routes up of varying length and difficulty.

When to Go

August to October

This is peak surfing season on the eastern seaboard, as offshore typhoons bring monster swells to places such as Baler, Pagudpud, Daet, Samar and of course Siargao, the country's top surf spot with its legendary Cloud Nine break. Heavy *habagat* (southwest monsoon) rains in most of the country also make this a great time for whitewater rafting.

December to March

The *amihan* (northeast monsoon) kicks up stiff, steady breezes, delighting sailors and turning Boracay and Pagudpud into kiteboarding and windsurfing havens. There are some decent waves this time of year along the western seaboard.

April to May

Stable weather means this is a great time for trekking as well as sea kayaking, island-hopping or other ocean-based activities. However, this is also the hottest time so bring plenty of water on those treks. Keep in mind that many waterfalls dry up during this time.

Taal Volcano It takes just 45 minutes to scale this diminutive crater (p98) within Taal Lake – itself a crater of a much larger volcano. Don't take it too lightly though: it's a brutally hot climb and one of the country's most active volcanoes.

Mt Apo The Philippines' highest peak, Mt Apo (p373; 2954m) dominates the horizon in southern Mindanao, tempting climbers to set out from nearby Davao.

Mt Halcon More a mountaineering expedition than a hike, Mindoro's Mt Halcon (p204; 2582m) is arguably the most challenging big peak in the Philippines.

Mt Kanlaon One of the Philippines' most thrilling volcano grunts is up Mt Kanlaon (p251; 2435m), one of Philippines' largest active volcanoes, on Negros. The climb takes you through forests teeming with bird species and wildlife.

Caving & Spelunking

The islands of the Philippines are pock-marked by some of the largest cave systems in Asia. Definitely not for the claustrophobic, the best spelunking adventures involve a combination of swimming through underground rivers, squeezing throughcrevasses and scrambling over ledges. Levels range from easy drifts through underground rivers to advanced caving with ropes and full equipment.

Where to Go

Catbalogan Langun-Gobingob Caves (Samar) The most expansive cave system in the Philippines, including one chamber the size of three football fields. The caves are surrounded by jungle, underground rivers and scores of waterfalls, and can be explored on a tour (p338).

Puerto Princesa Subterranean River National Park (p386) A good option for those not wanting to scramble around or swim underground rivers. Paddle boats drift silently through one of the world's longest navigable, river-traversable tunnels near a pristine stretch of jungle-backed coastline.

Sagada The four-hour Cave Connection (p141) tour takes you through a labyrinth of passages connecting two major caves via underground rivers.

Tuguegarao Northeast Luzon is home to a vast network of caves near the provincial centre of Tuguegarao. Walk through the Callao Cave (p159),

with seven chambers of limestone formations, or tackle the 12.5km-long Odessa-Tumbali Cave (p159), suitable for more advanced cavers.

Tabon Caves Home to significant anthropological remains, this fascinating series of caves (p388) near Quezon in Southern Palawan occupies a stunning coastal promontory.

Hiking

The major Philippine islands boast mountainous interiors with forests, bird life and spectacular views. The rice terraces and mountains of North Luzon are most popular for trekking, but there are jungles and mountains to be explored across the Visayas, Mindoro and Mindanao.

Where to Go

North Luzon This region's Cordillera Mountains (p129) are easily the country's top trekking destination. You'll find dazzling rice terraces throughout Ifugao, Bontoc and Kalinga – hiking among them is one of Southeast Asia's top trekking experiences. You can hike to stunning waterfalls out of Batad, Hungduan, Sagada or Pagudpud, and there are 2500m+ peaks to tackle throughout the region.

Puerto Princesa The lush tropical jungles of central Palawan are ripe for exploration. Hook up with Pasyar Travel & Tours (p380) for multiday expeditions led by forest guardians, or explore the lush rainforests and peaks (p387) around the Underground River in Sabang.

Camiguin This Northern Mindanao island (p350) is an adventure playground riddled with volcanoes and hiking trails leading to hot springs and spectacular waterfalls.

Around Manila Trails around Subic Bay (p110) allow you to visit indigenous Aeta groups. Mt Arayat (p107) near Angeles is a fun climb, while south of Manila you'll find dozens of peaks, led by Mt Banahaw (p104).

Dumaguete The perfect base (p257) for conquering the twin peaks of Mt Talinis or exploring the waterfalls and forests of Twin Lakes National Park (p258).

Puerto Galera Follow indigenous Mangyan guides to hidden waterfalls (p194), or scale the local peaks for panoramic views of Puerto Galera's (p194) jaw-dropping coastline.

Top: Mt Mayon (p179)

Bottom: Kayaking in El Nido (p396)

ALENA OZEROVA/SHUTTERSTOCK ©

Surfing

Stick 7000 islands in the middle of the Pacific and some decent-sized swell is going to make landfall somewhere. The typhoon season in the Philippines occasionally sees giant waves lash the entire length of the eastern seaboard, while west-coast surf hotspot San Juan reigns supreme in the dry season.

Where to Go

Cloud Nine The name of this legendary right-hander says it all. Despite increasing in popularity of late – some locals dub it 'crowd nine' – Siargao's signature wave (p362) remains the country's most legendary break.

La Union San Juan (p119) is the best surf spot on North Luzon's more consistent and beginner-friendly west coast. Here three- to five-footers pelt the sandy beach from November to March.

Baler The point break made famous in *Apocalypse Now* ('Charlie don't surf') hasn't changed – it's still guarded by palm trees in idyllic Baler (p155) and it's still fickle. But when it's on, it's surfing bliss.

Bicol Majestic (p184) on Catanduanes is the top wave in a region known for adventure sports. Bagasbas (p168), Camarines Norte, is another laid-back surfer hang-out.

Calicoan Island, Samar Home to four reef breaks collectively known as ABCD (p341), with both excellent right and left breaks. Otherwise hit the unexplored east coastline of Samar on a surfin' safari.

Sea Kayaking

The Philippines – and in particular Palawan – is heaven for sea kayakers, with thousands of kilometres of pristine coastline to explore.

Where to Go

Busuanga & the Calamian Islands A world-class sea-kayaking destination, with plenty of established operators based in Coron Town (p407). Take

---

MORE RELAXING PURSUITS

There are plenty of ways to enjoy the great outdoors in the Philippines that don't involve risking life and limb climbing volcanoes, flinging yourself down rapids or wiping out in crashing surf.

Island-hopping Boarding a trusty bangka and tooling around from island to island is a quintessential Philippine experience. Island-hopping tours are ubiquitous in places such as Palawan. Elsewhere you'll have to negotiate with local fishermen to take you out on a private tour.

Birdwatching Home to around 600 species of birds, 200 of which are endemic, the Philippines is a great country for twitchers. There's abundant bird life across the islands, including a variety of species of hornbill, birds of prey and kingfisher. Northern Sierra Madre and Mt Kanlaon Natural Parks are great for birds. Birding Adventure Philippines (www.birdingphilippines.com) is a good source of information and runs multiday tours.

Fishing The Philippines' waters teem with sailfish, tuna, trevally, wahoo, mahi-mahi and other sportfish. Siargao is one of the few places where you'll find organised operators. Elsewhere you'll have to find fishermen to take you out in their bangkas.

Golf There are several world-class courses in the Philippines. Although many of them are private, you can usually talk your way onto them if you're keen. Some more memorable choices include Manila's Club Intramuros Golf Course (p64), within the old walled city (and it's floodlit at night for an evening hit); scenic Ponderosa (p197), cut into the mountains of Puerto Galera; or a laid-back round in Siargao.

Sailing For those who like to take it slow and stay (relatively) dry, sailing is a great option. You can arrange excursions on big boats out of the yacht clubs in Puerto Galera, Subic Bay or Manila. Or take a relaxing sunset cruise on a *paraw* (traditional outrigger) or a luxury catamaran on Boracay's White Beach.

ONLINE RESOURCES

Volcano activity www.phivolcs.dost.gov.ph

Birdwatching www.birdwatch.ph

Rock climbing www.climbphilippines.com

Surfing www.surfingphilippines.com; www.surfistatravels.com

Golf www.golfingphilippines.com

off for a few days to explore sheltered bays and camp on idyllic islands, stopping often to snorkel on beautiful coral reefs.

El Nido Paddle to Cadlao Island (p403) in the glorious Bacuit Archipelago (p403), or pop over to the east coast to explore the Linapacan group of islands offshore.

Caramoan Peninsula Southeast Luzon's answer to El Nido, here you can paddle (p172) amid brooding karst formations and into secluded bays.

Hundred Islands Kayak is the best way to explore the curious mushroom-shaped islands of this national park (p118) in North Luzon's Lingayen Gulf.

River Sports

The rugged interiors of larger islands – Luzon, Negros, Mindanao, Panay, Leyte and Samar – feed scores of rivers that seethe with white water during the wet season. If you have your own kayak and are into first descents, there are remote, virtually unexplored rivers all over the big islands, especially North Luzon and Mindanao. There are plenty of mellow rivers to explore by kayak or stand-up paddleboard (SUP) as well.

Where to Go

Sagada, North Luzon One of the Philippines' best white-water-rafting sites, where you can tear down the raging gazpacho of the Chico River out of Sagada (p141) or Tabuk (p149).

Cagayan de Oro Take advantage of year-round white water (p348) in Mindanao, on rapids ranging from technical to gentle.

Tibiao River Test these tamer rapids in Antique (p233), western Panay, with a day kayaking excursion (p215) out of Boracay.

Pagsanjan Though your *bancero* (boatmen) will be doing all the paddling on this canoe trip (p105), you'll get to kick back and enjoy the scenery where *Apocalypse Now* was filmed before encountering fun little rapids (best done around July and August when the river is full).

Davao River Fun Grade 3 white-water rapids that peak around around June, bringing plenty of thrills and spills (p367).

Loboc, Bohol Explore this jade-coloured tidal river (p318) by SUP or kayak in search of waterfalls and fireflies.

Kiteboarding, Windsurfing & Wakeboarding

Catching barrels isn't the only way to have fun on a board in the Philippines, which is home to a world-class kiteboarding scene along with other action-packed water sports, including wakeboarding and windsurfing.

Where to Go

Boracay With a shallow lagoon protected by an offshore reef, steady winds from December to March, and state-of-the-art equipment for hire, Boracay's Bulabog Beach (p214) is an ideal place to learn kiteboarding and windsurfing.

Pagudpud (p128) The country's stiffest winds and sizeable surf create incredible conditions for advanced kiteboarders and windsurfers along Luzon's north coast from November to April.

Daet, Camarines Norte On Bagasbas Beach (p168) you'll find excellent kiteboarding conditions from November to March, with winds of 15 to 20 knots, and quality operators offering equipment hire and instruction.

El Nido The east coast of El Nido is rapidly emerging as a top kiteboarding destination, centred around the barangays of San Fernando and Sibaltan (p397).

CamSur Watersports Complex *Wake* magazine calls the home of the 2008 World Wakeboarding Championships, near Naga in Bicol, the best cable wakeboarding park (p169) in the world.

Plan Your Trip

Eat & Drink Like a Local

Kain na tayo – 'let's eat'. It's the Filipino invitation to eat, and if you travel in the Philippines you will hear it over and over and over again. The phrase reveals two essential aspects of Filipino people: one, that they are hospitable, and two, that they love to, well, eat. A melange of Asian, Latin, American and indigenous cooking, Filipino culinary traditions – hybridised and evolving – reflect the country's unique colonial history and varied geography.

Best Reading

Books

➡ *Memories of Philippine Kitchens* (Amy Desa and Romy Dorotan)

➡ *The Coconut Cookery of Bicol* (Honesto C General)

➡ *Philippine Food & LIfe* (Gilda Cordero-Fernando)

➡ *The Food of the Philippines* (Reynaldo Alejandro)

Online Resources

➡ www.filipinorecipe.com

➡ www.asia-recipe.com/philippines

➡ www.myfilipinorecipes.com

➡ www.blog.junbelen.com

Fun Fact

The longest barbecue on record, measuring 8km and using 50,000kg of fish, was held in Pangasinan in April 2014.

Food Experiences

Filipinos are constantly eating. Three meals a day just isn't enough, so they've added two *meryenda*. The term literally means 'snack', but don't let that fool you – the afternoon *meryenda* can include something as filling as *bihon* (fried rice sticks) or *goto* (Filipino congee) plus *bibingka* (fluffy rice cakes topped with cheese).

Filipino food has a somewhat poor reputation in both the West, where Filipino restaurants are rare, and Asia, where the cuisine is considered unimaginative and unrefined. This perplexes Filipinos, who are convinced their home-cooked comfort food is the greatest thing in the world. In truth, indigenous (Pinoy) food is neither as bad as its international reputation, nor as delicious as locals would have you believe. Of course, it all depends on your tastebuds.

The usual complaints about Filipino food are that it's too heavy, too salty and – especially – too sweet. Sugar is added in abundance to everything, from the hamburgers at Jollibee to locally rendered Thai food. But if you know what to order, or know a good cook, you'll find delights aplenty to satisfy the most discriminating tastebuds.

Influences on Filipino food include American (burgers, fast food); Chinese (*pansit*, *lumpia*, anything soy-based, stir frying); Mexican (tamales); and Spanish (*bringhe*, a version of paella most closely associated with Pampanga; any dishes sautéd with garlic, tomatoes and onions, flans, sofritos, fiesta foods).

Meanwhile, a new generation of Filipino chefs, restaurateurs and organic farmers are creating their own networks of like-minded foodies.

Meals of a Lifetime

Antonio's (p100) Country's top restaurant is worth the slog out of Manila to Tagaytay.

Van Gogh is Bipolar (p82) Manila's quirkiest restaurant offers mood-enhancing creations.

Kalui (p383) Delicious set seafood meals in a colourful setting in Palawan's capital, Puerto Princesa.

Cafe by the Ruins Dua (p135) Exotic specialties of North Luzon's Cordillera region.

Lab-as Seafood Restaurant (p261) Delicious fish and lots more on tap at this lively Dumaguete culinary colony.

Angelina (p297) Italian food done right on a distant Visayan beach.

Cheap Treats

➡ The eclectic Filipino dessert *halo-halo* is appropriately translated as 'mix-mix'.

➡ *Camaro* (fried crickets cooked in salt, vinegar and soy sauce) eating contests are held in Pampanga, where the dish is traditionally served.

➡ Exotic tropical fruits such as durians, mangosteens, rambutans, jackfruit and longans are sold at fruit stalls and street markets.

➡ *Bulalo* is a rich beef and marrow soup, while *tawili* is a tiny lake fish (found only in Taal Lake); both are popular snacks in the Batangas region.

➡ *Sisig* – sizzling grilled bits of pig jowl – is a tasty favourite Filipino bar snack. *Bopis* – pig's lungs, chopped and fried – is similar.

Dare to Try

➡ *Balút* (or 'eggs with legs' as it's also known) is a boiled duck egg containing a partially formed embryo – one of the Philippines' more exotic snacks.

➡ In some provinces, locals will cook anything under the sun *adobo*-style – rat, cat, bat, frog, cricket and *bayawak* (monitor lizard).

➡ *Aso* or *asusena* (dog meat) is popular in the Cordillera Mountains of North Luzon (as is 'Soup No 5' or bull-ball soup).

➡ To work up the courage to consume these local delicacies, down a few shots of *lambanog* (roughly distilled palm wine).

Staples & Specialities

If there were a national dish, it would undoubtedly be *adobo* – pork, chicken or just about any meat stewed in vinegar and garlic. It's delicious done right, but can be awfully salty and greasy if done wrong. Other dishes you'll find with striking regularity include *sinigáng* (any meat or seafood boiled in a sour, tamarind-flavoured soup), *kare-kare* (oxtail and vegetables cooked in peanut sauce), crispy *pata* (deep-fried pork hock or knuckles) and *pansit* (stir-fried noodles). *Ihaw-ihaw* eateries, serving *inahaw* (grilled meat or fish), are everywhere. *Lechón* (suckling pig roasted on a spit) is de rigueur at Filipino celebrations. Common appetisers include *lumpia* (small spring rolls, usually vegetarian) and the truly delicious *kinilaw* (Filipino-style ceviche).

Then there's the ubiquitous Filipino breakfast – rice (preferably garlic rice) with a fried egg on top, with *tapa* (salty beef strips), *tocino* (honey-cured pork), *bangus* (milkfish) or *longganisa* (sausages) on the side. For dessert, try *halo-halo*, a glass packed with fruit preserves, sweetcorn, young coconut and various tropical delights topped with milky crushed ice, a dollop of crème caramel and a scoop of ice cream.

Regional Specialities

In a country of such cultural, ethnographic and geographic diversity, it's no surprise that there's an equally diverse array of regional specialties. And staples such as *longganisa*, *lechón* and even *balút* are rendered in different ways. Of the regional cuisines, the spicy food of Bicol is probably most amenable to Western palates, while Filipinos consider Pampanga province in central Luzon the country's food capital.

Bicol

Bicolano cooking involves many varieties of *sili* (hot chilli pepper) and *gata* (coconut milk); anything cooked in *gata* is known as *ginataán*. Perhaps most well known is

FIESTA FOOD

Each village, town and city in the Philippines has its own fiesta, usually celebrated on the feast day of its patron saint, as determined by the Catholic calendar. Historically every household was expected to prepare food and serve it to anybody who appeared at the door. Nowadays, food is still prepared but on a greatly diminished scale, and only people who have been invited show up at the buffet table. The fare on such occasions varies regionally, but generally consists of pork, beef and chicken dishes, sometimes with some fish and seafood thrown in.

Kaldereta (beef or sometimes goat-meat stew), *igado* (stir-fried pork liver), fried chicken and, of course, *lechón* are some of the dishes you can expect to find at a fiesta. Sweet rice cakes, usually local delicacies, are served as dessert. Birthdays and other private parties are usually celebrated with a big plate of *pansit*.

Bicol *exprés*, a spicy mishmash of ground pork, *sili*, baby shrimps, onion, garlic and other spices cooked in coconut milk. Look for vendors sellling *pinangat*: green *gabi* (taro) leaves wrapped around pieces of fish, shrimp and/or pork. Another Bicol favourite is *candingga*, diced pork liver and carrots sweetened and cooked in vinegar. With all of these dishes and other main courses, you can expect to find *natong* or *laing*, a chopped, leafy green vegetable commonly served on its own as a side dish. And finally in the dessert department, pili nut, an alleged aphrodisiac, is popping up in cookies, pastries, marzipan, pies and ice cream.

Ilocos

To some, Ilocano cooking is a vegetarian's paradise. Its version of *pinakbét* with eggplant, tomatoes, okra and *ampalaya* (bitter melon) – cooked in layers in a pot like a vegetable lasagne or terrine – is possibly the best-known in the country. Its specific version of fish paste is called *bagoong* and goat or pig bile is sometimes used to flavour dishes.

Batanes

If you make it to these islands in the far north, be sure to try the following: *uved* balls, a surprisingly tasty dish (given the ingredients) made with bananas, mixed with minced pork and pig's blood; and *vunes*, which looks like a brown mess, but is actually chopped-up taro stalks cooked with garlic.

Cordillera

A warning, rather than encouragement: they eat pretty much everything in the Cordillera. Unless of course you get excited at the idea of eating python, a bundle of frogs and dog meat.

Mindanao

Northern Mindanao, around Cagayan de Oro, is known for its *kinilaw*, which is spiced with *tabon tabon*, a fruit native to northern Mindanao. Local foodies claim their city's *lechón baboy* (roasted pig), stuffed with lemongrass and other herbs and spices, is the tastiest. *Adobo* in Zamboanga is made with cream coconut; and *bulad* (dried fish), while popular everywhere in the country, comes in an especially large amount of varieties in southern Mindanao.

Negro

Inasal – basically grilled or roasted chicken marinated in lemongrass, *anchiote* (a peppery spice), *calamansi* (a citrus fruit) and garlic – has become something of a national dish and is most associated with Bacolod.

Pampanga

Dishes are often sweet and cooked with fermented sugar, while shellfish is frequently fermented in rice sauce. *Pinaupong manok*, steamed chicken stuffed with vegetables, is a Pampanga specialty beloved throughout the country.

How to Eat & Drink
Habits & Customs

➡ An everyday meal in the Philippines is a fairly informal occasion, though it can take on the trappings of a formal Western-style dinner in the houses of the rich.

Top: Market stall in Manila

Bottom: *Halo-halo*, a Filipino dessert

STUART DEE/GETTY IMAGES ©

VEGETARIANS & VEGANS

If you're vegetarian or vegan, you'll have a hard time eating out in the meat-mad Philippines. It's hard to find soy-based products outside of big cities, where Chinese merchants and restaurants sell tofu, soy milk etc. Beans in general don't figure prominently on the menu in the Philippines, thus getting adequate protein can be tricky. If you feel this is going to be a problem, then it's wise to stock up on these products before leaving Manila or Cebu.

➡ Boiled rice is the centrepiece of any meal.

➡ All dishes are usually served family-style on large plates in the middle of the table.

➡ *Calamansi* juice mixed with soy sauce is a commonly offered condiment.

➡ Generally Filipinos eat with a fork and a spoon (the latter is meant to double as a knife) and napkins tend to be super-thin and small – many visitors find both a little hard to get used to.

➡ 'For a while': an expression used in all settings, but in restaurants could mean your food is minutes or hours away from being served.

➡ Menus, especially in informal restaurants and rural areas, are theoretical versions of what could be served at any one time. It's not unusual for a good number of items to be unavailable.

Where to Eat & Drink

Although Filipinos love to eat out, you rarely need to book ahead outside of the trendiest restaurants in Manila and maybe Cebu.

Turu-Turò The basic Filipino eatery (literally 'point point').

Restaurants Manila and bigger cities have scores of international and Filipino restaurants. The best are outside of the malls.

Cafes International and Filipino coffee-shop chains are becoming more common, serving coffee and light bites to white-collar Filipinos.

Food parks These are wildly popular in Manila and trending in the provinces.

Markets Abundant. Good for affordable self-catering and sometimes for sampling regional specialities.

Fast food All too common everywhere.

Pubs and bars Common in cities and beach resorts. In more rural areas, karaoke (KTV) bars may be the only source of nightlife.

Menu Decoder

Names of dishes often describe the way they are cooked, so it's worth remembering that *adobo* is stewed in vinegar and garlic, *sinigáng* is sour soup, *ginataán* means cooked in coconut milk, *kilawin* or *kinilaw* is raw or vinegared seafood, *pangat* includes tomatoes in a light broth, and *inahaw* is grilled meat or fish (*ihaw-ihaw* denotes eateries that specialise in grilled food). The word for 'spicy' is *maangháng*.

Drinks

Alcoholic Drinks

➡ San Miguel (around P30) holds a virtual monopoly on the local beer market, though imported brands are also available. Red Horse is an extra-strong beer (7%) by San Miguel.

➡ In Manila and some resort areas, craft-beer breweries are becoming fashionable.

➡ Palatable (and cheap) spirits such as Tanduay rum are produced domestically and available at convenience stores such as 7-Eleven.

➡ Rural concoctions include *basi*, a sweet, portlike wine made from sugar cane juice, and *tuba*, a strong palm wine extracted from coconut flowers.

Non-alcoholic Drinks

➡ Tap water quality varies wildly; to be safe, carry a water bottle and fill up on purified water at restaurants.

➡ Carbonated soft drinks are ubiquitous, as are fruit juices; *buko* juice, said to be good for staving off dehydration, is young coconut juice with bits of translucent coconut meat floating in it.

➡ Decent ground coffee and espresso can be found in Manila and resort areas but more common is the three-in-one instant sachet variety.

➡ The popular little local citrus known as *calamansi* or *kalamansi* is used to make a refreshing cordial or added to black tea.

Regions at a Glance

The Philippines consists of three main island groups: Luzon, the Visayas and Mindanao. Between them they offer something for everyone: megacity madness in Manila, hill tribes in North Luzon, indigenous village life in Mindanao, surfing along the eastern seaboard of the entire country, and good snorkelling practically everywhere. The Visayas most embody the defining image of the Philippines: a dreamy desert island festooned with palm trees and ringed by white sand. Palawan is a region apart, a fantastic otherworld of unspoiled rainforests and surreal seascapes.

Manila

History
Nightlife
Food

The steamy, seamy capital is a little in-your-face for many first-time visitors, but if you can get underneath its surface it's a mix of fascinating museums, raucous nightlife, varied cuisine and undeniable energy.

p48

Around Manila

Diving
History
Trekking

Names such as Corregidor and Bataan evoke WWII like nowhere else. For climbers there's a bevy of accessible peaks to choose from, while the south coast of Luzon has some of the country's best diving.

p95

North Luzon

Outdoors
Culture
History

This region is intimidating in its diversity, with secluded bays where the surf's almost always up, romantic Spanish colonial enclaves and mountains sliced by rice terraces, inhabited by a staggeringly diverse range of indigenous tribes.

p113

Southeast Luzon

Food
Outdoors
Festivals

After searing your tongue on the spicy cuisine of Bicol, cool down by taking advantage of numerous water sports, or heat things up more with a volcano trek or by dancing at one of the region's rambunctious fiestas.

p165

Mindoro

Diving
Cultural Minorities
Remote Places

Diving or snorkelling at Apo Reef can't be beat, while Puerto Galera adds a party element to your diving experience. Elsewhere you can visit lost islands offshore and lost tribes in the impenetrable hinterlands.

p192

Boracay & Western Visayas

Beaches
Diving
Nightlife

Boracay is an intoxicating and fun draw with a world-class beach, but other destinations beckon: easygoing Siquijor and Sugar Beach; dive mecca Negros; happening Cebu; and vibrant Iloilo and Silay with their historic colonial-era mansions.

p211

Cebu & Eastern Visayas

Diving
Beaches
Wildlife

Cebu is the gateway to diving and beaches galore plus jungle adventures. Bohol has riparian pleasures and a little bit of everything else, while the forests and caves of Samar and Leyte are ripe for off-the-beaten-track exploration.

p277

Mindanao

Hiking
Water Sports
Culture

The southernmost island, blessed with rugged mountains, palm-lined beaches and a tapestry of distinctive cultures and cuisines, runs the gamut from cosmopolitan Davao to laid-back cool surf spot Siargao.

p342

Palawan

Beaches
Island-Hopping
Adventures

From exclusive private island retreats to simple beachfront bungalows, Palawan has it all. Get in the water to explore coral reefs and WWII shipwrecks, or trek through pristine jungle to reach waterfalls or isolated settlements.

p377

On the Road

North
Luzon
p113

Manila ⭐ Around Manila p95
p48

Southeast
Luzon
p165

Mindoro
p192

Boracay &
Western
Visayas
p211

Cebu &
Eastern
Visayas
p277

Palawan
p377

Mindanao
p342

Manila

🔗 02 / POP 12.95 MILLION

Best Places to Eat

➡ Sala (p79)

➡ Van Gogh is Bipolar (p82)

➡ El Chupacabra (p78)

➡ Locavore (p82)

➡ Corner Tree Cafe (p78)

Best Places to Stay

➡ Manila Hotel (p66)

➡ Henry Hotel (p70)

➡ Red Carabao (p70)

➡ Element Boutique Hotel (p70)

➡ Hive Hotel (p73)

Why Go?

Manila's moniker, the 'Pearl of the Orient', couldn't be more apt – its unappealing shell reveals its jewel only to those resolute enough to pry. No stranger to hardship, the city has endured every disaster humans and nature could throw at it, and yet today the chaotic metropolis thrives as a true Asian megacity. Skyscrapers pierce the hazy sky, mushrooming from the grinding poverty of expansive shanty towns, while gleaming malls foreshadow Manila's brave new air-conditioned world. The congested roads snarl with traffic, but, like the overworked arteries of a sweating giant, they are what keeps this modern metropolis alive.

As well as outstanding sightseeing, visitors who put in the effort will discover its creative soul – from edgy galleries to a lively indie music scene. Combine this with a penchant for speakeasy bars, artisan markets and single-origin coffees, and it's clear to see that Manila is not only one of Asia's most underrated cities, but one of its coolest.

When to Go
Manila

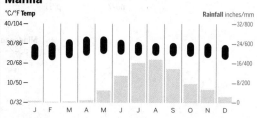

Dec–Feb
The coolest, most pleasant months.

Mar–Apr
Holy Week is no time for packed beach resorts, so spend it in Manila.

Jul–Aug
Some say it rains too much; we say it's the best time to escape the searing sun.

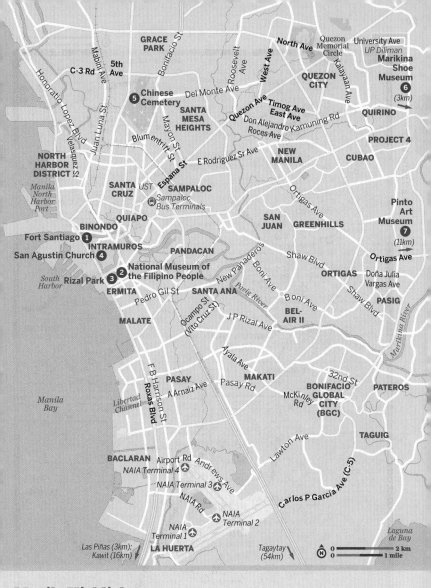

Manila Highlights

1 **Fort Santiago** (p53)
Hearing echoes of a lost past at this centuries-old Spanish fort.

2 **National Museum of the Filipino People** (p56) Getting a glimpse into the Filipino soul.

3 **Rizal Park** (p55) Taking the capital's pulse and enjoying free concerts.

4 **San Agustin Church** (p53) Admiring Manila's oldest church, a visual delight.

5 **Chinese Cemetery** (p57) Exploring eerie ghost-town-like streets and elaborate mausoleums.

6 **Marikina Shoe Museum** (p62) Gawking at Imelda Marcos' shoes – some 800 pairs of them.

7 **Pinto Art Museum** (p65) Being enticed by lush gardens, splendid views and unique art.

Greater Manila

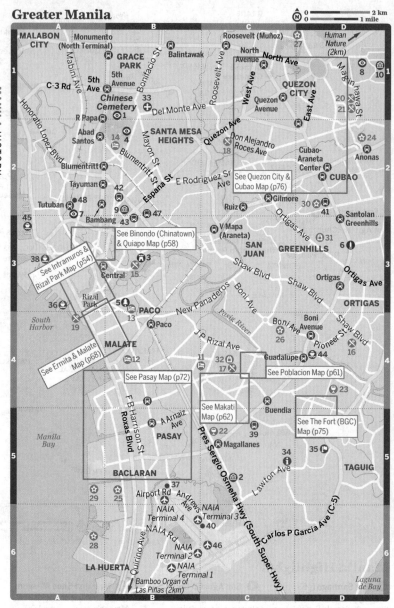

History

Manila was colonised by the Spaniard Miguel López de Legazpi in 1571 and blossomed into the jewel of Spain's empire in the Pacific. Its broad sweep of fertile lands made it more attractive than Cebu, which had been the capital.

King Philip II of Spain conferred on the city the illustrious title *Isigne y Siempre Leal Ciudad* (Distinguished and Ever Loyal City), but it continued to be called by its pre-

Greater Manila

Hispanic name of Maynilad (presumed to be from *may,* meaning 'there is', and *nilad,* a mangrove plant that grew in abundance on the banks of the Pasig River), which was later corrupted to Manila.

From the 19th century, it could be argued that Manila was something approaching a Paris of Asia. The 19th-century traveller Fedor Jagor described Manila as a splendid, fortified city of wide cobbled streets and regal town houses. It was a thriving trading centre and its multicultural mix provided a good entry point into China and other Asian countries.

In 1905 Daniel Burnham, the master planner of Chicago, was hired to produce a master plan for Manila. His grand vision included Roxas Blvd, which even today, under its somewhat shabby patina, echoes Lake Shore Dr in Chicago. The streets were lined with grand structures, many reflecting the best of art-deco design.

WWII changed everything. Many claim the city has never recovered. Rebuilding after the war was sporadic, and the city was never able to reclaim either its regional importance or its sense of self. Many locals complain about the scattered character of Manila; it's true that the various cities within the city feel disunified and there is no sense of a whole.

ℹ Orientation

Metro Manila is composed of 16 cities. From a tourist perspective, the important ones are the City of Manila ('downtown'), Pasay, Makati and Quezon City.

Gritty downtown Manila includes the touristy districts of Malate, Ermita, Intramuros, Quiapo and Binondo (Chinatown). Bordering downtown

Manila to the south is Pasay, a cultural precinct of sorts as well as a bus-station hub. The airport straddles Pasay and Parañaque.

Business hub Makati and its neighbour, Bonifacio Global City (universally known as 'BGC' or 'The Fort'), are cleaner, more organised and generally regarded as safer. A large chunk of Manila's expat community lives in Makati and The Fort, and the best restaurants and nightlife also tend to be in these two districts.

Well north of Makati is pleasant, youthful Quezon City, Metro Manila's most populous city with almost three million residents. 'QC' is a magnet foodies, barflies and live-music hounds.

As a tourist, you're best off tackling Manila one city at a time, otherwise you'll spend all your time in traffic. A city-by-city approach also allows you to get a better feel for the greater Manila metropolis, which really is a sum of its parts.

⊙ Sights

For a city that's not known as a major tourist draw, Manila sure has a lot to see. Because of its hugeness and its traffic you'll likely never see all of it – the best strategy is to explore one neighbourhood at a time. If you're short on time, focus on the downtown area. This is Metro Manila's epicentre, and also where the majority of the sights are. Of course what's best to see isn't always a traditional sight, rather it lies in the life of Metro Manila's varied barangays (neighbourhoods) – more than 1500 of them!

⊙ Intramuros

When Miguel López de Legazpi wrested control of Manila, he chose to erect his fortress on the remnants of the Islamic settlement by the mouth of the Pasig River. The walled city of Intramuros, as it came to be called, was invaded by Chinese pirates, threatened by Dutch forces, and held by the British, Americans and Japanese at various times, yet it survived until the closing days of WWII, when it was finally destroyed during the Battle of Manila – with all structures other than the San Agustin Church flattened.

From its founding in 1571, Intramuros was the exclusive preserve of the Spanish ruling classes. Fortified with bastions, the wall enclosed an area of some 64 hectares. Gates with drawbridges provided access to and from the outside world. Within the walls were imposing government buildings, stately homes, churches, convents, monasteries, schools, hospitals and cobbled plazas. The native populace was settled in surrounding areas such as Paco and Binondo, while the Chinese were kept under permanent supervision in ghettos called *parian*.

One can still feel a strong sense of history on a visit to Intramuros. Reconstruction began in 1951 to faithfully restore Intramuros' colonial architecture to its pre-war appearance and turn it into the tourist sight it is today. The residential areas within the walls have a friendly feel and provide a nice change

---

MANILA IN...

Two Days

Start with a tour (p65) of Intramuros followed by lunch. Take in Rizal Park (p55) and the National Museum of the Filipino People (p56). Head to Roxas Blvd (p59) for a sunset over Manila Bay, and dine and drink in Malate (p74).

On your second morning, head over the Pasig River to tour Binondo and Quiapo (p57). Start at Escolta St (p59) then wander around Chinatown (p74) and have lunch. Catch the LRT to the Chinese Cemetery (p57) and/or North Cemetery (p57). End the day with sunset drinks followed by dinner at the Sofitel Philippine Plaza (p70) or one of many rooftop bars (p85) around town.

Four Days

Base yourself in Makati if you're not already there. In the morning take in the engaging Ayala Museum (p60) then browse the upscale malls of the Ayala Center (p89) and have lunch. Have a massage (p64) then spend the evening in the gleaming Fort (p85) area (aka BGC).

On your final day, choose between a five-star brunch at the Sofitel Philippine Plaza (p70) and a short excursion out of town – the Marikina Shoe Museum (p62) and Pinto Art Museum (p65) are good options. By night, enjoy a fine meal then whoop it up in Makati's up-and-coming Poblacion district.

THE PRESIDENT'S RESIDENCE

Perched overlooking the Pasig River, **Malacañang Palace** (Map p50; ☑ 02-784 4286; malacanangmuseum@gmail.com; JP Laurel Sr St, San Miguel; ⊙ tours at 9am, 10am, 1pm & 2pm Mon-Fri) `FREE` dates to the mid-18th century, when it was built as the residence of a Spanish aristocrat before becoming the office of the Spanish and, later, American governors-general. It has been the official residence of the Philippine president since 1935.

Only the Museo ng Malacañang is open to tourists, and it's highly recommended for anyone who's interested in both political history and colonial architecture. To visit you'll need to book five business days in advance – which can be done by simply emailing the museum with your contact number, how many people are in your party and attached photocopies of all passports. Otherwise book a tour through Old Manila Walks (p65), which can arrange everything and combine a palace visit with an excellent walking tour of the area.

of pace from other parts of Manila. Anda St is a good street for a wander; many of the buildings still have Spanish–tile street names.

Most of Intramuros' walls, gates and bulwarks are accessible, and you can walk along the top of the ramparts for all or part of their approximately 4.5km length, with several places to ascend and descend.

Start your walking tour at the **Intramuros Visitors Center** (Map p54; ☑ 02-527 2961; ⊙ 8am-6pm) 🖉 inside the gate to Fort Santiago. They have an excellent free guided map of the walled city available on request. Next door is a cinema in a bomb-shelter cellar that screens a short film on the history of the area.

Kalesa (traditional horse-drawn carriages) are still used for transport in the area and provide an atmospheric way of getting around. They charge a fixed rate of P350 per carriage (good for four) for 30 minutes, or P500 per head for a 1½ hour tour.

★ Fort Santiago   FORT

(Map p54; Santa Clara St; adult/student P75/50; ⊙ 8am-9pm) Guarding the entrance to the Pasig River is Intramuros' premier tourist attraction: Fort Santiago. Within the fort grounds is an oasis of lovely manicured gardens, plazas and fountains leading to an arched gate and a pretty lily pond. Within is the beautifully presented Rizal Shrine (p56) museum, the building where Dr José Rizal – the Philippines' national hero – was incarcerated as he awaited execution in 1896. It contains various fascinating displays of Rizal memorabilia and a re-creation of his cell and the courtroom trial.

At the far end of the fort are outlooks over an industrial section of the Pasig River leading to **Baluarte de Santa Barbara**, a restored 18th-century Spanish military barracks where hundreds of Filipino and American POWs were killed in WWII; it's now the **Rizaliana Furniture Hall** (Map p54; P10), displaying Rizal's family furniture. Also of interest are various dungeon cell blocks, including one that Rizal spent his last night in. Brass footprints set into the pavement mark his final steps to the execution spot in Rizal Park (p56).

★ San Agustin Church   CHURCH

(Map p54; ☑ 02-527 4060; General Luna St) The San Agustin Church was the only building left intact after the destruction of Intramuros in WWII. Built between 1587 and 1606, it is the oldest church in the Philippines. The massive facade conceals an ornate interior filled with objects of great historical and cultural merit. Note the trompe l'oeil frescos on the vaulted ceiling. Be sure to check out the tropical cloisters as well as the slightly shabby gardens out the back.

The present structure is actually the third to stand on the site and has weathered seven major earthquakes, as well as the Battle of Manila. It's an active church and much in demand for weddings and other ceremonies.

You can access the church through the newly renovated **San Agustin Museum** (Map p54; adult/student P200/160; ⊙ 8am-noon & 1-6pm), a treasure house of antiquities that give the visitor tantalising glimpses of the fabled riches of Old Manila. Check out the vaguely Chinese–looking Immaculate Conception statue in ethereal ivory.

★ Casa Manila   MUSEUM

(Map p54; ☑ 02-527 4084; Plaza Luis Complex, General Luna St; adult/student P75/50; ⊙ 9am-6pm Tue-Sun) This beautiful reproduction of a Spanish colonial house offers a window into the opulent lifestyle of the gentry in the 19th century. Imelda Marcos had it built to

Intramuros & Rizal Park

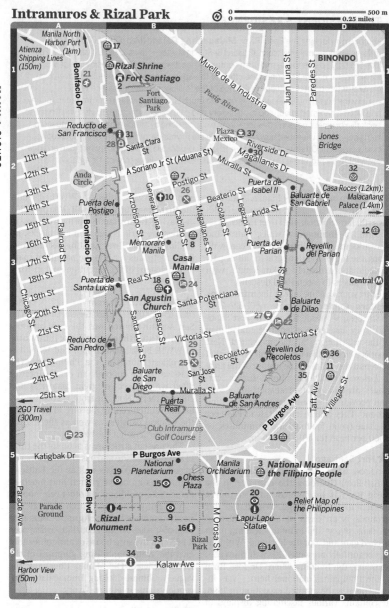

showcase the architecture and interior design of the late Spanish period, with lavish features throughout and some interesting items such as a double-seated toilet. The house may not be authentic but the stunning antique furniture and artwork are.

Manila Cathedral   CHURCH
(Map p54; cnr Postigo & General Luna Sts) First built in 1581 (and rebuilt seven times since, most recently in 1951 following its destruction in WWII), Manila Cathedral's present edifice looks suitably ancient with

Intramuros & Rizal Park

MANILA SIGHTS

its weathered Romanesque facade and graceful cupola. Inside are a gilded altar, a 4500-pipe organ and rosette windows with beautiful stained glass. Friezes on its bronze door depict the string of tragic events that led to the cathedral's destruction. The cathedral fronts Plaza de Roma, which was a blood-soaked bullring until it was converted into a plaza.

Ayuntamiento MUSEUM
(Old City Hall; Map p54; ☎02-524 7007; Plaza de Roma; P50; ⊙1hr tours at 11am & 4pm Tue & Fri) Once the grandest building in all of Intramuros, the Ayuntamiento was destroyed in WWII and spent years as a parking lot before a faithful re-creation of the original structure rose in 2010. Today it houses the country's Treasury Bureau, but its most impressive rooms – the Marble Hall and the Sala de Sessiones, where both the Spanish and American colonial governments held court – can be visited on a tour. No shorts, tank tops, miniskirts or flip-flops. Bring a valid ID.

Bahay Tsinoy MUSEUM
(Map p54; ☎02-527 6083; www.bahaytsinoy.org; cnr Anda & Cabildo Sts; adult/student P100/60; ⊙1-5pm Tue-Sun) The vast Bahay Tsinoy museum showcases the important role played by the *sangley*, as the Spanish called the Chinese, in the growth of Manila (*sangley* means 'itinerant merchant' in the locally prevailing Hokkien dialect). There are lifelike dioramas depicting Chinese and mestizo (mixed Spanish Filipino) life in the *parian* (Chinese ghettos), old coins and porcelain, and an excellent collection of photos.

◎ Rizal Park & Around

Still widely known as 'Luneta' (its name until it was officially changed in the 1950s), Manila's central Rizal Park (Map p54) is spread out over some 60 hectares of open lawns, ornamental gardens, ponds, paved walks and wooded areas, dotted with monuments to a whole pantheon of Filipino heroes. It's an atmospheric place to take a stroll, particularly late afternoon, early evening and on weekends. As the place where José Rizal was executed by the Spanish colonial authorities, it's also of great historical significance.

Here you'll find the **Rizal Monument**, fronted by a 46m flagpole and guarded by sentries in full regalia, which contains the hero's mortal remains and stands as a symbol of Filipino nationhood.

To one side of the monument you will find the **Site of Rizal's Execution** (Map p54; admission incl tour P20; ☉ 8am-5pm Wed-Sun); at the entrance is a granite wall inscribed with Rizal's 'Mi Ultimo Adios' (My Last Farewell). Eight tableaux of life-size bronze statues recreate the dramatic last moments of the hero's life. Evening light-and-sound presentations dedicated to Rizal usually take place here but are suspended indefinitely. When happening, they last 30 minutes and run every evening in both English and Tagalog.

In the middle of the park is the **Central Lagoon** (Map p54), a pool lined with busts of Filipino heroes and martyrs, and a dancing musical fountain that erupts in colourful explosions in the evening. Just north of the lagoon is the **open-air auditorium** (Map p54), where the long-running (and free) classical Concert at the Park kicks off at 6pm on Sun-

days. There's a free Filipino rock concert here at the same time every Saturday night.

The **visitors centre** (Map p54; ☉ 8am-5pm) at the park's Kalaw Ave entrance has a good map detailing the park's attractions and info on upcoming concerts and events.

★ **National Museum of the Filipino People**   MUSEUM
(Map p54; www.nationalmuseum.gov.ph; T Valencia Circle, Rizal Park; ☉ 10am-5pm Tue-Sun) **FREE** Within a resplendent neoclassical building, this superb museum houses a vast and varied collection, including the skullcap of the Philippines' earliest known inhabitant, Tabon Man (said by some to actually be a woman), who lived around 24,000 BCE. A large section of the museum is devoted to the wreck of the *San Diego*, a Spanish galleon that sank off the coast of Luzon in 1600, with salvaged items such as shell-encrusted swords, coins, porcelain plates and jewellery on display.

Other treasures include a large collection of pre-Hispanic artefacts and musical instruments, and displays on indigenous textiles.

National Museum of Fine Arts   MUSEUM
(Map p54; Padre Burgos Ave, Ermita; ☉ 10am-5pm Tue-Sun) **FREE** This proud museum contains many of the Philippines' signature works

---

JOSÉ RIZAL: THE MAN, THE MYTH, THE LEGEND

Despite living to only 35 years of age, Dr José Rizal (1861–96) – one of the Philippines' most revered figures – managed to pack a whole lot into his extraordinary life. The genius of the man is showcased at the modern **Rizal Shrine** (Map p54; Fort Santiago; adult/student P75/50; ☉ 9am-6pm Tue-Sun, 1-5pm Mon) inside Fort Santiago (p53), Intramuros. At this museum you'll learn that beyond being credited as the man responsible for forging the national identity of the Filipino people, in his short life he managed to speak 22 languages, found a political movement (La Liga Filipina), write two novels (most notably *Noli Me Tángere*; he was also an accomplished poet and essayist), become a doctor in ophthalmology, and gain recognition as an acclaimed artist (painter, sculptor and cartoonist cited as 'the father of Filipino comics'); he was also a world traveller and a fencing and martial-arts enthusiast. And if that's not enough, during his time in exile in Dapitan, in between discovering two species of frog and lizard (both named after him), he also won the lottery!

However it was only in death that Rizal *really* started to add to his extraordinary CV. Not only did his execution by firing squad in 1896 immortalise him as a martyr, elevating him to the status of national hero, it allowed him to add 'deity' to his list of achievements – dozens of cults known as Rizalistas in the Mt Banahaw area still worship him today as anything from the reincarnation of Christ to the messiah himself.

While detractors like to point out that his position as national hero was one bestowed upon him by American colonialists (who wanted the Filipino people to revere someone who preached non-violence), or that he was an aristocrat who spent more time abroad than in the Philippines (and was more fluent in Spanish than Tagalog) and had very little in common with the average Filipino, or that he was a womaniser – there's not much dirt on the man to take away from the greatness that is José Rizal.

of art, including Juan Luna's seminal *Spoliarium,* a colossal painting that provides harsh commentary on Spanish rule. It's in the old Congress building designed by Daniel Burnham.

National Museum of
Natural History   MUSEUM
(Map p54; www.nationalmuseum.gov.ph; Kalaw Ave, Rizal Park) FREE The natural history museum occupies the neoclassical heritage-listed sister building of the National Museum of the Filipino People. It features exhibits of taxidermy and Filipino artefacts.

Metropolitan Theater   HISTORIC BUILDING
(Map p54; Antonio Villegas St, Ermita) This stunning piece of art deco opened as the city's premier opera theatre under the Americans in 1931.

Manila City Hall   HISTORIC BUILDING
(Map p54; Padre Burgos Ave, Ermita) Looming east of Intramuros, the neoclassical city hall building is distinguished by an attractive clock tower that is beautifully illuminated at night. It was built in 1939–41, destroyed in the war, and rebuilt in 1946.

Binondo (Chinatown), Quiapo & Around

After centuries of suppression by the Spanish, Manila's Chinese population quickly rose on the economic and social ladder under more liberal administrations. Today the centre of the vibrant Chinese community is Chinatown, demarcated by the Arch of Goodwill (Map p58) and the Filipino–Chinese Friendship Arch (Map p58; Paredes St). The main street is Ongpin St, which straddles Binondo and Sta Cruz. It's lined with teahouses, goldsmiths, herbalists and shops selling moon cakes, incense, paper money to burn for ancestors and other curios.

These are some of the oldest parts of Manila, but sadly the few pieces of Spanish colonial architecture remaining are being rapidly torn down. Still, it remains the centre for trading, and there are numerous markets, especially in Quiapo.

★ Chinese Cemetery   CEMETERY
(Map p50; Rizal Ave Extension, Santa Cruz; 7.30am-7pm) FREE As in life, so it is in death for Manila's wealthy Chinese citizens, who are buried with every modern convenience in the huge Chinese Cemetery. It's far

from an ordinary cemetery and instead feels like a residential suburb with streets lined with mausoleums – some of which feature crystal chandeliers, air-con, hot and cold running water, kitchens and flushing toilets.

Hire a bicycle (per hour P100) to get around the sprawling grounds and consider hiring a guide for access to the best tombs. Tour guide Ivan Man Dy of Old Manila Walks (p65) does an excellent Chinese Cemetery tour.

Bahay Nakpil-Bautista   HISTORIC BUILDING
(Map p58; www.bahaynakpil.org; 432 A Bautista St, Quiapo; P80; 9.30am-4.30pm Tue, Thu & Sat) Built in 1914, this beautiful ancestral home is the former residence of Perona Nakpil, the widow of Andrés Bonifacio (father of the Philippine Revolution); she lived here after his death. As well as an insight into the grandeur of pre-war Manila, the museum provides a history of the Ilustrados and Katipunan – the anti–Spanish revolutionist movement.

North Cemetery   CEMETERY
(Map p50; Santa Cruz; tour guides approx P300) If you thought Manila's Chinese Cemetery was different, you clearly haven't made it to its abutting North Cemetery. While significant for being the burial place of many notable Filipinos, including numerous presidents and revolutionaries, it's on tourists' radars more as a place to observe the unique living arrangements of a community of some 6000 people who live here among the dead. It's a unique set-up, with many mausoleums doubling as houses, small shops and game arcades for kids.

Given the community is extremely impoverished, it's essential to come along with a guide who knows the area, either arranged through nearby Red Carabao (p70) hostel, Smokey Tours (p65) or at the cemetery entrance (though with the latter you're not guaranteed an English speaker).

Quiapo Church   CHURCH
(Map p58; Quezon Blvd, Quiapo) Quiapo Church is a 1933 replacement of an older structure destroyed by fire. One of Manila's best-known landmarks, Quiapo is the home of the Black Nazarene, an image of Christ believed to be miraculous. The life-size statue, carved from ebony, was first brought to Quiapo in 1767. Twice a year the revered image is carried on the shoulders of thousands of devotees in one of Manila's biggest religious festivals, the Black Nazarene Procession (p65).

Binondo (Chinatown) & Quiapo

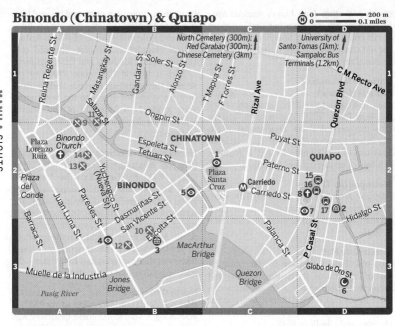

Binondo (Chinatown) & Quiapo

UST Museum   MUSEUM
(Map p50; http://ustmuseum.ust.edu.ph; Espana
Blvd, Sampaloc; P50; ◷1-5pm Mon, 8.30am-5pm
Tue-Fri) Housed in the superb American–era
main building of the University of Santo
Tomas, this museum lays claims to being
the oldest in Asia (the university's original
campus dates to 1611). The highlight is the
wonderful visual arts collection featuring
Filipino masters. Otherwise it's a mix of taxidermy, coins, textiles and religious artefacts.
The building also has a grim link to WWII,
having served as an internment camp that
held thousands of Allied soldiers for three
years under Japanese occupation.

Golden Mosque   MOSQUE
(Map p58; Globo de Oro St, Quiapo) The Golden
Mosque was constructed in 1976 as some-
thing of a welcoming gift for the late Libyan

leader Muammar al-Gaddafi, although his scheduled visit never happened. This is still the city's largest mosque and today it serves the growing Muslim community that has settled by the thousands in Quiapo.

Ermita & Malate

Baywalk STREET
(Map p68) Splendid sunset views of Manila Bay can be had from the pedestrian Baywalk that runs along Roxas Blvd. There's plenty of local colour here as well, although the vendors and food kiosks come and go.

1335Mabini GALLERY
(Map p68; ☎02-254 8498; www.1335mabini. com; 1335 Mabini St, Ermita; ☺2-6pm Tue-Sat, by appointment Sun) This gallery in the colonial Casa Tesoro mansion features changing shows of experimental art and installations in its 2nd-floor gallery. Other galleries and the beautiful antique shop Maria Closa (p88) also share the building, making it something of a hub for art and culture in Malate.

Malate Church CHURCH
(Map p68; cnr MH del Pilar & Remedios Sts, Malate) This attractive baroque-style church, built in 1588, is looking in fine fettle after an overhaul. This version of the church dates from the 1860s.

A greatly revered image of the Virgin Mary, called *Nuestra Señora de Remedios* (Our Lady of Remedies), is sited here.

ESCOLTA REVIVAL

In Manila's swinging pre–WWII years, Escolta St in Binondo was the capital's glamour strip, lined with beautiful buildings that housed upmarket department stores, cafes and theatres. Many of those buildings survived the war, but despite that Escolta's star faded and the area became downtrodden.

Today a group of artists and preservationists are gradually reviving Escolta. The area remains gritty, but galleries, cafes and creative spaces are bringing life back to the area, while a brace of museums celebrates the streets' fabled history, giving tourists a reason to visit.

The pre–WWII architecture is also a draw, given that the rest of Manila was mostly flattened. You'll find art-deco, beaux-arts and neoclassical design in the mix, along with some fine examples of 1950s and '60s modernism.

The best time to visit Escolta is during the quarterly **Block Party**, an artists' street fair with plenty of food, music and dancing thrown into the mix. It kicks off on a Saturday afternoon and lasts well into the evening. Check the Facebook page of **Escolta Block** (www.escoltablock.com) for the schedule.

The block party and much of Escolta's resurgence is the work of **98B COLLAboratory** (www.98-b.org), a cooperative of artists, writers and film makers that have set up shop in the 1920s, art-deco **First United Building** (Map p58). It established the **HUB Make Lab** (p88) in the same building, and hosts events, art exhibitions and talks in various spaces along Escolta St.

For a quick walking tour of Escolta, cross the Jones Bridge over the Pasig River and look for the spaceshiplike Commercial Bank & Trust Company Building (1969) at the corner of Nueva St (it's now a BPI bank branch). Walking northeast along Escolta St, you'll pass the wonderful art-deco Capitol Theatre (corner Yugchenko St), with the beaux-arts Calvo Building (1938) and **Calvo Museum** (Map p58; 2nd fl Calvo Bldg, 266 Escolta St; P50; ☺9am-5pm Mon-Fri, to 1pm Sat) roughly opposite. The museum houses a treasure trove of pre–WWII photographs and memorabilia.

Pop in for an ice cream at **Escolta Ice Cream & Snacks** (Map p58; 275 Escolta St; mains P100-150, ice cream scoops P30; ☺8.30am-8pm; ❄), then continue past the 1920s Burke Building (corner Burke St) to the First United Building – the epicentre of Escolta's resurgence with the HUB, **Den coffee shop** (Map p58; First United Bldg; dishes P175-250; ☺11am-9pm Tue-Sat; ❄ 🛜), **Fred's Revolucion bar** (Map p58; ☺1pm-midnight Mon-Sat), and the tiny **First United Community Museum** (Map p58; Escolta St; P50; ☺8am-6pm). Just east of here, roughly opposite Sta Cruz Church, is Escolta's most elaborate architectural jewel, the neoclassical Don Ramon Santos Building (Plaza Sta Cruz). It was built in 1894, expanded in 1937, and currently houses another BPI branch.

Pasay & Around

★ Metropolitan Museum of Manila
GALLERY

(Map p72; ✆02-523 7855; www.metmuseum.ph; Roxas Blvd, Bangko Sentral ng Pilipinas, Central Bank, Pasay; P100; ⊗10am-5.30pm Mon-Sat, gold exhibit to 4.30pm) The 'Met' is a world-class gallery tracing the evolution of Filipino art from the early 20th century to the present. Virtually all great Filipino painters from the last century are represented, while the selection of contemporary and experimental art is second to none in the Philippines. The ground floor has rotating exhibitions, while the wide-ranging permanent collection is on the 2nd floor. Guided tours (P500) can be booked ahead.

Cultural Center of the Philippines
HISTORIC BUILDING

(Tanghalang Pambansa; Map p72; www.cultural center.gov.ph; CCP Complex, Roxas Blvd, Pasay; galleries free, museums adult/student P30/20; ⊗gallery & museums 10am-6pm Tue-Sun) FREE The centrepiece of the CCP Complex is this bombastic building designed by noted Filipino architect Leandro Locsin. Inside attractions include the country's top performing arts theatre (p87), along with a brace of quality modern art galleries – **Bulwagang Juan Luna** on the 4th floor, and the smaller **Bulwagang Fernando Amorsolo** on the 5th floor, both with changing exhibits covering modernist and contemporary painters.

★ Bamboo Organ of Las Piñas
CHURCH

(✆02-825 7190; www.bambooorgan.org; Diego Cera Ave, Las Piñas; admission incl tour P100; ⊗8am-noon & 1-5pm) This famous organ, designated a national culture treasure, was built between 1816 and 1824 in the St Joseph Parish Church of Las Piñas on the southern fringes of Metro Manila. Those were lean times, so the Spanish priest Padre Diego Cera instructed that bamboo be used instead of more expensive metal for the majority of the organ's pipes. The horizontal trumpets are, however, made of metal. Tours of the church include a short organ concert and entrance to a small museum on-site.

Museo ng Sining
MUSEUM

(Museum of Art; Map p72; GSIS Bldg, CCP Complex, Pasay; ⊗8.30am-4.30pm Tue-Sat) FREE A classy gallery housing an extensive collection of contemporary and classic Filipino art.

Coconut Palace
NOTABLE BUILDING

(Map p72; ✆ext 3425 02-479 3500; Pedro Bukaneg St, CCP Complex) FREE The Coconut Palace was one of Imelda Marcos' great white elephant projects in the 1970s. It was so named because of the extensive use of coconut building materials in its construction. Nowadays the palace is used mainly for official functions. It's managed by the Government Service Insurance System (GSIS; www.gsis.gov.ph). Contact GSIS' Danny Martinez a few days in advance to schedule a free tour.

The Coconut Palace was unquestionably one of Imelda's wackiest schemes (and that's saying something). Hearing that Pope John Paul II was planning a visit to his flock in the Philippines, Imelda ordered that a grand palace be built. Huge teams of craftspeople laboured overtime to complete this edifice in time for the pontiff's arrival. As Imelda readied herself to throw open the door to welcome the pope, she got stiffed. After sternly chastising that the US$37 million cost could have gone to better uses, such as clean water for the people, the pope went elsewhere.

Poblacion, Makati & The Fort (BGC)

Makati's towers house the nation's major corporations and most of the major hotels. The heart of Makati was Manila's airport in the '30s and '40s: Ayala and Makati Aves were the runways, while Blackbird (p79) restaurant was the terminal.

The gleaming Fort (BGC) is like a mini-Singapore, with wide pavements, organised streets and vigilant police. Although it lies in Taguig, it's effectively an extension of Makati. It was part of nearby Fort Bonifacio before being sold off and developed, starting in the 1990s (hence the 'Fort' moniker).

★ Ayala Museum
MUSEUM

(Map p62; www.ayalamuseum.org; Greenbelt 4, Ayala Centre, Makati; adult/student P425/300; ⊗9am-6pm Tue-Sun) This gleaming museum features four floors of superbly curated exhibits on Filipino culture, art and history. At the heart of the collection is a brilliant exhibit consisting of 60 dioramas that succinctly, yet effectively, trace the nation's history, which kids will also love. The indigenous textile collection on the 4th floor is superb, and there are some exquisite pieces of pre-Hispanic gold jewellery and objects on display. The ro-

Poblacion

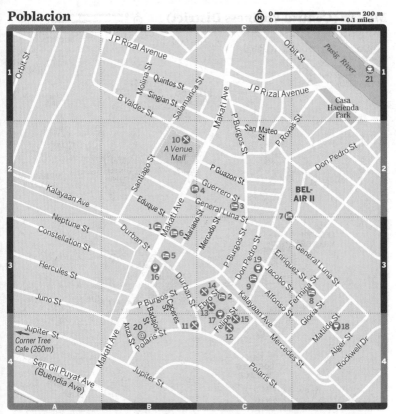

Poblacion

tating art exhibits tend to showcase Filipino masters such as Luna and Amorsolo.

Guided tours (P500) of the museum are highly recommended; book in advance.

Audioguides (P75) are also available. The excellent **Filipino Heritage Library** (Map p62; 6th fl, P100; ⊙9am-6pm Tue-Sat) – separate admission fee – is on the 6th floor.

Makati (Central Business District)

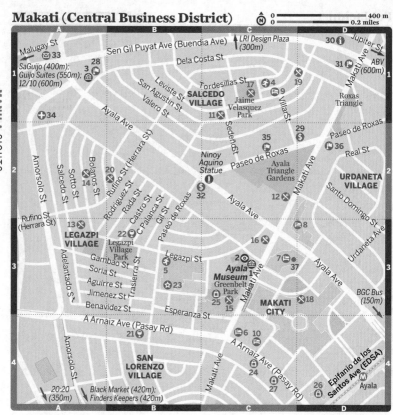

0 400 m
0 0.2 miles

★**Manila American Cemetery**   CEMETERY
(Map p75; Old Lawton Dr, BGC; ◷9am-5pm) A poignant and peaceful spot, this sprawling war cemetery on a grassy, beautifully manicured plot is the resting place of 17,206 soldiers killed in battle during WWII. In addition to hundreds of rows of perfectly aligned white crosses, there are several excellent open-air galleries with murals and descriptions of key battles.

Yuchengco Museum   GALLERY
(Map p62; www.yuchengcomuseum.org; Tower 2, RCBC Plaza, 6819 Ayala Ave, Makati; adult/student/child P100/50; ◷10am-6pm Mon-Sat) A mismatch among Makati's corporate highrises, this fantastic art and design gallery was established by prominent businessman and former UN diplomat, Alfonso Yuchengco. Set over three levels, its collection ranges from paintings by Filipino masters to contemporary art exhibitions.

Karrivin Plaza   GALLERY
(Map p50; 2316 Chino Roces Ave Ext, Makati) Busy Don Chino Roces Ave (Pasong Tamo) has evolved into an art district of sorts, and this hip collection of galleries, furniture shops and design labs is its shiny new showpiece. Galleries here include a branch of 1335Mabini (p59), the **Drawing Room** (drawingroomgallery.com) and **Art Informal** (www.artinformal.com). Most places are closed on Sundays.

◉ **Quezon City & Around**

★**Marikina Shoe Museum**   MUSEUM
(www.marikina.gov.ph/#!/museum; JP Rizal St, Marikina City; P50; ◷8am-noon & 1-5pm, closed holidays) A must for Imelda Marcos junkies is the Marikina Shoe Museum. There's the footwear of various Filipino luminaries on display here, but it's Imelda's shoes people come for – about 800 pairs of them, lined up

Makati (Central Business District)

MANILA SIGHTS

in rows behind glass cases. That's only about 25% of the hoard left behind in Malacañang Palace by the eccentric former First Lady.

Art In Island MUSEUM
(Map p76; ☑ 02-421 1356; 175 15th Ave, Cubao, Quezon City; adult/student P500/400; ⊗ 9.30am-9.30pm Tue-Sun) This is an art museum where you become the subject. It contains scores of three-dimensional murals and paintings designed to play tricks on your camera lens. Set it up right and you'll have a shot of yourself inside a snow globe, standing on your head, or gracing the cover of *Time* magazine.

Quezon Memorial Circle PARK
(Map p76; Elliptical Rd) The heart and soul of Quezon City is this vast park at the centre of a roundabout where several major avenues merge. There's all sorts of local flavour here – playgrounds, amusement park rides, restaurants, bazaars, and couples smooching in nooks. At the centre of it all rises the 36m art-deco **Quezon Memorial Shrine** (Map p76; ⊗ museum 8am-4pm Tue-Sun) FREE,

topped by three angels above the mausoleum of former president Manuel Quezon.

Ninoy Aquino Parks & Wildlife Center ZOO
(Map p76; Elliptical Rd, Quezon City; P100; ⊗ 8am-5pm) This park and wildlife rescue centre (open 9am to 4pm Tuesday to Sunday) runs a mini-zoo where confiscated animals and injured wildlife are nursed back to health. A few patients who never checked out are on display, including tigers, monkeys, pythons and various eagles and other birds.

**University of the
Philippines Diliman** UNIVERSITY
(UP Diliman; Map p50; http://upd.edu.ph; Quezon City) If you have a spare half-day, make the trip out to the lovely, leafy University of the Philippines Diliman campus. It has a genuine American university feel, and the 22,000-plus students fuel QC's active nightlife. It's a great place for a walk, bike or jog, and you'll find pick-up football and Ultimate Frisbee games most afternoons on the central field known as Sunken Garden.

It also has a decent art museum, the **Vargas Museum** (Map p50; ☑ 02-928 1927; www.vargas museum.wordpress.com; Roxas Ave; P30; ⊙ 9am-5pm Tue-Sat).

Activities

Walk-ins can use a few five-star hotel pools (which make a great place to while away an afternoon) but it will cost you P1000 and up. The Makati Shangri-La (p71) is a good choice, while the New World Manila Bay (p69) has a lap-length pool.

Club Intramuros Golf Course
GOLF

(Map p54; ☑ 02-526 1291; Bonifacio Dr, Intramuros; green fees incl club rental & caddy P2500) Just outside the walls of Intramuros in a uniquely urban venue, on what used to be the moat surrounding the city, you can play golf by day or by night at the quirky 18-hole, par-66 Club Intramuros Golf Course. Caddies cost P300, or you can obtain the shading services of an 'umbrella girl' for P350.

Prestige Cruises
BOATING

(Map p72; ☑ 02-832 8200; www.manilabaycruise. com; Esplanade Seaside Terminal, Seaside Blvd, Pasay; without/with buffet dinner P350/750) Evening cruises on Manila Bay kick off at 6pm and 8pm.

Spas
★I'm Onsen Spa
SPA

(Map p61; ☑ 02-755 7877; www.imonsenspa.com; I'm Hotel, Makati Ave, Poblacion, Makati; 1hr massages P1500-1800; ⊙ 10am-midnight Sun-Thu, to 2am Sat & Sun) The much-ballyhooed spa at the newly opened I'm Hotel (p72) is worth every bit of the hype. It takes up a full six floors, with all manner of treatments and room types to choose from.

MANILA FOR KIDS

Heading off to Manila with a child or two in tow? Not to worry. Many jet-setting parents are surprised to learn that the city is home to a fair number of kid-friendly activities and attractions. For more ideas check out **Manila for Kids** (www.manilaforkids.com).

Mind Museum (Map p75; ☑ 02-909 6463; www.themindmuseum.org; 3rd Ave, BGC; adult/student 3hr session P625/475, all-day passes P750; ⊙ sessions 9am-noon, noon-3pm & 3-6pm Tue-Sun) This excellent science museum succeeds in balancing education with fun, with plenty of cool interactive exhibits, including a planetarium, a printing press, various mind games and quizzes, environmental displays, model space craft and dinosaurs, and a shadow box.

Mall of Asia (p89) Several attractions here, including an IMAX theatre. Get here around sunset to stroll its atmospheric boardwalk lined with carnival rides, including the **MOA Eye** (Map p72; P150; ⊙ 3pm-midnight Mon-Fri, 10am-midnight Sat & Sun) Ferris wheel with amazing views over Manila Bay. Or beat the heat at the **Exploreum** (Map p72; www. exploreum.ph; admission P250, domed theatre shows P100-150; ⊙ 10am-10pm), an enlightening science museum filled with fun facts, educational video games and dozens of interactive exhibits. The Exploreum also has a modern planetarium with comfortable reclining seating.

Art In Island (p63) Kids and adults alike love this trick-of-the-eye specialist.

Star City (Map p72; ☑ 02-832 3249; www.starcity.com.ph; CCP Complex, Roxas Blvd, Pasay; unlimited rides P450; ⊙ 4pm-midnight Mon-Thu, 2pm-midnight Fri-Sun) A surprisingly decent amusement park in the heart of the CCP Complex, although it tends to get crowded on weekends. It has several thrilling rides including the signature Star Flyer roller coaster, although most rides last only 60 seconds or so.

Repertory Philippines (Map p62; ☑ 02-843 3570; www.repertoryphilippines.ph; OnStage Theatre, 2nd fl, Greenbelt 1, Makati; tickets from P450) Respected theatre company that produces child-friendly performances such as *Pinocchio* and *Seussical*.

Museo Pambata (Map p68; ☑ 02-523 1797; www.museopambata.org; Roxas Blvd, Ermita; P250; ⊙ 8am-noon & 1-5pm Tue-Sat, 1-5pm Sun) Both fun and charming, this hands-on museum has exhibits covering subjects as diverse as the environment, the human body and Old Manila, through the eyes of kids.

Neo Day Spa
MASSAGE

(Map p75; ☑02-815 8233; www.neo.net; cnr 26th St & 3rd Ave, BGC; 1hr massages P1200; ☺1-10pm) A pricier option than many others in Manila, but worth it.

The Spa
MASSAGE

(Map p62; ☑02-840 1325; www.thespa.com.ph; Greenbelt 1 Mall, Makati; 1hr massages from P1020; ☺noon-10pm) The Spa has immaculate facilities and a nice vibe. It's a chain with about a half-dozen other locations, including Bonifacio High St in The Fort.

Piandré
SPA

(Map p62; ☑02-817 8770; www.piandre.com; Tordesillas St cnr Toledo St, Salcedo Village; ☺7am-9pm Mon-Sat, 9am-5pm Sun) Professional waxing (no, really) and haircuts. Other outlets in The Fort and Greenbelt 1.

👉 Tours

There are a few truly excellent guided tours of Manila and they are a great way to get a feel for the city if time is short. Red Carabao hostel (p70) runs an excellent three-day cultural immersion package and also leads day tours for nonguests; its North Cemetery tour is highly recommended.

Old Manila Walks
WALKING

(☑02-711 3823, 0918 962 6452; www.oldmanila walks.com; tours P1000-1400) Tour leader Ivan Man Dy has a deep knowledge of Manila and its history and culture. He's an expert at ferreting out the city's often overlooked secrets, and is most known for his all-you-can-eat Chinatown foodie tours (P1200, 3½ hours), as well as a Chinese Cemetery tour (P650, two hours).

Smokey Tours
TOUR

(☑0917 578 5398, 02-622 1325; www.smokeytours. com; tours per person P950-P1200) Smokey's signature slum tours are highly educational, experiential, interactive forays into the barrios of Tondo, Manila's poorest district. This is not voyeurism; tours are led by underprivileged guides, and proceeds go to an NGO assisting with disaster relief and preparedness in slum areas. They have expanded and now do tours of the North Cemetery (p57), plus lighter market and bicycle tours.

Bambike
CYCLING

(Map p54; ☑02-525 8289; www.bambike.com; Plaza Luis Complex, General Luna St, Intramuros; 1/2½hr tours P600/1200; ☺10am & 3pm) Bambike runs guided cycling tours around Intra-

---

WORTH A TRIP

PINTO ART MUSEUM

This fantastic **museum** (☑02-697 1015; pintoartmuseum@yahoo.com; 1 Sierra Madre St, San Roque, Antipolo; adult/student P200/100; ☺9am-6pm Tue-Sun) in Antipolo, in the hills just east of Metro Manila, showcases some of the Philippines' best contemporary artists. There are six impressive galleries, outdoor art installations, and an indigenous arts wing where you can get an authentic Kalinga (North Luzon) tattoo. The beautifully landscaped grounds, with sweeping views of smog-choked Manila, are a welcome escape from the urban madness.

Figure on P450 each way for a taxi from Makati (50 minutes). Alternatively, take an Antipolo- or Tanay-bound jeepney or public van from SM Megamall in Ortigas. Get off at the Ynares Center and take a short tricycle ride or walk 1km to the museum.

---

muros on handmade bicycles with bamboo frames. Pedalling the laid-back backstreets of the walled city makes for a great way to cover expansive Intramuros, taking in all the main stops plus some less-visited gems. Prices include entrance fees, helmets and water.

Beyond Outdoor Adventures
CYCLING

(☑0917 838 1624; www.beyondoutdooradventures. com) Does excellent mountain bike tours outside Manila, with day and multiday routes and a nice range of top-of-the-line equipment to choose from. Destinations include the Daraitan River in the Sierra Madres (Rizal Province) and the Wawa Dam in Antipolo. They also do hiking tours to several peaks around Manila and beyond.

🎉 Festivals & Events

Black Nazarene Procession
RELIGIOUS

(☺9 Jan & Holy Week) The Black Nazarene, a life-size and highly revered statue of Christ in Quiapo Church (p57), is paraded through the streets in massive processions on 9 January and again during the week before Easter (Holy Week). Thousands of devotees crowd the streets carrying the image, believed to be miraculous, on their shoulders.

LOCAL KNOWLEDGE

VIVAMANILA

Nonprofit **VivaManila** (Map p58; www.facebook.com/vivamanila.org; Room 500, First United Bldg, Escolta St, Binondo) is an arts-and-culture organisation run by passionate locals who are on a mission to revive downtown Manila to its pre-war glory through a diverse combination of hipster initiatives, community building and art. It organises walking tours, street fairs, and urban design festivals in collaboration with art and design groups like **98B COLLaboratory** (www.98-b.org). Its Facebook page are a good source of information on music festivals, block parties, arthouse cinema premieres and gallery openings in Old Manila.

Fête de la Musique　　MUSIC
(◷ mid-Jun) Alliance Française organises this celebration of music annually on a Saturday in mid-June in Makati, with two main stages and more than 30 themed (reggae, blues, punk, etc) 'pocket' stages hosted by the best bars in Poblacion and elsewhere. Truly a smorgasbord for music lovers.

Fringe Manila　　ART
(www.fringemanila.com; ◷ Feb) This arts festival takes place over two to three weeks in February, with local artists and performers showcasing their talents in key galleries and theatres across Manila.

Bamboo Organ Festival　　MUSIC
(http://bambooorgan.org; ◷ late Feb) This festival sees an international roster of musicians from across the globe come to Manila for a week in late February to play and pay homage to the iconic Bamboo Organ (p60) in Las Piñas.

🛏 Sleeping

As one would expect from a megapolis of 13 million people, there is no limit to the range of accommodation you'll find in Manila. The five-star hotels are truly sumptuous. There's a decent rivalry between them and you can often bag a 'promo' rate (ie discount) well below those published, especially on weekends.

🛏 Intramuros & Around

White Knight Hotel Intramuros　　HOTEL $$
(Map p54; ☑ 02-526 6539; www.whiteknighthotel-intramuros.com; General Luna St, Intramuros; r P2000-3200; 🕸@🛜) A restored 19th-century heritage building that's part of the Casa Manila (p53) complex, White Knight makes a good choice for those wanting to stay within the solitude of the walled city. It has plenty of character, though feels a bit overdone with some flowery features.

★**Manila Hotel**　　HOTEL $$$
(Map p54; ☑ 02-527 0011; www.manila-hotel.com.ph; 1 Rizal Park; r from P9000; 🕸@🛜🌊) One of Asia's grand and regal hotels, where everyone from General MacArthur to the Beatles to JFK has spent the night. It's more than 100 years old, yet has kept up with the times brilliantly, adding elegant Filipino touches like capiz-shell dividers and two-poster beds to rooms that include every modern convenience imaginable, such as a flat-screen panel in the bath.

Bayleaf　　HOTEL $$$
(Map p54; ☑ 02-318 5000; www.thebayleaf.com.ph; cnr Muralla & Victoria Sts, Intramuros; incl breakfast r P5100-6100, ste P8700; 🕸@🛜) While a boutique hotel within Intramuros' old walls may not suit the area, the Bayleaf is rightfully popular for its rooms decked out in vibrant colour schemes with postmodern design and rainfall showers. It also has a busy restaurant and rooftop Sky Deck bar (p84). Book online for the best rates.

🛏 Ermita & Malate

★**Makabata Guesthouse & Cafe**　　GUESTHOUSE $
(Map p50; ☑ 02-254 0212; www.makabata.org; 2218 Leveriza St, Malate; incl breakfast dm P495-720, s P1050, d P1400-1800; 🕸) This training hotel provides at-risk youth with a chance to get a start in the hospitality industry. But it's more than just a feel-good story. Rooms boast an impressive traditional-meets-modern design, capiz-shell windows offsetting boutique wash basins and plasma TVs. Most rooms have balconies overlooking a colourful local neighbourhood 700m south of Remedios Circle. The cafe serves tasty light bites.

Bahay Kubo Hostel　　HOSTEL $
(Map p68; ☑ 02-243 7537; 1717 M Orosa St, Malate; dm P400-500, d P1500-3600; 🕸🛜) Helpful owners and homey if busy common spaces

are the hallmarks of this popular crash pad. The downstairs common area, open to the street, lends it a friendly neighbourhood feel, while upstairs is for lounging. Most of the six- to 14-bed dorms are air-conditioned and roomy enough, with big wooden lockers.

Stay
HOSTEL $

(Map p68; ☑ 02-525 1534; www.staymanila.com; 1750 Adriatico St, Malate; dm with fan/air-con P350/400, s/d from P690/790, tr P1350-1800; ✳@🛜) In the heart of Malate, Wanderers knows precisely what backpackers want and delivers with a mix of clean dorms and private rooms (some with balconies), excellent travel info and cooking facilities. The highlight is its grungy rooftop bar-restaurant–chill-out lounge, perfect for socialising with other travellers over cheap booze.

Pension Natividad
PENSION $

(Map p68; ☑ 02-521 0524; www.pensionnatividad. com; 1690 MH del Pilar St, Malate; dm P400, d without/with bathroom P1000/1100, d with air-con P1500; ✳🛜) Inside a beautiful art-deco building, this quiet, long-running pension is popular with Peace Corps volunteers and families. Consider staying elsewhere if you plan to party hard. The dorms are unisex and air-conditioned.

★ Amélie Hotel
BOUTIQUE HOTEL $$

(Map p68; ☑ 02-875 7888; www.ameliehotelmanila .com; 1667 Bocobo St, Malate; r incl breakfast P3900-5100; ✳@🛜⛲) A shot in the arm for Malate's hopeful revival, Amélie's greystone minimalism is the perfect antidote to the sweaty, steamy metropolis. The art-deco furniture barely fills the immense rectangular space of rooms. Head up to the rooftop plunge pool for happy hour and dial up drinks from the lobby bar 10 stories below.

Luneta Hotel
BOUTIQUE HOTEL $$

(Map p68; ☑02-875 8921; www.lunetahotel. com; 414 Kalaw Ave, Ermita; r P2900-4900, ste P6500; ✳🛜) The French Renaissance–style Luneta Hotel is symbolic of Manila's intent to return to its pre-war glory. Opened in 1918, the hotel survived WWII only to slip into decay. The elegant heritage-listed building has a range of excellent-value rooms that retain plenty of Old World flavour. The flashiest quarters have iron balconies overlooking Rizal Park.

1775 Adriatico Suites
HOTEL $$

(Map p68; ☑ 02-524 5402; www.adriaticosuites. com; 1775 Adriatico St, Malate; d/tw incl breakfast from P2200/2500, apt from P5000; ✳🛜⛲) Down a side street near Remedios Circle, this is your best bet for a quiet yet central midranger in Malate. There's a brand-new wing with snazzy doubles featuring attractive bed frames, cosy mattresses, desks and Netflix–enabled smart TVs. The pleasant pool and Jacuzzi are welcome amenities at this price point. The older wing consists mainly of apartments.

WHERE TO STAY IN MANILA

Choosing a hotel in Manila, sprawling megacity that it is, can be a daunting task, especially for first-time visitors. The key to accommodation enlightenment is to pick a district before settling on a hotel. A quick rundown of the major sleeping areas:

NEIGHBOURHOOD	FOR	AGAINST
Downtown (Intramuros)	Quiet, neighbourhood feel; close to main sights	Food options limited; nightlife non-existent
Downtown (Malate & Ermita)	Traditional tourist belt; close to main sights; 'authentic' Manila; cheapest budget accommodation	Beggars and scam artists; street-level destitution; restaurants are average; nightlife better elsewhere
Makati & The Fort (BGC)	Top restaurants; great nightlife; clean streets; modern hostels and hotels	Expensive; lacks character and too 'sanitised'
Pasay & Parañaque	Close to airport, cultural precinct and Pasay bus terminals	Close to busy Epifanio de los Santos Ave; loud, blighted; restaurants lacking
Quezon City	Less touristy, more local; good restaurants and bars; close to Cubao bus terminals	Far from everything except Cubao bus terminals

Ermita & Malate

0 — 200 m
0 — 0.1 miles

Rizal Park
Kalaw Ave

4

10

11

United Nations Ave

United Nations Ave

35

United Nations Avenue

Cortada St

27

Roxas Blvd

Alhambra St

A Flores St

36

Grey St

Bocobo St

M Orosa St

Taft Ave

8

Arquiza St

ERMITA

29

Padre Faura St

Padre Faura St

Paco Park (150m);
Oasis Paco Park Hotel (200m)

37 30

25

1

Santa Monica St

2

Adriatico St

Robinsons
Place

Taft Ave

Manila
Bay

31 20

R Salas St

United
Nations
Avenue

Pedro Gil St

Pedro Gil St

12

Pedro
Gil

34

Roxas Blvd

J Quintos Jr St

Mabini St

Adriatico St

Bocobo St

14

13

6

M H del Pilar St

24

23

Philippine
Kim Luan
Temple

Malvar St

7

Alonzo St

18

J Nakpil St

22

15

5

21

M Orosa St

Guerrero St

Vasques St

Hidalgo St

9

19

@ 32

17

Taft Ave

Rajah
Sulayman
Park

Remedios St

3

Remedios
Circle

Remedios St

16

33

MALATE

26

Madre Ignacia St

Adriatico St

San Andres St
Makabata Guesthouse
& Cafe (350m)

Leveriza
St

28

Buendia LRT Stop
& Bus Stations (2km);
Pasay Rotunda (4km)

Ermita & Malate

⊙ Sights
1 1335Mabini B3
2 Baywalk A3
3 Malate Church....................................... A7
4 Museo Pambata.....................................A1

🛏 Sleeping
5 1775 Adriatico Suites............................B6
6 Amélie Hotel...B5
7 Bahay Kubo Hostel C5
8 Best Western Hotel La Corona B2
9 Hop Inn Hotel Ermita............................A6
10 Luneta Hotel..A1
11 Miramar Hotel..A1
12 New World Manila Bay B4
13 Pan Pacific Hotel...................................B5
14 Pension Natividad.................................A5
15 Stay...B6

🍴 Eating
16 Aristocrat A7
17 Cafe Adriatico B6
18 Casa Armas..B6
19 Matoi...B6
20 Shawarma Snack Center B4

🍸 Drinking & Nightlife
21 Che'lu C6

22 Erra's Vest Ramen in Town B6
23 Oarhouse..C5
24 Pacific Lounge B5
25 Tap Station B3

🎭 Entertainment
26 Minokaua..B7

🛍 Shopping
27 Hiraya Gallery B1
    Maria Closa ....(see 1)
28 San Andres Public Market...................C7
29 Solidaridad Bookshop.......................... B2
30 Tesoro's B3

ℹ Information
31 Busy Bee Internet Cafe........................A4
32 Coreon Gate...B6
33 Ermita Post Office D7
34 Filipino Travel Center B5
35 Manila Doctors Hospital D1
36 US Embassy..A2

ℹ Transport
    Bicol Isarog Ermita......................(see 37)
37 Cagsawa Ermita B3

Best Western Hotel La Corona HOTEL $$
(Map p68; ☏ 02-524 2631; www.bestwesternhotel manila.com; 1166 M H del Pilar St, Ermita; d/ste incl breakfast from P3000/4300) Everything about this place is in direct contrast to the disorder of the streets outside. Rooms possess all mod-cons and border on boutique, with touches like inlaid brick panelling, big mirrors and contoured headboards. A P500 upgrade affords a big leap in comfort. One fuss: too many fabrics. Still, big online discounts turn this into tremendous value.

Oasis Paco Park HOTEL $$
(Map p50; ☏ 02-521 2371; www.oasispark.com; 1032-34 Belen St, Paco; d P2000-3000; ❄@🛜🏊) You come here mainly because it's relatively quiet and isolated, and because it's a rare Manila midranger with a decent pool – perfect after a sweltering day of sightseeing in nearby Intramuros. Rooms are generic motel-style; you may need to upgrade if you want a window. On-site is the delicious My Kitchen Italian restaurant.

Hop Inn Hotel Ermita HOTEL $$
(Map p68; ☏ 02-528 3988; www.hopinnhotel.com; 1850 MH del Pilar St, Malate; r without/with view P1900/2150; ❄🛜) This is a big (170-room), bright, no-nonsense hotel with cheery service

to match the decor. The colourful rooms are somewhat bare-bones but blissfully fabric-free and include a flat-screen TV, a long desk and a lone plastic chair. The 'view' rooms give a glimpse of the Manila Bay sunset but are louder than the standards.

Miramar Hotel HISTORIC HOTEL $$
(Map p68; ☏ 02-523 4484; www.miramarhotel. ph; 1034-36 Roxas Blvd, Ermita; s/d incl breakfast from P2600/2900, 12hrs from P1800; ❄@🛜) The rooms are a tad dated and dark but this 1930s art-deco masterpiece has undeniable flavour, including a classic facade, vintage elevators and four-storey hanging ceiling fans in the central atrium. Upgrade to the superior class if you want a more modern room. The 12-hour rates (for standard rooms only) are fantastic. Book direct to get the best deals.

★ New World Manila Bay HOTEL $$$
(Map p68; ☏ 02-252 6888; www.newworldhotels. com; 1588 Pedro Gil St, Malate; r from P7500; ❄@🛜🏊) The New World offers five-star amenities at a lower price (usually) than the competition. You can get a haircut, buy gourmet chocolate, play a game of roulette, enjoy a foot massage and swim laps in a giant pool (walk-ins P1000) without ever leaving the

building. The large, high-ceilinged rooms belong in a glossy magazine. Online specials approach P5000 for the standard rooms.

Pan Pacific Hotel HOTEL $$$
(Map p68; 02-318 0788; www.panpacific.com; cnr Adriatico & Malvar Sts, Malate; r from P8500; ✻@≋) This luxurious five-star business hotel is Malate's solitary choice for travellers requiring British–trained butler service. The particulars of each stay can be personalised online. Standard rooms include one of the following: free breakfast, free room upgrade or free airport transfer. Some rooms have bay views and TV-fitted baths. The glass elevators, which swoop over the pool, are attractions in themselves.

Santa Cruz

★**Red Carabao** HOSTEL $
(Map p50; 0998 573 3884; www.redcarabao philippines.com; 2819 Felix Huertas St; dm P450-500, r per person with fan/air-con P650/1050; ☺Sep-May; ✻@✺; ♿) With its innovative program of cultural immersion, Red Carabao Manila treads the line between hostel and tour. If you want in, you must commit to a multiday 'Urban Plunge', as they call it. You'll spend a day on a cultural tour of Intramuros and old downtown Manila sights, another on an excursion out of town, and one day doing charitable work.

Pasay

Orchid Garden Suites HOTEL $$
(Map p72; 02-516 0888; www.orchidgarden suites.com; 620 Ocampo St; incl breakfast d from P3000, ste P4500; ✻@✺≋) An elegant choice that's also convenient to Malate. The lobby and bar are in a 1930s art-deco mansion – one of Manila's finest pre-war architectural landmarks. Guests stay in a 1980s tower block built over the original mansion, or at the back in a newly added annexe. Rooms lack the charm of the lobby, but are big and functional.

★**Henry Hotel** BOUTIQUE HOTEL $$$
(Map p72; 02-807 8888; www.thehenryhotel. com; 2680 Harrison St; r/ste incl breakfast P6000/10,000; ✻@✺≋) We run out of superlatives when describing the two Henry Philippine properties – first the stunningly creative original in Cebu, and now this: a leafy 1948 Chinese estate converted into an irresistible oasis in back-alley Pasay. Spread over several structures, rooms retain the classical look while still possessing every modern convenience you might need.

★**Sofitel Philippine Plaza** HOTEL $$$
(Map p72; 02-551 5555; www.sofitelmanila.com; CCP Complex, Atang Dela Rama St; r incl breakfast from P9000; ✻@✺≋) This five-star masterpiece, with its meandering pool area right on Manila Bay, is the closest you'll get to a resort holiday in Manila. It's the same magnificent hotel that has presided over the CCP Complex for decades now. Other highlights are the bayside lawn/lounge area for sunset happy hours, and the stupendous buffet brunch at Spiral restaurant.

Makati & Poblacion

Makati's hip Poblacion area has emerged as Manila's flashpacker district, with more than a dozen hostels and 'poshtel's and myriad trendy bars and restaurants. The Central Business District around the Ayala Center is five-star territory, and you'll find a few decent midrangers there too.

Hilik Hostel HOSTEL $
(Map p61; 02-519 5821; www.hilikboutique hostel.ph; Mavenue Bldg, 7844 Makati Ave; incl breakfast dm P500-650, d P1100-1400; ✻✺) What distinguishes Hilik from the pack is its downright stylish private rooms, although you'll want to request one off noisy Makati Ave. The air-con dorms at Hilik ('snore' in Tagalog) are cramped but, like the kitchen and common area of this intimate hostel, immaculate.

★**Element Boutique Hotel** BOUTIQUE HOTEL $$
(Map p61; 02-805 1360; www.elementboutique hotelmakati.com; 4950 Guerrero St; incl breakfast d P2900-3800, ste P9000-9500) This functional and fashionable new French–run hotel adds another splash of originality to Makati's up-and-coming Poblacion area. The 14 rooms come in a mix of styles, but all are heavy on brushed concrete, recycled wood, pendant lamps and groovy furniture. Rooms are well sound-proofed and half have balconies. Downstairs is a beautiful, bright cafe.

★**La Casita Mercedes** B&B $$
(Map p61; 02-887 4385; http://lacasita mercedes.com; 5956 Enriquez St; incl breakfast s P1500-2200, d P2500-2900; ✻✺) ✔ This sophisticated addition to Poblacion occupies a beautifully restored 1930s house.

Step into an Old-World lobby of antique mirrors, filigreed transoms and gorgeous *machuka* (Mediterranean–style) tiles. The eight rooms, each with its own character, have touches like four-poster beds and original art-deco furniture. The neighbourhood wakes up early, so bring earplugs.

Z Hostel
HOSTEL **$$**

(Map p61; ☑02-856 0851; www.zhostel.com; 5660 Don Pedro St; dm P650-850, d incl breakfast P2430; ❄@⎙) This is Manila's number-one party address for groovy backpackers thanks to its rocking rooftop bar and chic ground-floor cafe. It's a huge space, with 130 beds over seven floors. The airy dorms are all en suite and boast sturdy iron-framed beds with personal charging stations.

Guijo Suites
HOTEL **$$**

(Map p50; ☑02-553 8998; www.guijosuitesmakati. com; 7644 Guijo St; ☻incl breakfast r P2400-2800, ste P3100-3900) Well removed from the busier parts of Makati, Guijo Suites is good value in a quiet location. Rooms are not fancy but are smart, with light-wood panelling, lime-green paint and rain showers. The tidy premiere suite, with two bedrooms and a kitchenette, is a nice deal for two people.

Clipper Hotel
HOTEL **$$**

(Map p61; ☑02-890 8577; www.theclipperhotel. com; 5766 Ebro St; s P1500-2500, d P2700-3000; ❄@⎙) The Clipper keeps it classy despite being steps away from seedy P Burgos St. The two quirky, windowless singles resemble boat cabins, with flat-screens built into the beds. The 12 roomy doubles are very white and bright, with parquet floors. Booking sites offer big discounts here.

Junction Hostel
HOSTEL **$$**

(Map p61; ☑02-501 6575; www.junctionhostels. com; cnr General Luna & Don Pedro Sts; dm P700-900, d without/with bathroom P1800/2800; ❄@⎙) Junction is an 111-bed poshtel with a distinctively urban feel. There are murals on the walls, industrial fixtures and boutique dorm rooms in a mix of styles and configurations. In the funky downstairs common area, baristas sling boutique coffee and imported beers to patrons hovered over their laptops. It could be Brooklyn.

Hotel Durban
HOTEL **$$**

(Map p61; ☑02-897 1866; www.hoteldurban.net; 4875 Durban St; r P1800-2900; ❄⎙) Makati's best midrange value is a tightly run ship. The immaculate rooms, with faux-wood panel-

ling, are more than adequate for the price, albeit most lack natural light. Upgrade to the top-floor 'deluxe' rooms, with windows.

★Makati Shangri-La
HOTEL **$$$**

(Map p62; ☑02-813 8888; www.shangri-la.com; cnr Ayala & Makati Aves; r P12,250; ❄@⎙⛱) With a soaring lobby lounge punctuated by floor-to-ceiling bay windows and sequoia-sized columns, the Shangri-La wins the award for Makati's most stunning interior. The rooms are masterpieces of originality, all swoops and swerves, coves and curved lines. You could throw a party on the California king beds. There are two tennis courts and a recently renovated swimming pool and bar.

★Raffles Makati
HOTEL **$$$**

(Map p62; ☑02-795 0755; www.raffles.com/ makati; 1 Raffles Dr; ste incl breakfast from P19,000; ❄@⎙⛱) Two five-star hotels in one skyscraper. The Raffles consists of 32 stunning suites on the 9th and 10th floors. They feature high ceilings, wooden floorboards, stand-alone baths with city views and on-call butlers. Its opulent palm-lined pool is straight out of a Beverly Hills mansion. Beneath the Raffles, the sister **Fairmont** (Map p62; ☑02-555 9888; www.fairmont.com/makati; d from P11,000; ⎙⛱) is just a small step down in luxuriousness.

Picasso
APARTMENT **$$$**

(Map p62; ☑02-828 4774; www.picassomakati. com; 119 Leviste St, Salcedo Village; r incl breakfast from P5000; ❄@⎙) Exuding rock-and-roll chic, this suave art hotel has serviced apartments and studios with mounted beds, floating staircases, space-age chairs and bright Picasso–inspired colour schemes. True to its name, the entire hotel doubles as a gallery, and it also has a gym and the Pablo 1B bistro cafe downstairs. The best rates are on their website.

Peninsula Manila
HOTEL **$$$**

(Map p62; ☑02-887 2888; www.peninsula.com; cnr Ayala & Makati Aves; r/ste from P9000/12,750; ❄@⎙⛱) With rooms that highlight the best of Philippine design, the Peninsula is a Makati veteran that nevertheless appears brand new. The cafe in the soaring lobby has a fine Sunday brunch and is a 24-hour destination for the city's business elite. A side note: a tank drove through the front doors here in 2007 during a foiled coup attempt.

Pasay

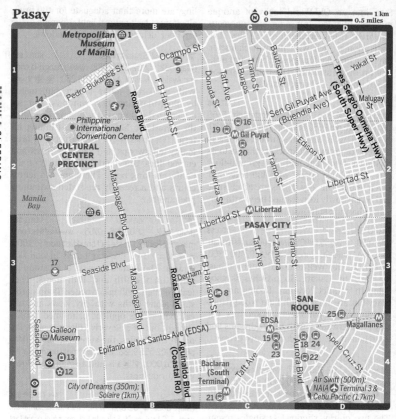

City Garden Grand Hotel

BUSINESS HOTEL **$$$**

(Map p61; ☑ 02-888 8181; www.citygardengrand
hotel.com; 8008 Makati Ave; d P4250-8000, ste
from P11,200; ✴❀☎) This 32-storey high-rise
is the smartest choice and best value in the
Poblacion area of Makati. Even the cheaper
rooms have desks, sleek TVs, polished wood
floors, shag rugs and floor-to-ceiling mir-
rors, plus surprising extras like bathrobes
and bathtubs. The spacious roof deck has a
pool and the swanky Firefly Bar (p84). Ser-
vice is exceptional.

I'm Hotel

HOTEL **$$$**

(Map p61; ☑ 02-755 7888; www.imhotel.com;
Makati Ave cnr Kalayaan Ave; r/ste incl breakfast
P6150/8850; ✴❀☎) With 34 floors and a
soaring glass-enclosed lobby, this Singapore
import is hard to miss. Six floors are given over
to the impressive I'm Onsen Spa (p64). The
other floors house several hundred modern,
business-standard rooms and kitchenette-
equipped suites. Up top is a rooftop restaurant, while the unique pool on the 3rd floor
practically hangs over Makati Ave.

The Fort (BGC)

Shangri-La at the Fort

HOTEL **$$$**

(Map p75; ☑ 02-820 0888; www.shangri-la.com/
fort; 30th St cnr 5th Ave; r incl breakfast from
P13,000; ✴@❀☎) This gleaming luxury ho-
tel signals The Fort's ambitions to become
Manila's new epicentre of business and com-
merce. It rises 60 storeys high, with condos
on the upper floors and a mix of hotel rooms
and serviced apartments beneath them. The
enormous rooms are equipped with both
baths and showers, and are adorned with
sculptures for art lovers.

★ Seda

HOTEL **$$$**

(Map p75; ☑ 02-945 8888; www.sedahotels.com;
cnr 30th St & 11th Ave; r incl breakfast from P8000;
✴@❀☎) One of the few hotel options in

Pasay

The Fort, this classy business hotel has large, stylish rooms with jumbo plasma TVs and bench seating. There's a gym, pool and computers in the lobby for free guest use. Weekends sometimes bring discounts. Also has the Straight Up (p84) rooftop bar.

🛏 Quezon City

Go Hotels Cubao　　　　　　　　HOTEL $
(Map p76; ☑02-687 7788; www.gohotels.ph; 840 Aurora Blvd; d from P1200; ❋@�) Yes it's cookie-cutter formulaic, but the exceedingly bright, clean rooms and gleaming lobby work perfectly if you're looking for a budget oasis near the bus terminals along gritty EDSA ring road in Cubao. Touches like plasma TVs and full-length mirrors are nice surprises at this price point.

★Hive Hotel　　　　　BOUTIQUE HOTEL $$
(Map p76; ☑02-806 1004; www.hivehotel.com; 68 Scout Tuazon St; incl breakfast d P3000-3750, ste P5300-6350; ❋�) ⏺ The lower-budget sister of Cocoon is hardly a downgrade. Rooms are slightly smaller, but efficiently designed with open closets and lovely room dividers in trademark purple-and-orange. Recycled hardwood floors, downy beds and noise-reducing felt wall panelling ensure you'll sleep soundly and in style. Adjoining rooms available.

Red Planet Quezon City　　　　HOTEL $$
(Map p76; ☑02-424 0567; www.redplanethotels.com; 100 Timog Ave; r from P1600; ❋@�) This ultra-clean chain hotel is a good, reliable choice. Rooms are compact but efficient, with quality beds and high-pressure showers. Rates fluctuate wildly – get in on the low end and it's a solid deal.

★Cocoon Boutique Hotel　BOUTIQUE HOTEL $$$
(Map p76; ☑02-998 3117; www.thecocoonhotel.com; 61 Scout Tobias St; incl breakfast d P4900-6300, ste P8400-11,900; ❋� ☲) ⏺ This is QC's most chic address for the wannabe hipster in you. The rooms are fit for the pages of *Wallpaper*, with beautiful 3m-long recycled-hardwood desks (and floors to match), lavish beds draped in Egyptian cotton, plenty of hang-out space and practical touches like bending-pipe reading lights and full-length mirrors. Throw in legit green credentials and you have a real gem.

B Hotel　　　　　　　BOUTIQUE HOTEL $$$
(Map p76; ☑02-990 5000; www.thebellevue.com; 14 Scout Rallas St; incl breakfast d P4500, ste P7500-9800; ❋☲) The T Morato area of Quezon City has suddenly become a mecca for Manila boutique hotels. Ian Schrager himself would admire the B's vintage industrial design, awash in grey slate, polished concrete and pendant lights. Rooms are spacious, and the pool here is the nicest in the area.

✖ Eating

Most of the best (and priciest) restaurants are in Makati and the Fort (BGC). Locally popular foodie hotspots include Quezon City's **Maginhawa St** area and **Kapitolyo** in Pasig City near Ortigas. They are lined with trendy eateries and food parks and make great targets for value-conscious DIY eaters. Self-caterers will find large supermarkets in the malls, although outdoor markets such as Malate's **San Andres market** (Map p68; San Andres St, Malate; ⊙7am-6pm) offer more colourful (and cheaper) grazing.

✖ Intramuros & Around

Patio de Conchita   FILIPINO $

(Map p54; Beaterio St, Intramuros; meals P75-150; ⊙10am-10pm) Patio de Conchita is an atmospheric *turu-turò* eatery within an ancestral house in the heart of Intramuros. Decent food and cheap beer make it popular with the after-work crowd, so it's a great place to enjoy some local colour.

Ilustrado   SPANISH, FILIPINO $$

(Map p54; ☑02-527 3674; 744 General Luna St, Intramuros; mains P400-500; ⊙11.30am-2.30pm & 6-9.30pm Mon-Sat, 9am-5.30pm Sun; ❋🕈) Set in a reconstructed Spanish–era house, this is fine dining of the stiff-upper-lip variety. Traditional Spanish Filipino dishes like paella join salmon, duck and lamb chops on the menu, which turns over monthly.

Harbor View   SEAFOOD $$

(Map p50; ☑02-524 1532; South Blvd, Rizal Park; mains for 2 from P450; ⊙11am-midnight) This longstanding and popular fresh seafood *in-ahaw* (grill) restaurant juts into Manila Bay. The breezes can be delightful on sweltering days, but check the wind direction as sometimes it sends the bay's insalubrious flotsam into malodorous piles along the piers. The fish is best enjoyed with a golden sunset and some amber refreshments.

Barbara's   FILIPINO $$

(Map p54; ☑02-975 7829; www.barbarasrestaurant andcatering.com; General Luna St, Intramuros; mains P200-500, lunch/dinner buffet P615/745; ⊙11.30am-9pm) In an elegant space within the Casa Manila (p53) complex, Barbara's does a buffet dinner that includes a cultural show (7.15pm) with traditional music and dances such as *tinikling* (traditional dance using sliding bamboo poles). The cultural show costs P350 if you order à la carte. This is white-tablecloth fine dining.

✖ Binondo (Chinatown)

The real reason to go to Chinatown is to eat! Food is Hokkien–influenced, reflecting the origin of its immigrants. Foodies should get in touch with Old Manila Walks (p65) for wonderful Chinatown walking/eating tours.

Polland Hopia Cafe   BAKERY $

(Map p58; Escolta St; snacks from P35; ⊙7am-7pm; ❋) A classic *Tsinoy* (Chinese Filipino) bakery marked by an awesome 1950s-style neon sign on Escolta St. Thin-crust *hopia* – dense sweet cakes filled with mung beans or *ube* (purple yam) – is the name of the game. Plenty of other savoury surprises await, plus air-con.

Dong Bei Dumplings   CHINESE $

(Map p58; 642 Yuchengco St; mains P100-200; ⊙7am-9pm; ❋) Their handmade dumplings – you can see them being made in the window – are a northern Chinese variety, in contrast to the Hokkien (southern) cuisine that prevails in most of Chinatown. Simple and delicious.

New Quan Yin Chay   VEGETARIAN $

(Map p58; Ongpin St cnr Salazar St; dishes P75-100; ⊙7am-9pm) An unassuming *turu-turò* style vegetarian place in the heart of Chinatown, serving stewed or barbecued fake meat plus dim sum. The fried cashew 'shrimp' is a speciality.

Quik Snack   CHINESE $$

(Map p58; Caravajal St; mains P120-250; ⊙9.30am-5.30pm) Also known as Amah (Grandma) Pilar's after its founding matriarch, this Chinatown institution has been serving its trademark *ku-tsai-ah* (Chinese empanadas), *lumpia* (spring rolls) and noodle soup for more than 50 years. It's hidden on atmospheric Caravajal St, a narrow alley that doubles as a wet market.

Sincerity   CHINESE $$

(Map p58; 497 Yuchengco St; mains P150-200; ⊙9am-9pm) Famous across Manila for its fried chicken and other home-style Hokkien cooking; run by a third-generation family.

✖ Malate, Ermita & Pasay

The best restaurants are in Malate around Remedios Circle and J Nakpil St, where there's plenty of neighbourhood colour to observe if you can bag a streetside perch.

The Fort (BGC)

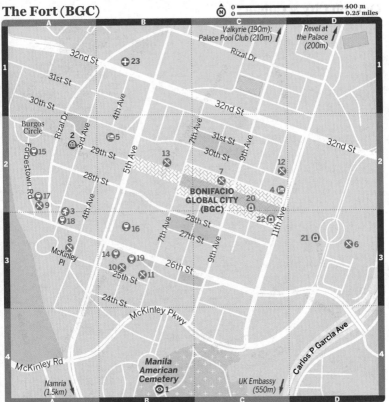

Valkyrie (190m);
Palace Pool Club (210m)

Revel at
the Palace (200m)

Namria
(1.5km)

UK Embassy
(550m)

Quezon City & Cubao

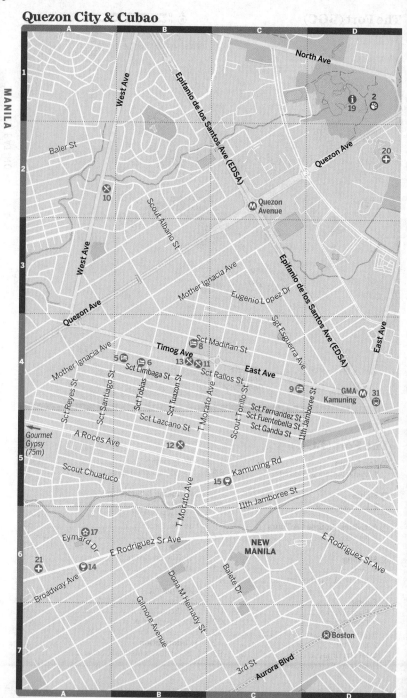

Quezon City & Cubao

◎ Sights
1	Art In Island	F6
2	Ninoy Aquino Parks & Wildlife Center	D1
3	Quezon Memorial Circle	E1
4	Quezon Memorial Shrine	E1

🛏 Sleeping
5	B Hotel	B4
6	Cocoon Boutique Hotel	B4
7	Go Hotels Cubao	E6
8	Hive Hotel	B4
9	Red Planet Quezon City	C4

✖ Eating
10	Coffee Empire	A2
11	Eighteen Bistro	B4
12	Greens Vegetarian Restaurant and Cafe	B5
13	Señor Pollo	B4

🍸 Drinking & Nightlife
14	Big Sky Mind	A6
15	Catch 272	C5
	Craft Coffee Revolution	(see 14)
	Cubao Expo	(see 18)
	Fred's Revolucion	(see 18)

★ Entertainment
16	Araneta Coliseum	F6
17	Philippine Educational Theater Association	A6

⬤ Shopping
18	Cubao Expo	F6

ⓘ Information
19	Biodiversity Management Bureau	D1
20	PCSSD Hyperbaric Chamber Manila	D2
21	St Luke's Medical Center	A6

ⓘ Transport
	Amihan Bus Lines	(see 23)
22	Araneta Bus Terminal	F6
23	Araneta Center Busport	F7
24	Bicol Isarog Cubao	E7
	Cagsawa Cubao	(see 23)
25	Coda Lines	E6
26	Dagupan Bus Co	E6
27	Dominion Bus Lines	E6
28	Genesis Cubao	E6
29	Partas Cubao	E7
30	Victory Liner Cubao	E6
31	Victory Liner Kamias	D4

Shawarma Snack Center   MIDDLE EASTERN $

(Map p68; 485 R Salas St, Ermita; shawarma P60-75, meals P85-300; ⏱24hr; ✠) It doesn't sound like much, but this streetside eatery serves the richest and most flavourful falafel, *mutabal* (eggplant dip), hummus and kebabs in downtown Manila.

Cafe Adriatico   INTERNATIONAL $$

(Map p68; 1790 Adriatico St, Malate; mains P200-400; ⏱7am-3am; ✠🖥) An old-time Malate favourite, this romantic corner bistro is worth a splurge for original multicultural fare with Spanish, English, American and Italian options, and the people-watching on Remedios Circle.

Dampa Seaside   SEAFOOD $$

(Map p72; Macapagal Blvd, Pasay; meals P300-500; ⏱11am-10pm) A real local experience (and institution), here you trawl the attached wet market for your desired ingredients (preferably seafood) and then choose one of several sleeves-up restaurants on the premises to cook your selection the way you like it. The prices are all very reasonable, and close seating quarters ensure that it's a social affair.

Aristocrat   FILIPINO $$

(Map p68; www.aristocrat.com.ph; cnr Roxas Blvd & San Andres St, Malate; mains P200-400; ⏱24hr) Aristocrat began life in 1936 as a mobile snack cart and is so iconic that it has its own historical marker. A replica of the old Ford canteen is incorporated into the front window. It serves a huge range of Filipino food, but chicken barbecue is the speciality. Branches have sprung up all over the country but you want this one.

Matoi   JAPANESE $$

(Map p68; 1767 Mabini St, Malate; mains P150-300; ⏱8am-2am; ✠) This authentic Japanese eatery is divided into two parts: a tiny seven-seat sushi bar operated by the owner/chef and open from 5.30pm daily; and the main restaurant, with good-value lunch sets of ramen, *tonkatsu* and other Japanese staples. Shoot for dinner in the sushi bar, which comes with various free appetisers.

Casa Roces   SPANISH, FILIPINO $$

(Map p50; ☎02-735 5896; www.casaroces.com; 1153 JP Laurel St, cnr Aguado St, San Miguel; mains from P280; ⏱10am-10pm) This laid-back yet classy bistro is a good stop for lunch or a *meryenda* (snack) if you're on a tour of the Malacañang Palace (p53). Dishes are Spanish

Filipino, including an authentic Catalonian tapas selection. Excellent cakes too.

★Casa Armas   SPANISH $$$

(Map p68; ☎02-526 1839; 573 J Nakpil St, Malate; tapas P180-400, mains P350-700; ⏱11am-midnight Mon-Sat, 6pm-midnight Sun) Foodies have been enamoured with this cavernlike Spanish restaurant for years; it's best known for tapas favourites such as *calamares a la plancha alioli* (grilled calamari with garlic sauce) and *gambas al ajillo* (sizzling prawns in garlic and oil). Also does excellent paellas, affordable *bocadillos* (baguettelike sandwiches), and of course sangria.

✕ Makati & Poblacion

Trendy Poblacion is ground zero for foodies and cafe freaks – some call it 'Williamsburgos', a dig on its seedy central street (P Burgos) and its alleged similarity to Brooklyn.

Beni's Falafel   MIDDLE EASTERN $

(Map p61; ☎02-621 6163; A Venue Mall, B Valdez St Entrance; dishes P130-225; ⏱24hr; ✠🖥) Everything on the menu of this unassuming Yemeni–owned eatery is original and done to perfection. The *shakshuka* (eggs poached in a spicy tomato sauce) and Beni's falafel are our faves. Shawarmas are served out of neighbouring Beni's Grill. There's another Beni's branch in Mall of Asia (p89).

Tambai   FUSION $

(Map p61; Felipe St; dishes P70-300; ⏱6pm-midnight; ✠🖥) Quick but highly original Japanese–infused Filipino snacks served on the street or in a small air-conditioned room at the back. Try the to-die-for beef-rib *laki-tori* sticks.

★Corner Tree Cafe   CAFE $$

(Map p50; ☎02-897 0295; www.cornertreecafe.com; 150 Jupiter St; mains P250-350; ⏱11am-10pm; ✠🖥🅿) ✐ The Corner Tree provides a tranquil escape from busy Jupiter St, not to mention heavenly vegetarian fare that even diehard meat-eaters will love. The soups, stews, spinach filo triangles and smoothies are our favourites, or try the tofu walnut burger or vego chili. Vegan and gluten-free options available.

★El Chupacabra   MEXICAN $$

(Map p61; 5782 Felipe St; tacos P110-170; ⏱11am-3am Mon-Thu, to 3am Fri-Sun; ✠) Bringing the Mexican street-food craze to Makati, El Chupacabra is a grungy open-air taqueria cooking up a mouthwatering selection of soft-corn tortilla tacos. Go for the spicy chipotle shrimp or *sisig* (sizzling grilled pork) tacos. It's wildly popular so expect to wait in the evenings (no reservations). Grab a margarita in the meantime.

Mantra
INDIAN $$

(Map p62; ☑ 02-776 0318; Bolanos St, Legazpi Village; mains P275-500; ⊙ 11am-2.30pm & 6-11pm) Mantra represents the very best of contemporary Indian cuisine in the Philippine capital, serving divine dhal and other vegetarian dishes and plenty of meat mains such as succulent lamb curries. It's in a dimly lit, minimalist space with outdoor and indoor seating in the heart of Makati's business district.

12/10
JAPANESE $$

(Map p50; ☑ 0915 663 2823; 7635 Guijo St; dishes P250-500; ⊙ 6-11pm Mon-Sat; ☀ 🛜) This is a sleek Japanese *izakaya* (drinking spot) run by a Filipino chef in Makati's arty Guijo St neighbourhood. There are fancy cocktails and Japanese whisky, but the focus is on small plates of contemporary fusion fare like salmon *kushiyashi* (salmon skewers with truffle teriyaki sauce) and the signature *katsu sando* (fried pork cutlet sandwich).

TimHoWan
HONG KONG $$

(Map p62; Glorietta 3; small plates P120-170; ⊙ 10am-10pm; ☀) Michelin–starred in Hong Kong, this dim sum institution was an instant smash upon opening in Manila. It's a more sanitised experience than its hole-in-the-wall parent, but the signature BBQ pork buns leave nothing to be desired. We also love the vermicelli rolls, but really you can't go wrong here.

Commune
CAFE $$

(Map p61; www.commune.ph; 36 Polaris St; light meals P150-320; ⊙ 8am-midnight Mon-Sat, 11am-10pm Sun; ☀ 🛜) Commune sources its own coffee beans from around the Philippines – the beans of the month are written on a large blackboard wall, along with the schedule of community happenings in their event space upstairs. Good espressos, Aeropress and cold drips, as well as sandwiches, salads, Filipino breakfasts and other light bites.

Kite Kebab Bar
MIDDLE EASTERN $$

(Map p61; 5772 Ebro St; mains P200-400; ⊙ 11am-4am; ☀ 🛜) Mediterranean street food is the name of the game here. Besides the basics (hummus, keema) you'll find original surprises like Wagyu kebabs, lamb ribs and ox brain, all delicious. The attractive space in the heart of Poblacion invites lingering with a single malt or beer, or build your own wrap for a takeaway lunch.

★ Sala
FUSION $$$

(Map p62; ☑ 02-750 1555; www.salarestaurant.com; Makati Ave cnr Ayala Ave; mains P500-1500; ⊙ 11am-2pm & 6-11pm Mon-Fri, 6-11pm Sat & Sun) Arguably Manila's finest restaurant for almost 15 years, this refined European bistro is headed by Scottish chef-owner Colin Mackay, who also runs Blackbird. It features top-level service and an ever-changing selection of fusion dishes and creative desserts. The five-course tasting menu (P2900) is a good choice.

Blackbird
INTERNATIONAL $$$

(Map p62; ☑ 02-828 4888; http://blackbird.com.ph; Nielson Tower, Ayala Triangle; mains P600-1000; ⊙ 11am-11pm; ☀) Blackbird is set up inside the art-deco Nielson Tower, a historic 1937 airport control tower, with dining in the old terminal. The menu is international fusion – you can expect the likes of prawn Scotch egg served on betel leaf with sambal, gourmet burgers, Mussaman lamb shank or vegetarian lasagna filled with portobello mushrooms, asparagus, fontina cheese and truffle oil.

Apartment 1B
EUROPEAN $$$

(Map p62; ☑ 02-843 4075; Sedeño St cnr San Agustin St; mains P450-1500; ⊙ 7am-11pm Tue-Sun; ☀ 🛜) A dependable expat fave hidden in the Makati residential district Salcedo

---

A FOODIE'S WEEKEND PARADISE

On weekends, those who love artisan food and laid-back farmers markets will want to check out **Salcedo Community Market** (Map p62; Jaime Velasquez Park, Salcedo Village, Makati; ⊙ 7am-2pm Sat) on Saturday and the **Legazpi Sunday Market** (Map p62; Rufino St, Legazpi Village, Makati; ⊙ 7am-2pm Sun) the next day. Close to 150 vendors set up shop with a dizzying array of local specialities from food-crazy regions such as Ilocos, Pampanga and Bicol, as well as French, Thai and Indonesian offerings and heaps of organic produce. Several local restaurants are also represented here.

JE/IM/SHUTTERSTOCK ©

Filipino breakfast (p41)

joy the ubiquitous Filipino breakfast – rice with a
ed egg accompanied by *bangus* (milkfish).

Donsol (p180), Southeast Luzon

nce a sleepy fishing village, people now flock to
nsol to spot whale sharks, dive the Manta Bowl
drift among fireflies on the Ogod River.

Makati, Manila (p60)

akati used to be Manila's airport, but now the
ldings house the nation's major corporations
d most of the major hotels.

Ifugao people, Banaue (p149)

e Ifugao people, once headhunters, built the
e terraces and are also skilled wood carvers.
eir carved *bulol* (sacred wood figures) are a
ilippine icon.

3

VM/EER/SHUTTERSTOCK ©

Village, Apartment 1B is known for delicious stick-to-your-ribs continental cuisine and huge, hangover-slaying breakfasts (served 7am to 3pm) such as *croque madame*, steak and eggs, and the famous eggs Benedict. Another branch is in a gorgeous space at the Henry Hotel (p70) in Pasay.

The Fort (BGC)

Mercato Centrale
MARKET $

(Map p75; 7th Ave cnr 25th St; mains P100-300; ⊙6pm-3am Thu-Sat) Mercato Centrale is a pop-up food park of sorts that sees close to 50 vendors appear every weekend (and Thursdays) in one of the few vacant lots left in The Fort. It's a lively scene, with most regions of the Philippines well represented along with international stalls and a beer tent.

Tomatito
TAPAS $$

(Map p75; ☑02-805 7840; 30th St cnr 11th Ave; tapas P250-500; ⊙11am-1am; ❄🛜) A big, open, bustling new bistro that dishes out self-described 'sexy' small plates like the signature salmon TNT, *albondigas* (homemade meatballs) and nachos with runny eggs. They have a fine selection of both ceviche and sangria, great gazpacho, and floor-to-ceiling windows that ensure you'll be seen in this trendy spot.

Fowl Bread
CHICKEN $$

(Map p75; Bonifacio High St, cnr 9th Ave; mains P200-300; ⊙8am-midnight) Manila's most famous chicken sandwiches include a slab of signature crispy chicken skin (spicy preferred). Or order garlic noodles topped with cheeseburger potstickers – excellent value, especially with a side of chicken skin (P25). It's a diminutive open-air place with a tiny air-conditioned room at the back, so expect lines at peak hours.

★ Las Flores
SPANISH $$$

(Map p75; ☑02-552 2815; 1 McKinley Pl; mains P400-4000; ⊙11am-2am) With a slick industrial interior and an authentic menu of Catalonia-inspired tapas and mains, Las Flores is justifiably one of Manila's most popular restaurants. Paella (five types) serves two. Steaks – including a Basque variety – are a speciality. They offer cava by the glass, sangria and inspired cocktails.

★ Locavore
FILIPINO $$$

(Map p75; ☑02-796 2017; www.locavore.ph; 5-7AB Forbeswood Parklane; mains 300-700; ⊙9am-2pm; ❄🛜) Locavore uses locally sourced ingredients to stunning effect, creating French-inspired takes on Filipino classics like Bicol *exprés, kaldereta* (beef stew) and of course *halo-halo* (various fruit preserves served in shaved ice and milk). The signature *lechón* (roast suckling pig) and oyster *sisig* is to die for. This place will instantly change your perception of Filipino food. An institution, it does not take reservations, so there's often a wait.

Mecha Uma
JAPANESE $$$

(Map p75; ☑02-964 9605; http://mechauma.ph; 25th St cnr 6th Ave; meals P800-2000; ⊙6-11pm Mon-Sat; ❄) Manileños are crazy about Japanese food, and nobody has caught that wave like top chef Bruce Ricketts at Mecha Uma. A US-trained Filipino, he procures the best tuna and other ingredients for his small plates, which might include hand rolls, *aburi* sushi or mini Japanese-style tacos. Bag a seat for the *omakase* (tasting menu) at the chef's table (reservations essential).

Wholesome Table
FUSION $$$

(Map p75; ☑02-867 0000; www.thewholesometable.com; Bonifacio High St, BGC; mains P250-750; ⊙11am-11pm Mon-Thu, 8am-11pm Fri-Sun; ❄🛜🍴) 🌿 It's all about healthy cuisine here, much of it locally sourced from organic, grass-fed creatures and/or plants. The menu is all over the place, incorporating European (especially Italian) and Asian influences in equal measure. A portion of proceeds from the tasty, filling 'power bowls' supports underprivileged communities, and myriad power shakes are on offer too.

Another branch in **Salcedo Village** (Map p62; ☑02-848 7777; Leviste St cnr Dela Costa St; mains P250-750; ⊙7am-11pm; ❄🛜🍴) 🌿 in Makati.

Quezon City & Around

Quezon City has cutting-edge restaurants and food parks around Maginhawa St, and excellent coffee roasters scattered throughout the city.

★ Van Gogh is Bipolar
CAFE $$

(Map p50; ☑0922 824 3051; 154 Maginhawa St, Quezon City; mains P300-500; ⊙noon-5pm & 6pm-midnight; ❄) Every bit as interesting as it sounds, this chaotic restaurant inhabits a tiny space packed with curios and artworks. It's run by artist Jetro, who cooks entirely original, delicious food in a riotous atmosphere that'll likely see you dine wearing a flamboyant hat (grab one from the hat-stand). Dinners are three- to five-course set meals, while lunch is à la carte.

Jetro established the place as a sanctuary to assist with non-pharmaceutical treatment of his bipolar condition. The shoes-off dining room emits a lovely lemongrass fragrance, and cooking incorporates natural ingredients with reputed mood-enhancing properties. It's (fittingly) prone to close for days or weeks at a time, so call ahead. VGB led the emergence of Maginhawa St as a hotbed of Manila's culinary scene.

Soru Izakaya
JAPANESE $$
(Map p50; ☑ 02-738 2543; 140 Maginhawa St, Quezon City; mains P220-350; ⏱ 11am-11pm; ✷ 🛜)
Soru is a slick new Japanese bistro known for mouthwatering *aburi* (torched) sushi in the heart of QC's Maginhawa foodie district. It also has great ramen, barbecued meat skewers, teppanyaki, tempura and a good selection of sake and Japanese whisky. Professional service too.

Greens Vegetarian
Restaurant and Cafe
VEGETARIAN $$
(Map p76; 92 Scout Castor St, Quezon City; mains P175-225; ⏱ 11am-10pm; 🍴) Earthy and laidback, Greens serves wonderful vegetarian and vegan fare, including eggplant parmigiana and delicious logic-defying meatless *sisig* (usually sizzling grilled pork).

Eighteen Bistro
FUSION $$
(Map p76; ☑ 0917 595 0018; 51B Scout Rallos St, Quezon City; mains P300-400; ⏱ 11am-10pm; ✷) This intimate bistro has just four tables and – fittingly – 18 dishes on the menu. Small plates are the speciality – go for the baked prawn casserole and a salad. There are just four mains, among them beef bourguignon. Wine by the glass (P220) is *very* generously poured.

Gourmet Gypsy
FUSION $$
(Map p50; ☑ 02-662 0880; 25 A Roces Ave, Quezon City; mains P300-800; ⏱ 10am-2pm & 6-10pm; ✷ 🛜) The food is mostly Mediterranean-inspired, with Indian and Vietnamese tastes thrown in. Opt for the Moroccan braised chicken, try an original flatbread pizza, splurge for the osso buco or go healthy with a vegetarian 'Buddha bowl'.

Cafe Kapitan
SPANISH, FILIPINO $$
(JP Rizal St, Marikina City; mains P185-325; ⏱ 9.30am-6.30pm; ✷) Just up the road from the Marikina Shoe Museum (p62), this a good spot for a lunch break within the at-mospheric late-17th-century former home of Kapitan Moy, the Chinese founder of the Marikina shoe industry. Food is heavily Spanish–influenced.

Charlies Grind & Grill
BURGERS $$
(Map p50; 16 East Capitol Dr, Pasig; burgers P200-370; ⏱ noon-1am) This institution in the well-regarded food district of Kapitolyo near Ortigas cooks up Manila's best burgers – go for the double black Angus burger topped with a cheese-stuffed portobello patty if you really want a mouthful. Other offerings include pulled-pork sandwiches and black truffle fries, washed down with imported or local beer.

Señor Pollo
LATIN $$
(Map p76; 49 Scout Rallos St, Quezon City; mains P175-250; ⏱ noon-11pm) The speciality here is, naturally, chicken – we prefer it roasted with a couple of sides. Nachos, quesadillas, margaritas and local craft beer on tap (P120) are also part of the mix. There is another branch in **Poblacion, Makati** (Map p61; Ebro St; mains P175-250; ⏱ 11am-1am).

🍷 Drinking & Nightlife

You're rarely far from a drinking opportunity in Manila. Malate is popular with university kids and backpackers and, along with The Fort (BGC), is the centre of Manila's gay nightlife. Makati is where the expats hang out, along with more and more travellers. Music lovers focus their love on Quezon City.

🍸 Downtown Manila

You'll find the college crowd chugging cheap suds curbside just west of Remedios Circle on Remedios St in Malate – dubbed the 'Monoblock Republic' because of the preponderance of brittle plastic furniture. Malate is awash with big live-music venues, indoor or outdoor, featuring exuberant cover bands. These are a fun way to absorb local colour; just be on the lookout for hidden 'entertainment' charges. Karaoke bars are everywhere; some of them are less than wholesome.

★ Oarhouse
BAR
(Map p68; www.oarhousepub.com; 1688 Bocobo St, Malate; ⏱ 5pm-late Mon-Fri, 3pm-late Sat & Sun; 🛜) Around since 1977, the Oarhouse is a Malate treasure, attracting an intelligent, boozy crowd of regulars, comprising

ROOFTOP HANG-OUTS

To get a different perspective on Manila, head up to one of the city's rooftop bars to escape street-level chaos and enjoy some great views.

Sky Deck (Map p54; Muralla & Victoria Sts, Intramuros; ⊙5pm-1am; 🔊) Perched atop the Bayleaf hotel in Intramuros, with 360-degree views of the metropolis. Come for sunset post-sightseeing. Happy hour (5pm to 9pm) features all-you-can-drink San Miguel for P550. Live acoustic bands some nights.

Firefly Roofdeck Bar (Map p61; 8008 Makati Ave, Poblacion, Makati; ⊙10am-2am) This elegant rooftop lounge is 32 storeys up at the City Garden Grand Hotel. It has nearly 360-degree views of Makati, a wide-ranging cocktail and craft beer menu and decent food, including themed buffet nights.

Pacific Lounge (Map p68; cnr Adriatico & Malvar Sts, Pan Pacific Hotel, 21st fl, Malate; cocktails incl nibbles P250; ⊙6am-11pm) Hidden 21 floors above Malate, this five-star hotel's rooftop bar is open to nonguests. Hang out in its garden oasis (complete with gazebo and footbridge) or head indoors for suave city views; drink all you can for P800 during happy hour (6am to 8pm), which includes a buffet of nibbles.

Straight Up (Map p75; cnr 30th St & 11th Ave, BGC; 🔊) A classic Manhattan–style roof bar atop the Seda Hotel in The Fort (BGC), with great city views and two-for-one cocktails from 5pm to 7pm.

students, journalists and foreigners who often linger until the sun comes up. Serves the coldest beer in town and plays great music. Serves craft beer, good burgers and great chilli, plus a nightly barbecue.

Erra's Vest Ramen in Town
BAR

(Map p68; 1755 Adriatico St, Malate; ⊙24hr) Erra's is your classic Southeast Asian streetside shack luring folk from all corners of the galaxy to quaff cheap San Miguel and – as its quirky name implies – slurp the house ramen (P60 to P90).

Che'lu
GAY

(Map p68; 1802 Maria Orosa St, Malate; ⊙9pm-4am, to 6am Thu-Sat) This long-running club is one of the few places with staying power in Malate's gay district. With much cheaper drinks than the places in the Fort, it draws a decent crowd most nights and really gets raucous starting from Thursday.

 Makati & Poblacion

Poblacion – also known as the P Burgos area after its central street – is where most people go out in Makati these days. P Burgos St itself remains a red-light district, but the surrounding streets now brim with white-collar Filipinos and expats enjoying a burgeoning dining and drinking scene. Elsewhere, speakeasies are a local speciality, and

you'll find swanky rooftop bars and grungy music venues as well.

★ Long Bar
COCKTAIL BAR

(Map p62; 1 Raffles Dr; ⊙noon-2am) Inspired by the Singapore original, this lobby-level watering hole at the Raffles Makati (p71) has an unbeatable happy hour – all-you-can-drink beer, wine and cocktails (including the signature Singapore Sling) for P870 from 5pm to 8pm. The lacquered, suitably lengthy bar is a real treasure. Discarded peanut husks pile up on the floor.

★ A Toda Madre
BAR

(Map p61; www.atmrestaurant.com; Durban St cnr Makati Ave; ⊙5pm-2am) This snazzy tequila bar and Mexican eatery carries a rotating selection of close to 85 different tequilas and mezcals, Mexican beers and several types of margarita (order it with Don Julio or Casa Noble *reposado*). The hand-pressed, double-wrapped soft corn-tortilla tacos are delicious – try the *barbacoa* (slow-cooked beef) off the specials menu.

Z Roofdeck
BAR

(Map p61; 5660 Don Pedro St; ⊙5pm-late) There's no doubt where the top backpacker party spot in Manila is. Z Hostel's (p71) roof deck draws hot local and foreign DJ talent and is popular with locals and expats too. Happy hour (5pm to 8pm Monday to Thursday) brings P58 local beers – purchase credit on an RFID bracelet to pay for your drinks.

★ **Pura Vida**   BAR
(Map p61; Don Pedro St cnr Jacobo St; ⊘6.30pm-2am Mon-Sat) Owned by a Costa Rican, Pura Vida brings a dash of laid-back Caribbean attitude to the heart of Poblacion, with occasional reggae bands, *arroz con camarones* (rice with prawns), mojitos and a decidedly global crowd lapping it all up. Downstairs is **Polilya** (Map p61; ⊘6.30pm-2am Tue-Sun; 🖼), the uber-classy new taproom of craft brewer Engkanto.

20:20   COCKTAIL BAR
(Map p50; La Fuerza Plaza, Chino Roces Ave; ⊘7pm-3am Wed-Sat) Enter and be greeted by a towering rack of top-shelf spirits rising from the bar. This is a good sign. The positives hardly stop there, what with groovy DJs, funky light installations, creative bar food and a sophisticated crowd cosied up to the bar or nestled at dimly lit tables.

Curator   BAR
(Map p62; 134 Legazpi St, Legazpi Village; cocktails from P400; ⊘6.30pm-2am) The place for those who take their alcohol seriously, the award-winning Curator serves up an changing menu of original cocktails made by mixologists who know their stuff. Drinks are pricey, but use quality ingredients. Single-origin coffees and sandwiches are served in the cafe out front (open 7am to 10 pm).

Joe's Brew   BAR
(Map p61; Mathilde St cnr Jacobo St; ⊘5pm-1am Tue-Sun) This minute space is the taproom of one of Manila's leading craft brewers. Try their Fish Rider Pale Ale accompanied by brisket or poutine (French-Canadian dish of chips with gravy) from the attached **Holy Smokes** smoke house.

H&J   BAR
(Map p61; 5781 Felipe St; ⊘2pm-7am Mon-Fri, 24hr Sat & Sun; 🖼) This long-running pub is wildly popular among expats for watching live sport on TV, and usually features a live band or two on weekend nights.

Finders Keepers   BAR
(Map p50; www.facebook.com/finderskeepersmnl; Sabio St cnr Chino Roces Ave; ⊘8pm-late Tue-Sun) This dimly lit speakeasy is hidden within a nondescript warehouse under the ultra-cool **Black Market club** (Map p50; www.blackmarketmnl.com; ⊘9pm-3am Wed-Sat). Once you've found it, grab a stool at the long bar for quality cocktails or lounge on a couch.

🍷 The Fort (BGC)

BGC (aka The Fort) is Manila's upscale party zone. The big superclubs are here, and you'll also find plenty of fancy cocktail bars and

---

CRAFT BEER DENS

The craft beer revolution has reached Manila, as local beer aficionados ply their craft to cater to a thirsty new generation of drinkers. Here are some places that specialise in Filipino craft beer:

The Bottle Shop (Map p75; 26th St cnr 3rd Ave, BGC; ⊘1pm-2am Mon-Sat; 🖼) Manila's best selection of craft beer. Huge range of domestic and international brews available (both on tap and bottled), including Rogue and other US Pacific Northwest brands.

Big Bad Wolf (Map p75; Forbestown Rd, Burgos Circle, BGC; ⊘11am-1.30am; 🖼) Reminiscent of a hipster bar in Portland, Big Bad Wolf is split over two levels with comfy couches, a cool soundtrack and blackboard menus with an excellent selection of craft beer from around the country.

Tap Station (Map p75; Forbestown Rd, BGC; ⊘5pm-late) A happening, down-to-earth, open-air craft beer specialist near Burgos Circle. They have 25 beers on tap (pints P225 to P295), including a few Belgian varieties. Happy hour (6pm to 9pm) means two-for-one on the house pilsner. Another branch in **Ermita** (Map p68; Adriatico St cnr Padre Faura St, Ermita; 330ml beer P120-200; ⊘5pm-2am Mon-Sat, to 11pm Sun).

Batala Bar (Map p62; 830 A Arnaiz Ave, 2nd fl, Makati; ⊘3pm-midnight Tue-Sun; 🖼) 🍃 Superb selection of craft beer, both in bottles and on tap, creative cocktails, and a locavore-leaning menu. They also peddle locally made fair-trade wares and support environmental and other good causes with frequent fundraisers and art exhibitions.

craft beer places, none of them cheap. The area south of Burgos Circle (Forbestown Rd) is an active drinking zone, with many bars and cafes offering outdoor seating.

★ **Bank Bar** BAR
(Map p75; RCBC Tower, 26th St; ⊙5pm-2am Mon-Fri, 7pm-3am Sat & Sun) Self-described as a 'drinking den', this sophisticated secret bar is well hidden behind a 7-Eleven in The Fort. It has a huge selection of spirits, craft cocktails and bar snacks, plus a roving martini trolley that delivers customised concoctions.

★ **Nectar** GAY & LESBIAN
(Map p75; ☑0917 542 8831; The Fort Strip, 5th Ave; admission P500; ⊙10pm-4am Tue-Sat) Recently opened in the heart of The Fort, this is Manila's top LGTB nightclub. No flamboyant drag shows here, just hunky dancers and top DJs holding court in front of a heaving crowd that draws plenty of heteros as well. Tuesday is lesbian night.

Valkyrie CLUB
(Map p50; www.thepalacemanila.com; 9th Ave cnr 36th St) This superclub draws top local and international DJs to spin in a humongous space in The Fort. It's under the same management as the equally popular nightclub **Revel at the Palace** (Map p50; ☑0917 550 8888; admission incl 2 cocktails Wed & Thu P800, Fri & Sat P1500; ⊙10pm-late Mon-Sat); **Palace Pool Club** (Map p50; ⊙11am-3am), known for pool parties; and a chichi beer hall.

Unit 27 BAR
(Map p75; 26th St cnr 7th Ave) A regular old bar and cafe by day, Unit 27 morphs into a party playground for a well-heeled, gay-friendly clientele by evening. Thursday and Friday are the big nights, when top DJs spin and it's elbow-to-elbow. The action begins at midnight.

Quezon City & Cubao

★ **Cubao Expo** AREA
(Map p76; Gen Romulo Ave, Cubao; ⊙5pm-late) A precinct of cool bars, cheap eats and boutiques, Cubao X is a must for anyone interested in Manila's underground scene. Venues come and go, but boozy communist-themed bar **Fred's Revolución** (Map p76; ⊙6pm-midnight Tue-Sun) is one constant. It hums with alternative rock and serves a few craft beers.

Catch 272 BAR
(Map p76; T Gener St cnr Kamuning Rd, Quezon City; ⊙7pm-late Tue-Sun) A bohemian hang-out with suitably tattooed bartenders slinging original drinks like the signature 'baywalker'

MANILA'S THIRD-WAVE COFFEE

Coffee is something Manila's new generation likes to take seriously. Quezon City leads the way, with several professional coffee roasters, but Makati and The Fort (BGC) are catching up. All of the following source single-origin, fair-trade beans. A few of them roast on-site, and they all have excellent food as well.

Coffee Empire (Map p76; www.coffeeempire.com.ph; 74 West Ave, Quezon City; mains P200-400; ⊙9am-1am) A chic, industrial open-plan warehouse setup with hessian sacks of single-origin green beans on display in the glassed-in 'green room', plus drawers of roasted beans for sniffing. You can observe roastings on Wednesdays and Saturdays, and they also do cuppings (check the website).

Craft Coffee Revolution (Map p76; 66c Broadway Ave, Quezon City; ⊙8am-11pm; 🛜) Next door to Big Sky Mind, Craft Coffee Revolution is everything a coffeehouse should be, with wooden-crate furniture where patrons can enjoy single-origin espressos or 24-hour cold-steeped coffee.

Yardstick (Map p62; ☑02-624 9511; www.yardstickcoffee.com; 106 Esteban St, Legazpi Village, Makati; mains P300; ⊙7am-11pm Mon-Sat, 8am-6pm Sun; ▣🛜) Doubles as a wholesaler of single-origin beans and La Marzocco equipment. It's in a bright, airy space with a roasting area out back and a glassed-in facility for frequent cuppings and coffee workshops. Brewed coffee is steam-pumped.

Hineleban Cafe (Map p62; 830 A Arnaiz Ave, Makati; ⊙7am-9pm Mon-Fri, 9am-8pm Sat & Sun) 🖋 Specialises in single-origin coffee that is locally sourced – mainly from Bukidnon (Mindanao). Aeropress, pour-over, French press and siphon all available.

(a salted-rim Long Island iced tea of sorts). There's great live music on Friday and Saturday – try to catch local favourite Kapitan Kuman. It serves delicious pub food like seaweed and parmesan chicken tenders.

Big Sky Mind   BAR
(Map p76; Broadway Ave, New Manila, Quezon City; ☺9pm-5am Tue-Sun) Manila's most famous dive bar has been around since 1999. All sorts of characters show up to sit on second-hand furniture, swap yarns and listen to classic Pinoy rock music. It really gets hopping around 2am. There's tasty bar food, and first-timers are encouraged to try the 'welcome shot' (just ask for it).

☆ Entertainment

Live Music

★ SaGuijo   LIVE MUSIC
(Map p50; ☎02-897 8629; www.facebook.com/saGuijo.Cafe.Bar.Events; 7612 Guijo St, Makati; admission after 10pm incl a drink P150-200; ☺6pm-2am) A wonderfully decrepit dive bar with a jam-packed roster of indie, punk and new-wave bands that kick off at 10.30pm. Check Facebook for their schedule.

Tago Jazz Cafe   JAZZ
(Map p50; ☎0922 357 5896; www.facebook.com/tagojazzcafe; 14 Main Ave, Cubao; ☺9pm-3am) A fantastic and intimate jazz lounge hidden off the grid in Quezon City. They put on top local musicians plus the occasional imported guest, and their open jazz jams (usually Sunday) draw some real talent. Thursday is for bebop. There may be a small (P100) admission fee for higher-profile acts.

'70s Bistro   LIVE MUSIC
(Map p50; www.the70sbistro.com; 46 Anonas St, Quezon City; admission around P150; ☺7pm-late Mon-Sat) A long-running Quezon City bar, '70s Bistro is known for getting some of the best reggae acts in the country, plus classic Pinoy rock bands that have been around almost since the 1970s, like the Jerks. Check their Facebook page for the schedule.

Conspiracy Garden Cafe   LIVE MUSIC
(Map p50; ☎02-453 2170; www.facebook.com/conspiracy.garden.cafe; 59 Visayas Ave, Quezon City; admission P100-150; ☺5pm-2am Mon-Sat) This is a longstanding, character-filled venue attracting an older, sit-down crowd for more acoustic-oriented gigs. The garden is a good place to chill with a dark San Miguel. Gigs start around 10pm; check their Facebook page for the schedule.

Salon de Ning   LIVE MUSIC
(Map p62; Peninsula Manila Hotel, Makati Ave, Makati; ☺7pm-2am Tue-Sat) Hidden away inside the luxurious Peninsula hotel (p71), this is a 1930s Shanghai–style drinking den full of dark nooks and hidden spaces. Themes range from bohemian lounge to air zeppelin cockpit to Thrilla in Manila (ie, boxing). Live music kicks off nightly on the central stage.

Minokaua   LIVE MUSIC
(Penguin Cafe; Map p68; 1951 Adriatico St, Malate; ☺from 5pm Tue-Sat) In the space of the old Penguin Cafe, once Malate's prime boho magnet, the Minokaua puts exceptional musical talent on stage.

Performing Arts

Cultural Center of the Philippines   PERFORMING ARTS
(Map p72; ☎02-832 1125; www.culturalcenter.gov.ph; CCP Complex, Roxas Blvd, Pasay; performance prices vary; ☺box office 9am-6pm Tue-Sat, 1-5pm Sun performance days) Manila's major cultural guns perform here, including Ballet Philippines, the nation's premiere dance troupe; Philippine Philharmonic Orchestra, the nation's main classical orchestra; and Tanghalang Pilipino, a theatre group that performs classic and original local work.

Club Mwah!   CABARET
(Map p50; ☎02-535 7943; www.theclubmwah.com; Venue Tower, 652 Boni Ave, Mandaluyong City; tickets P750; ☺dinner 7.30pm, show 9.30pm Fri & Sat) The best of the city's drag stage shows take place at the opulent Club Mwah!, an incredibly shiny, sparkly and simply fabulous place with obvious Las Vegas interior-design influences. On par with anything in Bangkok, it gets a huge thumbs-up for choreography and creativity.

Philippine Educational Theater Association   THEATRE
(PETA; Map p76; ☎02-725 6244; www.petatheater.com; 5 Eymard Dr, Quezon City; tickets from P800; ☺shows 10am, 3pm &/or 8pm Fri-Sun) This 'open' theatre group does both comedy and tragedy, most of it original. Arguably Manila's best troupe, but check whether performances are in English. Also hosts festivals and workshops.

Arenas

Mall of Asia Arena   CONCERT VENUE
(Map p72; Diokno Blvd, Pasay) Venue for high-profile concerts and shows; Madonna and Britney Spears have played here.

Araneta Coliseum
LIVE MUSIC

(The Big Dome; Map p76; www.smataraneta coliseum.com; Gen Roxas Ave, Cubao) Manila's iconic arena was the site of the 'Thrilla in Manila', possibly the most famous boxing match of all time. Today it hosts big PBA (Philippine Basketball Association) games, other sporting events and a hotchpotch of touring international bands.

Cinemas
Manila's malls boast hundreds of cinemas, many of them state of the art. Hollywood blockbusters are often shown in the Philippines at the same time as their US release, yet it costs only P120 to P200 to watch a movie here. There's an IMAX at Mall of Asia.

Casinos
Three world-class casinos have opened in recent years in Manila, which is shooting to become something of a 'Macau South': **Solaire** (Map p50; ☑02-888 8888; www.solaireresort. com; 1 Asean Ave, Entertainment City, Parañaque; ⊘24hr), **City of Dreams** (Map p50; ☑02-800 8080; www.cityofdreamsmanila.com; Asean Ave, Entertainment City, Parañaque; ⊘24hr) and **Okada** (Map p50; ☑02-888 0777; www.okadamanila.com; New Seaside Drive, Entertainment City, Parañaque). The latter is the newest and most ambitious, occupying 43 hectares of reclaimed Manila Bay waterfront. You'll easily spot the metallic colossus and its record-setting fountain (it's the world's largest dancing fountain) when flying into Manila at night.

If you want to have a punt, the three big boys occupy the so-called 'Entertainment City' in Parañaque, and the tables are open 24 hours a day. Aside from gambling, they offer the usual range of Vegas–style entertainment: variety shows, concerts, celebrity restaurants and clubs. Solaire in particular draws high-profile musicians and quality drama to its impressive **Theater at Solaire**. Okada's **Cove** is a sprawling indoor beach club.

🔒 Shopping

🔒 Downtown Manila

★ **Silahis Arts & Artifacts** GIFTS & SOUVENIRS
(Map p54; 744 General Luna St, Intramuros; ⊘10am-7pm) This is almost more of a cultural centre than a shop. Intricately woven baskets, wooden Ifugao *bulol* statues for guarding rice, textiles and other crafts from around the country are sold next to beautiful antiques.

Upstairs **Tradewinds Books** (Map p54; ⊘10am-7pm) specialises in Philippine history, culture and biography.

★ **Solidaridad Bookshop** BOOKS
(Map p68; 531 Padre Faura St, Ermita; ⊘9am-6pm Mon-Sat) Owned by the Filipino author F Sionil José, Solidaridad has a masterfully curated collection of both Western and Eastern non-fiction, international magazines such as the *New Yorker*, and hard-to-find Filipino history titles and documentaries.

HUB Make Lab
MARKET

(Map p58; www.98-B.org/hubmakelab; First United Bldg, Escolta St, Binondo; ⊘11am-8pm Tue-Sun) The HUB is basically a happy place for creators and entrepreneurs. You'll find all sorts of things being sold out of funky cubicles: wacky fashion accessories, vintage items, ice cream 'experiments' (soy sauce and bacon, anyone?), desktop succulents (ie miniplants)...and of course plenty of art – the artists' group 98B COLLABoratory is just upstairs.

Manila Collectible Co
GIFTS & SOUVENIRS

(Map p54; ☑0917 861 3011; Fort Santiago, Intramuros; ⊘9am-8pm) This funky shop specialises in hand-spun textiles and accessories produced by indigenous groups across the Philippines. It also sells fair-trade organic coffee, Philippine cigars, local 'wines', flavoured pili nuts and pure cacao.

Tesoro's
GIFTS & SOUVENIRS

(Map p68; www.tesoros.ph; 1325 Mabini St, Ermita; ⊘11am-8pm) The speciality here is *pinya* (fabric woven from pineapple fibres) products - especially embroidered *barongs* (from P9500), but there are also lacquered coconut-shell products, baskets, bags, coffee, dried mangoes and a few rare books on Philippine culture. Also has branches in **Makati** (Map p62; 1016 A Arnaiz Ave; ⊘9.30am-9pm Mon-Sat, 10am-7.30pm Sun) and the airport too (Terminal 1 and 3) for last-minute gift shopping.

Maria Closa
ANTIQUES, ARTS

(Map p68; www.mariaclosa.com; 1335 Mabini St, Ermita; ⊘9am-6.30pm Mon-Sat) This high-end gallery shop is one for serious collectors with quality hand-crafted furniture, sculpture and artefacts from around the country.

Hiraya Gallery
ART

(Map p68; www.hiraya.com; 530 United Nations Ave, Ermita; ⊘9am-5pm Mon-Sat) This long-established commercial gallery has a museum-quality selection of Filipino contemporary art. Names to look out for are Norberto Carating, Eric Guazon and young Batanes artist Randalf Dilla.

Mall of Asia MALL
(Map p72; Manila Bay, Pasay; ⊘10am-10pm) One of the top 10 largest malls in the world, with the usual retail shops and a zillion restaurants, plus an Olympic–sized ice rink and an IMAX theatre. Come early evening for its oceanfront carnival rides and stay for the impressive weekend fireworks shows over Manila Bay.

Makati

★**Balikbayan
Handicrafts** GIFTS & SOUVENIRS
(Map p62; www.balikbayanhandicrafts.com; 1010 A Arnaiz Ave; ⊘9am-8pm Mon-Sat, 10am-8pm Sun) Set over three levels, this is the kind of place that pulls in tourists by the busload. The merchandise is of good quality, considering how much of it they have. The speciality is beautiful glazed coconut dishware and decorative balls, among many other products.

★**Greenbelt** MALL
(Map p62; Ayala Centre; ⊘11am-9pm) This is the high end of the Ayala Centre, with scores of cafes and restaurants around a central park area. There are five sections (Greenbelt 1 to Greenbelt 5), each with its own character.

Lemongrass House COSMETICS
(Map p62; Dusit Thani Hotel; ⊘9am-10pm) This well-regarded Thai import peddles all-natural oils, sunscreen, after-sun gel and an effective lavender-and-citronella mozzie repellent, among many other fragrant soaps and lotions, all sourced from small suppliers in Thailand.

LRI Design Plaza DESIGN, ART
(Map p50; www.lridesignplaza.com; 210 Nicanor Garcia St; ⊘10am-7pm Mon-Sat) A conglomeration of art galleries and contemporary furniture showrooms showcases all that's chic in the capital's art and design world.

The Fort (BGC)

Echo Store COSMETICS, FOOD
(Map p75; www.echostore.ph; Serendra Mall, McKinley Pkwy; ⊘9am-9pm) ✹ Specialises in fairtrade, locally sourced products (including coffee and handicrafts) and chemical-free beauty/health items. Its cafe serves tasty organic and sustainable dishes.

Fully Booked BOOKS
(Map p75; www.fullybookedonline.com; 902 Bonifacio High St; ⊘11am-11pm) Manila's most comprehensive bookshop, with a great travel section and an outstanding selection of fiction and non-fiction (all in English). There are branches in most malls across Manila, but fans of Tintin will want to check out this flagship branch in The Fort.

Bonifacio High Street SHOPPING CENTRE
(Map p75; btwn 5th & 11th Aves) This upscale open-air strip mall spans three long blocks in The Fort (BGC), with loads of good restaurants and upmarket fashion labels, plus art installations and frequent weekend festivals. It leads to the **Fiesta Market** (Map p75; McKinley Pkwy, BGC; ⊘10am-9pm) outside Market! Market! mall, with open-air eateries and regional cuisine.

MANILA SHOPPING

QUIAPO MARKET FERVOUR

Lovers of markets and mayhem should cross the Quezon Bridge over the Pasig River to Quiapo Church (p57), home of the Black Nazarene (p65).

The main reason to go to Quiapo, however, is not to see the church but to witness what's happening on and around the church square, **Plaza Miranda** (Map p58). Here and in the surrounding markets every manner of product is sold to a throng of humanity.

Most notorious are the dubious apothecary stalls selling herbal and folk medicines, as well as amulets (carved stones and medallions believed to have magical powers). Showing admirable initiative, vendors will tell you that the 'Pampa Regla' potion is good for everything from weight loss to curing erectile dysfunction, depending on how you look.

Particularly colourful are the stalls around Carriedo St, which sell thickly padded bras, hardware, porn DVDs and just about anything else. Nearby under **Quezon Bridge**, the area known as **Ilalim ng Tulay** (literally 'under the bridge'), you can find really cheap junk for tourists. Across the road at the recently modernised **Quinta Market & Fish Port**, vendors peddle seafood, meat, vegetables, fruit and other foodstuffs.

Quezon City & Around

★ **Cubao Expo**   VINTAGE
(Map p76; Gen Romulo Ave, Cubao) Über-hip assortment of bars, kitschy shops and galleries selling everything from old LPs to retro toys and housewares.

★ **Greenhills Shopping Center**   MARKET
(Map p50; www.greenhills.com.ph; Ortigas Ave, San Juan; ⊙10am-8pm) Somewhat like an indoor/outdoor flea market, Greenhills has stall after stall selling DVDs and brand-named clothing of questionable legitimacy. But snoop around here and you'll find quality antiques and the best selection of genuine pearls in the country.

Human Nature   COSMETICS
(www.humanheartnature.com; 463 Commonwealth Ave, Quezon City; ⊙9am-6pm Mon-Sat) 🌿 The flagship shop of this social enterprise selling all–Filipino, chemical-free beauty and health products. Also sells local coffee beans, with free cups of brewed coffee. Does excellent work in helping poorer communities.

ℹ️ Information

INTERNET ACCESS

Coreon Gate (Map p68; 1774 Adriatico St, Malate; per hour P60; ⊙24hr) Bright, clean internet cafe that doubles as a high-speed–wi-fi-enabled co-working space. There's another branch in Makati (Map p61; Polaris St, Makati; per hr P60; ⊙24hr).

MEDICAL SERVICES

Metro Manila has several large private hospitals that are gaining traction for medical tourism.

Makati Medical Center (Map p62; 📞02-888 8999; www.makatimed.net.ph; 2 Amorsolo St, Makati)

Manila Doctors Hospital (Map p68; 📞02-558 0888; www.maniladoctors.com.ph; 667 United Nations Ave, Ermita)

St Luke's Medical Center (Map p75; 📞02-789 7700, emergency 02-789 7810; www.stluke. com.ph; 32nd St, BGC) Metro Manila's most modern hospital. Also in **Quezon City** (Map p76; 📞02-723 0101, emergency 02-727 2328; 279 E Rodriguez Sr Ave, Quezon City).

POST

Ermita Post Office (Map p68; Hidalgo St, Malate; ⊙8am-5pm Mon-Fri) Most convenient to Malate's tourist belt.

Makati Central Post Office (Map p62; Sen Gil Puyat Ave, Makati; ⊙8am-5pm Mon-Fri)

Manila Central Post Office (Map p54; Magallanes Dr, Intramuros; ⊙6am-6.30pm Mon-Fri, 8am-noon Sat) This beautiful American–era landmark lords over the Pasig River near Intramuros. Offers full services.

MONEY

Malate and Ermita are peppered with money changers, and most malls and all four airport terminals have them too. These offer better rates than banks.

Citibank main office (Map p62; 8741 Paseo de Roxas, Makati; ⊙ATM 24hr) Allows withdrawals of P15,000; also has an ATM at NAIA Terminal 3.

HSBC main office (Map p62; 6766 Ayala Ave, Makati) Allows P40,000 ATM withdrawals. Additional outlets at Power Plant Mall in Rockwell (Makati) and on 5th Ave in The Fort.

SAFE TRAVEL

Manila is probably no more dangerous than the next city, but it can still be dodgy, and foreigners are sometimes targeted by petty criminals and car-jackers.

➡ Be on your guard if walking around on your own at night, especially in rough districts like Tondo.

➡ Pickpocketing is rampant on the MRT/LRT and on major bar strips, where drunk tourists make easy prey.

➡ Traffic is the big annoyance in Manila; you'll probably spend half your time either stuck in it or talking about it. Leave extra time to get to airports, bus stations and dinner dates.

➡ Noise, crowds and air pollution are other major annoyances.

TOURIST INFORMATION

Department of Tourism Information Centre (DOT; Map p62; 📋02-459 5200; www.visit myphilippines.com; JB Bldg, 351 Sen Gil Puyat Ave, Makati; ⊙7am-6pm Mon-Sat) The tourism office has helpful staff, city maps and information for trips around Manila. There are also smaller DOT offices at the various NAIA terminals.

ℹ️ Getting There & Away

AIR

All international flights in and out of Manila use one of the three main terminals (Terminal 1, Terminal 2, Terminal 3) of **Ninoy Aquino International Airport** (NAIA; Map p50; www.miaa.gov. ph) in Manila's south, while many domestic flights use a fourth, domestic terminal (Terminal 4).

The four terminals share runways, but they are not particularly close to each other, so pay very close attention to which terminal you are flying into and out of; if you go to the wrong terminal it could take you 30 minutes to correct your mistake and you could miss your flight. For more information see the Transport chapter (p443).

'Airport Loop' shuttle buses and vans (P20, 7am to 10pm) link the four terminals, but they are slow and sporadic, so take a taxi if you're in a hurry.

Note that several Asian discount carriers fly to **Clark International Airport** (DMIA; ☑ 045-599 2888; http://crk.clarkairport.com) in the Clark Special Economic Zones, a two-hour drive north of Manila.

Airlines

Manila is well connected to the world via international carriers and the two main national carriers (Philippine Airlines and Cebu Pacific).

For domestic flights Philippine Airlines, Cebu Pacific and Air Asia are the main airlines and serve the key provincial centres from Manila. Newish player Skyjet has good rates on a few useful routes, while rapidly expanding Air Juan runs tiny sea and/or wheeled planes on a few niche routes. Air Swift monopolises the Manila–El Nido route.

One-way domestic flights cost P1000 to P3500 (including taxes) on most routes, provided you book in advance. Flight times range from 45 minutes for short hops such as Manila to Caticlan, to 1½ hours for flights from Manila to southern Mindanao.

The following airlines fly domestically in and out of Manila. All have ticket offices at their terminal of departure or around town:

Air Juan (☑ 02-718 8111; www.airjuan.com) Daily seaplanes to Puerto Galera (P5500, 20 minutes) at 7.10am, hopping to Boracay on Mondays, Tuesdays, Thursdays and Saturdays.

Air Swift (☑ 02-318 5942; http://air-swift.com) Serves El Nido from its own separate terminal near Terminal 4.

AirAsia (☑ 02-722 2742; www.airasia.com; NAIA Terminal 4) Flights to Caticlan (for Boracay), Cebu, Davao, Kalibo, Puerto Princesa, Tacloban and Tagbilaran.

Cebu Pacific (Map p50; ☑ 02-702 0888; www. cebupacificair.com; NAIA Terminal 3) Primary domestic budget carrier with dozens of routes out of Manila.

Philippine Airlines (PAL; ☑ 02-855 8888; www.philippineairlines.com; NAIA Terminal 2) Flagship carrier with scores of domestic routes.

Skyjet (☑ in Manila 02-863 1333; www.skyjetair. com; NAIA Terminal 4) Serves Batanes, Coron, Caticlan and Siargao.

BOAT

The flashy **Manila North Harbor Port** (Map p50; ☑ 02-588 9000; www.mnhport.com.ph; Piers 4 & 6, Tondo), northwest of Binondo, is the departure and arrival point for all domestic ferry travel. The South Harbor is now used for cargo and international cruise ships.

It's best to take a taxi to/from North Harbor, as Tondo district isn't a place for a foreigner to be wandering around with luggage, and public transport routes are complicated.

2GO Travel (Map p50; ☑ 02-528 7000; http://travel.2go.com.ph; Pier 4, Manila North Harbor Port) is the major shipping line handling interisland boat trips from Manila. It has an excellent website for checking schedules and reserving tickets. Tickets can be purchased online, and through travel agents, major malls or its main branch in **Rizal Park** (The Hub @ Kilometer Zero, Rizal Park). For ferries to Caticlan (for Boracay), you'll need to head to Batangas pier.

Atienza Shipping Lines (Map p50; ☑ 0999 881 7266; 1st St, cnr Muelle de Tacoma, Tondo) has ferries to Coron town, Palawan, Tuesday at 8pm and on Thursday and Saturday at 4pm (P1000 to P1150, 16 hours). Atienza also sails to El Nido on Friday at 4pm (P1700 to P1850, 25 hours) via Linapacan in the Calamian Islands.

BUS

Getting out of Manila by bus is harder than you might expect, as there is no central bus terminal. Instead, myriad private operators serve specific destinations from their own terminals.

The two main 'clusters' of terminals are known as **Cubao**, which is in Quezon City near the corner of EDSA and Aurora Blvd; and **Pasay**, which is along EDSA near the LRT/MRT interchange at **Pasay Rotunda** (Map p72; cnr EDSA & Taft Ave).

Two harder-to-reach clusters are **Sampaloc**, north of Quiapo near the University of Santo Tomas (UST); and **Caloocan** in the far north of Metro Manila.

Wherever you are heading, it's worth paying a little extra for buses that take the modern expressways heading north and south out of Manila. Getting stuck on a 'local' bus could add several hours to your trip.

Better yet, shoot for the comfortable 27-seat 'deluxe' express and/or sleeper buses that serve major Luzon hubs including Baguio, Vigan, Laoag, Tuguegarao, Naga and Legazpi. It's recommended to book these, and the direct night buses to Banaue, a day or more ahead.

Bus Companies

Amihan Bus Lines (Map p76; ☑ 0917 508 9724; Araneta Center Busport, Cubao)

Bicol Isarog Terminals in **Ermita** (Map p68; ☑ 02-525 7077; Padre Faura Center, Padre Faura St, Ermita) and **Cubao** (Map p76; ☑ 02-727 8194; 599 EDSA, Cubao)

BSC San Agustin (Map p72; Pasay Rotunda, cnr Taft Ave & EDSA)

Cagsawa Terminals in **Ermita** (Map p68; ☑ 02-525 9756; Padre Faura Center, Padre Faura St, Ermita) and **Cubao** (Map p76; Araneta Center Busport, Cubao)

BUSES FROM MANILA

DESTINATION	TIME (HR)	PRICE (P)	COMPANY	FREQUENCY
Alaminos	5½	393	Dagupan, Five Star, Victory Liner (Cubao)	hourly
Baguio (air-con)	6-7	450	Genesis, Victory Liner	frequent
Baguio (deluxe)	4	760	Genesis, Victory Liner	6-7 daily
Balanga	3-4	210-400	Genesis	frequent
Baler	4-6	air-con–deluxe 450-700	Genesis (Cubao)	air-con 7am & noon, deluxe 12.30am-5.30am
Banaue	8-9	490-530	Ohayami	2-4 night buses
Batangas	2-2½	170	Ceres, DLTB, Jam	every 20min
Bolinao	7	350-470	Dagupan, Victory Liner (Cubao)	6-7 buses daily
Clark Airport	2-3	350	Philtranco	8 daily
Dau (Angeles)	1½-2½	139-150	Most companies	frequent
Iba	5-7	376	Victory Liner	6-7 daily
Laoag	8-12	air-con–sleeper 550-850	Fariñas, Florida, Maria de Leon	frequent
Legazpi	10-12	air-con–sleeper 850-1100	Amihan, Bicol Isarog, Cagsawa, DLTB, Philtranco	mostly night buses
Lucena	4-5	220	DLTB, JAC, Jam	frequent
Naga	8-10	air-con–deluxe 670-900	Amihan, Bicol Isarog, Cagsawa	mostly night buses
Sagada (via Banaue)	11	air-con–deluxe 720-980	Coda Lines	8pm & 9pm
San Jose (Mindoro)	12	900	Dimple Star, Roro Bus	7 daily
San Fernando (La Union)	6	378-436	Dominion, Partas	hourly
San Pablo (for Mt Banahaw)	2½-3	127-150	DLTB, Jac, Jam	every 30min
Santa Cruz (for Pagsanjan)	2½-3	140	DLTB, Jac	frequent
Solano (for Banaue)	8	320	Florida, Victory Liner	frequent
Subic Bay (Olangapo)	3-4	air-con–express 200-245	Victory Liner	frequent
Tagaytay	3	83-92	BSC San Agustin, DLTB	every 30min
Tuguegarao	12	air-con–deluxe 600-900	Florida, Victory Liner (Kamias, Pasay)	hourly
Vigan (air-con)	10-11	550	Dominion, Partas	hourly
Vigan (deluxe)	8-9	750-850	Partas	night buses

Ceres (Map p72; cnr Taft & Sen Gil Puyat Aves, Pasay)

Coda Lines (Map p76; ☏ 0927 559 2197; HM Transport Terminal, EDSA, Cubao)

Dagupan Bus Co (Map p76; ☏ 02-727 2330; cnr EDSA & New York Ave, Cubao)

Dimple Star (☏ 0908 700 7769; South Rd cnr EDSA, Cubao)

DLTB (Map p72; ☏ 02-564 7777; cnr Taft & Sen Gil Puyat Aves, Pasay)

Dominion Bus Lines (Map p76; ☏ 02-727 2350; cnr EDSA & New York Ave, Cubao)

Fariñas Transit (Map p50; ☏ 02-731 4507; Lacson Ave cnr Laong Laan Rd, Sampaloc)

Five Star Bus Lines (Map p72; ☏ 02-853 4772; Aurora Blvd, Pasay)

Florida Bus Lines (Map p50; ☑ 02-789 5894, 02-781 5894; https://gvfloridatransport. com.ph; cnr of Earnshaw St & Lacson Ave, Sampaloc)

Genesis (Joybus) Terminals in **Pasay** (Map p72; ☑ 0933 852 7686; Pasay Rotunda, Pasay) and **Cubao** (Map p76; ☑ 0933 852 7688, 02-709 0544; cnr New York Ave & EDSA, Cubao).

Jac Liner (Map p72; ☑ 0922 853 1891; www. jacliner.com; cnr Taft & Sen Gil Puyat Aves, Pasay; 🖀)

Jam Liner (Map p72; ☑ 0917 526 0008; www. jam.com.ph; cnr Taft & Sen Gil Puyat Aves, Pasay; 🖀)

Maria de Leon Trans (Map p50; ☑ 02-731 4907; Gelinos St cnr Dapitan St, Sampaloc)

Ohayami (Map p50; ☑ 0927 649 3055; www. ohayamitrans.com; cnr Fajardo St & Lacson Ave, Sampaloc)

Partas Terminals in **Pasay** (Map p72; ☑ 0917 825 9423, 02-725 1756; Aurora Blvd, Pasay) and **Cubao** (Map p76; ☑ 0917 825 9423, 02-725 1756; 816 Aurora Blvd, Cubao).

Philtranco (Map p72; ☑ 02-851 8077, 0917 860 4418; www.philtranco.com.ph; cnr EDSA & Apelo Cruz, Pasay)

Roro Bus (Map p50; South Rd, Cubao)

Victory Liner Terminals in **Pasay** (Map p72; ☑ 02-833 5019; EDSA), **Cubao** (Map p76; ☑ 0998 591 5054, 02-727 4534; cnr EDSA & New York Ave), **Kamias** (Map p76; ☑ 02-920 7396; cnr EDSA & East Ave, Quezon City) and **Sampaloc** (☑ 02-559 7735; www.victoryliner. com; 551 Earnshaw St).

Bus Terminals

Araneta Center Busport (Map p76; ☑ 02-588 4156; Gen Romulo Ave, Cubao; ⊙ 5am-10pm) Hub for express Bicol–bound buses.

Araneta Bus Terminal (Map p76; Times Sq Ave, Cubao) For cheaper 'ordinary' (no air-con) buses to Bicol (frequent).

ⓘ Getting Around

TO/FROM THE AIRPORT

As there are no direct public transport routes from either of the four terminals to Malate or Makati, bite the bullet and take a taxi, especially if you have a bit of luggage. The airport is quite close to the city and, barring traffic, you can get to Malate or Makati by taxi in 20 minutes. Uber is also a good option from the airport.

You have three options for taxis: first are white prepaid 'coupon' taxis that charge set rates of P600 to P700 to Malate or Makati. These will actively solicit you the minute you step outside the arrivals hall.

Feel free to ignore them for the second option: yellow airport metered taxis, which have a flag-fall of P70 (regular metered taxis on the street have a P40 flagfall). Your total bill to Malate should be about P200, closer to P250 if you're travelling to Makati. To find the yellow cab rank at the three main terminals, walk straight and then to the right.

The third option is regular metered taxis. There is a rank of these at Terminal 4, but at the other three terminals you must walk up to departures to find one (relatively easy). These can be preferable when the lines for the yellow metered cabs are very long (common). They also save you P50 to P80 to Makati or Malate.

The 'Airport Loop' shuttle bus takes you to Pasay Rotunda in Baclaran (P20, every 20 minutes), from where you can find onward public transport (taxi, jeepney or MRT/LRT). At the three main terminals, walk straight and then to the right for Airport Loop buses.

BUS

The most useful bus from a tourist's perspective is probably the **BGC Bus** (Map p50; cnr EDSA & McKinley Rd, Makati) that links Makati and The Fort. Departures are every 10 minutes or so from the terminal on EDSA in Makati to various points in BGC. Another bus links Makati (from Makati Ave, opposite the Peninsula Hotel) and **Quiapo** (Map p58).

Local buses can be handy along EDSA as an alternative to the MRT. Depending on the journey, ordinary buses cost from P10 to P15; air-con buses cost from P10 to P25.

CAR & MOTORCYCLE

Due to traffic and unorthodox local driving habits, renting a self-drive car or motorcycle to get around Manila is not recommended. On the other hand, a rental car is a great way to visit the attractions outside Metro Manila, many of which are hard to reach by public transport.

A car and driver is another option, and will set you back P2500 to P4000 per day. Arrange one through your hotel or negotiate with a cab driver.

For those who want to drive themselves, car-rental companies, including **Avis** (Map p62; ☑ 02-462 2881; www.avis.com.ph) and **Nissan** (☑ 02-886 9931; www.nissanrentacar.com), have offices at the airport terminals and some major hotels. Rates start at about P3000 per day

FERRY

The Pasig River Ferry is an interesting if slow way of travelling between Intramuros and Makati. You'll pass the classic Post Office (p90) building, Malacañang Palace (p53) and a few other interesting spots on the way. From **Plaza Mexico** (Map p54; Riverside Dr, Intramuros) in Intramuros to the **Hulo** (Map p61; Coronado Ave, Mandaluyong) or **Guadalupe** (Map p50; JP Rizal Ave, Makati) stations near Makati takes almost 1½ hours and costs P50.

ⓘ AIRPORT TAXI SCAMS

Most problems with taxi drivers occur at the airport. Some tips:

➡ Taxi drivers who actively approach you at the airport may be out to scam you; stick to the ranks – and under no circumstances follow a driver on foot to a car waiting outside the airport.

➡ Watch out for rigged taxi meters at the airport, including the yellow airport cabs. The first five minutes in a properly metered taxi in normal Manila traffic should not bring the meter past P50 to P60 (P90 to P100 in the airport cabs). If it's racing up a lot faster that, you're being played.

JEEPNEY

For the uninitiated, Manila jeepneys can be a challenging experience. The long-wheel-base jeeps offer a bewildering array of destinations and, though these destinations are written on signboards stuck in the window, few people arrive exactly where they intend to on their first jeepney ride. However, if you stick to the more common routes, you shouldn't go too far astray.

Heading **south** (Map p58) from Quiapo Church, jeepneys to 'Baclaran' pass **City Hall** (Map p54), then traverse Ermita/Malate along MH del Pilar St, continue close to the CCP, cross EDSA and end up at the Baclaran LRT stop. From Quiapo Church you can also take 'Kalaw' jeepneys to Ermita.

Heading north from Baclaran, jeepneys pass along Mabini St or Taft Ave, heading off in various directions from **Manila City Hall** (Map p54):

➡ 'Divisoria' jeepneys take Jones Bridge, passing close to the office of the Bureau of Immigration, and end up at Divisoria Market.

➡ 'Monumento' jeepneys pass the Manila Central Post Office and roll over the MacArthur Bridge before passing the Chinese Cemetery and the Caloocan bus terminals.

➡ 'Quiapo' and 'Cubao' jeepneys take Quezon Bridge, passing **Quiapo Church** (Map p58). 'Cubao via España' jeepneys continue to the Cubao bus stations via UST and the Sampaloc bus stations.

KALESA

Horse-drawn carriages known as kalesa are still a form of public transport in some rural areas, but in Manila they're confined to Chinatown, Intramuros and Malate, where they're mainly used to take tourists for a ride (sometimes in the figurative sense). Agree to a price beforehand, and make it clear that the price is per ride, not per person. The Intramuros drivers charge a flat fee of P300 for trips around the walled city.

LRT & MRT

The LRT and MRT trains are an excellent way to soar over and past traffic. Unfortunately, coverage of the city is far from comprehensive, and they are basically unusable at rush hour, when hour-long lines are common. If you do manage to get on a train, it can be a tight squeeze to say the least, and pickpocketing is common.

Fares are P12 to P15, depending on distance. Transferring between train lines means leaving the station and lining up anew for another ticket.

TAXI

Taxis in Manila are cheap and plentiful. Flagfall is a mere P40 for the first kilometre, plus P3.5 for every 300m (or two minutes of waiting time) after that. A 15- to 20-minute trip rarely costs more than P150 or so.

Most taxi drivers will turn on the meter; if they don't, politely request that they do. If the meter is 'broken' or your taxi driver says the fare is 'up to you', the best strategy is to get out and find another cab (or offer a low-ball price).

It can be almost impossible to get a cab during rush hour; be prepared to offer P50 to P100 on top of the metered rate. When riding in taxis, do as your driver does and lock your doors.

Uber is popular in Manila and charges similarly low rates.

TRICYCLE

Motorised tricycles are useful for short hops around town. Short journeys should cost from P40 to P50, depending on how well you bargain.

Electronic 'E-trikes' are starting to appear in Intramuros and Chinatown. They are a quieter, greener option if you can find one.

Push tricycles, or pedicabs, are a cheaper alternative in a few areas, such as Malate.

Around Manila

Best Places to Eat

➡ Antonio's (p100)

➡ Kinabuhayan Cafe (p104)

➡ Feliza Taverna y Café (p102)

➡ Red Bus (p100)

➡ Aling Taleng's Halo Halo (p105)

Best Places to Stay

➡ Sonya's Garden (p99)

➡ Alvin & Angie Mt Pinatubo Guesthouse (p112)

➡ Lilom Resort & Gallery Cafe (p104)

➡ Paradores del Castillo (p102)

➡ Tagaytay Garden Mountain Breeze (p98)

Why Go?

Banned from travelling the rest of the country, cooped-up Manileños rediscovered the splendors of the surrounding provinces during the pandemic.

The area south of Manila has fantastic hikes, championship golf courses, and fabulous Lake Taal, with diminutive Taal Volcano bubbling in its middle. The coastline of South Luzon presents dramatic cliffs and sandy beaches, with several islands offshore that can be explored by boat, plus superb scuba diving in Anilao.

Head north and you'll find the most notorious volcano of them all, Mt Pinatubo, in the underrated Zambales Mountains. The freeport of Subic Bay offers a diverse range of activities, from diving to hiking, and the surrounding Bataan Peninsula is a fascinating historic site.

This is one area of the Philippines where it makes sense to rent a car, as everything is accessible from Manila and public transport routes are notoriously slow and complex.

When to Go
Manila

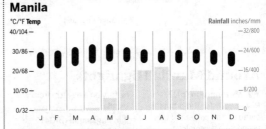

Dec–Feb
The coolest months are particularly welcome.

May
Local peaks become places of refuge in the height of the hot season.

Aug–Oct
Some surf on the Zambales Coast within range of Subic.

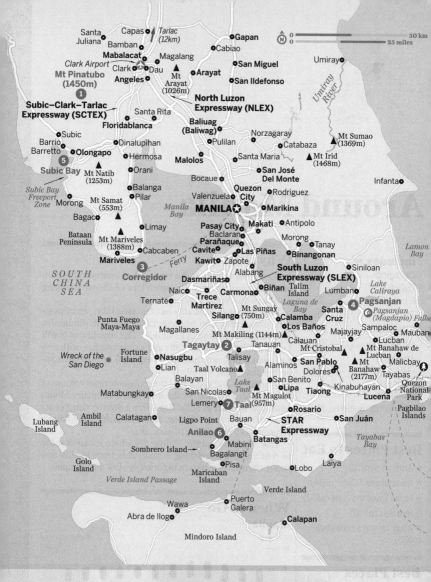

Around Manila Highlights

1 Mt Pinatubo (p112) Rising early for the dramatic climb up the caldera of this brooding active volcano.

2 Tagaytay (p97) Enjoying stellar views of Taal Volcano and sumptuous cuisine in this laid-back hilltop town.

3 Corregidor (p97) Immersing yourself in WWII history on a day trip from Manila.

4 Pagsanjan (p104) Paddling along the heart of darkness up the Pagsanjan River to Pagsanjan Falls.

5 Subic Bay (p109) Going to extremes amid the virgin forests and sunken wrecks in and around Subic Bay.

6 Anilao (p103) Spending a weekend diving in the best conditions close to the capital.

7 Taal (p101) Wandering the relaxed streets of Taal, lined with heritage ancestral houses.

CORREGIDOR

The island of Corregidor (Corrector), 48km southwest of Manila and often referred to as 'The Rock,' is a popular day trip from the capital. In the decades after WWII many visitors were history buffs and veterans, but now it's mostly locals who venture out here to enjoy the scenic island and its sweeping views.

⊙ Sights & Activities

There are, as you'd expect, numerous war monuments and ruins on the island. Significant sights include General MacArthur's HQ, the mile-long barracks, gun batteries and the Spanish lighthouse, which offers views over Manila Bay. Also worthwhile is the understated and formal Japanese Cemetery.

Admission to all of the above is included in the packages run by Sun Cruises, Corregidor's main tour operator. Tours are conducted on open-sided buses modelled on the electric trolleys used by the Americans. Otherwise there are walking tours (P1800 not including lunch).

If you opt to take the ferry but not join the Sun Cruises tour, you can sign up for a more engaging, personalised tour with Old Manila Walks (p65).

Completed in 1932 after 10 years of construction, the Malinta Tunnel complex is built into the side of a hill and was used by the Americans as a bombproof bunker, for ammunition storage, and also as a hospital. The tunnel spans 250m, with numerous laterals branching off, one of which was used as General MacArthur's HQ.

The American-built Pacific War Memorial, at the island's highest point (210m), is a shrine to the thousands from both sides who died in the conflict.

🛏 Sleeping & Eating

Corregidor Inn INN $$

(☏ 0917 527 6350; www.corregidorphilippines.com; s/d incl breakfast P1500/2000; ❄ ❄) This attractive hotel has timber floors, fine coastal views, rattan furniture and capiz windows, as well as a pool and restaurant. Book through Sun Cruises.

ⓘ Getting There & Away

Sun Cruises (Map p72; ☏ 02-831 8140; www.corregidorphilippines.com; Esplanade Seaside Terminal, Seaside Blvd, Pasay; ferry only weekday/weekend P1400/1500, excursion incl lunch & tram tour weekday/weekend P2550/2750, walking tours P1800; ⊙ 6.30am-4.15pm) has the market cornered for trips to Corregidor. Ferries depart daily at 7.30am from the Esplanade Seaside Terminal just north of the Mall of Asia; you should return to Manila by 4.15pm, unless you stay overnight. The price includes lunch and a comprehensive tour of the island.

The only other way to get to Corregidor is to charter a bangka (wooden outrigger boat) from Cabcaben (P3500, 30 minutes) on the Bataan Peninsula – ask at Cabcaben Beach for Villa Carmen Resort. The boat captain will wait for the return trip, but you'll need to organise your own transport and tours on the island.

SOUTH OF MANILA

The South Luzon Expressway will take you south of the city to some popular weekender attractions.

Tagaytay & Lake Taal

☐ TAGAYTAY 046, TALISAY 043 / POP 71,200

Strung out along a high ridge overlooking stunning Lake Taal and the multiple craters of active Taal volcano, Tagaytay is a thoroughly absorbing town where you could easily spend a couple of days admiring the views, hiking the volcano, sailing on the lake and dining out in style.

About 600m below Tagaytay, Lake Taal and Volcano Island lie within a prehistoric volcano crater measuring roughly 75km around. This ancient crater forms Tagaytay Ridge, where the town is haphazardly draped like a set of Russian matryoshka dolls. Taal

---

ⓘ TRIP PLANNER

Most places around Manila can be visited as a day trip, but considering the time spent getting in and out of the city, it's better to allow a minimum of two days.

One day If time is short, start early. Good day trips include Corregidor, the canoe trip at Pagsanjan, and Tagaytay.

Two days Possibilities include Tagaytay with a detour to Taal village, scuba diving at Anilao, hiking at Mt Banahaw and climbing Mt Pinatubo.

Three days+ Combine some of the above trips, or head to the burgeoning activity centre at Subic Bay and the Bataan Peninsula.

Volcano in turn encircles its own little crater lake, itself containing a small island.

Lying just 60km south of Manila, Tagaytay is everything the capital is not: cool, clean, gorgeous and oxygenated. The nature of the town changes dramatically on weekends, though, when the Manila hordes arrive and traffic jams appear.

◎ Sights & Activities

★ Taal Volcano HIKING

(adult/child P50/100; ☺ 6am-6pm) Once you've enjoyed the sight of mist tickling Taal Volcano from afar, it's time to get up close and personal. Notoriously dusty and hot, this is neither a difficult climb nor a particularly rewarding one, but there are decent views back down to the lake and Tagaytay Ridge.

By far the most popular of several possible hikes is the well-worn, 35-minute trail from the village straight up to the main crater, with its dark green lake. Along the way are 14 Stations of the Cross and the inevitable drink stalls selling coconut water and even beer. If you're not up for the walk, you can hire a tired-looking horse for P500. Pay your admission fee at the village where the boats dock and ask directions to the path.

The bulk of Volcano Island emerged from the lake during a savage eruption in 1911, which claimed hundreds of lives. Since then frequent eruptions have sculpted and resculpted the island's appearance. With more than 47 craters and 35 volcanic cones, Taal Volcano remains one of the world's deadliest volcanoes. The main crater is in the middle of the island (the obvious cone visible from the ridge is Binitiang Malaki, which last erupted in 1715). The most active crater is Mt Taburo, on the west side, which released dramatic lava flows in the late 1960s and mid-1970s.

The launch point for bangkas out to Volcano Island is the lakeside town of Talisay, where dozens of operators vie for the attention of arriving tourists. The official rate is P2000 for the whole boat (20 minutes; up to six people) but if you hire direct from a boat owner or lakeside resort (rather than a tout) you can expect to pay P1500. The best place to arrange this is at one of the ramshackle resorts or bangka depots that line the lakefront west of Talisay proper.

More adventurous hiking options on Volcano Island include all-day treks up Mt Taburo or the south ridge of Taal's main crater, from where there's a trail leading down to the crater lake. Few guides make these trips; they charge around P500, plus a bit extra for a bangka ride around to the south side of the island (P3000 for up to six people).

People's Park in the Sky VIEWPOINT

(P30; ☺ 7.30am-6.30pm) Improbably perched on a mound of earth at Tagaytay's eastern end, this is Ferdinand Marcos' unfinished summer home. It's a derelict yet strangely intriguing ruin, with a decrepit Greek-style amphitheatre, viewpoints and souvenir stalls. A weather tower and telecommunications tower are newer additions. The 360-degree view of the area alone is worth the trip up. It's 8.5km east of the Tagaytay Rotunda. Jeepneys (P8) go here from Olivarez Plaza, or a tricycle charges P150.

Sky Ranch AMUSEMENT PARK

(☎ 02-862 7704; www.skyranch.ph; weekday/weekend P80/100; ☺ 10am-10pm Mon-Fri, 8am-10pm Sat & Sun; ☝) The centrepiece of this ridge-top amusement park is the 63m-high Sky Eye (P150) Ferris wheel, visible for miles when illuminated at night. There are another 20 or so rides of varying thrills and a dozen dining options.

Taal Lake Yacht Club BOATING

(☎ 043-773 0192; www.tlyc.com; Barangay Santa Maria, Talisay; ☺ 8am-7pm) The local sailing club in Talisay hires out Hobie 16 catamarans (per day P3800), single-sail Toppers (per day P1800) and tandem sea kayaks (per hour/day P400/1200) for a unique way of getting out onto the lake. It also arranges sailing lessons (per day P2500). It's 1km west of the Tagaytay road junction.

⊨ Sleeping

The widest choice of accommodation (and restaurants) is along the ridge in Tagaytay, overlooking the lake and volcano. If you want to stay on the lake in Talisay, choices are more limited and the lakeside resorts are relatively rundown, but you're within easy reach of the volcano.

⊨ Tagaytay

★ Tagaytay Garden

Mountain Breeze HOSTEL $

(☎ 0977-816 0773; 730 Calamba Rd; dm/d/tr P450/1000/1400) Tagaytay's best budget option enjoys an excellent location just a few hundred metres from the rotunda. As well as clean dorms there are a few compact pri-

FABULOUS FARMS

Two very different 'farms' are worth seeking out in the rural back blocks out of Manila.

Hidden away a 1½-hour drive north of Quezon City, the volunteer-run **GK Enchanted Farm** (☑ 0916 225 3363, 02-533 2217; www.gk1world.com; Angat, Bulacan; day tours incl lunch P695-995) is attempting to alleviate poverty by fostering young local entrepreneurs in impoverished communities. It's possible to visit on a day tour or spend the night. On a day tour you'll see a range of demonstrations and observe what it's doing in terms of permaculture, ecodesign etc. Accommodation (dorm beds P800, double rooms P2500 to P3500) is in comfortable lodgings and there is an infinity pool you can laze around. Or you can stay nearby at the pleasant **Oasis Boutique Hotel** (☑ 0956 130 5238; GK Enchanted Farm, Angat, Bulacan; s/d incl breakfast P2500/3500) ✍.

Near Lipa City, a two-hour drive south of Manila, **Farm at San Benito** (☑ 02-884 8074, 0918 884 8078; www.thefarm.com.ph; Barangay Tipakan; r US$200-1800; ❋@🛜🏊) is a peaceful wellness and detoxification centre enveloped in jungle. Besides a bevy of detox and spa treatments, the resort has a mouthwatering vegan restaurant, tropical hardwood and bamboo suites and luxurious villas.

vate rooms (the triples are more spacious), a small kitchen and a garden from where you can almost see Taal Lake. Rates for triples increase at weekends.

Our Melting Pot
HOSTEL **$**

(☑ 915-774 0864; www.ourmeltingpottagaytay.com; 75 Smokey Hill; dm P450, d with/without bath P1050/970, tr P1400; 🛜) Our Melting Pot is one of Tagaytay's best budget options, hidden down a quiet residential street just off the main ridge road. Rooms and dorms are spotless (most have shared bathroom so book ahead for the en-suite room), there's a homely lounge and a kitchen and breakfast is included. No air-con.

★ Keni Po
HOTEL **$$**

(☑ 046-483 0977; www.keniporooms.blogspot.com; 110 Calamba Rd; d P1200-1500; ❋🛜🏊) Rooms at this valleyside place, 3.5km east of the rotunda, are a steal. The double-storey hotel with a bright-yellow, Thai–style facade is immaculately kept with a lovely pool in the back garden. Rooms feature minibars, cable TV and shared balconies.

Tagaytay Econo Hotel
HOTEL **$$**

(☑ 046-483 4284; www.tagaytayeconohotel.com; Calamba Rd; r incl breakfast P2580-4500, ste P5500; ❋@🛜) This well-maintained place, 2.7km east of the rotunda, is good value. It overlooks the lake but sits on an intersection, so noise is a potential problem. Pricier rooms are further from the road and have lake views.

★ Sonya's Garden
B&B **$$$**

(☑ 0917 533 5140; www.sonyasgarden.com; Barangay Buck Estate, Alfonso; cottages s/d incl breakfast & dinner P5000/6000, d weekends P6800; ❋🛜) Alongside its lovely restaurant (p101), Sonya's runs an exquisite B&B set among a beautiful flower garden. In grand cottages, rooms are expansive and rustic with thick rugs, and no TV to detract from the tranquillity. Yoga, meditation and a full range of spa services are on offer. It's a fair way out of town; look for the well-marked turn-off before MC Mountain Home Apartelle, 13km west of the rotunda.

Joaquin's
B&B **$$$**

(☑ 0917-503 7122, 046-483 0463; www.joaquins bedandbreakfast.com; Aquinaldo Hwy; d incl breakfast Sun-Thu P4800-6800, Fri & Sat P5800-7800; ❋🛜) A lovely rustic-style B&B where the eight suites have sublime views of the lake and volcano from private balconies, rooms open up to high ceilings, and there are polished floorboards and arty touches throughout. There's a large dining deck with requisite views and an intimate, family feel.

🛏 Talisay

Talisay Green Lake Resort
RESORT **$$**

(☑ 043-773 0247; www.taal-greenlakeresort.net; Barangay Santa Maria; d/tr/villa P1500/2000/3500; ❋🛜🏊) A solid choice on the lake, with a popular air-con restaurant and a murky swimming pool. Rooms could do with a refurb, as could the overgrown garden, but the thatched nipa huts on the waterfront are a nice touch.

San Roque Paradise Resort
RESORT $$

(☑ 043-773 0271; Barangay Buco; r P1500-3000; ✳ @ 🎧) In a well-kept compound in Talisay, this is a good option for a lakefront stay. The 10 rooms are clean and there's a four-bed apartment. The friendly family management can organise meals and boat trips, and there's a swimming area on the lake.

Club Balai Isabel
RESORT $$$

(☑ 0906-518 5491; www.balaiisabel.com; r/villa from P5550/7000; ✳ 🎧 🛥) Talisay's most up-market resort sits on the waterfront near the junction of the main Banga–Tagaytay Rd. Stylish rooms and villas (up to four bedrooms) have all the usual mod cons as well as artworks and private verandahs. The resort boasts three pools, a day spa, kayaks and jet skis for hire, beach volleyball and a quality restaurant serving local lake fish.

🍴 Eating

Tagaytay features some of the Philippines' best restaurants, most of them strung out along (or just off) the ridge road. Tagaytay is renowned for *bulalo* (a rich beef and marrow soup) and *tawili* (tiny lake fish found only in Taal). There's relatively little of culinary interest in Talisay.

Java Jazz Cafe
CAFE $

(☑ 0917-483 7399; 442 Calamba Rd; coffee P50-100, mains P99-199; ⊙ 9am-9pm Mon-Fri, 9am-10.30pm Sat, 8am-10pm Sun; 🎧) This vibrant little cafe and gallery does good breakfasts, sandwiches, pizza, Filipino coffee and light lunches. There are three basic but good-value double rooms down below (fan/air-con P980/1400 including breakfast).

Mushroomburger
FAST FOOD $

(☑ 046-483 1330; www.mushroomburger.ph; Aguinaldo Hwy; burger meals P72-115; ⊙ 7.30am-11pm; 🍴) This Tagaytay institution is fast food with a difference, renowned for its cheap and tasty vegie mushroom burgers (as well chicken and rice dishes). It's 300m west of Taal Vista Hotel.

★ Red Bus
DINER $$

(Calamba Rd; burgers P180-210; ⊙ noon-10pm) The coolest place to dine in Tagaytay is on a stool outside the red Kombi van just east of the rotunda. The Red Bus diner specialises in burgers (try the wasabi burger), but also does burritos, quesadillas and nachos, and serves beer (P60).

★ Bag of Beans
BAKERY $$

(www.bagofbeans.ph; 115 Aguinaldo Hwy; pies P135-155, mains P310-575; ⊙ 6am-10pm; 🎧) Dine among hanging angel's trumpets, begonias and other exotic flowering plants on the garden patio of this superb bakery-restaurant specialising in English-style pies, breakfasts, coffee and scrumptious desserts. It's 6.5km west of the rotunda. There are two other branches (Athena and Charito) on the highway closer to the rotunda.

★ Josephine
FILIPINO $$

(☑ 046-413 1801; Km 58 Aguinaldo Hwy; mains P195-550; ⊙ 8am-9pm Mon-Fri, 7am-10.30pm Sat & Sun; ✳ 🎧) Views don't come much better than those at Josephine, a long-running favourite with huge convex windows providing spectacular lake panoramas. It's known for its weekend buffet breakfast (P255) and lunch (P450) but has a broad menu of Filipino classics and seafood dishes. The bar does excellent cocktails. It's 3km west of the rotunda.

Mahogany Market
FILIPINO $$

(Mahogany Ave; mains P200-700; ⊙ 6am-midnight) Mahogany Market, with its undercover produce market and whiffy meat market, is the place to sample inexpensive regional dishes. Upstairs from the meat market you'll find food stalls serving the local specialities *bulalo* and *tawili*. This is the best and cheapest place to try either, though they cater to groups – *bulalo* is P350 for three people.

Leslie's
FILIPINO $$

(☑ 046-438 7899; Aguinaldo Hwy; mains from P300; ⊙ 6am-midnight; 🎧) Leslie's is the most famous of several large Filipino *inahaw* (grill) restaurants along the central ridge where you can sample *tawili* and *bulalo*. The standard servings are intended for groups of three to 10, which doesn't leave much choice for solo travellers or couples. The restaurant offers some outstanding lake views if you get a seat or hut at the back. It's 1.8km west of the rotunda.

★ Antonio's
INTERNATIONAL $$$

(☑ 0917 899 2866; www.antoniosrestaurant.ph; Barangay Neogan; mains P1500-2200; ⊙ 11.30am-1pm & 5.30-8pm Tue-Sun; ✳ 🎧) One of the finest restaurants in the country, this upscale French-Euro-Filipino eatery offers the chance to rub elbows with politicians and oligarchs over delightfully presented dishes from foie-gras raclette to roast suckling pig –

if you can get a reservation. Seating areas include some lovely tables in elegant dining rooms overlooking lotus ponds and a lush tropical garden. Also has a superb garden cocktail bar, the Lanai Lounge.

★ **Sonya's Garden**   BUFFET $$$
(☑ 0917 532 9097; www.sonyasgarden.com; buffet P683; ⊙ 11am-7pm) 🏃 One of Tagaytay's most beloved restaurants, serving buffet lunches and dinners. It features homemade pasta, fresh bread, desserts and produce grown in a sprawling garden that practically envelops diners. Reservations recommended.

ℹ Information

There are several internet cafes (P20 per hour) around Olivarez Plaza.

Talisay Tourism (☑ 043-773 0238; www.talisaybatangas.gov.ph; 2nd fl, Municipal Office, Talisay-Tanauan Rd, Talisay; ⊙ 8am-5pm Mon-Fri) Has a map and basic information on surrounding sights.

ℹ Getting There & Away

San Agustin buses from Pasay Rotunda in Manila rumble through Tagaytay (P78 to P120, two hours, every 30 minutes) on their way to Nasugbu or Calatagan. To return to Manila, hail a bus from the streetside shed at Olivarez Plaza or Mendez Crossing in town.

Those wanting to stay in Talisay can also catch a bus heading to Batangas City and jump off at Tanauan (P95, 1½ hours); get a jeepney/tricycle for the 15km from there.

ℹ Getting Around

Frequent jeepneys traverse the ridge road from one end of town to the other (P8). A short trip by tricycle costs around P50.

To get to Talisay from Tagaytay take a jeepney (P35, 25 minutes, hourly) or tricycle (P300, 30 minutes) straight downhill from the Talisay turn-off, 4km east of the rotunda.

Taal

☑ 043 / POP 56,300

Often overlooked by travellers (and not to be confused with Lake Taal or Taal Volcano), this charming historic township is famous for its heritage-listed colonial buildings. Its relaxed streets are lined with ancestral houses, and it makes a lovely overnight escape from Manila. Having been awarded the status of a heritage-listed town ensures Taal's magnificent 19th-century buildings remain intact and several have been con-

AGUINALDO MANSION

History buffs should venture 20km south of Manila to view this museum in **Aguinaldo Mansion** (☑ 0917 851 9819; www.nhcp.gov.ph/baldomero-aguinaldo-shrine; Tirona Hwy; ⊙ 8am-5pm Tue-Sun), in the town of Kawit. Here the revolutionary army of General Emilio Aguinaldo proclaimed Philippine Independence on 12 June 1898 – a triumph soon quashed by the Americans. The alluring mahogany-and-nara-wood house, built in 1849, is now a shrine, and you can tour Aguinaldo's private rooms and see his much-loved bowling alley.

verted into excellent museums, B&Bs and restaurants. Numerous shops sell the town's famous embroidery and *balisong* (butterfly knives), though be aware the latter are illegal in many countries.

◉ Sights

★ **Basilica of St Martin de Tours**   CHURCH
(Agoncillo St; ⊙ 6am-7pm) Originally built in 1759, before being destroyed and rebuilt between 1849 and 1865, this truly massive baroque-style basilica is one of the largest and oldest Catholic churches in Asia. It dominates Taal Park at its base.

★ **Marcela Mariño &
Felipe Agoncillo House**   MUSEUM
(☑ 0917-656 4170; 14 Agoncillo St; admission by donation; ⊙ 9am-5pm Tue-Sun) One of Taal's most engaging house museums, this was the home of Dona Marcela Mariño, who married local lawyer and independence activist Felipe Agoncillo. In 1898, at the request of General Emilio Aguinaldo, Marcela was the principal seamstress of the first Philippine national flag. A guide will take you through the various galleries, explaining the history of the families and the evolution of the flag.

Galleria Taal   ARCHITECTURE
(☑ 0918 912 4051; 60 Agoncillo St; adult/student P100/50; ⊙ 8am-5pm) Galleria Taal is a good example of a well-preserved ancestral house, but far more impressive is the museum containing a vast collection of vintage cameras collected by Manny Barrion Inumerable. There's also a good gallery of family and antiquarian photographs.

Leon & Galicano Apacible Museum
MUSEUM

(☑043-408 2045; 59 Agoncillo St; admission by donation; ☺9am-5pm Tue-Sun) This beautiful old 19th-century colonial home has been converted into a museum with six galleries tracing the lives of siblings Leon and Galicano Apacible. Leon was a lawyer, judge and military commander against the Spanish, while Galicano became a political activist and a senior Filipino diplomat.

🛏 Sleeping & Eating

★ Paradores del Castillo
HERITAGE HOTEL $$

(☑043-740 4060; www.paradoresdetaal.com; 28 Calle Dr H Del Castillo; d/tr incl breakfast from P2500/4000; ❀🛜🏊) This early-20th-century house is Taal's finest hotel. Rooms are quaint, individually decorated and well equipped (only the cheapest double has a shared bathroom). Outside is a lovely sprawling lawn and garden with views of Lemery, a terrace, a swimming pool and an excellent Italian restaurant and bar.

Villa Severina
B&B $$

(☑0917 501 8060; villa.severina@yahoo.com; 55 Illustre St; r incl breakfast P2500; ❀🛜) This charming 1870 ancestral house has four rooms decked out in period features, each a different configuration and theme pertaining to French colonial cities (Pondicherry, Hanoi, Martinique) and to Paris (the two upstairs rooms share a bathroom). It has lovely common areas, hardwood floors, a well-equipped kitchen and breakfast included, served on its attractive outdoor terrace.

Conchita B&B
B&B $$

(☑0927 722 8463, 043-722 8463; Calle Antonio de las Alas; r incl breakfast per person P850; ❀🛜) This guesthouse, almost opposite the basilica, isn't as historic as some but has a homey feel and the two upstairs doubles (sharing a bathroom) are cosy and functional.

Don Juan Boodle House
FILIPINO $$

(☑047-740 1828; www.donjuan.taal.ph; Calle Diokno St; mains P110-299, boodle for 2 from P499; ☺8am-9pm Mon-Fri, 7am-9pm Sat & Sun; ❀🛜) Adjacent to the Taal Market, Don Juan specialises in *boodle* – a shared banquet served on a banana leaf and comprising variations on *adobo* and Taal regional specialities such as *sinaing na tulingan* (native mackerel) and *tawili* (freshwater lake fish). If you're not in a *boodle*-fighting group, go for one of the rice dishes or *inahaw* (grill) plates.

★ Feliza Taverna y Café
FILIPINO, SPANISH $$$

(☑043-740 0113; 6 Agoncillo St; mains from P300; ☺11am-10pm Tue-Thu, 10am-10.30pm Fri-Sun; ❀🛜) The former residence of Felisa Diokno – secretary to the first president of the Philippines, Emilio Aguinaldo – is now a fine dining restaurant and B&B. The beautiful dining room has capiz windows and is full of antiques and memorabilia, and there's a lovely rear courtyard garden. The food is top-notch Filipino Spanish, mixed with local specialities.

ℹ Information

Taal Tourist Office (☑0917 501 8060; www.taal.gov.ph; Agoncillo St; ☺8am-5pm) is located beside the steps to the basilica. Head here for a map of the town's heritage-listed colonial buildings.

The excellent website www.taal.ph has a comprehensive overview of things to see, and places to eat and shop.

ℹ Getting There & Away

The town is 2km off the main road between Batangas and Tagaytay. From Manila take the Jam bus from Cubao to Lemery (P180, three hours), from where you can take a tricycle (P70).

Batangas

☑043 / POP 329,874

The busy industrial port of Batangas is a major transport hub, both for buses and for ferries to Puerto Galera and a few other ports on Mindoro and Romblon. There's little else of interest to travellers.

There's no need to stay overnight unless you are unfortunate enough to miss the last ferry. If you get stuck, try **Travellers Hotel** (☑043-723 2309; New Access Rd; s/d P900/1200; ❀🛜), a nondescript but comfortable and reasonably priced option with clean rooms fitted with cable TV and air-con. It's one of several hotels about 1km from the port.

ℹ Getting There & Away

BOAT

Super Shuttle Roro (☑032-4127688; http://supershuttleroro.com) Has weekly long-distance boats to Cebu (P1200, 24 hours, Tuesday) and twice-weekly to Calapan.

Boracay

2Go Travel (☑043-702 5525; http://travel.2go.com.ph; Terminal 2) Sails daily to Caticlan (from P1250, 10 hours) at 9pm.

Abra de Ilog & Calapan (Mindoro)

FastCat (☑ 043-702 6983; www.fastcat.com.ph; Terminal 2) Calapan (P190 to P300, 1½ hours, 16 daily)

Montenegro Lines (☑ 043-740 3201; Terminal 3) Abra de Ilog (P260, 2½ hours, six daily); Calapan (P240, 2½ hours, every two hours)

Starlite Ferries (☑ 043-723 9965; www.starliteferries.com) Calapan (P199, three hours, 12 daily)

SuperCat (☑ 032-233 7000; www.supercat.com.ph; Terminal 3) Calapan (P175 to P280, one hour, 10 daily fastcraft, from 6am to 8pm)

Puerto Galera (Mindoro)

From terminal 3, speedy bangka ferries to Puerto Galera town (P230, one hour), Sabang (P230, one hour) and White Beach (P270, 1¼ hours) leave regularly throughout the day until about 5pm.

Starlite Ferries has roll-on, roll-off ferries to Puerto Galera at 10am and 6pm (P180, two hours), which are a better option than a bangka if the sea looks rough.

Panay Island & Romblon

Montenegro Lines Departs 5pm daily to Odiongan (P762, eight hours). On Monday, Thursday and Saturday the same boat continues on to Romblon town (P954, 12 hours).

Navios Shipping (☑ 0908 146 2243; Terminal 3) Heads to Romblon (P850, 10 hours) on Sunday and Wednesday at 5pm.

BUS

Most Batangas-bound buses from Manila go to the pier but double-check with your driver. Make sure you get on an express bus to the pier via the speedy SLEX and STAR expressways (P180, 1½ hours). These are signed 'Batangas Pier' and/or 'derecho' (straight). Pick up buses to Manila right at the pier.

Anilao

☑ 043 / POP 28,680

Anilao, 30km west of Batangas on a small peninsula, is where the Philippines' first scuba-diving operators started back in the '60s. While it has since been overtaken by places such as Alona Beach (Bohol), it remains an extremely popular weekend destination for Manila-based divers.

The area empties out during the week, when resorts will be understaffed (so don't expect high levels of customer service). If you're not a diver, there's not a whole lot to keep you entertained, although you can go snorkelling and the fine views and midweek solitude might appeal to some.

Anilao is the generic tourist name for the 13km peninsula that extends south from Anilao village (a barangay of Mabini). The dive resorts are strung out along the rocky western edge of the peninsula, linked by a winding sealed road.

🏃 Activities

Anilao is famed for its colourful corals and rich species diversity, which yield excellent macrophotography. There are good dive sites scattered around Balayan Bay and around the Sombrero and Maricaban Islands. Most resorts offer diving and some form of certification program; expect to pay around P900/1500 for one/two dives, plus equipment hire.

🛌 Sleeping

As well as dozens of dive resorts along the coast, there are resorts and hotels patronised by nondivers with decent accommodation and occasionally a pool.

Arthur's Place Dive Resort   RESORT **$$**
(☑ 09197167973; www.arthursplacediveresort.com; d with fan/air-con P1500/2500, cottage P3800; ❄️🛜) One of the few dive-oriented places that approaches the budget category, Arthur's has very liveable rooms with little patios around a grassy courtyard. To treat yourself, splash out on the family cottage directly on the waterfront. Dive packages start at P1775 in a group of four. It's 9.5km south of the turn-off in Anilao village.

Dive Solana   RESORT **$$**
(☑ 0908 876 5262; www.divesolana.com; s/d/tr per person incl meals from P5250/4250/3917; 🛜❄️) The refurbished Solana is a good choice for those seeking some R&R, with its swimming pool, swim-out pontoon and all-inclusive packages. All of the cottages are well appointed and ocean facing. As well as scuba diving, staff can arrange snorkelling, kayaking and island-hopping. It's 10km south of the Anilao village turn-off.

Dive & Trek   RESORT **$$**
(☑ 0910 936 4556, 02-851 8746; www.diveandtrek.com; r incl unlimited diving & meals per person from P5000, nondiver per person P4000; ❄️❄️) Accessible only by boat, this is the place to really get away from it all. The unlimited diving and snorkelling on the house reef doesn't hurt either; gear rental is an extra P1000. The simple, comfortable rooms are in a pair of hillside bamboo-and-nipa complexes.

★**Lilom Resort & Gallery Cafe** RESORT **$$$**
(http://lilomresort.wixsite.com/lilom-resort; r/cottage per person incl meals P3000/3500; 🅟 🛜) Seafront Lilom is not a dive resort but a relaxing retreat and dining experience, with all meals and a sunset cocktail included in the rates. There are four rooms in the main house, and a couple of garden cottages, all neatly decorated with a rustic-chic vibe, but the best deal is the private cottage (Satcho's) with a verandah facing the lovely garden.

ℹ Information

Mabini Tourist Office (📞 043-410 0607; ⏱ 8am-5pm) On the pier in Anilao; can help with information and transport.

ℹ Getting There & Away

To get to Anilao from Manila, take a bus to Batangas pier and get off just before the bridge leading over to the pier. From here frequent jeepneys head west to Mabini (P30, 30 to 45 minutes) from where you can take a tricycle the last 2km to Anilao town.

From Anilao proper, tricycles cost P40 for short trips, or P150 to P200 to the far resorts.

Mt Banahaw

Descriptions of the vast dormant volcanic cone of Mt Banahaw (2177m), which looms over the entire southwest Luzon region, are almost always accompanied by the term 'mystic'. The mountain is said to be inhabited by a host of deities and spirits – most famously Filipino revolutionary hero and poet José Rizal, who was executed by the Spanish in 1896. A group called the 'Rizalistas' believe that Rizal was the reincarnation of Christ. At least 75 cults have taken up residence on the mountain's lower reaches, dedicating their lives to the spirits of Rizal and others that dwell in Banahaw's crater.

🏃 Activities

Though Mt Banahaw offers some of the most impressive hiking in southern Luzon, the summit is off-limits to trekkers indefinitely to prevent environmental damage caused by unchecked trekking and mass pilgrimages up the lower slopes of the mountain. Contact **Biodiversity Management Bureau** (BMB; Map p80; 📞 02-924 6031; http://bmb.gov. ph) in Quezon City to see if the mountain is open and to enquire about permits. The main trailheads for both Mt Banahaw and Mt Cristobal are near the village of Kinabuhayan. Besides Mt Banahaw, Mt Cristobal and Mt Banahaw de Lucban, another good hiking option in this mountainous region of southwest Luzon is flora- and fauna-rich Mt Makiling near Los Baños. Leeches are rampant on all of these peaks in the wet season.

🛏 Sleeping & Eating

★**Kinabuhayan Cafe** GUESTHOUSE **$$**
(📞 0916 221 5791; Dolores; r incl meals P3000; 🅟) The new incarnation of this B&B is on an ancestral farm about 5km from the tiny town of Dolores. Currently there's just one cottage, but the main reason to venture out here is the food. Charismatic and slightly eccentric owner Jay Herrera crafts superb home-style banquet meals using fresh local ingredients in his makeshift kitchen. Book ahead.

★**Bangkong Kahoy Valley** RESORT **$$**
(📞 0929 149 6458; http://bangkongkahoy.com; Kinabuhayan; camping P100, 4-7 person cottages P2000-3000, villas P3500; 🛜) In a spectacular setting wedged between Mts Banahaw and Cristobal, this fantastic ecoresort consists of a camping area and a range of open-air nipa cottages and villa-style rooms. It's run by a passionate environmentalist who can arrange walks, birdwatching and other activities. The resort grows its own organic vegetables for the rustic restaurant.

ℹ Getting There & Away

The Mt Banahaw region is best explored by private vehicle. The long drive around the base of Mt Banahaw via San Pablo, Tiaong, Tayabas and Lucban is one of the prettiest in the country, with the misty mountain and its foothills – Mt Banahaw de Lucban (1875m) and Mt Cristobal (1470m) – constantly looming.

Otherwise take a Jam Liner bus from Manila's Buendia LRT to San Pablo or Tiaong (towards Lucena; P150, three hours), get off at the Dolores turn-off and pick up a jeepney or tricycle.

Pagsanjan

📞 049 / POP 42,164
The town of Pagsanjan (pag-san-*han*), in Laguna Province 100km southeast of Manila, is best known for the popular canoe trips up the Pagsanjan River to Pagsanjan (Magdapio) Falls. It's a long way to come for a canoe trip, but if you're exploring the Mt Banahaw region it's an essential detour. The town benefits from its pleasant riverside location, but, apart from the Our Lady of Guadalupe Church, there's not a lot to see.

🏃 Activities

Pagsanjan Falls
CANOEING

(Magdapio Falls) The sole reason to come to Pagsanjan is for the river trip to Pagsanjan Falls, where some of the final scenes of Francis Ford Coppola's epic Vietnam War movie *Apocalypse Now* were filmed. Two hard-working *bangceros* (boaters) paddle you upriver for 1½ hours through a dramatic gorge hemmed by towering cliffs and vegetation to the small but powerful falls.

At the top, the *bangcero* will take you under the 10m-high falls on a bamboo raft into the 'Devil's Cave', an exhilarating and unnerving moment as you pass directly through its high-pressure cascade.

On the return journey you let the water do the work on the fast and exciting downstream adventure. The height of the wet season (August to October) is the best time to ride the rapids. Timing is everything: towards the end of the dry season the low water level means there's more dragging over boulders than riding rapids; if the water level is too high, you may not be able to go all the way to the falls. At any time of year it's best to avoid weekends, as half of Manila seems to descend on Pagsanjan. Bring a plastic bag for your camera, and prepare to get wet.

To arrange your falls trip, secure a canoe (P1250 per person) from the tourist office in the centre of town next to the plaza. A minimum of two people is required (boats fit three passengers); if you're travelling solo the tourist office will do its best to pair you with another (or you can pay double). Only *bangcero* licensed and employed by the town government are allowed to operate boats.

Riverside guesthouses and resorts such as La Vista will also organise a boat for you for an extra fee, with the advantage that they'll pick you up.

It's customary and expected to tip your *bangcero*; P100 per person is suggested.

🍴 Sleeping & Eating

La Vista
GUESTHOUSE $

(☑ 049-501 1229; 2 Garcia St; d P950; ❄️🛜) Right on the river in town, 150m west of the bridge, friendly, family-run La Vista has five clean air-con doubles and loungey common areas, and is the best budget choice. It caters to short stayers coming for the waterfall trip with a 12-hour rate (P450) and a three-hour rate (P350) in a house across the street.

Willy Flores Guesthouse
GUESTHOUSE $

(☑ 0948 601 2086; Garcia St; r with fan P500) More a homestay than guesthouse, this very basic place is cheap and run by an affable family with knowledge of the area. Breakfast is P60 extra. It's 400m west of the bridge in the centre of town.

★ Aling Taleng's Halo Halo
FILIPINO $

(☑ 0916-309 3683; 169 General Luna St; halo-halo P110, mains P120-370; ⏱ 9am-8pm; 🛜) This restaurant-bar right by the bridge has been making its signature *halo-halo* – that iconic icy Filipino dessert – since 1933, and is locally famous for it. It's also an excellent place for a meal of the usual Filipino classics or an evening cocktail.

Emin & Milas
FILIPINO $

(Rizal St; mains P70-160; ⏱ 10am-10pm) This simple canteen is the place for cheap, filling and authentic Filipino dishes.

★ Calle Arco
FILIPINO $$

(☑ 049-501 4584; 57 Rizal St; mains P170-300; ⏱ 10am-10pm; ❄️) Easily the best restaurant in town, atmospheric Calle Arco adds uniquely Pagsanjan touches to Filipino fare, along with pizza and pasta. Try the chicken *sisig* (spicy and sour grilled meat) fajitas. There's an attached Parisian-themed cafe and a breezy alfresco dining area to complement the more formal restaurant.

ℹ️ Information

Pagsanjan Tourist Office (☑ 049-501 3544; http://pagsanjan.gov.ph; General Taino St; ⏱ 8am-5pm) This is the place to organise boat trips and pick up local information.

ℹ️ Getting There & Away

There are no direct buses to Pagsanjan, but regular DLTB and Greenstar buses link Manila (P140, 2½ hours) with nearby Santa Cruz. The Santa Cruz bus terminal is on the highway about 5km west of Pagsanjan; frequent jeepneys run to/from Pagsanjan (P10).

Pick up jeepneys to Lucena and Lucban heading east along the main road in Pagsanjan.

Lucban

☑ 042 / POP 51,475

Tucked away in the foothills of Mt Banahaw, the pleasant mountain town of Lucban boasts an impressive stone **church** (A Racelis Ave) surrounded by usually quiet cobbled streets. It comes alive for **Pahiyas** on 15 May, the annual harvest festival and feast of San Isidro Labrador. Locals compete for a prize by covering their houses in fruit, vegetables and wildly elaborate multicoloured rice-starch decorations called *kiping*. Giant papier-mâché effigies are marched through the streets to the town church.

Colonial-style **Patio Rizal Hotel** (☑042-540 2107; patiorizal@yahoo.com; 77 Quezon Ave; d incl breakfast P2300-3500, ste from P3700; ❄ ☎) is one of Lucban's best, with a decent range of rooms with cable TV, friendly staff and a super-central location (parking can be a problem). There's an excellent streetside cafe and bar overlooking a small plaza. **Cafe San Luis** (☑042-540 2122; cnr San Luis & Regidor Sts; mains from P190; ⊗8am-midnight) is an attractive open-air garden bistro in Lucban's backstreets serving Filipino dishes, pizza and cold beers. Live music on weekends.

Pick up regular jeepneys or minivans from the central stop on A Racelis Ave to Lucena (P30, 45 minutes), from where frequent buses go to Manila, Batangas and Naga. Jeepneys also run to Pagsanjan (P45, one hour).

Lucena

☑ 042 / POP 236,500

Lucena, capital of Quezon Province, is a southern transport hub and the closest city to the departure point for ferries to Marinduque island. It's a congested, gritty place with no particular attractions, but the Dalahican port for Marinduque is actually 5km south of the city proper (Manila-bound buses meet the boats) and the main highway skirts to the north, so unless you get stuck or lost it's unlikely you'll even need to venture in.

🛏 Sleeping

Fresh Air Hotel & Resort   HOTEL **$**
(☑042-710 2424; Tagarao St, Isabeng; r P400-1100; ❄ ☎ ☎) Popular with family day trippers for its pools and kids' playground, this is a fading but inexpensive resort out on the road towards Batangas. Rooms and cottages are passably clean and there's a restaurant with a limited menu.

Queen Margharette Hotel   HOTEL **$$**
(☑042-373 7171; www.queenmargharettehotel.com; Diversion Rd, Domoit; d incl breakfast P1200-2900, ste from P3500; ❄ ☎ ☎) About 2km from the bus station on the outskirts of town is one of Lucena's best value deals. The large complex features rooms well back from the road, a pool area with slide, a spa, a bar and a restau-

rant serving buffet breakfast. The standard rooms are eminently affordable and clean. There's a second branch in the city centre.

ℹ Information

Quezon Tourism Office (☑042-373 7510; Merchan St; ⊗8am-5pm Mon-Fri) Provincial tourist information.

ℹ Getting There & Away

Getting in and out of Lucena can be slow going but the extension of the South Luzon Expressway from Santo Thomas cut travel time from Manila to less than two hours.

BOAT

Boats to Marinduque depart from Dalahican port, 5km south of Lucena. Your nostrils will tell you that Dalahican port is not only a major port for travellers, but also for fishing. There's a P30 terminal fee.

At the time of research there were no longer fast-craft ferries, only roll-on, roll-off.

Starhorse Shipping (☑0948 548 0767) has four departures to Balancan (P260, 2½ hours) in Marinduque, while **Montenegro Lines** (☑047-373 7084) has eight departures. Montenegro also has an inconvenient 2am ferry to Cawit (P350) on Tuesday and Saturday. **Kalayaan Shipping** has two weekly ferries (Sunday and Wednesday) to Romblon (P700, 17 hours).

BUS

JAM Liner and JAC Liner buses meet ferries, then head to Manila's Buendia LRT stop in Pasay (P176, 3½ hours).

From Grand Central, 5km north of town on Diversion Rd (National Hwy), **Lucena Lines** (☑0922 852 2096) and JAC Liner head to Manila (Pasay, P210 to P258, four hours) every 20 minutes. There are also frequent buses to Daet (P315, five hours) and Legazpi (P480, eight hours).

Jeepneys (P8) connect Grand Central with Lucena's centre, from where you need to catch another string of jeepneys via SM Mall to Dalahican port. A tricycle to the port from Lucena costs from P50 to P75.

On the road to Batangas, near the Fresh Air Hotel & Resort, you can flag down frequent ordinary Supreme Lines buses to Batangas.

NORTH OF MANILA

Most travellers merely pass through the area north of Manila on the way to North Luzon, but attractions here include the resort Freeport Zone at Subic Bay and the notorious volcano Mt Pinatubo.

Angeles & Clark Airport

☑ 045 / POP 411,600

Clark, 80km northwest of Manila, is the former site of the US Air Force's base, in use from 1903 until the eruption of Mt Pinatubo forced their hasty departure in 1991. Since then the base has been developed into the site of an international airport and the Clark Freeport Zone – a somewhat refined enclave comprising a business district, estates, casinos, golf courses, duty-free shops and upcoming restaurants. It's also used as a base by the Philippine Air Force.

Unless you have a flight from Clark Airport or a bus transfer at Mabalacat terminal in Dau there's no pressing reason to visit Clark or Angeles; the latter is synonymous with the sex industry in the Philippines. The 10,000 girls and women working the strip of tacky clubs and bars are only the vestiges of the time before the closure of the airbase, when it was estimated 10 times as many were employed.

◎ Sights & Activities

★ Clark Museum　　　　MUSEUM
(☑ 045-599 2854; Clark Parade Grounds; adult P200, student & child free; ◎9am-4pm Tue-Sun) On the edge of the former American parade grounds, this well-presented museum details the history of Clark from 1901 up to its development of the Freeport Zone. It includes some great military memorabilia, photos and displays on Mt Pinatubo's dramatic eruption, and info on the indigenous Aeta. A highlight is the 4D theatre screening four times a day.

Mt Arayat National Park　　TREKKING
(P75) The volcanic cone of Mt Arayat (1026m) is a local trek that's doable in a half-day from Clark or Angeles. Take a jeepney at the Mabalacat/Dau terminal heading to Arayat town, then take a tricycle to the park entrance, where you pay your fee and pick up a guide (mandatory). There are villas from P1200 if you feel like staying the night. A locally run 'Revive Mt Arayat National Park' Facebook page has more information.

Angeles City Flying Club　　SCENIC FLIGHTS
(☑ 0916 456 8588; www.angelesflying.com; trial instruction flight from P2466) For sublime views take a trial ultralight flight with an instructor over Pampanga, taking in its verdant rice paddies and Mt Arayat, with this well-established company located 25 minutes' drive from Angeles in Magalang.

SAN FERNANDO CRUCIFIXION CEREMONY

The industrial town of San Fernando – not to be confused with San Fernando (La Union), northwest of Baguio – is the capital of Pampanga Province.

About the only reason people come here is to see devout Christians taking part in a crucifixion ceremony every Easter. At noon on Good Friday, in barangay San Pedro Cutud, masochistic volunteer devotees are nailed to wooden crosses and whipped till they bleed.

Victory Liner has buses to San Fernando from its Cubao terminal in Manila (P105, one hour, every 30 minutes). Be aware that buses from Manila to points further north take the NLEX; take a bus heading to Olongapo via San Fernando.

🍴 Sleeping & Eating

There's no truly budget accommodation recommendable in Clark or Angeles, but Clark has a number of top-end hotels.

Red Planet Hotel　　　HOTEL $
(www.redplanethotels.com; Don Juico Ave; d P1200; ▣🖙) On busy Don Juico Ave, Red Planet is a relatively new accommodation option, efficiently run with immaculate modern rooms. Flat-screen TVs, powerful showers and in-room safes give it a midrange feel at a budget price.

Clark Hostel　　　HOSTEL $$
(☑ 045-599 7500; http://clarkhostelphil.com; Ninoy Aquino Ave; d from P2300; ▣🖙) Even the hostels are pricey in Clark. This HI-affiliated place behind a 7-Eleven has no dorms, just fading doubles with bathroom and aircon, but it's super central (near the Parade Grounds), secure and cheaper than surrounding hotels.

Park Inn by Radisson　　BUSINESS HOTEL $$$
(☑ 045-598 7000; Manuel A Roxas Ave, SM City Clark; d from P3400; ▣🖙🏊) Between Clark and Angeles, this high-rise is one of the better-value top-end hotels near the Freeport Zone. The 154 rooms are more functional than luxurious, but neatly decorated, and the pools and gym are in good shape. It's 8km from the airport, next to the giant SM City Mall.

BATAAN PENINSULA

For WWII veterans of the Pacific campaign, few places have such bitter associations as the Bataan Peninsula. Both sides saw some of their darkest moments in the jungles around Mt Mariveles.

Few are left who experienced the Bataan Death March firsthand, a grisly affair that began when 70,000 US and Filipino troops surrendered to the Japanese in April 1942. The victors marched the prisoners, many sick and injured from months of fighting, 90km from Mariveles to San Fernando, Pampanga, where they were loaded into box cars and brought by train to the Camp O'Donnell POW camp, now the Capas National Shrine (p112). Along the way some 15,000 to 25,000 American and Filipino troops perished.

The peninsula's most poignant site is the **Dambana ng Kagitingan** (Shrine of Valour; Mt Samat Rd; P50; ☺8am-5pm) on Mt Samat near Balanga. Atop the mountain is a 90m-high crucifix with battle scenes carved around its base. You can take a lift (which operates from 8am to noon and from 1pm to 5pm) to the top of the cross, where there is a long viewing gallery with fine views out over Mt Mariveles, Manila Bay and the South China Sea.

From the base of the cross, steps lead 50m down the hill to the shrine proper, where the stories of the Battle of Bataan and the ensuing Death March are carved into a marble memorial wall. In a bunker beneath the shrine is the excellent and blissfully air-conditioned **Battle of Bataan Museum** (☺8am-noon & 1-5pm) FREE, with an impressive range of weaponry on display, battles scenes depicted in drawings and dioramas, and a brilliant relief map of the Bataan Peninsula.

Every 9 April, a national holiday known as Araw ng Kagitingan (Day of Valour), relatives of American, Japanese and Filipino veterans of the battles and Death March (plus the last remaining veterans) gather at the shrine and pay tribute to the thousands who fell in the surrounding jungles.

To get to the shrine by road, travel to Balanga, linked by Genesis and Bataan Transport buses from Pasay Rotunda in Manila (P210, four hours) via Angeles' Mabalacat/Dau bus terminal. You can also take a Victory Liner bus to/from Olongapo (P70, 1¾ hours).

From Balanga head south a few kilometres then turn right (west) off the highway toward Bagac. From the turn-off it's 4.5km to the Mt Samat turn-off, then another 7km up a steep but well-paved road to the cross. Tricycles wait at the Mt Samat turn-off (P300 round trip). You can also reach the Mt Samat turn-off from Balanga on a Bagac-bound jeepney (P10).

Hiring a van in Balanga for a half-day trip to Mt Samat costs P1500. Staff at the **Gap Plaza** (☑047-633 2761; www.gapplaza.com; cnr Capitol Dr & Sampaguita St, Balanga; d incl breakfast P2300-3000; P ❋ ☎) can arrange transport and tours. The hotel is the pick of the central hotels in Balanga, with spotless rooms with cable TV and an attached eatery, Cafe Nicole.

At time of research a ferry service was poised to resume (and had already made a test run) between the Esplanade Seaside Terminal in Manila and Orion port just south of Balanga. The MV *XGC Express* (www.magicleaf.ph) was scheduled to run four times daily each way on weekdays and twice on weekends, taking only 45 minutes.

The **Bataan Tourism Center** (☑047-237 4785; www.bataan.gov.ph; Capital Compound, Balanga) has an excellent website detailing where to find historical WWII sites and other places of interest.

Yakiniku Kosyu Japanese Grill JAPANESE $$
(☑045-499 1026; Santos St, Clark Freeport Zone; mains P180-650; ☺11.30am-11pm) Overlooking the Parade Grounds, this Japanese restaurant is set inside a converted historical barn house with decor mixing traditional *izakaya* (Japanese pub-restaurant) with colourful kitsch. It does excellent sushi and barbecue dishes and has some garden cabanas.

Iguana's MEXICAN $$
(☑045-893 3654; Don Juico Ave; mains P160-300; ☺11am-10pm Tue-Sat; ❋ ☎) Located approximately halfway between Clark Airport and Angeles (within the Freeport Zone), Iguana's is one of the Philippines' best Mexican restaurants with great margaritas and beer-battered fish tacos.

ⓘ Getting There & Away

AIR

Clark International Airport (DMIA; ☑ 045-599 2888; http://crk.clarkairport.com) is in the Clark Special Economic Zone and used by Asian low-cost airlines, which serve the following cities, among others:

Dohar Qatar Airways

Hong Kong Cebu Pacific

Kuala Lumpur Air Asia

Seoul Jin Air, Korean Air

Singapore Cebu Pacific

In theory air-con shuttles meet all flights and drop passengers off either at the Clark Freeport Zone main gate (P30) or the Mabalacat (Dau) bus terminal (P50). If these aren't around, look for a jeepney to the main gate, or take an over-priced fixed-rate taxi (P450/500 to Mabalacat/Angeles).

BUS

The cheapest way to get to Manila is to head to the main Mabalacat bus station in Dau, around 3km from Clark's main gate, where you'll find scores of buses heading to Manila (fan/air-con P115/150, 1½ hours). There are also buses to Olongapo (P140, one hour) and just about anywhere else in North Luzon. Most depart only when they're full.

Otherwise Philtranco runs eight direct, air-con buses daily from Clark to Manila (Pasay, P350, two hours). Victory Liner has three daily buses to Cubao.

Getting to Banaue is trickier. If you're comfortable changing buses, the recommended route is Dau–Cabanatuan–Solano–Lagawe–Banaue. The alternative is to backtrack to Manila and get the direct night bus to Banaue, or take a Victory Liner bus to Baguio (P300, three hours) and pick up a connection there.

A constant stream of jeepneys connects Dau and Angeles, a five-minute journey.

Subic Bay & Olongapo

☑ 047 / POP 325,949

Until 1992, Subic Bay was the base for the huge 7th Fleet of the US Navy – the largest outside the USA. The adjoining town of Olongapo was known for its sex industry, and not much else.

Though the US Navy has recently returned to Subic Bay on a semipermanent (and small-scale) basis, these days authorities are busy trying to remould the Subic Bay Freeport Zone (SBFZ), as the former military base is now known, into a legitimate business hub and family-friendly tourist destination. To that end, it's popular with weekenders from Manila for its theme parks, jungle trekking, water sports and wreck diving.

◉ Sights & Activities

The Freeport Zone has a relaxed feel devoid of jeepneys and tricycles, and a pleasant waterfront strip of restaurants, bars and hotels. The same can't be said for the busy hub of Olongapo, which offers no reason to hang about other than to catch a bus. The pungent canal that divides Olongapo and the Freeport Zone feeds a slow-and-steady stream of raw sewage into Subic Bay. The Americans dubbed it 'Shit River' and it still goes by that moniker today.

Diving

Wreck diving is one of the big adventure draws in Subic. Of the seven wrecks commonly visited by divers, the USS New York (at a depth of 28m) is the most impressive. The battle cruiser was built in 1891 and was scuttled by American troops in 1941 to keep it out of Japanese hands. The *New York* wreck is penetrable, but this is a huge ship and it is easy to get fatally lost in the endless corridors and passageways. Appropriate training and an experienced guide are vital.

Other wrecks in the harbour include *El Capitan* (20m), a well-preserved site favoured by photographers for its intactness, penetrability and prolific marine life; and the *San Quintin* (16m), home to larger fish such as wrasse, tangs, glasseyes and sweetlips. Both *El Capitan* and *San Quintin* are suitable for beginners. Advanced divers might try the LST (Landing Ship, Tank), an American landing craft at 37m.

The *Oryuku Maru* (Hell Ship; 20m), in which 1600 US prisoners of war were imprisoned and mistakenly killed during an air attack, was off-limits to divers at the time of research.

Visibility in Subic is not what it is elsewhere in the country. The best time for water clarity is from February to April. Dive prices aren't bad – P1000 to P1500 for a dive, and P16,000 to P18,000 for an open-water course.

Subic Scuba 719 (☑ 047-252 9528; 664 Waterfront Rd, SBFZ; ⊙ 8am-5pm) is a laid-back place with knowledge about the wrecks.

Ecotourism

Illegal logging was nonexistent in the Freeport Zone during the American years and as a result the area has some fantastically pristine jungle trekking. The Subic Bay Tourism

Department can help steer you to walks in the large rainforest south of the SBFZ (you'll need a private vehicle to reach the area), which also has excellent birdwatching.

A unique activity in Subic Bay is the opportunity to learn jungle survival skills from the indigenous Aeta ('Aeta' is the term given to the indigenous Negrito population in the area), who were employed to teach US service officers how to survive in the jungle.

The Cubi district (near the Subic airport) is home to the biggest known roosting site of the world's largest bats: the Philippine fruit bat and the golden-crowned flying fox. Dubbed the 'Bat Kingdom', the roosting site moves around from year to year but it isn't hard to find; just follow your ears around dusk as hundreds of bats take to the sky.

Tree Top Adventure
ADVENTURE SPORTS

(☑ 047-252 9425; www.treetopadventureph.com; Cubi, SBFZ; admission P100-1000; ⊙ 8am-4.30pm Mon-Fri, to 5pm Sat & Sun) The mix of treetop activities offered by this organisation, such as obstacle courses, rappelling, ziplines and freefalls, are a great way to get intimate with Subic's beautiful forest. Also trekking opportunities.

Jungle Environment Survival Training Camp
ADVENTURE SPORTS

(JEST; ☑ 047-252 1489; www.jestcamp.com; Cubi, SBFZ; from P450; ⊙ 8.30am-5pm) If you can gather a group of five people, JEST Camp can arrange a number of different activities, ranging from basic demonstrations to hardcore multiday survival courses where you build your own shelters and gather water from vines. You'll also find a bird park and other activities here.

Pamulaklakin Forest Trail
ECOTOUR, TREKKING

(☑ 0921 682 7175; Binictican Dr, SBFZ; 2hr tours P250; ⊙ 8am-5pm) A more grassroots option as opposed to the more commercial JEST Camp nearby, at the Pamulaklakin trailhead an Aeta guide can lead you into the forest to teach you fire making and other handy jungle survival techniques. Ask about longer ecology tours and overnight trips (P500).

Horseriding

El Kabayo Stables
HORSE RIDING

(☑ 0998 553 3925, 047-252 1050; http://elkabayo stables.com; El Kabayo Rd, Binictican; horse riding 30min/1hr P370/770; ⊙ 8.30am-5pm) People with equestrian instincts make the trip from Manila just to come here. It has plenty of horses, lessons and riding options around

Subic Bay, including a one-hour ride to El Kabayo waterfall.

Beaches

Most of Subic's beaches just south of the SBFZ are enclosed in developed resorts with entrance fees, such as **Camayan Beach Resort** (☑ 047-252 8000; http://camayanbeachresort. ph; SBFZ; day use adult/child P300/250; ⊙ 24hr) and **All Hands Resort** (☑ 047-250 2270; www. allhandsbeach.com; SBFZ; P550; ⊙ 24hr), and are popular with rowdy day trippers on weekends, but they are decent enough if you want to laze on a beach close to Manila.

Barrio Barretto (northwest of the SBFZ) has a nice stretch of sand, but as a sleazy sexpat hang-out it's best avoided. There are some nice beaches further north in Zambales, including Anawanigin Cove, but these are best reached by rented car. The palm-lined stretch of sand that runs along Waterfront Beach isn't considered suitable for swimming due to pollution from the nearby port.

🛏 Sleeping

The Cabin
GUESTHOUSE $

(☑ 047-250 3042; www.thecabinsubic.com; Schley Rd, SBFZ; dm/d P650/1050; ❄ 🛜) In a town of pricey accommodation, this cosy faux-log lodge is the only true budget choice and it comes as a welcome surprise, tucked away down a quiet backstreet but close to the action. Dorms and private rooms (shared bathroom) are cramped but modern, clean and all-round good value.

Subic Travelers Hotel
HOTEL $$

(☑ 047-252 1688; www.subicbaytravelershotel.com; cnr Aguinaldo & Raymundo Sts, SBFZ; d/f incl breakfast from P3000/4500; 🅿 ❄ 🛜 🏊) In central Subic, this hotel is one of the better uppermidrange places in town. There's a Mediterranean feel about the pool and cafe, while the expansive rooms are every bit business class, with soft beds, cable TV and artworks. Professional, welcoming staff top it off.

Herbie's Mansion
HOTEL $$

(☑ 047-252 7350, 0917 863 0677; Waterfront Rd, SBFZ; d weekday/weekend P1700/1900; ❄ 🛜) It's no mansion, but Herbie's offers familyfriendly, no-frills rooms in the heart of the Waterfront. Good value for the location.

Lighthouse Marina Resort
HOTEL $$$

(☑ 047-252 5000; www.lighthousesubic.com; Waterfront Rd, SBFZ; r incl breakfast P6000-8000, ste P9000; ❄ 🛜 🏊) Streets ahead of most places in Subic Bay in terms of comfort, design, service – and price. The spacious rooms are truly luxurious, with supersized flat-screen TVs, minibars and room service, and the hotel amenities, from pool to restaurant, are top. Even if you're not staying, call into the London Music Bar for a cocktail.

✖ Eating & Drinking

★ Vasco's
PUB FOOD $$

(☑047-252 1845, 0919 830 9387; www.vascos resort-museum.com; Lot 14, Argonaut Hwy, SBFZ; mains P250-360; ⊙24hr; P🕿) Popular with the expat community and with a breezy deck looking back over the bay, this 'pirate' bar and restaurant is a prime drinking spot and grill restaurant. To get here from the CBD take an 'Airport-Cubi' Winstar (P9). Aussie owner Brian Homan is an accomplished shipwreck explorer who has been diving in the Philippines forever.

Rachi Curry Corner
INDIAN $$

(☑047-252 3663; Santa Rita Rd; shwarma P55-75, mains P275-350; ⊙10am-10pm) Jovial Nepalese owner Ram serves up large portions of delicious South Asian specialities, including lots of veg dishes, as well as bargain Middle Eastern shwarma and falafel at this intimate Indian restaurant.

Xtremely Xpresso Cafe
COFFEE

(☑047-252 3681; www.xtremelyxpresso.com; 1 Dewey Ave, SBFZ; ⊙6am-midnight; 🕿) The best coffee and cafe experience in Subic. There's a full range of meals, including thin-crust pizzas, and it gets busy at lunch and dinner. Come early for your caffeine fix.

Roofdeck
BAR

(Terrace Hotel, Waterfront Rd, SBFZ; P300; ⊙10am-midnight) Head to the Terrace Hotel's rooftop bar for ocean vistas, a dip in its infinity pool and a cocktail. The P300 entrance fee is redeemable against food and drinks.

Pier One
LIVE MUSIC

(249 Waterfront Rd, SBFZ; ⊙10am-2am; 🕿) This huge semi-open-air waterfront place next to Lighthouse Marina Resort has live bands every night, usually playing foot-tappable Filipino pop. Also a popular bar and grill with pool tables.

❶ Information

Subic Bay Tourism Department (☑047-252 4123; www.sbma.com; 2nd Fl, Subic Bay Exhibition & Convention Center, Efficiency Ave,

SBFZ; ⊙8am-5pm) Information on activities, accommodation and restaurants.

VisitSubic (www.visitsubic.com) Useful travel information for the area including accommodation, theme parks and transport.

❶ Getting There & Away

If you're heading to/from Manila take **Victory Liner** (☑222 2241; cnr W 18th St & Rizal Ave, Olongapo) express buses with 'via SCTEX' placards to shave an hour off the trip (P245, three hours), departing every hour until early afternoon. Otherwise there are slower buses to Cubao hourly (P207, four hours). There are also frequent buses north to Iba (P140, two hours) and Baguio (P449, six hours). The Victory Liner terminal is in Olongapo, a 10-minute jeepney ride from the SBFZ.

❶ Getting Around

'Winstar' buses are unique to the SBFZ and perform the role that jeepneys perform elsewhere. They leave from the Transport Terminal near SBFZ main gate and travel within the Freeport Zone.

In Olongapo, blue jeepneys for Barrio Barretto and Subic town are signed 'Castillejos'. Red jeepneys serve the bus terminal.

Taxis operate along Waterfront Rd, and while pricey for individual trips (around P400), for the day it works out to be around P300 per hour – so P2400 for eight hours to explore the Subic region.

Mt Pinatubo Region

For centuries, the residents of Angeles took the nearby volcanoes of Mt Pinatubo and Mt Arayat for granted. That changed suddenly on 15 June 1991, when Pinatubo, the larger of the two volcanoes, literally blew itself apart, sending a column of ash and rock 40km into the air. The mountain lost 300m in height, and fine dust and fist-sized fragments of rock rained down on nearby Angeles, Clark Airbase and Subic Bay. Compounding the catastrophe, a savage typhoon chose this moment to lash northern Luzon, turning the ash into lethal lahar (mobile volcanic mud), which flooded downhill from the volcano with dire consequences. In Zambales Province, to the west of Mt Pinatubo, lahar flows rerouted rivers and sank entire villages under newly formed Lake Mapanuepe.

❂ Sights & Activities

In the wet season, try white-water rafting (from P1500 per person). Trips involve a one-hour jeep from Santa Juliana then around two hours rafting on a 7km course. Contact Alvin & Angie Mt Pinatubo Guesthouse.

CLIMBING MT PINATUBO

While the journey up Mt Pinatubo (1450m) is one of the country's most accessible adventures, be aware that it's closed in inclement weather. Given the fragility of the lahar cliffs (prone to landslides), it shouldn't be attempted if conditions are unfavourable. Flash floods during the remnants of a 2009 typhoon swept away a convoy of jeeps, killing seven. After the accident, the mountain was closed for a spell, and when it reopened new rules were enforced ensuring excursions to the summit begin between 6am and 8am (usually dependent on when military exercises are being held). For this reason organised excursions to Pinatubo start very early – predawn in Manila and just a little after that in Angeles.

It's only possible to climb Mt Pinatubo with a guide and 4WD. While many choose to go on organised excursions with Angeles- or Manila-based tour companies, it's easy enough to spend a night in Santa Juliana and arrange it all independently – giving you the advantage of staying at the foot of the volcano to avoid the super-early wake up.

The main point of contact for the climb is the **Santa Juliana Tourism Council** (📱 0906 462 3388) or Alvin & Angie Mt Pinatubo Guesthouse, who can advise you on bookings, logistics and safety matters. Call in advance to make sure they're allowing climbs on the day you want to go up.

Costs vary according to group size, but if you arrange it independently a group of four or more can expect to pay around P2000 per person (including lunch). The tourist office and Alvin are both good at matching independent travellers with other groups. Otherwise, if you want to go alone, expect to pay P5000. For Manila- and Angeles-based tour companies you'll pay significantly more.

After climbing Pinatubo, there are also some interesting Aeta villages in the area you can visit; get in touch with Alvin at Mt Pinatubo Guesthouse.

Capas National Shrine   MEMORIAL
(Filipino/foreigner P20/40; ⏱8am-5pm) This Camp O'Donnell POW camp was where the American and Filipino soldiers who endured the notorious WWII Bataan Death March were transported. At the heart of the 22-hectare memorial park is the Capas National Shrine, a 70m needle-shaped obelisk and the Wall of Heroes, standing solemnly at the end of the boulevard.

🛏 Sleeping & Eating

There are two excellent family guesthouses in Santa Juliana.

★ Alvin & Angie
Mt Pinatubo Guesthouse   GUESTHOUSE $
(📱09292490865,09198614102;www.mt-pinatubo.weebly.com; Santa Juliana; dm P350-500, s/d incl breakfast P1000/1200; 🌬🛜) Run by super-friendly Alvin and Angie, this laid-back guesthouse is the place independent travellers head to to arrange their volcano trek. It's a relaxing spot set among fruit trees in a rural village, with 14 rooms (a mix of bunks and doubles) and delicious home-cooked meals (P150).

Allan Bognot's
Pinatubo Guesthouse   GUESTHOUSE $
(📱0919 934 9474; Purok 5, Santa Juliana; dm/s/d incl breakfast P500/1100/1400; 🌬🛜) This stylish and homey guesthouse features rooms in the main family house and new chalet-style rooms at the back, all equipped with private bathroom and air-con. The guest kitchen and common lounge are good places to meet other travellers, and there's also a decent restaurant.

ℹ Getting There & Away

To get to Santa Juliana from Manila take any North Luzon–bound bus heading to Capas (fan/air-con P140/180), from where you then take a tricycle direct (P300); otherwise from Capas you could try for a jeepney to Patling (P30), and then a tricycle to Santa Juliana (P60). Regular buses to Capas also leave Mabalacat bus terminal in Dau, Angeles (P50, 45 minutes).

North Luzon

Best Places to Eat

➡ Cafe by the Ruins Dua (p135)

➡ Log Cabin (p144)

➡ Angel & Marie's (p121)

➡ Pension Ivatan (p162)

➡ La Preciosa (p127)

Best Off the Beaten Track

➡ Sierra Madre (p158)

➡ Babuyan Islands (p161)

➡ Itbayat Island (p164)

➡ Hapao & Hungduan (p154)

➡ Adams (p128)

➡ Lake Mapanuepe (p117)

Why Go?

A region that invites intrepid exploration, North Luzon encapsulates a nation in miniature. Surfers race waves onto sunny beaches, where whites sands are lapped by teal waters. Machete-carrying mountain tribespeople are quick to smile and quicker to share their rice wine. Impenetrable jungle hides endemic critters. In Spanish colonial cities, sunlight breaks through seashell windows. Far-flung islands with pristine landscapes greet few visitors.

For many travellers, the lure is the emerald rice terraces of the Cordillera, a mountain range that hides hanging coffins and mummies. Trekking is a prime activity, but caving, mountain biking and rafting are other adrenalin-fuelled activities that shape the North Luzon experience. Culturally, this is the Philippines at its most diverse; the peoples of the mountains, Zambales, Ilocos and Batanes, are notable for a melange of language and ritual, and share a genuine and consistent friendliness to visitors.

When to Go
Sagada

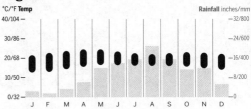

Nov–May
The best weather the Philippines has to offer – you'll have lots of company!

Apr–Jul
The heat is on but the crowds are down.

Jul–Oct
Rice terraces are green, but typhoons can be a problem.

North Luzon Highlights

1 Batad (p152)
Being awestruck by this rice-terrace amphitheatre then trekking to others that rival it.

2 Kalinga Province (p147)
Hobnobbing with former headhunters and meeting a famous tattoo artist.

3 Sagada (p140)
Shimmying, climbing and swimming into deep caves before hiking to hanging coffins.

4 Batanes Islands (p160) Exploring the end of the world to experience Ivatan culture.

5 Pagudpud (p128) Kitesurfing windy waves or chilling on the sublime white-sand beaches.

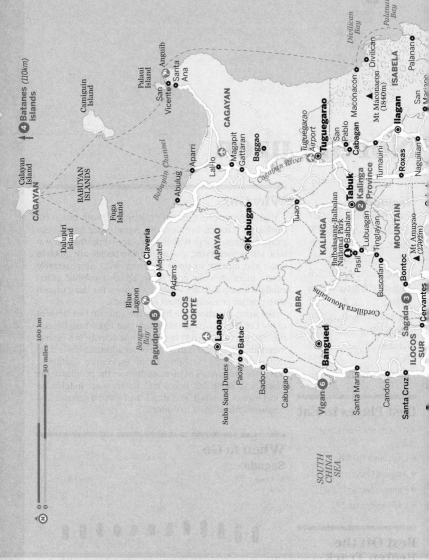

↑ **4 Batanes** (110km) **Islands**

PHILIPPINE SEA

POLILLO ISLANDS

Northern Sierra Madre National Park

Sierra Madre Mountains

QUIRINO

AURORA

NUEVA VIZCAYA

NUEVA ECIJA

BULACAN

QUEZON

BENGUET

LA UNION

PANGASINAN

ZAMBALES

TARLAC

PAMPANGA

BATAAN

METRO MANILA

RIZAL

CAVITE

LAGUNA

North Luzon Expressway (NLEX)

South Luzon Expressway (SLEX)

6 Mestizo District
(p122) Step back in time in this lovely quarter of Spanish Colonial Vigan.

7 Kabayan
(p138) Hiking steep vegetable terraces to ancient mummy caves.

8 San Juan
(La Union) (p119) Learning to surf and then partying on the beach.

9 Baguio (p131)
Taking in music, fine food and cool mountain air.

Language

Myriad languages are spoken in North Luzon, including dozens of dialects in the Cordillera alone. It's most confusing in Kalinga, where just about every village has its own dialect. In the Cordillera, people are far more likely to understand Ilocano or English than the national language, Tagalog.

In the lowlands, the principal languages are Tagalog and Ilocano, which is the predominant language not only in Ilocos but also in Cagayan, Isabela and La Union. Other common dialects include Pangasinan and Sambal, the language of the Zambales people, while the people of the Batanes speak Ivatan.

ⓘ Getting There & Away

Regular flights connect Manila with Laoag, Tuguegarao and Basco (Batanes); Vigan with Basco; Tuguegarao with Basco, Palanan and Maconacon; and Cauayan (Isabela Province) with Palanan and Maconacon. Air-con buses link Manila with major North Luzon cities, and comfortable deluxe buses run to a growing number of destinations.

Luzon's more remote regions, such as the Cordillera and the northeast part of the island, are very reachable by an assortment of reasonably frequent public transport options.

If driving off the beaten track, keep in mind you'll need a good 4WD; some of the roads that cut through Kalinga Province are not for the faint of heart. Lack of parking spots and traffic jams are a common problem in most cities and towns. You can rent cars in Manila.

ZAMBALES COAST

The Zambales Coast lies between a rock and a wet place. The rock? The angry massif of Mt Pinatubo. The wet? Well, the sea of course, which has some fine surfing especially around Pundaquit and Liw-iiwa (sometimes called 'Liwa'), and often as not the rains that unrelentingly lash this 100km of coastline every summer. Outside this season, uninhabited offshore islands and beach resorts are popular as offbeat weekend getaways with folks from Manila.

Southern Zambales Coast

This corner of Luzon still very much retains a chilled-out backpacker vibe with its wave-lapped beaches on the hot, dry coastline bordering San Antonio, San Narciso

and San Felipe. **La Paz** is the most built-up area and gets lots of big groups staying at its resorts. **Liw-iiwa** is known for its mellow, sandy-bottom surf break (although it can get big) and hosts a groovy, beach-bum scene. **Pundaquit**, with its fishing-boat-strewn beach, feels more untouched, although it has a few quiet, midrange places to stay; it's also the jumping-off point to get to the remote yet often busy camping spots on hourglass-shaped **Capones Island** and the stunning white-ash-sand **Anawangin Cove**. As the area is only a five-hour bus ride from Manila, it's gaining popularity with Filipino tourists, especially university students.

If the surf is flat it's a good time to hire a bangka from Pundaquit for island- and beach-hopping (P1300 for up to four people).

Don't miss an ecotour with **MAD Travel** (Make a Difference Travel; www.madtravel.com; Circle Hostel, Liw-iiwa; tours per person incl meals P1500; ⊙7am-7pm Sat) to meet the Aeta tribespeople and help reforest their lands. After the eruption of Mt Pinatubo in 1991, this area was covered with volcanic ash, making it nearly impossible to farm. The tour takes you to the village by ox-cart to meet the friendly families, who are thrilled to have help in their efforts. Expect to be treated like family and be spoiled with delicious local cooking.

🛏 Sleeping & Eating

Camping is very popular on this coast and everything gets busy at weekends and on holidays. Try **Crystal Beach Resort & Campsite** (☑047-222 2227; www.crystalbeach.com.ph; La Paz; r with fan/air-con from P1700/2750, camp sites P550, tent rental P750; ❄), which also has surf lessons and board rental.

Circle Hostel   HOSTEL $

(☑0917 861 1929; www.zambales.thecirclehostel.com; Liw-iiwa; hammocks P450, dm P550) This original, colourful backpacker and surfer hostel in Liw-iiwa is a great place to connect with a young crowd of fellow wave riders and make friends with the lovely staff. Lodgings consist of varying levels for the budget-conscious, with the thatch-walled, very basic dorms being the upmarket option. Lockers are available and the vibe encourages lingering, both in and out of the sea.

Kilabot Surfing   RESORT $

(☑0930 509 5122; Liw-iiwa; huts P800) If you've come to Liw-iiwa to surf but want your own space, these basic beachside *kubos* (thatched huts) are the answer.

Mommy Phoebe's Place FILIPINO $
(Liw-liwa; mains P80-220; ☺6am-late) Mommy Phoebe can stuff you full of her delicious *pansit, bagnet* and whatever else she's got cooking that day; cool you off with fresh, icy juice shakes; and sell you quality surfing supplies.

ℹ Getting There & Away

From Olongapo or Manila, take any bus heading towards Iba; get off at San Felipe for Liw-liwa, San Narciso for La Paz or San Antonio for Pundaquit. You'll then need to take a tricycle from these towns to your beach of choice (P50 to P80).

From Pundaquit, a 25-minute bangka ride to Capones Island or Anawangin Cove costs P1000.

Iba & Botolan

☏ 047 / POP 108,210

The neighbouring towns of Iba and Botolan, about 45km north of San Antonio, make convenient bases for hikes in the Zambales Mountains or decent-enough places for an overnight stopover.

The main trek around here is the ascent up mist-shrouded **Mt Tapulao** (High Peak; 2037m), the highest mountain in the Zambales range. You can walk or take a 4WD most of the way up the mountain along a mining road that terminates about an hour's walk from the summit.

The 18km mining road originates in barangay Dampay, a 40-minute tricycle ride (P170) from the small town of Palauig, 14km northwest of Iba.

🛌 Sleeping & Eating

Botolan Wildlife Farm GUESTHOUSE $$
(☏0917 829 5478, 0917 734 2206; www.botolan wildlifefarm.com; Botolan; s/d P1500/1800) Located at the foot of the Zambales Mountains and run by Swiss zoologist Martin Zoller, this is a humane sanctuary for an array of rescued beasts, with guest rooms overlooking the animal pens and the mountains. To get here, take a tricycle (P90) 4km east from a well-marked turn-off on the National Hwy, just south of Botolan centre.

Palmera Garden Beach Resort RESORT $$
(☏0908 503 1416, 047-811 1886; www.palmera-garden.com; Iba; r P1600-4400; ❀🌐🏊) This Swiss-owned resort, 2km north of Iba, is the most service-oriented in the area. The rooms are clean, air-conditioned and utterly unmemorable, but there's access to a pleasant stretch of beach and a pool surrounded by blooming flowers. The restaurant serves the likes of Currywurst alongside Filipino standards.

Rama Beach Resort RESORT $$
(☏0917 523 7262; www.ramabeach.com; Botolan; d P1900-2600; ❀🌐) There's pretty accommodation and a nice restaurant with a library and a pool table at this Australian-owned resort, on a quiet stretch of beach 8km south of Botolan proper. Turtles nest here from October to February, and the owners arrange trips to nearby caves.

ℹ Getting There & Away

Victory Liner (☏047-811 1392) has frequent buses (hourly from 5am to 6pm) from Iba south to Cubao and Pasay in Manila (P375, five to six hours) via Olongapo (P107, two hours). It has

---

WORTH A TRIP

LAKE MAPANUEPE

When Mt Pinatubo (1450m) erupted in 1991, lava flows dammed the Mapanuepe River flowing out of the Zambales range. Slowly rising floodwaters forced residents of Aglao and Bajaoen to flee to higher ground. Unfazed, locals rebuilt their villages on the shores of newly minted Lake Mapanuepe, nestled in the Zambales Mountains about 15km east of San Marcelino.

These villages are only accessible by boat and remain quite traditional – the Aeta people wearing the indigenous G-strings (loincloths) are still a common sight.

In the middle of Lake Mapanuepe is the **sunken church** of Bajaoen, easily identifiable by its maroon cross sticking out of the water – an unsettling sight.

There are one or two jeepneys per day to Aglao from San Marcelino (45 minutes), but the last one returning from Aglao is at noon. A bangka to the sunken church from the 'port' in Aglao should cost about P900. All buses travelling between Olongapo and Iba stop in San Marcelino.

departures every 30 minutes north to Santa Cruz (P108, 1½ hours).

North of Iba

If you're into island-hopping and beach camping, head to the border of the Zambales and Pangasinan Provinces. Off Santa Cruz, **Hermana Menor Island** is fringed by a postcard-worthy white beach with some decent snorkelling just offshore. The island is privately owned, but bangka excursions there and to neighbouring **Hermana Mayor Island** are possible through **SeaSun Beach Resort** (☑ 0917 409 3347; Santa Cruz, Barangay Sabang; d/f P2000/4000; ❄), which fronts a pleasantly secluded sliver of beach with views of both Hermana Menor and Hermana Mayor. Rooms run the gamut from bare-bones fan rooms (P800) to fancier digs with minibars and satellite TV. The resort is 1.5km off the main road – spot the well-marked turn-off 2km south of Santa Cruz.

Just south of here, **Potipot Island** is more accessible and more popular. It has a white beach where you can camp. SeaSun Beach Resort can arrange trips out here for P800.

Victory Liner has frequent buses south to Iba and Olongapo and north to Alaminos and Lingayen. Local buses (no air-con) run up and down the same road through the day.

LINGAYEN GULF

This pretty pocket of water, a scattershot of emerald islands on azure and turquoise, dominates the coastline of Pangasinan province.

Conservation efforts are underway to restore the coral reefs that have been severely damaged by dynamite and cyanide fishing. There is no shortage of beach resorts scattered along the coastline from Bolinao to San Juan (La Union), a popular surfer hang-out.

Bolinao & Patar Beach

☑ 075 / POP 82,090

Bolinao has a palpable end-of-the-road feel to it – unsurprising, as it is basically located at the end of everything. Depending on your point of view, local beach resorts can feel romantically isolated or a bit forlorn.

Patar Beach, a long stretch of narrow sand linking Bolinao with barangay Patar, situated 18km to the south, is popular with weekenders from Manila and makes for a relaxing stopover. The best beach for swimming is White Beach in Patar proper, overlooked by the towering Spanish-built Cape Bolinao Lighthouse.

The 17th-century **Church of St James** in the town plaza is notable for the rare wooden *santos* (religious statues) on its facade, and it's well worth paying a visit to the **University of the Philippines Marine Science Institute** (☑ 075-554 2755; www.msi.upd.edu.ph/bml; P15; ☺ 8am-5pm Mon-Fri) if you have any interest in the fragile marine ecology of Lingayen Gulf. Researchers cultivate coral-producing giant clams and transplant them to Hundred Islands National Park and as far away as Australia and Malaysia.

Treasures of Bolinao (☑ 0921 564 2408, 075-696 3266; 2-person villa P4000; ❄☞☞) is as opulent as Bolinao (indeed, this part of Luzon) gets. Located some 17km from Bolinao proper, the resort features posh villas, upmarket coconut cottages, and cavernous, exquisitely furnished suites with ocean views. The beach down here is powder-sugar soft.

Frequent buses (P56), jeepneys and vans (P65) shuttle to Alaminos (one hour) from Bolinao. A tricycle to the resorts on Patar Beach should cost around P175 one way, depending on how far you are going.

Hundred Islands National Park

☑ 075

This **national park** (☑ 075-551 2145; www.hundredislands.ph) off the coast of Alaminos actually consists of 123 separate islets. Over the centuries the tides have eaten away at the bases of some of these limestone islands, giving them a striking mushroom-like appearance.

Unfortunately, the Hundred Islands may be too popular for its own good. Visitors and fishing have taxed the local ecology, thus it can be difficult finding the right island where the coral hasn't been damaged by dynamite fishing or typhoons. While many visitors 'do' the islands in a day, the Hundred Islands rewards those who take the time to snorkel, swim and lounge on the beaches over a few days.

Environmentally, the situation has improved since the Alaminos city government took control of the park in 2005. Speedboats patrol in search of illegal fishers, while the University of the Philippines Marine Science Institute in Bolinao has been repopulating the decimated giant-clam population.

Of the scattering of 123 limestone islets and islands shrouded in greenery, some are craggy and cliff-y, and others have pleasant stretches of beach (though litter is a problem on the most popular islands), calm waters for snorkelling, caves to explore and plenty of avian life. The only three islands with facilities are Quezon Island, Governor's Island and Children's Island and domestic tourists make a beeline for these; the rest are uninhabited and you can have them to yourself.

The beaches on Quezon, Governor's and Children's Islands are nothing special, although **Governor's Island** has a nice lookout point and the calm, shallow waters surrounding **Children's Island** are ideal for children.

One of the most remote islands, **Cathedral Island** is known for its variety of seabirds; on **Marcos Island** you can practise cliff-diving from a 20m rock tower. **Cuenco Island** is bisected by a cave that passes right through it and tiny **Martha** are beautiful – the beach between the two tiny islets is only reachable during high tide.

Island Tropic (☑ 0906 469 7888, 075-551 4913; www.islandtropichotel.com; Lucap Wharf; d/f incl breakfast P1600/2400; ❊ ☎) has motel-style accommodation with a breezy restaurant upstairs and a block of spacious, clean but bland concrete rooms. **Maxine by the Sea** (☑ 075-696 0964; www.maxinebythesea.com; Lucap Wharf; d/q/f P2110/2950/4020, mains P250-800; ❊ ☎) is a breezy sea-view seafood restaurant; steer clear of the overly ambitious dishes and go for the signature squid and catch-of-the-day *kinilaw* (ceviche). The seven rooms are also the best in town, especially if you can nab the one, lower-priced double.

ⓘ Information

Hundred Islands National Park Office
(☑ 075-203 0917, 075-551 2505; www.hundredislands.ph; Lucap; ☺ 24hr) is the place to go for everything from information to boat hire.

ⓘ Getting There & Around

To reach the park, you first have to get to the town of Alaminos and then take a tricycle (P80) to Lucap Wharf to pay the park entrance fee (P80 day entry or P120 overnight) at the Hundred Islands National Park Office.

Five Star and Victory Liner have frequent bus departures from Alaminos to Pasay, Manila (ordinary/air-con P380/490, 5½ hours), and to Santa Cruz (P180, two hours), where you transfer to Olongapo. Victory Liner also has buses

to Baguio (P230, four hours, three daily). For La Union and north up the coast you'll need to take a bus or van (P68) to Dagupan and transfer there.

Bolinao is reachable by frequent jeepney (P45), bus (P56) or air-con van (P65).

The air-con van station is in Alaminos City about 500m from the Victory Liner Station, near the Red Ribbon cake shop.

The park now only offers service boats (day/overnight P1400/3000), which run except in very special cases. These give you free rein as to which islands you get to visit and how long you'd like to spend on each one.

Boats run from Lucap Wharf to the islands between 6am and 5.30pm.

San Juan (La Union)

Surfers, look no further. Most travellers heading here are bound for barangay Urbiztondo in San Juan, an unassuming beach town 6km north of San Fernando that gets the country's most consistent waves from November to March. During the season a legion of bronzed instructors offer beginners some of the world's cheapest surf lessons (P400 per hour) on perfect learners' waves that stroke the shore.

Barangay Montemar, 1km north of San Juan is a much quieter stretch of beach, and is isolated from barangay Urbiztondo's restaurants and services. The resorts there are happy to call you a tricycle (P50), however, and it's easy to go back and forth between the two villages.

⊙ Sights & Activities

Surfing instructors are easily found through barangay Urbiztondo's lodgings, which also rent boards (P200 per hour). The best beginners' break is usually at the 'cement factory' in Bacnotan, 6km north of San Juan. Urbiztondo's main beach break and neighbouring Mona Lisa Point tend to get bigger waves. Cartile Point and Darigayos are other favourite local breaks that are further out.

A popular day trip when the surf is flat, **Tangadan Falls** is a P500 tricycle ride from San Juan, then an hour's hike (P150 guide fee).

🛏 Sleeping

Most surf-inclined travellers stay in barangay Urbiztondo, a stretch of coast 3.5km south of San Juan proper, while sol-

San Juan (La Union)

0 — 1 km
0 — 0.5 miles

South China Sea

TABOK

Tangadan Falls (8km)

MONTEMAR

SAN JUAN

National Hwy

URBIZTONDO

San Fernando (5km)

itude seekers should head to tiny barangay Montemar.

★ Flotsam & Jetsam Hostel   HOSTEL $

(☑ 0917 802 1328; www.flotsamandjetsamhostel. com; dm from P650; ✳🛜) Artistic touches abound at this surfboard-strewn beach-front hostel; it's the kind of place where guests spontaneously jam on guitars, and the thatched-roof bar heaves with bronzed young surfers even in the low season. Choose between rooming in a thatch-walled, fan-cooled dorm; a 'sea suite'; or a converted RV. The 'spicy Nikki' by the resident 'alcohol alchemist' will lay you flat.

Vessel Hotel   HOSTEL $

(www.vesselhostel.com; dm P980; ✳🛜) If you want a dorm bed but sleep is still important to you, this should be your first choice. The multistorey, modern building is right in town and has air-conditioned rooms, each with an assortment of large, wooden bunks, desks, lights and a little bit of privacy. You can check the surf from the breezy rooftop hang-out area.

Sunset German Beach Resort   RESORT $

(☑ 0917 921 2420, 072-888 4719; www.sunset germanbeachresort.com; d with fan/air-con P800/1100, ste P2100; ✳🛜) Cosy, attractive rooms with exposed brickwork, a quiet beach that gets OK surf, and a German owner who makes his own German sausage. The owner has an interesting take on life in rural Philippines and expects you to eat at his restaurant. The resort turn-off is 1km north of San Juan.

Circle Hostel   HOSTEL $

(☑ 0917 832 6253; www.launion.thecirclehostel. com; hammocks P350, dm P450-550) Staying at this colourful, chilled-out hostel is kind of like staying at a friend's place: you come, you surf, you relax with your fellow wanderers on beanbags in the common area, you befriend the wonderful staff and end up lingering for days. Bed down in the very basic thatched dorms with mosquito nets or sleep in a hammock.

San Juan Surf Resort   RESORT $$

(☑ 072-687 9990, 0917 887 5470; www.san juansurfresort.com.ph; d/q with air-con from P1800/2600, 2-person villa P1800; ✳🛜) Run by Aussie Brian Landrigan, a nearly 30-year veteran of the area, this resort started as beach shacks but is now an upmarket surfers' village, ranging from spartan standard rooms and multi-person 'villas' to the spacious 'de luxe'.

There's a popular open-air restaurant near the sand and the professionally run multiday surf-school packages come highly recommended.

Kahuna Resort   RESORT $$$

(☑ 072 607 1040; www.kahunaresort.com; d incl breakfast P5265-7020; ✳🛜🏊) This is the swankiest choice in the area. Understated bungalows have slate tile floors, bamboo-and-wood details and cool bathrooms, many with a window-full of potted plants. There's an infinity pool overlooking the beach, and everything sits in manicured tropical gardens.

✖ Eating & Drinking

There is a great selection of restaurants in barangay Urbiztondo, ranging from Greek and Mexican to hole-in-the-wall Filipino. The bigger resorts have on-site restaurants, generally of decent quality.

★ **Angel & Marie's** FILIPINO $$
(☏0917 723 3253; mains P99-199; ⏱5.30-10pm Mon-Fri, 6am-10pm Sat & Sun) Run by a friendly pair of local surfers, this great little thatched restaurant in the middle of Urbiztondo has a loyal following thanks to its beautifully prepared, healthy banana pancakes, *pinakbét* (mixed vegetable stew), and grilled meats and fish. If the place is closed when you show up at the weekend, it means the surf's up!

★ **El Union** CAFE
(⏱9am-9pm Mon-Fri, 7am-10pm Sat & Sun) The size of a thimble, yet bustling and decidedly hip, this cafe takes care of surfers' caffeine-related needs via great espresso drinks (P100 to P140), masala chai and an assortment of creative hot and cold beverages. Nosh on grilled cheese sandwiches, pancakes and awesome skillet cookies.

ℹ Getting There & Away

You can try to flag down buses from the side of the road in barangay Urbiztondo, but many will be full and so won't stop. To avoid a long wait, take a tricycle to the bus station in San Fernando (P20).

From San Fernando, **Partas** (☏072-242 0465; Quezon Ave, San Fernando) serves Manila (P436, seven hours, hourly), Pagudpud (P484, seven hours), Laoag (P367, five hours) and Vigan (P235, three hours). Cheaper, more frequent ordinary buses head to Laoag and Vigan in San Fernando from the Quezon Ave stop in front of the town plaza.

Minibuses to Baguio (P82, 1½ hours) leave twice hourly from Governor Luna St in San Fernando.

If heading towards Dagupan, Lingayen or the Zambales Coast, your best bet is to take any Manila- or Baguio-bound bus to Agoo (P65). From Agoo hop on a bus to Dagupan (P70), where you'll have to change buses once again to get to the coast.

ILOCOS

Vigan

♩077 / POP 53,880

One of the oldest towns in the Philippines, Vigan is a Spanish Colonial fairy tale of dark-wood mansions, cobblestone streets and clattering *kalesa* (horse-drawn carriages). In fact, it is the finest surviving example of a Spanish Colonial town in Asia and a Unesco World Heritage site. But outside of well-restored Crisologo St (closed to vehicular traffic) and a few surrounding blocks, it's also a noisy Filipino town like many others. In the places where history feels alive, you can smell the aroma of freshly baked empanadas wafting past antique shops, explore pottery collectives and watch sunlight flicker off capiz-shell windows.

History

Located near where the Govantes River meets the South China Sea, Vigan became a convenient stop on the Silk Route, which linked China, the Middle East and Europe, and a thriving trading post where gold, logs and beeswax were bartered for goods from around the world and where Chinese settlers intermingled with the locals.

In 1572, Spanish conquistador Juan de Salcedo (the grandson of Miguel Lopez de Legazpi, one of the first conquistadors) took possession of the bustling international port. De Salcedo became the lieutenant governor of the Ilocos region, and Vigan became the centre of the politics, religion and commerce in the north. The rise of the mestizos led to considerable tension, and Vigan became a hotbed of dissent against the Spanish when, in 1762, Diego Silang captured the city and named it the capital of Free Ilocos. He was eventually assassinated (the Spanish paid Silang's friend, Miguel Vicos, to shoot him in the back), and his wife, Gabriela Silang, took over. The first woman to lead a revolt in the Philippines, she was eventually captured and publicly hanged in the town square.

The city avoided destruction in WWII when Japanese troops fled the city just ahead of American carpet bombers, who aborted their mission at the last second.

◉ Sights

Vigan has two main squares located near each other at the north end of town: Plaza Salcedo, dominated by St Paul Cathedral,

Vigan

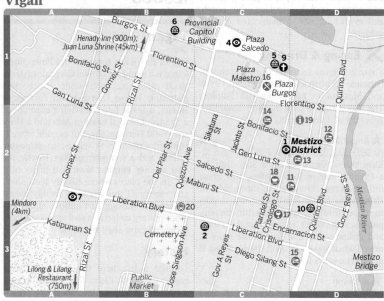

Vigan

◉ Top Sights

◉ Sights

🛌 Sleeping

✖ Eating

🍸 Drinking & Nightlife

ℹ Information

ℹ Transport

and the livelier Plaza Burgos, where locals stroll and hang out. The Mestizo District is centred on nearby Crisologo St. The main commercial drag is congested Quezon Ave, which runs south to the public market.

★ Mestizo District HISTORIC SITE

The Mestizo District, or Kasanglayan ('where the Chinese live'), is a grid of streets hemmed in between Plaza Burgos and Liberation Blvd and bisected by the beautifully preserved

Crisologo St. You can wander in a daze among ancestral homes and colonial-era architecture. The mansions here are beautiful and architecturally unique, marrying two great aesthetic styles: Chinese and Spanish.

The latter were once Vigan's colonial masters; the former were merchants who settled, intermarried and, by the 19th century, became the city's elite. In fact, Spanish and Chinese are themselves limiting terms when it comes to describing Vigan architecture.

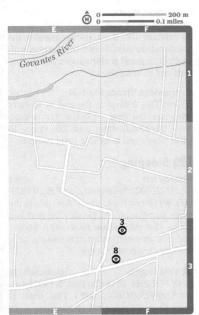

Spain itself has either influenced or been influenced by Mexico, the Caribbean and North Africa, and these regions also make their presence known in the form of airy verandahs, leafy inner courtyards and wrought-iron balconies. At the same time, Asia makes an appearance with dark wooden accents, polished floors, sliding capiz-shell windows and *ventanillas* (ventilated walls).

In most mansions, the ground floor has stone walls and is strictly for storage and/or work, while the wooden 1st floor, with its large, airy *sala* (living room), is for living. The capiz-shell windows are as tall as doors, while the wide window sills are good spots for a siesta. The capiz is a flat bivalve found in the coastal waters of the Philippines. It came into fashion in the 19th century because it was cheaper than glass and sturdy enough to withstand typhoon winds and rain. Light shines through capiz in a particular way that is almost impossibly romantic.

While a couple of mansions have been converted into B&Bs or museums, most are private homes. Two houses to look out for are the Quema House, with its original furnishings and decor, and the Syquia Mansion on Quirino Blvd, the former holiday home of Vigan native Elpidio Quirino, the Philippines' sixth president, who was born in

the nearby provincial jail. This is one of the best-preserved historical homes, and a good place to get a sense of the traditional interior of a Chinese–Spanish mansion at the end of the 19th century.

Magsingal Museum   MUSEUM
(⊙ 8am-4pm Tue-Sun) **FREE** This branch of Vigan's Padre José Burgos National Museum, located 11km north of Vigan in Magsingal, displays an absorbing collection of Ilocano relics. An ancient-looking belfry (1732), part of the remains of a ruined old church, still stands in front of the museum.

St Paul Cathedral   CHURCH
(Burgos St; ⊙ 6am-9pm) This church was built in 'earthquake baroque' style (ie thick-walled and massive) after an earlier incarnation was damaged by quakes in 1619 and 1627. The construction of the original wooden, thatched church is believed to have been supervised by Juan de Salcedo, lieutenant governor of the Ilocos region, in 1574.

Pottery Factories   WORKSHOP
(Gomez St; ⊙ hours vary) Prior to the arrival of the Spanish, Chinese settlers pioneered a still-active pottery industry. You can visit a couple of pottery factories on Gomez St. The 50m-long kiln at RG Jar, which was made in 1823 and can hold nearly 1000 jars, is a wonder to behold. Local potters let you create your own misshapen ceramics at the pottery wheel.

Magic Fountain   FOUNTAIN
(Plaza Salcedo; ⊙ 7.30pm) Every night at 7.30pm during peak tourist season, the fountain in the middle of Plaza Salcedo bursts into a music and light show. It gets crowded and is fantastically kitsch; you can watch the waters dance to the latest hip-hop and Disney tunes.

**Padre José Burgos
National Museum**   MUSEUM
(Ayala Museum; Burgos St; P20; ⊙ 8.30-11.30am & 1.30-4.30pm Tue-Sun) Built in 1788, this museum is in the ancestral home of Father José Burgos, one of the three martyr priests executed by the Spanish in 1872. It houses an extensive collection of Ilocano artefacts. Make sure to see the series of paintings by the locally famed painter Don Esteban Villanueva depicting the 1807 Basi Revolt, housed in the old jailhouse.

Crisologo Museum   MUSEUM
(Liberation Blvd; by donation; ⊙ 8.30-11.30am & 1.30-4.30pm) The Crisologos, Vigan's most

prominent political dynasty, have converted their ancestral home into this strangely compelling family shrine. In addition to the mildly interesting family photos, personal effects, period furniture and an impressive collection of indigenous Filipino headgear, you may spot the blood-stained pair of trousers from Floro Crisologo's assassination in 1972, and the old Chevy that Governor Carmeling Crisologo was in when she was (unsuccessfully) ambushed by gunmen in 1961.

Museo San Pablo   MUSEUM
(⊘9am-noon & 2-5pm Tue-Sun) FREE The Museo San Pablo, behind the altar of St Paul Cathedral, is a good place to see old *santos* (religious statues). Make sure to have a look at the wonderfully aged photo collection of a German pharmacist who lived in Vigan for a number of years in the late 1800s.

Syquia Mansion Museum   MUSEUM
(Quirino Blvd; P30; ⊘9am-noon & 1.30-5pm Wed-Mon) The Syquia Mansion on Quirino Blvd was recently turned into a museum filled with old furniture and exhibits dedicated to the life of Vigan native Elpidio Quirino, the Philippines' sixth president. Quirino was born in the nearby provincial jail, where his mother worked. He rose to political prominence after marrying into the fabulously wealthy Syquia family.

🎊 Festivals & Events

Viva Vigan Festival of the Arts   CULTURAL
(⊘May) A grand celebration of the town's cultural heritage takes place in the first week of May. There is street dancing, a fashion show, a *kalesa* parade and, of course, lots of food.

VIGAN WEAVERS

Vigan weavers are known for using *abel*, a locally produced cotton fabric, to hand-weave shawls, tablecloths, napkins and *barong* (traditional Filipino shirts). In barangay Camanggaan, just a 10-minute tricycle ride southeast of Vigan, you can watch *abel* hand-weavers in action at **Rowilda's Weaving Factory**, which is actually just a house, or its neighbour, **Cristy's Loom Weaving**.

High-quality *binakol* (blankets), including some antique blankets from nearby Abra Province, are for sale at many shops lining Crisologo St.

Vigan Town Fiesta   CULTURAL
(⊘Jan) A weeklong festival held around 25 January, the fiesta commemorates the town's patron saint, St Paul the Apostle, with a parade, musical performances, beauty contests and cultural shows.

Kannawidan Ylocos Festival   CULTURAL
(⊘Jan) This festival at the end of January celebrates the best of Ilocos Sur culture, from traditional dress and folk dance to tribal rituals and marching band contests.

🛏 Sleeping

Henady Inn   HOTEL $
(☑077-722 8001; National Hwy; dm P250, d P800-1375; ✳) Out on the highway right where the buses drop you off, the Henady has four-bed dorms that will please those on a budget and/or early-morning arrivals looking for a few extra hours of shut-eye.

★ Villa Angela   HISTORIC HOTEL $$
(☑077-722 2914; 26 Quirino Blvd; d/q incl breakfast from P1600/3800; ✳🖥) This hotel is more than 135 years old and retains every morsel of its old-world charm. The spacious rooms, fabulous antique furniture – which includes wooden harps and king-sized *nara*-wood canopy beds – and colonial-style lounge were good enough for Tom Cruise and Willem Dafoe when filming *Born on the Fourth of July* in the vicinity of Vigan in 1989.

Hotel Veneto de Vigan   HOTEL $$
(☑077-674 0938; www.hotelvenetodevigan.com; cnr Bonifacio & Governor A Reyes Sts; d/f from P2459/5316; ✳🖥) The renovated exterior of this historical wooden building hides light, bright, modern rooms with particularly comfortable beds and polished floors. Some of the stairs are break-neck steep, but the staff are wonderfully friendly and helpful, and we love the colourful mural in the lobby. Avoid the 'annex' rooms, which are poor value.

Grandpa's Inn   HOTEL $$
(☑077-674 0686; 1 Bonifacio St; d from P2280; ✳🖥) Grandpa's feels like a medieval mansion and has an impressive array of decent-value digs. All rooms have brick walls, capiz-shell windows, wooden beams, antique furnishings and rustic style; there are a couple of rooms where you can sleep in a *kalesa*. Drawbacks include thimble-sized bathrooms and street noise; earplugs are a boon.

AROUND VIGAN

A Unesco World Heritage site 38km south of Vigan, the massive baroque **La Nuestra Senora de La Asuncion Parish Church**, built in 1769, is unique. It has an imposing brick facade and sits alone on a hill – rather than in the town square like most Spanish churches – overlooking the town of Santa Maria, giving it a Wild West kinda vibe. It's not hard to see why it was used as a fortress during the Philippine Revolution in 1896.

Take any Manila-bound bus to Santa Maria. It's a long ride (80 minutes) for a short visit but if you're lucky you may catch a wedding or other event.

It's worth stopping in Badoc, halfway between Vigan and Laoag (about an hour by bus), for a peek inside the **Juan Luna Shrine** (www.nhcp.gov.ph; ⊘ 8am-5pm Tue-Sun) FREE in the restored ancestral home of Juan Luna, arguably the Philippines' greatest painter. The knowledgeable curator will introduce you to the history of the Luna family and tell the stories behind the paintings. The museum is near the Virgen Milagrosa Church.

Gordion Inn HOTEL **$$**

(☑ 077-674 0998; www.vigangordionhotel.com; cnr V de los Reyes & Salcedo Sts; s/d/ste from P2500/2800/7000; ❉ 🛜) This bright blue-and-yellow B&B looks much more posh from the outside than in, but offers smart, spacious rooms in an excellent central location. The breakfast buffet is a good introduction to Filipino favourites.

★ **Hotel Luna** BOUTIQUE HOTEL **$$$**

(☑ 077-632 2222; www.hotelluna.ph; cnr V de los Reyes & General Luna Sts; d/ste from P5000/11,000; ❉ 🛜 ▣) Vigan's most striking hotel is a 19th-century mansion that's all exposed stone, original wooden floors and crystal chandeliers, with original paintings and sculptures of Filipino artist Juan Luna throughout. The standard rooms are compact, carpeted and quiet, and we love the split-level loft suite with a free-standing tub and rain shower. The elegant Comedor serves fantastic Ilocano dishes.

✖ Eating

The Ilocos region is known for its food, and local specialities include *pinakbét* (mixed vegetable stew), *bagnet* (deep-fried pork knuckle) and *poqui-poqui* (a roasted eggplant dish).

Street Stalls STREET FOOD **$**

(Plaza Burgos; snacks P50) For quick, cheap Ilocano fare, check out the collection of street stalls that lines Florentino St along Plaza Burgos. These specialise in local empanadas filled with cabbage, green papaya and *longganisa; okoy* (deep-fried shrimp omelettes) and *sinanglao* (beef soup).

★ **Lilong & Lilang Restaurant** ILOCANO **$**

(Hidden Garden; ☑ 077-722-1450; www.hiddengardenvigan.com; Barangay Bulala; mains P40-120;

⊘ noon-9pm) Nestled at the heart of lush gardens crossed with a nature trail, this thatched-roofed, plant-festooned restaurant is a great bet for Ilocano dishes such as Vigan empanadas, *poqui-poqui, warek-warek* (pork innards with mayo) and the more conventional *bagnet, pinakbét* and mega fruit shakes. During busy weekends it hads set meals only (P180) and you'll have to queue.

Cafe Uno ILOCANO **$$**

(1 Bonifacio St; mains P140-260; ⊘ 9am-11.30pm; ❉ 🛜) Head to this popular place for Vigan *longganisa* (the local sausage) and very fatty *bagnet*. If you're feeling more adventurous, go for the 'seasonal specialities' such as *nga abuos* (mountain ants) or *tokak* (frog). The shakes and cakes are worth a stop, too. It's across from Grandpa's Inn and has an air-con annex in the inn itself.

🍷 Drinking & Nightlife

BarTech CLUB

(Crisologo St; ⊘ 6pm-late) BarTech is conservative Vigan's concession to nightlife. On the inside it resembles a New York lounge misplaced in Ilocos. Most nights you'll be serenaded by live, local, acoustic music.

Coffee Break Vigan CAFE

(3 Salcedo St; ⊘ 10am-10pm) Cute little cafe that makes for an excellent frappuccino-fuelled respite from the heat. Its pesto pasta also hits the spot.

❶ Information

Ilocos Sur Tourism Information Centre

(☑ 077-722 8520; www.ilocossur.gov.ph; 1 Crisologo St; ⊘ 8am-noon & 1-5pm) Highly informative staffers give out maps of Vigan in the ancestral home of poet Leona Florentino.

❶ Getting There & Away

Vigan's Mindoro Airport offes flights to the Batanes and more connections are expected in future.

Buses to Manila (P700, nine hours) are plentiful. Try **Dominion Bus Lines** (☑ 077-722 2084; cnr Liberation Blvd & Quezon Ave) to Cubao and Sampaloc, or **Partas** (☑ 077-722 3369; Alcantara St) to Cubao and Pasay. Partas has three nightly 29-seat deluxe express buses (P805, eight hours), as well as frequent buses to Laoag (P165, two hours), a daily bus to Pagudpud (P245, five hours) and buses to Baguio (P334, five to seven hours, three daily). It also runs buses south to San Fernando (La Union; P235, four hours).

Many more buses bound for Laoag and Manila stop at the Caltex Station on the National Hwy just outside Vigan. South-bound buses go via San Fernando (P235, 3½ hours), with departures roughly every two hours.

❶ Getting Around

Vigan is one of the few remaining towns in the Philippines where *kalesa* are still in use (P150 per hour). Whole-day tours will cost you around P1000, but pick your driver wisely, as English is not always strong. A tricycle ride should cost P12 within town (more at night).

Laoag

☑ 077 / POP 111,120

Laoag is a town with some history behind it, but this is only evident in a few locations; you'll have to head far out of town to see many of the sights and this can be very time consuming without your own transport. Laoag largely comes off as a noisy step to something better, although the nearby beaches and Unesco heritage church make it a worthwhile stop for many. This remains loyal Marcos country, and around here the former dictator is still referred to somewhat reverently as 'President Marcos'.

◎ Sights & Activities

Museo Ilocos Norte   MUSEUM
(www.museoilocosnorte.com;   General   Antonio Luna St; P30; ⊙9am-noon & 1-5pm Mon-Sat, from 10am Sun) Housed in the historic Tabacalera warehouse, the Museo Ilocos Norte is one of the better ethnographic museums in the Philippines. It houses a large collection of Ilocano, Igorot and Itneg traditional clothing, household utensils, ceremonial objects and more. At the end of the hall is a replica *ilustrado* (19th-century ancestral house).

★**Paoay Church**   CHURCH
(San Agustin Church) Nineteen kilometres southwest of Laoag is North Luzon's most famous church. Unesco World Heritage-listed Paoay Church was built in classic earthquake-baroque style, with a towering belfry and massive brick reinforcements running along its sides. Begun in 1704 and finished 90 years later, it's architecturally unique: an incongruous yet beautiful blend of Gothic, Chinese, Japanese and even Javanese influences.

Sinking Bell Tower   LANDMARK
(Bonifacio St) Laoag's main architectural attraction is the Sinking Bell Tower, with what is presently a hobbit-sized doorway. Built by Augustine friars to accommodate men on horseback, it is gradually sinking into the soft riverside loam.

St William's Cathedral   CHURCH
(Juan Luna Rd) The Italian Renaissance–style St William's Cathedral was built in 1880.

Sand Dunes   DUNES
Located along the coast near Laoag, the seemingly endless sand dunes sprawl south all the way to Paoay. Access is easiest to the La Paz stretch, only 15 minutes from the city. The Suba dunes near the Fort Ilocandia resort is where scenes from Mad *Max* and *Born on the Fourth of July* were shot.

Fort Ilocandia rents out 4WDs and you can also go sandboarding with **Ilocos Sand Adventures** (☑ 0915 456 1133, 0908 885 3669; www.ilocossandadventures.com; 4WD ride plus unlimited sandboarding per person P2500).

🛏 Sleeping

Laoag is a popular getaway for folks from Manila, so reserve in advance for weekends and holidays.

Laoag Renzo Hotel   HOTEL $
(☑ 077-770 4898; http://laoagrenzohotel.tripod. com; F Guerrero St; r from P1200; ❄🛜) With a surprisingly grand lobby full of woodcarvings, Renzo is Laoag's best bargain. Its lemon-scented en-suite rooms are spacious, cool and quiet. If you've got a lot of luggage, the trudge to the top floor is a good workout.

Java Hotel   HOTEL $$
(☑ 077-770 5596; www.javahotel.com.ph; General Segundo Ave; r/ste from P3000/4100; ❄🛜🏊) The petrol station in the parking lot isn't really in tune with the 'Balinese-Moroccan' theme, but the spacious rooms are decorated

in warm ochres and yellows with wicker furniture. Ilocano dishes and sushi grace the menu at the thatch-roofed restaurant. Perks include a gym and tennis court.

Isabel Suites   HOTEL **$$**
(☑ 077-770 4998; General Segundo Ave; s/d/tr from P1000/1650/2150; ❄ 🛜) A study in austerity, the rooms at the Isabel are generally small, but the beds are comfy and the tiled floors sparkle. The soundproofing is quite good for a central hotel on the main street, which means you might be able to sleep until 6.30am instead of 6am.

✕ Eating & Drinking

★ La Preciosa   ILOCANO **$$**
(☑ 077-773 1162; Rizal Ave; mains P120-220; ⊘ 8am-11pm) Laoag's best-loved restaurant is highly recommended for its large portions of delicious Ilocano specialities such as *pinakbét* (mixed vegetable stew), crispy yet tender *bagnet, dinardaan* (offal simmered in pig's-blood gravy) and delectable *sarabasab* (grilled pork liver in papaitan sauce). The sweets don't let down the side either: go for the carrot cake or the decidedly non-Ilocano velvet cupcakes.

Saramsam
Ylocano Restaurant   ILOCANO **$$**
(cnr Gomez Ave & Giron St; mains P75-220; ⊘ 11am-11pm) Surrounded by the owner's antique collection, you can sample the superlative *pinakbét* and *poqui-poqui* pizza (which we suppose can be loosely classed as fusion), as well as the restaurant's unusual signature pasta with mango. Portions are sizeable, so come ravenous.

Johnny Moon Cafe   CAFE
(Gen Antonio Luna St; ⊘ 10am-9pm) 'Johnny Moon' is a play on Juan Luna, the renowned Filipino artist whose bold replica works decorate the interior of this cafe inside the La Tabacalera Ilocano Lifestyle Center. The food is only so-so, but we love the fruit shakes (P90) and alcohol-infused coffees.

❶ Getting There & Away

PAL Express and **Cebu Pacific** (www.cebupacific air.com) fly daily to Manila from the airport 7km west of town. Airport jeepneys (P20, 15 minutes) leave from Fariñas St; most are marked 'Laoag-Gabu'.

There's no shortage of buses to Manila (from P797, 10 to 12 hours). Companies include **Partas** (☑ 077-771 4898; Gen Antonio Luna St) and **Fariñas Trans** (☑ 077-772 0126; www.farinas trans.com; FR Castro Ave). Superdeluxe express buses (up to P965) tend to run overnight.

Fariñas Trans also runs to Baguio (P466, eight to 10 hours), and Partas has frequent buses to Baguio (P466, seven hours) and Pagudpud (P123, 1½ hours). All buses heading south stop in Vigan (P165, two hours).

GMW/GV Florida (☑ 077-771 7382; Paco Roman St) has several daily buses to Tuguegarao (P455, seven hours) via Pagudpud (P107, 1½ hours) and Claveria (P189, three hours). Minibuses to Pagudpud (P100) leave every 30 minutes from behind the Provincial Capitol Building.

Laoag–Batac–Paoay jeepneys leave from Hernando Ave.

THE MARCOS LEGACY

Many Filipinos equate the 20-year rule of Ferdinand Marcos with martial law, repressions of civil liberties, imprisonment and torture of opposition and embezzlement of public funds on an epic scale. In spite of that, the Marcos family continues to be very popular in this part of Luzon, with Marcos' legacy 'enshrined' in several locations.

Marcos Museum (by donation; ⊘ 8am-6pm) The house where Ferdinand Marcos was born on 11 September 1917 takes pride of place in the small village of Sarrat, 15km east of Laoag. Displays embellish the former dictator's legal career. The nearby Santa Monica Church hosted the wedding of Marcos' youngest daughter in 1983 – at a price tag of more than US$10 million.

Malacañang of the North (P30; ⊘ 9am-noon & 1-4pm Tue-Sun) In a peaceful location next to the scenic Paoay Lake, the opulent former estate where the Marcos family spent their holidays is open to the public. The impressive house, with its cavernous *sala* (living room), capiz-shell windows and other colonial touches, provides a glimpse into the family's lavish lifestyle; the golf course where the Marcos used to tee-off now belongs to Fort Ilocandia.

Laoag–Nagbacalan–Paoay jeepneys take the coastal road to Paoay (45 minutes) via the Fort Ilocandia turn-off and Malacañang of the North (30 minutes). They depart from Fariñas St.

Pagudpud & Around

☑ 077 / POP 23,770

Pagudpud is the stuff of glossy postcards: white-sand beaches, swaying green palms, water that shimmers through every cool shade of blue. There are singing frogs at night and friendly locals by day. A clutch of stylishly renovated hotels and the best kite-surfing in the Philippines, giving Pagudpud cred as 'the next big thing on the surfing cir-cuit', have put this lonely stretch of coastline on the tourist map, although it mercifully remains sleepy compared to the likes of Bo-racay. If you're looking for blue water and white sands in North Luzon, make this your first stop.

⊙ Sights

Pagudpud actually consists of several beaches, strung along Luzon's northern edge and hemmed in by windmill-clad headlands. Coconut-palm-backed **Saud Beach** is where most resorts are to be found. Busy **Blue Lagoon** is a few headlands east. Deserted **Pansian Beach** is still further on, near the border of Cagayan Province. Kiteboarders' favourite **Caparispisan Beach** is a few kilo-metres down the road from Saud.

Kabigan Falls   WATERFALL
(P110) Kabigan Falls is 120m of crashing white water and a cool, clear pool for swim-ming. It's accessible via group tours run by all hotels or via private tricycle hire (around P700 return from Saud Beach). The falls are a 30-minute walk from the highway turn-off and the admission price includes a guide.

Stingray Memorial   MEMORIAL
In secluded Caunayan Bay, this memorial commemorates the mission of American submarine USS *Stingray*, which delivered weapons to Ilocano guerrillas, thus play-ing a decisive role in the Japanese defeat in WWII. The memorial itself is just a ce-ment block with an anchor on top but the surrounding scenery of palms, secluded white beach and rice fields makes it worth the trip.

🛏 Sleeping

Accommodation rates drop precipitously in low season (June to December). A lot of basic homestays have opened in the village that abuts Saud Beach – follow the road past the big bend near Saud Beach Resort.

All the resorts have attached restaurants. Most of them are quite good and specialise in amazingly fresh seafood.

🛏 Saud Beach

**Evangeline
Beach Resort**   RESORT $$
(☑ 0908 863 7564, 077-655 5862; www.evan gelinebeachresort.net; d P2100-4500; ❄ 🛜)
Evangeline's feels more like a B&B than a hotel. The multi-storied house is built like a heritage home, with heavy wood floors. The bedrooms, furnished with tasteful wooden beds and dressers, feel homey and warm. We particularly liked the smaller, top-storey

---

WORTH A TRIP

ADAMS

The former rebel stronghold of Adams nestles between jungle-covered mountains and is accessible via a rough 14km road that starts near Pansian Beach, off the coastal highway. All dirt trails and rickety bridges, Adams offers some good trekking, including a popular two-hour hike to the 25ft **Anuplig Falls**, which have a wonderfully clear pool beneath, and a stretch of the Bulu River is open for inner-tubing.

Adams gets few visitors, despite its spectacular location, but there are a few homestays popping up, including **Ilyn's Homestay** (☑ 0920 661 0632; r P1000), which has been getting rave reviews for its food, or you can enquire about camping at the Municipal Hall. Local food delicacies include deep-fried frogs, organic vegies and *buos* (boiled fire-ant eggs).

You can get out to Adams on your own steam: motorbikes from Pagudpud cost around P250, or take an east-bound bus from Pagudpud and ask to get off at the Adams stop just before the Pansian Bridge (about 20 minutes). Motorcycles that wait there can take you the rest of the way to Adams.

double. Evangeline's is set back a couple of minutes' walk from the beach, but its excellent seafood restaurant is beachfront.

Northridge Resort
RESORT $$

(📞0921 415 9545; d P1000-1500; ✳🛜) Here's a simple but very friendly family-run option with clean, well-kept doubles at the rocky south end of Saud Beach. It's good value; there's swimming out the front; and the white sand is only a few minutes' walk away.

Apo Idon
RESORT $$$

(📞0917 510 0671, 077-676 0438; www.apoidon.com; r/ste from P8000/10,000; ✳🛜🏊) The fanciest resort along Saud Beach, this is a Spanish-style confection with grand staircases, bright colours, stained-glass windows and Mediterranean-inspired tiles. The unique rooms feature Ifugao art, private verandahs and Western-style mod cons. It's right on the beach. Prices drop around 40% when it's slow.

Saud Beach Resort
RESORT $$$

(📞0917 519 5495; www.saudbeachresort.com; d/tr from P3619/3949; ✳🛜) Location, location, location. The rooms may be clean, good-sized and have wood floors and nice verandahs, but it's the perfect stretch of alabaster sand and a veritable ocean swimming pool out the front that makes this place shine. Service is professional, and there are plenty of bamboo hammocks strewn between coconut palms for you to lounge the days away in.

🛏 Caparispisan

⭐Kingfisher Resort
RESORT $$

(📞0927 525 8111; www.kingfisher.ph; tiki huts/casita/ste P2500/7000/12,000; ✳🛜) In splendid isolation 10km along a partially paved road from Saud Beach, Kingfisher caters to active travellers, with kitesurfing and windsurfing available between October and March, and paddleboards and kayaks for rent when seas are calmer. Lodge in basic tiki huts or treat yourself to their swanky casita. The chilled beach vibe makes it difficult to leave. Three-night minimum stay.

🛏 Blue Lagoon

Casa Consuelo
RESORT $$

(📞0918 990 5385; www.facebook.com/CASA CONSUELO; d incl breakfast P3200; ✳🛜🏊) Tucked at the far, quiet end of Blue Lagoon, this chilled-out, family-run place has 14 tiny yet chic rooms overlooking Dos Hermanos rocks and a slim white beach – you can swim from here to the area's best snorkelling. Enjoy perfect sunrises; take a dip in the petite infinity pool; and enjoy the delicious, fresh seafood served in the restaurant.

Kapuluan Vista Resort
RESORT $$

(📞077-676 9075, 0920 952 2528; www.kapulanvistaresortandrestaurant.com; dm per person P650, d from P3700, all incl breakfast; ✳🛜🏊) Towards the more low-key end of Blue Lagoon, this fading yet strangely stylish place sits in front of the beach's best surfing waves. Polished cement and white-painted rooms are minimalist chic, and the restaurant has bleached wood tables graced with tiny oil lamps. Surfboards (P350 per hour), SUPs (P300 per hour) and surfing instruction (P200) are available.

❶ Getting There & Away

The highway is spectacular in spots. If you're coming from Laoag or continuing on towards Claveria, get a seat on the left side of the bus.

Frequent buses travel the coastal road to Laoag (P123, two hours) and Tuguegarao (P350, five hours). You'll have to flag one down from the main highway.

There are also two daily Florida buses from Pagudpud to Manila (P700).

THE CORDILLERA

To many travellers, North Luzon is simply the Cordillera. These spiny mountains, which top out at around 2900m, are beloved, worshipped and feared in equal doses by those who witness them and those who live among them.

The tribes of the Cordillera, collectively known as the Igorot, have distinct traditions that have survived both Spanish and American occupation and that add a culturally rich dimension to the already bounteous attractions of the region. Banaue's renowned rice terraces have been dubbed 'the eighth wonder of the world', while lesser-known but no less spectacular terraces exist throughout Ifugao, Mountain Province and Kalinga. Rice terraces aside, the mountains throw down the gauntlet to hikers, bikers, cavers and other fresh-air fiends.

The Cordillera

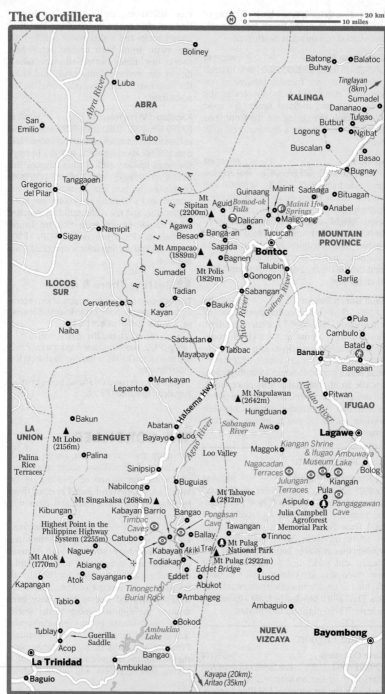

Baguio

📞 074 / POP 345,370 / ELEV 1540M

This is the Philippine's upland, pine-clad retreat from the heat and dust of the lowlands, albeit not a very tranquil one. Baguio (bah-gee-oh) is a university town that boasts one of the Philippines' largest student populations (250,000), and is also a crossroads between hill tribe culture and lowland settlers. For most travellers, Baguio serves as the primary gateway to backpacker bliss up north in Sagada, Banaue and Kalinga.

Sadly, thousands of jeepneys, taxis and tricycles are responsible for almost unbearable levels of smog in the city centre, and long-time Baguio dwellers wax nostalgic about the days before SM Mall marred every view and traffic clogged every street. Away from the traffic-snarled city centre, Baguio is airy and pleasant. If you're returning from the mountains, the small-scale urban mayhem, nightlife and burgeoning restaurant scene are actually refreshing.

◉ Sights

★**BenCab Museum**   MUSEUM
(www.bencabmuseum.org; Km 6 Asin Rd, Tadiangan; adult/student P120/100; ⏱9am-6pm Tue-Sun) This superb museum dedicated to the life, times and work of artist Benedicto Reyes Cabrera (BenCab) is as fascinating as the man himself. The gallery is a mix of high glass panes that slant light into modern art colonnades offset by walls of traditional animist wood carvings, *bulol* (sacred wood figures), psychedelic works by Leonard Aguinaldo and ceremonial *hagabi* (carved wooden benches).

★**St Louis University Museum**   MUSEUM
(Magsaysay Ave; ⏱8am-12.30pm & 1.30-5pm Mon-Sat) FREE This campus museum is run by Isekias 'Ike' Picpican, one of the country's foremost authorities on the history and culture of the Cordillera people. You can spend hours examining weapons, funereal artefacts, tribal costumes, musical instruments such as the nose flute, woodcarvings, and photographs of various rituals and sacrifices, but it helps if Ike is around to explain their context.

Lourdes Grotto   MONUMENT
Established by the Spanish Jesuits in 1907, the Lourdes Grotto sits at the top of 252 steps in the hilly western part of town. From the top, there's a nice view of the city's rooftops. Even better views are to be had from the top of Dominican Hill, a short walk from the grotto up Dominican Hill Rd.

Camp John Hay   AREA
A Japanese internment camp for Allied prisoners of war in WWII, and then a US military rest-and-recreation facility, 246-hectare Camp John Hay has been reinvented as a mountain resort with restaurants, hotels, shops, a fantastic golf course and a handful of scattered sights sprinkled amid rolling hills and stands of Benguet pines.

The Historical Core, with the attractively landscaped **Bell Amphitheatre** and some walking trails, incorporates the site where General Yamashita surrendered to the Americans; **Tree Top Adventure zipline**; and the **Cemetery of Negativism** (open 9am to 5pm), a twee but entertaining graveyard that's supposed to boost your positive thinking.

Camp John Hay is very spread out, and jeepneys are not allowed in, so your best bet is to commandeer a taxi.

Tam-awan Village   ARTS CENTRE
(☎0921 588 3131, 074-446 2949; www.tam-awanvillage.com; Long-Long Rd, Pinsao; adult/student P50/30, workshops per person P450; ⏱8am-6pm) 🌿 Nine traditional Ifugao homes and two Kalinga huts were taken apart then reassembled on the side of a hill at this artist colony. Spending the night in one of these huts (single/double P500/1000) is a rare treat. You can participate in art workshops, learn dream-catcher or bead making, and enjoy indigenous music and dance demonstrations.

Baguio Mountain Provinces Museum   MUSEUM
(Governor Pack Rd; adult/student P40/20; ⏱8am-5pm Mon-Sat) This museum is a great introduction to the Igorot ('mountain people') of the Cordillera and the harmful 'savage highlander'/'cultured lowlander' divide, introduced by the Spanish. Each display focuses on an indigenous group, and you'll see spears, *bolos* (machetes) of Kalinga headhunters, accounts of Ibaloi mummification practices and a Kabayan mummy, and a compelling exhibition on the history of Baguio.

Baguio

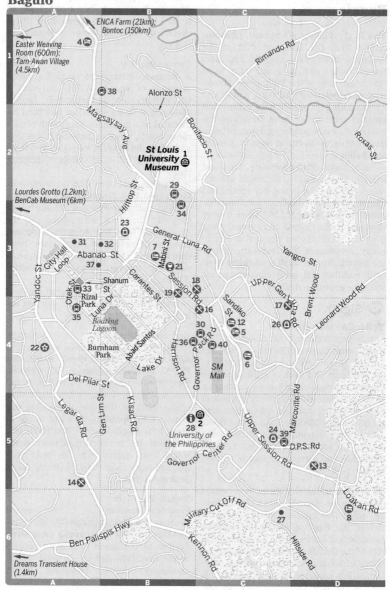

ENCA Farm (21km);
Bontoc (150km)

Easter Weaving
Room (600m);
Tam-Awan Village
(4.5km)

Alonzo St

St Louis
University
Museum

Lourdes Grotto (1.2km);
BenCab Museum (6km)

Abanao St

Shanum St
Rizal Park

Boating Lagoon

Burnham Park

Del Pilar St

University of
the Philippines

Governor Center Rd

SM Mall

Dreams Transient House
(1.4km)

Ben Palispis Hwy

Kennon Rd

Loakan Rd

NORTH LUZON BAGUIO

Sleeping

Consider staying out of the centre to escape Baguio's notorious noise and air pollution; however, staying in the centre makes it easy to walk to many of the town's great restau-rants. Be sure to ask for the 'promo rate' (or just a discount) in the low season.

Baguio Village Inn GUESTHOUSE $
(☑074-442 3901; 355 Magsaysay Ave; s/d from P400/750; ☎) Beyond the Slaughterhouse

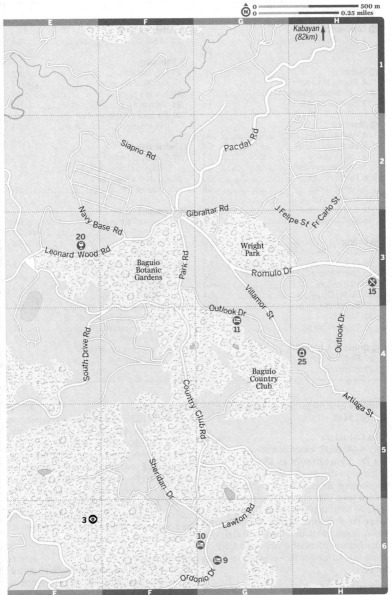

Terminal, this warm and inviting back-packer special is reminiscent of cosy pine-wood guesthouses in Sagada. Rooms in the new annex at the back are pricier but you'll find they are quieter.

YMCA Hostel   HOSTEL $
(☎074-442 4766; Post Office Loop; dm/d P400/1420) The 'Y' boasts huge, bright dorm rooms and some colourful private rooms with soft beds and flat-screen TVs, which are pretty good value. It's very

Baguio

centrally located, just off Session Rd, opposite SM Mall.

Villa Cordillera
LODGE $$
(☑ 074-442 6036; www.villacordillera.com; 6 Outlook Dr; d/tr/q P1600/2400/3200; ☎) There's a cabin-in-the-woods feel to this lodge overlooking Baguio Country Club. Well removed from the centre, it's so quiet (unless the live band is playing) you'll hardly realise you're in Baguio. Rooms are spiffy, with wood floors, walk-in wardrobes and spacious bathrooms (that could use a facelift). Make sure to sample the scrumptious raisin bread.

Mile Hi Inn
HOSTEL $$
(☑ 074-446 6141; Mile Hi Center, Loacan Rd; dm/d/tr P650/2300/2700; ☎) Mile Hi's motto is 'clean, cosy, comfy', and frankly it would be hard to argue with that. Located in Camp John Hay's duty-free shopping centre, it has simple, tiled, four-bed dorm rooms and golden-hued doubles.

Casa Vallejo
HOTEL $$
(☑ 074-424 3397; www.casavallejo-baguio.com; Upper Session Rd; d with fan/air-con from P2371/3761, f from P3125; ❄@) Situated in a classic historical building that harks back to the turn of the (20th) century, this understated hotel boasts a grand dining area with dark wood accents and attentive staff. The rooms don't quite fulfill the promise of the exterior, but they are comfortable, carpeted and come with reliable hot showers. Ask for a room away from the road.

Forest Lodge
HOTEL $$
(☑ 074-422 2075; www.campjohnhayhotels.ph; Loakan Rd; d/tr from P3522/4013; ☎) The spacious, wood-panelled interior of this large lodge at the heart of Camp John Hay leaves you with a vague feeling that there ought to be a ski slope nearby. Instead, you have pine-scented air; spacious, business-traveller-oriented rooms with full amenities; and access to the gym and spa that Forest Lodge shares with Manor Hotel.

City Center Hotel
HOTEL $$

(☎074-422 3637; www.baguiocitycenterhotel.com; cnr Session Rd & Mabini St; d/f P2100/3200; ❄🖥) Though modest in their furnishings, these rooms are brand new and in a couldn't-be-more-central-if-you-tried location. Perks include power showers and cable TV.

Bloomfield Hotel
HOTEL $$

(☎074-446 9112; www.bloomfieldhotel.com; 3 Leonard Wood Rd; d/ste from P2140/3390; ❄🖥) This snazzy spot near SM Mall has tastefully austere rooms with inviting beds, polished wooden floors and colourful prints. The suites, with king-sized beds, are worth the splurge.

Dreams Transient House
HOTEL $$

(☎0933 522 5671; Km 4 Palispis (Marcos) Hwy; d/f P1000/3500; ❄) It's a bit out of the centre but this is one of the best midrange deals in town: clean, spacious and equipped with flat-screen TVs. It's located under the Baguio Craft Brewery; have your own wheels or expect to use a lot of taxis.

Forest House
BOUTIQUE HOTEL $$$

(☎074-447 0459; www.foresthouse.ph; 16 Laokan Rd; d/tr incl breakfast from P3700/5850; 🖥) Consisting of just four rooms, named after the owner's children, this boutique spot is rustic without getting tacky and offers either mountain or garden views from its windows. The wood-panelled rooms don't lack for luxurious touches (we particularly like Kahlil's Room). The excellent on-site bistro serves superlative *bagnet, pinakbét* and other classics, and a generous breakfast is included.

🍴 Eating

Baguio has arguably the best dining in the Philippines, pound for pound. The Mile Hi Center in Camp John Hay has several good eating options, plus there's the usual cluster of fast-food joints near SM Mall. Kisad Rd is lined with Korean restaurants.

Oh My Gulay!
VEGETARIAN $

(☎0939 912 7266; 4th fl, La Azotea Bldg, Session Rd; mains P130-155; ⊙11am-8pm Tue-Thu, to 9pm Fri & Sat, to 7pm Sun & Mon; 🌱) Step into an enchanted, multilevel garden, with wooden carvings, plants, bridges, water features and little nooks to hide in. The delicious vegetarian menu tempts with vegie burgers, open-faced sandwiches, salads, omelettes, pastas and more. Mediterranean flavours dominate. It's a bit hard to find on the 4th floor of the La Azotea Building (and there's no sign).

Volante Pizza
INTERNATIONAL $

(82 Session Rd; 6in/10in pizzas from P89/182; ⊙24hr) Catering to night owls, revellers with postdrinking munchies and a loyal lunchtime crowd, this informal spot serves surprisingly good pizza, fried chicken and heaped po'boy sandwiches.

★ Cafe by the Ruins Dua
FUSION $$

(☎074-442 4010; 225 Upper Sessions Rd; P120-380; ⊙7am-9pm; 🖥🌱) The clean white, vaguely colonial decor makes one of North Luzon's best meals taste even swankier. Local specialities such as carabao (water buffalo) cheese, *etag* (smoked pork), mountain rice and jackfruit are woven into a seasonal menu inspired by dishes from around the world. Live music and poetry readings pop

NORTH LUZON BAGUIO

WORTH A TRIP

ORGANIC FARMING IN BENGUET

Fulfill your farming fantasies as a WWOOF (World Wide Opportunities on Organic Farms; www.wwoof.com.ph) volunteer on the Cosalan family's organic **ENCA Farm** (☎0919 834 4542, in the US +1 425 698 5808; www.encaorganicfarm.com) in Acop, Benguet, 21km north of Baguio. Marilyn Cosalan's family has been farming for generations using indigenous Ibaloi methods. Both short-term visitors (P50) and volunteers can check out the farm.

The Cosalan family lost its original *kintoman* (red) rice farm in nearby Itogon to unchecked copper mining, which destroyed hectares of farmland and killed several rivers in southern Benguet in the Marcos era. Having won back their land in legal battles, the family now grows beans, lettuce, broccoli, carrots, radish and coffee. Volunteers usually do about eight hours of farm work per day. Accommodation is in rustic but cosy lodgings on-site for just P250 a night; visitors can also camp overnight (P150).

Contact Marilyn or take a Baguio–Acop jeepney from the Dangwa terminal (one hour); it's a 3km walk to the farm.

up on occasion and there's an all-around intellectual, bohemian vibe.

Chaya
JAPANESE $$

(☑074-424 4726; 72 Legarda Rd; mains P180-390; ⊙10am-9pm) Baguio's best Japanese restaurant feels like a cosy living room, with its handful of tables close together between wood-panelled walls decorated with tapestries, plants and colourful bottles. There's also a casual outdoor area. Choose from fresh sashimi, delicious ramen, well-presented tempura and classic sushi rolls. There are ice-cream confections for dessert. You'll definitely need to reserve in advance.

Solibao
FILIPINO $$

(www.solibao.com; Session Rd; mains P130-330; ⊙noon-10pm; ☑) The casual Session Rd branch of a venerable Baguio institution provides a belt-loosening course in Filipino classics. Choose from beef *kare-kare* (meat cooked in peanut sauce), crispy *dinguan* (pork fried with chilli and pig's blood) and *pinakbét*, as well as its signature *palabok* (noodles smothered with shrimp and meat sauce), green mango salad and more.

Rose Bowl
CHINESE $$

(☑074-442 4213; Upper General Luna Rd; mains P140-850; ⊙10am-10pm) A local institution for decades, the Rose Bowl serves the best Chinese food in town. Its extensive menu runs the gamut from chop suey to expensive delicacies featuring abalone and lobster. Bring friends, as portions are meant for sharing.

NO SPITTING MOMA

Those red puddles you keep seeing are not the aftermath of violent skirmishes; nor do the crimson smiles of Cordillera men betray a fondness for cannibalism. Betel-nut chewing (*moma* in the local lingo) is a longstanding tradition among the mountain tribes; the men typically chew the nut wrapped in mint leaves, with an added pinch of lime (ground-up shells work well to create a lime powder). The effect is mild euphoria, increased stamina, and a sense of well-being, paired with the side effect of mouth cancer. The Philippines government has been trying (ineffectually) to suppress the habit, which explains the 'No Spitting of Moma' signs you see everywhere.

Chef's Home
MALAYSIAN $$$

(☑0916 444 5756; 13 Outlook Dr S; P280-950; ⊙11am-2.30pm & 6-8.30pm Mon-Sat) Get to this homey, simple and very popular place early for a table. If you've been pining for mainland Southeast Asian flavours, you'll love the tom yum seafood soup, crispy green papaya salad, squid curry and yummy *char koay teow* (fried noodles). The seafood dishes are much pricier than the meat. Cash only.

Hill Station
FUSION $$$

(☑074-424 2734; www.hillstationbaguio.com; Upper Session Rd; mains P295-595; ⊙7am-10pm; ☜☑) The menu at this refined restaurant reads like a fantasy tour of the world: mutton Berbere (lamb stew), Australian tenderloin steak, and smoked paprika roasted salmon. Some dishes work better than others; custom cocktails hit the spot, along with the lemon pie and homemade ice creams. A sign in the hotel suggests not turning up in your pyjamas, so dress appropriately.

🍷 Drinking & Nightlife

Baguio Craft Brewery
MICROBREWERY

(Palispis (Marcos) Hwy; ⊙5pm-2am; ☜) Baguio's entry on the ever-growing ledger of Philippine craft-brew houses is worth the mild slog out of the centre. You'll be rewarded by around 20 different types of craft beers (from P160), fine mountain views from the rooftop terrace, and toothsome wings, fish tacos and other bar snacks (mains P300 to P350).

Rumours
BAR

(56 Session Rd; ⊙11am-11pm) An institution that draws a nice mix of tourists, expats, local students and random barflies. Some of the speciality drinks will, in no uncertain terms, lay you flat (cocktails P85 to P150).

Red Lion Pub
PUB

(☑074-422 9135; 35 Leonard Wood Rd; ⊙24hr; ☜) You can find a drinking buddy or billiards partner any time of day at this expat fave. Good steaks and ribs too (mains P150 to P600).

☆ Entertainment

18 BC
LIVE MUSIC

(16 Legarda Rd; ⊙6.30pm-late) In a city where live music seemingly wafts out of every window, this dive opposite Prince Plaza Hotel consistently features Baguio's best original live music, from jazz and blues to reggae. Annoyingly, no shorts or flip-flops allowed.

🔓 Shopping

★ Sabado's ARTS & CRAFTS
(16 Outlook Dr; ⊘8am-5pm) Though non-descript from the outside, Sabado's is an Aladdin's cave of genuine indigenous treasures. Poke around in the semi-gloom and you may find Kalinga spears, Ifugao head-gear, hollow sticks used for carrying water in the jungle, a plethora of woven containers and wood carvings, as well as antique *bulol*.

Mt Cloud Bookshop BOOKS
(Upper Session Rd; ⊘10.30am-8pm) Arguably Luzon's hippest bookstore, with a fantastic selection of Western and Filipino titles, and a trend towards historical and ethnographic nonfiction, although there are plenty of novels also. Located below Casa Vallejo.

Teresita's Antiques
and Furniture ARTS & CRAFTS
(☑074-442 3376; 90 Upper General Luna Rd; ⊘9am-6pm) Teresita's largely caters to serious collectors, with antique *bulol* out of financial reach of casual shoppers. There's also a good selection of Igorot textiles and beads, carved wooden items, vintage offering boxes and wooden lime containers that used to be part of betel-nut-chewing paraphernalia. There's another outlet at Mines View Park, which sells mainly mass-produced contemporary carvings.

City Market MARKET
(Magsaysay Ave; ⊘6am-7pm) Baguio's city market is a 3-sq-km maze of 'useful things', where vendors sell everything from fruit to live poultry to low-quality crafts and souvenirs. Be prepared to haggle. There are some good eating options – find a spot that's crowded, pull up a stool, point at something that smells good and chow down.

Narda's TEXTILES
(www.nardas.com; 151 Upper Session Rd; ⊘8am-7pm) Started by Bontoc weaver Narda Capuyan, this flagship store carries a broad selection of high-quality, locally made items, from traditional *barong* to bags, blouses, scarves and table runners. These threads recently wowed the audience at the World Eco-Fiber Textile fashion show in New York.

Easter Weaving Room TEXTILES
(☑074-442 4972; www.easterweaving.com; 2 Easter School Rd) Easter Weaving Room makes genuine Igorot weavings and traditional garments, as well as contemporary menswear and womenswear. Also sells everything from hand-woven bookmarks to *tapis* (woven wraparound skirts). In the basement factory you can watch the women hard at work at their looms.

ℹ️ Information

Bureau of Immigration Baguio Office (BOI; ☑074-447 0805; www.immigration.gov.ph; 38 Military Cut Off Rd; ⊘8am-5pm Mon-Fri) Just out of the city centre, for all your visa extension needs.

Cordillera Regional Tourist Office (☑074-442 7014; Governor Pack Rd; ⊘8am-5pm Mon-Fri) Information on tours and treks throughout the Cordillera, and maps of town.

ℹ️ Getting There & Away

The nonstop, 25-seater buses run by **Victory Liner** (☑074-619 0000; Utility Rd) to Pasay (P750, five hours, one to five daily) are a quick and very comfortable option. Just as nice are the 29-seater Joybuses run by **Genesis** (☑074-422 7763; Governor Pack Rd) that run both to Pasay (P730, six hours, frequent) and Cubao (Manila; P720, six hours, frequent). All these buses take the fast SCTEX (Subic–Clark–Tarlac Expressway). Reserve bus tickets ahead of time. Victory and Genesis also have slower buses to Manila about every 20 minutes (P455, seven hours); Victory accepts credit cards.

Victory Liner also runs to Iba and Zambales (P357, three to 4½ hours, four daily) from its Governor Pack Rd Terminal.

Partas (☑074-444 8431) has hourly buses to San Fernando (La Union; P104, 1½ hours) and to Vigan (P334, five to seven hours) from 8am until about 6pm, with some buses continuing to Laoag (P466). Minibuses to San Fernando (P80) leave frequently from the **Plaza jeepney area** east of Rizal Park.

Lizardo Trans (☑074-304 5994) has hourly trips to Sagada (P250, five to seven hours) departing from 6am to 1pm from the **Dangwa Terminal** (Magsaysay Ave), and four buses to Baler (P312 to P360, eight hours) via San Jose departing from 4am and 1pm from the **Slaughterhouse Terminal** (Magsaysay Ave). Also from the Slaughterhouse Terminal, **D'Rising Sun** (☑0910 709 9102) has buses to Bontoc (P240, six hours, hourly from 6am to 4pm); and A-Liner runs to Kabayan (P180, 3½ hours) daily at 7am. There's also a minivan that typically heads to Kabayan around 4pm (but is not to be relied on).

Ohayami (Shanum St) and **KMS** (Shanum St) each have daily trips to Banaue (P490, nine to 11 hours) along the paved southern route, via San Jose, departing around 7am and from 6pm or

ⓘ FINDING A GUIDE

While you can visit most of Kabayan's attractions with little chance of getting lost, local guides are professional and courteous and can clue you in on all sorts of cultural background that would otherwise go over most travellers' heads. At research time, guides were arranged either by Pine Cone Lodge, the Kabayan National Museum or at the **Municipal Tourism Office** (☑0917 521 5830; ☺8am-noon & 1-5pm Mon-Fri) and fees were standardised for Tinongchol Burial Rock (P500), Pongasan Cave (P1000), Timbac Caves (P1500) and Mt Pulag via Akiki (p140; P2400).

You can hire a private car with driver for P800 to sights around town and to the trailheads for Tinongchol Burial Rock and Pongasan Cave; this cuts several hours off the walking times along the roads. If you're hiking up to Timbac Caves with all your gear, guides can share your burden for P100 per kg.

7pm. A faster way to Banaue is to take a direct air-con van from the Dangwa terminal (P360, seven hours) via Ambuklao Rd.

ⓘ Getting Around

The easiest way to get around is by taxi, which are cheap, plentiful and invariably honest with their meters. Jeepneys to Asin Rd leave from Abanao St near City Hall. For Tam-awan, take a jeepney from the corner of Kayang and Shagem Sts (P8).

Kabayan

☑074 / POP 1390 / ELEV 1200M

Nestled amid dramatic, rice-terraced slabs of mountain terrain and watched over by its world-famous mummies, Kabayan remains an appealing, refreshingly untouristed spot, where villagers get up at dawn and silence falls with the evening darkness.

Even if mummified mortal remains aren't your thing, Kabayan is a nice place to hike around the dramatically sloped rice terraces and marvel at the star-filled night sky. Kabayan is also the centre of Ibaloi culture, and many Ibaloi traditions and animistic beliefs linger, especially in the surrounding hills. The area is also known for strong Arabica coffee and tasty red *kintoman* rice.

◉ Sights

Opdas Mass Burial Cave CAVE
(suggested donation P50) On the southern edge of town (in someone's backyard), this spooky charnel house has hundreds of skulls and bones between 500 and 1000 years old lined up on a stone ledge. It's suggested that the deceased either died during a smallpox epidemic brought by the Spanish or were entombed en mass through the years due to their low social status.

It's signed from the road. Make sure to ask permission in the green house on the left.

Kabayan National Museum MUSEUM
(☺8am-noon & 1-5pm Mon-Fri) ⓕⓡⓔⓔ This compact museum is a good introduction to this part of the Cordillera. Ask the friendly curator to explain the difference between traditional clothing of the rich and poor; show off a backpack used to carry pigs and a female mummy; explain local death rites; and point out the Kankanay and Ikalahan ritual artefacts and plants used in the mummification process.

Tinongchol Burial Rock CAVE
(donation P30) About 3km northwest of Kabayan, near barangay Kabayan Barrio, is the Tinongchol Burial Rock, where several coffins have been leveraged into cuts in a boulder. It's a one-hour walk along a footpath that starts behind Kabayan's national museum through stunning mountain scenery. After crossing the river, ascend the paved road; the Rock is signposted off to your left.

Bangao Mummy Caves CAVE
(P30) The forests around Kabayan hide dozens of mummy caves that only Ibaloi elders can locate; the nearest site where you can see some (not terribly well-preserved) mummies is Bangao in the foothills of Mt Tabayoc (2812m), 7km north of Kabayan.

You'll find the most interesting is **Pongasan Cave**, a 45-minute climb straight up from Bangao, where you'll find five coffins with mummies.

🛏 Sleeping & Eating

Pine Cone Lodge   GUESTHOUSE $
(☎ 0929-327 7749; r without bathroom P300-750) The best of the very few places to stay in town, this friendly, airy guesthouse at the end of the village, overlooking the river, offers spacious and surprisingly posh wood-panelled rooms with shared bathrooms. Jertrude, your host, is an excellent cook and can whip up breakfasts or local specialities on request.

Rockwood Cafe   FILIPINO $
(mains P70-100; ⏰ 7am-6pm Nov-Apr) Tastefully done up with pinewood and stone, this cafe serves organically grown coffee and vegetables, and sells locally produced souvenirs such as lemongrass oil, tea and shoulder bags woven by nearby Kabayan Weaving.

Ba-Jon'z   FILIPINO $
(mains P60-80; ⏰ 7am-7pm) The busiest and most reliably open restaurant in Kabayan offers a fresh buffet selection of around 10 dishes that range from stir-fried vegetables to more challenging choices like stewed pork intestines. Finish off your meal with an ice cream from the chest freezer.

ℹ Getting There & Away

Kabayan is linked to Baguio's Slaughterhouse Terminal by bus (P135, 3½ hours); it departs Baguio at 10am and Kabayan at around 8.30am daily. The paved winding mountain road up to Kabayan is absolutely gorgeous but very prone to landslides.

Three daily vans run to/from Abatan (P150, two hours) between 9am and 1pm, from where you can catch a van to Sagada (P95, 2½ hours). If you miss the van from Abatan to Kabayan, you can also hire a private vehicle and driver to take you for P2000. Enquire at the Abatan police station.

For a more adventurous escape, hike to Timbac Caves and walk out to the Halsema Hwy, where you can flag down a bus going south to Baguio or north to Bontoc or Sagada.

MEETING TIMBAC'S MUMMIES

The centuries-old mummification procedure practised by the Ibaloi is different from that of the nine other cultures that have practised mummification worldwide, because here the internal organs were left intact. According to Ibaloi oral history, the corpses were dried using the heat and smoke of a small fire, then meticulously bathed in herbal preservatives. Tobacco smoke was periodically blown into the abdominal cavities to drive out worms and to preserve the organs. The whole process is said to have taken up to a year. The curator at the University Museum in Baguio disputes this, saying that the process, as remembered by the Ibaloi elders, didn't work when it was attempted in 1907 and that no family could have afforded not to work for an entire year, which the death rites would have demanded.

The Ibaloi stopped mummifying their dead by the 20th century because the practice was discouraged by the Americans as unhygienic. The mummies have been frequently stolen and vandalised over the years, so the main caves are now under lock and key.

The best-preserved Ibaloi mummies – complete with tattooed skin – are found in the **Timbac Caves** (P100). Located about 1200m above Kabayan proper, these are Kabayan's most sacred caves, and locals customarily make offerings of gin before entering them. Unfortunately, the mummies here are deteriorating so the caves have been closed since 2016 as experts find a better way to protect them. They will open again, so ask around.

The most rewarding and culturally sensitive way to experience the unique folkways of the Cordillera is to hike from Kabayan to the caves with a guide. It's a strenuous, beautiful four- to six-hour hike that follows the 4WD track (though your guide will take a steep shortcut through the rice terraces).

When you reach the caves themselves, your guide will get the key from the caretaker, who lives above the caves, and then open the coffins to let you see the mummified mortal remains. The mummies, ranging from adult to small child, are entombed in the traditional foetal position and the sight is vaguely unsettling.

Some travellers bypass the Kabayan hike by taking a Baguio–Sagada bus, getting off at the signposted turn-off for the Timbac Caves and walking 3.5km along the paved road. This is an easier way, but by going without a guide, you risk offending local sensibilities and there's no guarantee that the caretaker will be in.

Mt Pulag National Park

Mt Pulag (2922m), sacred to the Ibaloi and Kalanguya peoples, is the highest peak in Luzon and anchors the Cordillera's largest national park. The **Protected Areas Office** (PAO; ☑0919 631 5402) in Ambangeg, 1½ hours south of Kabayan, doubles as the park's visitor centre. There's a hefty P1000 park entrance fee for nonresidents, payable here or at other points of entry.

From the visitor centre a rough road climbs 11km to the start of the Grassland Trail near the Department of Environment & Natural Resources (DENR) ranger station, where you must hire a guide (P600), or else bring one with you from Kabayan to navigate the final three hours to the summit.

Visibility is best in March and April, and the area sees regular heavy downpours from June to November.

An interesting two-day alternative route to the main Grassland Trail up Mt Pulag is the Akiki Trail – also known as the 'killer trail' – which starts 2km south of Kabayan in Todiakap, a sitio of Duacan. From the trailhead it's two hours to Eddet River and another six hours to the 'cow country' campsite. You can camp there or continue on another four hours and camp at the 'saddle grassland' campsite. It's just 30 minutes from there to the Mt Pulag summit. A guide for this route costs P1200 per day.

There are still longer routes up Mt Pulag that take you around the back of the mountain through Tawangan or Lusod, home of the Kalanguya. Call the PAO or ask guides in Kabayan for details.

❶ Getting There & Away

To get to the PAO office/visitor centre, jump off your Baguio–Kabayan bus in Ambangeg. If coming by bus from Baguio, you'll arrive too late to launch an assault on Mt Pulag, as it's often raining by 2pm, so plan to sleep a night in Kabayan and start early the next morning.

Sagada & Around

☑074 / POP 1670 / ELEV 1477M

Sitting among mist-shrouded mountains, tiny Sagada is the closest thing the Philippines has to a Southeast Asian backpacker mecca, yet it's possible to find tranquillity along its many hiking trails and get your adrenalin pumping on adventures in the depths of its caves. There's a mystical element to this village, a former refuge for intelligensia fleeing dictatorship: the centuries-old coffins high up along limestone cliffs lie close to the sky, and days and nights are peaceful thanks to the lack of tricycles or much other traffic.

If you're lucky, your visit will coincide with a *begnas* (traditional Kankanay community celebration), when women wear *tapis* (woven wraparound skirts) and older men don G-strings and gather in the *dap-ay* (outdoor patio); chickens are sacrificed, gongs are played and general merriment ensues. Sagadans are of Applai (northern Kankanay) ancestry and their native language is Kankanay.

◉ Sights

★**Echo Valley Hanging Coffins** HISTORIC SITE
Sagada's most popular attractions are the hanging coffins of Echo Valley: some are centuries old while others are only a few years old. Most are high up the sheer rock face, leading you to wonder how this was originally done. It's a short trek (P200) of less than half an hour to get down to the coffins via the trail that runs by the cemetery, but people do get lost without a guide.

The chairs, also attached to the rock face, are the funereal chairs that the bodies were originally strapped to during a traditional burial; the smallest coffins are those that accommodated bodies laid out in foetal position. The newer coffins with crosses blend the old ways with modern Christianity, and some locals still prefer to be buried this way.

Lumiang Burial Cave CAVE
Lumiang Burial Cave is a 10- to 15-minute walk south of the main village, towards Ambasing, well signposted along the left-hand fork in the road. Steep steps lead down to an enormous, lichen-furred cave where more than 100 coffins are stacked at the entrance; the oldest coffin is believed to be about 500 years old.

Many are carved with images of lizards – symbols of long life and fertility. Across the road from the steps, peer down at another cave featuring more coffins. Animistic Applai elders continue to be entombed in the caves surrounding Sagada – if they can afford it. The gods demand the sacrifice of more than 20 pigs and three times as many chickens for the privilege of being buried in the caves.

If you decide to do the challenging Cave Connection, you'll start in this cave.

Sumaging Cave   CAVE

The exhilarating Sumaging Cave, or Big Cave, is the most popular of Sagada's caves. Its immense chambers are home to otherworldly rock formations with fanciful names such as 'King's Curtain' and the more literal 'Cauliflower'. You'll need a guide (P500) to tour the cave (roughly two hours); the guide will provide a gas lantern.

It's quite slippery in parts and you'll get wet; wear river sandals or other shoes with nonslip soles. It's a 45-minute walk south of Sagada. The Cave Connection adventure ends here.

Ganduyan Museum   MUSEUM

(P50; ☉1-6pm) This small museum is packed with an anthropologist's dream of sculptures, jewellery and other Kankanay artefacts. Be sure to chat to the owner, the son of the late founder Christina Aben, who is a font of information about local culture and history. Ganduyan is the traditional Kankanay name for Sagada.

Demang   VILLAGE

South of the centre, the small village of Demang is now a barangay of Sagada but was the area's original settlement and remains Sagada's cultural and traditional heart. Most of Sagada's dap-ay (outdoor patios) are in Demang and most begnas (traditional Kankanay community celebrations) are held here. If you happen to be invited to one, bring a gift such as bread or a chicken.

Echo Valley Lookout   VIEWPOINT

You'll pass the Echo Valley lookout on the way to the Echo Valley Hanging Coffins. You'll probably hear people shouting into the valley before you get there. The local joke is that if you shout out in Tagalog, it will come back to you in English.

🏃 Activities

Sagada has a wealth of top-notch hikes. To get around anywhere in Sagada, arrange a guide with the tourist information centre (p144) or contact the rival Sagada Genuine Guides Assocation (p144); the latter in particular takes trekking and customer service seriously. Their livelihood relies on tourism, and they do their best to take care of each and every one of their charges.

★ Cave Connection   CAVING

This thrilling cave adventure is suitable for the reasonably fit and courageous. Cave Connection is an underground passage that links Sumaging and Lumiang Caves. The three- to four-hour tour (P800) involves crawling through tiny tunnels (smaller folks have an advantage), making vertical descents that involve jamming your limbs into the rock, swinging on ropes and swimming through underground pools.

Trekking sandals are a really good idea, as are waterproof torches, though your guide will carry a lantern. Be warned that caving during rainy season, when there is a risk of flash flooding, can be highly dangerous (people have died) and is not recommended.

Bomod-ok Falls   HIKING

Banga-an is where the excellent 45-minute walk to the impressive Bomod-ok Falls (Big Waterfall) begins. You'll need a guide (P650), as the walk traverses rice terraces and access is sometimes restricted because of with the planting and harvest season traditions.

Two daily jeepneys go from Sagada to Banga-an, but they aren't much use to day trippers as they both depart mid-afternoon. Walk or hire transport via the tourist office (P650 return) instead. Jeepneys from Banga-an to Sagada depart early in the morning.

Mt Sipitan   HIKING

Sagada's highest mountain, Mt Sipitan (2200m) is said to be rife with hunters' booby traps; don't try it without a guide (P1600). The majority of this rigorous, full-day hike, which starts near not-quite-idyllic Lake Danum on the way to Besao and ends in Banga-an, is through mossy forest.

Mt Kiltepan   HIKING

There are superb panoramic views of the rice terraces and surrounding mountains from Mt Kiltepan (1636m), which is about a 40-minute walk (or 10-minute drive) from town. Take the road heading east out of town for 2.5km and turn left at a Petron Station. Weekend mornings see hundreds of domestic tourists in vans crowd the viewpoint for sunrise starting at about 4.30am.

Sagada Outdoors   RAFTING

(☑ 0919 698 8361; www.sagadaoutdoors.com; rafting trips per person from P2500) This excellent outfit, run by an American who invests tourism dollars back into the local community, offers a wide range of rafting and kayaking trips up the Chico River, as well as thrilling canyoning expeditions close to Sagada. The rafting season is between September and December. The company's outdoor gear shop is on the 1st floor of the public market.

Sagada

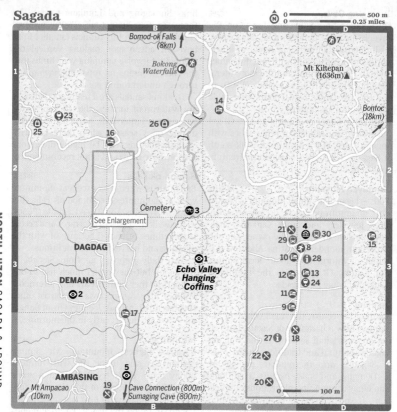

N
0   500 m
0   0.25 miles

Bomod-ok Falls (8km)

Bokong Waterfalls 6

14

26

23

25

16

Mt Kiltepan (1636m)

Bontoc (18km)

7

Cemetery

See Enlargement

3

DAGDAG

Echo Valley Hanging Coffins 1

21 4 30
29
8
10 28
12 13 24
11
9

15

DEMANG

2

17

27 18

22

AMBASING

5

19

20

Mt Ampacao (10km)

Cave Connection (800m);
Sumaging Cave (800m);

0   100 m

Mt Ampacao   HIKING

Mt Ampacao (1889m), 10km south of town beyond Ambasing, can be traversed with a three-hour loop hike that also takes in Lake Danum. A guide costs P1200.

Bokong Waterfalls   HIKING

Around a 30-minute walk from town are the small Bokong Waterfalls, where you can take a refreshing dip. To get here, follow the road east out of town and take the steps just after Sagada Weaving on the left. Follow the path through the rice fields down to a small river. Cross the river and continue upstream to the falls.

🛏 Sleeping

★ Misty Lodge & Cafe   LODGE $

(📱 0926 123 5186; mistylodgeandcafe@rocketmail. com; r without bathroom per person P300; 🖥) It's definitely worth the 15-minute walk east out of town to stay (or dine) at this gem. The eight rooms are sizeable and swathed in radiant blond wood, and the owner is a fountain of smiles and helpful information. A fireplace crackles in the cafe, where you can enjoy gourmet pizzas, real Australian beef burgers, good wine, coffees and desserts.

Sagada View Homestay   GUESTHOUSE $

(📱 0919 702 8380; sagadahomestay@yahoo.com. ph; s/d from P350/650; @🖥) This sprawling place is friendly, eminently affordable and loaded with character born of its polished pinewood. The righteous views are unfortunately becoming blighted by construction but they're still pretty, and this place catches some cooling mountain breezes.

Canaway Resthouse   GUESTHOUSE $

(📱 0918 291 5063; s/d P400/700; 🖥) You'll find exceptional-value, bright, big rooms here, with friendly service, clean sheets and reliable hot showers in the attached bathrooms. Wi-fi comes and goes.

Sagada

◉ Top Sights
1 Echo Valley Hanging Coffins	B3

◉ Sights
2 Demang	A3
3 Echo Valley Lookout	B2
4 Ganduyan Museum	D3
5 Lumiang Burial Cave	B4

◎ Activities, Courses & Tours
6 Bokong Waterfalls	B1
7 Mt Kiltepan	D1
8 Sagada Outdoors	D3

⬡ Sleeping
9 Canaway Resthouse	C3
10 Davey's Inn & Restaurant	C3
11 George Guesthouse	C3
12 Green House	C3
13 Masferré Inn & Restaurant	D3
14 Misty Lodge & Cafe	C1
15 Rock Inn	D3
16 Sagada View Homestay	B2
17 Treasure Rock Inn	B4

⊗ Eating
18 Bana's Cafe	C4
19 Gaia Cafe	B4
20 Lemon Pie House	C4
21 Log Cabin	C3
22 Sagada Brew	C4
Yoghurt House	(see 11)

◎ Drinking & Nightlife
23 Brewery	A1
24 Moon House	D3

⬡ Shopping
25 Sagada Pottery	A2
26 Sagada Weaving	B2

ⓘ Information
27 Sagada Genuine Guides Association	C4
28 Tourist Information Center	D3

ⓘ Transport
29 Coda Lines	C3
30 GL Lizardo	D3

Davey's Inn & Restaurant GUESTHOUSE $
(📱 0939 506 1914; s/d P350/500; 🛜) The simple doubles, better than most in town, are fine value. Davey's overlooks the plaza in the middle of town and has a big fireplace in the downstairs cafe.

Green House GUESTHOUSE $
(📱 0999 903 7675; r per person P200; 🛜) Not only is this about the cheapest guesthouse we've found here, but it's also one of the warmest and quietest, set up on the hill over the south road. The simple rooms have plenty of rustic charm.

George Guesthouse GUESTHOUSE $
(📱 0920 948 3133; s/d from P300/500) The George is located in a brightly tiled building, and while its rooms are simple, the doubles come with TVs and shower's reliably flow with hot water – a huge boon for chilly nights and post-hike stiff muscles. Wi-fi in the restaurant only.

Treasure Rock Inn GUESTHOUSE $
(📱 0920 272 5881; r per person P300; 🛜) 'Aunty Mary' runs this spick-and-span guesthouse with killer views of Sagada's famed cliffs from its simple rooms. The location 1km south of town ensures peace and quiet – except when the nightly videoke or acoustic live music ramps up (but only until 9pm). Also has an annex with a few en-suite rooms.

The path here runs through a gnarly-treed, Brothers Grimm–like copse.

Masferré Inn & Restaurant GUESTHOUSE $$
(📱 0918 341 6164; http://masferre.blogspot.co.uk; d/tr/q/ste P1800/2500/3000/4500; 🛜) Sagada's most upmarket option is adorned with the awesome, powerful prints of the late Sagada-born photographer Eduardo Masferré, who recorded the lives of the Cordillera people. As for the lodgings, the rooms are well appointed; the views are stellar; the water is hot; and the restaurant (open for breakfast, lunch and dinner) makes excellent use of the superb local vegetables.

Rock Inn HOTEL $$
(📱 0905 554 5950, 0928 213 1149; www.rockfarmsagada.com; dm/d/tr/q P450/1300/1500/1800; 🛜) If you don't mind long walks, consider this option in a citrus grove 2km from the town centre. It has a huge, beautiful banquet hall and top-notch doubles overlooking a tranquil rock garden and *dap-ay*. Bare-bones shoestringers can opt to stay in the attic (P300).

✕ Eating

Bana's Cafe CAFE $
(mains P100-170; ⊙ 6.30am-8pm; 🛜✦) Oriented towards trekkers, Bana's specialises in coffee, omelettes and delicious homemade

yoghurt. Its narrow balcony overlooks a gorge and catches the morning sun.

Gaia Cafe
VEGETARIAN $

(mains P125-175; ◷7am-7pm; ✎) Hidden in the woods 1.6km south of the centre past the Lumiang Cave entrance, Gaia serves locally sourced vegan fare (plus a few egg dishes) amid pine trees and in view of rice terraces. It's easily the nicest setting for a meal in Sagada, and the food is good enough to please carnivores as long as no one's too hungry.

Lemon Pie House
FILIPINO $

(pie slices P30; ◷8am-8pm; ✎) Filipino standards are well represented here, and there are brave stabs at international dishes, but the eponymous lemon pie is where this place really shines.

★Log Cabin
INTERNATIONAL $$

(☏0915 671 7949; mains P190-290; ◷6-9pm) One of Sagada's many wonderful surprises is this aptly named eatery that feels like a cosy ski lodge, with a roaring log fire and a fleece-clad foreign crowd. Treat yourself to the likes of roast meats with local vegies or pasta, complemented by a short wine list. Place your order before 3pm during peak season, and always reserve in advance.

★Sagada Brew
FUSION $$

(meals P200; ✎) All clean lines, floor-to-ceiling glass and blond-wood furnishings, Sagada Brew strives to be the most sophisticated cafe in the village, which it does well. Stuffed peppers sit alongside rosemary pepper chicken and waffles on its diverse menu. You may find yourself lingering over a freshly brewed coffee or beautifully steeped wild herb tea – it's that kind of place.

Yoghurt House
FUSION $$

(snacks P100, mains P160-240; ◷8am-8.30pm; ✎) Enjoy your banana pancake out on the balcony at breakfast; get some of the great oatmeal cookies to go; or linger over pasta and chunky sandwiches on homemade bread or baguettes. If you've been craving vegies, the tangy yoghurt sauce is the best thing in town to top the locally grown, seasonal crop.

🍷 Drinking & Nightlife

Brewery
BREWERY

(◷from 4pm) Located in the pine forest a few kilometres out of Sagada on the road to Besao, this place serves up locally brewed beers (pints P150 to P280) with strong (and arguably overpowering) flavours of local violet rice, banana, coffee, pine bark and more. Imbibe around the fire pit or indoors to occasional live music.

Moon House
BAR

(◷4-10pm) Bring all your Jah love to this Rasta-inspired micro bar where you'll be chatting with everyone else in no time over beer, shots and cocktails. The slightly inebriated staff will blush when they have to tell you that the place closes at 10pm for local rules. Karaoke downstairs.

🛍 Shopping

Sagada Pottery
CERAMICS

On the main road to Besao, Sagada Pottery creates labour-intensive earthenware pottery that takes 30 hours to fire. Potters will show off their skills for a small fee (P100 or so) and you can try your hand at the craft for an additional P100. It's 1.5km north of Sagada.

Sagada Weaving
ARTS & CRAFTS

(◷7am-6pm) Produces backpacks and money belts, as well as traditional loincloths, table runners and more, all in the traditional patterns of the region. It's about a 20-minute walk from the centre of town along the road to Besao.

ℹ Information

There's an ATM next to the tourist information centre that only works half the time. We've heard reports from travellers (and one of our authors) that it can charge your account even if you get no money out of it; bring plenty of cash.

Sagada Genuine Guides Association (SAGGAS; ☏0916 559 9050; www.saggas.org) Head here for help with serious hikes.

Tourist Information Center (Municipal Building; ◷7am-5pm) Pay your P35 environmental fee here. Rates are fixed for guides and private jeepney hire.

ℹ Getting There & Away

Jeepneys run hourly to Bontoc (P45, one hour); the last one leaves at 1pm. **GL Lizardo** (Sagada Public Market) has hourly buses to Baguio (P250, seven hours) until 1pm.

Coda Lines (☏0929 521 3247; Sagada Public Market) runs a bus to Manila (P720, 13 hours) via Banaue at 2pm.

One direct van to Banaue leaves daily at around 1pm. Otherwise connect in Bontoc for more transport to Banaue.

Bontoc

📞074 / POP 3790 / ELEV 900M

Bustling Bontoc is one of the most important market towns and transport hubs in the Cordillera. It's an excellent place to arrange a guide if you're looking to get out to the rice terraces of Maligcong and Mainit or stay in the former headhunter villages of Kalinga, so you'll likely find yourself staying a day or two. Today you can still glimpse the occasional elderly woman with tattooed arms and snake vertebrae headgear or elderly men wearing a traditional G-string, particularly during the **Lang-Ay Festival** in the first week of April, when locals parade through the streets in traditional clothing.

◎ Sights

★ Bontoc Museum   MUSEUM
(P70; ⊘8am-noon & 1-5pm Mon-Sat) At this wonderful museum, powerful black-and-white photos are interspersed with indigenous art, representing each of the region's main tribes. You may spot Kalinga head-hunter axes, *gansa* (gong) handles made with human jawbones, and *fanitan* (baskets used for carrying severed heads).

Other items include delicately etched nose flutes, snake-spine headdresses of Bontoc women, bark raincoats of the Ifugao, traditional woven loincloths worn by men from each Cordillera group, and bamboo pipes used as containers for rice-wine offerings.

🛏 Sleeping & Eating

For a modicum of comfort you have to cross the bridge to the quiet eastern side of the Chico River, but if you're here to organise a trek, get some money or catch a bus, it's easier to stay in the town centre.

Archog Hotel   HOTEL $
(📞0917 695 9036, 0918 328 6908; r P600-1200; 🛜) The Archog is the closest thing Bontoc has to a business hotel. The clean doubles without bathrooms are a decent deal. It's a P8 tricycle ride across the bridge from town.

Churya-a Hotel & Restaurant   HOTEL $
(📞0999 994 6726; Halsema Hwy; d without bathroom P300, d/tr with bathroom from P700/1000; 🛜) This can-do, extremely centrally located guesthouse with a social common area and cafe overlooking the main street isn't ageing gracefully but it's the best choice in town. If you're much above 170cm tall, you may have to sleep in a foetal position.

★ Anayah's   FILIPINO $
(Halsema Hwy; P60-135; ⊘7am-7pm Mon, Tue & Thu-Sat; 🍴) Step into friendly Anayah's to find local dishes jazzed up with additional vegetables and flair, homemade yoghurt, freshly squeezed juices, and other surprises such as really good vegetarian hamburgers. There's usually a buffet with the dishes of the day, or the cooks are happy to prepare special-order vegetarian meals. Everything is fresh and delicious.

Cable Cafe   FILIPINO $
(Halsema Hwy; mains from P80; ⊘7am-3pm & 6-10pm) This dimly lit bar serves large portions of *lechón kawali,* chicken wings and other local faves, alongside nightly live music – OK, it's mostly '80s pop and Pinoy love songs – and beer.

Goldfish Cafe   INTERNATIONAL $
(Halsema Hwy; mains P100-150; ⊘8am-7.30pm; 🛜🍴) Goldfish takes a stab at 'cosmopolitan', with chocolate French toast and omelettes sharing the menu with pesto pasta, (rather sweet) pad thai and fancy coffees in hip, brightly lit surroundings with strong wi-fi. The food isn't great but it's a nice spot to hang out.

🛍 Shopping

Market   MARKET
(Halsema Hwy; ⊘6am-9pm) A covered market with fruits, vegies, grains and all manner of foods for sale. If severed pigs' heads aren't your thing, steer clear of the meat section, at the back to the left. The restaurant stalls, where you can sit down for a meal, are fortunately on the other far side of the building.

Mountain Province Trade Centre   TEXTILES
(Halsema Hwy; ⊘8.30am-6pm) Has woven materials from Sagada, Sadanga and Samoki, all with their own distinctive styles. Located on the 2nd floor.

ℹ Information

Municipal Tourism Office (📞0949 623 4913; Halsema Hwy; ⊘8am-5pm Mon-Fri) Very helpful, offers maps, and can suggest trekking routes and connect you with guides.

PNB The only ATM in town that accepts foreign cards (Visa only).

ℹ Getting There & Away

Vonvon bus makes the trip to Banaue (P150, 2½ hours) at 10am and 2pm. Jeepneys to

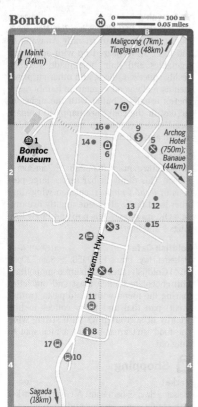

Bontoc

⊚ **Top Sights**
1 Bontoc Museum A2

🛏 **Sleeping**
2 Churya-a Hotel & Restaurant A3

🍴 **Eating**
3 Anayah's B3
4 Cable Cafe B3
5 Goldfish Cafe B2

🛍 **Shopping**
6 Market B2
7 Mountain Province Trade
   Centre B1

ℹ **Information**
8 Municipal Tourism Office A4
9 PNB B2

ℹ **Transport**
10 Dadance Bus Terminal A4
11 D'Rising Sun Bus Terminal A3
   Jeepneys to Banaue .... (see 8)
12 Jeepneys to Barlig, Kadaclan
   & Natonin B2
13 Jeepneys to Mainit B2
14 Jeepneys to Maligcong A2
15 Jeepneys to Sagada B3
16 Jeepneys to Tinglayan B2
17 Vonvon Terminal (Buses to
   Banaue) A4

Banaue leave when full, usually around noon (P150). A few morning vans (P150) leave when full from the same station as the jeepneys to Sagada.

D'Rising Sun has hourly buses to Baguio (P240, six hours) from 5.30am until 4pm.

Jeepneys depart every hour to Sagada (P60, one hour) from 8am to 5.30pm; note the last trip is unreliable, so take an earlier one if possible.

There's at least one bus and one jeepney every day to Tinglayan (P200, two hours); the best option is usually to catch the 9am bus, which continues to Tabuk (P300, five hours).

Maligcong is served by jeepneys (P30, 30 minutes) at 8am, noon, 2pm and 4pm, with return journeys at 7am, 2pm and 4pm.

Jeepneys tackle the rough roads to Mainit (P55, one hour) at 7.30am, 4pm and 5pm; Barlig (P110, 1½ hours) at 1.30pm; and Kadaclan (P130, four hours) at 11am, 1pm and 3pm. Jeepneys head to Natonin (P170, six hours) via Barlig and Kadaclan at 11am, as does an early-morning Dadance bus.

Around Bontoc

Maligcong & Mainit

The towering, sprawling stone-walled **rice terraces** of Maligcong rival those of Banaue and Batad elsewhere in the Cordillera, but draw only a fraction of the visitors. Mainit has some scalding **hot springs** that periodically pop up in random places, several interesting **ato** (*dap-ay* or outdoor patio) and backyard **mausoleums** adorned with carabao horns – a symbol of the deceased's wealth.

It's a steep two-hour grunt from Maligcong to Mainit, up and down a 300m spine. You can also hike to Bangaan, near Sagada, from Mainit via Dalican (six hours over very steep terrain). Both hikes require a guide.

If you need to overnight, rudimentary guesthouses are popping up all over Mainit. **Geston's** (r per person P250), in Mainit, and **Terraces View** (r per person P250), a short walk from Maligcong, are good options; you'll find clean rooms, hard beds and, in the case of Geston's, a couple of hot-spring pools.

Maligcong is a 30-minute tricycle ride (around P30) up Maligcong Rd from Bontoc; Mainit is about an hour up Ginaang Rd (around P100). A steep dirt track links the two villages and takes around two hours to walk.

Barlig, Kadaclan & Natonin

East of Bontoc, the secluded, rarely visited villages of Barlig, Kadaclan and Natonin have magnificent **rice terraces**. From Barlig it only takes around four hours to summit this region's highest peak, **Mt Amuyao** (2702m). The walk from Barlig to Batad, over Mt Amuyao, is one of the best two-day hikes in the Cordillera. Natonin to Mayoyao is a two- or three-day trek. Guides typically charge P800 per day and can be found in Barlig's Municipal Hall or in Bontoc.

There are a few extremely basic guesthouses and homestays in the villages; our favourite is the curiously named **Sea World** (r per person P250) in landlocked Barlig.

Ask the Municipal Tourism Office (p145) in Bontoc about transport options and guides.

Kalinga Province

The Spanish may have toppled the mighty Inca, Aztec and Mayan empires, and conquered the lowlands of the Philippines, but they never took Kalinga. While the practice of headhunting ceased decades ago, the proud inhabitants of these mountain villages have a justified reputation as fierce warriors and even now people occasionally get killed in tribal disputes. The loincloths and full-length arm tattoos boasted by older women are on the way out, but the machetes worn on the hips of most men are not just for show, and tattoos inked across a man's biceps are testimony to his having taken part in a skirmish.

Animals are frequently sacrificed in *cañao* (ritual feasts); traditional law still trumps the contemporary world; and yet, surprisingly, the Kalinga people also have a fondness for American country music. You'll hike along ancient mountain trails to villages enveloped in rice terraces as spectacular as those in renowned Ifugao to the south.

Tinglayan

📞 074 / POP 1100 / ELEV 900M

Three hours north of Bontoc on the Chico River, Tinglayan is the starting point for treks in Kalinga. It's a small, friendly village

without too much going on, and most people stay just long enough to find a guide before trekking off into more remote villages. Arrange in advance with a guide such as Francis Pa-In (p148) or turn up at either of the guesthouses where they will rustle up a guide for you. If you're coming from the south, it's worth setting up a guide with the excellent Municipal Tourism Office (p145) in Bontoc or with any guide organisations in Banaue or Sagada. Guide rates average P1000 per day.

🏃 Activities

Kalinga's main attraction lies in the scenic treks among the steep rice terraces between its numerous indigenous villages and in interaction with the locals. There are several exceptional routes in the Tinglayan area – some are half-day forays into nearby villages, others are multiday grinds terminating as far away as Tabuk or Abra Province. Local guides will arrange accommodation and transport to the trailhead where necessary.

Among villages where you can still encounter the traditional way of life are **Sumadel**, a nine-hour hike from Tinglayan, and **Dananao**, a three-hour hike from Sumadel, which is best combined with another three-hour trek to **Tulgao**, near where you'll find hot springs and a 30m waterfall. One early-afternoon jeepney goes most of the way to Tulgao (40 minutes) from Tinglayan.

> ### ℹ️ TRIBAL WARS
>
> Tribal wars occasionally break out between villages in Kalinga, Bontoc, and Mountain Province. The Philippine government leaves it up to the tribal elders to resolve disputes, some of which go back centuries and are over water rights, hunting rights and so on. The last thing mountain tribespeople want to do is involve tourists in their internal quarrels; still, travelling with a local guide is essential, because they're tuned in to the local grapevine and can help you avoid trouble spots as well as prevent you from offending local sensibilities.
>
> Gifts go a long way in Kalinga, and your guide will help you stock up on matches (the most popular item), washing soap and packets of nuts for the kids.

Another excellent one-day hike is **Ngibat–Botbot–Logong–Buscalan**; alternatively, your guide can arrange motorcycle transport from Tinglayan to Tulgao, from where the walk to Buscalan via Botbot and Logong takes around four hours. You have to be in reasonably good shape and prepared to negotiate a few short, steep sections on most trails. Botbot's blacksmith can supply you with machetes in wooden scabbards. Buscalan is a beautiful village with pretty stone-walled rice terraces and a few traditional houses, home to world-famous Whang-Od, the last *mambabatok* (traditional Kalinga tattoo artist).

East of the Chico River, **Tanudan** municipality sees fewer visitors than the villages west of Tinglayan. This is extremely isolated and rugged terrain.

For a shorter walk, try the **Tinglayan–Ambuto–Liglig–Tinglayan** loop, which takes you through some small rice terraces, as well as villages where a few indigenous houses remain.

One of Kalinga's most experienced guides, Francis Pa-In (☑ 0915 769 0843) is like a local version of Billy Crystal, telling silly jokes and leaving laughter in his wake. He knows everyone in the region, but he likes to flirt with the ladies so single female travellers may not feel comfortable with him.

🛏 Sleeping & Eating

Sleeping Beauty Resthouse   GUESTHOUSE $
(r per person from P400) Tinglayan's swishest option, conveniently located on the main road, has en-suite rooms with hot water, as well as basic digs with shared facilities. There's a little restaurant serving a few dishes of the day and cold drinks.

Luplupa Riverside Inn & Restaurant   GUESTHOUSE $
(r per person P250-400) Hard to miss due to the giant sign on its roof, this basic guesthouse is used to hosting international travellers. Meals available on request. It's down the hill across the bridge from the main road.

Good Samaritan Inn   FILIPINO $
(mains P60; ⏲ 11am-7pm) Buses between Bontoc and Tabuk pause here, in the middle of Tinglayan, for a meal stop. Expect large helpings of the dish of the day and a very crowded dining room.

ℹ Getting There & Away

The daily Tabuk–Bontoc bus passes through heading north to Tabuk at around 11am and south to Bontoc around 10.30am (P100 each way). Two buses run each way during peak season. There is also at least one daily jeepney heading to both Bontoc and Tabuk for the same price. For the best views, sit on the roof.

KALINGA'S CELEBRITY TATTOO ARTIST

It's estimated that more than 150,000 people each year make the pilgrimage to remote **Buscalan** to get tattooed by a tiny, strikingly beautiful woman who is claimed to be more than 100 years old. It all began around 2009 when the then-unknown **Maria Whang-Od** (also spelled Fang-Od) was included in the *Tattoo Hunter* documentary series. Since then she's been the subject of several documentaries, TV appearances and magazine articles.

Whang-Od is the last *mambabatok*, a traditional Kalinga tattoo artist. In her time she would have tattooed headhunters and tribal women. Today she wakes up at dawn to prepare her soot-based ink and pomelo-thorn needles to tattoo a selection of Kalinga symbols on tourists who come from as close as Bontoc and as far away as Europe. In 2016 she became an official National Living Treasure of the Philippines.

Traditionally *mambatok* are of the same bloodline but Whang-Od had no children, which is why she is considered the last of her trade. Fortunately she has trained her grand-nieces Grace Palicas and Elyang Wigan in the art. If you go to Buscalan to get a tattoo you may end up getting inked by one of them instead of Whang-Od, if she has too many people to cope with on her own or is feeling under the weather. The younger women's vision is better and their work produces cleaner and more regular lines. If you get tattooed by the nieces you can probably still have Whang-Od tattoo her three dot 'signature'. Expect more pain and blood with this traditional technique than modern tattooing, and understand that there's no antiseptic or sterilisation.

To get to Buscalan, ask to get off your Tinglayan-bound transport at barangay Bugnay, then hike two hours to the village (follow the crowd) or get one of the motorcycles (P100) waiting at this stop to take you to the Buscalan trailhead. It's a 40-minute, steep walk from here. There's a guesthouse in the village that charges P250 per person.

Tabuk

📞 074 / POP 110,640 / ELEV 200M

The capital of Kalinga Province is a flat, dusty, sweltering university town on the banks of the Chico River. There's not much happening here, but **Chico River Quest** (📞 0917 750 2913, 0917 804 3468; www.chico riverquest.com; lower/upper Chico River trips incl transport & accommodation P4000/7000) runs rafting trips from Tinglayan from June to early January. The lower Chico River Ullalim run is a straightforward Grade III, while the upper river Mataguan run passes through the Chico River gorge, with some challenging Grade VI rapids.

For accommodation, try **Davidson Hotel** (📞 0926 412 6018; Provincial Hwy; d/tr from P1050/1400; ❄ 🛜 ⛱).

Victory Liner has a daily bus to Manila (P750, 10 hours), but you're better off taking one of the frequent vans to Tuguegarao (P119, 1½ hours), from where onward connections north or south are plentiful.

Vans leave from the station on Kalinga-Cabayan Rd to Tinglayan (P100, two hours), in theory from 7am to 1pm, although the later ones are iffy so get there early. Jeepneys to Bontoc (P200, five hours) leave from the same area at 6am, 7am and 8am. A 7am and 8am bus to Bontoc (five hours) and jeepneys to interior Kalinga villages originate in barangay Dagupan, 7km north of town.

Banaue

📞 074 / POP 1390 / ELEV 1200M

Hemmed in on all sides by dramatic rice terraces, Banaue is directly accessible from Manila and can sometimes get overwhelmed by visitors. It's hard to blame them: the local mud-walled rice terraces are pleasingly different from the stone-walled terraces in most of the Cordillera. World Heritage listed, they're impressive not only for their chiselled beauty but because they were introduced around 2000 years ago by the Chinese.

The Ifugao people, once headhunters, built the terraces and were as skilled at carving wood as they were at carving terraces. Their carved *bulol* (sacred wood figures) are a Philippine icon, albeit a misunderstood one: *bulol* are rice guardians, not rice gods, as many would have you believe.

While Banaue remains the cultural and tourism centre of Ifugao culture, it's easy to lose the crowds by escaping to remote villages such as **Cambulo** and **Pula**, which have their own incredible rice terraces.

◎ Sights & Activities

★ **Museum of Cordillera Sculpture** MUSEUM
(P100; ⊙ 8am-6pm) This museum showcases a collection of Ifugao woodcarvings, and what a collection it is. Ritual objects and antique *bulol* line the vast hall, among displays of weaponry, fertility carvings and smoked human skulls attached to carabao horns. There are also some fascinating old books that you can read here, including a 1912 *National Geographic* on Ifugao headhunters.

Banaue Museum MUSEUM
(P50; ⊙ 8am-5pm) The Banaue View Inn runs this museum, which contains books written decades ago by anthropologist Otley Beyer and Igorot artefacts collected by his son William. Displays over two floors include jewellery, weaponry, traditional dress and headgear, and photos of Banaue in the early 20th century. Beyer's massive ethnography of the Igorot people is a must-peruse for anyone with even a passing interest in anthropology.

Tam-an, Poitan, Matanglag & Bocos HIKING
Hikes between these villages traverse rice fields in the immediate vicinity of Banaue and make for an easy half-day's walk. They can be done without a guide, provided you frequently ask for directions. You'll see traditional Ifugao houses in all of these villages.

The 45-minute hike from Tam-an to Poitan starts near Banaue Hotel's swimming pool and follows a century-old irrigation canal. Once you reach Poitan, ascend to the road, go left towards Banaue, then turn right at a staircase a few minutes later and start climbing. In 30 minutes you'll reach Matanglag, where a few bronzesmiths work. From here it's another half-hour to Bocos, known for its woodcarving. From Bocos you can descend to Banaue or head north across yet more rice terraces and end up at the viewpoint.

🛏 Sleeping

Options on Main Rd suffer road noise until around 10pm but are a good choice if you have errands to run or want to explore on foot. Places further up in the hills will mean hailing a tricycle to get around. Most lodges have wi-fi of varying quality.

Banaue

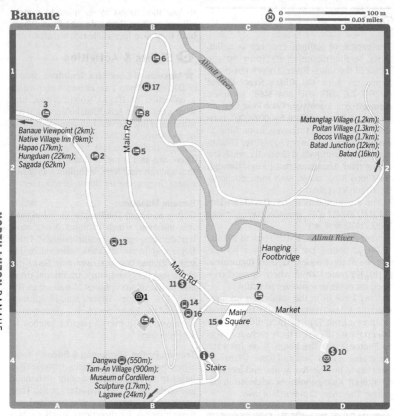

N 0 — 100 m
0 — 0.05 miles

Alimit River

Banaue Viewpoint (2km);
Native Village Inn (9km);
Hapao (17km);
Hungduan (22km);
Sagada (62km)

Main Rd

Matanglag Village (1.2km);
Poitan Village (1.3km);
Bocos Village (1.7km);
Batad Junction (12km);
Batad (16km)

Alimit River

Hanging
Footbridge

Main Rd

Market

Main
Square

Dangwa (550m);
Tam-An Village (900m);
Museum of Cordillera
Sculpture (1.7km);
Lagawe (24km)

Stairs

★ **Banaue Homestay** GUESTHOUSE $
(☑ 0929 197 4242, 0920 278 7328; www.banaue homestay.weebly.com; d P600-1200; ☜) Staying at this spotless, homey guesthouse up from the main town is like staying with family. You get to know your fellow guests and get plenty of individual attention and advice; the views from the rooms are splendid; and the meals rival anything you may sample elsewhere in Banaue. Very popular year-round; book well in advance.

7th Heaven's GUESTHOUSE $
(☑ 0908 467 4854; d P1000) Located 500m up the road from the main town, 7th Heaven's has rooms that are basic but clean and cheery. Each has its own bathroom but these are outside the rooms, not en suite. Angle for a room with a view! The wonderful cafe (open from 7am to 8pm) has the best views in town.

Randy's Brookside Inn GUESTHOUSE $
(☑ 0917 577 2010; r per person incl breakfast P250; ☜) Not only is Randy a great and know-ledgeable host whose brain you may wish to pick about all things Banaue, but he runs a ship-shape guesthouse with some of the cheapest rooms in town, and throws in a free breakfast.

Uyami's Greenview Lodge GUESTHOUSE $
(☑ 074-386 4021, 0920 540 4225; www.ugreen view.wordpress.com; s/d from P500/1000; ☜) The Greenview is one of the most popular places in town, which is unsurprising since it covers the backpacker bases: a decent restaurant, mostly functioning wi-fi and guides loitering on the doorstep. The cheapest rooms are windowless cells; opt for a 'de-luxe' with own bathroom and partial view of the terraces. It's a bit pricier, than the competition but worth it.

Banaue

Banaue View Inn   GUESTHOUSE $
(☑ 074-386 4078, 0916 694 4551; d/tr/f
P1000/1200/1500; 🖥) This inn sits at the top
of Magubon hill, overlooking the town and
the rice terraces. Rooms are pleasant and
clean, and service is friendly. Ask the owner,
Lily, to regale you with stories about her
grandfather, renowned Yale anthropologist
Otley Beyer, who wrote extensively about
Ifugao culture, or her father, William, a
swashbuckling antiques dealer who had 16
children.

People's Lodge   GUESTHOUSE $
(☑ 0935 189 5455; s/d from P400/800; @🖥)
This centrally located spot has a huge variety of rooms, and a popular restaurant with
rice-terrace views and a balcony, which most
of its neighbours lack.

Sanafe Lodge & Restaurant   GUESTHOUSE $$
(☑ 0939 939 0128, 0918 947 7226; www.facebook.
com/pg/sanafelodge; s/d from P850/1100; 🖥)
Sanafe Lodge has extremely cosy rooms, and
the best-looking restaurant in the centre. The
'deluxe' double rooms are pretty posh (for
Banaue), if a bit overpriced, but have mini-
balconies with terrace views. The restaurant
serves the likes of fried *bangus,* and has a
splendid leafy patio, and bar stools that stare
straight at the terraces (a happy-hour must).

Native Village Inn   HUT $$
(☑ 0908 864 6658, 0916 405 6743; www.native
village-inn.com; 2-person huts from P1500) These
lovely Ifugao huts, situated 9km out of town,
offer incomparable views of Banaue and the
surrounding rice terraces. Each hut sits on
its own plateau. There's a shared kitchen and
latrine-like bathrooms, so expect a camping-
like experience. Guests have access to two
mini-museums inside huts, which have extensive collections of *bulol* and smoked Japanese skulls tied to carabao horns.

ℹ Information

Banaue Tourist Information Center (☑ 0906
770 7969; ⊙ 5.30am-5pm Mon-Fri, to 3pm Sat
& Sun) Manages a network of accredited guides
and maintains the definitive list of guide and
private transport prices to selected locations.
Guides average P1200 for full-day hikes.

Landbank Very beat-up ATM next to Banaue
Town Hall; bring extra cash just in case.

Money Changer (2nd fl, Old Banaue Market;
⊙ 8am-6pm Mon-Sat, 2-6pm Sun) To exchange
your foreign cash.

Post Office The main post office is near the
entrance to Banaue Hotel.

ℹ Getting There & Away

Ohayami (http://ohayamitrans.com) buses
depart at 6.30pm and 7pm for Manila (P490,
nine hours) via Cubao. It's a P25 tricycle ride
from the Ohayami bus station to the town centre. **Dangwa** (☑ 0918 522 5049; www.phbus.
com/florida-bus) also runs a more comfortable
bus to Manila (P530, nine hours) departing at
8pm in high season only; Florida buses may
take over this run in future. In high season buy
your tickets well ahead of time – in person, or
online if travelling with Ohayami. The earliest
Manila-bound bus of the day is the 5pm **Coda
Lines** (P490, nine hours).

If you prefer daytime travel take a frequent
jeepney to Lagawe (P40, one hour), then another
to Solano (P80, 1¼ hours), and from there catch
a frequent Manila (Sampaloc)-bound bus (P355,
seven hours).

For Baguio, Ohayami has a 5am departure
and Coda Lines a 6pm (both P430, eight hours).
Vans also run to Baguio from the main square
between 7am and 1pm, and there's an unreliable
5pm departure (P415, eight hours).

For Vigan, the least complicated way (at least 12
hours) is to take an Ohayami or Coda Lines bus to
Baguio, get off in Rosario, La Union, and transfer to
a north-bound bus. Buses also run to Tuguegarao
via Cauayan City, which takes approximately the
same amount of time as the more direct Banaue–
Bontoc–Tabuk–Tuguegarao route.

NORTH LUZON BANAUE

A **bus to Bontoc** (P150, 2½ hours) leaves at 11am and a couple of additional buses pass through. A jeepney to Bontoc (P150) departs at 8am.

One direct van to Sagada leaves daily at around 8.30am (P300, three hours) from a departure point roughly two minutes' walk downhill from Uyami's Greenview Lodge. Coda Lines runs high-season buses to Sagada at 4.30am (P300, three hours); otherwise connect to Sagada in Bontoc.

Most jeepneys leave from the main square.

Around Banaue

Batad

✍ 074 / POP 1150

Given the proliferation of hugely picturesque rice terraces all over the Cordillera, winning the 'best terrace' competition is no mean feat. While these particular rice terraces are not necessarily the most beautiful, it's difficult not to gawp in awe when you reach the ridge overlooking Batad's 'amphitheatre' of rice, because as far as stages go, it's certainly very dramatic.

This backpacker hotspot is for now only accessible on foot (hence the lack of crowds from Manila), but this may soon change, as a road towards the village is being paved. If Batad is too 'on the beaten track', you can also escape to remoter surrounding villages such as **Pula** and **Kambulo**.

◉ Sights & Activities

There are many hikes in the area, and the Banaue Tourist Information Center (p151) or any guide can recommend longer treks. Batad has a network of guides called the Batad Environmental Tour Guides Associa-

tion. Twenty per cent of all fees collected by these guides goes towards restoring the rice terraces. Not all hikes around Batad require guides, but most do, and besides, you'll find their local knowledge a huge asset, especially for locating local craftspeople.

If you're feeling in need of pampering, ask your guesthouse about getting an excellent massage for P350 an hour. You may need it after walking the steep hills all around you.

Tappia Waterfall   WATERFALL

It's a 40-minute gruelling but worthwhile hike across the terraces and a steep descent to the 21m-high Tappia Waterfall, where you can sunbathe on the rocks or swim in the chilly water. *Do not attempt to swim under the falls;* the waterfall has claimed several lives. The falls are so strong that the pool is full of white caps.

Banaue Viewpoint–Pula–Cambulo–Batad   HIKING

This is a reasonably strenuous hike that passes through jaw-droppingly impressive rice-terrace scenery. Most people tackle it over two days, with an overnight stop in Pula, and a guide is mandatory. Your tricycle will stop on the way at Banaue Viewpoint then drive on to Awan-Igid where the trail starts.

From here to Pula it's a four- to six-hour hike; from Pula to Cambulo it's two or three hours; and another two hours from Cambulo to Batad.

The path to Pula cuts through jungle, the only part of the trail that doesn't involve rice terraces. Pula itself is a tiny collection of Ifugao houses on a hilly outcrop. Just outside of Pula, there's a waterfall and a deep swimming pool under a bridge. The trail from Pula

IFUGAO'S RICE TERRACES

The Ifugao rice terraces are incredible any time of the year, but they are at their best one to two months before harvest, when they become bright green before gradually turning gold. Around planting time, the terraces take on a barren, naked look that is also appealing. In Banaue (p149), the best viewing period is from June to July (before harvest) and February to March (cleaning and planting time). In Batad, which has two plantings a year, the fields are at their greenest from April to May and October to November. This is no longer set in stone, though: with the weather patterns changing over the past few years, the best time for planting has become less predictable, so make enquiries in advance if you have your heart set on watching the lifeblood of the Philippines grow.

Five Ifugao rice terraces are included on the Unesco Word Heritage list: Batad, Bangaan, Mayoyao, Hungduan (p154) and the Nagacadan terraces near Kiangan. Of those, Batad's are the most famous, but Mayoyao gives Batad a run for its money. Mayoyao is accessible from Banaue (three hours), or Santiago (five hours) in Isabela Province.

Around Banaue

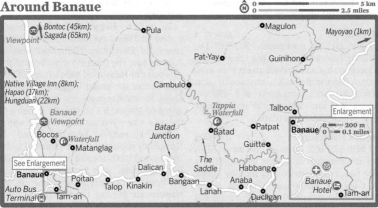

to Cambulo follows a winding river, with terraces carved high into the mountains.

If you take this route, you might plan on spending a night in Pula, where the simple Pula Village Inn will put you up for P250 per night; in Cambulo there are a handful of guesthouses, the best being the immaculate Hiker's Homestay (p154).

Batad–Bangaan   HIKING
This 2½-hour hike is the recommended route out of Batad. You'll take in the tiny village of Bangaan with it's Unesco rice terraces and some fantastic vistas en route.

From Batad, take the path towards Batad Saddle. About a minute after you pass the Main Viewpoint, there's a fork in the trail. Take the smaller, lower footpath to the left. From there it's pretty much smooth sailing, but do pay attention to the trail, as it tends to disappear here and there. You'll enjoy stunning panoramas of the mountains and rice terraces, bisected by a river hundreds of metres below. Eventually you'll walk through a rice terrace and hit the main road at Lanah, from where it's 2km to Bangaan Family Inn, which overlooks Bangaan, and another 1.5km from there to Batad junction. Many people arrange a tricycle to meet them at Lanah, which cuts out the walking time on the road.

Pula–Mt Amuyao   HIKING
From Pula it's a taxing seven-hour climb up the region's highest peak (2702m). You'll need a guide (P1200 per day) and have to be in seriously good shape. Be prepared to sleep at the radar station at the summit. Amuyao is much easier to scale from Barlig, near Bontoc, which is a three-hour hike from Pula.

🛏 Sleeping

Mobile phone reception barely reaches Batad, and most of its guesthouses usually cannot be contacted by phone. During March to May especially, accommodation can fill up, so get in early in the morning.

Most lodgings are on the ridge overlooking the rice terraces, and are nicer, breezier places to stay than the options in the village proper below. Expect basic wood-panelled rooms and shared bathrooms. Room prices are per person.

Ramon's Place   GUESTHOUSE $
(r per person P200-300) More characterful than most, Ramon's offers lodgings in an Ifugao hut (one/two people P500/800) and basic rooms of varying sizes. The gregarious host will dress you up in traditional Ifugao clothing, give you a rice-wine-making demo and feed you curry, salads and pizza at his terrace restaurant.

Batad Pension & Restaurant   GUESTHOUSE $
(📱 0918 964 3368; r per person P250) Eight little rooms are on offer at this small, friendly place. There's reliable hot water in the shared bathrooms, and the guesthouse is decorated with the works of the skilled woodcarver whose children now run it. You can also pick up some traditional cloth, woodcarvings and rice wine at the little shop.

Waterfall Side Lodge   GUESTHOUSE $
(r per person P200) The most isolated lodge in Batad is also one of the most beautiful, situated just by Tappia Waterfall. There are two rooms and fantastic views wherever you

turn. But you'll half-kill yourself going up and down the uber-steep steps.

Hillside Inn
GUESTHOUSE $

(📞 0936 131 1724; r per person P200-250) The Hillside has clean rooms, hot showers and a lovely verandah on which to eat your *malawach* (Yemeni flatbread), *shakshuka* (eggs scrambled with tomatoes) and Filipino mains. You can even splurge on a double with private bathroom (P900).

Hiker's Homestay
HOMESTAY $

(📞 0939 6357 055; Cambulo; r per person P250) An absolute gem of a place sitting above a rice paddy and overlooking the tiny village of Cambulo. The owner Conchita single-handedly keeps everything immaculate and cooks up excellent food. The tiny rooms have quality sheets and rice-terrace views.

Rita's
GUESTHOUSE $

(📞 0910 842 3076; r per person P200) Rooms here might be pokey, but they come thoughtfully equipped with mosquito nets, and chirpy Mr Romeo, with his red betel-nut smile, is quite a character.

ⓘ Getting There & Away

From Banaue, it's 12km to Batad junction, where a beautifully paved road runs right up to the 'saddle' high above Batad and continues towards the village. From the end of the paved road, it's a 20-minute hike downhill to Batad. Work on the road paving continues at a slow pace, and will eventually link to the village, so walking time may decrease in future.

The easiest and most popular method to get to Batad is to hire a tricycle in Banaue; get it to drop you at the end of the paved road and have it pick you up again at a set time when you plan to leave (P1400 return trip). You can organise a tricycle at the Banaue Tourist Information Center (p151) the moment you step off your bus in Banaue (during daylight hours).

Another option is to take the jeepney that heads from Banaue to Batad Saddle at 3pm (P150). From there you'll have to walk 40 minutes to the village. To return to Banaue, the same jeepney runs from Batad Saddle at 9am.

Hapao & Hungduan

POP 3860 / ELEV 1001M

Spread out over the valley floor, the rice terraces in Hapao and Hungduan are some of the most dazzling in the region, and you'll likely escape other tourists entirely. Aside from the superlative terraces, you can trek to waterfalls, stay in local homestays and climb historical mountains.

To walk to **Bogya Hotsprings** beside a river in Hapao (population 2200), a barangay of Hungduan 17km northwest of Banaue, take the concrete steps behind the viewpoint in Hapao and turn left at the bottom. Follow the paved irrigation canal for about 10 minutes until you reach a small group of houses. It's another 15 minutes to the river, where you can cool off in the water.

Five kilometres beyond Hapao is Hungduan poblacion (town centre; population around 1500), the site of the spectacular **Bacung spider web terraces**. The main trailhead for the seven-hour climb up **Mt Napulawan** (2642m), the final hiding place of General Yamashita at the end of WWII, is also here. You can arrange a guide and camping equipment for this climb through **Jascel** (📞 0926 380 2090; jascelpic@yahoo.com), who runs the Hungduan Guides Association. She can be found at Bugan's Homestay, a small guesthouse on the highway near the Mt Napulawan trailhead. Additional guesthouses are in the town center near the municipal hall (rooms start at about P400).

About 7km beyond Hungduan, in barangay Abatan, a trail provides access to two spectacular waterfalls. The first waterfall, 20m **Tobac Falls** (Balentimol Falls), is a steep 15-minute from the highway. Beyond here you can continue walking straight up for almost two hours along the Abatan Trail to reach **Mungkilat Falls**, a 40m cascade roaring off Mt Napulawan. You'll need a guide to get here. The Abatan Trail, which continues to the summit of Mt Napulawan, is impassable during much of the rainy season.

Jeepneys to Banaue leave Hungduan (P80, two hours, 22km) and Hapao (P70, one hour, 17km) around 8am and return between 3pm and 5pm. There is at least one jeepney per day to/from each town.

Hapao is within tricycle range of Banaue (return P800, 1½ hours) and it's a 45-minute ride between the Hapao and Hungduan.

Kiangan

📞 074 / POP 1690 / ELEV 1200M

Kiangan is where Ifugao and American troops helped force Japanese general Yamashita, the 'Tiger of Malaya', to make his informal surrender in WWII. Most people visit, however, to ogle the World Heritage-listed Nagacadan Terraces and Julongan

Terraces that are about 10km west of town, accessible by tricycle. You can also hike up into the Nagacadan terraces and then descend to Maggok village (three hours).

◉ Sights & Activities

Julia Campbell Agroforest Memorial Park
PARK

(☑ +1 512-305-3367, in US +1 210-859-4342; www.bantaicivetcoffee.com) In the Pula barangay of Asipulo town, the 48-hectare organic coffee farm, Bantai Civet Coffee, is a WWOOF (www.wwoof.com.ph) project that specialises in a rare and expensive type of coffee derived from the excrement of the coffee-bean-eating civet. The farm is part of the Julia Campbell Agroforest Memorial Park, named after the US Peace Corps volunteer who was murdered locally.

Volunteers and visitors can stay in a small Ifugao village (P300).

Jeepneys to barangay Pula (P80, two hours) run from Lagawe via Kiangan.

Whereas most commercial coffee plantations are on clear-cut plots, here trees have been planted amid natural forest. It is precisely this natural environment that draws shade-loving civets, which means the farm has both an economic and an ecological motive for preserving native forest.

War Memorial Shrine
LANDMARK

(P30) A short ride up from the village proper, this pyramid-shaped shrine marks the spot where Japanese general Yamashita surrendered on 2 September 1945, only to be hanged for war crimes shortly afterwards.

Pangaggawan Cave
CAVE

Pangaggawan Cave is a three-hour hike from Kiangan; there are several other caves in the vicinity.

Ifugao Museum
MUSEUM

(☺ 8am-noon & 1-5pm Mon-Fri) FREE Across the lawn from the War Memorial Shrine is the Ifugao Museum, which houses an absorbing collection of Ifugao artefacts, from household utensils and headhunting *bolos* (machetes) to intricately carved *pakko* (wooden spoons). The centrepiece is a huddle of *bulol* (sacred wood figures, or rice guardians).

✿ Festivals & Events

Bakle'd Kiangan
CULTURAL

If you arrive here around the last weekend of August, you may be able to participate in the Bakle'd Kiangan, a local festival that celebrates a bountiful rice harvest; during this time, locals don traditional dress and consume plenty of *binakle* (rice cakes) and *baya* (rice wine).

⌨ Sleeping

Kiangan Youth Hostel
HOSTEL $

(☑ 0910 324 3296; dm/d P250/400) Has passable rooms if you don't mind the Dickensian orphanage vibe.

★ Ibulao, Ibulao Bed & Breakfast
B&B $$

(☑ 0917 553 3299; www.facebook.com/ibulao ibulaobedandbreakfast; treehouse P600, dm/s/d P500/1600/1800; ❋ 🛜) Roberto and Teresa Kaludgan, both doctors, have built a house fit for the pages of *Architectural Digest* at the junction of the Lagawe–Kiangan road. The vast, beautiful family room with native hardwood accents is built right into the rock foundation, and guests can choose between a treehouse, an Ifugao hut and comfortable air-con rooms. No walk-ins; book ahead.

❶ Getting There & Away

From Banaue, take a jeepney to Lagawe (P40, 25 minutes, every 20 minutes until 4pm), then tricycle onwards to Kiangan (P100).

Coda Lines has a 5.30pm direct daily bus from Kiangan to Manila's Cubao bus station.

NORTHEAST LUZON

Get yourself to northeast Luzon and you're deep in the Filipino frontier. Hill tribes, huge swathes of forest, small towns connected by smaller lumber tracks – you won't find many Filipinos, let alone foreigners, out this way, with the exception of those in hip surfing town and weekend getaway Baler. The Cagayan River, the country's longest inland waterway, cuts a swathe through this famously fertile region. East of the river are the Sierra Madre, among the country's most impenetrable mountains, home to wild and woolly Northern Sierra Madre Natural Park.

Baler
☑ 042 / POP 39,560

Baler (bah-*lehr*) has never needed city walls for protection; the Sierra Madre and the Philippine Sea cut the capital of Aurora Province off from the outside world. Today Baler is best known as the location of the surfing scene in the film *Apocalypse Now*. The minuscule waves on display in that scene are

NORTH LUZON BALER

a testament to the area's fickleness, but the surfboards that were left here, post-filming, have kick-started a lively surfing scene.

⊙ Sights & Activities

Most people come to Baler to surf. If the water's flat, you can spend the day checking out **Museo de Baler** (Quezon Park; P30; ⊙8am-5pm), the **Catholic Church** (Quezon Park) and nearby beaches.

Sabang Beach
SURFING

The town hosts the Aurora Surfing Cup every February on Sabang Beach, an endless strip of fine dark sand extending north from Baler proper to Charlie's Point, the river-mouth break that spawned the famous 'Charlie don't surf' line in the film *Apocalypse Now*.

Dicasalarin Cove
HIKING

From Digisit, 5km south of Cemento Wharf, a hiking trail leads through the jungle south to an isolated white-sand beach at Dicasalarin Cove. It's a two- to three-hour hike (take a guide), or hire a bangka (P1300 return) near the San Luis River mouth at Sabang Beach.

Ditumabo Falls
HIKING

Ditumabo Falls (Mother Falls), which drop 15m into a small reservoir above an unfinished hydroelectric dam, are easily accessible from Ditumabo, 12km west of Baler.

DON'T MISS

SURF'S UP

Baler gets some of the biggest waves during the September–March season (though it's possible to surf year-round, particularly if you're a beginner). Here are our top five breaks:

Sabang Beach Left and right breaks and no reefs to snag beginners.

Dicasalarin Point Consistent reef breaks for pros and left and right beach breaks for newbies.

Cemento Reef Powerful right reef break for pros, used for surfing competitions.

Lobbot's Point, Dipaculao Left and right beach breaks suitable for beginners and intermediate surfers.

Dalugan Bay, San Idefonso Shallow left-hand reef break, best for pros.

Walk or take a tricycle (P100) 2km along an unpaved track to the trailhead, from where it's a straightforward 30- to 45-minute hike to the falls up a creek bed next to a water pipeline.

🛏 Sleeping

★Circle Hostel
HOSTEL $

(📞0917 501 0235; http://baler.thecirclehostel. com; Buton St; hammocks/dm/r P400/500/1250; 🛜) 🍃 Our favourite of this surf hostel chain, Circle has mastered a chilled-out surfer vibe where you'll make friends in minutes and never want to leave. The bamboo dorms are rickety and the 'cuddle rooms' spartan, but with a skate half-pipe in the middle of the common space and a lively kitchen area you won't care.

Elaine MM Lodge
GUESTHOUSE $

(📞0919 537 9405; r P800; ❄) Beachfront cheapie with colourful, basic, fan-cooled rooms and a 2nd-floor balcony that wraps around the building (so best hope you get on with your neighbours). Toilet seats appear to have gone AWOL; there are handy buckets and scoops in the bathrooms to shower with.

Aliya Surf Resort
HOTEL $$

(📞0917 982 6626, 0939 939 0844; www.aliya surfcamp.com; t/q from P2688/3584; ❄🛜🏊) This three-storey, ever-expanding concrete building by the sea offers bright rooms with modern clean beds, hot water and working internet. There's a surf-gear rental shop, a lively beachfront cafe and an infinity pool right over the beach. Central and good value.

Bay's Inn
HOTEL $$

(📞0908 982 3509; d with fan/air-con P1200/1600; ❄🛜) Bay's has a lively beachfront location, with rooms that are clean but uninspiring, unlike the bay views from their windows. The restaurant does a reasonable job of capturing the surfer ethos, with yummy fish tacos and loud music.

Costa Pacifica
HOTEL $$$

(📞0917 853 6040, 0917 857 4424; reservations@ costapacificabaler.com; r P9000-13,000 ste P15,000; ❄🛜🏊) With its swimming pools, manicured grounds and hammocks strung between palm trees, this waterfront hotel is Baler's fanciest. Gigantic white tiled rooms are decorated with floral wall art reminiscent of a kindergarten classroom. The chic Beach House restaurant serves excellent fish tacos, ribs and Filipino favourites. Service is inconsistent, however.

Baler

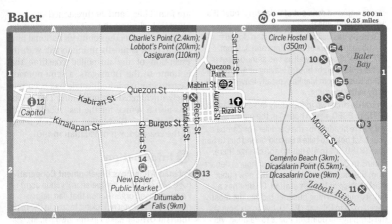

Baler

⊙ Sights
1 Catholic Church	C1
2 Museo de Baler	C1

⊕ Activities, Courses & Tours
3 Sabang Beach	D2

⊟ Sleeping
4 Aliya Surf Resort	D1
5 Bay's Inn	D1
6 Costa Pacifica	D1
7 Elaine MM Lodge	D1

⊗ Eating
8 Charlie Does	D1
9 Gerry Shan's Place	B1
10 Good Food	D1
11 Shack	D2

ⓘ Information
12 Provincial Tourism Office	A1

ⓘ Transport
13 Genesis Bus Terminal	C2
14 Main Bus Station	B2

✕ Eating

★ Charlie Does   INTERNATIONAL $
(Buton St; meals P95-200; ⊙10am-5pm; 🛜📶)
This groovy place is a surfing fashion boutique combined with a book exchange (you're welcome to chill out and read), a hip gallery, coffee counter and vegetarian restaurant. We recommend the fresh vegetable omelette and peanut-butter iced coffee (better than it sounds). You can also stay here in a hammock (P250) or in rooms made from recycled shipping containers (P1500 to P3500).

Good Food   INTERNATIONAL $
(Buton St; mains P60-120; ⊙10am-10pm) Perfect for filling hungry bellies post-surf, Good Food dishes up soulful fish tacos, burgers, burritos and plates of tasty pork or freshly-caught fish with rice. There's even a tofu option for vegetarians. It's just a concrete floor with a roof and some plastic tables but the food will make your taste buds sing.

Shack   INDIAN $
(📞0929 611 2607; Muldong St; meals around P200; ⊙7am-8pm Wed-Mon) This thatched roof restaurant in Baler town elicits wide-eyed hyperbole from all who have eaten here. An Indian chef on the scene means flavours are authentic and servings are big. Expect a warm reception but beach-paced service.

Gerry Shan's Place   FILIPINO, SEAFOOD $$
(Quezon St; buffet P199; ⊙11am-11pm) Gerry's place is famous for its buffet, which is particularly seafood-heavy, with touches of Chinese cuisine and a welcome bit of spice.

ⓘ Information

The friendly **Provincial Tourism Office** (📞042-209 4373; off Quezon St; ⊙8am-noon & 1-5pm Mon-Fri), part of the Provincial Capitol Compound, has maps of the area and can help you find a bangka or hiking guide. It also has information on exploring the scenic Aurora coastline north of Baler around Casiguran and Dilasag.

ⓘ Getting There & Away

Buses to Baler, both from Manila via Cabanatuan and from Baguio via San Jose, take the sealed road via Pantabangan. If you have your own 4WD, you can take the more direct and more scenic unpaved road out of Palayan (though it's prone to landslides).

Genesis has daily deluxe, nonstop 'Joybuses' to Cubao in Manila at 1pm, 2pm and 3.30pm (P730, six hours) as well as two semi-deluxe buses (P450, eight hours) leaving at 4.30am and noon. Buses from Manila typically leave for Baler early in the morning.

Lizardo runs two to four daily buses to Baguio (P312 to P360, seven hours) in the morning.

If you're heading for the Cordillera or Zambales, your best bet is to take a Baguio-bound bus to San Jose (P180, 3½ to 4½ hours) and change there.

Vans to Cabanatuan (P270, four hours) depart from the main bus station near the new public market. Also at the bus station, D'Liner has a rickety mid-morning bus that tackles the mostly paved road to Dilasag (P450, five to six hours), the jumping-off point for boats to Palanan, via Casiguran.

San Jose

While San Jose is little more than a crossroads town with no real attractions, it's a connection between the Cordillera, the west coast, the east coast and northeast Luzon, with buses passing through. ATMs and fast-food joints line the National Hwy.

If you must overnight here, well-run **Hotel Francesko** (☑ 044-958 0988; r from P1200; ❄ ⑤) offers bland en suites at the north end of San Jose along the National Hwy.

If coming from Banaue, you can catch one of the three daily Lizardo Trans buses heading to Baler (P140, three to four hours) along main Bonifacio Ave. If you're coming from Baler and want to head up to Tuguegarao and the north coast, hop on a north-bound bus along the north–south National Hwy that intersects with east–west Bonifacio Ave.

Northern Sierra Madre Natural Park

Shielded by the mountains, untamed by roads, and accessible only by tiny planes, by boats dependent on the mercy of the sea or by foot, this final wild frontier is the most pristine and naturally diverse part of North Luzon.

The Northern Sierra Madre takes up a whopping 3600 sq km (almost the same size as Switzerland) and incorporates the longest mountain range in the Philippines. It's a hugely exciting area for naturalists, since more than 60% of the country's plant species

are found here, and 29 threatened species of animal, including the critically endangered Philippine eagle, the country's national bird.

The park is mostly uninhabited, with the exception of the unspoiled coastline that is home to the Dumagats, a semi-nomadic Negrito group whose lifestyle has been relatively unchanged for millennia. This region was also a refuge for the last rebels during the Philippine Revolution, who took refuge in the coastal town of Palanan in 1901.

❶ Information

Palanan Wilderness Development Cooperative (☑ 0928 341 5375; amgpalanan@yahoo.com) Palanan-based organisation that can help arrange a guide if you're looking to trek in the park.

Tourism Officer Based in the town hall in Palanan, Myrose Alvarez (☑ 0906 721 1016) is the superhelpful tourism officer who has plenty of info on the park in general and can assist with organising a homestay in Palanan (where there is no commercial accommodation).

❶ Getting There & Away

AIR

Palanan, the main gateway to the park, is connected to Cauayan by daily **Cyclone Airways** (☑ Cauayan 078-652 0913; www.cyclone-airways.com) and thrice-weekly **Sky Pasada** (☑ 02-912 3333; www.skypasada.com) flights, while **Northsky Air** (☑ 078-304 6148; www.northskyair.com) flies to Palanan from Tuguegarao on Wednesdays and Sundays. All three airlines also serve Maconacon (daily except Thursdays). Flights tend to leave early in the morning, take around 30 minutes to either town and cost around P2200 one way.

BOAT

There are two boat routes into the park. One involves taking a weekly boat from San Vicente port near Santa Ana (10 hours) to Maconacon and then a second boat from Maconacon to Palanan (P600, four to five hours). Alternatively, take a bus to Dilasag either from Baler (seven hours, three daily) or from Santiago (10 to 12 hours, daily around 5am) and then catch a boat to Palanan from there (P600, one daily, six to eight hours). There are a few simple guesthouses in Dilasag if you need to spend the night. Boat routes are notoriously weather-dependent.

ON FOOT

From San Mariano, reachable by direct Victory Liner bus from Manila, it's possible to trek all the way to Palanan. It's only 45km, but due to trail conditions the trek typically takes at least five days; arrange a guide via the Palanan Wilderness Development Cooperative.

Tuguegarao

☎ 078 / POP 153,500

The only thing that puts the 'wow' in Tuguegarao (too-geg-uh-row), the political and commercial capital of Cagayan Province, is the country's largest cave system 25km east of the city. Otherwise, most travellers take one look at the tricycle-asphyxiated streets and make a beeline either for Pagudpud and Saud Beach to the northeast or the Kalinga Province out west.

◎ Sights & Activities

★ Callao Cave
CAVE

(P20) The most accessible part of the area's immense 25km limestone cave complex is the seven-chambered Callao Cave. The cave is reached by 184 slippery steps. Several sinkholes illuminate the cavernous chambers, the largest of which houses a little chapel. Compulsory guides (P100) are supposed to protect the cave from vandalism.

To get here, catch a jeepney (P50) from Don Domingo Market, just north of the city, or make the return trip by tricycle (P500, with waiting time).

A must-do excursion if you're in the area is to hire a bangka (P700) near Callao Cave and head 15 minutes upriver to watch the exodus of tens of thousands of bats as they pour out of the caves for a flight over the Pinacanauan River at dusk. If it's raining, the bats won't come out. You can rent kayaks (P200 per hour) from Callao Caves Resort, across the Pinacanauan River from Callao Cave.

Odessa-Tumbali Cave
CAVE

Estimated to be at least the second-longest cave system in the country at 12.5km (it still hasn't been explored to its terminus), Odessa-Tumbali Cave is for advanced cavers only. It can only be visited with permission from the tourist office in Tuguegarao and you must be accompanied by guide. Access requires a 7km hike from Callao Cave, followed by a 30m rappel into a sinkhole.

Adventures & Expeditions
NATURE

(☎ 078-844 1298, 0917 532 7480; 29 Burgos St) Run by veteran guide Anton Carag, the company offers kayaking trips on the Pinacanauan, where clean green waters cut through the limestone cliffs. This involves taking a bangka 5km upstream, then navigating the return trip via no-flip kayaks over light rapids. Adventures & Expeditions also organises multiday caving, kayaking and rafting trips on the Chico River in nearby Kalinga Province.

🛏 Sleeping

Hotel Carmelita
HOTEL $

(☎ 0917 572 2777, 078-844 7027; 9 Diversion Rd; s/d/f from P350/600/1030; ❄ 🛜 🌊) On the pro side, this hotel is close to the main bus terminals, has a pool, and its restaurant serves some of the best pizza and coffee in town. Plus, the rooms are as cheap as chips. Cons? The bathrooms need a facelift and the aircon in the budget rooms is reminiscent of a jet taking off (bring earplugs).

Hotel Joselina
HOTEL $

(☎ 078-844 7318, 0917 553 7930; http://hotel joselina.com; Aguinaldo St; s/d/f from P750/900/1000; ❄ 🛜) Remarkably good value for a central, efficiently run business hotel. Joselina has employed better interior designers than most of the competition: its compact, unfussy rooms are decorated with a bit of flair in warm yellows and browns, and have good beds and creature comforts.

Hotel Lorita
HOTEL $$

(☎ 078-844 1390; www.hotellorita.com; 67 Rizal St; s/d from P1000/1700; ❄ 🛜) Tuguegarao's best deal, especially if you bump up to the huge, rear-facing 'matrimonial deluxe' rooms. Rooms are surprisingly modern and well kitted out, and quiet to boot. The staff nearly trips over itself trying to help rare foreign visitors. The downstairs restaurant serves delicious Ilocano and Chinese dishes and there's a trendy cafe attached.

ℹ Information

Department of Tourism Office (DOT; ☎ 078-373-9563, 0918 909 2326; www.dotregion2.com.ph; 2 Dalan na Pavvurulun, Enrile Ave; ⊙9am-6pm) Has all the info you need, plus you can book caving permits here.

Sierra Madre Outdoor Club (SMOC; ☎ 0917 272 6494; www.facebook.com/Sierra-Madre-Outdoor-Club-Inc-SMOC-Inc; 2 Dalan na Pavvurulun, Enrile Ave) The people to talk to if you're looking for more adventurous cave excursions.

ℹ Getting There & Away

PAL Express and Cebu Pacific (http://cebu pacificair.com) have daily flights to/from Manila (one hour) from the airport, 2km north of the city centre. Sky Pasada (www.skypasada.com)

flies to Basco, Batanes and Maconacon (Northern Sierra Madre Natural Park).

Victory Liner (✅ 078-844 0777), **Baliwag** (✅ 078-844 4325) and **Florida Liner** (✅ 078-846 2265; Diversion Rd) are the most comfortable options to Manila (P750, 12 to 13 hours), with twice-hourly departures. GMW has buses to Laoag (P455, seven to eight hours) via Claveria and Pagudpud (P350). Afternoon Dangwa and Dalin buses serve Baguio (11 to 12 hours).

From the Tuguegarao van terminal, 2.5km north of the centre, air-con vans run regularly to Tabuk (P119, 1½ hours), Santa Ana (P180, three hours), Santiago (P160, three hours) and Claveria (P180, 3½ hours).

Santa Ana

✅ 078 / POP 32,900

Near the eastern tip of an infrequently visited part of the north coast, the fishing town of Santa Ana acts as a gateway to the Northern Sierra Madre Natural Park and also as one of the jumping-off points to the equally remote Babuyan Islands. While there's little to detain you in the town proper, **Anguib Beach** is as pristine as they come and easily reached by bangka from the port of San Vicente (P1500 return), 6km north of Santa Ana. Also accessible via a 15-minute bangka ride is **Palaui Island** (P800 return), which has a sedate pace of life, no lodgings and a beautiful three-hour walking trail from the village of Punta Verde to Cape Engaño and its still-functioning Spanish lighthouse.

Santa Ana is a big name in game-fishing circles, with Babuyan Strait rich in marlin, dorado and sailfish. The fishing season is between March and June, and you can arrange sports-fishing trips through the **Philippine Game Fishing Association** (✅ 0927 320 7261; www.pgff.net).

Between February and May the Babuyan Strait is also a good place to go whale-watching; look for everything from humpback, pilot and pygmy killer whales to spotted dolphins and bottle-nosed dolphins.

There are a number of places to stay, but we like **Jotay Resort** (✅ 078-372 0560, 0906 478 1270; www.jotayresort.com; r/ste from P1350/2800; ❋🐾❄) for its above standard rooms.

❶ Getting There & Away

Lal-lo International Airport services the area.

Large pumpboats leave weekly for Maconacon in the Northern Sierra Madre Natural Park from San Vicente pier.

Direct Guardian Angels buses connect Santa Ana to Manila (14 to 15 hours, two daily), while GMW Trans runs to Vigan (12 to 13 hours, two daily) via Laoag. Frequent air-con vans head south to Tuguegarao (P180, three hours).

BATANES ISLANDS

At the far northern reach of the Philippines, Batanes is a group of 10 islands floating off the corner of the map near Taiwan. Only three of these specks are permanently inhabited: the main island, Batan; tradition-rich Sabtang; and remote Itbayat. Island landscapes alternate between greenery-clad extinct volcanoes, rugged cliffs, rolling hills, verdant pastureland and turquoise-wave-fringed white slivers of beach.

Batanes gets battered by typhoons on a regular basis. The locals, most of whom are of indigenous Ivatan stock and converse in Ivatan, have designed their houses to be typhoon-tough, positioned slightly underground with metre-thick limestone walls and bushy roofs made out of *cogon* grass.

You may notice the wig-like headpiece that increasingly few Ivatan women wear; it is called a *vakul*, and it's made from abaca and the fibre of the voyavoy palm, found only in Batanes. The men wear a *kanayi* (vest made from voyavoy). Both protect the wearer from the sun and rain.

❶ Getting There & Away

Northsky Air (✅ 078-304 6148; www.north skyair.com) Small plane (Cessna 402 and BN Islander) flights from Tuguegarao to Basco and Itbayat. Mondays, Wednesdays and Fridays only; same day return.

PAL Express (www.philippineairlines.com) Flights from Manila to Vasco (1¾ hours), daily except Mondays and Fridays, returning to Manila daily except Mondays and Sundays.

Sky Pasada (www.skypasada.com) Three weekly flights between Tuguegarao and Basco and one weekly flight between Vigan and Basco.

Skyjet Airlines (www.skyjetair.com) The only jet flights between Manila and Basco (1¼ hours). Mondays and Fridays only.

Batan Island

✅ 078 / POP 11,980

Virtually all visitors to Batanes enter through Batan, the commercial centre and site of the provincial government. You'll want to spend at least a day circumnavigating the island, taking in the fabulous scenery, driving

BABUYAN ISLANDS

Clearly visible from the mainland, yet off the beaten path, the Babuyan Islands are 24 volcanic creations, some of which sport rugged cliffs and caves, while others are fringed with white-sand beaches and the most achingly blue, crystal-clear waters imaginable. Only the five largest islands are inhabited: **Fuga**, **Dalupri**, **Calayan**, **Babuyan** and **Camiguin**, and their residents lead quiet, pastoral lives, with limited electricity and little contact with the mainland. Volcanic Camiguin is known for its hot springs; the undeveloped islands of Fuga and Dalupri have beautiful white-sand beaches but no electricity or accommodation; developed Calayan has an incredible natural cove.

April to June is the best time to visit. The Babuyan Channel is generally too rough for crossings from December to March and during peak typhoon season (August to October); April is traditionally the calmest month..An airport on Calayan Island was completed in 2019 and has improved access to the islands dramatically.

A passenger ferry **MV Eagle** (☑ 0939 921 6181, 0906 8356 715) sails from San Vicente Port in Santa Ana to Calayan (P800, four to five hours, three weekly) via Camiguin (P500, two to three hours), weather permitting.

Otherwise, bangkas head out to the islands from Claveria and Aparri several times weekly. You can also either hire a private bangka in San Vicente, Aparri or Claveria (around P8000 return) or try to snag a space on a *lampitaw* (cargo boat) from one of the ports for around P600; prepare for exposure to the elements and a potentially hairy crossing.

Irregular bangkas link Calayan with the other inhabited Babuyans, and you can hire bangkas to jump between the islands.

its hilly roads and visiting its villages. Batan is blessed with ample natural beauty, but doesn't have the raw Ivatan culture of Sabtang Island.

ⓘ Getting There & Away

Batan Island is connected by air to Tuguegarao with Sky Pasada (www.skypasada.com) and Northsky Air (www.northskyair.com), and Manila with PAL Express (www.philippineairlines.com) and Skyjet Airlines (www.skyjetair.com). Sky Pasada also run one weekly flight to/from Vigan.

Batan Island is also connected by sea to Sabtang (p164). with ferries departing from Ivana on Batan; and to Itbayat (p164), with ferries from Basco.

ⓘ Getting Around

There are several ways to negotiate the island, including tricycles and jeepneys. Most lodgings and plenty of tour operators have bicycles for rent (P25 per hour) and you can hire mountain bikes from Dive Batanes (P250 per day). Riding the southern loop takes around six hours, not including stops; you have to be in decent shape and carry plenty of water.

Several lodgings have scooters or motorbikes for hire (P150 per hour); if yours doesn't, try the Petron petrol station or the Municipal Tourism Office (p162) in Basco.

Basco

With its wealth of accommodation options and a few decent restaurants, Batanes' compact capital makes an excellent base for exploring the rest of Batan Island. Awash with bougainvillea and shrouded in greenery, Basco's streets are a pleasure to walk. Abad St is the main drag; it really comes to life in the evenings with fragrant smoke rising from half-a-dozen streetside grills.

North of Basco, **Mt Iraya** (1009m), a dormant volcano that last erupted in CE 505, can be climbed in about five hours and descended in three, though the summit is usually obscured by clouds. Your hotel can help you find a guide (P1200).

🛏 Sleeping & Eating

⭐**Time Travel Lodge** GUESTHOUSE **$**
(☑ 0929 166 9838, 0939 623 8979; www.facebook.com/Timetravel-Lodge-BATANES; r with/without air-con P1500/600; ❄🛜) Half-hidden behind a wall and blooming shrubbery, this white-and-blue, colonial-style guesthouse has six rooms, all with kitchens and en-suite bathrooms. The immaculate front garden has a thatch-roofed, open-air dining/hang-out area. Chill out in the whimsically painted Adirondack chairs on your verandah with

a cold drink from the honesty refrigerator (take what you want and pay later).

Crisan Lodge
GUESTHOUSE $

(📞 0915 849 0178; crisonpensionhouse@gmail. com; Dita St; r per person from P400; ❄ 🛜) Run by friendly Mon and Crisan, this very central guesthouse above a chaotic grocery store offers small rooms, a guest kitchen and a small restaurant. It's an incredibly friendly place and you'll feel like part of the community.

Dive Batanes Lodge
HOTEL $$

(📞 0939 922 4609; www.divebatanes.com; r P2600-3600; ❄ 🛜) The rooms at this diving lodge are all warm hues and floral-patterned linens. There are numerous activities on offer, from diving trips off the south end of the island to snorkelling outings and mountain biking. Dive Batanes is located just off Chanarian Beach, 3km south of Basco.

★ Fundacion Pacita Batanes Nature Lodge
HOTEL $$$

(📞 0939 901 6353, 0917 855 9364; www.funda cionpacita.ph; ste P10,000-18,500; ❄ 🛜) You pay the price of luxury here, but you're rewarded with staying in an exquisite bohemian arts mansion perched on a bluff overlooking a stormy ocean. Think bold colours, exposed stone walls, tree-trunk beams, luxurious bed linens and carved wooden features. The on-site, equally quirky Cafe Tukon serves inventive meals made from the freshest local ingredients. Two-night minimum.

★ Phil's Brew
CAFE $

(⊘3.30-9pm) Watch the hours pass in this magical cafe in the garden of a traditional stone Ivatan home. Owner Imee makes all her own treats, including *tres leches* sponge cake, chocolate cake and *suman* (an Ivatan dessert made from cassava and sweetened coconut). The brewed coffees and espresso drinks are a godsend, and guests are encouraged to chat with each other. Drinks P75 to P120.

Beehon
FILIPINO $

(P60-300; ⊘7am-9pm) Opens reliably and has a great menu of basic Ivatan specialties to try; it easily becomes a regular haunt when in Basco. Try the *paco* (fern) salad, grilled fresh fish and filling Filipino breakfasts. All the dishes are a little bland but Beehon's setting under a thatched roof and local smiles make it a winner.

Ela Food House
FILIPINO $

(National Rd; mains from P60; ⊘7am-10pm) Basic little eatery on the corner of National and Lopez. The mother-and-daughter dream team cooks up classics such as *lechón kawali* (deep-fried pork belly) and crispy *pata* (deep-fried pork hock or knuckles), as well as fresh fish and a handful of Ivatan dishes.

★ Pension Ivatan
FILIPINO, IVATAN $$

(Main Rd; mains P150-450; ⊘noon-10pm; 🍴) This thatched oasis is, hands down, the best place in town to sample Batanes' specialities – from coconut crab and *kinilaw* (ceviche) to *uved* balls (banana root balls with bits of garlic and fish) and *vunes* (fried gabi stalks).

ⓘ Information

Municipal Tourism Office (📞 0929 846 8395; www.batanes.gov.ph; National Rd) Helpful tourist office on the ground floor of the Municipal Hall compound. Can help arrange guides around the island and has info on Sabtang and Itbayat Islands.

There's also a small information point at the airport.

Northern Loop

On this route, you'll take in the **Basco Lighthouse** just north of Basco; it's possible to climb it for stellar views of the coast. Further north, a new road leads to a short walking path up the crest of one of the **Vayang Rolling Hills**, where Itbayat and Dinem Islands are visible on the horizon on clear days.

Retrace your steps to Basco and head southeast up to the **Tukon Chapel** (Mt Carmel Chapel; suggested donation P20), an appealing stone church built by the Abad family. Further uphill it is **PAGASA Weather Station**, a giant golfball-like weather station with great 360-degree views; it's also reachable via a 1½-hour walk or a tough 30-minute bike ride from Basco. You'll see Fundacion Pacita, a magnificent stone house perched on a bluff, about 500m down the hill from here. The beautiful hotel is closed to outside visitors unless you dine at the restaurant. Further east, towards Valugan Boulder Beach, are the **Dipnaysupuan Tunnels**, built deep into the rock face by the occupying Japanese during WWII using forced local labour; you can explore the tunnels with a torch.

On the east coast, **Valugan Boulder Beach** is strewn with exercise-ball-sized boulders. Fishing at this sacred port is only

Batanes Islands

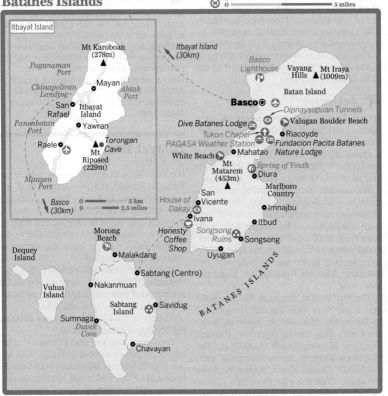

allowed from March to May so that the fish populations can be maintained.

Southern Loop

The island's main road, National Hwy, hugs the twists of the coastline south of Basco.

Just south of Mahatao, with its cluster of traditional houses, you'll find **White Beach**, a cove that's generally considered safe for swimming. Continuing south you'll pass through **Ivana**, the jumping-off point for Sabtang Island and home to the 1877 Unesco-listed **House of Dakay**, the oldest stone house in the Batanes. Right near the pier is the **Honesty Coffee Shop** (⊙8am-6pm), a great little place where you drop your money in the box and help yourself to drinks. The road flattens out on the way to southernmost **Uyugan**, where there are a few traditional houses.

The road then turns north, passing by a sweeping bay and the **Songsong ruins**

of stone houses demolished by a tidal wave. Passing through Itbud and Imnajbu, the road climbs to green, rolling pastureland populated by undomesticated carabao and cattle. This is Racuh Apayaman, better known as **Marlboro Country**. From here there are fantastic views of Batan's eastern coastline and Mt Iraya. You'll then reach an intersection, where the left fork leads to Mahatao (3km) and the right to the dorado-fishing village of **Diura** (1.5km). At Diura, pay P50 to register and then take the 20-minute walk to the refreshing **Spring of Youth**.

Sabtang Island

📞 078 / POP 1620

Travelling to Sabtang, you may feel as if you've left the Philippines entirely. Ivatan culture survives virtually intact here. The *vahay* (limestone houses) and their bushy roofs have been well preserved, and a few older women still work in the fields in their *vakul* (headpiece). Dramatic headlands, white beaches and a striking mountain interior round out Sabtang's feast for the eyes.

On arrival, visitors must pay a P200 fee at the **Municipal Tourism Office** (☑ 0918 488 2424; Centro; ⊙ 8am-5pm).

🏃 Activities

From Sabtang (aka Centro), where the ferry docks, head south on the road to **Savidug** (6km). Just south of Savidug look for a grassy *idjang* (fortress), which dates to pre-Hispanic times; there is a great hilly viewpoint overlooking a pristine cove, too.

It's another 4km from Savidug to picturesque **Chavayan**, which the local authorities have nominated as a World Heritage site because of its exceptionally well-preserved traditional Ivatan architecture. Hand-woven *vakul* and *kanayi* (vests made from voyavoy palm) can be bought at the **Sabtang Weavers Association**, along the main road.

The road ends in Chavayan, but you could take a two-hour walk through the interior to **Sumnaga**. Most people, however, backtrack with their tricycle from here through Centro to **Morong Beach** to check out the **Mayahaw Cave**, a Japanese hideout during WWII. There's also a **zipline** here for the brave. Continue past incredible coastal vistas to traditional **Nakanmuan**, where coconut-crab catchers live. From here you can then continue on to Sumnaga, an authentic fishing village with stone houses up to the shoreline and flying fish hanging out to dry on clotheslines. Take a walk further about 10 minutes to the perfect arc of white sand strewn with colourful fishing boats at **Duvek Cove**; it's reminiscent of a Polynesian paradise.

🛏 Sleeping

There are currently around 12 homestays on Sabtang. Our favourites are the authentic Itbayat **Cervillon Ancestral Home** (☑ 0919 323 9304; Savidug; r P250) in Savidug, and **Lighthouse Guesthouse** (☑ 0921 496 7233; r per person P500), which sits on a scenic bluff next to the out-of-commission lighthouse and has access to its own private beach. Your guide or the Municipal Tourism Office can help set you up at all the guesthouses on the island.

ⓘ Getting There & Away

Weather permitting, round-bottomed *falowa* boats make at least one daily trip between Ivana on Batan Island and Centro (P100 return, 30 to 45 minutes), the first departing from Ivana around 7am; the return from Centro is in the afternoon only, usually around 2pm. Sometimes another afternoon trip is added. If you're desperate, a *falowa* will make a special trip for a minimum of P3000. Be warned: this crossing can be rough.

Itbayat Island

☑ 078 / POP 2870

It's a thrilling 15-minute plane ride from Basco to Itbayat, the Philippines' final inhabited frontier. Unlike its Batanes siblings, this platform of an island has no beaches; it rises vertically out of the depths, cliff-fringed all the way around. This is an island to do a whole lot of walking and enjoy authentic culture and wild nature.

Itbayat has electricity between 6am and midnight. If the weather acts up you could get stranded here for a few days, so build some flexibility into your schedule.

Visitors to the island have to pay P100 at the Municipal Treasurer office.

Guides can help you find a homestay. The mayor (at the municipal building) will let you stay in Mayan's **Municipal Hall Guesthouse** (dm P150) which has kitchen access. Homey and comfortable **Cano Homestay** (☑ 0919 300 4787; r P250), is run by former tourism officer Faustina Cano, who will treat you like family and tell you all about the island.

ⓘ Getting There & Away

Every now and then, and if the weather is good, **Northsky Air** (☑ 078-304 6148; www.north skyair.com) runs eight-seater flights between Basco and Itbayat (P1875, 15 minutes) usually on Mondays, Wednesdays and Fridays at 11am. The landing strip is near Raele, 10km south of Mayan.

M/B Ocean Spirit (☑ 0920 664 0137) and **M/B Itransa** (☑ 0908 502 2814) *falowa* ferries depart Basco for Itbayat around 6am and 7am (P450, three to four hours), landing at either Chinapoliran Port (halfway along the west coast) or Panenbatan Port in the southwest, and returning around noon. This is a rough crossing at the best of times and may be cancelled altogether when seas are particularly perilous.

Southeast Luzon

Why Go?

Southeast Luzon is one of the more overlooked parts of the Philippines, but those travellers who do make it here will find a wildly varied and unusual part of the country, where you're likely to encounter anything from creatures of the deep (in Donsol and Ticao) to Easter-time Romans and self-flagellation (Marinduque), cowboys rounding up both steers and crabs (Masbate), and *Survivor* locations (Caramoan peninsula).

Surfers make the trek down here, drawn to the waves whipped up by the fierce winds in Southeast Luzon's outer reaches, while adventurous travellers look to the active volcanoes of Mayon, Isarog and Bulusan. Departing the tourist trail to island-hop *Survivor* film locations and making the well-worn journey to snorkel with whale sharks in Donsol are highlights. Dive in!

Best Places to Eat

➡ Smalltalk Cafe (p177)

➡ Kusina sa Plaza (p190)

➡ Bob Marlin (p171)

➡ Blossoms (p184)

Best Places to Stay

➡ Balai Tinay Guesthouse (p175)

➡ Carmen (p170)

➡ Bagasbas Lighthouse (p168)

➡ Mayon Backpackers Hostel (p175)

➡ Ticao Island Resort (p188)

When to Go
Naga City

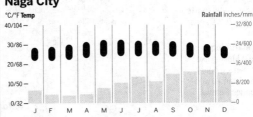

Apr & May	May–Jul	Aug–Nov
Festival time in Legazpi and Masbate.	Sunny (and hot!) time of year, ideal for island-hopping and diving.	Surf's up in Catanduanes and Bagasbas; kitesurfing also takes off.

Southeast Luzon Highlights

1 Donsol (p180) Snorkelling alongside Bicol's gentle whale sharks.

2 Mt Mayon (p179) Riding an ATV near the base of Mt Mayon, Bicol's prettiest volcano.

3 Legazpi (p174) Sampling the best of Bicol's spicy cuisine.

4 Masbate (p185) Getting off the beaten track at this 'Wild East' island, with its cowboys and crab races.

5 Catanduanes (p182) Riding the legendary Majestic surf break on this remote island.

6 Caramoan Peninsula (p171) Exploring the uninhabited islands, beaches and *Survivor* locations of this pristine peninsula.

7 Ticao Island (p188) Diving with manta rays at the Manta Bowl.

8 Naga (p169) Wakeboarding, wakeskating and waterskiing at CamSur Watersports Complex (CWC) near Naga.

9 Marinduque (p190) Making like a Roman legionary at this island's wild Moriones Festival.

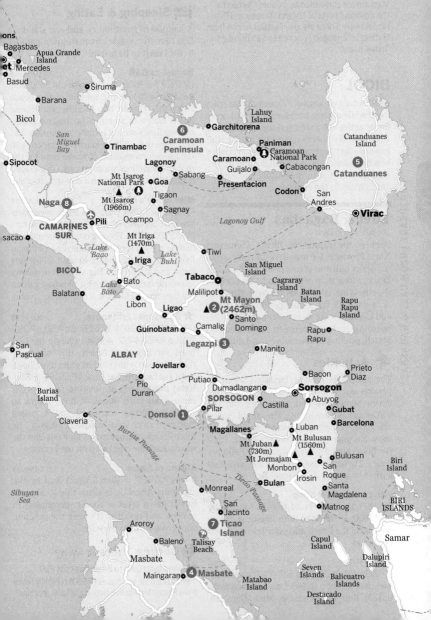

PHILIPPINE
SEA

Calagua
Islands

ons
Bagasbas
et   Apua Grande
Mercedes   Island
Basud

Siruma

Barana

Bicol

San
Miguel
Bay

Sipocot

Tinambac

Lahuy
Island

Garchitorena

Caramoan
Peninsula **6**

Paniman
Caramoan Caramoan
National Park

Catanduanes
Island

Lagonoy
Sabang
Guijalo
Cabacongan

Mt Isarog
National Park Goa

Naga **8**

Tigaon

Presentacion

Codon

San
Andres

Catanduanes **5**

Virac

Pili

Mt Isarog
(1966m)

Sagnay

CAMARINES
SUR

Ocampo

Lagonoy Gulf

sacao

Lake
Baao

Mt Iriga
(1470m)

Tiwi

San Miguel
Island

BICOL

Iriga

Lake
Buhi

Cagraray
Island

Batan
Island

Rapu
Rapu
Island

Balatan

Lake
Bato

Bato

Libon

Tabaco

Malilipot

Ligao

Mt Mayon **2**
(2462m)

Santo
Domingo

Rapu
Rapu

San
Pascual

Guinobatan

Camalig

Legazpi **3**

Manito

ALBAY

Jovellar

Bacon

Prieto
Diaz

Burias
Island

Pio
Duran

Putiao

Dumadlangan

Sorsogon

Claveria

Donsol **1**

Pilar

SORSOGON

Castilla

Abuyog

Gubat

Barcelona

Magallanes

Luban

Mt Juban ▲
(730m)

Mt Bulusan
(1560m)

Bulusan

Burias Passage

Monreal

San
Jacinto

Mt Jormajam ▲
Monbon

Bulan

San
Roque

Santa
Magdalena

Biri
Island

Irosin

Matnog

BIRI
ISLANDS

Sibuyan
Sea

Aroroy

Baleno

Ticao **7**
Island

Talisay
Beach

Diego Passage

Capul
Island

Samar

Masbate

Maingaran

Masbate **4**

Matabao
Island

Seven
Islands

Balicuatro
Islands

Dalupiri
Island

Destacado
Island

ℹ Getting There & Away

There are daily flights from Manila to Legazpi, Masbate, Naga and Virac (Catanduanes).

Numerous (mainly overnight) buses run from Manila to Southeast Luzon's cities – it takes at least 15 hours to get to Legazpi.

The islands of Marinduque, Catanduanes and Masbate are connected by frequent ferries to the mainland ports of Lucena, Tabaco and Pilar, respectively. There are also FastCat ferries from Matnog in Sorsogon Province to San Isidro on Samar island.

BICOL

Bicol is famous among Filipinos for its spicy food, while among travellers it's best known for its active volcanoes and the whale sharks of Donsol. But there's quite a bit more to this less-travelled region: explore barely visited beaches, island-hop on a bangka and experience some of the most unusual and exuberant festivals in the country.

Daet & Bagasbas

📞 054 / POP 104,800

Daet is the capital of Bicol's Camarines Norte Province; for travellers it's really just a transport hub and access point for Bagasbas Beach, a long strip of grey sand 4km north of the city. When conditions are right, Bagasbas draws surfers for its temperamental waves and kitesurfers for its consistent winds. Kiteboarding season is between November and March, peaking in December and January.

🏃 Activities

The surfing is best at Bagasbas when typhoons churn up the Pacific's waters between September and November, but the waves are inconsistent. The small waves are good for beginner surfers, though, and most lodgings hire out boards (from P200 per hour) and arrange instruction (P400 per hour). There are good breaks for advanced surfers in nearby San Miguel Bay.

Hang Loose Surf Shop   SURFING
(📞 0909 531 2869; board hire per half/full day P500/800; ⏰ 6am-5pm) Enthusiastic staff hire boards on the beach and offer lessons (P400 per hour).

Mike's Kites   KITESURFING
(📞 0995 458 9995, 0949 622 0749; www.mikes-kites.com; 2hr intro US$60, 1-day kiteboard rental US$20) Run by American Mike Gambrill, Mike's offers kiteboarding lessons with a certified instructor, hires out equipment and arranges surfing, island-hopping, paragliding and wakeboarding trips. Kiteboarding season in Bagasbas is between November and March; Mike's is usually closed out of season so call ahead.

🛏 Sleeping & Eating

A handful of guesthouses and one standout hotel line the single street running parallel to the beach in Bagasbas.

Bagasbas B&B   GUESTHOUSE $
(📞 0929 545 8955; d with fan/air-con P600/800, q P1500; ❄🖥) In the middle of the beach strip, this simple but friendly guesthouse has a clutch of small, clean budget rooms on two floors with a rooftop restaurant and bar topping it off. Breakfast is included with the air-con rooms and, if you're here for the day, the travellers wash-up rate (five hours) is just P300. There's even a day spa attached.

Mike & Joy's Kite Bar   BUNGALOW $
(📞 0949 622 0749, 0995 458 9995; www.mikes-kites.com; Bagasbas Rd; d fan/air-con bungalow from P1000/800; ❄🖥) The seasonal bar-restaurant here is a good spot for Western and Filipino food, beer and the chance to meet fellow surf bums and kitesurfers. The air-con bungalows are comfortable and front a pleasant garden but they tend to fill up fast during kite season.

★ Bagasbas Lighthouse   RESORT $$
(📞 0917 510 1856, 054-731 0355; dm P550, d P1750-2950, q P3950-4450; ❄🖥🏊) Clearly the best hotel on Bagasbas Beach, this nautically themed resort, shrouded in vegetation, has a great **restaurant-bar** (mains P155-195; ⏰ 8am-10pm) overlooking an inviting pool. Rooms range from fairly standard hotel rooms to small but funky converted trailer rooms (and even an en suite backpacker dorm). The more luxurious front rooms look out over the waves. Karaoke cranks up on weekends.

Kusina ni Angel   FILIPINO $
(mains P60-300; ⏰ 10am-9.30pm) Run by the charming Angel de la Cruz, this local institution has a creative menu specialising in seafood and noodles. It's near the junction where you pick up tricycles.

ℹ Getting There & Away

Tricycles from Daet to Bagasbas cost P50.

Philtranco air-con buses (P550) typically leave from Pasay, Manila five time daily for Daet (nine hours). From Daet, DLTB and Superlines buses run frequently to Manila from their own terminals along the Mahalika Diversion Rd. Regular buses also go to Lucena (P315).

There are frequent morning minivan services to Naga (P180, three hours) from the Central Terminal along Vinzons Ave.

Naga

☑ 054 / POP 196,000

Naga is a busy student city, home to Bicol's oldest university and an impressive range of cafes, bars and malls. Of greater interest to travellers is the volcano-related hiking, biking and climbing in Naga's vicinity, and the nearby wakeboarding park. In September, thousands of devotees come to Naga for the Peñafrancia Festival in celebration of the Virgin of Peñafrancia, Bicol's patron saint. Book accommodation at least two months in advance.

⊙ Sights & Activities

Naga Cathedral   CATHEDRAL
(St John the Evangelist; Barlin St) The 19th-century Naga Cathedral, with its imposing Romanesque facade, is a major city landmark. It's fronted by the equally imposing Porta Mariae, a triumphal arch built in 2010 and dedicated to Our Lady of Peñafrancia.

**Holy Rosary Minor
Seminary Museum**   MUSEUM
(off Elias Angeles St; ⊙9am-noon & 2-5pm Mon-Fri, 8am-noon Sat) FREE If you can't make the **Peñafrancia Festival** (⊙Sep), this little museum may be the next best thing. Located adjacent to the city-dominating cathedral, the exhibits here consist of pictures and glass displays of religious pageantry and some entertaining dioramas of the main procession.

Naga City Museum   MUSEUM
(Burgos St; ⊙8am-noon & 2-5pm Mon-Fri) FREE This small museum, located on the 3rd floor of the campus of the University of Nueva Caceres, is ethnographic in focus, filled with crafts, tools and other artefacts of pre-colonial Bicol and covering the history of the Philippines as a whole.

★ CamSur
Watersports Complex   WATER SPORTS
(CWC; ☑054-477 3344, 0917 895 4156; www.cwc wake.com; Provincial Capitol Complex Cadlan, Pili; wakeboarding 1/2/4hr P165/330/460, full-day P750, night rate per hr P325; ⊙8am-6pm Mon-

Wed, to 9pm Thu-Sun) CWC is a state-of-the-art outdoor cable-ski water-sports complex, where overhead cables do the work of speedboats, towing boarders around the purpose-built water park, complete with jumps, rails and slides. It's fun to watch experienced riders doing tricks and flips, and beginners are welcome to have a go, with gear hire and instruction. It's 12km south of Naga in Pili.

Kadlagan Outdoor Shop & Tours   CLIMBING
(☑0919 800 6299; kadlagan@yahoo.com; 2nd fl, SM Mall, Ninoy & Cory Ave) Local guide Jojo Villareal is one of the best sources of information about climbing Mt Isarog and other Naga-based adventure activities. The outdoor shop in SM Mall stocks camping and climbing equipment.

🛏 Sleeping

Budget and midrange options are in the city centre, while the more upmarket hotels are found on and off Magsaysay Ave, a 10-minute tricycle ride north.

Hillary & Andrew Hostel   HOSTEL $
(☑0998 845 5248; hillaryandandrew_hostel @yahoo.com.ph; 32 Barlin St; s/d/tr from P600/850/1400; ❄🛜) It's more of a budget hotel than a backpackers' joint but this is the clear budget standout in Naga, a friendly place with a restaurant-bar, streetside verandah and occasional live music. Cheapest rooms are en suite but tiny and windowless; you only need to pay a bit more for something spacious. It's a short walk from the iconic Naga Cathedral.

Naga Regent Hotel   HOTEL $$
(☑054-472 2626; www.nagaregenthotel.com; Elias Angeles St; dm/s/d/ste incl breakfast from P500/900/1400/2800; ❄🛜) There's a lot to like about this affordable business-class hotel. From enormous suites with polished wooden floors down to spacious dorms with sturdy bunks, it embraces the divide between budget and midrange with something for everyone. The central location is a bonus.

Eurotel Naga   HOTEL $$
(☑054-472 5321; www.eurotel-hotel.com; cnr General Luna St & Riverside Rd; d/ste incl breakfast from P1750/2500; P❄🛜) Spotless business hotel in a central location overlooking the river. Expect funky wall-to-wall prints of famous European landmarks, stuccoed ceilings in the suites and compact twins and doubles with mod cons aplenty.

Naga

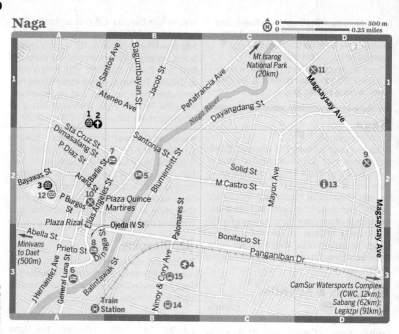

Naga

★ **Carmen**　　　　　BOUTIQUE HOTEL $$$
(☏054-472 5888; www.thecarmenhotel.com.ph; Peñafrancia Ave; d P7500-8500, ste P13,000; ❅⛱☄) Naga's newest hotel sits comfortably at the top of the posh pile, with 45 ubermodern and spacious rooms with floor-to-ceiling windows and cloudlike beds. There's an attractive pool deck, a gym and the oh-so-cool rooftop Sky Lounge with perfect city views. Street noise is muted by a thoughtful exterior design. Discounted online rates can be less than half those listed.

✗ Eating

Come evening, food stalls pop up around the lively squares that dot downtown. A good cluster of vendors collects near the San Francisco church off Peñafrancia Ave, and more upmarket restaurants are along Magsaysay Ave. Otherwise try the popular food court at SM Mall.

Geewan　　　　　BICOLANO $
(☏054-473 3030; www.geewan.ph; Burgos St; mains P65-150; ⊙9am-9pm; ❅) This Bicolano cafeteria-style joint is justifiably popular with locals thanks to its extensive and inexpensive array of dishes such as *lechón* (roast suckling pig), *pinangat* (taro leaves, chili, meat and coconut milk) and *bangus* (milkfish), all consumed on genuinely comfy

seats in an arctic air-con environment. Many dishes are already prepared and on display in food warmers.

★**Bob Marlin** FILIPINO $$
(☑054-473 1339; www.bobmarlin.ph; Magsaysay Ave; mains P175-320; ⊙11am-1am) Bob Marlin is locally renowned as the best spot in town to chow down on crispy *pata* (deep-fried pork knuckle). Other Filipino dishes such as *inahaws* (grills) also hit the spot, and it's a sociable and entertaining place for a beer and a night out on the busy Magsaysay strip.

Red Platter FILIPINO $$
(☑054-472 9933; www.redplatter.ph; Magsaysay Ave; ⊙10am-10pm Mon-Sat, 9am-10pm Sun; ❄️ 🔊) One of the more upmarket independent restaurants on the Magsaysay strip, Red Platter is semiformal in atmosphere but high quality in presentation. The focus is Filipino grills, seafood and rice dishes, but pizza, pasta and snacks such as nachos also grace the menu.

❶ Information

Downtown Post Office (University of Nueva Caceres; ⊙8am-5pm Mon-Fri)
Naga City Visitors Center (☑054-473 4432; www.naga.gov.ph/tourism; cnr Miranda Ave & Maria Cristina St; ⊙8am-noon & 1-5pm Mon-Fri) Inside the City Hall complex.

❶ Getting There & Away

AIR

The airport is in Pili, 14km south of Naga. Cebu Pacific and PAL fly daily (from P3500, one hour) between Manila and Naga.

BUS & JEEPNEY

All bus services use Naga's **central bus terminal** (Ninoy & Cory Ave), just south of the SM City Mall. Cagsawa has air-con night buses that go directly to Ermita in Manila (10 to 13 hours), while **Isarog** (☑0908 851 2649; https://bicol isarog.com) and Amihan go to Cubao (P760) and Philtranco goes to Pasay (P630). Most air-con and deluxe services are at night. Raymond bus has several daily services to Caramoan (P220, five to 5½ hours) and one overnighter to Cubao.

Jeepneys and air-con minivans leave from the **jeepney terminal** (Carnation St) 200m east of SM City Mall. There are frequent minivans to Legazpi (P140, 2½ hours), Tabaco (P180, two hours) and Sabang (P100, 1½ hours). Jeepneys head to Panicuason (P25, 30 minutes) and Pili (P15, 20 minutes).

Minivans (Felix Plazo St) to Daet (P180, two hours) leave from the LCC Transport Terminal behind LCC Mall until 9pm. Jeepney also operate from this terminal.

Mt Isarog National Park

Dominating Camarines Sur's landscape is Mt Isarog (1966m), Bicol's (dormant) second-highest volcano. From Panicuason (pan-ee-*kwa*-sone), a steep, half-hour walk along a rough road (passable if dry, but a regular car will struggle) leads to the entrance of **Mt Isarog National Park** (P50; ⊙park office 8am-4pm). Pay admission at the base of the mountain. To the right, a short walk leads down some very steep stone steps to Malabsay Falls, where you can swim with a view of Mt Isarog – the experience is amazing. At Panicuason, **Mt Isarog Hot Springs** (P100; ⊙7am-6pm) has five natural hot-to-tepid pools – a nice way to relax after a trek in the park. The springs are a 1.3km walk off the main road, just before the road to the national park.

Officially a licensed guide and permit (US$10) are required for the two-day return trek up Mt Isarog. Visit the tourist office at city hall in Naga, or talk to Jojo at Kadlagan Outdoor Shop (p169). The hike up takes you through the last virgin tropical forest in Luzon; the trek can be done in one day if you're very fit (check first as this may change), but the permit allows for two days. As you get higher, the vegetation turns to mossy forest, then sparse grassland and stony alpine shelves closer to the summit. Traditionally, early March to late May has been the best time, weather-wise, to climb. More than one trail snakes its way up the volcano: trekkers typically hike up either the popular trail from Panicuason, or the less-used and more environmentally friendly trail starting at Consocep. Jojo at Kadlagan Outdoor Shop can also help with permits and hiring camping gear.

❶ Getting There & Away

To travel to Mt Isarog from Naga, take a jeepney to Panicuason. Note that the last jeepney back to Naga leaves Panicuason around 5pm.

Caramoan Peninsula

The mountainous, thickly jungled Caramoan peninsula is only 50km or so from Naga, but it might as well be worlds away. Best approached by boat, it can feel as if you're arriving at the *Jurassic Park* island, with its jagged cliffs, teal sea and pristine strips of sand. The northern coast has a sprinkling of grey-sand beach resorts, the main one being

Paniman, which serve as a starting point for island-hopping or relaxation.

The Caramoan is remote enough to have been the location for filming of US, French, Israeli, Danish, Serbian and other versions of *Survivor*, but the peninsula has become ever more accessible with the paving of the road (it's still better to get here by boat). It's off the tourist radar but on weekends Filipinos come from the cities for island-hopping adventures, so don't expect to have it all to yourself.

Activities

Floating between the jungle-tufted limestone crags and golden strips of sand that make up the island archipelago off its north coast is one of Caramoan's biggest attractions. Any guesthouse or resort can arrange a full day of island-hopping with swimming and snorkelling from P1500 to P2000, depending on how many islands you visit; or haggle with the fishers in Bikal or Paniman Beach and commandeer a bangka for a similar price.

Highlights include pretty little Matukad with a hidden lagoon, accessible only by swimming under some rocks; Lahos, popular with Survivor crews; plus postcard-perfect Aguirangan. The V-shaped Sabitan Laya offers long stretches of white sand and a limestone outcrop at the base of the V – there's good snorkelling here. Tinago has a secluded cove that's perfect for sunbathing, while Pitogo is another Survivor location. The largest of the dozen or so islands, and one of the closest to Paniman, is Lahuy, with beaches, local gold panners and a fruit-bat colony. Tabgon is set among onshore mangroves and, with a 500-step climb up to an enormous statue of Mary of Peace, it's a popular place of pilgrimage for Filipinos.

Caramoan Kayaks
KAYAKING

(☑ 0947 524 5858; www.cki-inn.com; Guijalo; 1hr/day P150/1900) The owners of CK Inn offer sea kayaks for hire and can guide paddlers around the islands, or else provide camping equipment if you fancy staging a mini-*Survivor* scenario on an uninhabited island all by yourself.

Sleeping

Caramoan town, about 7km from Paniman Beach, has a number of hotels but a better option is to head to the coast at Paniman or one of the secluded beach resorts. If you're intent on living out your *Castaway* fantasy

by staying on an uninhabited island, you can rent tents from CK Inn, near Guijalo, and Residencia de Salvacion.

Residencia de Salvacion
B&B $

(☑ 0939 310 1135; http://residenciadesalvacion.weebly.com; Paniman Beach; r incl breakfast P1000-1500; ❋ 🛜) At the southern end of Paniman Beach, near the mouth of the Manapo River, Residencia de Salvacion is excellent value with a handful of tidy cabins and rooms. Home-cooked meals and island-hopping trips available (from P1500).

Casita Mia Bed & Breakfast
B&B $$

(☑ 0917 819 5150; www.casitamia.com.ph; Guilajo Rd, Caramoan town; d with/without full board P3500/2700; ❋ 🛜) This local take on a Spanish-style hacienda, hiding in a quiet area south of the town proper, is the most impressive option in Caramoan town, with immaculate, stylish rooms and a leafy garden. It offers all-inclusive bed, board and boat packages that introduce you to the uninhabited islands.

Breeze & Waves
GUESTHOUSE $$

(☑ 0918 913 9623; myrna.rodriguez@yahoo.com.ph; Paniman Beach; d/tr P1500/1700) The best of the midrange guesthouses on Paniman Beach, Breeze & Waves has eight spacious rooms with shared verandah or balcony over two floors, as well as a breezy restaurant. The owners have a small flotilla of bangkas for island-hopping trips.

Gota Village Resort
RESORT $$

(☑ 0920 967 2942; http://caramoanislands.com; Gota Beach; 2-person cabins P2500-3000; ❋ 🛜) Gota Village is the sprawling seafront resort at Gota Beach, about 5km from Caramoan town (P120 and 20 minutes by tricycle). These 50 wooden chalet-style cabins are not fancy for the price and tend to be booked solid by *Survivor* crews in summer, but the location is superb and they offer a huge variety of activities.

CK Inn
B&B $$

(☑ 0947 524 5858; http://ck-inn.one; Guijalo; d/tr/f from P1400/1700/3800; ❋ 🛜) Although removed from the peninsula's northern coast, sea-facing CK is handily located just south of Guijalo port (ask for Harvey at the port) and the helpful owners specialise in peninsula tours and kayaking. The family-run guesthouse has clean rooms, free breakfast and a wonderfully secluded location. The family room can accommodate eight people.

BICOLANO CUISINE

Filipino food is roundly vilified as the bland, poor cousin of internationally renowned Asian cuisines such as Thai and Vietnamese. Bicol, with its smorgasbord of fiery dishes, is the country's answer to that criticism.

Coconut is a key Bicolano ingredient. Anything cooked in coconut milk is known as *ginataán*. *Pusít* (squid) cooked in coconut milk is thus *ginataán pusít* (and it's highly recommended). *Ginataán santol* (a pulpy fruit) and *ginataán* jackfruit are also tasty. The other key ingredient in Bicol cuisine is *sili* (hot chilli pepper). There are many varieties of *sili*, among them the tiny but potent *labuyo*, which you can order in bars mixed with tender, almond-shaped pili nuts.

Two of the most popular savoury delights are Bicol *exprés* and *pinangat*. The former is a spicy mishmash of ground pork, *sili*, baby shrimp, onion, garlic and other spices cooked in coconut milk, typically served with rice. *Pinangat* is green *gabi* (taro) leaves wrapped around small pieces of fish, shrimp and/or pork, and a chopped, leafy green vegetable known as *natong (laing)*, which is also commonly served on its own as a side dish. Lastly, there's the surprisingly palatable *candingga* – diced pork liver and carrots sweetened and cooked in vinegar.

The ubiquitous pili nut – an alleged aphrodisiac – has a strong presence in the dessert department, popping up in biscuits, pastries, marzipan, pies and ice cream.

Caramoan Garden
RESORT $$
(☎0919 882 1879; www.caramoangarden.com; Bikal; r from P2000; 😨🤍😨) Near the Bikal boat landing about 5km from Caramoan town, this appealing resort has spacious rooms (which can accommodate four people), a swish pool and the usual package of activities.

Las Casa Roa Hostel
GUESTHOUSE $$
(☎0917 937 2227; Alvarez Rd, Caramoan town; d/f P1550/1850; 😨🤍) In an ancestral family home, this is a guesthouse rather than a hostel, with 13 neat and comfy rooms, two dining rooms and inviting common areas with rattan furniture. It's at the end of a small street just off the main road through Caramoan town.

★Hunangan Cove
RESORT $$$
(☎0920 967 2942; http://caramoanislands.com; Hunangan Cove; d P5000-7500, ste P10,000; 😨🤍) Fronting a private strip of beach around the corner from Gota Beach, this cluster of seven luxurious thatched-roof cottages is the standout resort in this part of Caramoan. Each one is tastefully decorated and equipped with a TV and DVD player, while the suite has two bedrooms, a kitchen and a dining room. If you're not staying here you can admire it from your island-hopping bangka.

✖ Eating & Drinking

Caramoan town has a couple of cafes and there are several basic restaurants at Paniman. Otherwise you can eat at your guesthouse.

Bay Sand Food Stop
FILIPINO $$
(Paniman Beach; mains P150-275; ⊙7am-10pm; 🤍) At the entrance to the beach, you can relax on solid wooden furniture (as opposed to plastic chairs) under a thatched roof at this breezy restaurant serving breakfast, seafood, Filipino and local dishes such as Bicol *exprés*.

Barako Coffee Shop
COFFEE
(National Rd, Caramoan town; drinks P15-54; ⊙11am-8pm) Fresh-ground Filipino coffee, flavoured coffees and icy frappés are the speciality at this open-fronted main-street stall.

ℹ Information

There's one international ATM in Caramoan town. The **tourist office** (☎0930 811 8406; caramoan.tourism@gmail.com; ⊙8am-5pm Mon-Fri) is upstairs in the Municipal Hall compound on the main street in Caramoan town. Harvey from CK Inn operates a small tourist desk at Guijalo port from 8am to 4pm.

ℹ Getting There & Away

Although you can reach Caramoan by road, a quicker option is the boat from Sabang port.

BOAT
Coming from Naga, take an air-con minivan to Sabang (P120, two hours). From Sabang, 'Harry' boats (large bangkas) leave at 7am, 8am, 9am and 11am for Guijalo port (P120, two hours).

One Harry boat sails daily between Guijalo and Cabcab on Catanduanes (P100, 1½ hours), departing Guijalo at 11am and Cabcab at 9am.

On arrival to Guijalo, you have to register and pay a P30 environmental fee. From Guijalo port, it's a 15-minute tricycle ride to Caramoan town (P150) and 30 minutes to Paniman (P300).

If you miss the scheduled ferry between Guijalo and Catanduanes, you can hire a bangka at Condon (Catanduanes) to ferry you across the 'typhoon highway' (from P1500 per bangka, 1½ hours). This is not to be attempted during rough seas, as the journey can be very dangerous.

BUS

The road between Sabang and Caramoan (90km) is paved but narrow, winding and slow going. Raymond bus runs at least six daily services to and from Naga (P220, 5½ hours) and, if you're a real masochist, two buses go all the way to Manila (P875, 15 hours, two daily). From Caramoan, the bus departs at 7am from next to the market and passes along the main street.

From Legazpi or Tabaco, take a jeepney to Tigaon, switch to another jeepney to Sabang and then either catch the last boat to Guijalo or connect with the Raymond bus.

Tabaco

☑ 052 / POP 133,900

In the northern shadow of Mt Mayon and with equally good volcano views, for travellers Tabaco is mainly a departure point for ferries to Catanduanes. However, it lacks the urban charms and modern outlook of Legazpi. The central city is noisy and traffic clogged, but the pier is only a few blocks to the east.

🛏 Sleeping & Eating

JJ Midcity Inn   HOTEL $

(☑ 052-742 5136; www.jjmidcityinn.com; Herrera St; s/d/tr P850/1000/2800; ❄ 🤖) Supercentral on a noisy street, JJ Midcity makes for a perfectly comfortable stay, and reduced 12-hour rates make it even more affordable if you're just waiting for a ferry. Cheaper rooms are snug and most are windowless, but they're very clean with bright splashes of colour. The top floor cafe (breakfast included with full room rates) and bar is good, with city views, cocktails and occasional karaoke.

Gardenia Hotel   HOTEL $$

(☑ 052-487 8019; www.tabacogardeniahotel.com; Riosa St; d incl breakfast P900-1400; ❄ 🤖) One of Tabaco's neat and serviceable lower midrange options, Gardenia has large, clean doubles, volcano views and a relatively quiet location behind the market. Windowless rooms are quieter than the streetside ones. The in-house Japanese **restaurant** (mains P150-400; ⏰ 11am-2pm & 5-11pm) makes a change from Filipino food and the pier is only three blocks away.

Hotel Fina   HOTEL $$

(☑ 052-487 8885; www.hotelfina.com; AA Berces St; s/d/tr incl breakfast P1700/2500/3500; ❄ 🤖 🍴) Tabaco's best hotel boasts a rooftop infinity pool with super views of Mt Mayon, and top-end features such as in-room safes and minibars. Rooms are contemporary with supremely comfortable beds, and there's a good restaurant and bar.

Vista Garden   FILIPINO $$

(☑ 0917 303 7515; Morayta St; mains P140-300; 🤖) This open-air restobar is a great little oasis for a casual meal in the heart of busy Tabaco. Filipino and Bicolano cuisine and cold beer.

❶ Getting There & Away

BOAT

Daily ferries run from Tabaco Pier to Virac (air-con/ordinary P300/230, four hours) at 6.30am and to San Andres (P250/200, three hours) at 7am and 1pm. Although the San Andres ferry is faster, if you're heading to Virac the travel time works out the same.

BUS

Cagsawa, Philtranco and Raymond Tours run buses to and from Cubao, Manila (air-con/deluxe from P850/1100, 12 hours) from the Tabaco City Terminal on Ziga St. Frequent minivans (P50, 40 minutes) and jeepneys (P36) go to and from Legazpi, while minivans to Naga (P180, three hours) leave from beside the city hall on Rizal St.

Legazpi

☑ 052 / POP 196,560

Legazpi is the capital of Albay Province but its real claim to fame is its location at the foot of active Mt Mayon (2462m), justifiably dubbed the world's most perfect volcano. It's a relaxed enough place; the main city streets are clogged with traffic and shopping malls, but step even a few blocks away and you find yourself observing quiet houses drowning in greenery, pecking chickens and tricycle drivers napping in the shade.

Legazpi is divided into Albay District and Legazpi City. Albay is a better place to stay, while the city has the appealing seafront area. Mayon is visible from many places in the city; for the best views head up to Lignon Hill or to Daraga and Cagsawa.

⊙ Sights & Activities

Legazpi is a good base for exploring the nearby adventureland of Bicol. Most hotels can set you up with vans and drivers; the going rate for day tours within Albay Province is around P3000 to P3500, but inexpensive day tours of Legazpi proper are available through Bicol Adventure ATV (p179).

Lignon Hill Nature Park   HILL
(☑ 0922 883 6722; P25; ⊙ 5am-10pm) For one of the best panoramic views of brooding Mt Mayon and the city, head up Lignon Hill. It's a steep, but paved, 20-minute walk up the hill; tricycles generally won't do it. At the top you'll find a park, a cafe, an observation deck and a bunch of activities including ziplining (P250), a hanging bridge (P300) and minigolf.

Sleeping Lion Hill   HILL
(Legazpi Blvd) The view that holds everyone's attention in Legazpi is of Mt Mayon, but there's another beautiful panorama many visitors miss: the pretty port of Legazpi itself. Legazpi Blvd, behind Embarcadero, leads directly to Sleeping Lion Hill, located near the waterfront. Its rump-ish rise does bear a vague resemblance to a snoozing cat. The 30-minute ascent goes up a rough path and culminates in a great view of the waterfront and nearby islands.

Embarcadero   PIER
(☑ 052-480 4333; Legazpi Blvd; ⊙ 10am-8pm Mon-Thu, to 9pm Fri-Sun) Legazpi's ambitious waterfront mall and entertainment complex is already looking a bit tired, with empty shops and a forlorn feel. The location is fabulous though, with a palm-tree-lined seafront walk, a Skywalk for Mt Mayon views and valiant attempts at being an adventure centre with a bungee trampoline, a zipline and a go-karting track. Embarcadero is connected to the LCC Mall in the city centre by free electric jeepneys.

**Mayon Naturalist
Eco-Guides of Albay**   HIKING
(Manega; ☑ 0915 422 4508; pinangat2001@yahoo.com) This local NGO consists of a group of highly experienced outdoor enthusiasts and guides who can help organise guided trips throughout the Bicol region, including Mt Mayon climbs.

Your Brother Travel & Tours   ADVENTURE SPORTS
(☑ 052-742 9871; www.mayonatvtour.com; Pawa Rd; ATV tours P599-4000) This longstanding outfit runs ATV tours behind Lignon Hill along lava trails towards Mt Mayon. This is the best option for ATV adventures if you don't want to go out to Cagsawa. It also offers a variety of adventure tours around Legazpi.

✪ Festivals & Events

Magayon Festival   FIESTA
(⊙ May) This month-long festival centres on Albay, with nightly street markets and pop-up bars and music stages around Peñaranda Park. There's a show, such as a chilli-eating contest or dance performance, on the main stage most nights.

🛏 Sleeping

★ **Mayon Backpackers Hostel**   HOSTEL $
(☑ 052-742 2613; http://mayonbackpackers.wordpress.com; Diego Silang St; dm with fan/air-con P350/450, d/q P1200/1400; ❋@ ☎) The only legitimate hostel in Legazpi is the clear top budget choice, with cramped but comfy four-, six- and eight-bed dorm rooms with en suite and lockers, and a few sought-after private rooms in a separate building. There's a basic common kitchen and free breakfast is served in the upstairs dining room. Good views of Mt Mayon from the tiny rooftop area.

Legazpi Tourist Inn   INN $
(☑ 052-480 6147; legazpitouristinn@yahoo.com.ph; V&O Bldg, Quezon Ave; s/d with fan P600/700, with air-con P1200/1400; ❋ ☎) The 3rd-floor Tourist Inn is the best of the budget places in Legazpi City, with cramped but clean rooms with private bathrooms, TVs and lots of mirrors. The attached Veranda Cafe (7am to 7pm) makes up for a lack of common areas.

★ **Balai Tinay
Guesthouse**   B&B $$
(☑ 052-742 3366, 0917 841 3051; http://balaitinay.weebly.com; 70 Gapo St; d/tr/f incl breakfast P1500/2000/3000; ❋ ☎) This welcome family-run oasis of peace sits on a quiet little street in Albay and is easily the best midrange guesthouse around. The eight compact en suite rooms are spotless and the tranquil common areas are great for meeting other guests. Naturally there's a balcony for Mayon viewing. Head right along the riverside path from Albay Central School.

Apple Peach House   BOUTIQUE HOTEL $$
(☑ 052-481 1725, 0906 591 8210; cnr Marquez & Rosario Sts; r incl breakfast P2500-3500, ste P3800; ❋ ☎) Apple Peach is designed in that contemporary minimalist whitewashed style that you'll either love or hate. Still, the

Legazpi

Lignon Hill Nature Park (4.5km)

Legazpi (2km; see main map)

Albay District (2km; see inset)

SOUTHEAST LUZON LEGAZPI

Legazpi

◎ Sights
1 Embarcadero	D4
2 Sleeping Lion Hill	D4

◎ Sleeping
3 Apple Peach House	A3
4 Balai Tinay Guesthouse	B2
5 Hotel St Ellis	C3
6 Hotel Villa Angelina	A3
7 Legazpi Tourist Inn	C3
8 Mayon Backpackers Hostel	A3
9 Tyche Boutique Hotel	C3

◎ Eating
1st Colonial Grill	(see 14)
10 Sibid-Sibid	C1
11 Smalltalk Cafe	B2
12 Waway Restaurant	B1

◎ Drinking & Nightlife
13 La Mia Tazzza Coffee	B2

◎ Shopping
14 Pacific Mall	B4

◎ Information
15 Provincial Tourism Office	B2

◎ Transport
Cagsawa	(see 16)
Isarog	(see 16)
16 Legazpi Grand Central Terminal	A4
Peñafrancia	(see 16)
Philtranco	(see 16)

austere charcoal-and-white rooms on three floors are ruthlessly clean, with comfortable beds and powerful showers – go for one at the front for Mayon views. On the ground floor is a chic Chicos Cafe (6am to 9.30pm) with chess-board tables and a stylish bar.

Hotel

Villa Angelina
HOTEL **$$**

(☑052-736 0515; hotelvillaangelina@gmail.com; 32 Diego Silang St; d/ste/f P1800/2500/3000; ❄🛜) Villa Angelina is an ancestral home in a central but quiet location a couple of blocks south of Albay's main street. Second-floor rooms are reached via a sweeping staircase – ask for one of the north-facing rooms opening onto a shared balcony with views of Mt Mayon. Friendly staff but no restaurant.

Tyche Boutique Hotel
HOTEL **$$**

(☑052-480 5555, 0917-559 0566; www.tyche boutiquehotel.com; cnr Rizal & Governor Forbes Sts; r/ste inc breakfast from P2700/3000; ❄🛜) The 'boutique' tag may be stretching things but this central, modern hotel has clean and compact rooms decked out in classic creams and browns, and the staff are helpful. The attached restaurant serves a good mix of Filipino and Chinese dishes with seafood a speciality. 'Tyche' is pronounced 'tay-keh'.

Hotel St Ellis
HOTEL **$$$**

(☑052-480 8088; www.hotelstellis.com; Rizal St; d/ste incl breakfast from P4750/6650; ❄🛜🏊) Legazpi's smartest central city hotel has 40 spacious rooms with slightly stuffy '70s decor in browns and whites but a high degree of comfort. There's a good restaurant, an indoor pool on the 2nd floor, a day spa and professional staff. It's in a relatively quiet street just off the main drag.

✖ Eating & Drinking

Legazpi has some of the best Bicolano food in the region, with a crop of good restaurants and cafes in Albay and in the city.

The best place for a sunset or evening drink is the collection of ramshackle restaurants and bars lining the seafront south of the city centre along Legazpi Blvd. The best strip faces pungent black-sand Puro Beach.

Most restaurants also serve alcohol and there are numerous videoke joints in the city centre.

★ Smalltalk Cafe
BICOLANO **$$**

(Doña Aurora St; mains P120-290; ⊙11.30am-10pm; ❄🛜✏) This quaint little Albay eatery defines the notion of Bicol-fusion cooking and draws in travellers and locals like a tractor beam. The menu covers 'small talk', 'big talk' and, of course, 'sweet talk'. Consider the Bicol *exprés* pasta, Mayon stuffed pizza or paella Valencia. Save room for the pili-nut pie or the apocalyptic Red Hot Lava: with *sili* ice cream.

Kim's Bowl
FILIPINO **$$**

(☑052-480 2882; F Imperial St; P185-355; ⊙9am-9.30pm; 🛜) Open-air Kim's is a classic Filipino garden restaurant where big plates of crispy *pata* are shared among friends, along with *bulalo* (a rich beef and marrow stew), Bicol *exprés* (a fiery pork dish), *kare-kare* (meat cooked in peanut sauce) and *lechón kawali* (deep-fried pork belly). Seafood and chicken dishes are also a hit. Beer available.

1st Colonial Grill
BICOLANO **$$**

(Pacific Mall; mains P150-360; ⊙10am-9pm Mon-Thu, 9am-9pm Fri-Sun; 🛜) This chain grill place has found a new home in the Pacific Mall (and other mall locations around town). It feels a little impersonal but still serves up good Bicolano dishes such as *tinapa* rice (rice with smoked fish flakes and green mango) and five-spiced chicken, and is famous for its unusual ice-cream flavours, such as *sili* (chili) and pili nut.

Sibid-Sibid
SEAFOOD **$$**

(☑052-480 3030; 328 Peñaranda St; mains P70-415; ⊙10am-9pm; 🛜) A wonderful open-air bamboo-and-thatch restaurant 1km north of Legazpi City, Sibid-Sibid specialises in highly original, Bicol-inspired seafood concoctions like fish Bicol *exprés* and a superb *pinangat* (meat with taro leaves and coconut milk).

La Mia
Tazza Coffee
COFFEE

(☑052-820 1808; 733 Rizal Ave; ⊙9am-midnight Sun-Thu, 8am-1am Fri & Sat; 🛜) Legazpi's best coffee shop is a relaxed place for a cappuccino, a frappé and other assorted caffeine needs.

🛍 Shopping

Pacific Mall
MALL

(☑052-480 6027; Landco St; ⊙10am-9pm Mon-Thu, 9am-9pm Fri-Sun) In a city of malls, Pacific Mall is the biggest and busiest. Along with retail shops there's a good range of restaurants, a food court and a cinema.

ℹ Information

Legazpi's unofficial tourism website, Wow! Legazpi (http://wowlegazpi.com), is a good portal.

Adjacent to the Astrodome Complex in Albay, the **Provincial Tourism Office** (☑ 052-481 0250; www.albay.gov.ph; Aquende Dr; ⊗ 8am-5pm Mon-Fri) offers local information and a free city map.

❶ Getting There & Away

AIR

Cebu Pacific and PAL each fly at least once daily to/from Manila (1¼ hours). The airport is just 3km west of the city centre and 2km north of Albay (P50 by tricycle to either).

BUS

From the **Legazpi Grand Central Terminal** (Terminal Rd; ⊗ 24hr), overnight air-con and deluxe services to Manila (around P800 to P1100, 12 to 15 hours) depart between 6.30pm and 8.30pm. 'Ordinary' (non air-con) buses depart throughout the day, both to Manila (P500) and to local destinations such as Sorsogon and Tabaco.

Cagsawa (☑ 052-235 0381) runs comfortable night buses to Ermita and Cubao in Manila. **Isarog** (☑ 0908 851 2651; https://bicolisarog.com) and **Peñafrancia** (☑ 052-435 3012) head to Cubao, while **Philtranco** (☑ 052-742 0331; www.philtranco.net) serves Pasay.

Across the street from the bus terminal, there are frequent minivans during daylight hours to and from the following destinations:

Donsol P75, 1¼ hours, until 5pm

Naga P140, 2½ hours

Pilar P70, one hour

Sorsogon P100, 1½ to two hours

Tabaco P40, 40 minutes

❶ Getting Around

Hundreds of jeepneys ply the route between Legazpi City and Albay District, continuing on to Daraga. The main jeepney terminal is next to the bus stand.

Tricycles around town cost P20 to P50. You can hire mountain bikes (P300 per day) and mopeds (P650) from Bicol Adventure ATV.

Around Legazpi

Daraga & Around

☑ 052 / POP 126,600

Daraga, a bustling market town and transport hub 12km southwest of Legazpi, is renowned for the baroque-style Daraga Church and the nearby Cagsawa ruins. Both, along with a couple of hours quad biking, make it well worth a day trip from Legazpi.

◉ Sights & Activities

Daraga Church   CHURCH
(Santa Maria St; ⊗ 5am-6pm) Set on a hill splendidly overlooking Mt Mayon is the baroque-style Nuestra Senora de la Porteria church in Daraga, constructed from volcanic rock in 1773 and with detailed sculpted reliefs on the columns. Surviving residents of Cagsawa moved to this parish after their church was buried in the 1814 Mayon eruption.

Cagsawa
Church & Ruins   CHURCH
(adult/child P20/10; ⊗ 6am-7.30pm) A couple of kilometres northwest of Daraga is the most classic of Bicol's panoramas: the stand-alone greenery-topped belfry of the sunken Cagsawa Church against the backdrop of Mt Mayon. Twelve hundred people took refuge here from divine wrath in the form of 1814's violent eruption and were entombed alive, suggesting that the Creator is matchless in irony. Come early to avoid day trippers.

Hoyop-Hoyopan Cave   CAVE
(admission incl guide & lantern P300; ⊗ 6.30am-6pm) Pottery dating from 200 BCE to CE 900 has been found in this easily accessed limestone cave, set on a quiet hillside above a pretty rural valley. Guides are available at the entrance; tips are expected.

Calabidongan Cave   CAVE
Located around 3km from Hoyop-Hoyopan Cave, the more challenging Calabidongan Cave (literally, Cave of the Bats) is for more adventurous, confident spelunkers as its partially flooded interior requires you to swim a short distance within the cave. It can only be accessed when water levels allow (typically from March to June). Guides (P500) at Hoyop-Hoyopan can arrange transport; exploration of Calabidongan's subterranean depths takes a couple of hours.

Bicol Adventure ATV   ADVENTURE
(☑ 0919 228 7064, 0917 571 4357; www.bicoladventureatv.com; Cagsawa; Cagsawa Trail P399, Lava Trail from P950; ⊗ 5am-5pm) There are numerous ATV (quad bike) outfits lining the entry road to Cagsawa Church, but Bicol Adventure is one of the original and best with rides in the foothills of Mt Mayon on ATVs ranging from 150cc to powerful 500cc and Terracross vehicles. You'll ride through rivers and across plains and mountainous terrain.

MT MAYON

The perfect cone of Mt Mayon (2462m) rises dramatically from the flat Albay terrain, and can be seen from as far away as Naga and Catanduanes. The volcano's name derives from the Bicol *daragan magayon* (beautiful single lady), and the Philippines' most active volcano is a cantankerous beauty at that, responsible for over 40 deadly eruptions since 1616. The most recent eruption was in 2018 when more than 50,000 people were evacuated from a 7km exclusion zone around the mountain.

While thankfully the 2018 eruption did not claim any lives, the last victims of Mt Mayon were four German hikers and a local guide, killed by a minor belch of ash and rock during their ascent of the peak in 2013. In 2006, after lava flows subsided, a biblically proportioned Typhoon Durian triggered mudslides on Mt Mayon that killed more than 1000 people, while in 1993, 77 people were killed by eruptions. The deadliest eruption to date took place in 1814, destroying the Cagsawa Church and killing over 1200 people.

Due to the risk of volcanic activity, the summit of Mt Mayon is off limits to climbers. Before the 2018 eruption it was possible to trek to Camp 2 (1400m) and beyond to 'Rabbit's Ear' at around 1750m; check before travelling for updated conditions. Climbers pass through varied terrain: boulder-strewn desert, grassy plain and forest. You must take all gear (tents, warm clothes) and food with you; there are water sources along the way, but purification tablets are a must.

There are three routes up the volcano: one from Legazpi's Buyunan barangay, one via Santo Domingo's Centennial Forest, while the most popular route runs from Bonga in San Roque barangay. The best (and driest) time to hike is usally between March and September. A guide for a Mayon hiking package costs from P6000 for a two-day climb and P4500 for a one-day climb. This fee covers all food, transport, gear and porters: Bicol Adventure ATV and Your Brother Travel & Tours (p175) can arrange guides, equipment and transport.

Mt Mayon is carefully monitored by the Philippine Institute of Volcanology and Seismology (PhiVolcs; www.phivolcs.dost.gov.ph). It strongly recommends you don't climb beyond 1800m. Go much higher and you'll be overwhelmed by the sulphurous gases.

❶ Getting There & Away

From Legazpi take any Daraga–bound jeepney (P9) along Rizal Ave. Jeepneys heading to Camalig, Guinobatan or Ligao can drop you at the Cagsawa ruins; a tricycle from Daraga costs P50.

Sorsogon

☏ 056 / POP 168,100

The eponymous capital of Bicol's southernmost province lies in a beautiful area of off-track beaches, natural springs and rice fields that sprawl beneath jungle-clad volcanoes. Sorsogon city itself is not particularly beautiful or appealing, but it's a good base for trekking on the province's highest volcano, Mt Bulusan, and it provides transport links to the rest of the province. The liveliest time to be in Sorsogon is during the mid-October Kasanggayahan festival, which celebrates the history of the city through beauty pageants, parades, music and bangka races.

Of the numerous beaches within striking distance of Sorsogon city, the most popular is Rizal Beach, 24km southeast.

🛏 Sleeping & Eating

Villa Kasanggayahan GUESTHOUSE $
(☏056-211 1275; Rizal St; r P1000-1600; ❄ 🛜) The lovely garden, green walls, breezy balconies and outdoor sitting areas make this quiet place a good budget choice. Rooms are spacious but in need of a bit of redecorating – the more expensive rooms sleep up to six people. The guesthouse hides behind a tall gate just off the main street.

★ Fernandos Hotel HOTEL $$
(☏056-255 0833; www.fernandoshotel.com; N Pareja St; d/tr without bathroom P1100/1350, d/tr/q with bathroom from P1600/1800/2000; ❄🛜❄) Fernandos is the best hotel in town, not least because the friendly owners Cecilia and Angie Duran are a great source of information and provincial tours. The cheaper rooms are small with common

bathroom, but above that rooms are spacious and tastefully decorated, with some fronting the brand-new pool. Next to the lobby, the lounge has an occasional resident pianist.

Fernando 168 Bistro BICOLANO $$
(☑ 056-421 5212; N Pareja St; mains P120-200; ☺8am-10pm Mon-Sat; ☎) This restaurant next door to Fernandos Hotel (p179) serves excellent Bicolano dishes and grilled seafood.

ⓘ Information

For tours of the area, camping-gear hire, guides for climbing Mt Bulusan, arranging private transport and general info, the owners of **Fernandos Hotel** (p179) are your go-to people.

ⓘ Getting There & Away

The jeepney terminal is next to the massive St Peter & Paul Cathedral that resembles the Capitol Building, while buses leave from the stands next to the City Hall. Jeepneys run to most Sorsogon Province destinations, including Bulan, Barcelona, Bulusan and Matnog. For Donsol, you have to take a jeepney to Putiao (P40, 45 minutes) and get on another jeepney to Donsol (P40, one hour).

Regular buses/minivans to Legazpi (P60/80, 1½ to two hours) leave from a separate stand two blocks west. The main bus terminal is about 1km east of the centre. Inconveniently timed buses depart to Manila from here – it's easier to get to Legazpi and take a bus from there.

Bulusan Volcano National Park & Around

South of Sorsogon is **Bulusan Volcano National Park** (P30; ☺7am-5.30pm). Just inside the park, Bulusan Lake is a popular picnic spot, and there's a 1.8km walking trail around the crater lake. You can hire kayaks (P100 per person). When the mist is lying low over the forest and the birds are singing, it's a lovely, peaceful spot and the clear, still water makes for an inviting swim. Climbers must go with a guide; contact **Bulusan Volcano Mountaineering** (☑0939 377 3502; wildboarsphil@yahoo.com; Bulusan Lake Rd), or Fernandos Hotel (p179) in Sorsogon.

A successful conquest of Mt Bulusan deserves a soak in the Palogtoc Falls, accessible by a 500m walk from a trailhead off the main road between the park entrance and San Roque (it's also on the Bulusan–Irosin jeepney route). It features a gorgeous cold-water pool fed by falls beside a shady river,

with just a few low-key bamboo and nipa huts. Nearby, the soda-water **Masacrot Springs** (P35) offer the same sort of pool, but with concrete huts and videoke.

ⓘ Getting There & Away

The entrance to the park is near San Roque, about 10km west of Bulusan town. A day trip to the lake is feasible if you don't want to take an organised tour; take one of the infrequent jeepneys from Sorsogon to Bulusan (P50, 1½ hours). In Bulusan, look for the Bulusan–Irosin jeepney; this will drop you at the park-entrance track 6km from town, and you can walk the 2km in from here. Alternatively, hire a tricycle from Bulusan directly to the lake (about P300, including waiting time).

Donsol

☑056 / POP 47,560
Until the 'discovery' of whale sharks off the coast here in 1998, Donsol, about 45km southwest of Legazpi, was a sleepy village in one of Sorsogon's more remote areas. In 1998 a local diver shot a video of the whale sharks and a newspaper carried a story about Donsol's gentle *butanding*. Since then Donsol has become one of the Philippines' most popular tourist locations, though the permanence of its shark population is now in question.

🏃 Activities

Whale-Shark Spotting
Swimming with these huge, blue-grey, silver-spotted creatures is a truly exhilarating experience. You do need to use fins and be a decent snorkeller to keep up with them!

Whale sharks migrate here between November and June, with the peak months generally being March and April (avoid busy Easter week), but in the last several years sighting haven't always been consistent. Whale-shark spotting is also subject to the vagaries of weather – if the sea is rough or a typhoon is on the way, the boats will not go out. Be sure to check the weather conditions to avoid disappointment.

When you get to Donsol, head to the Butanding Visitors Center (p182), along the coast road about 1.5km north of the river bridge (P40 by tricycle from town).

There are three spotting sessions daily at 7.30am, 11am and 2pm, depending on visitor numbers. The first trip is the most popular so it pays to register the day before to maximise your chances of getting on a boat. Registration fee is P300, and the boat costs P3500 for six people for a three-hour tour. The centre may close earlier (in the day or the season) if the weather is bad or if there are no visitors.

Only snorkelling equipment is allowed; scuba diving is prohibited. Snorkelling equipment is available for hire (P300 per session) at the visitor centre complex. Each boat has a spotter and a Butanding Interaction Officer (BIO) on board – tip them a couple of hundred pesos, especially if you've had a good day. Before setting off, you watch a video briefing on how to behave around the sharks: namely, no touching, and avoid their powerful tails.

When a shark is spotted, your BIO will direct you into the water: be prepared, as the experience can be fleeting if the whale shark is on the move. The experience is quite regimented – it has to be for the well-being of the animals, given the number of visitors and the need to rotate boat crews – and access to the whale sharks is limited to a maximum of 30 boats per day.

Diving

Donsol is a good base for exploring the Manta Bowl off Ticao Island and other macro dive sites closer to shore. There are a couple of dive outfits and some resorts have their own dive centres with a floating population of experienced freelance dive masters.

Bicol Dive Center   DIVING

(☑ 0921 929 3811, 0906 801 6852; www.bicol divecenter.com; 3-dive trips from P4500) Long-standing diving operator offering PADI certification course (P19,000), five-day, four-night Ticao adventures (P26,600), and the standard three-dive day trip to San Miguel and the Manta Bowl (from P4500).

Other Activities

The beach is merely a thin strand of grey sand but there are some good swimming areas in front of the resorts. Nonguests can use the pool at Vitton resort (p182) for P200 (free if you spend P300 in the restaurant).

A popular evening experience is to spend a couple of hours on the Ogod River after dusk, watching the myriad tiny, gently floating lights of the fireflies. Boat trips cost P1250 for a maximum of five people, and leave from Ogod. A tricycle from Donsol costs P200 including waiting time.

🛏 Sleeping & Eating

Budget lodgings and homestays can be found in Donsol town proper, but a better option is one of the resorts or budget guesthouses stretching out along several kilometres of coastal road, starting beyond the bridge just west of Donsol. During the off-season, from June to mid-November, most of the accommodation closes down.

Victoria's Guest House   B&B $

(☑ 0936 153 6990; www.victorias-guesthouse-donsol.com; Purok 1; d with shared bath P600, cottages P1000; ☎) The four bamboo and thatch cottages and two 'tree house' rooms here are a classic backpackers bolthole set in a lovely garden back from the coast road. Just north of the bridge, it's near enough town to wander there on foot, but far enough away to experience tranquillity. There's no restaurant but Julia's Bar in front serves food.

Dancalan Beach Resort   RESORT $

(☑ 0999 445 0030; dm P500, d/tr with fan P800/1200, with air-con P1500/2000; ☀☎) This excellent budget standby is right next to the visitors centre so you don't have to go far for whale-shark interaction. The fan rooms and two-bed dorms are great value, while the air-con rooms, with shiny white tiles, blond-wood bed frames and patios, are immaculate. The little beachfront sit-outs and restaurant make it an easy place to hang around.

WHALE SHARKS OF DONSOL

The mangrove forests that skirt the Donsol River are a rich source of nutrients that feed the microscopic plankton which, in turn, was bringing whale sharks to Donsol in huge numbers. Over the last decade, however, there had been a drop in whale-shark sightings around Donsol. This prompted concern from the WWF that the shark population was being affected by climate change: the rising temperature of the water and damage to the mangrove forests was impacting on the sharks' primary source of food, the plankton, and keeping them in deeper waters. Or perhaps the fact that some boat drivers and tourists were disregarding shark-interaction rules and touching the animals was distressing the sharks and driving them away. Sightings can be inconsistent, but authorities reported a rise in numbers from 2018, with sightings of between two and five sharks most days.

Giddy's Place
RESORT **$$**

(☑ 0917 848 8881; www.giddysplace.com; 54 Clemente St; d/f from P2500/3500; ☺ Nov-May; ✱ ☞ ☲) Giddy's is far and away the best guesthouse in Donsol town proper. It's a sociable place with a good bar and restaurant, cable TV, modern, clean en suite rooms, an on-site spa and a pool. Its dive centre is a one-stop shop with PADI courses and dive tours. Accept credit cards.

Vitton & Woodland Resorts
HOTEL **$$**

(☑ 0917 544 4089; Woodland dm P500, r from P1800, Vitton d/f P2300/3700; ☺ closed Jul-Oct; ✱ ☞ ☲) Twin resorts a couple of hundred metres apart north of the visitors centre. Vitton is the more upmarket, a sprawling resort with rooms in a large building and more private cottages, along with a pool and restaurant. At the older Woodland, backpackers are catered for with four-bed dorm rooms.

Aguluz Homestay
HOMESTAY **$$**

(☑ 0998 886 1779; razormarilyn@yahoo.com; San José St; r with fan/air-con from P1000/1700, deluxe r P2000; ✱ ☞) Run by the energetic Marilyn, Aguluz is the 'fancy' homestay option in Donsol, with excellent home-cooked food and small but tidy rooms. Only the two 'deluxe' rooms have private bathroom and air-con, while the other four share a bathroom and have either fan or air-con.

Elysia Beach Resort
RESORT **$$$**

(☑ 0917 547 4466; www.elysia-donsol.com; r P3150-3550; ☺ mid-Nov–Jun; ✱ ☞ ☲) At this northern end of the coast road, Elysia is Donsol's fanciest resort but it's still pretty down-to-earth and good value. There are attractively manicured garden cabanas with thatched roofs and the air-con rooms orbiting the pool are bright, spacious and come with cable TV. The open-sided restaurant and cocktail bar is as good as anything around.

BARacuda
SEAFOOD **$$**

(mains P100-400; ☺ 5pm-late) One of the few independent restaurants along the resort strip, BARacuda is a popular waterfront hang-out in season with an extensive cocktail and beer menu and fresh fish, prawns and crab from the local market on the grill.

❶ Information

There's a DBP ATM in the community college just off Rizal St in the town proper.

Butanding Visitors Center (Donsol Whaleshark Interaction Center; ☑ 0919 707 0394, 0927 483 6735; ☺ 7am-4.30pm) The Butanding Visitors Center, along the coast road about 1.5km north of the river bridge (P40 by tricycle from town), should be your first stop in Donsol – this is the only place where you can organise a whale-shark-spotting boat trip. There are three spotting sessions daily at 7.30am, 11am and 2pm, depending on visitor numbers.

❶ Getting There & Away

Jeepneys and buses stop at the terminal on Hernandez St, in the southwest corner of town.

There are direct air-con minivans to and from Legazpi (P75, one hour) that leave when full until about 2pm. Jeepneys (P60) go via Pilar and take at least twice as long. If you miss the last minivan, make your way to Pilar via jeepney, and connect with more frequent minivans and buses there.

Pilar

Pilar is a port town 7km northeast of Donsol from where daily ferries connect the mainland with Masbate and Ticao islands. It's also useful for jeepney connections between Donsol and Legazpi. Boats are met by air-con vans bound for Legazpi and Daraga. Otherwise, there's nothing to hold your attention.

❶ Getting There & Away

Minivans meet ferries at the port bound for Legazpi (P70, one hour). Jeepneys go to Donsol (P25, 30 minutes) and Legazpi (P35, one hour).

Montenegro Lines runs three daily fastcraft (P396, two to 2½ hours) from Pilar to Masbate at 8am, noon and 3.30pm, returning at 4.30am, 8am and noon. Two slower roll-on, roll-off ferries (P257, four hours) depart at 10pm and 4am, returning at 10am and noon.

Several large bangkas depart daily for Monreal or San Jacinto on Ticao Island (P140, two hours).

CATANDUANES

☑ 052 / POP 261,000

Catanduanes, aka 'Land of the Howling Winds' for its typhoons, is well off the tourist radar for most travellers but is a magnet for intrepid surfers looking to ride the famous Majestic surf break.

Few other foreign travellers make the trip here to explore the sedate fishing villages, the jagged, beautiful coastline and the caves and waterfalls of the interior. Storms roll in from July to November, when heavy rains are eagerly absorbed by lush rainforests that have been mercifully preserved due to both Catanduanes' isolation and its sparse population.

Catanduanes

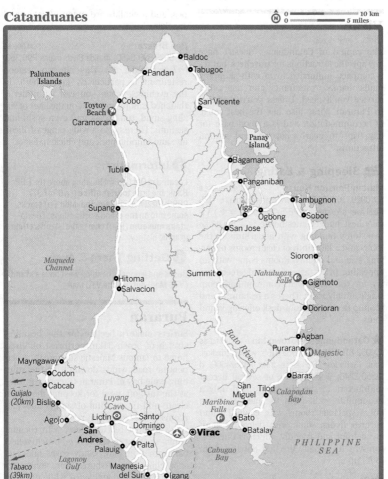

Palumbanes Islands

Baldoc
Tabugoc
Pandan
Cobo
San Vicente
Toytoy Beach
Caramoran
Panay Island
Tubli
Bagamanoc
Panganiban
Supang
Tambugnon
Viga
Ogbong
Soboc
San Jose
Maqueda Channel
Sioron
Hitoma
Summit
Nahulugan Falls
Gigmoto
Salvacion
Dorioran
Bato River
Agban
Puraran
Majestic
Mayngaway
Codon
Baras
Cabcab
San Miguel
Tilod
Calapadan Bay
Guijalo (20km)
Bislig
Luyang Cave
Maribina Falls
Agojo
Lictin
Santo Domingo
Bato
Virac
San Andres
Batalay
PHILIPPINE SEA
Palauig
Palta
Lagonoy Gulf
Magnesia del Sur
Igang
Cabugao Bay
Tabaco (39km)
Tabaco (60km)

SOUTHEAST LUZON CATANDUANES

Getting There & Away

AIR

Cebu Pacific flies Monday, Wednesday, Friday and Sunday from Manila to Virac (from P7300, 1¼ hours). The airport is 3.5km from town, P50 by tricycle.

BOAT

Regina Shipping Lines (☑ 052-811 1707; ordinary/air-con P195/260) has three ferries a day between Tabaco and San Andres, 17km west of Virac (ordinary/air-con P200/250, three hours). The boats leave Tabaco at 7am, 10am and 1pm, then make the return journey at 7am, 8am and 1pm. Virac–bound jeepneys

(P25, 45 minutes) and tricycles (P150, 25 minutes) meet the ferry in San Andres.

Another two roll-on, roll-off (RORO) ferries sail between Tabaco and Virac at 6.30am and noon.

Getting Around

From Virac's bus and jeepney terminal (p184), there are several daily departures to Pandan (P180, five hours), Bagamanoc (P120, two hours), Baras (P80, one hour), Codon (P50, one hour) and other destinations.

Ask at the tourist office or your lodgings about hiring a van (up to P5000 per day) or a motorcycle with driver.

Virac

📱 021 / POP 73,650

The capital of Catanduanes doesn't have any specific attractions for travellers, but it's a compact, unhurried town with shopping malls, banks, restaurants and any other service you'll need. Unless you're heading to Puraran, Virac also has the best range of accommodation and is a good base for day trips to nearby beaches and natural attractions.

🛏 Sleeping & Eating

Marem Pension House GUESTHOUSE $

(📱 0929 162 0000; www.marem.com.ph; 136 Rizal Ave; s/d/ste from P675/855/900; ❋ 🔊) Virac's best budget guesthouse is a mazelike two-storey building with aquariums in the lobby and a labyrinth of clean rooms of varying size and quality. Rooms come with an appealing price tag – true budgeteers can try for the fan-cooled, common-bathroom single at only P250. There's a restaurant and rooftop deck and a tour desk offering island tours.

⭐ **Catanduanes Midtown Inn** HOTEL $$

(📱 052-811 4165, 0947 563 8165; www.catmidinn.com; San José St; s/ste from P985/4500, d P1350-2240; ❋ @ 🔊) One of several decent midrangers in the city centre and only a two-minute walk from the pier, Midtown offers spacious rooms with cable TV and parquet floors, some with balconies. Staff are helpful and friendly, which is one reason why it's usually the first hotel in town to fill up.

⭐ **Blossoms** BICOLANO $

(Salvacion; mains P65-200; ⏱ 7am-10pm Mon-Sat; ❋ 🔊) Blossoms has the air of an English tearoom downstairs, with its tempting cake display, quaint furniture and cheery ambience. Upstairs is a more modern air-con dining space. The food is uniformly good – from its signature Blossom Bicol *exprés* to fish rolls, burgers, pasta, pizza, *pansit* canton (stir-fry noodles) and more.

Café de Au CAFE $

(Salvacion; coffee P50-85, mains P65-120; ⏱ 8am-10pm Mon & Sat, 9am-9pm Tue-Fri; 🔊) This friendly and relatively hip coffee shop is a place to linger; apart from free wi-fi there are board games and a guitar. It's all about the coffee, though, with locally grown and roasted beans, refreshing frappés, and a chalkboard menu of cakes and snacks.

Sea Breeze SEAFOOD $$

(📱 0929 399 8450; Imelda Blvd; mains P90-350; ⏱ 7am-midnight; 🔊) This alfresco seafood restaurant is particularly atmospheric in the evenings, when you can sit under a thatched canopy and feast on the likes of sizzling squid, tuna steak and even sushi and sashimi. There's also a wide range of Bicolano and Filipino pork and chicken dishes.

ℹ Information

Located in Old Capitol Building above the DBP Bank, the little **tourist office** (📱 0947 377 9999; Rizal Ave; ⏱ 8am-5pm Mon-Fri) stocks some info on the island's attractions. The upstairs **museum** (P50) charts the island's ethnographic history.

ℹ Getting There & Away

Buses and jeepneys heading west have a **stand** (VTC Mall) outside the VTC Mall.

Puraran

Surfers make a beeline for this beautiful stretch of beach 34km northeast of Virac, home to famous Majestic surf break. A serpentine road winds downhill to the stunning wide bay of Puraran (there's a P10 fee at the turn-off, used for keeping the beach clean) and the handful of simple huts and rooms in the beachfront resorts.

It's a super relaxed place, with coconut palms swaying in the breeze, beach volleyball games in play, sandy coves and reef snorkelling just offshore. Even nonsurfers bask in the casual ambience, while pro surfers flock to Puraran for the international surfing competition (8 to 11 October).

🏃 Activities

Surfing members of the local family are happy to give advice; hire out longboards (P200 per hour), shortboards (P150 per hour or P500 per day) and boogie boards (P50 per hour); organise surfing lessons (P350 per hour with guide); or arrange a boat to take you around the headland to the north to another good surfing and snorkelling spot.

⭐ **Majestic** SURFING

A reef break 200m offshore, powerful Majestic is no beginner's wave. Like most breaks on the country's Pacific coast, Majestic usually only works when there's a typhoon lurking offshore during the *habagat* (southwest monsoon), between July and October. The *amihan* (northeast monsoon) kicks up powerful onshore breezes from October to March, making conditions too choppy for all but the pros.

🛏 Sleeping & Eating

There are three resorts on the beach here, each run by members of the same extended family. Book ahead from July to October.

Puraran Surf Camp (📞0921 664 1933; www.puraransurf.com; dm/s/d/f 400/600/700/1800; ❄), **Majestic Puraran** (📞0929 424 3818, 0929 481 0068; www.majesticpuraran.com.ph; cottages P700, r with air-con P1000-1500; ❄) and **Pacific Surfers' Paradise** (📞0906 507 1883; pacificsurfersparadiseresort@yahoo.com.ph; cottages P800, f with air-con P1500; ❄ 🛜) offer a variety of beachfront cottages and air-con rooms, along with basic restaurants, garden hammocks and surfing equipment hire.

ℹ Getting There & Away

The quickest way to get here is to hire a van (around P1300 one way, one hour); tricycles will do the same trip for around P800 one way.

There is one daily jeepney from Virac to Gigmoto via Puraran (P50, two hours). It waits for the arrival of the roll-on, roll-off ferry in Virac and leaves around 11am. The resorts can arrange tricycle rides (P150) to Baras where it's easy to hop on a bus or jeepney (P50) to Virac, although public transport only runs in the mornings on weekends.

Around Catanduanes

Catanduanes' attractions are scattered around the island. Some of the more accessible include the popular **Maribina Falls** (P10; ⏰8am-5pm), which drain into a series of refreshing pools, 4km northeast of Virac; the vast **Luyang Cave**, near the village of Lictin, en route to San Andres; the long, pristine stretch of **Toytoy Beach** near Caramoran, its coral formations good for snorkelling; and **Nahulugan Falls**, impressive cascades of water in the jungle, inland from Gigmoto.

MASBATE

📞056 / POP 892,393

Masbate Island is the largest and most developed of the three main islands comprising Masbate Province. It's mostly devoted to ranching, which, together with a certain reputation for lawlessness, has earned the island the moniker 'the Wild East'. The main visitor draw is the raucous annual rodeo (p187) in April in Masbate Town; some travellers are also drawn by the relative lack of infrastructure, an absence of tourist hordes, inland scenery that alternates between pastureland and jungle-shrouded mountains and a smattering of offbeat attractions.

Masbate Province incorporates the satellite islands of Ticao, with its renowned diving destination of Manta Bowl (p188), and wilder, remoter Burias.

ℹ Getting There & Away

AIR

PAL and Cebu Pacific each have one flight daily between Masbate and Manila. The **airport** (📞056-333 3007; Airport Rd) is conveniently in Masbate city centre.

BOAT

Masbate Town is an important shipping port. Roll-on, roll-off (RORO) ferries sail from Masbate to Pilar and Cebu City, from Mandaon to Mindoro, Sibuyan and Caticlan, from Milagros to Iloilo City, and from Cawayan to Bogo. Check out the shipping movements board in the Port Authority office at Masbate pier for full, up-to-date weekly schedules.

Large bangkas go several times a day from Pilar to Monreal or San Jacinto on Ticao Island (P150, two hours) and between Bulan and San Jacinto.

Montenegro Lines (📞043-723 6980; fastcraft/RORO P396/257) runs three daily fastcraft (P396; two to 2½ hours) from Masbate to Pilar run at 4.30am, 8am and noon, returning from Pilar at 8am, noon and 3.30pm. Two additional slower RORO ferries (four hours) depart at 10am and noon, returning from Pilar at 10pm and 4am. Also runs daily RORO services at noon from Cataingan, Masbate, to Bogo, Cebu.

Masbate Town

📞056 / POP 95,400

A knobby peninsula surrounded by water on three sides, Masbate Town greets you with a bustling port area and a compact grid of streets clogged with yellow tricycles. There are few attractions in the town proper, but just a few minutes' tricycle ride away the chaos lessens, and busy streets give way to mangroves and beaches.

Masbate

0 ——— 50 km
0 ——— 25 miles

Sights & Activities

Buntod Sandbar
BEACH

(📞0920 433 8512) The Buntod sandbar, protruding from the sea about 7km east of town, is part of the Bugsayon marine sanctuary and accessible only by boat. You can hire a bangka (around P500 return for up to four people, including waiting time) from in front of Rendezvous Resort northeast of town, to take you to take you to the sandbar (20 to 30 minutes each way), where you can hire snorkelling gear (P100) and kayaks (P200 per hour).

Pawa Mangrove Nature Park
NATURE RESERVE

(🕐sunrise-sunset) Pawa Mangrove Nature Park consists of some 300 hectares of mangroves threaded through with a 1.3km boardwalk. It's a lovely, quiet place for a stroll, and there's a good chance you'll spot flocks of wading birds, especially at low tide. A tricycle from town will cost P100 with waiting time,

or take a jeepney to Maingaran and follow the track past the Santos Elementary School.

Sleeping

Balay Valencia
HOTEL $

(📞056-333 6530; Ibañez St; s/d/tr incl breakfast with fan P500/600/700, with air-con P700/850/1000; ❄️🛜) This well-maintained ancestral house, with lattice breezeways, has nine simple but clean en suite rooms that represent the best budget deal in town. The central location on Ibañez St is a bonus, close to night food stalls and main-street shops. Wi-fi (P50) comes and goes like a stray cat.

GV Hotel
HOTEL $

(📞056-333 6844; Danao St; d with fan/air-con 625/825, f P1650; ❄️🛜) Rooms at this anonymous hotel are a bit claustrophobic and basic but it's a short walk from the port – convenient if you're making an early getaway. More expensive rooms have cable TV and hot water. Surprisingly quiet given the location.

MASBATE'S RODEOS

Masbate's wild west reputation is helped along by two of its biggest annual events – Filipino takes on the rodeo. In the second week of April Masbate hosts a four-day rodeo, which seeks to celebrate its cattle and ranching industry with cowboys and cowgirls coming from all over the island. The event includes bull-riding contests and steer-dogging. Note that animal welfare groups say the latter, in particular, can involve risk of neck injury to the animal. Rodeo organisers have stated the festival adheres to all welfare regulations, and that a veterinarian ensures animals are in good condition throughout.

In the town of Aroroy on a full moon in May, the Aroroy Wacky Rodeo pits brave cowboys against a particularly cantankerous creature, the crab. Events include crab races, crab catching, parades, dancing, and the mass consumption of the aforementioned crab. The coveted Miss Crab prize goes to the town's beauty queen.

Legacy Suites   HOTEL $$
(☑ 056-582 0210; Purok 8; s/d/st/f P1350/1600/2600/3000; ❄ ☎) At the northern end of the city, sea-facing Legacy trumps most of Masbate's dreary midrangers with spotless, though slightly fading rooms, friendly staff and an inviting restaurant and bar downstairs. The waterfront location feels a little desolate but it's not far from the centre.

MG Hotel   HOTEL $$
(☑ 056-333 5614; Punta Nursery; s P950, d P1050-1650; ❄ ☎ ☲) MG promises a lot but the backyard pool is a little murky and the restaurant permanently closed. Still, the top-floor rooms are big and airy, with huge beds and small balconies overlooking the water. The poolside rooms are smaller and cheaper. It's an easy walk from the Butando landing point and a P20 tricycle ride from Masbate port.

✖ Eating & Drinking

The best place for entertainment is the small strip of bars and music cafes along Ibañez St.

★ **Ham's Cup**   FILIPINO $
(☑ 056-582 0205; Ibañez St; breakfast P120, mains P50-80; ☺ 7am-midnight; ☎) This excellent contemporary little cafe in Masbate's 'eat street' serves good coffee, set breakfasts such as Spanish sardines, inexpensive pasta and burgers, as well as beer and cocktails.

Mina's Crib Cafe   CAFE $
(Quezon St; snacks P48-110; ☺ 10am-10pm; ☎) Like a little doll's house for young adults, Mina's is a quirky cafe with cribs in place of booths or seats and loud music playing. Good place for a coffee, smoothie or sandwich and to meet local youth.

Tio Jose   AMERICAN $$
(☑ 0915 298 0852; Ibingay St; mains P120-450; ☺ 11am-11pm; ❄ ☎) Although styled on an American diner, with booth seating, memorabilia, and nachos, fries and hot dogs on the menu, Tio Jose also does a fine line in Filipino dishes, from crispy *pata* to *kare-kare* and sizzling platters. Cocktails and cold beer too.

❶ Information

Masbate Tourism Office (☑ 0906 212 5684; http://masbatecity.gov.ph; Municipal Rd; ☺ 8am-5pm Mon-Fri) Upstairs in the City Hall compound, three blocks north of Quezon St.

❶ Getting There & Around

From the integrated terminal off Diversion Rd, just south of the port, there are frequent jeepney and air-con van departures for Aroroy, Mandaon, Cataingan via Palanas, Esperanza and Balud.

Around Masbate Island

Masbate Island's attractions are easily reachable by public transport from Masbate Town. Points of interest include the oldest lighthouse in the province, in the gold-mining and fishing town of Aroroy, and the immense Kalanay and Batongan caves near the port of Mandaon, complete with underground river (ask about guides at the Mandaon town hall). A jeepney trip to Mandaon is worth it for the views of the mountains and rolling countryside alone. Southeast of Masbate Town, Uson features some surviving wooden Spanish houses, while Palanas, further east, has similar ancestral houses, but with traditional thatched roofs. Finding these spots requires a bit of DIY spirit and as for finding a place to stay, your best bet is to make a beeline for the town hall.

Ticao Island

Ticao feels on the edge between laissez-faire island time and impending tourism development. For now, the sweet, rotting scent of copra weaves through the trees and – except in the few small townships – concrete barely interrupts the bamboo and thatch structures. The island's one road bumps and winds and slopes its way through villages such as Batuan, where you can stop and check out the mangrove boardwalk.

In Monreal, hire a bangka for the day (P2500 to P3000) and head along the coast to see the 30m-tall Catandayagan Falls or lovely Talisay Beach, both on the west coast.

🛏 Sleeping

There are a couple of cheapies in San Jacinto and Monreal, but the standouts are the two resorts just north of San Jacinto.

★ Ticao Island Resort   RESORT $$$
(📞0917 506 3554, 02-893 8173; www.ticao-island-resort.com; s/d/tr P2200/3600/5100, 1-/2-/3-person cabanas P4000/5500/7200; ❋🛜) In Tacdogan, about 8km north of San Jacinto, nine plush cabanas front a perfect and secluded cove, while four fan-only budget rooms huddle off the beach. Divers will enjoy the island's proximity to the famed Manta Bowl dive site, while nondiving guests can go horse riding, kayaking and fishing or learn the secrets of Bicolano cooking. Full board included.

Altamar Ticao Island Beach Resort   RESORT $$$
(📞0906 324 3034, 0915 599 5517; www.ticaoaltamar.com; San Jacinto; 2-person cottages P3500-4000, ste P6000; ❋🛜) Secluded Altamar consists of a series of tastefully decorated beachfront cottages, most built for couples.

Staff are attentive and dish up some seriously delicious food, and the friendly owners can arrange diving, massages and other activities.

ℹ Getting There & Away

Three bangkas a day go between Lagundi pier and the 'fish port' in Masbate Town (P90, one hour).

Daily ferries run between Monreal and Pilar (P150, two hours). The last trip is around 1pm. There are five daily ferries (P120, one hour) from Bulan in Sorsogon Province to San Jacinto.

MARINDUQUE

📞 042 / POP 234,520

Soporific Marinduque is a heart-shaped island, appropriately positioned at the heart of the Philippine archipelago. Bound by a scenic 120km sealed ring road, the islands seems to truly come to life only during the Moriones Festival (p190) at Easter. The rest of the year visitors must content themselves with the laid-back charm of its villages, beautiful scenery, dormant Mt Malindig volcano, a handful of beach resorts, hot springs in the interior and wildlife-filled caves.

ℹ Getting There & Away

AIR
Cebu Pacific operate flights to/from Manila out of Marinduque airport.

BOAT
Most passenger boats (from Dalahican) land at Balanacan, 30 minutes north of Boac. Arrivals are met by tricycles (P200 to Boac), and also jeepneys and air-con vans (P50), departing for Boac, Santa Cruz, Torrijos and Buenavista.

Montenegro Shipping Lines (📞0917 867 2337) Operates roll-on, roll-off (RORO) ferries between Lucena and Balanacan daily at 6am, 8am, 10am, 5pm and 11pm (P260, three hours).

MANTA BOWL

March to May are the peak months to dive the Manta Bowl, a 17m to 22m atoll dive where you hook at the bottom to take a rest from the strong currents. It provides the perfect conditions for a manta-ray cleaning station, where mantas positively queue up for cleaner wrasse to remove parasites from their skin. Whale sharks may be seen here too, as well as occasional thresher sharks and hammerheads, while Tuna Alley attracts sheer walls of tuna and barracuda. Manta Bowl is an advanced dive, though operators will take divers with less than 20 dives under their belt as long as they pay for a dive master to go one-to-one with them. Geographically part of Masbate, it's logistically easier to dive with one of the regular trips from Donsol on mainland Southeast Luzon, or by staying at one of the resorts on Ticao Island. Contact Bicol Dive Center (p181) or Fun Dive Asia (📞0927 490 7041; 3-dive trips P4000; ⏰7am-7pm) in Donsol.

Marinduque

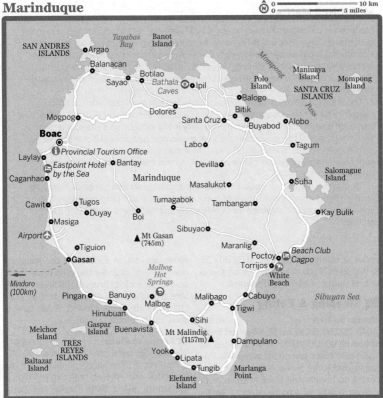

N 0 —— 10 km
0 —— 5 miles

(map)

SAN ANDRES ISLANDS
Argao
Balanacan
Tayabas Bay
Botilao
Sayao *Bathala Caves* Ipil
Banot Island
Mompong
Polo Island
Maniuaya Island
Mompong Island
SANTA CRUZ ISLANDS
Balogo
Mogpog
Dolores
Bitik
Santa Cruz Buyabod Alobo
Puss
Boac
Provincial Tourism Office
Labo
Tagum
Laylay *Eastpoint Hotel by the Sea* Bantay
Devilla
Suha
Salomague Island
Caganhao
Marinduque
Masalukot
Cawit Tugos
Tumagabok
Tambangan
Duyay Boi
Masiga
Airport
Sibuyao
Kay Bulik
Tiguion
▲ Mt Gasan (745m)
Maranlig
Gasan
Poctoy
Torrijos *Beach Club Cagpo*
Mindoro (100km)
Malbog Hot Springs
White Beach
Sibuyan Sea
Pingan Banuyo
Malbog
Malibago Cabuyo
Hinubuan
Tigwi
Melchor Island
Gaspar Island Buenavista
Sihi
TRES REYES ISLANDS
Mt Malindig (1157m) ▲
Dampulano
Baltazar Island
Yook Lipata
Tungib
Marlanga Point
Elefante Island

Starhorse Shipping Lines (📞 0921 274 5340) Operates eight RORO ferries daily between Lucena and Balanacan (P260, three hours).

Boac

📞 042 / POP 54,730

Centred around its impressive cathedral-fortress, Marinduque's laid-back capital has considerably more character than most Filipino towns. Its narrow streets are lined with 19th-century ancestral houses in various states of repair, with capiz-shell windows and upstairs verandahs spilling over with flowers. If you're not staying at one of the coastal resorts, this is the best base for exploring the island.

👁 Sights & Activities

Boac Cathedral   CHURCH
(San Miguel St; ⏰ 5am-6pm) The focal point of the town, this stone cathedral dates back to the 17th century and its fortified ramparts testify to its role as local refuge during the Moro pirate raids. Above the main doors is a niche containing the 1792 statue of the Blessed Virgin, credited with driving away the pirates with storms and saving the town from natural disasters.

National Museum Marinduque   MUSEUM
(Mercader St; ⏰ 8am-noon & 1-5pm Mon-Fri) FREE The highlights of this concise museum include its collection of *moriones* masks, Ming-dynasty ceramics retrieved from the the seabed near Gaspar Island, and *kalutang,* one of the earliest native musical instruments.

**Dream Favor
Travel & Tours**   OUTDOORS
(📞 0918 993 1605, 042-332 0371; 21 Santol; ⏰ 8am-5pm) This local outfit can tailor guided tours around the island, including caving, trekking, island-hopping and snorkelling, or

MORIONES MANIA

Marinduque's Moriones Festival began in 1807 when Padre Dionsio Santiago, a Mogpog parish priest, organised a play based on the story of Longinus (or Longino), one of the Roman centurions assigned to execute Christ. A drop of Christ's blood miraculously restored sight in Longinus' blind right eye during the crucifixion. Longinus instantly proclaimed his faith, whereupon he was chased around town, captured and summarily beheaded.

These days, a fabulous Easter festival combining folk mysticism with Catholic pageantry turns Marinduque's streets into a colourful reenactment of those events, over the seven days of Holy Week. Each municipality in Marinduque holds its own festival, in which hundreds of *moriones* don centurion masks and costumes and arm themselves with wooden swords, spears and shields. The masks take months to prepare and are kept secret from even close friends and family so that the *moriones'* true identity is never known.

Throughout the festival week *moriones* take to the streets and run amok, engaging in sword fights, dances and sneaky pranks on bystanders, with Longinus hiding behind spectators before undergoing a mock beheading and his 'lifeless' body being paraded around.

provide a minivan and driver (P3500) for the day. Even if you don't take a tour, this is the best source of island information.

🛏 Sleeping & Eating

Tahanan Sa Isok   HOTEL **$**
(📞 042-332 1231; 5 Canovas St; s/tw/f incl breakfast from P1000/1200/1800; ❇ 🛜) Located on a quiet side street just off Magsaysay St, this creeper-clad stone house is the most characterful and best-value place in town, with 15 clean rooms of varying sizes, a pretty garden restaurant and a very helpful front desk. There are original artworks on display and *moriones* masks made by provincial jail inmates available for purchase.

Hotel Zenturia   BOUTIQUE HOTEL **$$**
(📞 0917 305 2689; hotelzenturia@gmail.com; Magsaysay Rd; r P1500-2500, ste P3000; ❇ 🛜) Zenturia is immaculate. In stark white four-storey buildings, rooms offer contemporary comfort with muted tones, super-soft beds, cable TV, gleaming bathrooms and private balconies. The 10 rooms are all similar in decor but get bigger as the price goes up. A rooftop cafe is planned but hadn't opened at the time of review.

Boac Hotel   HOTEL **$$**
(📞 042-332 1121; theboachotel@yahoo.com; Nepomuceno St; s/d/ste/f P1200/1500/2000/2500; ❇ 🛜) In a great location near the cathedral, Boac promises a load of character in the downstairs lobby, with arty decor, vintage photos, *moriones* masks and traditional headgear adorning the walls. The upstairs

rooms are not as endearing: the standard ones are tiny, so go for the suite if you value space. Fan-cooled cheapies (P600) are available if you're on a desperate budget. The attached **cafe** (mains P80-450; ⏰ 7am-8pm) is good and breakfast is included.

⭐ **Kusina sa Plaza**   FILIPINO **$**
(Mercader St; buffet plate P65, mains P30-240; ⏰ 7am-7pm; 🛜) The hugely popular place has two sides, one offering buffet-style Filipino specialities, along with noodle and pasta dishes, the other a fast-food cafe doing burgers, pizzas, coffee and juices.

Good Chow   FILIPINO **$**
(Mercader St; mains P45-165; ⏰ 7am-7pm) Cheerful snack bar serving *siopao* (steamed buns, P25), pizza and Filipino standards.

ⓘ Information

The **PNB** (Reyes St; ⏰ 24hr) has the town's ATM; bring cash, especially during the Moriones Festival.

The **Provincial Tourism Office** (📞 042-332 1498; ⏰ 8am-5pm Mon-Fri) is located in the Capitol Building complex, 2km out of town on the main road south.

ⓘ Getting There & Away

Jeepneys and minivans run from the ferry dock in Balanacan to Boac (P50, 30 minutes).

From Boac, jeepneys head south to Gasan (P25, 30 minutes) and Buenavista (P45, one hour). Frequent jeepneys also head northeast to Mogpog (P10, 10 minutes), Balanacan (P50, 30 minutes), Santa Cruz (P70, one hour) and Torrijos (P120, two hours).

Gasan & the West Coast

The 17km from Boac to Gasan is popular with visitors, thanks to a motley selection of beach resorts peppering the thin strip of grey sand. The beach becomes broader, brighter and lined with fishing boats as you head south of Gasan town proper.

In Gasan you can hire a boat to visit the pretty Tres Reyes Islands (named Melchor, Gaspar and Baltazar after the biblical kings), visible from the mainland; expect to pay around P1500 for a few hours of island-hopping. Gaspar Island is a marine reserve and you can snorkel off the northern beach, but you'll need to bring your own equipment.

The main round-island road leaves the coast at Buenavista and winds over the mountains to the east coast before continuing up to Torrijos. The alternative coastal route between Buenavista and Tigwi is a scenic drive. A single jeepney runs between Buenavista and Lipata, so your only option is to hire a van for a day in Boac or haggle with the Buenavista tricycle drivers.

🏃 Activities

The five-hour hike up and down the perfect cone of Mt Malindig (1157m) follows a usually clearly marked trail from Sihi, a barangay of Buenavista. Take a tricycle to Sihi from Buenavista (P400 return) or any jeepney towards Torrijos (P30). Ask in Sihi whether a permit is required, as there's a military post halfway up the volcano.

Malbog Hot Springs   HOT SPRINGS
(P70; ⊙7.30am-10pm) A couple of kilometres inland from Buenavista are the Malbog Hot Springs, where a series of bathing pools have been constructed to tap the sulphur-scented water and a modest resort welcomes day and overnight visitors.

🛏 Sleeping & Eating

Eastpoint Hotel by the Sea   HOTEL **$$**
(☑042-332 2229; www.eastpointhotel.com; r P1000-3000; ❄❀🐾) Halfway between Boac and Gasan, this quirky place comes with well-furnished and very good-value rooms around a neat garden. The larger rooms sleep up to seven. The restaurant overlooking a small strip of grey beach serves delicious home-cooked dishes if ordered in advance. There's a van available for island tours and a wellness centre for pampering.

Barbarossa Pub   FILIPINO, INTERNATIONAL **$$**
(San José St; mains P160-380; ⊙9am-9pm) This German-owned bar-restaurant in Gasan is popular with a mix of expats and locals thanks to its German sausages, tasty takes on Filipino standards and pizza and pasta. The heavy wooden furniture gives it a pub feel and you can order cold draught beer (P88).

❶ Getting There & Away

Daily bangkas sail from Gasan pier to Pinamalayan (P280, three hours) on Mindoro at 8am.

Frequent jeepneys run from Boac to Gasan (P25, 30 minutes).

East Coast

The east coast is the wilder side of the island, with less infrastructure and just a few resorts. Most travellers head to Torrijos and the beaches near Poctoy. Coming from the north you'll also pass through Santa Cruz, a larger town than Boac, with an imposing church and the popular Rejano's bakery. From the town's Buyabod Port it's possible to hire a bangka to outlying islands such as Maniuaya Island.

The whitest and longest beach in Marinduque is the aptly named **White Beach** (P30) in Poctoy, lapped at by teal waters and with views of Mt Malindig's conical snout. You'll find some day-use cottages here, and it gets pretty busy on weekends.

🛏 Sleeping

There's one resort of note on the east coast and some basic holiday rentals in Torrijos. About 2km north of Poctoy is the appealing **Beach Club Cagpo** (☑0921 993 2537; www.beachclubcagpo.com; Poctoy; dm P350, d with fan P1000-1250, d with air-con P1350-1500; ❄🐾), with private beach. Spacious oceanfront rooms and one cottage are sparse, clean and comfortable; the cramped dorm is for real shoestringers or groups, with no linen supplied. The bar-restaurant serves decent grilled fish, pizza and Filipino dishes. A 125cc motorbike is available for hire – ideal for exploring the island.

❶ Getting There & Away

Torrijos and Poctoy are most easily accessible from the north via Santa Cruz. Jeepneys from Balanacan and Boac run to Santa Cruz (P60, one hour) via Mogpog, with some continuing on to Torrijos (P120, two hours).

Mindoro

Best Places to Stay

➡ Pandan Island Resort (p209)

➡ El Galleon Beach Resort (p198)

➡ Verde View Villas (p198)

➡ Apo Reef Club (p210)

➡ Sunset at Aninuan (p200)

Best Hikes

➡ Mt Halcon (p204)

➡ Mt Iglit-Baco National Park (p208)

➡ Sablayan Prison Farm & Rainforest (p209)

➡ Talipanan Falls (p194)

Why Go?

There are two sides to this large island just south of Luzon: Puerto Galera, and the rest of Mindoro. Puerto Galera is a dive mecca that lies at the heart of the Verde Island Passage – one of the world's most biologically diverse underwater environments. It's essentially an extension of Luzon.

The rest of Mindoro is an untamed hinterland of virtually impenetrable mountains populated by the indigenous Mangyan tribespeople. Those who like to get way off the beaten track need look no further. Off the west coast, accessible from the towns of Calintaan and Sablayan, underwater wonderland Apo Reef is populated by sharks and stingrays.

Most folks travel to Mindoro via land and sea from Manila. At the south of the island, Roxas and Bulalacao are jumping-off points to Caticlan (for Boracay).

When to Go
San José

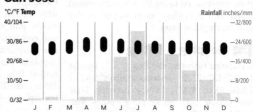

Apr & May
Rainy season has yet to begin and winds are at their calmest at Apo Reef.

Feb–Apr
The driest months and the best season for climbing Mt Halcon.

Oct & Nov
Another transitional period wind-wise, meaning flat seas for divers.

Mindoro Highlights

1 Apo Reef (p210)
Swimming with turtles, sharks, wrasses and other sea critters at this incredible protected marine park off Sablayan.

2 Puerto Galera (p194)
Exploring the pretty coves, waterfalls and beaches of this resort town, and diving into its underwater wonders.

3 Mt Iglit-Baco National Park (p208) Observing the headcount of critically endangered *tamaraw* (native buffalo) and visiting Mangyan villages.

4 Sablayan Prison Farm & Rainforest (p209) Visiting bird-laden rainforests and lakes, led by prisoner-guides.

5 Mt Halcon (p204)
Launching an assault on Mindoro's highest peak – the country's ultimate climb.

6 Malasimbo Music & Arts Festival (p198) Taking in the Philippines' premier open-air music event in Puerto Galera.

❶ Getting There & Away

You can fly into San José, but most visitors to Mindoro arrive by boat from Batangas in Luzon.

BOAT

Luzon The usual tourist route to Mindoro is by fast bangka from Batangas to Puerto Galera. There's also a fleet of fast and slow craft connecting Batangas with Calapan, while roll-on, roll-off (RORO) car ferries link Batangas with Abra de Ilog (for Sablayan).

Marinduque Bangkas leave for Gasan at 8am every morning from Pinamalayan (P280, three hours) on Mindoro's east coast.

Panay and Romblon Roxas in southern Mindoro Oriental is linked by frequent car ferries to Caticlan (for Boracay) and a daily ferry to Odiongan, Romblon. A bit further south, Bulalacao has two daily fast ferries to Caticlan.

Palawan At the time of research, the only boats to Palawan were sporadic bangkas from San José to Coron and the Cuyo Islands.

BUS

If travelling from Manila, it's common to travel by bus straight through to Calapan or Abra de Ilog and points south, with your bus rolling onto a car ferry for the Batangas–Mindoro leg.

❶ Getting Around

The road around Mindoro is paved these days and traversed by a sizeable fleet of buses, vans and jeepneys. However, there is no road link between Puerto Galera and Abra de Ilog in the north of the island; travel between the two is by boat.

Puerto Galera

🎵 043 / POP 32,520

Just a few hours' travel from Manila, this gorgeous collection of bays and islands is one of the country's top dive destinations. Puerto Galera is Spanish for 'port of the galleons'. Its deep natural harbour, sheltered on all sides, was a favoured anchorage well before the Spanish arrived in 1572, and today it remains a favoured anchorage for long-term yachties and short-term vacationers.

Puerto Galera (PG) typically refers to the town of Puerto Galera and the resort areas surrounding it – namely Sabang, 5km to the east, and White Beach, 7km to the west. Each area has its own distinct character, spanning the range from sleaze to sophistication; you'd be well advised to choose carefully.

◉ Sights

Talipanan Falls   WATERFALL

(Map p196) Much less touristy than the area's famous Tamaraw Falls, Talipanan Falls is a short walk from the village of Talipanan. Hire a Mangyan guide (P200) in the Iraya-Mangyan village just off the main road in Talipanan. From here a track behind the school winds for about 30 minutes uphill and through forest to the swimmable, two-tiered falls. Early in the morning you stand a good chance of seeing monkeys.

Tamaraw Falls   WATERFALL

(P30; ☉7am-5pm) This waterfall drops 30m from a forested ravine into splash pools off the main Puerto Galera–Calapan road, 13km out of town, then flows out again in another series of falls. It gets busy at weekends, so go during the week when crowds are more moderate. Jeepneys headed for Calapan will drop you here (P25, 30 minutes).

Tukuran Falls   WATERFALL

(P50) Tukuran Falls is a series of gentle cascades and turquoise-toned swimming holes accessed from the village of Calsapa, about 45 minutes south of Puerto Galera. They are refreshing and photogenic, but go early in the morning or late in the day to avoid the tour vans that frequent the place, thanks to a newly sealed access road to the trailhead. A guide (P300) is mandatory for the 30-minute walk from the trailhead.

🏃 Activities

Around Puerto Galera, diving reigns supreme (with drinking a close second). Campbell's (p199) beach resort in Small La Laguna is among several resorts that rent out **paddle boards**. Landlubbers will find plenty to do as well. Renting a motorbike and driving along PG's spectacular coastline is a favourite activity, and there are plenty of **waterfalls** to check out along the way. The falls can dry up a bit from March to May.

Beaches

The best beaches in the area are the western beaches of **Aninuan** and **Talipanan**. They are much quieter and classier than nearby White Beach – for now. Talipanan in particular is developing rapidly. **White Beach** is decent in its own right, but suffers from tasteless development and high-season crowds.

Sabang's filthy little beach is hardly worthy of the name. Head around the point to much better **Small La Laguna** or, further on, pretty **Big La Laguna**.

About 5km south of town towards Calapan, **Dulangan Beach** is a locals' favourite, with jet skis and wakeboards for rent. It's easily combined with a trip to Tamaraw Falls.

Diving & Snorkelling

Puerto Galera offers prime underwater real estate. Special critters that live among the coral include frogfish and mandarin fish, pygmy sea horses, ghost pipefish and nudibranches. Some of the best diving is around Verde Island, a few kilometres offshore.

Dive prices vary wildly, so shop around (although quality and safety should always trump price). Expect to pay between P1000 and P1800 for a dive, including equipment, with discounts available if you do six or more dives. An open-water course will set you back P15,000 to P20,000.

Many of the top dive sites are well suited for snorkelling. Most dive operators offer a snorkel option. P1200 is the going rate for a three-hour tour.

Asia Divers   DIVING
(Map p200; ☑0917 814 5107; www.asiadivers.com; Small La Laguna) Highly professional. Also manages top technical dive outfit **Tech Asia** (Map p200; ☑043-287 3205; Small La Laguna).

Capt'n Gregg's Dive Shop   DIVING
(Map p200; ☑0917 540 4570; www.captngreggs. com; Sabang; fun dives incl equipment P1400) Long-established, reliable dive operator.

EACY Dive   DIVING
(Environmental Awareness for Children & Youth; Map p196; ☑0916 794 5624; www.eacydive.org; Aninuan) ◢ This dive shop is associated with the Stairway Foundation (www.stairway foundation.org), which runs a host of programs for disadvantaged youth. Proceeds from the shop go towards programs to promote environmental awareness among project kids, beach cleans and more. Equipment is provided by local NGO Scuba for Change (www.scubaforchange.com).

Blue Ribbon Divers   DIVING
(Map p200; ☑0917 893 2719; www.blueribbon divers.com; Small La Laguna; fun dives incl equipment P1200) Excellent dive outfit with good rates.

Pacific Divers   DIVING
(Map p196; ☑0920 613 5140; http://pacificdivers. net; White Beach; fun dives with/without equipment P1400/1200) The most professional dive outfit on White Beach.

Big Apple Dive Shop   DIVING
(Map p200; ☑0919 449 8298; www.divebigapple. com; fun dives incl equipment P1100) Attached to the resort of the same name, Big Apple has some of the most competitive dive prices in Puerto Galera.

Octopus Divers   DIVING
(Map p200; ☑0919 379 0811; www.mac-octopus divers.com; Sabang) A longstanding and well-regarded operator. It's behind Papa Fred's restaurant.

Tina's Reef Divers   DIVING
(Map p200; ☑043-287 3139; www.tinasreefdivers. com; Sabang) Good choice for budget divers, with prices starting at P1000 per dive including equipment.

MINDORO PUERTO GALERA

PUERTO GALERA'S TOP DIVE SITES

Here are some of the best dive sites in the area, according to resident dive instructors:

Hole in the Wall (Map p196) to **Canyons** (Map p196) Big fan corals, sweet lips (groupers), tuna and jacks at a max depth of about 27m. Location: Escarceo Point, 3km east of Sabang.

Sinandigan Wall (Map p196) Multilevel dive with lots of nudibranches and other macro-life, plus some swim-throughs. Start at 42m and gradually make your way up. Best in the morning. Location: off Sinandigan Point, 3km east of Sabang.

Monkey Beach (Map p196) Multilevel dive starting at 30m and gradually ascending all the way to 4m. Great fish life, sponges, gorgonian fans and lots of different corals. Nearby lies the **Monkey Wreck** in 20m, suitable for advanced divers. Location: five minutes east of Sabang Beach.

Verde Island Dropoff A big wall that goes all the way down to 70m. Lots of jacks and pelagics. Heavy currents make this more suitable for advanced divers. Location: Verde Island.

Washing Machine Heavy currents wash over underwater canyons at 18m. You get washed downstream then climb back through the canyons, pulling yourself by the rocks. An adventure dive with lots of pelagic life when it's running heavy. Location: Verde Island.

Puerto Galera Beaches

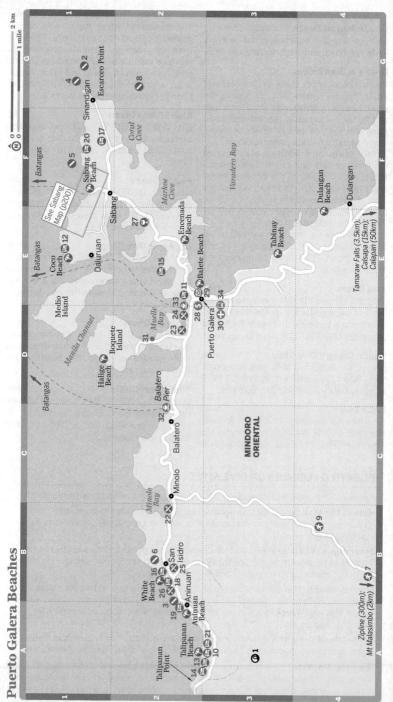

Tamaraw Falls (3.5km);
Calsapa (15km);
Calapan (50km)

Zipline (300m);
Mt Malasimbo (2km)

MINDORO
ORIENTAL

See Sabang
Map (p200)

Puerto Galera Beaches

Sailing

A few sailboats operating out of Puerto Galera harbour are available for half-day, full-day or sunset cruises. Check the noticeboard at the yacht club for listings. Kareem of **Freedom Kite Surfing** (☑ 0917 642 6740; www.freedom-kitesurfing.com) rents out a 44ft luxury catamaran from May to October and can arrange kitesurfing safaris.

Puerto Galera Yacht Club   BOATING
(Map p196; ☑ 043-287 3401; www.pgyc.org; Puerto Galera Town) Keen or even novice sailors can head over to the Puerto Galera Yacht Club, which will team you with an experienced sailor for its 'Wet Wednesday' afternoon fun races (P600). Start time is 1pm. It rents out Laser sailboats (P1700 for two hours) and Hobie catamarans (P2250 for two hours), and can also help you charter a bigger boat for a half-day cruise (P4000).

Golf

Ponderosa Golf & Country Club   GOLF
(Map p196; ☑ 0915 507 6348; www.puertogalera golf.com; Minolo; 9 holes incl equipment & caddy P1350) Golfers can swing on one of the quirkiest courses you'll find anywhere, the diminutive and dramatic Ponderosa Golf & Country Club, cut into a steep mountain 500m above PG town.

Sto Niño Mini Golf   MINIGOLF
(Map p196; National Hwy, Santo Niño; adult/child P250/150; ☺ 9am-6pm) Arguably the country's finest minigolf course is found here, with fresh felt and a few creatively designed holes. It's nestled beside the Puerto Galera Yacht Club.

Trekking

It's possible to climb **Mt Talipanan** (1130m) and nearby **Mt Malasimbo** (1215m), which lord over Puerto Galera to the south. Both require about four hours to ascend and a few hours to get down, so start early. Find guides at the Mangyan village in Talipanan – the same guides that lead shorter hikes to Talipanan Falls (p194). Much larger Mt Halcon (p204) must be tackled out of Baco or Calapan to the south of Puerto Galera.

Other Activities

Hash House Harriers   RUNNING
(Map p200) Every Saturday at 3.30pm, the local branch of the Hash House Harriers meets at Capt'n Gregg's (p198) for a fun run followed by a drinking session.

Zipline   ADVENTURE SPORTS
(Map p196; ☑ 0917 506 2280; per ride P600) This dramatic zipline drops 250m vertical in the shadow of Mt Malasimbo.

MINDORO PUERTO GALERA

✖ Festivals & Events

Malasimbo Music & Arts Festival MUSIC
(www.malasimbofestival.com; ☉Mar) Malasimbo
Festival is a marquee open-air music festival
featuring bands and electronic acts. It draws
a mix of top Pinoy talent and a few international groups, performing in a jaw-dropping
natural amphitheatre up near Ponderosa
Golf Club in the foothills of Mt Malasimbo.

⌷ Sleeping

Location is everything in PG. Sabang is the
noisy party zone but is closest to the dive
sites; adjoining Small La Laguna and Big
La Laguna are much quieter. Puerto Galera
town is noisy by day, quiet by night. White
Beach draws mostly local tourists as well as
a smattering of loyal expats and the odd lost
backpacker. Aninuan and Talipanan feel the
most remote and have the best beaches.

⌷ Sabang

Sabang struts its stuff along the eastern
shore. By day it's relaxed; around sunset a
metamorphosis takes place as watering holes
open, barflies settle in, music cranks up, and
all types – and we mean all types – of nightlife emerge. The cheapest lodging is on the
hillside at the eastern end of Sabang Beach,
where you also might find a homestay for
P500 to P700.

★**Capt'n Gregg's Dive Resort** LODGE $
(Map p200; ☎043-287 3070, 0917 540 4570; www.
captngreggs.com; Sabang; r with fan P800-1200,
with air-con P1200-1900; ✺🖥) This Sabang institution has been the best value in town for
more than 25 years. The compact but cosy
wood-lined 'old' rooms, right over the water,
still have the most charm and are also the
cheapest.

★**Reynaldo's Upstairs** GUESTHOUSE $
(Map p200; ☎0917 489 5609; rey_purie@yahoo.
com; Sabang; r P900-1200; ✺🖥) Run by the
nicest family you'll ever meet, Reynaldo's
has a splendid mix of more-than-passable
budget fan rooms and large 'view' rooms
with kitchenettes and balconies on a hillside.

**Paddy's Bar &
Backpacker Hostel** GUESTHOUSE $
(Map p196; ☎0977 184 5540; Sinandigan; dm/d
with fan P250/400, d with air-con P450-700; 🖥🖥)
About 1km east of Sabang (P20 by motorbike), Paddy's is Puerto Galera's only legitimate hostel. It has basic doubles, spacious
if stuffy five-bed dorms in stand-alone huts,

and a well-stocked Irish bar overlooking a ravine. Two slightly fancier rooms are fronted
by a newly added plunge pool.

★**El Galleon Beach Resort** RESORT $$
(Map p200; ☎043-287 3205; www.elgalleon.com;
Small La Laguna; d incl breakfast US$59-110, villas
US$110-315; ✺🖥🖥) Elegant hut-style rooms
with wicker furniture and verandahs creep
up a beachfront cliff and around a pool.
There's a fine restaurant and a technical dive
school on the premises, not to mention the
Point Bar, one of the country's best bars. For a
modest splurge, ask about the incredible vil-
las at their neighbouring Waimea Suites.

Steps Garden Resort COTTAGE $$
(Map p200; ☎0915 381 3220, 043-287 3046; www.
stepsgarden.com; Sabang; d P1600-2750; ✺🖥🖥)
A delightful cluster of stand-alone cottages
with private balconies in an overflowing and
colourful garden, this resort sits high above
the beach. It has a lovely pool, breezes and
views, and is away from the noise. And yes,
there are a lot of steps.

Mermaid Dive Resort RESORT $$
(Map p200; ☎0916 439 8132; www.mermaid
resort.com; Sabang; d US$65-115, ste US$130-195;
✺🖥🖥) Reliable Mermaid is off the beach
but this shouldn't worry you. It seals off the
noise better than most places in Sabang, and
the rooms more than make up for the lack
of an ocean view – even the cheapest have
oodles of space, plush beds, sufficient furni-
ture and all the mod cons you need.

★**Verde View Villas** VILLA $$$
(Map p196; ☎0998 558 4739; www.verdeview
villas.com; Sinandigan; d weekday/weekend from
P4600/5600; ✺🖥🖥) The views from this
hilltop property 1.5km east of Sabang are
nonpareil. Four luxurious pool-front rooms
boasting Apple TVs stare straight at magnificent Verde Island to the east. At the back
there's a four-room complex with equally
impressive views of Batangas to the north. A
steep walk down the hill takes you to a private beach, where there's great snorkelling.

⌷ Small La Laguna

Small La Laguna offers a better chance of a
quiet night's sleep than Sabang, and has a
nicer beach to boot.

★**La Laguna Villas** RESORT $$
(Map p200; ☎043-287 3696; www.llv.ph; Small La
Laguna; r from P3100, ste from P6000; ✺🖥🖥)
These luxury hillside villas are a steal, es-

pecially when low-season discounts kick in. Most rooms have working kitchenettes and at least two rooms are outfitted with quality beds, polished wood floors and flat-screen TVs (although not all rooms have balconies to take full advantage of the luscious views).

Blue Ribbon Dive Resort — RESORT $$
(Map p200; ☐ 0917 893 2791, 043-287 3561; www.blueribbondivers.com; Small La Laguna; r P2000-2200, bungalows P2400; ❀ ☎ ≋) This place is popular with divers, who get a 10% discount on accommodation. The large rooms are set around a small pool at the back. They are more functional than fashionable, but have TVs, and most have private terraces. Out the front a lively beachfront bar and restaurant sometimes has live acoustic music.

🛏 Big La Laguna

One beach east of Small La Laguna, Big La Laguna is even further removed from Sabang's noise, and the beach is the best in the area.

Campbell's — RESORT $$
(Map p200; ☐ 043-287 3466, 0917 558 7547; www.campbellsbeachresort.com; Big La Laguna; dm US$14, d US$44-88, ste US$130-220; ❀ ☎) The westernmost place on Big La Laguna beach, right at the water's edge, is its best all-rounder. The standard rooms are nothing special, but upgrade to the deluxe and you'll reap plump sea views from your balcony, a flat-screen TV and comfy linens. It has a good bar too, with a high-def TV and a Sunday into-the-water golf shoot-out.

Coco Beach Island Resort — RESORT $$$
(Map p196; ☐ 0917 883 9334; www.cocobeach.com; r P4500-5500, ste P9000-12,500; @ ☎ ≋) Around the point from Big La Laguna, this giant resort sprawls along a private beach and through the jungle, offering up dark but attractive standard rooms and luxurious hillside suites. All rooms are constructed of native materials; some are reached by 250 steps. There are two pools, a few restaurants, and activities galore.

🛏 Puerto Galera Town

Some visitors prefer the comparative calm of the waterfront around Muelle Pier in Puerto Galera town to the busy resort areas of the beaches. It's where yachties tend to drop an-

chor. There are several chic higher-end options on private coves just out of town.

Kalaw Place — VILLA $$
(Map p196; ☐ 043-442 0209; www.kalawplace.com.ph; Palangan; r P1900-3800; ☎) If privacy is your goal, look no further than this classy hilltop place on a private cove between PG town and Sabang. The 10 old-style rooms, with capiz-shell windows, lack air-con and TVs but are breezy and have balconies with sea views. Walk down to the bar and swimming area by the water.

Badladz Dive Resort — RESORT $$
(Map p196; ☐ 0939 914 8819; www.badladz.com; Muelle Pier; d P1490-1890; ❀ ☎) In a great location slap on PG harbour, Badladz has a well-regarded dive shop, functional if unspectacular rooms, and a good restaurant (mains P250 to P400) with views and tasty Mexican faves such as *huevos rancheros*.

🛏 White Beach & Around

White Beach fills up with groups of Manileños on weekends and in the March–May 'summer' season. Accommodation is geared towards large families and is substantially overpriced for individual travellers. At weekends, rates in this area go up further than published rates. A better option is to continue west to mellower Aninuan or Talipanan beaches, although resorts there are subject to the same neurotic price fluctuations.

★ Amami Beach Resort — BEACH RESORT $$
(Map p196; ☐ 0908 206 8534; www.amamibeachresort.com; Talipanan; r with fan/air-con P1000/1800; ❀ ☎) Run with gusto by a hospitable Italian-Filipino family, this is the best value resort on Talipanan Beach. The native-style rooms are simple but tasteful affairs with mozzie nets and hot water. Most are off a long shared verandah behind the excellent restaurant (mains P180 to P250). Walk-in guests net the best rates.

Veronica's Inn Bed & Breakfast — RESORT $$
(Map p196; ☐ 0977 727 2014; www.veronicasinn.wordpress.com; Talipanan; d weekday/weekend P2300/3000; ❀ ☎ ≋) At the far east end of Talipanan Beach, Veronica's is a real find. The eight rooms are austere, but with great common areas upstairs and down – plus a swimming pool, free kayaks, darts and a

Sabang

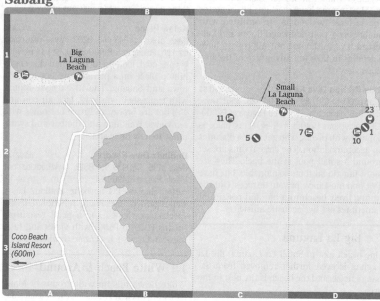

pool table – you won't be hanging out in your room much. At weekends the whole place is often booked out by groups.

Lenly's Cottages
COTTAGE $$

(Map p196; ☎0915 664 4104; www.lenlys.com; White Beach; with fan/air-con from P1500/2500; ☑) Behind a row of concession stands, this is something of an oasis in central White Beach. You get your own private bamboo bungalow with a balcony set around a courtyard.

D'Mountain Beach Resort
BUNGALOW $$

(Map p196; ☎0906 362 5406; www.mountain beachresort.com; Talipanan; d with fan/air-con from P1000/2000; ☒☑) This long-running family-owned place consists of a cluster of bungalows and beach houses at the quiet east end of Talipanan Beach. We prefer the fan rooms, in a long wooden row house with thatched walls and a long, lazy verandah.

Summer Connection
HOTEL $$

(Map p196; ☎043-287 3688; www.summercon nection.net; White Beach; r from P2500; ☒☑☒) Down at the preferable and quieter west end of White Beach, this is a decent all-around option. It's a sprawling concrete place with a good swimming pool and functional rooms illuminated by attractive

hanging lights. The Beach Frog Bar, a White Beach happy-hour fave, is out the front.

★Sunset at Aninuan
BEACH RESORT $$$

(Map p196; ☎0920 931 8924; www.aninuanbeach. com; Aninuan; r P5500-10,000; ☒☑☒) Sunset is as reliable as it gets if you're looking for a stand-alone beach resort in Puerto Galera. The cheapest rooms are uneventful, but a small upgrade nets you luxurious quarters with king beds, ample furniture, tasteful handicrafts and hangings, and private balconies facing the sea. Free kayak use.

Infinity Resort
RESORT $$$

(Map p196; ☎0917 792 6353; www.infinityresort. com.ph; Talipanan; r/ste from P9800/14,000; ☒☒) With a mountain backdrop and a glorious infinity pool fronting the beach, Puerto Galera's fanciest resort makes a stunning first impression. Rooms are in split-level villas; book them individually or take the entire villa. They have all comforts imaginable and are beautifully designed with intricate wood flourishes and coved ceilings.

✗ Eating

Puerto Galera has a great dining scene, with the waterfront restaurants of Sabang leading the way, although prices are high by

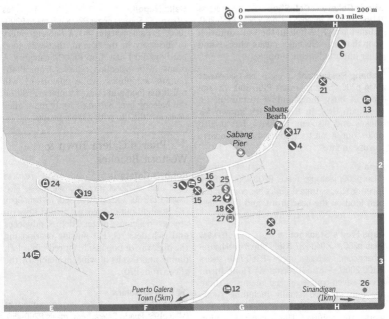

Sabang

Activities, Courses & Tours
1 Asia Divers	D2
2 Big Apple Dive Shop	F3
Blue Ribbon Divers	(see 7)
3 Capt'n Gregg's Dive Shop	F2
Hash House Harriers	(see 3)
4 Octopus Divers	H2
5 Tech Asia	C2
6 Tina's Reef Divers	H1

Sleeping
7 Blue Ribbon Dive Resort	D2
8 Campbell's	A1
9 Capt'n Gregg's Dive Resort	F2
10 El Galleon Beach Resort	D2
11 La Laguna Villas	C2
12 Mermaid Dive Resort	G3
13 Reynaldo's Upstairs	H1
14 Steps Garden Resort	E3

Eating
15 Bella Napoli	G2
16 Mira's Bakery & Deli Shop	G2
17 Papa Fred's Steakhouse	H2
18 Sabang Restaurant	G2
19 Tamarind Restaurant	E2
20 Teo's Native Sizzling House	G3
21 Tina's	H1

Drinking & Nightlife
22 Aquabest	G2
23 Point Bar	D2

Shopping
24 Frontier Handicrafts	E2

Information
25 Western Union	G2

Transport
26 Alex Motorcycle Rental	H3
27 Jeepneys to PG Town	G3

Philippine standards. Several resorts also have worthy eateries, including El Galleon (p198) and Capt'n Gregg's (p198) in the Sabang area; Badladz (p199) in PG town; and Amami Beach Resort (p199) and Infinity Resort in Talipanan.

Sabang & Around

Teo's Native Sizzling House FILIPINO $
(Map p200; Sabang; mains P85-300; ⊙24hr)
Open-air place with a comprehensive menu of sizzling dishes, Filipino classics, steaks and budget meals.

Mira's Bakery & Deli Shop
DELI $$

(Map p200; Sabang; sandwiches P150-200; ⊘6am-10pm; 🖘) A hole-in-the-wall sandwich shop that also sells fancy meats, cheeses and other imported picnic supplies.

Sabang Restaurant
INTERNATIONAL $$

(Map p200; Sabang; mains P100-300; ⊘7am-11pm) A busy, longstanding restaurant on the main drag in Sabang. It's known for shakes and discount brekkies, but it also doles out a pretty good range of hearty European fare.

Tina's
GERMAN, FILIPINO $$

(Map p200; Sabang; mains P200-450; ⊘8am-10pm; 🖘) Swiss-tinged Tina's has some of the best food on the beachfront, and the prices are good for PG. Do try the schnitzel.

Papa Fred's Steakhouse
STEAK $$$

(Map p200; ☑043-287 3361; http://steakhouse-sabang.com; Sabang; mains P350-750, steaks P1100-2000; ⊘8am-11.30pm; 🖘) Hone in on Fred's seven-course special menus – there are four choices, usually including steak, seafood or a combination of the two. They're worth the splurge. The à-la-carte section sees fondue, Bavarian pork and good wines orbit a core of steaks. Bonus points for the waterfront location.

★Tamarind Restaurant
INTERNATIONAL $$$

(Map p200; Sabang; mains P350-1000; ⊘7am-11pm; 🖘) Tamarind lures you in with the scent of steaks and seafood being fired up on its open-air barbecue – try the carabao (water buffalo) steak or the prawns à la tamarind. Filipino faves, pasta, schnitzel and many wines also grace the menu. It has a great waterfront location.

Bella Napoli
ITALIAN $$$

(Map p200; Sabang; pizzas P260-450, mains P300-1000; ⊘11am-midnight; ※) A Sabang eatery to file away in the 'Damn, that was good but how did I just drop P1500?' category. A robust wine selection (glasses from P140) tempts oenophiles, while epicureans will relish the food and relaxed ambience. Sit on the balcony over Sabang's seedy main alley or escape the din with a table inside.

✕ Puerto Galera Town & Western Beaches

Robby's Cafeteria
ITALIAN $$

(Map p196; National Hwy, opposite Muelle Pier; mains P150-300, pizzas P200-360; ⊘8am-9pm; 🖘) Straight-out-of-Bologna owner Roberto creates delicious pizzas, deli sandwiches and rich desserts. Eat outside overlooking the highway, or pop inside for red-tablecloth dining amid walls of wine, available by the glass (from P70).

★Puerto Galera Yacht Club
INTERNATIONAL $$

(Map p196; Puerto Galera Town; meals P290-450; ⊘noon-9pm, closed Mon in low season) This is a hidden gem, perched among the trees on the west edge of Muelle Bay. Sunset drinks and a barbecue are the traditional way to celebrate Friday, while 'Wet Wednesdays' mean all-you-can-eat curry for just P289.

★Arcobaleno Pizzeria & Ristorante
ITALIAN $$

(Map p196; National Hwy, Minolo; ⊘9am-9pm) It doesn't look like much – basically a lean-to with just a few tables – but the medium-crust pizza here is the best in Puerto Galera, heaped with mozzarella and fresh toppings.

THE IRAYA-MANGYAN OF TALIPANAN

Shrewd observers will notice two things when they wander into Talipanan's Iraya-Mangyan village. For one, it's in the lowlands (the vast majority of Mangyan people live in the mountains). For another it's relatively well-off; the grounds are well kept, the houses neat, and there's even a community centre filled with brand-new computers. It's a far cry from most Mangyan villages, which are shockingly poor.

The Mangyan people living have come along way since being driven out of the hills several decades ago amid fighting between the government and the Communist New People's Army rebels. The land they settled on, along the beach just north of **Talipanan Beach** (Map p196), was owned by one of the Philippines' richest families, the Ayalas.

Through their Ayala Foundation, the Ayalas instituted a comprehensive sustainable-livelihoods program, including support for health care, education and nutrition within the community. The foundation also helped the village revive the craft of hexagonal *nito* (woody vine) basket weaving. Visiting the village today, you will see weavers hard at work and can purchase their beautiful *nito* products.

There's a tall Italian staffing the kitchen and a simple menu of pizza, pasta and salads. The pizzas feed two, making this excellent value.

Rumulus FUSION $$
(Map p196; White Beach; meals P245; ⊙10am-10pm) The eponymous Filipino chef at Rumulus serves some of PG's best food out of a nondescript shack 100m behind White Beach. It's all about the specials here – three new ones per day, usually consisting of fresh fish and/or meat and potatoes, plus an Asian curry or stir-fry. Fresh ingredients are bought each morning from the local market.

★**Veranda** INTERNATIONAL $$$
(Map p196; White Beach; mains P300-700; ⊙11am-10pm) Veranda pushes all the right buttons – delicious food, chilled-out ambience, a groovy soundtrack and good service. The creatively diverse menu leans towards French (pâté, coq au vin) and Italian (pizza), with hints of Asia (Thai pomelo salad), and also includes steaks and fresh seafood. Veranda occupies an enviable spot at the much quieter far western end of White Beach.

🍷 Drinking & Nightlife

Almost everywhere has a happy hour, anytime between 2pm and 7pm.

★**Point Bar** BAR
(Map p200; El Galleon Beach Resort, Small La-guna) Our favourite bar, the Point Bar is a mellow sunset-and-beyond meeting place with great views and eclectic music. It's one of the few bars in town where solo women travellers can feel comfortable.

View Point BAR
(Map p196; ⊙9am-9pm) Atop a ridge on the winding road between PG town and Sa-bang, View Point overlooks jaw-droppingly beautiful Dalaruan Cove, about 2km west of Sabang. Come for the views and stay for English faves such as steak and mushroom pies (mains P200 to P300).

Aquabest WATER STATION
(Map p200; Sabang; ⊙8am-7pm) Water refills: P5 for a 1L bottle.

🛍 Shopping

Frontier Handicrafts GIFTS & SOUVENIRS
(Map p200; Sabang; ⊙6.30am-9pm) A really good souvenir store tucked in among the restaurants. Lots of wooden Ifugao (North Luzon) statuettes plus local handicrafts.

ℹ️ Information

There's a Max Bank on the main road out of town in Sabang that takes some international cards, but it's often offline. If you can't manage to get cash in PG, you'll have to go to Calapan or Batangas, so stock up before you come.

PNB (Map p196; National Hwy; ⊙9am-4pm Mon-Fri) Has the only ATM in the area, but it's not always reliable; also changes dollars (but not euros or travellers cheques).

Post Office (Map p196; E Brucal St, Puerto Galera Town; ⊙8am-4.45pm Mon-Fri)

Puerto Galera Hospital (Map p196; ☎0917 302 3312; Puerto Galera Town)

Western Union (Map p200; Sabang; ⊙7.30am-11pm) Changes cash and gives cash advances for a 7% fee.

ℹ️ Getting There & Away

AIR

Air Juan (Map p196; ☎0917 625 9628; Puerto Galera Town) sea planes now connect Puerto Galera with Manila (from P4500, 20 minutes). Daily departures are at 7.10am from Manila and 1pm from Puerto Galera. On Mondays, Tuesdays, Thursdays and Saturdays there is a flight to Caticlan (for Boracay) at 8am (from P6000, 30 minutes). The return trip is at noon.

BOAT

Frequent bangka ferries connect Batangas on Lu-zon with all three Puerto Galera resort hubs (P230 to P250, one to 1½ hours). Be aware that the last trip to Batangas from **Sabang Pier** (Map p200) leaves at 2pm. From White Beach the last trip is usually 3pm, and from **Muelle Pier** (Map p196) in Puerto Galera town it's 3.30pm. You'll pay a P50 environmental fee on arrival, and modest terminal and security fees on departure from either side.

The irregular roll-on, roll-off (RORO) car ferry to Batangas departs from the **Balatero Pier** (Map p196; ☎043-287 3541), 2.2km west of PG town, at 5am and 3pm.

Also from Balatero, there's a 10.30am bangka every day to Abra de Ilog (P200, one to 1½ hours).

Heavy winds or bad weather often close the Verde Island Passage to Batangas-bound bangkas, especially during windy months from December to February.

JEEPNEY & VAN

Jeepneys (P80, 1½ hours, every 45 minutes until 4pm) and air-con vans (P100, 1¼ hours, hourly until 6pm) service Calapan, 48km southeast of PG town, along a winding road with spectacular views across Verde Island Passage. Both depart from the ambitiously named **Puerto Galera Grand Terminal** (Map p196) just south of the Petron station in PG town. To reach Roxas, you must transfer in Calapan.

ℹ Getting Around

Regular **jeepneys** (Map p200) connect Sabang and PG town during daylight hours (P25, 25 minutes). A tricycle between the two is P150 (more at night); from Sabang to Talipanan it's P350. A tricycle from Puerto Galera town to White Beach costs P150. Motorcycle taxis ('singles') are cheaper.

You can rent motorcycles in Puerto Galera at a cluster of shops around **Alex Motorcycle Rental** (Map p200; ☑ 0908 144 8884; Sinandigan Rd) east of the public market.

Calapan

☑ 043 / POP 133,900

The bustling administrative capital of Mindoro Oriental, Calapan is a feeder port for Batangas, Luzon, and – as far as most visitors are concerned – one of the stops on the bus–boat route between Manila and Boracay. It is also a good base for hiking formidable Mt Halcon and for getting to know a little about Mangyan culture.

◉ Sights & Activities

Mangyan Heritage Center   CULTURAL CENTRE
(☑ 043-441 3132; www.mangyan.org; St Augustine Bldg, Sto Niño St; ☺8.30am-5pm Mon-Fri, by appointment Sat & Sun) ✐ This research center and library is a trove of books, archival photos and old news clippings about Mangyan

culture. Its souvenir shop sells baskets, wild honey, Mangyan mouth harps (P20), Mangyan woven shirts and bags, and greeting cards in Mangyan script – all directly traded at fair prices. They'll enlighten you about the eight main Mangyan tribes and even teach you how to write in Mangyan script.

Mt Halcon   TREKKING
Mt Halcon (2582m), looming over Calapan from the west, is thought by many to be the most challenging peak in the Philippines. Treks should be arranged weeks in advance, as access to the mountain is strictly controlled. Only 20 climbers per day are allowed at each of the two entry points. The hiking season is mid-January until the end of May; the mountain is closed at other times. The standard trip is two days up, two days down.

You'll need to secure permits (P350) from the **municipal tourism office** (☑ 0918 913 4437; emily_naling@yahoo.com; Baco; ☺8am-5pm Mon-Fri) in Baco, the next town north of Calapan. The **Apâk Outdoor Shop** (☑ 0916 241 1780; richard.alcanices@yahoo.com; Quezon Dr), staffed by Richard of the Mt Halcon Mountaineering Association (MHMA), can handle this for you, or to go it alone contact Emily in the Baco tourism office. A Basic Mountaineering Course Certification is required for the climb; the MHMA offers two-day courses.

MANGYAN PEOPLE

The Mangyan people were the first settlers of Mindoro, arriving around 800 years ago. A proto-Malay people, derived from the same ethnic stock as the majority Malay, they comprise eight linguistically similar tribes spread along the length of the island's mountainous interior. It's estimated they make up about 10% of Mindoro's population.

The Mangyan people have preserved their culture to a much greater extent than many other indigenous groups. Many tribespeople still wear traditional dress, such as the ba-ag (loincloth) worn by males. Animism – belief in the spirits that inhabit nature – remains a potent force in Mangyan cosmology, though now it often has some Christian influence.

Most Mangyan people are swidden farmers. During the dry season farmers burn scrub and forest to clear the ground and fertilise the soil; a succession of crops is then planted, including tubers, maize, pulses and 'mountain' rice (a dry rice variety). In the wet season, if there is enough game, pigs, monkeys, birds and other small animals are hunted. On market days the people then descend to the lowlands to trade crops and handicrafts with non-Mangyans.

Mangyan people have a long history of being persecuted by newcomers to the island or being involuntarily caught up in their wars. The Spanish punished them for their close relations with the Moro people, and the Americans put them to work on sugar estates or forced them into reservations. Recently, Mangyan people have been caught in the crossfire in conflicts between the Philippine Army and the New People's Army (NPA).

That they are still able to hold on to their culture despite centuries of incursions from outsiders is a testimony to vitality and tenacity. To find out more, visit the Mangyan Heritage Center in Calapan.

🛏 Sleeping & Eating

There are several hotels near the pier, some of which offer short-stay rates. These make sense if you are transiting via ferry. Otherwise you're better off in the centre.

★ Don Amando's Inn   LODGE $
(☑ 0998 954 6823; cnr San Agustin & G Paras Sts; d P350-650, tr P850; 🛜) More like a cosy hostel than an inn, superfriendly Don Amando's is the perfect choice for a group of climbers. It has a lovely communal kitchen and common area, nine no-frills but clean rooms, and a relatively quiet location near the old town plaza.

Calapan Bay Hotel   HOTEL $
(☑ 043-288 1309; calapanbayhotel@ymail.com; Quezon Dr; d P1100-1500; ❄🛜) Just a 10-minute walk west of the pier, this waterfront hotel has 11 large, cheerful rooms and a terrace where you can dine while admiring the offshore islands. Pick a room far from the road.

Filipiniana Hotel   HOTEL $$
(☑ 043-286 2624; www.filipinianacalapan.com; M Roxas St; r P1750-3500; ❄🛜🏊) Helpful staff, spacious if time-worn rooms, functional wi-fi, a large pool and a location opposite the Xentro Mall make this the top choice for business travellers to Calapan. Ask for the 'promo rate'.

Cargo Grill   FILIPINO $
(JP Rizal St, Tawiran; burgers from P110; ⊘ 10am-midnight) The speciality at this bar and grill is carabao meat. It's served in many forms, most popularly carabao burgers. It's 2km south of the city centre in the Tawiran district, right next to Café del Jardin.

Night Market   MARKET $
(dishes P50-80; ⊘ from 6pm) The night market, on a lane near the City Market in the centre, is great for local budget meals.

★ Café del Jardin   FILIPINO, JAPANESE $$
(JP Rizal St, Tawirin; mains P120-400; ⊘ 11am-9pm; ❄🛜) This blissfully air-conditioned, traditionally decorated cafe is the best dining option in Calapan. In addition to coffee drinks and the full range of Filipino specialities, there's a Japanese menu with udon curry and sashimi. It fronts the Bimas Hotel on the main drag 2km south of the city centre.

Dutch Cafe   CAFE $$
(JP Rizal St; mains P170-300; ⊘ noon-11pm; ❄) A colourful cafe serving coffee drinks, light meals, sandwiches and burgers. It's in a strip of bars and restaurants practically on the grounds of the Filipiniana Hotel.

ℹ Getting There & Away

BOAT
The pier is 2km from the town centre (P20 to P30 by tricycle). The only destination from Calapan is Batangas, Luzon.

Tickets can be purchased on the spot at the pier. The impressive **FastCat** (☑ 0998 845 3285; www.fastcat.com.ph) boats are the most reliable (P190 to P300, 1¾ hours); **SuperCat** (www.supercat.com.ph; Town Pier) and **OceanJet** (☑ 0925 802 9400; www.oceanjet.net) also run fastcraft (P200 to P335, 1½ hours, seven daily).

Trips dwindle after 8pm, although FastCat has additional late-night and early-morning trips. Slower roll-on, roll-off (RORO) car ferries run around the clock (P200, 2½ hours).

BUS & JEEPNEY
Jeepneys to Puerto Galera (P80, 1½ hours, every 45 minutes) leave mainly from the jeepney terminal next to the Flying V petrol station on JP Rizal St, 1km south of Calapan. You can also simply wait for a passing jeepney in Tawiran (south of the centre) at the Puerto Galera road junction.

Vans to Puerto Galera depart from the Calapan City Market on Juan Luna St (P100, 1¼ hours, every 45 minutes). Trips dry up after 5pm.

Also from the Calapan City Market, vans leave to Roxas (P180, 2¾ hours) via Pinamalayan (P100, 1½ hours). Roxas-bound vans also depart from Xentro Mall and the city pier. Frequent vans serve San José (P500, 5½ hours) via Bulalacao.

Roxas & Around
☑ 043 / POP 53,200

Roxas is a dusty little spot with ferry connections to Caticlan. Few travellers stay here intentionally, but some get stuck when the notoriously flaky ferries cancel trips. If you have some time to kill, stroll into the centre and check out the lively **market**, best on Wednesday and Sunday mornings, when villagers come to sell their wares.

Maur Hotel (☑ 043-289 2493; elalm99@yahoo.com; Dangay Pier; r with fan P500, with air-con 6hr/12hr/24hr P700/1300/1500; ❄), at the pier, is the best all-rounder in town.

ℹ Getting There & Away

BOAT
Roxas' Dangay pier is about 3km from the centre (P10 by public tricycle or P50 for a special trip). Vans arriving from points north do drop-offs at the pier before heading into the centre.

If you are heading to Caticlan (P420 to P480, four hours), call the **Ports Authority** (☑ 043-289 2813) at the pier to check the RORO (car

MINDORO ROXAS & AROUND

WORTH A TRIP

BUKTOT BEACH

About 30km south of Roxas you'll encounter a gorgeous sweep of white sand and calm water at Buktot Beach. Visit during the week and you'll have it to yourself. Weekends occasionally draw crowds. From a well-marked turn-off 10km south of Mansalay, it's 1.7km to the beach.

You can sleep on the sand if you're so inclined, or head to nearby **RC Farm & Resort** (☑ 0915 251 2164; rcfarmresort@ yahoo.com.ph; National Hwy; r with fan/ air-con P700/1100; ✱ ☎ ✖), which has a few cute concrete cottages set around a tidy courtyard and a small pool. It's 1km south of the Buktot Beach turn-off.

ferry) schedule, as it changes often and departures are infrequent during the day. **Starlite Ferries** (☑ 0947 596 2493; www.starliteferries. com; Dangay Pier) usually has an 11am departure. **Montenegro Lines** (☑ 0909 856 6559) has between one and three daytime departures, but times vary – 10am, noon, 2pm and 4pm are possible times. Montenegro, Starlite and other companies run several late-night trips.

Starlite Ferries also has daily services to Odiongong, Romblon (P250, 2½ hours, 5pm).

BUS

Vans to Calapan (P180, 2¾ hours) via Pinamalayan (P100, 1¼ hours) meet the ferries at the pier. More vans depart from several points in the town centre throughout the day.

Going south, vans leave roughly hourly from the centre to Bulalacao (P80, one hour) and San José (P250, 2½ hours) until 4pm or so.

From the highway, passing Roro Bus and Dimple Star buses head south to San José and north to Calapan and Manila (P650, nine hours – with a little help from a ferry). Usually a bus passes every two hours or so in either direction.

Bulalacao

☑ 043 / POP 39,100

This unassuming coastal town is surrounded by lost coves and practically uninhabited islands ripe for exploring. South Drive Resort organises island-hopping trips, rents out motorbikes (per day P800) and has a car for hire. Many Mangyans come to town on market days (Tuesdays and Saturdays). A new fast-craft ferry to Caticlan means that a few more travellers are trickling through these days. Note, there is no ATM in Bulalacao.

🛏 Sleeping & Eating

Tambaron Green
Beach Resort   BEACH RESORT $
(☑ 0919 993 4987; www.tambaron.com; dm/d P350/1500) A cheap dorm on a private island? Count us in. It's rote basic – just some mattresses in a musty cottage – but you might have it to yourself. Private rooms are likewise basic but face the sea. There's decent snorkelling and you can hike to several private white-sand beaches, so it's unlikely you'll be spending much time in your room.

Meals are available. Hire a bangka from Bulalacao (P700, 30 minutes).

J Felipa Lodge II   LODGE $
(☑ 0908 867 5162; d with fan P500, with air-con P1200-1500; ✱ ☎) This exceptional deal is nestled amid manicured gardens on the water 2km west of town near the RORO terminal. Fan rooms can sleep four in two queen beds, but lack sinks. Request mosquito nets.

South Drive Resort   GUESTHOUSE $$
(☑ 0928 503 3327; tr P1000-2500; ✱ ☎) This resort slinks down a hillside about 1km beyond the new RORO terminal. The nipa huts, hung with shells and surrounded by a light screen, are the highlight (albeit they don't allow much privacy). They are flush with a small beach. Air-con rooms are up on the hill.

This is easily the best place to eat in town as well. Highlights include steamed crab.

ℹ Getting There & Away

FastCat (☑ 0998 845 3317; RORO Pier) serves Caticlan (for Boracay) by speedy car ferry twice daily at 10am and 10pm (P375 to P500, three hours). The reverse trips leave at 3am and 3pm.

Vans for San José pass through the van terminal every hour or so (P100, 1¼ hours), while more comfortable buses to San José pass along the main highway every two hours (P140, 1½ hours).

Additional vans meet the ferries and head to San José as well as to Calapan (P250, four hours). Manila-bound buses are another option for connecting to Roxas and Calapan.

San José

☑ 043 / POP 143,430

The southernmost town in Mindoro Occidental, San José has a cluster of three pretty islands – **White**, **Ambulong** and **Ilin** – just offshore. It's notable for having an airport, and its position as a transport hub is what brings most travellers through. It also has the only ATMs in Mindoro Occidental, so it's

San José

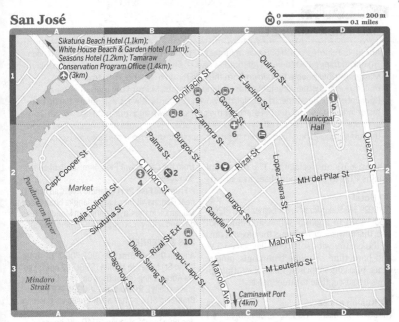

Sikatuna Beach Hotel (1.1km);
White House Beach & Garden Hotel (1.1km);
Seasons Hotel (1.2km); Tamaraw
Conservation Program Office (1.4km);
(3km)

the place to restock your cash. Long, dark-sand **Aroma Beach** begins about 1.5km northwest of the centre. It's clean and good for walking, with decent swimming at high tide and karaoke action by night.

🛏 Sleeping & Eating

The centre is noisy and fumy, so we recommend staying northwest of the centre along Airport Rd or on Aroma Beach – just a short tricycle ride (P10) from town.

★ Seasons Hotel
HOTEL **$$**

(☑ 0909 371 0799; www.seasonsmindoro.com; Airport Rd; r incl breakfast P1600-2600; ❄ 🛜) With 40 business-standard rooms, this new hotel is far better than anything in the noisy centre and just a short tricycle ride into town. You get plenty of mod cons here, including bedside lighting panels and tightly made beds, and it also boasts San José's best restaurant.

It's a short walk to Aroma Beach and a two-minute ride to the airport.

White House Beach & Garden Hotel
HOTEL **$$**

(☑ 0999 138 5854; whitehousephilippines@gmail.com; off Airport Rd; r P2500-3500; ❄ 🛜) This Aroma Beach option is more like the well-to-do mansion of a classy relative than a hotel. The style is luxurious, with balconies and

San José

🛏 Sleeping
1 JD Hotel C2

🍴 Eating
2 Kusina ni Lea B2

🍸 Drinking & Nightlife
3 Chowder C2

ℹ Information
4 Metrobank B2
5 Municipal Tourism Office D1
6 Westmin Hospital C2

ℹ Transport
7 Dimple Star C1
8 RORO Bus B1
9 Vans to Roxas & Calapan B1
10 Vans to Roxas & Calapan B3

huge marble bathrooms (and bidets!). However, it is somewhat sleepy and overpriced.

Sikatuna Beach Hotel
HOTEL **$$**

(☑ 043-491 2182; www.sikatunabeachhotel.com; off Airport Rd; d P1350-1450; ❄ 🛜) This rambling place on Aroma Beach has a mix of rooms (some windowless) around a courtyard that's popular for local weddings. The main draw is its proximity to the ocean,

BAIT FRIDAY MARKET

About 45 minutes south of Roxas, a fantastic **Friday market** (Bait, Mansalay; dawn-noon Fri) called *tianggе* – Mangyan for 'market day' – is held in Bait, a barangay of Mansalay. Mangyan tribespeople trek down from the hills for up to five hours to trade tubers, maize, rice and other vegetables for lowland products. Many of the men wear *ba-ag* (loincloths), while women don colourful woven garments. Always ask before taking photos of individuals. The market starts at the crack of dawn and runs until noon or so. To get here, turn right (west) off the National Hwy about 6km south of Mansalay and follow the rough road 2.7km (you'll need to ford a couple of streams in the rainy season).

otherwise it's unspectacular. The restaurant (mains P175 to P400) specialises in seafood.

JD Hotel   HOTEL $$
(☑ 0929 561 3694; Rizal St, cnr Gomez St; d P1200-1750; ❋ 🛜) In a gaudy yellow-and-blue high rise, this newcomer harbours the nicest rooms in the centre, with soft beds, flat-screen TVs and borderline boutique bathrooms, among other pleasant surprises. Like all central options it's susceptible to street noise.

★ Kusina ni Lea   FILIPINO $
(Sikatuna St; mains P80-150; ⊙6am-10pm; ❋) Kusina has air-con (a rarity in San José), friendly service and a good seafood selection, including sweet-and-sour *lapu-lapu* (grouper), sashimi and grilled squid.

Chowder   PUB
(Rizal St; ⊙24hr) This centrally located resto-bar draws raucous live-music acts by night and serves buckets of beer and Filipino food (mains P50 to P150) around-the-clock.

ℹ Information

Metrobank (C Liboro St)
Municipal Tourism Office (☑ 0929 448 8315; www.sanjoseoccidentalmindoro.com; Municipal Compound, Rizal St; ⊙8am-5pm Mon-Fri) Very helpful office providing ideas on things to do around San José.
Westmin Hospital (Sikatuna St)

ℹ Getting There & Away

AIR
Cebu Pacific (www.cebupacificair.com) has an early-morning flight from Manila to San José. The **airport** (Airport Rd) is 2km northwest of the centre

BOAT
Weather permitting, **Bunso Lines** (☑ 0936 626 3789, 0912 127 8081; Manolo Ave, Caminawit) runs bangka ferries to Coron town in northern Palawan (P800 including lunch, six hours) on Tuesdays, Thursdays and Saturdays at 9am

from the Caminawit Pier, 4km south of central San José.

From the **Fish Port** (Manolo Ave, Caminawit) near Caminawit Pier, cargo bangka boats head to Manamok in the Cuyo Islands on Monday, Tuesday and Friday mornings (P800, nine hours).

BUS & JEEPNEY
Air-con **Dimple Star** (☑ 0908 700 7769; Bonifacio St) buses to Manila (P900, 12 hours) go via Abra de Ilog (eight trips daily) or Calapan (seven daily); **RORO Bus** (☑ 0995 168 7699; Bonifacio St) also has a few buses via Calapan. North-bound buses get you to Calintaan (P60, one hour) and Sablayan (P140, 2½ hours). East-bound Dimple Star buses transit Bulalacao (P170, 1½ hours) and Roxas (P250, 2½ hours).

Similarly priced vans, with several departure points including C Liboro St and Bonifacio St, are another option to Calapan (six hours). Cheaper jeepneys and rickety ordinary buses are slower options to Calintaan or Sablayan.

Mt Iglit-Baco National Park

Travellers who trek to this remote area may be rewarded with a sighting of the wild *tamaraw,* the Philippines' endangered native buffalo. The national park is made up of grassland (the favoured habitat of the *tamaraw*), Mangyan slash-and-burn areas, and forested ridges. Conservation efforts within the park are paying off: *tamaraw* counts have risen steadily over the last several years, from 253 animals in 2002 to 401 in 2017.

To catch sight of a *tamaraw* you'll need to hike. It's straightforward to arrange a hike in the park, but because of the protected status of the wild animals you need to sign in and get permits (free) from the **Tamaraw Conservation Program Office** (☑ 0917 855 6396; tcp.denroccmin04@gmail.com; off Airport Rd, Aroma Beach, San José; ⊙8am-5pm Mon-Fri). The office will call the park entrance in Mantancob in Calintaan municipality, so that a guide (P350 including food) and porter (optional, P500) are waiting for you. If you can't make it to the park office or want to arrange a permit outside of office hours, call project head June Pineda (☑0999 995 6625), who will tell you everything you need to know about visiting the national park.

From Mantancob (Station 1) it's roughly a three-hour hike to the Iglit Station (Station 2) bunkhouse, where you can stay overnight. Alternatively, continue on a further two hours to the Magawang Station (Station 3), where there's a newer bunkhouse and a viewing platform from where you will hopefully observe *tamaraw* gambolling on the plains below. Bring a mosquito net and bedding. December to April are the best climbing months, and in April you may coincide with and observe the annual *tamaraw* count. Access is difficult to impossible during the rainy period from July to September.

Another possible day hike is from the **Gene Pool** station in Manoot to the Mt Magawang viewing platform (about four hours), but this trail is not well kept and not possible in the wet season.

❶ Getting There & Away

Take one of the few direct jeepneys to Poypoy from San José that go to the park entrance in Mantancob, or take a bus to Calintaan (P60, one hour) and a tricycle to Mantancob (P75, 35 minutes).

Sablayan

☑ 043 / POP 83,170

A welcome sight after the long journey from either the north or the south, rural and friendly Sablayan sits astride the Bagong Sabang River. It has a lively market and makes a good base for several worthwhile terrestrial excursions. The main attraction here is Apo Reef, one of the country's best dive sites, about two hours offshore.

◉ Sights & Activities

Sablayan Prison Farm
& Rainforest   PARK
(P50) A wonderfully quirky experience, this penal colony 40 minutes out of town offers much more than a chance to meet and greet prisoners in their element. Various prisoner-guided excursions in the lush forests around the farm are offered, and you can even sleep within earshot of snoring prisoners in the prison guesthouse. You must secure an environmental permit (P55) from the Ecotourism Office in Sablayan to enter the prison

grounds, and then pay the separate admission price at the prison proper.

A half-day of activities might combine an hour or so guided hike in Siburan rainforest with a visit to Libuao Lake, some time talking to prisoners at the central subprison and a visit to Pasugi subprison, where you can buy prisoner-made handicrafts.

Sleeping at the guesthouse requires written permission in advance; arrange this through the Ecotourism Office.

Ecotourism Office   TOURS
(☑043-458 0028, 0915 995 3895; www.sablayan. net; Town Plaza, P Urieta St; ⊙8am-5pm) This tourist office is unique in that it actually runs tours. Apo Reef day or overnight snorkelling trips are the big draw, and staff can also arrange excursions to Sablayan Prison Farm & Rainforest, Mt Iglit-Baco National Park and a two-day forest trek covering several Mangyan villages.

Sablayan
Zipline Adventure   ADVENTURE SPORTS
(☑0917 813 2554; one way P500; ⊙8am-noon & 1-5pm) Sablayan may seem like a strange place for allegedly the world's longest island-to-island zipline (about 1.5km), but here it is. It's a motorised zipline that runs from the port area to South Pandan Island. You can either then pay for the reverse trip or take a bangka (P30). Rock-wall climbing (P50) and rappelling (P50) are also available.

🍴 Sleeping & Eating

★ Pandan Island Resort   BEACH RESORT $
(☑0919 305 7821; www.pandan.com; budget r P900, bungalows P1800, q cottages from P2600; ☎) This postcard-perfect, privately owned resort island is a low-key tropical paradise. It's on a long, curving white-sand beach, and has a combination of comfortable bungalows and rudimentary budget rooms with shared bathrooms. Solar-powered electricity keeps the fans whirring all night. Tasty buffet meals cost P470 and guests are required to take at least one; full board is P1000.

Sablayan Adventure Camp   CABIN $
(☑0917 813 2554; www.sablayanadventurecamp. com; dm P350, r P1500-2500; ❄☎) Navigate the back roads south of town and you'll arrive at this rambling complex among coconut palms on a dark-sand beach. There's a restaurant and adequate air-con and fan rooms. It has a dive shop for Apo Reef trips, and SUPs and kayaks are available; kayaking to South Pandan Island is also possible.

WORTH A TRIP

APO REEF

At 35 sq km, **Apo Reef Natural Park** (environmental fee snorkellers/divers P650/2450) is the largest atoll-type reef in the Philippines. Not to be confused with Apo Island off the south coast of Negros, the park has crystal-clear waters that abound with life, including 285 species of fish and 197 species of coral.

This is the only readily accessible dive site in the Philippines where snorkellers and divers alike are practically guaranteed heavy pelagic (large fish) action – mostly white-tip and black-tip sharks, reef sharks, wrasses, jacks and tuna. You also stand a chance of seeing hammerhead sharks, whale sharks and manta rays out here. The three islands of the reef play host to a variety of turtle and bird species, including the endangered Nicobar pigeon.

The best time to make the trip to Apo Reef is when the seas are at their flattest – April, May, October and November. The journey is very rough during the windy December–March period. At the height of the southwest monsoon (July–September) it's often impossible to get out to the reef and some operators shut down, so be sure to call ahead.

At the time of research five local operators were doing mostly overnight dive and snorkelling trips to Apo Reef: Pandan Island Resort (p209), Gustav's Place, Sablayan Adventure Camp (p209) and Pentagon Diving in Sablayan; and Apo Reef Club in Calintaan. Individuals or couples looking to split costs with other divers are advised to contact the Ecotourism Office (p209) in Sablayan, which can sometimes set you up with a group through one of the four Sablayan-based operators.

The Ecotourism Office also runs day or overnight snorkelling trips to Apo Reef. These cost P8000 per group for the boat (up to 15 people, two hours each way); plus the environmental fee; P1000 per day for a guide; and P300 for full snorkelling equipment (including fins). Bring your own lunch, water and snacks. Overnight trips involve sleeping in hammocks or on the floor of the open-air park ranger station on Apo Island, or on boats.

MINDORO SABLAYAN

Gustav's Place
BEACH RESORT $$

(☑ 0939 432 6134, 0939 432 6131; www.gustavsplace.com; r with fan P800-1400, with air-con P2200; ❄ 🖀) Located out on Sablayan's wide gray-sand beach, Gustav's has a genuinely remote quality. The 13 rooms are simple thatched concrete affairs, some stand-alone, others in a central house. Pricier digs have air-con and hot water. Activities offered include forest walks, kayaking and, of course, diving. From the public market, cross the footbridge and walk 1.5km north along the beach.

⭐ Apo Reef Club
BEACH RESORT $$

(☑ 0917 815 2499; www.aporeefclub.com; r incl half-board per person with fan P1650, with air-con P2310-2950; ⊙ Oct-May; ❄ @ 🖀 ⊠) This Swiss-owned resort 30km south of Sablayan is closer to San José than resorts in Sablayan, potentially allowing you to depart from Manila on an early-morning flight and be diving at Apo Reef the same day. You get big buffet meals and smart, shiny concrete beachfront cottages to go along with more rustic nipa huts and simpler 'backpacker rooms'.

Camalig
FILIPINO $

(C Salvo St; mains P130-350, snacks P50-100) Easily the best restaurant in town, Camalig serves freshly prepared curries and other Filipino food under a soaring nipa canopy. It's just off the National Hwy opposite the town plaza, behind a Card Bank.

❶ Getting There & Away

To easiest way to get to Sablayan is to fly to San José then take a van or bus north.

Alternatively, take a boat to Abra de Ilog, the dusty northern gateway to Mindoro's west coast, from either Batangas (P260, 2½ hours, every three hours) or Puerto Galera (P200, one to 1½ hours, daily at 10.30am). Hop in a waiting air-con van at the pier in Abra de Ilog and head south to Sablayan (P225, 3½ hours).

Direct **Dimple Star** (Map p50; South Rd cnr EDSA, Cubao) buses to Sablayan from Manila (P800, nine hours, every three hours) are also an option. Leaving town, air-con buses rumble through town every three hours or so on their way to Manila (P800, nine hours), and in the other direction to San José (P140, 2½ hours). Air-con vans are somewhat more frequent in both directions.

❶ Getting Around

You can rent motorbikes (P500 per day) at the *habal-habal* stop north of the public market, which fronts the Sabang River near the Emily Hotel.

Boracay & Western Visayas

Best Places to Eat

➡ Albason Ihaw-Ihaw (p232)

➡ Buto't Balat (p237)

➡ Lab-as Seafood Restaurant (p261)

➡ JD&G Italian Food (p274)

Best Places to Stay

➡ Lind (p219)

➡ Cabugan Adventure Resort (p241)

➡ Kookoo's Nest (p257)

➡ Coco Grove Beach Resort (p268)

➡ Aglicay Beach Resort (p271)

Why Go?

Western Visayas tends to attract three types of visitors. The most common is the holidaymaker drawn by Boracay's gorgeous White Beach and the fiesta hubbub that surrounds it: a collection of resorts, restaurants, bars, masseuses and tour touts lined up along one great stretch of sand. And as the latest tour group will attest, it's the perfect place for that selfie in the waves. Next comes the diver drawn to world-class undersea destinations, from Romblon Island in the north to Dauin and Apo Island in the south. Finally there's the off-the-beaten-track traveller braving endless miles of roadside shacks to discover the region's discrete rewards, including mountain trekking and cave exploration, pockets of vibrant nightlife in cities such as Iloilo, some fascinating architectural history, alluring beach resorts and oases of fine food. If you have the endurance to hit them all, pack your compass, snorkel, ear plugs and motion-sickness tablets.

When to Go
Bacolod

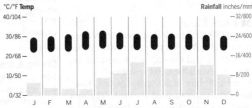

Dec–Apr
These months offer the best diving conditions.

Jun–Oct
Tropical storms and occasional typhoons make this the off-season for a reason.

Oct–Jun
High tourist season. Bring your wallet to Boracay.

BORACAY

♫ 036 / POP 30,100

While only 7km tall and at its bikini line 500m wide, tiny Boracay is the Philippines' top tourist draw, fuelled by explosive growth and a tsunami of hype. Alas, it all got to be too much for the poor little island, and in 2018 Boracay was famously placed in 'rehab' – closed for six months to ease the strain on its fragile environment and fix up the infrastructure.

Boracay version 2.0 was unveiled in November 2018, with cleaner beaches, wider roads and a green streak. The island effectively closed again during the pandemic, allowing the few who visited a chance to experience the island with no crowds. Even when the crowds do return – and they will –there are areas where you can still hear whispers of the fabled 'Old Boracay.'

◉ Sights

Believe it or not, Boracay has other beaches that are almost as pretty as White Beach, if not quite so endless. A scenic walk around the headland at the island's north end brings you to lovely and secluded **Diniwid Beach**, where you'll find excellent accommodation and dining. On the north tip of the island, pretty **Puka Beach** is popular in the off-season and has a few eateries. Some of the best *puka* jewellery (popular necklaces, anklets and bracelets made from the tiny shells of the cone snail) is found in the handicraft stalls here. Other northern beaches are well off the package-tourist radar and nearly deserted. The formerly hard-to-reach **Ilig-Iligan Beach**, in the northeast, looks on to a couple of scenic limestone islets that are snorkelling distance from shore. However, much of it is now essentially property of the Newcoast development.

★ White Beach   BEACH
(Map p220) With its glorious, powdered-sugar sand, White Beach is the centre of the action in Boracay and the only sight most visitors ever see. Beach locations are defined relative to three former boat stations, where bangkas from Caticlan used to arrive. The area south of Station 3, known as Angol, contains most of the budget accommodation, including a few remnants of Old Boracay.

Mt Luho View Deck   VIEWPOINT
(Lapus-Lapus Rd; P120) Looming high above the east coast, this viewpoint has stunning views across the island, though the steps up were designed for giants. The lush cross-country road linking it with the main road is quite a contrast to the coast.

🏃 Activities

You can try your hand at a broad range of outdoor activities. Annoyingly, touts will tout these (Zorbs? 4WDs? Helmet dives? Banana boats?) in your face, every few metres along White Beach. Daily games of football, volleyball and ultimate Frisbee kick off late afternoon on White Beach. Yoga classes are common. For more far-flung adventures, consider a tour to Antique Province or take a bangka to Romblon Province.

Sailing
Sunset *paraw* (traditional outrigger sailboat) trips are a quintessential Boracay experience. Trips start at P800 per hour for up to five or six passengers, and you can usually haggle. Boats depart from Station 1 and 3 in season (October to June), and from Bulabog Beach in the off-season (June to October). D'Boracay Sailing offers a much more personalised and luxurious experience.

D'Boracay
Sailing   BOATING
(♫ 0906 308 8614; www.boracay-sailing.com) MAHAL, a 13m luxury catamaran, is the passion project of Lilyan and Steve, a Chinese-American couple who run sunset cruises, including wine, beer and canapes ($100 per person). They can also organise half- and full-day trips (US$170/245 per person) or customise overnights for groups of four. Reserve online.

Red Pirates   BOATING
(Map p220; Station 3, White Beach; per boat P800) Red Pirates' supersized *paraw* (12-person capacity) does the standard cruises off White Beach, plus longer trips to secret spots around northern Panay and Carabao Island.

Diving & Snorkelling
Diving around Boracay pales in comparison with more renowned hotspots such as Puerto Galera, but there are some OK spots around. **Yapak**, off the northern tip, is a sheer soft-coral-covered wall running from 30m to 65m. Big-fish lovers adore this spot, though depth, currents and surface chop restrict it to advanced divers. There are also drift dives and cave dives. **Crocodile Island**,

Boracay & Western Visayas Highlights

1 White Beach (p212) Catching sunsets on Boracay's deservedly famous beach with a drink or two in hand.

2 Apo Island (p255) Snorkelling or diving with sea turtles in the marine sanctuary's colourful reef.

3 Malumpati Cold Spring (p232) Tracing the aquamarine water back to its mysterious source in the jungle of Panay.

4 Danjugan Island Marine Reserve & Sanctuary (p254) Kayaking around this ecotourist's dream.

5 Siquijor (p264) Cruising the island's circumference at your own speed on a motorbike.

6 Romblon Town (p272) Crashing the expat happy hour in this charming town.

7 Baybay Beach (p230) Chowing down on fresh seafood at a humble waterfront eatery.

8 Sipaway Island (p253) Exploring this unspoiled island by motorcycle.

9 Ariel's Point (p215) Cliff diving into pristine waters on this day trip from Boracay.

10 Mt Kanlaon Natural Park (p249) Refreshing yourself in this park's cool mountain resorts.

Boracay

Kitesurfing & Windsurfing

During the height of the *amihan* (northeast monsoon; December to March), excellent conditions and decent prices (about P19,000 for a 12-hour certification course) make Bulabog Beach on the east side of the island the perfect place to learn kitesurfing. The action shifts to White Beach during the *habagat* (southwest monsoon; June to October), when heavy onshore chop makes it more of an expert's sport. Water-sports businesses rotate location accordingly.

Boracay was an Asian windsurfing mecca long before kitesurfing was even invented, but now windsurfers are in the minority on Bulabog Beach. The season is the same for both. Per-hour board-rental prices are around P700 to P1300, and private 1½-hour lessons are about P3000.

It's not hard to find a good-quality short or longboard to rent in high season.

Habagat
KITESURFING

(Map p220; ☑ 036-288 5787; www.kiteboracay.com) Located at White Beach from May to October; get info from Steakhouse Boracay, near Boracay Beach Club (p219) or Aissatou Beach Resort (p222) on Bulabog Beach.

Hangin'
KITESURFING

(Map p216; ☑ 036-288 3766; www.hanginkite.com; Bulabog Beach) Most of the year this is located on Bulabog Beach in front of a hotel of the same name. It has good equipment and instruction.

Freestyle Academy
KITESURFING

(Map p216; ☑ 0915 559 3080; www.freestyle-boracay.com; Bulabog Beach) One of the best kitesurfing operations.

Isla Kitesurfing
KITESURFING

(Map p216; ☑ 036-288 5352; www.islakitesurfing.com; Bulabog Beach) Lessons, equipment, trips and accommodation from a veteran operation, one of the biggest in Boracay.

Reef Riders
WINDSURFING

(Map p216; ☑ 0908 820 2267; www.reefriders-watersports.com; Bulabog Beach) Has the best equipment and teachers for lessons. Also offers SUP lessons, rental gear and trips around Boracay and Aklan province on Panay.

Adventure Windsurfing
WINDSURFING, KITESURFING

(Map p220; ☑ 036-288 3182; www.adventure-windsurfing-boracay.com; Bulabog Beach) Well-

off the small beach at Tambisaan, is a popular snorkelling destination in good weather.

There are many, many dive centres on Boracay; walk-in prices are usually P1900 per dive with full gear, and P22,000 for an open-water diving certificate. The quality of equipment and instruction is high, and fly-by-night operations fail. Nevertheless, always exercise caution with rental dive equipment. Dive resorts on White Beach offer diving vacations.

Calypso Diving
DIVING

(Map p220; ☑ 036-288 3206; www.calypso-boracay.com/diving; Station 3) PADI five-star development centre for instructors, part of the upscale Calypso Resort (p219).

Fisheye Divers
DIVING

(Map p216; ☑ 036-288 6090; www.fisheyedivers.com; Station 1) This PADI dive centre operates three dive boats, including one live-aboard. It also does free diving lessons.

regarded instruction and equipment for both windsurfing and kitesurfing.

Funboard Center Boracay
WINDSURFING, KITESURFING

(Map p216; ☑036-288 3876; www.windsurfasia.com; Bulabog Beach) Offering equipment and multilingual courses in windsurfing and kitesurfing.

Parasailing

You can't overlook the increasing popularity of this 15-minute activity: just look at the sky off White Beach. There are several providers competing for business, but if you're going to hang from a parachute over the water it behoves you not to skimp. Go at sunset!

Diamond Watersports
WATER SPORTS

(Map p216; ☑036-288 6621; flight P2000) Perhaps the best known in the business for parasailing. Prices halve during low season.

Massage & Spa

You've come to the land of the spa treatment. But where to go amid all these options? It pays not to skimp in this department. White Beach is chock-a-block with groups of women in associations offering inexpensive full-body, back and foot massages right on the beach. Quality can be hit or miss.

★Mandala Spa
SPA

(Map p220; ☑036-288 5857; www.mandalaspa.com; Angol; 90min signature massage P2995, yoga P400; ☺10am-10pm) 🖉 Located on a lush hilltop on the edge of Angol, yet worlds away from White Beach, this spa immerses you in nature, providing a wonderfully tranquil ambience. You can come for a treatment, or a more extended retreat that includes an entire detox program. Uniquely, a tree is planted in your name for every night's stay.

Chi
SPA

(☑036-288 4988; www.shangri-la.com; Shangri-La Resort; 75min signature massage P5800; ☺10am-10pm) Located within the enormous Shangri-La Resort, Chi is a sanctuary within a sanctuary. There are four different treatment villas, each named after a Tibetan village, complete with Asian design flourishes – you'll want to move in. Treatment options are more limited than the competition, but enough to wash all cares away; their focus is removing blockages from your 'chi', or living energy.

Tours

★Tribal Adventures
ADVENTURE

(Map p216; ☑0920 558 7188, 036-288 3207; www.tribaladventures.com; Sandcastles Resort, Station 2, White Beach) Offers a host of well-organised and professionally run adventures on mountainous mainland Panay, including kayaking trips in Tibiao. The day trip is the most popular (P3700 per person in groups of five or more, 6am to 6pm) and involves kayaking on the Tibiao River (March to May not ideal because of low water) and hiking to the Bugtong Bato Falls.

★Ariel's Point
SWIMMING

(☑036-288 6770; www.arielspoint.com) Located on the mainland of Panay and a 40-minute bangka ride away, but only accessible as part of a tour from Boracay, this cliff-jump complex is increasingly popular. Trips (P2500 per person) depart at 11.15am from Ariel's House (Station 1, White Beach), returning at 5pm, and include all the snorkelling, jumping and kayaking you could want, plus food and drinks.

🛏 Sleeping

Boracay has every form of accommodation under the sun, including dive hotels (White Beach) and kitesurfer hotels (Bulabog Beach). Backpackers are well served by an increasing number of hostels, many congregating in the area between the pond by D'Mall and Bulabog Beach. New hotels are mushrooming everywhere, but especially

> ### ℹ THE SEASON MATTERS
>
> Boracay has two seasons of weather, and hence tourism. The high season is defined by the *amihan* (October to June), when wind blows from the northeast, the waters off White Beach are calm and rain is scarce. The island consequently fills with visitors and prices are high. The low season arises from the *habagat* (June to October), when the wind blows from the west, buffeting White Beach amid frequent showers. Businesses erect unsightly windscreens, walking paths flood and detritus blows ashore. Rates drop accordingly and hotels renovate. Note that wind sports operate year-round, but rotate east and west with the season.

White Beach North & Around

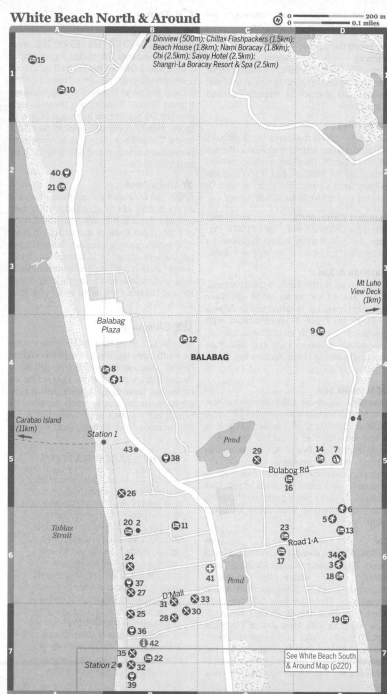

0   200 m
0   0.1 miles

Diniview (500m); Chillax Flashpackers (1.5km);
Beach House (1.8km); Nami Boracay (1.8km);
Chi (2.5km); Savoy Hotel (2.5km);
Shangri-La Boracay Resort & Spa (2.5km)

15

10

40

21

Balabag
Plaza

12

BALABAG

Mt Luho
View Deck
(1km)

9

Carabao Island
(11km)

Station 1

8
1

4

43

38

Pond

29

14 7

Bulabog Rd

16

26

Tablas
Strait

20 2

11

5
6

24

23

Road 1-A

13

17

34
3
18

37
27

41

Pond

D'Mall

31

33

25

28 30

36

42

19

35

22

Station 2

32

39

See White Beach South
& Around Map (p220)

White Beach North & Around

BORACAY & WESTERN VISAYAS BORACAY

on the northern end of the island – this can feel isolating. Whether that's good or bad depends on taste.

Angol (South of Station 3)

You can still find good-value rooms in Angol, where some say the spirit of the 'Old Boracay' survives. There are really no drawbacks to staying down here; it's an easy, pleasant walk to central White Beach.

Orchids LODGE $
(Map p220; ☑ 0917 242 0833, 036-288 3313; www.orchidsboracay.com; Angol; r incl breakfast P1000-2600; ❄ 🛜) And ageing complex of bamboo and nipa rooms at the end of a narrow alleyway set in quiet little garden with orchids all over. Stand-alone cottages are more appealing than the rooms.

★ Hey! Jude South Beach HOTEL $$
(Map p220; ☑ 0917 861 6618, 036-288 2401; www.heyjude-boracay.com; Angol, White Beach; d incl breakfast P3200-7000; ❄ 🛜) The minimalist style and variety of rooms – the priciest open to the sea – are just right. The low-key break-

fast by the White Beach Path is the ideal start to the day. Add helpful staff and an attractive price and you simply can't beat this for value.

Dave's Straw Hat Inn COTTAGE $$
(Map p220; ☑ 036-288 5465; www.davesstrawhatinn.com; r with fan/air-con P1800/3100; ❄ 🛜) Old-timey Boracay feel with blue tin roofs and bamboo set in a leafy, secluded garden at the end of a narrow alleyway off White Beach. Air-con rooms have private verandahs and some charm, the fan rooms much less so. Dave scores points for the breakfasts, especially the discus-sized pancakes, but doesn't take credit cards.

Boracay Pito Huts BUNGALOW $$
(Map p220; ☑ 0922 820 9765; boracaypitohuts@yahoo.com; bungalow P3200; ❄ 🛜) Inside the white-sand enclosure concealed behind a stockade fence like an Old West fort lies a Boracay gem. With an A+ for originality, these seven ('pito') huts have a winning, modern design, with angled walls and twilight interiors, an alluring complement to the bright beach beyond. Each sleeps three with P500 for an extra bed.

Melinda's Garden
BUNGALOW $$

(Map p220; ☎ 036-288 3021; www.melindasgarden.com; r with fan P1600, with air-con P2500-3500; ❄ 🛜) If you're looking for old Boracay, this nearly 30-year-old institution offers nipa huts in a private courtyard, although they're dim and a bit musty. The upper-storey rooms (P1500) are atmospheric, with rattan hammocks on balconies where you can easily blow an entire afternoon. Located at the end of a narrow alleyway off White Beach.

🛏 Central White Beach (Stations 1-3)

If you stay here you are committed to being in the thick of things. The trappings of Boracay's success are everywhere: resorts, restaurants, bars, beach vendors, touts, masseuses, souvenir shops, transvestites and petty thieves. That said, most resorts are set well back from the beach, so you can still get a decent night's sleep.

You'll pay a slight premium for staying on this stretch, but there's a complex of budget resorts around Tans Guesthouse, roughly behind **Summer Place** (Map p216; Station 2; P200; ⏰ 11am-late), that pack in the local tourists. Overseas visitors usually prefer Angol.

Frendz Resort
HOSTEL $

(Map p216; ☎ 036-288 3803; www.frendzresortboracay.com; Station 1; dm P300, r with fan/air-con P1200/1600; ❄ @ 🛜) A lively bar (open to 11pm), cheap cocktails and a young backpacker crowd make long-running Frendz the party people's choice. Dedicated beach beds (a two-minute walk) complement your stay, as does free beer upon arrival and free pasta nights Wednesdays and Sundays. The single-sex dorms are cosy but lack air-con.

Trafalgar Garden Cottages
BUNGALOW $

(Map p220; ☎ 036-288 3711; trafalgarboracay@hotmail.com; s/d with fan P350/500, d with air-con P1000; ❄ 🛜) This leafy little village of basic budget rooms is close to the main road yet not as noisy as you might think. There's a family vibe, public kitchen and lounge area and it's only a short walk to the beach.

Tans Guesthouse
HOTEL $$

(Map p216; ☎ 0917 723 4570; www.tghboracay.com; s/d/q incl breakfast P2500/3500/4000; ❄ 🛜) Tans has a wide variety of rooms, of all styles and quality, spread over a couple of locations. Best considered by groups for the large rooms with kitchens.

★ Nigi Nigi Nu Noos
RESORT $$$

(Map p220; ☎ 036-288 3101; www.niginigi.com; d incl breakfast P6200-7200; ❄ 🛜) The polygonal two-storey cottages, set in a lush garden, have huge rooms, balconies and loads of Balinese atmosphere; they're easily the most elegant choice on this stretch of beach if you like tropical style. An old-school Boracay bar, popular with expats, is on the beach.

Sandcastles
APARTMENT $$$

(Map p216; ☎ 036-288 3207, 0920 558 7188; www.boracaysandcastles.com; White Beach; 1-bedroom apt P6000-11,000; ❄ @ 🛜) The large one- to two-bedroom apartments (44 sq metres to 200 sq metres), recently renovated, are a comfortable mix of rustic and modern with fully stocked kitchens and nicely appointed living rooms. The costlier beachfront rooms have patios that open directly on to White Beach. Heavily discounted (up to 50%) in low season; rather pricey otherwise.

BORACAY'S ENVIRONMENTAL CHALLENGE

Boracay's small size and rapid development have put it under particularly intense environmental pressure. Problems include an inadequate sewage system, frequent electricity brownouts, waste-management problems and a lack of regulatory enforcement. A Beach Management Program has been put in place, but enforcement is erratic, to say the least. The indoors antismoking policy is backed up by fines and a wind farm has gone up in the hills above Caticlan. Silent E-Trikes are competing with their much more numerous, loud and polluting tricycle brethren.

However, most structures are closer to the shoreline than allowed, even granted the continued erosion of the beaches. One new sewage treatment plant opened in Manoc Manoc, in the southern part of the island, and another is scheduled to open in Yapak in the north. However, green algae blooms along White Beach from February to May and sewage emptied not far off Bulabog Beach are a couple of visible indicators of problems to come.

Calypso Resort RESORT $$$
(Map p220; ☑ 036-288 3206; www.calypso-boracay.com; d P3680-8600; ✳@☞) Nicely appointed deluxe rooms with an inviting contemporary-meets-local design and great views define this dive-centric hotel. It offers walk-in discounts.

🛏 North of Station 1

Any promotional photo of Boracay you've seen was probably taken at this heavenly stretch of White Beach. At low tide the expanse of white sand seems infinite, and the sunset *paraw* action – a Boracay trademark – is particularly intense. As are the prices. The further north you go, the lower the density of the resorts.

★ Lind RESORT $$$
(Map p216; ☑ 0998 847 9465, in Manila 02-835 8888; www.thelindhotels.com; White Beach; d incl breakfast P19,000-36,000; ✳☞☲) Ibiza meets Miami Beach meets Filipino hospitality at this smoothly run boutique resort at White Beach's private northern end. Aesthetically, it's Boracay's best, instantly Instagrammable, especially the rooftop infinity pool with perhaps the best sunset views on the island. Each of the 119 rooms has its own balcony, some with small private pool. There are three top-flight restaurants.

Boracay Beach Club HOTEL $$$
(Map p216; ☑ 036-288 6770; www.boracaybeachclub.com; d incl breakfast P5500-6000, ste P7600; ✳☞☲) The 'BBC' is across the road from White Beach, but don't let that deter you. It has a lovely pool area with plenty of shade less than a minute's walk from the beach. Standard rooms are comfortable, if compact. Unfortunately, views from ground-floor rooms are limited, but ocean views can be had from the hotel's beach restaurant.

Sea Wind RESORT $$$
(Map p216; ☑ 036-288 3091; www.seawindboracay.ph; near Station 1; d incl breakfast P5000-9000; ✳@☞☲) A bit of old Boracay on an exquisite patch of sand on a quiet part of White Beach. However, Sea Wind, which has expanded in waves, is a jumble. The rooms adjoining reception have an attractive vintage feel, though road noise can be an issue. Villas across the street are gems and the super-deluxe rooms are worth the price.

FRIENDS OF THE FLYING FOX

One of Boracay's iconic scenes is the nightly migration of hundreds of enormous flying foxes (fruit bats) across the sky. This includes the large flying fox, the common island flying fox and the endangered golden crowned flying fox, the world's heaviest bat. These amazing creatures also perform a vital function, as the seeds they extrude plant trees as they go, accounting for 95% of forest regrowth on cleared land. The local bat population has plunged in the face of development, from 15,000 in 1986 to only 3000 in 2016. The **Friends of the Flying Foxes Boracay** (☑ 036-288 1239; www.fb.com/friendsoftheflyingfoxesboracay) is attempting, despite setbacks from private developers, to create a reserve in the north of the island. Part of their efforts includes regular bat counts, which anyone is welcome to join.

Discovery Shores RESORT $$$
(Map p216; ☑ 036-288 4503; www.discoveryshoresboracay.com; d P25,000; ✳☞☲) Discovery Shores established the standard for White Beach contemporary style and luxury. The fantastic modern design, like a small white city, is open and spacious, especially in the multilevel rooms, which are more like chic lofts. From the private beach you'll flow into the bar, past the stylish pool and into the lobby as if borne on a wave.

Hampstead Boutique Hotel Boracay BOUTIQUE HOTEL $$$
(Map p216; ☑ 036-288 2469; www.hampsteadboracay.com; d P4600; ✳☞) If you want to be near White Beach, but prefer peace and quiet, this artsy boutique hotel a short walk from Station 1 is a good choice. Well-appointed rooms, including robes and espresso machines, a rooftop bar, spacious light-filled public spaces and some outstanding art make for a stylish getaway. It is, however, a very steep walk up the driveway.

🛏 Diniwid Beach

Continue north from White Beach along the narrow concrete path that hugs the point, and you get to peaceful and quiet Diniwid

White Beach South & Around

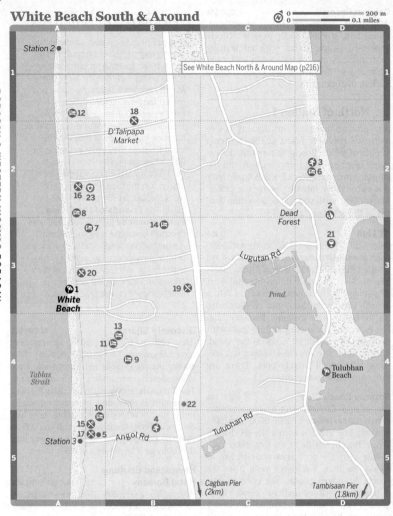

Station 2

See White Beach North & Around Map (p216)

D'Talipapa Market

Dead Forest

Lugutan Rd

White Beach

Pond

Tablas Strait

Tulubhan Beach

Tulubhan Rd

Angol Rd

Station 3

Cagban Pier (2km)

Tambisaan Pier (1.8km)

Beach. It's a beautiful spot, highlighted by a strip of the softest white sand you'll find anywhere and an extraordinary collection of hillside bungalows perched over the sea. There's development happening on the access road to Diniwid, which leads up to City Mall and then to Newcoast.

Chillax Flashpackers
HOSTEL $

(☑ 0908 603 7463; www.chillaxflashpackers.com; Diniwid Rd; dm P450-550, d P1500; ❄ �︎ ☎) Far from the White Beach action, especially if travelling by vehicle, Chillax, true to its name, is a hostel best considered by those

looking for peace and quiet. White, minimalistic and stylish, Chillax is built out of shipping containers with a great rooftop pool. Not carrying any baggage? You can reach Chillax walking north from White Beach.

Beach House
BEACH RESORT $$

(☑ 036-288 2278; cja1025@yahoo.com; Diniwid Beach; d incl breakfast P3000-4000; ❄ @ ☎) Beautifully situated on quiet Diniwid Beach, and one of the best value places, Beach House's rooms are stylish and clean. Beachfront rooms are worth the price.

White Beach South & Around

★ **Diniview** BUNGALOW $$$
(☎ 0917 799 2029; www.diniviewboracay.com; villas P9000-15,000; ❄☎☲) High up the green valley behind Diniwid Beach, these five private hillside villas look ready for an architectural magazine photo shoot. The owner has lavished attention on every detail of the design and decoration; think 'high-end tropical'. Each sleeps four to six, and comes with everything you can imagine, including all mod cons and a fully stocked kitchen.

★ **Nami Boracay** RESORT $$$
(☎ 036-288 6753; www.namiresorts.com; Diniwid Beach; r incl breakfast P9350-13,725; ❄☎) Perched above a fantastic beach like a deluxe treehouse, Nami offers privacy, breathtaking views and a bamboo elevator to save your legs. The 12 luxury rooms have their own outdoor Jacuzzis above the ocean, while the restaurant has an eclectic menu offering everything from Filipino and Asian fusion to burgers and goat's-cheese filet mignon. A honeymooner favourite.

Banyugan Beach

Shangri-La Boracay
Resort & Spa RESORT $$$
(☎ 036-288 4988; www.shangri-la.com/boracay/boracayresort; Yapak; r P1500-15,900, 1-bedroom villa P29,000-38,000; ❄☎☲) There's no doubt about it: this is Boracay's most impressive resort. Occupying the northwest tip of the island, it offers everything you might wish for: two private beaches (including beautiful Banyugan Beach), huge pool, tropical lodge,

beach bar, massive gym, impressive spa etc. But here's the rub: this self-contained world could be absolutely anywhere in the tropics.

Bulabog Beach

Across Boracay's narrow middle from White Beach – just a 10-minute walk from D'Mall, the pedestrian arcade at White Beach's mid-point – is water-sports haven Bulabog Beach, with its laid-back, mellow community vibe. The water here isn't as clean, as some of Boracay's sewage is released offshore. However, a large number of outstanding new accommodation options have opened here in recent years. Rates rise during the December–March kitesurfing season. During low season a charming bangka fleet beaches itself.

Mad Monkey Hostel HOSTEL $
(Map p216; www.madmonkeyhostels.com/boracay; Bulabog Beach Rd; dm/d P800/3000; ❄☎) The party rarely stops at this fun and raucous hostel with whitewashed, simply furnished rooms a short walk from Bulabog Beach. Because of its popularity and relatively large size for a hostel, service can feel impersonal. But for the socially minded you can't beat the pool and bar area and daily activities and trips – many involve drinking.

W Hostel Boracay HOSTEL $
(Map p216; ☎ 036-288 9059; 2nd fl, Gill & Park Bldg, Rd 1-A; dm P500-950, d incl breakfast P2300; ☎) You'll think you're in an alien spaceship at this sleek addition to the Bulabog hostel scene. It has washed concrete hallways, fluorescently lit room numbers and efficiently designed if bare-bones bunk rooms (trippy

spray-painted wall murals add colour). An equally slick kitchen and the large flat-screen TV with video games is a nice touch.

Partying happens on the astroturfed rooftop with a plunge pool good for cooling off post- or midbender.

MNL Hostel
HOSTEL $

(Map p216; ☑0917 702 2160; www.mnlhostels. com; Rd 1-A; incl breakfast dm P500-580, d P1550; ✴@🛜) This high-rise hostel a block or so from Bulabog Beach is clean and intelligently designed (eg private outlets and pull-out lockers), if slightly claustrophobic, with sleeping in pod-like dorm beds. Nice views from the rooftop lounge, and two good restaurants occupy the street-level floor.

★Pahuwayan Suites
RESORT $$

(Map p216; ☑036-288 1449, 0917 322 0497; www. pahuwayansuites.com; d P3000-4500; ✴🛜) Little Pahuwayan, at the end of an alleyway on Bulabog Beach, is one of the best-value spots on the island, offering spacious, stylish rooms with private sea-facing porches and balconies. Floors and walls are brushed concrete, the bathrooms have boutique touches and beds are way above average. Lounge chairs and even a little sheltered cabana are on the beach.

Jeepney Hostel & Boracay Kite Resort
HOSTEL $

(Map p216; ☑0947 777 3551; www.jeepneyhostel boracay.com; Bulabog Rd; incl breakfast dm P400-700, d P1200-2000; ✴🛜) Off Bulabog Beach, Canadian-owned Jeepney caters to hard-living kitesurfers with regular parties, a kitesurfing centre and a sports bar (open 24 hours). Choose from polished-bamboo dorm beds – a step above others in terms of character – in the hostel or the kite resort's clean and colourful private rooms. A small above-ground pool occupies the central courtyard.

★Palassa Private Residences
BOUTIQUE HOTEL $$$

(Map p216; ☑036-288 2703; www.palassaprivate residencesboracay.com; Bulabog Beach; studio incl breakfast P5900, 1-bedroom apt incl breakfast P5900-8900; 🛜🏊) When talented local artist Antonio Gelito San Jose Jr allowed this small, stylish hotel to be constructed on his land, he did so with the proviso that his beachfront art studio be incorporated into it. The owners went a step further and hung his colourful portraits in every other-

wise minimalist room. Every stay includes a complimentary one-hour massage.

Aissatou Beach Resort
BOUTIQUE HOTEL $$$

(Map p220; Habagat Kiteboarding Center; ☑0917 492 1537, 036-288 5787; www.kiteboracay.com; Bulabog Beach; d P1600; ✴🛜) The 10 rooms at this German-run kitesurfing centre are well maintained and generously fitted out with handcrafted furniture and locally commissioned art. Number 12, a fantastic upper-floor, water-view one-bedroom, is one of the best deals around. Private chaise longues line the beach out front.

Hangin Kite Center & Resort
RESORT $$$

(Map p216; ☑036-288 2527; www.kite-asia.com; Rd 1-A, Bulabog Beach; r P3000-5000; ✴🛜) The ground-floor garden and upper-floor sea-view rooms here are good (value is debatable in high season, while low-season rates are deals), but minimally furnished, with tile floors, flat screens and bathrooms with rainwater showers. And when the day is done, you can relax at the Hang Out bar, a popular watering hole.

Boracay Private Mountain Casitas
COTTAGE $$$

(Map p216; ☑0977 855 0596; www.facebook. com/boracayprivatemtcasitas; Bulabog Mtn Rd; r P5100-6500) These thatched-roof cottages offer panoramic (and perfect sunrise) views over Bulabog Beach and southern Boracay. They're a bit dated, but that's part of the charm – you've definitely taken a step back in time. Studio rooms occupy one floor in a two-storey cottage, so you'll have neighbours, but there is one private *casita*. It's a real hike up, particularly in the heat.

🛏 Newcoast

More than 5000 rooms are coming online at this massive development, including the Savoy Hotel, a Marriott Courtyard and a Hilton, at the northern end of the island. Condos, themed to other parts of the world, will be part of this new minicity which will make up 12% of the island and have access to its own private beach. Shops and restaurants will follow. There's already a City Mall (9am to 9pm), the island's first indoor mall.

Savoy Hotel
RESORT $$$

(☑0917 828 4663, 036-286 2800; www.savoy hotelboracay.com; Newcoast; d P5000-8000; ✴🛜🏊) The first hotel to open as part of the massive Newcoast development, the

Savoy is a large high-rise complex with two resort-style pool areas, a stylish lobby and restaurant, but small rooms with Ikea-level furnishings that seem out of step with its ambitions.

Carabou Island

Carabao Island

White Beach Divers RESORT $$
(☎ 0939 774 7410; www.carabao-island.com; Lanas, Carabao; d with fan/air-con P1500/2600; ☎) A retreat from Boracay, this beachfront resort offers clean basic rooms with sea-facing porches, homemade cooking and professional dive services; there's a good wall reef a short swim from shore.

✕ Eating

White Beach Path is one long fantastic food court – half the fun of dining is taking a walk here at sunset. An impressive variety of ethnic restaurants is clustered around D'Mall, the busy pedestrian arcade at White Beach's midpoint. Most upscale resorts have restaurants, some excellent. Korean is the dominant cuisine, followed by Filipino and then a wide variety of international fare.

✕ Angol & Station 3

★ Sunny Side Cafe CAFE $$
(Map p220; ☎ 036-288 2874; www.thesunnysideboracay.com; White Beach; meals P225-395; ☎ 7.30am-10pm; ☎) Make a beeline here in the morning for large, fluffy pancakes (a half-order is all you'll need) and the *roesti* (crumbled chorizo, poached eggs, sour cream and arugula on a fried potato frittata) and strong espresso drinks. Repeat visits will likely follow for inventive twists on classics such as the bacon and mango grilled-cheese sandwiches or shrimp and spinach ravioli.

★ Nagisa Coffee Shop JAPANESE $$
(Map p220; Angol, White Beach; mains P140-330; ☎ 6.30-11pm) Open-air nipa-style Nagisa serves affordable sashimi, okonomiyaki and a P100 snack menu.

Street Market INTERNATIONAL $$
(Map p220; Station X, Main Rd; mains P250-590; ☎ 11am-11pm) Chic and stylish, built below the construction site for a big new resort, is this small food court with Mexican, Japanese, pizza, seafood and Southeast Asian outlets. Seating is in central alcove area with astroturf and floor cushions.

★ Cowboy Cucina INTERNATIONAL $$$
(Map p220; Angol, White Beach; mains P250-600; ☎ 7am-11pm; ☎) This small place has American West decor and expertly prepared burgers, steaks and chilli, plus a dash of Mexican fare and the island's best ribs, all eaten with your toes in the sand. There are some vegie options, a kids' menu and a Sunday roast buffet. Chow down!

✕ Central White Beach

Crazy Crepes CRÊPES $
(Map p216; crêpe P105-150; ☎ 10am-11.30pm) Bubblegum-coloured box on the beach in front of D'Mall offering a variety of sinful dessert crêpes, the perfect complement to a meal. There's another branch on White Beach.

Red Bean Halowich DESSERTS $
(Map p216; D'Mall; ice cream P70-150; ☎ 9am-midnight) Especially popular with Korean tourists, this place selling shaved ice and fruit topped by soft-serve mango ice cream, a twist on the traditional *halo-halo*, always has a long line. A few other varieties, including just soft-serve mango, are on the menu.

★ Plato D'Boracay SEAFOOD $$
(Map p220; D'Talipapa Market; cook to order P150-250; ☎ 8am-9pm) Choose fish, lobster, prawns and other freshly caught shellfish from the D'Talipapa wet market just a few feet away and this family-style grill will cook them. While the resulting prices don't necessarily undercut the White Beach seafood barbecues on the beach by much, it feels satisfying to cut out at least one step on the food-production chain.

Jammers FAST FOOD $$
(Map p216; D'Mall, White Beach; sandwiches P150-345; ☎ 24hr) Satisfying and quick sandwiches, tacos and burgers on a prime patch of real estate, worth including on a late-night bar crawl.

Cozina SPANISH $$
(Map p216; ☎ 036-288 4477; www.lacozina.ph; White Beach; mains P220-460; ☎ 7am-11pm) Stylish beachfront spot with a pan-Latino menu featuring tacos, pulled-pork sandwiches, chorizo bolognese linguini and paella. Wash it down with a mojito or pitcher of sangria and chocolate churros for dessert.

Heidiland DELI $$
(Map p216; D'Mall; ☎ 7am-7pm) Amazingly well-stocked deli offers beach-picnic supplies,

along with sandwiches, bread and gourmet imports. After another rice breakfast, you'll be caressing that jar of Nutella.

Real Coffee & Tea Cafe
CAFE $$

(Map p216; Station 1; breakfasts P200-350; ⊙7am-7pm; 🖉) This old-timer's favourite is a rebuke to the slick chains that have spread throughout Boracay, but the winning recipe remains the same: signature *calamansi* cupcakes, creative tea and coffee, exotic drinks and home-style American cooking. A stool at the front of the upper-storey location facing Station 2 is good for people-watching.

★ Lemon Cafe
INTERNATIONAL $$$

(Map p216; 🖉036-288 6781; D'Mall; mains P300-550; ⊙7am-11pm) Fresh and healthy define this colourful and vibrant D'Mall cafe, which serves big salads, creative sandwiches (eg smoked turkey with apples and celery on ciabatta), classic eggs-Benedict brunches, tropical juices and tasty quiches. At P550, the lunchbox special – soup of the day, green salad, choice of sandwich or rice dish and dessert – is a wise choice.

Aplaya
MEDITERRANEAN $$$

(Map p216; mains P350-600; ⊙9am-1am) This open-air Mediterranean restaurant and mellow beach bar feature beanbag chairs on the sand, a massive tropical drinks menu, ambient grooves, shisha pipes and endlessly creative cuisine – it can capture you here for hours. Just make sure you include sunset.

True Food
INDIAN $$$

(Map p216; 🖉036-288 3142; White Beach, near D'Mall; mains P350-670; ⊙7am-midnight) Desultory service aside, head to the 2nd floor with its floor cushions and airy (hot when no breeze) dining space for excellent set vegetarian and meat meals of Indian and Pakistani dishes. The falafel sandwich (P250) is a good choice if pinching those pesos.

Aria Restaurant
ITALIAN $$$

(Map p216; 🖉036-288 5573; White Beach; mains P288-573; ⊙11am-11.30pm) Aria has a prime people-watching location on the beach path at D'Mall's entrance. The stylish and modern dining room serves homemade pasta such as wonderful *tagliatelle con tartufu* (white truffle) and excellent thin-crust pizza. Beach seating is across the White Beach pathway.

Dos Mestizos
SPANISH $$$

(Map p220; 🖉036-288 5786; tapas from P300; ⊙11am-11pm) Outstanding Spanish cuisine infused with local flavours – including sophisticated tapas, authentic paella, bean soups and hearty stews – makes this an island treat favoured by other restaurateurs. The amiable owner is steeped in Boracay's fascinating modern history. See the wall of photos depicting the 'founders of modern Boracay'; each one has a story behind it.

Cyma
GREEK $$$

(Map p216; D'Mall; mains P360-700; ⊙10am-11pm; 🖉) This popular and cramped Greek restaurant is known for grilled meat, appetisers such as flaming *saganaki* (fried salty cheese) and outstanding salads. Affordable gyros are available for thriftier diners.

✕ Bulabog Beach

Smoke 2
FILIPINO $

(Map p216; Bulabog Beach; P120-180; ⊙7am-11pm) There's no competition if you want a good-value Filipino-style dining experience on Bulabog Beach. Caters to locals and budget-minded travellers with grilled fish, steak, noodle and soup dishes.

English Bakery
BAKERY $

(Map p216; breakfasts P100-200; ⊙7am-11pm) Geared to locals and backpackers on a budget, this is a good spot for freshly baked bread and on-the-run breakfasts such as bacon, egg and cheese sandwiches (P130).

🍷 Drinking & Nightlife

Evenings on White Beach kick off with one long happy hour, mostly from around 4pm or 5pm to between 7pm and 9pm. Nearly every White Beach restaurant has seating, often beanbags or lounge chairs on the sand, and doubles as a bar (usually with poi performances to thumping pop music). Many bars stay open until between 1am and 3am.

★ Epic
CLUB

(Map p216; www.epicboracay.com; MOS nights P100; ⊙10pm-3am) This flashy club with its world-class DJs remains the most popular of the beach discos, and is also known for its Wednesday-night table-football matches. By day, it's a bar and grill; happy hour lasts from noon to 10pm – far longer than you will.

★ Area 51 Secret Party Facility
CLUB

(Map p220; 🖉0917 886 2548; Lugutan Beach; cover P100-200) Apart from having one of the greatest club names ever, Area 51 is (low voice) the only underground party spot on the island. Its schedule is appropriately linked to the phases of the moon, ie there are full-moon and black-moon parties each month, as well as others in high season.

Exit Bar
BEACH BAR
(Map p216; Station 2, White Beach; ⊗5pm-2am) This chilled-out watering hole made from driftwood with a thatch nipa roof is popular with old-school expats, and as they're a colourful lot, that's not a bad thing.

Bom Bom
BAR
(Map p216; Station 2, White Beach; ⊗8am-2am) With nightly acoustic, often reggae or bongo-infused live music, laid-back Bom Bom is one of the best spots to kill time between dinner and late-night dancing.

White House Beach Lounge
BEACH BAR
(Map p216; www.whitehouseboracay.com; north of Station 1; ⊗7am-10pm) A shot of Ibiza, this all-white beach bar, the first north of Station 1, is also the venue for big rave parties in season.

Pub Crawl
PUB CRAWL
(☑0906 207 5343; www.pubcrawl.ph; P990; ⊗7.30-11.30pm Mon, Wed, Fri & Sat) Organises pub crawls of big groups all outfitted in complimentary yellow T-shirts.

Nigi Nigi Nu Noos
BAR
(Map p220; ⊗10am-midnight) The legendary Mason jars of Long Island iced tea (two-for-one during happy hour, 5pm to 7pm) and *weng weng* (rum, gin, tequila, vodka and Cointreau with orange and pineapple juice) more than capably kick-start any evening. And you may stay for the juicy steaks. Popular with old-school expats and anyone looking to watch a little Australian Rules football.

Jonah's Fruit Shakes
JUICE BAR
(Map p216; Main Rd; shakes around P110; ⊗7am-11pm) Amid plenty of competition, Jonah's boasts the best shakes on the island – the avocado and banana mix is sensational. Also has an extensive menu of Filipino faves.

❶ Information

EMERGENCY
Police station (Map p220; ☑036-288 3066) Located just off White Beach.

MEDICAL SERVICES
For serious ailments, diving boats can provide fast transport to the mainland. Patients are then taken to Kalibo or flown to Manila.

Boracay Lying-In & Diagnostic Center (Map p216; ☑036-288 4448; D'Mall; ⊗24hr) The expats' private clinic of choice.

MONEY
ATMs are as numerous as beach touts, especially in D'Mall, along Main Rd and even on the beach path along White Beach. Many resorts handle foreign exchange.

TOURIST INFORMATION
Department of Tourism (DOT; Map p216; ☑036-288 3689; dotr6@boracay@gmail.com; D'Mall; ⊗8am-5pm) Has a few brochures and updated ferry schedules out of Caticlan, Kalibo and Iloilo. Otherwise of limited use.

Filipino Travel Center (Map p216; ☑036-288 6499; www.filipinotravel.com.ph; G/F Plaza Santa Fe Commercial Bldg, Balabag; ⊗9am-6pm) One-stop shop for all air, boat and land transport questions; can book tickets. Also offers transfers from Kalibo (P650) and Caticlan (P550) airports. Possibly worth considering for Kalibo, but not for Caticlan.

VISAS
Bureau of Immigration (BOI; Map p220; ☑036-288 5267; Main Rd; ⊗8am-5pm Mon-Fri) If there are no complicating circumstances, the immigration officer here vows first-time renewals take no longer than 10 minutes.

❶ Getting There & Away

AIR
The island of Boracay has no commercial airport. However, **Caticlan Airport** (Boracay Airport) is just across the strait on the mainland of Panay, only a 10- to 15-minute boat ride away. Cebu Pacific (www.cebupacificair.com) and Philippine Airlines (www.philippineairlines.com) offer many flights daily to Manila and Cebu. And two small airlines, Air Swift (www.air-swift.com) and Air Juan (www.airjuan.com) service important routes to Palawan: Air Swift to Busuanga (Coron) and Air Juan to El Nido.

However, flights fill up during high season and so the alternative is the airport in Kalibo, 1½ to two hours by road to Caticlan. In addition to Cebu Pacific and Philippine Airlines, with flights from Manila and Cebu, there are several other airlines servicing domestic routes. In general, flights tend to be somewhat cheaper and Kalibo receives many international flights from a number of cities in China and Korea, as well as Kuala Lumpur, Malaysia; Hong Kong, Singapore and elsewhere.

There is talk that Caticlan Airport will be improved and expanded to receive international flights in the near future. What that would mean for tourism on Boracay is hard to conceive.

BOAT

A fleet of bangkas shuttles people back and forth between Caticlan and Boracay (P25 for pump-boat, P75 environmental fee and P100 terminal fee; 15 minutes) every 15 minutes between 5am and 7pm, and then as the need arises between 7pm and 10pm (sometimes later if a ferry is late). All boats arrive at Boracay's **Cagban Pier**, where a queue of tricycles awaits to take you to your hotel. They cost P25 per person or P150 per tricycle (more if you are going north of Station 1).

From June to November, brisk southwesterly winds mean you'll often be shuttled round the northern tip of Caticlan to Tabon, where the same fleet of boats will take you to Boracay's alternative pier at **Tambisaan**.

If you arrive after the last regular bangka has departed, you will have to charter a private bangka or sleep at one of the basic pension houses in town.

VAN

It's difficult to justify since it's such an easy trip to do on your own, but there are companies offering all-inclusive round-trip transfers from Caticlan Airport to your hotel, via a combination of van and boat. Price ranges from P800 to P1500 per person, depending on location. Call **Southwest** (☑ 0999 997 5770) or **Island Star Express** (☑ 0917 623 9796; www.islandstarexpress.com). Many hotels outsource these services, or have their own, sometimes complimentary, service; ask for a better deal.

❶ Getting Around

To get from one end of White Beach to the other, either walk, take a pedicab along the walking strip (P10 to P100) or flag down a tricycle along the main road. Tricycles cost only P10 provided you steer clear of the 'special trips' offered by stationary tricycles (P100). Try a silent E-Trike – its roominess feels luxurious and you'll be making a small effort at promoting sustainability.

PANAY

POP 4,400,800

For most visitors to the Philippines, Panay is the island they land on in order to get to the famous White Beach on Boracay. But what does Panay have to offer? Think of it as distinct provinces, as the locals do. In the northwest, Aklan Province (which includes Boracay) is best known for hosting the amazing Ati-Atihan Festival in its capital, Kalibo. Northeast, Capiz Province, has long been known for the fishponds dotting its capital, Roxas, and for the seafood on nearby Baybay Beach. Antique, on the west coast, is the least developed province, making ex-

BOATS & BUSES FROM CATICLAN

Boats

Car ferries to Caticlan from Roxas (Mindoro) and to Batangas (for Manila) are serviced by **2GO Travel** (☑ Manila 02-528 7000; www.travel.2go.com.ph), and Carabao Island is a short boat ride away. The other important routes are to Tablas Island, Romblon.

DESTINATION	FARE (P)	DURATION	DAILY FREQUENCY
Carabao (Lanas)	85	1hr	1
Carabao (San José)	75	45min	1
Roxas (Mindoro)	430-460	4hr	5-6
Batangas	1000	10hr	1, except Tue
Tablas (Odiongan)	300	2hr	Thu & Sun
Tablas (Looc)	300	2½hr	1

Buses

DESTINATION	COMPANY	TYPE	FARE (P)	DURATION (HR)	FREQUENCY
Iloilo	Ceres	bus	350	6	hourly
Iloilo	various	van	400	4	morning
Kalibo	Ceres	bus	107	2	hourly
Kalibo	various	van	100-200	1½	hourly
Kalibo	various	jeepney	80	2½	intermittent
Antique	Ceres	bus	250	3½	every 2hr

ploration doubly interesting; ecotourism is taking hold among its lovely mountains and crystal-clear rivers. Iloilo Province, to the east, has the most sophisticated city on Panay, and also the nearby island of Guimaras, with aquamarine waters and mango farms. All this can be stitched together by circumnavigating Panay on its excellent road network.

Getting There & Away

AIR

The main airports are in Iloilo in the south, and Caticlan, the gateway to Boracay, and Kalibo (an alternative gateway to Boracay) in the north.

Caticlan is planning to expand its airport to become an international hub for western Visayas. Several important routes between Caticlan and Palawan are now serviced by Air Juan (www.airjuan.com) and Air Swift (www.air-swift.com).

All the airports are serviced by Cebu Pacific (www.cebupacificair.com) and Philippine Airlines (www.philippineairlines.com) with flights to Manila (hourly) and Cebu (two to three daily); Cebu Pacific also has direct flights between Iloilo and Cagayan de Oro on the northern coast of Mindanao. Kalibo has international connections to cities in China, Korea, Malaysia, Singapore and Taiwan.

BOAT

You can reach a host of islands from the main ports of Caticlan, Kalibo, Roxas, Iloilo and Dumangas. Two of the more important routes, both serviced by **2GO Travel** (☑ Manila 02-528 7000; www.travel.2go.com.ph), are between Iloilo and Bacolod on the island of Negros, and from Iloilo to Cagayan de Oro on the northern coast of Mindanao. Also, boats from Caticlan and Roxas reach Tablas and Sibuyan islands respectively, in Romblon.

Kalibo

☑ 036 / POP 84,600

The capital of Aklan Province, Kalibo is primarily an alternative port of entry to Boracay and the site of the granddaddy of all Philippine festivals, the raucous Ati-Atihan Festival in January. At other times of the year it's a fairly typical loud and congested Philippine provincial city draped in spaghetti-like electrical lines.

Aklan was settled in 1213 by Malay settlers from Borneo. The local dialect is Aklanon. It's one of the Philippine's youngest provinces, having broken away from neighbouring Capiz in 1956.

◉ Sights

★ Bakhawan EcoPark   PARK
(☑ 036-262 8862; bakhawan_ecopark@yahoo.com; P150; ◎8am-5pm) Five minutes from town in New Buswang (P20 per person by tricycle), this 120-hectare park is the base for a mangrove reforestation project begun in the late 1980s. Visitors can check out intertidal ecology from an 850m boardwalk which ends in a lagoon (kayaks are for rent), while enjoying birdsong and mud critters. It's a welcome green escape from the polluted city.

Museo It Akean   MUSEUM
(☑ 036-268 9260; Martelino St; P20; ◎8am-5pm Tue-Sun) This little downtown museum, in a nicely restored school building located between the market and Pastrana Park, offers a rare look at Aklan history, culture and traditions. It is worth the visit as it only takes 30 minutes and there is nothing else like it in the area.

★ Festivals & Events

Ati-Atihan Festival   CULTURAL
This fantastic festival is the nation's biggest and best Mardi Gras, it most likely dates back to the days of the Borneo settlers. Described by its promoters as a mix of 'Catholic ritual, social activity, indigenous drama and tourist attraction', it's a weeklong street party raging from sunrise to sundown, peaking on the third Sunday of January.

🛏 Sleeping

Most people are only in transit to Boracay depending on the time of flight. But for an overnight only, there are a handful of acceptable options. During Ati-Atihan you should book months in advance and expect to pay two to five times the normal price.

Papierus Pensionne   HOTEL $
(☑ 036-268 5285, 0915 478 6408; www.papieruspensionne.com; 647 Osmeña Ave; d P950-1100; ❄️🛜) Tucked back from a busy main road with a quiet, if dishevelled, central patio, is this good-value choice with clean rooms, polished floors and comfortable beds. It has friendly staff and is accustomed to foreign travellers staying only one night.

Ati-Atihan
County Inn   HOSTEL $
(☑ 036-268 6116; atiatihancounty@yahoo.com; D Maagma St; dm/d/tr/q P150/840/960/1400; ❄️🛜) Just a few blocks south of city centre,

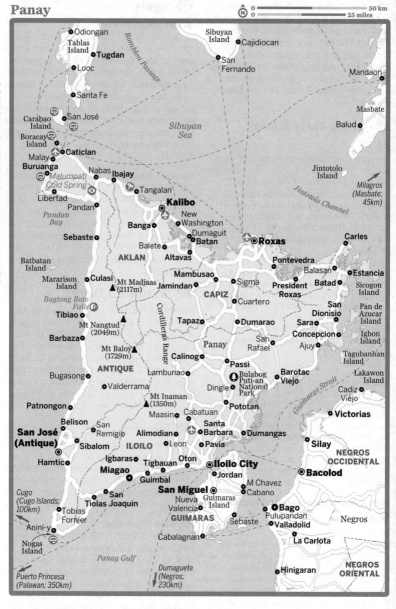

this government-run hotel offers good value, particularly during the Ati-Atihan Festival, when its rates don't change.

The basic rooms are clean and air-conditioned, while the 16-bed fan dorm is spotless.

★ **Marzon Hotel** HOTEL **$$**
(☏036-268 2188; www.marzonhotelkalibo.com; Quezon Ave Ext; d/tr/q incl breakfast P1800/2352/3136; ❄️🛜🏊) Kalibo's top hotel, this extremely well-appointed place is only five minutes from the airport (and around

2.5km from the city centre). It's a five-storey complex with a contemporary coffee shop, as well as a restaurant with al fresco dining by the 25m pool. The rooms are kept shiny, but with little thought given to decor.

✗ Eating & Drinking

★ Kitty's Kitchen
INTERNATIONAL $$

(☑ 033-268 9444; Rizal St; dishes P150-310; ⊘10.30am-9pm; ❀ 🛜) A contemporary design with plush banquette tables means Kitty's is an oasis of comfortable dining in the city centre. The menu runs the gamut from Mexican to Kansas City ribs and especially good pies and cakes for dessert.

★ Manobo Grill
FILIPINO $$

(☑ 0920 904 4540; barangay Tambak, New Washington; mains P180-400; ⊘9am-10pm) Feast on big servings of Filipino specialities such as *bulalo* (bone marrow and beef-shank soup) and steamed seafood at long rows of picnic tables at this open-air spot. Look for the row of fluttering colourful flags on the inland side of the waterfront road.

Roz & Angelique's Cafe
FILIPINO $$

(☑ 036-268 3512; Quezon Ave; mains P200-325; ⊘10am-10pm Tue-Sun) This pleasant homey restaurant attached to an inn of the same name is known for its crispy *pata* (deep-fried pork leg) and all-you-can-eat Sunday meals (P350). The menu is heavy on comfort foods, Filipino and otherwise, such as *pansit bihon* (thick- or thin-noodle dish) and lasagna.

Primavera
ITALIAN $$$

(☑ 036-268 3533; 19 Martyrs St; mains P225-995; ⊘10am-10pm; 🛜) With big portions, a long specials menu, outdoor seating and a wine list, this restaurant a few blocks east of Pastrana Park feels like an oasis of sophistication in Kalibo. Think classic pastas (frustratingly, a third of the options weren't available on our visit), steaks and sandwiches.

★ Kubo Bar
BEER GARDEN

(☑ 0999 395 7035; Osmeña Ave; ⊘10am-midnight) Live acoustic music most nights, cheap buckets of beer and an extensive menu of Filipino fare (P250 to P450) are on tap at this open-air bamboo pavilion just off the highway.

Lorraine's Tapsi
CAFE

(Mabini St; ⊘10am-11pm Sun-Thu, to 1am Fri & Sat) This roadside cafe with its tiki-hut feel is popular with foreigners. It serves decent Filipino food and ice-cold beers and has weekend DJs.

ⓘ Information

Bureau of Immigration (BOI; ☑ 036-268 3164; ABL Sports Complex, Osmeña Ave; ⊘8am-5pm Mon-Fri) Handles visa renewals.

Kalibo Tourism Office (☑ 036-262 1020; kalibotour@yahoo.com; 2nd fl, Municipal Hall, United Veterans Ave; ⊘8am-5pm Mon-Fri) Helpful staff can arrange local tours and help find you a room if everything is booked out for Ati-Atihan.

ⓘ Getting There & Away

Travellers bound for Boracay can fly straight to Kalibo from various Asian cities. Service is seasonal, however, and highly dynamic.

At the airport, tricycles charge a flat P150 to take you to the centre of Kalibo. Alternatively, you can walk 500m out to the highway and flag down a tricycle or jeepney for P10.

BUSES FROM KALIBO

DEPARTS	DESTINATION	FARE (P)	DURATION (HR)	DAILY FREQUENCY
Ceres Bus Terminal	Caticlan	87-105	1¾	frequent
Ceres Bus Terminal	Iloilo	230-250	4	frequent
Ceres Bus Terminal	San José, Antique	200	4	4 Fri-Mon
various, city centre	Caticlan	100	1½	frequent
various, city centre	Iloilo	200	3-3½	frequent
various, city centre	Roxas	120	1½-2	frequent

WORTH A TRIP

ISLAS DE GIGANTES

Comprising eight islets and two large islands, **Gigantes Norte (North Gigantes)** and **Gigantes Sur (South Gigantes)**, a little archipelago off the northeastern tip of Panay, makes for a great bout of island exploration. The islands are all quite different and equally alluring, offering attractive beaches, caves, a turquoise lagoon and more scallops than you've ever seen. Three spots to check out are Antonia Beach, Bantigue Sandbar and Tangke Saltwater lagoon. The only economical way to get here is from Estancia harbour (one hour from Roxas, three hours from Iloilo, four hours from Bantayan), where four bankgas serve various villages (P80). These depart at 1.30pm and return at 9am.

Gigantes Sur is the only island with accommodation. The western side has several similar beach resorts, with basic huts running P1000 to P1800 for four people. A better choice is **Gigantes Hideaway** (☑0918 468 5006, 0999 325 4050; Gigante Sur; dm/cottage/bungalow P200/1000/1500), in the main fishing village. While it has no beach, this well-run resort has nice nipas and a good restaurant. Its package deal is a good-value way to approach the islands. Transport from Estancia, a full day of island-hopping, two nights' accommodation and all meals is P2300 per person for three people. Or get in touch with **Las Islas Travel & Tours** (☑0917 709 3856, 036-521 0725; www.lasislas.ph); it can organise all-inclusive trips starting in Roxas, beginning at P3000 per person for three days and two nights.

The port is at Dumaguit, about 20km southeast of the city.

Buses leave from the **Ceres Bus Terminal** (☑0917 771 1230; Osmeña Ave), a shed on the outskirts of town. Vans depart from several points in the centre, the main cluster being near La Esperanza Hotel at the corner of Toting Reyes and Quezon Ave.

Roxas

☑036 / POP 167,000

Welcome to the self-described 'seafood capital of the Philippines'. The busy capital of Capiz Province and commercial capital of northern Panay, Roxas ships out tonnes of seafood daily, much of it from a huge network of local fishponds. A large development, Pueblo de Panay, has expanded the city's footprint to include a transport terminal and Robinsons Place mall. There are a few beach resorts to choose from, some very cheap seafood at Baybaby Beach and a handful of sights, including a growing network of huge religious statues.

◉ Sights & Activities

Baybay Beach   BEACH

About 3km north of downtown Roxas is this 7km grey-sand beach lined with eateries and picnic shelters. It varies greatly in width depending on the location and tide. Watch fishers unloading their catch at dawn and again at dusk. It's most lively at night when the waterfront is filled with families and couples out for a stroll.

Cadimahan   PARK

(P10) This mangrove park with bamboo walkway is 3½km northwest of the city centre (P25 by tricycle). It has two-hour tours on bamboo rafts pulled by paddleboats (P1800 for 10 to 15 people), with the addition of a back and foot massage as you go. Every Sunday there's a 9am boat tour good for those not in large groups (P100 per person).

Sacred Heart of Jesus Shrine   MONUMENT

(Pueblo de Panay) Occupying a hilltop location about 1.5km from the bus terminal is this enormous nearly 132ft-tall statue of Jesus. Originally the hands were supposed to be outstretched in welcome, but the sculptor made them vertical for technical reasons, creating an 'I surrender' look. You can climb inside to the top. The site offers great views of the region, including the many fishponds that go unseen at sea level. A statue of Mary is visible when approaching Roxas from the east.

Ang Panublion Museum   MUSEUM

(☑036-522 8857; Hughes St; ⊙9am-5pm Tue-Sun) FREE Originally built as a water-storage tank, this quirky museum on the plaza will give you a quick (30-minute) introduction to the city. A *Heritage Walk* booklet will lead you around the nearby area.

✦ Festivals & Events

Sinadya sa Halaran Festival   CULTURAL
(☉ early Dec) A colourful four-day event that celebrates the Immaculate Conception. It includes a solemn candlelit parade on the Roxas River.

Capiztahan   CULTURAL
(☉ Apr) Three-day festival celebrating the founding of Capiz, culminating in a parade of lights and fireworks. The highlight for many is the food, featuring traditional delicacies from all over the province.

🛏 Sleeping

⭐ **Roxas President's Inn**   INN $$
(✆ 0917 803 2277, 036-621 0208; www.roxaspresidentsinn.com; cnr Rizal & Lopez Jaena Sts; s/d from P1180/1800; ❈ 🛜) A mix of old-world charm and modern amenities, this is the best place to stay in the centre. The downside, of course, is street noise. Rooms are comfortable and spacious; some even come with an easy chair. There are only two economy singles.

Hotel Veronica   HOTEL $$
(✆ 036-621 0919, 0939 904 3317; www.hotelveronica.com.ph; Sacred Heart of Mary Ave; r P2000-2400; ❈ 🛜) This upscale hotel in Pueblo de Panay is the place to stay for quick access to Robinsons Place mall and the bus terminal. A restaurant with live music and a rooftop pool will give you something to do.

🍴 Eating & Drinking

Baybay Beach is lined with more than a dozen good-value seafood restaurants. Most of the offerings are the same – a variety of fresh catch cooling on ice – and the best strategy is simply to walk this stretch until you see a place that strikes your fancy.

Cebrew   CAFE $
(Gaisano Arcade, opposite Gaisano Mall; drinks & snacks P50-125; ☉ 11.30am-2am Mon-Thu, to 3am

BORACAY & WESTERN VISAYAS ROXAS

BOATS & BUSES FROM ROXAS

Boats

DEPARTS	DESTINATION	COMPANY	TYPE	FARE (P)	DURATION	FREQUENCY
Culasi Seaport	Odiongan	Super Shuttle	RORO	650	7hr	Mon, Wed & Fri
Culasi Seaport	Batangas	Super Shuttle	RORO	800	15hr	Wed & Sat
Culasi Seaport	Manila	2GO & Super Shuttle	ferry	1000	21hr	Mon, Wed & Sat
Culasi Seaport	Romblon City	2GO	RORO	1990	5hr	3pm Sat
Culasi Seaport	Batangas	2GO	RORO	958	14hr	3pm Wed & Sat
Culasi Seaport	Odiongan	various	bangka	350	4hr	varies; call port
Culasi Seaport	Sibuyan (San Fernando et al)	various	bangka	350	5hr	9am daily
Banica Wharf	Masbate (various ports)	various	bangka	250-500	2-7hr	daily
Banica Wharf	Olotayon	various	bangka	150	30min	8am daily

Buses

The buses below depart from the Integrated Transport Terminal and run hourly.

DESTINATION	COMPANY	TYPE	FARE (P)	DURATION
Iloilo City	Ceres Liner	bus	180	3hr
Kalibo	Acacia & GM's Tours	van	120	1½hr
Caticlan	Acacia & GM's Tours	van	220	3hr
Estancia	Acacia, GM's Tours & Ceres Liner	bus, van	vans P75, bus P110	1½-2hr

Fri & Sat, to midnight Sun; 🐦) A comfortable and cool escape from the noise and sounds of the city. Cappuccinos here are extremely milky lattes sprinkled with cinnamon, but the frappes, brownies and ice cream are tasty.

★ **Albason Ihaw-Ihaw** SEAFOOD **$$**
(Babybay Beach; mains P250-450; ⊗ 9am-10pm) A feast for the eyes and stomach, choose your catch, including squid, sea urchin, prawns and a variety of freshly caught fish, from the display and then your cooking method. Several rows of picnic tables are housed in a pavilion overlooking the beach.

Wayfarer Restaurant BAR
(Baybay Beach; ⊗ 7am-midnight) An upscale and stylish spot for a sundowner (P150 for a rum and coke) with tables on a lawn just off the beach. The open-sided pavilion has a pool table (P20 per game) and there's a good, if relatively pricey, menu (P175 for burgers to P800 for a sirloin steak). Service can be slow and indifferent.

❶ Information

The widely distributed *EZ Map Panay* includes a Roxas city map that's much better than anything offered by the tourist offices.
City Tourism Office (📞 036-621 5316; ⊗ 8am-5pm Mon-Fri) This oft-unstaffed office is located at the back of the civic-centre building. Best to try the provincial office instead.
Provincial Tourism Office (📞 036-621 0042; capiz.tourism@gmail.com; 2nd fl, Capitol Bldg; ⊗ 8am-5pm Mon-Fri) Helpful, friendly and a good source of ideas for things to do.

❶ Getting There & Away

Airline offices are at the **airport** (📞 036-621 2249), a five-minute tricycle ride (P15) north of central Roxas. **Culasi Port** (📞 036-522 3270) is about 3km west of Baybay Beach. The small Banica pier is east of town. All land connections are through the **Roxas City Integrated Transport Terminal** (Acacia Terminal; Sacred Heart of Jesus Ave) in Pueblo de Panay a few kilometres south of the town centre (P25 by tricycle).

Antique Province

This province of rugged peaks and jungle rivers hugging Panay's west coast – pronounced an-TEE-kay – has an excellent road connecting Caticlan (and Boracay) at one end and the southern tip of Panay at the other. Tibiao in particular has become an adventure getaway from Boracay. Other attractions, most notably in Pandan, are spread out, so it helps to have your own vehicle, or base yourself at a resort that provides tours. The area around Tobias Fornier and Anini-y on the southwestern tip of Panay feels like a well-tended hideaway with a handful of great-value beach resorts.

San José de Buenavista, aka 'San José Antique', is the provincial capital and a transport hub, but its logged streets offer little to the traveller apart from the province's only ATMs and a Robinsons Place mall.

❶ Getting There & Away

Frequent Ceres Liner buses run between Iloilo and San José de Buenavista – from here you'll have to transfer to another bus heading north. The wait shouldn't be long. Or you can hop in a minivan; these leave when full and are much quicker but tend to be overpacked and much less comfortable. From Caticlan, Ceres Liner buses and minivans run south to San José – just ask your driver to let you off anywhere along the way.

The most convenient option is your own transport or with an organised tour arranged in Iloilo or Boracay.

Pandan

📞 036 / POP 34,300

A popular day-tour destination 32km from Caticlan (the jumping-off point for Boracay), Pandan is an excellent base for ecotourists interested in pursuing off-the-beaten-track adventures, most especially for the increasingly well-known **Malumpati Cold Spring & Bugang River**.

One of the most striking natural features in western Visayas, the astonishing Malumpati Spring and Bugang River emerges from nowhere in the midst of the jungle, with perfectly clear turquoise water, before flowing to the sea. It's considered a spring, but given the volume of water and the number of caves in the region an underground river might also be at work.

The river is signed off the national road. You come first to Malumpati Health Spring Resort (P10 entrance), which has some basic pensions (rooms P1000), two ziplines (P200) of 200m and 300m and a diving board. The source of the river is a 30-minute walk upstream. Guides (required) are P200. Wear water shoes. From here you can also take a bamboo raft downstream (P450 per person for five people), which is a lot of fun.

TOBIAS FORNIER & ANINI-Y

This area on the southwestern tip of Panay feels like a well-tended hideaway; you'll notice the difference right away. Tourism is focused on a handful of beach resorts that offer great value and there's some excellent diving in the area. However, only one resort, **Dive House** (☑0920 952 8869; www.thedivehouse.com; all meals, lodging & 2-3 dives per day P6500; ❉☎) in Anini-y, offers a fully operational, professionally run dive shop with good-value packages and trips to Nogas Island. It's a charming lodge built from reused materials; walk-in rooms cost P1500. Nearby is the **Sira-an Hot Spring**, a series of developed pools perched on a rocky waterfront. If you don't want to take a dip, you can appreciate the views and fine grilled fish at the **Kanza Grill** on the same property.

As you round the southern tip of Panay and head north to Tobias Fornier, you can break up a trip with a stay at one of two places: **Dalaag Campsite & Resort** (☑0926 448 1063; www.fb.com/dalaag; Poblacion Norte; cottages with fan/air-con P600/1500; ❉), which is a sprawling complex with a huge pool and water slide, aimed at everyone from backpackers to local families; or charming **Punta Hagdan** (☑0916 795 0264; krissy347@ yahoo.com; Paciencia; d P500-1250), with some excellent budget rooms, a cook-to-order kitchen and rental kayaks in a park-like setting by the sea – the perfect spot to refresh if you've been travelling awhile.

Phaidon Beach Resort (☑036-278 9901, 0929 599 2308; www.island-dreams.com; Pandan; d incl breakfast P2750-4300; ❉☎) is both a great place to stay and adventure-travel HQ. Owned by a Filipino-Austrian couple, this very private resort has its own white-sand beach, a small pool, a sea-view restaurant, some smallish bungalows, and a great line-up of adventures including trekking, birdwatching, river boating, islands and especially diving. Tours range from P800 to P3500. Credit cards accepted.

Dramatically sited at the mouth of the Bugang River, **Rose Point Beach Resort** (☑0946 242 4524; Pandan; bungalow P1200-2800; ❉☎) offers a restaurant-bar and simple bungalows, but you're really staying here for the lovely views across Pandan Bay to the mountains, and the chance to kayak upriver.

Tibiao

☑036 / POP 26,800

Thanks to an especially scenic river, beautiful waterfalls, some offshore islands and its proximity to Boracay – Caticlan is only about 1½ hours (85km) from here – the area around Tibiao is a popular destination for outdoor adventures. The town of Tibiao itself has branded all the activities around the Tibiao River the **Tibiao EcoAdventure Park** (TEA Park; www.facebook.com/ tibiaoecoadventurepark; Km 172, National Rd; P50). Mt Madjaas (2113m), Panay's highest peak, is a challenging climb and relatively unexplored.

For the Tibiao version of couch potato try one of the area's distinctive **kawa hot baths**. But instead of being mesmerised by the TV, you have jungle views and the sounds of the rushing river. And instead of an easy chair you're baking in a giant metal vat of herb-infused water heated from a fire below. It's relaxing, meditative and muscle-soothing. A few places offer the experience but Kayak Inn might have the most naturalistic setting where the baths are perched over the Tibiao River.

Bugtong Bato Falls is a series of seven scenic cascades at the end of the TEA Park road that can be ascended one by one, offering some fine swimming holes (the third tier is especially good). The first fall (around 60ft) is reached after a 30-minute hike alongside pretty rice terraces; get your required guide at the barangay booth (P100 for five people). Climb a steep stairway to reach the upper falls. Rappelling might be possible here again in the near future.

Katahum Tours & Fish Spa (☑0917 450 3121; www.katahum.com; 1-day TEA Park tour P1750) offers well-run trips to Seco and Mararison islands, the Bugang River and Malumpati Cold Spring, TEA Park (includes beginner kayaking) and caves. A unique offering, lambaklad fishing, involves going out with local fishers at daybreak and hauling up nets full of migratory fish, particularly tuna.

🛏 Sleeping & Eating

Kasa Raya Travellers Inn   INN $
(📞0917 524 7875; kasaraya@gmail.com; Km 172, barangay Importante; d P900; 🛜) There's a warm familial vibe at this native-style inn set on the edge of a rice paddy. Rooms are basic and the restaurant serves excellent food. You can arrange adventure trips here.

Kawa Inn   INN $
(📞0917 450 3121; barangay Malabor; d with fan/aircon P1400/1600) Sharing space with the Tibiao fish spa, these basic bamboo rooms have nice colourful native-style textiles, though rooms can be dim.

★ Kayak Inn   INN $$
(📞0922 701 4648; www.tribaladventures.com; barangay Tono; dm/d P250/1500) This property run by **Tribal Adventures** (📞Boracay 0920 558 7188; TEA Park; 🚐), a highly recommended tour company based in Boracay, is perched over the Tibiao River and has basic bamboo cottages. True to its name, the main activity on offer is whitewater kayaking, though any other Tibiao adventure activity can be organised here. If not on a Tribal Adventure trip, it's best to make advance enquiries.

Bugtong Bato Falls Inn   BUNGALOW $$
(📞0998 980 4726; Bungtong Bato Falls; bungalow P2500) These three two-floor nipas sleep six and are in an atmospheric spot facing the last cascade of the falls. Bring your food and definitely bargain beforehand.

Iloilo

📞033 / POP 448,000

Panay's largest city is just right. It's big enough to offer a scaled-down version of the urban comforts you get in Manila, yet small enough to remain accessible and down-to-earth. Ilonggo, the people of Iloilo, are rightfully proud and connected to their city's past and invested in its future.Come here for fascinating history, buoyant nightlife and a side trip to rural Guimaras island.

Badly fading grandeur defines the congested old city, which is basically everything south of Iloilo River and east of its tributary, the Dungon River. The future is being cast to the north and west, in the Mandurriao district, from the riverside Esplanade and vibrant Smallville complex and on to the Megaworld Iloilo Business Park near the ever metastasising SM City mall.

👁 Sights & Activities

Iloilo has seven districts, each with its own plaza. These plazas offer pleasant strolls and some impressive historic sites, particularly churches. Of note are the huge **Metropolitan Cathedral** in Jaro, the seat of the Catholic diocese in western Visayas, and the adjacent **Jaro Belfry**; lovely **St Anne's Church** on Molo Plaza, 1km west of the centre; and downtown **San Jose Church** (Plaza Libertad, btwn Dela Rama & Zamora Sts).

★ Casa Mariquit   HISTORIC BUILDING
(Santa Isabel, Jaro; by donation; ⏲9am-7pm) **FREE** A massive banyan tree looms atmospherically over the entrance to this grand home built in 1803 by Philippines VP Fernando Lopez (Mariquit was his wife's nickname). Photos of meetings with Emperor Hirohito, Chiang Kai-shek, Generalissimo Franco, Lyndon Johnson and others are a fascinating step back in time. You can turn up without prior notice, however you might need to shout to get a caretaker's attention.

HISTORIC MANSIONS

Scratch the skin of Iloilo, and you'll find an architectural wonder that goes amazingly uncelebrated. Iloilo has an impressive number of historic mansions from the 19th and early 20th centuries, the legacy of a far more prosperous era, when the city had the highest concentration of millionaires outside Manila. Owned by prominent families largely in the sugar and textile businesses, they were abandoned in the face of war and economic collapse. Sadly, these beautiful examples of Spanish and American architecture are going to rot.

Most of the houses are in Jaro, although they also appear by the city's plazas. Stately **Nelly's Garden** (📞033-320 3075; www.facebook.com/nellygardeniloilo; E Lopez St; per person P200, minimum P1000), built in 1928, and resembling the White House, and ornate **Villa Lizares** (MacArthur Dr, Jaro), built in 1937 and now a school, are two of the grandest. For a general overview, take the unique heritage tour offered by **Panay Tours** (📞0917 536 6779; www.fb.com/cafepanay; Festive Walk, Megaworld, Mandurriao) 🖊.

Bulabog Puti-An
National Park   NATIONAL PARK

Spelunkers take note: this 847-hectare old-growth forest 33km north of Iloilo has dozens of caves, of which six are open to the public, all within 3km of the park entrance. It also has about 40km of trails and the Nautod Wall, a popular rock-climbing site. Secure a guide (P200) at the park office (p239).

The park office also rents two basic open-air cottages (suggested donation P250), or you can pitch your tent. There's plenty of drinking water, but bring your own food. And do beware of the deadly green pit viper, which likes to curl around the tree by the ranger's hut.

The park entrance is a rough tricycle (P120, 20 minutes) or single (motorcycle taxi; P100, 10 minutes) ride from the town of Dingle: take the Iloilo–Kalibo bus to Pototan or Tabugon, and continue by tricycle (P10 to P15). There are also slow and infrequent jeepneys to Dingle from the Tagbac terminal in Iloilo. The rock-climbing area is 2km off the road between Dingle and the National Hwy; contact the Iloilo Mountaineering Club for more detailed information.

City Hall   VIEWPOINT
(Plaza Libertad; ⊙ 8am-6pm Mon-Fri) FREE For the best view of the old city, climb to the roof above the 7th floor – ask the guard for permission. You'll be surprised how different it appears. There are nice views to Guimaras too.

Museo Iloilo   MUSEUM
(Bonifacio Dr; P50; ⊙ 9am-5pm Mon-Sat) Offers a worthwhile display on the indigenous Ati (Negrito) people and a collection of old *pinya* (pineapple fibre) weavings, for which the area is famous. It also has treasure plucked from sunken ships and jewellery unearthed from Spanish burial sites.

✦ Festivals & Events

★ **Dinagyang Festival**   CULTURAL
Celebrating the Santo Niño with outrageous costumes and dances, this three-day, Mardi Gras–style party takes place in the fourth week of January. If you miss it, see the colourful exhibition at City Hall.

Paraw Regatta   SAILING
A race from Iloilo to Guimaras in traditional sailing outriggers (*paraw*), held the third weekend in February.

DON'T MISS

LA PAZ MARKET

In addition to the fascinating sights and smells of a rambling public market, **La Paz Market** (cnr Rizal & Huervana Sts; ⊙ 24hr) contains two local legends. Batchoy, a popular concoction of broth, onion, rice noodles, beef, pork and liver, was invented here, and Netong's Bachoy is the place to try some. Just around the corner, **Madge Cafe** (⊙ 5am-6pm Mon-Sat, to 1pm Sun) has been serving roasted Iloilo coffee since the 1940s. The pictures of visiting local celebs and the personal coffee mugs of the president and other notable figures tell the tale.

Like markets? Check out the chaotic **Central Market** (Rizal St; ⊙ 4am-8pm) too. The dried-fish stalls go on forever.

🛏 Sleeping

GO Hotel   HOTEL $
(☎ 033-335 3376; www.gohotels.ph; Robinsons Pl; r P1000; ❄ ⓢ) Sterile and charmless, about what you'd expect for a chain hotel attached to Robinsons Place mall. However, the simply furnished rooms are clean and modern and it's a good deal, especially if you book in advance for large discounts.

★ **Smallville 21**   HOTEL $$
(☎ 033-501 6821; www.ann2.net/hotels/smallville21; Diversion Rd, Smallville; r P2400-3300; ❄ ⓢ) Spacious and clean, if not particularly stylish, rooms with above-average mattresses, the Smallville 21 is all about location. Smack in the middle of Smallville, which means noise can be an issue from some rooms, and within walking distance of the Shops at Atria.

Injap Tower Hotel   HOTEL $$
(☎ 033-370-7111; www.injaptowerhotel.com.ph; Diversion Rd; r incl breakfast P2300-4000; ❄ ⓢ ⓢ) This high-rise towers over its competition for value. Rates are low for the amenities such as robes, 46in flat-screen TVs and a 21st-floor restaurant (mains P250 to P380) that affords unrivalled panoramic city views. There's a small pool and a spa, but the lobby is tiny. A pedestrian overpass connects it to the massive SM City Mall (p239) across the street.

Iloilo City

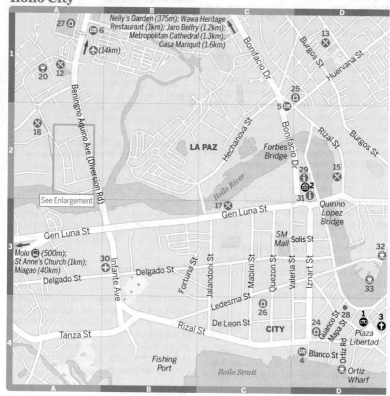

Nelly's Garden (375m); Wawa Heritage Restaurant (1km); Jaro Belfry (1.2km); Metropolitan Cathedral (1.3km); Casa Mariquit (1.6km)

(14km)

Beningno Aquino Ave (Diversion Rd)

LA PAZ

Hechanova St

Bonifacio Dr

Forbes Bridge

Iloilo River

Rizal St

Burgos St

See Enlargement

Gen Luna St

Quirino Lopez Bridge

Gen Luna St

Molo (500m); St Anne's Church (1km); Miagao (40km)

Infante Ave

Delgado St

Delgado St

Fortuna St

Jalandoni St

Mabini St

Quezon St

Valeria St

Iznart St

SM Mall

Solis St

Ledesma St

Rizal St

De Leon St

CITY

Tanza St

Fishing Port

Iloilo Strait

Guanco St

Mapa St

Ortiz Rd

Plaza Libertad

Blanco St

Ortiz Wharf

Grand Dame Hotel HOTEL $$
(☎033-320 5252; www.facebook.com/thegrand damehotel; cnr Rizal & Huervana Sts; r incl breakfast P2000-4000; ❄☎) If you want to experience a bit of old Iloilo, then Grand Dame's location with La Paz Market (p235) directly across the street and historic Jaro just to the north is a good one. While there are a few try-hard touches in the lobby which mean to evoke European sophistication, the rooms are tastefully and comfortably furnished.

Circle Inn HOTEL $$
(☎033-508 0000; www.circleinn-iloilo.com; Iznart St; r P1400-2400; ❄☎❄) While a downtown waterfront location sounds good on paper, there's not much going on here at night. On the plus side, the deluxe rooms with balconies get good light and the pool is nice enough for a dip.

MO2 Westown Hotel HOTEL $$
(☎033-509-0303; www.mo2westowniloilo.com; Glicerio Pison Ave, Smallville; d P2000-3500; ❄☎❄) This chain's icon, a sombrero and palm tree, suggests something akin to Club Med. And the pool area, with a small slide and faux statuary, tries to evoke a beach resort. While it may not succeed on that score, it does offer professional service, well-maintained rooms with contemporary features and a central Smallville location. It also has its own bar complex.

★ **Richmonde Hotel** BUSINESS HOTEL $$$
(☎033-328 7888; www.richmondehoteliloilo.com. ph; cnr Megaworld Blvd & Enterprise Rd; d incl breakfast P3500; ❄@☎❄) The city's newest upscale hotel is also the slickest and most luxurious – that is, until the next one goes up nearby. It has contemporary and stylish furnishings, a sleek lobby and pool area and maybe the city's best buffet breakfast.

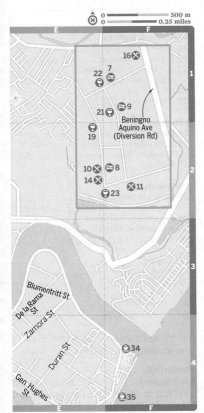

Seafood lovers should head 10km west out of town to Arevalo, where several seafood buffets await with picnic-table seaside dining. Most 'Arevalo' jeepneys get you here.

★**Buto't Balat** FILIPINO **$$**
(Pison Ave; mains P120-175; ⊗10.30am-11.30pm) Even with SM City across the street, mall-themed restaurants feel worlds away at this atmospheric thatch-roofed pavilion. Munch on Ilonggo specialities such as *tinuom* (chicken in banana leaves) and seafood – most serve two to three healthy appetites – amid soft and romantic lighting hanging like branches from trees.

There are branches in Jaro Plaza and Dalon Solis Ave, just over a block from the Iloilo River, close to the city centre.

★**Wawa Heritage Restaurant** INTERNATIONAL **$$**
(☑033-321 0315; E Lopez St; meals P135-150; ⊗11am-2pm & 5pm-midnight; 🖘) Situated amid the historic homes of Jaro, this charming locavore's delight feels like a 19th-century living room, and serves a tasty and inexpensive mix of Filipino, Chinese and Spanish 'heritage dishes'. The eclectically designed homey ambience is a welcome alternative to the mall-like feel of other Iloilo restaurants.

★**Breakthrough Restaurant** SEAFOOD **$$**
(dishes P150-300; ⊗7.30am-9pm) An enormous, wonderfully atmospheric open-air restaurant by the ocean. Select your victims from huge tanks or mounds of ice, then have the chef cook it all for you. Expect to wait.

DoVa INTERNATIONAL **$$**
(Javellana St; mains P150-350; ⊗9am-9pm) Known for its all-day brunch, this atmospheric modern cafe across from La Paz Market is a real green shoot, featuring music, views and nicely presented Western meals with Filipino twists. Way above the competition.

Bluejay Coffee & Co CAFE **$$**
(Ayala Technohub, Smallville; mains P140-240; ⊗7am-midnight; 🖘🍽) More comfortable and stylish than the average Iloilo coffee shop, Bluejay has booths and comfy couches to enjoy hot and cold espresso drinks and a simple menu of sandwiches and pasta. Good for breakfast as well.

Pyt Stop FILIPINO **$$**
(Diversion Rd; mains P220-400; ⊗11.30am-2pm & 5-9pm) Choose from more than half a dozen 'boodle fight' set menus (P1400 to P1700, good

Skinetics Wellness Center BOUTIQUE HOTEL **$$$**
(☑033-320 8726; www.skinetics.com.ph; Boardwalk Ave, Smallville; r incl breakfast P3500-6509; ❉🖘) This strange hybrid high-rise – part therapeutic spa, part cosmetic clinic and part boutique hotel (all on separate floors) – is aimed at the medical-tourism industry, but can be taken piecemeal. Standard rooms are business class, with comfy beds, wood panelling and some heavy and colourful furnishings. The reasonably priced spa is equally professional.

✗ Eating

One approach to eating out here is to wander around a complex such as Smallville's **Boardwalk** (⊗11am-11pm), the **Shops at Atria** (cnr Pacencia Pison & Donato Pison Aves; ⊗10am-10pm) or the SouthPoint expansion of SM City Mall (p239), which all have many restaurants.

Iloilo City

for eight), where heaping serves, laid out on banana leaves in the centre of the table, are enjoyed sans utensils. It's good for groups only. Just outside the Smallville entrance.

Freska FILIPINO $$
(📞 0923 745 8542; Ayala Technohub, Smallville; mains P120-380; ⊙ 11am-3pm & 5pm-1am) The theme is traditional Ilonggo seafood, with snapper and shellfish taking pride of place on the menu, and a great all-you-can-eat lunch and dinner buffet (P300). Best of all, it has broken the San Miguel monopoly, offering a broad selection of foreign beers.

Salt Gastro Lounge AMERICAN $$
(📞 033-335 4529; Gen Luna St; mains P255-320; ⊙ 10.30am-11.30pm; ❄ 🛜) The New York City photos, US licence plates, New Jersey fried chicken (who knew this was a Jersey speciality?) and peach cobbler are all meant to evoke America. Even if the style and taste of the dishes don't exactly match their inspiration, they're still tasty, and it's a stylish and comfortable place to eat.

Troi Oi VIETNAMESE $$
(Boardwalk, Smallville; mains P120-220; ⊙ 11am-11pm) Featuring Vietnamese street food such as banh mi and a variety of pho dishes in a pleasantly designed room with colourful umbrellas hanging from the ceiling. Upbeat

and friendly service – the waitstaff might spontaneously break into a song or dance.

Muelle Deli & Restaurant INTERNATIONAL $$$
(135-B Rizal St; mains P350; ⊙ 11am-11pm Tue-Sun) Filipino–owned, Swiss–managed and with a German chef, this riverfront spot serves hearty steaks and sausages. The outdoor patio, with riverfront views, is as good a place as any to forget the urban bustle, especially at sunset.

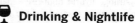

🍷 Drinking & Nightlife

Iloilo's nightlife hub is Smallville and the surrounding area. Clubs come and go and many bars have live acoustic music or DJs. Some cater to Iloilo's sizeable student population. Admission is free on weekdays and up to P200 weekends, when closing time is 2am to 4am; some clubs only open Wednesday to Saturday. Downtown is mostly dark and dead at night.

Zyron CLUB
(📞 033-301 6484; R Mapa St; ⊙ 9pm-3am Tue-Sun) If you like wild evenings, or at least the occasional pyjama or foam party, Zyron, at the western end of the Esplanade, is your place. You can't miss it: the entrance is an enormous wolf's mouth.

Red Paprika BAR
(Boardwalk, Smallville; ⊙10am-2pm & 4pm-1am)
This open-air Asian place is known for its
house cover band, Binhi, which plays 'old-
ies but goldies' Monday to Wednesday and
Friday.

Aura Chill Out Lounge CLUB
(2nd fl, the Ave, Boardwalk Ave; ⊙9pm-4am
Thu-Sat) This dance club with resident DJ
attracts mostly students and young professionals. Entrance fee for men is no problem:
two beers. No flip-flops.

MO2 Ice CLUB
(Smallville; ⊙5pm-4am) A complex combining
a dance club, KTV lounge and open-air bar,
part of the larger MO2 resort. No flip-flops.

Brewery Gastropub PUB
(☑033-393 4038; Pison Ave; ⊙4pm-midnight)
Nearly 100 imported beers, plus several craft
brews on tap, are available at this contemporary spot close to SM Mall and Smallville. It
has an interesting menu as well, including
Filipino specials and dishes such as lamb
with mashed potatoes and raspberry sauce.

JLK Music Lounge & Bar LOUNGE
(☑0947 607 0129; Red Sq Bldg, Smallville; ⊙7pm-
2am) Head splitting from the clubs? For a
truly chilled-out experience, submerge into
the cool blue lighting and retro tunes of this
Smallville lounge.

🛍 Shopping

Robinsons (Ledesma St, btwn Mabini & Quezon
Sts; ⊙9am-9pm) is the big downtown mall,
while **SM City** (Diversion Rd; ⊙9am-8pm)
beyond Smallville on Benigno Aquino Ave

is at least twice as large and has more upscale shops. There are a couple of good
local markets and a few places selling high-
quality handicrafts outside the city centre.

★**Camiña Balay nga Bato** ARTS & CRAFTS
(Lola Rufina Heritage Curio Shop; ☑033-336 3858;
20 Osmeña St, Arevalo; ⊙8am-6pm) This beautifully restored Spanish home (1865) offers
private tours of the upstairs living area (P150,
minimum five people) and a downstairs shop
where the ancient art of weaving *hablon*
cloth is practised. The shop sells *hablon* skirts
(*patadyong*) and a rare, if limited, selection
of other local handicrafts and food. Soup and
homemade hot chocolate are available.

ℹ Information

Bureau of Immigration (BOI; ☑033-336
9603; 2nd fl, Customs House Bldg, Aduana St;
⊙8am-5pm) Issues visa extensions.
Bulabog Puti-An National Park Office
(☑0917 353 6864; Bulabog Puti-An National
Park)
Department of Tourism (DOT; ☑033-337
5411; www.westernvisayastourism.com.ph;
Capitol Grounds, Bonifacio Dr; ⊙8am-5pm
Mon-Fri) Extremely large office with helpful
staff.
Provincial Tourism (☑033-228-4910;
bombette14@yahoo.com; 2nd fl, Old Provincial
Capitol Bldg) Can provide transport information and suggestions for travelling throughout
the province. Both tourist offices are planning
to move to the renovated Old Capitol Building,
Casa Real (cnr Gen Luna & Muelle Looney),
next door.
Iloilo Doctors Hospital (☑033-777 0209;
www.iloilodoctorshospital.com; West Ave) The
most modern hospital in town.

WORTH A TRIP

MIAGAO CHURCH

The relaxed coastal town of Miagao (mee-*yag*-ow), 40km west of Iloilo City, makes for an
excellent day trip. The city is primarily known as the site of the elegant honey-coloured
Miagao Church (Miagao; ⊙5am-6pm Tue-Sun), the only Unesco World Heritage site in
the Visayas. Built from 1787–97, the baroque church served as a fortress against Muslim
raiders, and has striking pyramidal towers. Damaged over the years by fighting, fire and
earthquakes, it was finally restored to its rococo glory in 1962. The fabulous bas-relief
sandstone facade depicts St Christopher strolling through a tropical forest of coconut
palms and papaya trees with baby Jesus. For lunch there's the multtipurpose **Sulu
Garden** (☑033-513-9017; www.sulugarden.com; National Hwy, Miagao; mains P155-275;
⊙9am-10pm), which manages to combine a Japanese teahouse with a fish farm, butterfly
hatchery, artists' studios and sushi restaurant. In the town hall, Miagao's helpful tourist
office has ideas for local excursions, including caves, lakes, interesting rock formations
and cool fern forests.

BORACAY & WESTERN VISAYAS ILOILO

ℹ️ Getting There & Away

AIR

Iloilo Airport is 18km north of town in Santa Barbara. Cebu Pacific (www.cebupacificair.com) and Philippine Airlines (www.philippineairlines.com) serve Manila (hourly) and Davao (daily) and have several flights a week to Cagayan de Oro, General Santos, Puerto Princesa, Singapore, Seoul and Hong Kong. The domestic departure tax is a relatively hefty P200 and P700 for international flights. Airport shuttle buses (P70, 30 minutes) depart from the Travellers Lounge at **SM City** (p239) from 4am to 6pm. They leave when full so allow plenty of time, maybe at least two hours before your flight. A taxi from the city centre runs between P350 to P400.

BOAT

Fastcraft to Bacolod operate out of the Lapuz Terminal (**Iloilo River Wharf**), as do the roll-on, roll-off ferries (RORO) to Guimaras and Puerto Princesa. The frequent RORO to Bacolod operates from Dumangas, 20km north of Iloilo City (P80 per person, P1000 per car, two hours).

Small pumpboats to Jordan Port on Guimaras leave frequently throughout the day from Ortiz Wharf.

The big malls have ticketing offices open 9am to 8pm daily. Boat tickets can be bought at the pier.

BUS & JEEPNEY

A taxi from the city centre to the Ceres Terminal in barangay Tagbak costs around P200.

ℹ️ Getting Around

Hire cars, either self- or driver-driven, are readily available through your hotel. Figure on P2500 per day for an air-con van to cruise around the countryside, excluding petrol.

BOATS & BUSES FROM ILOILO

Boats

DEPARTS	DESTINATION	COMPANY	TYPE	FARE (P)	DURATION	FREQUENCY
Iloilo River Wharf	Bacolod	Weesam Express, FastCat, Ocean Jet	fastcraft	250-600	1hr	hourly
Port San Pedro	Manila	2GO	ferry	1243	27hr	Sun, Wed & Thu
Port San Pedro	Cagayan de Oro	2GO	ferry	1113	14hr	Sat
Port San Pedro	Bacolod	2GO	ferry	595	4hr	Sun
Port San Pedro	Cebu	Trans-Asia, Cokaliong	ferry	760-800	13hr	Tue-Sun
Ortiz Wharf	Jordan Port, Guimaras	various	bangka	14-28	25min	every 30min
Parola Wharf	Buenavista, Guimaras	various	bangka	29	20min	every 30min
Lapuz Terminal	Jordan, Guimaras	FF Cruz	RORO	70 plus vehicle	1hr	every 2hr
Lapuz Terminal	Cuyo/Puerto Princesa	Milagrosa, Montenegro	RORO	950-1220	12/24hr	Thu & Sat

Buses

DEPARTS	DESTINATION	FARE (P)	DURATION (HR)	FREQUENCY
Ceres Terminal	Kalibo	300	4-5	hourly
Ceres Terminal	Caticlan	420	5-6	hourly
Ceres Terminal	Roxas City	180-205	2¾	hourly
Ceres Terminal	Antique (via Miagao)	275	5	every 30min
Ceres Terminal	Carles	300	2-2½	hourly
Molo Terminal	San José, Antique	110 (to San José)	3 (to San José)	daily

GUIMARAS

🎵 033 / POP 174,600

Just a short boat ride from Iloilo City, rural Guimaras is a world away. Known for its sweet mangoes, this is an island of winding roads (ideal for motorbikes), picturesque rice paddies, coral islets and a handful of low-key resorts. A sizeable wind farm has gone up on the eastern side of the island and stories are circulating of a proposal to build a bridge linking the island to Iloilo. However, development, for better or worse, is sure to come slowly. For its size, Guimaras harbours a good number of nice resorts – beach, island and nature resorts – most very moderately priced. If you want to play castaway for a few days, it makes an ideal getaway.

👁 Sights & Activities

Navalas   VILLAGE
Navalas has the only heritage church on the island – quaint Spanish-era **Navales Church** (1880) is made of coral blocks blackened by the years. The much-photographed summer retreat of the wealthy López family, **Roca Encantada** (Enchanted Rock), lies nearby, just off Navalas beach. Navalas is a P400 tricycle ride from Jordan.

Mountain Bikers Hub   MOUNTAIN BIKING
(🎵 0936 994 8528; tommartirguim@yahoo.com) Owned and run by mountain-biking enthusiast Tommy Martir, this is the only place to rent mountain bikes on the island, apart from a few resorts. Tommy also acts as a guide – something to consider, as it's easy to get lost. Ask for him near Jordan Port; bikes are around P500 per day.

Spring Bloom Farm   TOUR
(🎵 0908 821 1289; btwn Km 100 & Km 101; tour P150; ⊙ 7.30am-4pm Mon-Fri) Operating five organic farms totalling 32 hectares of bananas, papayas, cashew, pineapple and more. Offers personal and recommended tours with a day's notice, but the real treat is sitting in the farm's charming cottage sipping fresh *calamansi* juice.

🎉 Festivals & Events

Manggahan Sa
Guimaras Fiesta   FOOD & DRINK
(⊙ Apr/May) The island's main festival honours the much-admired mango just after harvest time. A parade and carnival are held in San Miguel, as well as a mango-eating contest that sent the last winner (13kg!) to hospital.

Ang Pagtaltal Sa Guimaras   RELIGIOUS
(⊙ Good Fri) Jordan's Easter ceremony draws crowds to Guimaras every Good Friday.

🛏 Sleeping & Eating

🛏 San Miguel & Around

Valle Verde Mountain
Spring Resort   RESORT $
(🎵 0918 594 0958; d with fan P550-800, air-con P1500; ❋ ≋) This budget hilltop retreat is a refreshing change from the beach. Accommodation is very basic, nay rundown, and the spring-fed pool a bit green, but there are wonderful views of a jungle-covered valley with Lawi Bay in the distance. Turn off the highway 6km south of San Miguel and proceed 1km down a rough road (P100 by tricycle from San Miguel).

⭐**Camp Alfredo**   RESORT $$
(🎵 0908 123 2977; Ring Rd, after Km 101; cottage P2500; ❋ ≋) Midway between San Miguel and Nueva Valencia, this nature resort is superbly done. Set in an attractive forest with concrete pathways and a running stream, it offers a beautiful open-air dining pavilion, and an even more beautiful horizon pool that can easily capture your entire day. If not, there's always the 325m zip-line course (P425 for visitors).

Cabaling Beach Resort   RESORT $$
(🎵 0949 490 9206; www.cabalingbeachresort.com; Cabaling; r with fan/air-con P1800/3100; ❋) This resort on its own peninsula south of Espinosa has nice facilities, but don't walk the beach to reach it – call ahead for a bangka pick-up (P2000 for the boat from Iloilo). You'll find huge rooms with big balconies – the bamboo cottages have more character – on an attractive cove with a narrow beach and a nice horizon pool.

Celian Seafood   SEAFOOD $$
(San Miguel; mains P220-400; ⊙ 9am-9pm) On the side of the road at the northern end of town is this open-air pavilion serving freshly caught seafood.

🛏 South Coast

⭐**Cabugan Adventure Resort**   RESORT $
(🎵 0939 921 5908, 0917 321 0603; www.fb.com/cabuganadventureresort; near Lucmayan; r with

Guimaras

Guimaras

fan P900-1200, air-con P2200, all incl breakast;
❄) Our favourite budget resort in western Visayas, Cabugan is a particular kind of earthy tropical paradise. The resort hides on a spit of white sand between a headland and a huge coral rock; think of Scaramanga's lair in *The Man with the Golden Gun*. On one side a sea of islets, on another a private bay.

★ **Magic Island Resort**   RESORT $
(☎0910 624 3770; www.fb.com/magicisland resortguimaras; near Lucmayan; cottage incl 3 meals, boat transfer & 90min island-hopping for 2 people P3500; ❄🛜) This tiny resort island – you can walk around it in 10 minutes – sits in an alluring sea of coral islets. Very well managed, it offers superb food and accommodation of various kinds, including two-floor 'Vietnamese houses' (P300) and comfy waterfront cottages. Rooms surprise with their light, cleanliness and Western bathrooms. Canoes are available, too.

⭐ **Jannah-Glycel Beach House** INN $$
(☑0929 281 6498, 033-582 1003; www.jannah glycelbeachhouse.com; Alubihod Beach; r P1450-1800; ☀🅰) Serving primarily European and North American guests, this private water-front villa sits at the very quiet end of Alubi-hod Beach – at high tide there's no beach to speak of. The simply furnished rooms have balconies, though many face one another, and there's an attractive seaside garden. Bangkas take you island-hopping directly from the beach.

Costa Aguada Island Resort RESORT $$
(☑0999 382 7702, 034-433 7373; costaaguada@ gmail.com; r with fan/air-con P1500/2250; 🅰) This resort on Inampulugan, a large island 30 minutes off the southeast coast, is a good place to play Robinson Crusoe – in style. The 68 bamboo and nipa cottages are spacious, the open-air restaurant serves fresh seafood and there are four nearby islands to explore. Or you can just sit by the pool.

Isla Naburot Resort RESORT $$$
(☑0918 909 8500; www.fb.com/islanaburot; cot-tages P5990) Occupying its own island, this absolutely private resort is one of the best offshore options. Those who fantasise about being a castaway (no internet, no air-con and limited electricity) will enjoy the eight cottages made from natural materials, in-cluding pebbles, shells and discarded parts of other houses. Each rustic structure is well designed and comfortable.

ℹ Information

Tourist office (☑0999 332 1727; www. guimaras.gov.ph; Jordan Port; ⊙6am-6pm)

Can answer basic questions and suggest accommodation. Transport rates for all island destinations are posted here.

ℹ Getting There & Around

There's no airport in Guimaras. Visitors arrive by sea from Iloilo City and Negros (Pulupandan and Valladolid), each with roll-on, roll-off ferry (RORO) service.

The tourist office at Jordan Port can help you hire a tricycle (P250 to Alubihod Beach) or multi-cab to any resort. Public jeepneys link Jordan with San Miguel (P15), but aren't convenient for most resorts, which often lie several kilometres off the highway.

If only around for a day, your best bet is rent-ing a motorbike (P500) from outside the tourist office.

NEGROS

POP 4.1 MILLION

With its rugged mountain interior, un-spoiled beaches, underwater coral gardens and urban grooves, Negros has the most to offer in western Visayas after Boracay. This is particularly true of its southern coast, stretching from Danjugan Island around the tip to Bais, where diving is big business. Here the natural base is Dumaguete, a funky col-lege town and expat hang-out. In the north, Bacolod has culinary treats, nearby Silay is a living museum of historic homes, and the cool mountain resorts of Mt Kanlaon are a refreshing alternative to the beach.

When travelling, it makes sense to think of Negros in north–south terms, however politically, it's divided into two provinces

BOATS FROM GUIMARAS

DEPARTS	DESTINATION	COMPANY	TYPE	FARE (P)	DURATION	DAILY FREQUENCY
Jordan Port	River Wharf, Iloilo	FF Cruz	RORO	50	30min	4 Mon-Sat, 2 Sun
Sebaste Port	Pulupandan, Negros	Montenegro	RORO	80	1hr	9am & noon
Jordan Port	Ortiz Wharf, Iloilo	various	bangka	14	15min	every 20min
MacArthur's Wharf	Parola Wharf, Iloilo	various	bangka	15	15min	every 20min
Cabalagnan Port	Valladolid, Negros	various	bangka	150	2hr	1
Cabano Wharf	Pulupandan, Negros	various	bangka	70	45min	10am & 3pm

lying on either side of a central mountain range. To the west lies Negros Occidental – its capital is Bacolod and language Ilonggo. To the east is Negros Oriental, with its capital Dumaguete, and where people speak Cebuano.

ⓘ Getting There & Away

Bacolod and Dumaguete airports are serviced by Cebu Pacific (www.cebupacificair.com) and Philippine Airlines (www.philippineairlines.com) from Manila and Cebu City. Bacolod and Dumaguete are also the island's major ports, although a number of smaller towns are also accessible by boat. Ferries connect Negros to Cebu, Bohol, Mindanao, Panay and Siquijor. Getting around the island is easy: there are good roads and virtually nonstop bus services (Ceres Bus Liner is the major company) around the coast.

Bacolod

⌀ 034 / POP 562,000

Once the hub of a sugar industry, these days Bacolod is known for its food and convenience as a transport hub. Sprawling and clogged with traffic, its appeal isn't readily apparent. However with a limited and targeted stay you can enjoy yourself. There are a few sights of historic interest and good restaurants, and it's a useful base for Mt Kanlaon Natural Park or the nearby historic district of Silay.

◉ Sights & Activities

Permits for trekking in nearby Mt Kanlaon Natural Park are obtained in Bacolod, at the Office of the Park Superintendent (p248).

★ Negros Forests & Ecological Foundation   ZOO
(⌀ 034-433 9234; www.negrosforests.org; South Capitol Rd; adult/child P15/25; ⊙ 9am-noon & 1-4.30pm Mon-Sat) A zoo with a difference, this foundation seeks to preserve endangered animals endemic to Negros. It houses mostly birds, including an extraordinary collection of rare and colourful hornbills that alone justifies a visit. There are also flying foxes, Visayan leopards and endangered local deer.

San Sebastian Cathedral   CATHEDRAL
Worth a look is this impressive 19th-century cathedral built from coral stone (quarried from Guimaras) across from the city's central plaza. It's especially striking at night when its two bell towers are illuminated.

RUINS   HISTORIC BUILDING
(⌀ 034-476 4334; www.theruins.com.ph; P80; ⊙ 8am-8pm) Set among cane fields on lovely manicured grounds, the RUINS is an early-20th-century Italianate mansion originally built by a local sugar magnate in honour of his deceased wife. During WWII, US soldiers set it on fire to prevent the advancing Japanese army from occupying it. Three days later, after the fire subsided, only a haunting skeletal concrete frame remained. If you visit at sunset, its neoclassical columns and stately carved arches make fantastic photographic backdrops.

Negros Museum   MUSEUM
(⌀ 034-433 4764; Gatuslao St; adult/child P50/25; ⊙ 9am-6pm Mon-Sat, cafe 10am-10pm Tue-Sun) Houses an eclectic collection, from a room dedicated to the sugar industry to one containing toys from around the world. Don't miss the fake cannons used to scare the Spanish, including coconut cannonballs. It also has an art gallery, a gift shop and an outdoor cafe.

✵ Festivals & Events

MassKara Festival   CULTURAL
On the weekend nearest to 19 October each year, the city goes crazy with the MassKara Festival, with participants wearing elaborate smiley masks and dancing in the streets.

⤶ Sleeping

11th Street Bed & Breakfast Inn   GUESTHOUSE $
(⌀ 034-433 9191; bb11st@yahoo.com; 11th St; s/d/tr incl breakfast P600/1000/1500; ❄ 🛜) On a relatively calm and quiet side street, just off busy Lacson, this B&B has no-frills rooms (single standards are claustrophobic) with a leafy courtyard and friendly service.

★ Suites at Calle Nueva   BOUTIQUE HOTEL $$
(⌀ 0917 677 8000, 034-708 8000; www.thesuites atcallenueva.com; 15 Nueva St; s/d incl breakfast P1000/1500; ❄ 🛜) With a touch of Spanish-Colonial style, this centrally located boutique hotel is the best value in town. The rooms are every bit as comfortable as a high-end hotel with comfy beds and couches, flashes of colour and sparkling bathrooms with modern fittings. Generous buffet breakfast included.

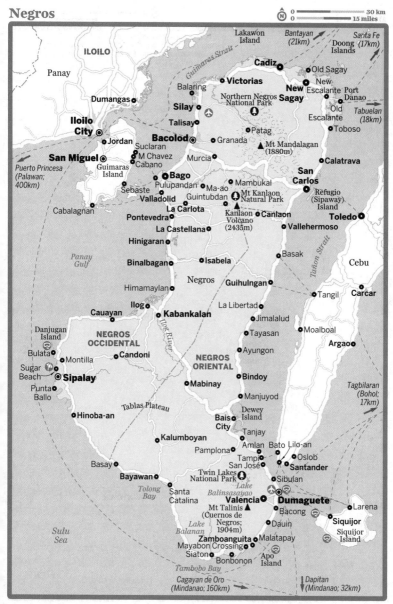

★ **Nature's Village Resort** RESORT $$
(☎034-495 0808; www.naturesvillageresort.net;
Talisay City; r P1800-2400, ste P4200; ❄🛜🏊)
🏖 Located by the highway outside Talisay
City, between Bacolod and Silay, this unique

3-hectare resort combines sustainable hos-
pitality with rustic, high-quality accommo-
dations. However, the building and rooms
aren't especially naturalistic or homespun;
ones in the east wing feature charming

Bacolod

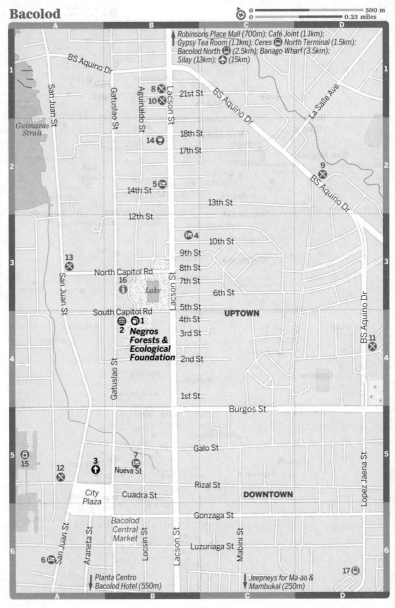

wall murals painted by local artists. The adjoining Village Restaurant is excellent, and partly supplied by an on-site organic farm.

Planta Centro Bacolod Hotel HOTEL **$$**
(☑034-468 0400; www.bacolodplantahotel.com; cnr Araneta & Roxas Sts; d incl breakfast P1800-3500; ❄❅☀) Bright yellow and somewhat grand in appearance, the Planta is a comfortable and good-value choice. However, not much is within walking distance. Popular with conferences, weddings and families, you can expect professional and courteous

Bacolod

service and business-class-quality rooms. Ask for one with lots of light. Breakfast is above average.

MO2 Westown Hotel   HOTEL **$$**
(☏034-709 8899; www.mo2westownhotel.com; cnr San Juan & Luzuriaga Sts; d P2000; @ 🛜 ≋) Within walking distance of SM City, a plus in these parts, the Westown offers spacious rooms with especially comfortable beds and rooms with plenty of light. The small pool and lounge area are surprisingly stylish and there's a coffee shop attached.

L'Fisher Hotel Complex   HOTEL **$$**
(☏034-433 3731; www.lfisherhotelbacolod.com; cnr 14th & Lacson Sts; d P2000-5000, ste P7000; ✳@🛜≋) This centrally located mall-like complex combines three hotels with a range of shared facilities, the most important being an attractive rooftop pool. The lobby is promising, but the carpeting and furnishings are in need of updating and air-conditioning can be loud; ask for a recently renovated room. There are four restaurants, including a nice street-front cafe.

✗ Eating

★Malaspina Inasalan   BARBECUE **$**
(Lopez Jaena St, Villa Monte; mains P30-55; ⊙4-9pm Mon-Sat) An otherwise ordinary-looking street-food eatery has been propelled into a foodie destination for locals of all stripes who claim it serves the best barbecue chicken in the city, nay, in all of Negros. Since its popularity has grown, the menu now also includes pork and fish.

Manokan Country   FILIPINO **$**
(Rizal St; chicken P70; ⊙11am-9pm) This long strip of basic open-air eateries is known for serving the city's famous chicken *inasal* (marinated in lemon and soy, and barbecued on charcoal). Cheap beer and oysters (P35 per plate) don't hurt either. They're fairly interchangeable, with similar dishes on display, but a good strategy is to go where others are already gathered.

★Pala Pala   SEAFOOD **$$**
(North Capitol Rd; ⊙3pm-late) Shrimps, crabs, squid, fish and scallops, fresh from the sea, are displayed at this large market-like shed. After buying your catch, head to one of the next-door eateries, such as D' New Hyksos Tulahan, who will then prepare your meal in whatever method you choose (*sinigáng,* steamed, grilled, fried, *kinilaw* etc). Cooking fees start from P120 per kilogram.

21 Restaurant   FILIPINO **$$**
(www.21restaurant.com; Lacson St; mains P175-360; ⊙10am-11pm) Crisp white tablecloths, professional waiters and an appetising menu set the tone for this classy and reasonably priced restaurant. It's known for its *bachoy* (concoction of broth, onion, rice noodles, beef, pork and liver) and seafood, such as the grilled squid stuffed with lemongrass.

Fresh Start   VEGETARIAN **$$**
(www.freshstartorganic.com; Robinsons Pl Mall; mains P175-375; ⊙10am-9pm; ✎) This health-conscious restaurant with its own organic farm behind it is a vegetarian delight. Combine a vegie wrap with a bottle of Bog's

Brew, a rare example of local craft beer. There's another outlet in Ayala Mall.

C's   CAFE $$
(☑034-433 3731; cnr Lacson & 14th Sts; mains P210-380; ☺7am-10pm; ☎) An authentic patisserie run by a French chef, with an ever-changing selection of gourmet treats, including delicious churros and good espresso drinks.

365 Modern Cafe   INTERNATIONAL $$
(☑034-435 2351; cnr BS Aquino Dr & Kamagong St; mains P185-325; ☺9am-10pm Mon-Thu & Sun, to 11pm Fri & Sat) Gas-station-adjacent restaurants don't normally offer anything more than day-old hot dogs, but this restaurant located in a Fuelstar station harbours a skilled chef who dishes out superb brick-oven pizza, beautiful pasta and Chinese dishes such as beef-brisket noodle soup and authentically prepared dim sum.

Inaka   JAPANESE $$$
(Lacson St; meals P100-750; ☺10am-4pm & 6-10pm Tue-Sun) Tastefully decorated, Inaka has an authentic Japanese menu with a good sushi and sashimi selection and a teppanyaki chef. Vegetarians will want to try tofu steak with mushroom rice (P250). If it's full, try nearby **L'Kaisei**, which has an identical menu.

🍷 Drinking & Nightlife

⭐**Palms at 18th St**   BAR
(☺noon-late) Small, lively outdoor compound with more than a half-dozen eateries doubling as bars; great spot for a bucket of beers.

Gypsy Tea Room   BAR
(Art District; ☺2pm-2am) Offers a scarily cheap drinks menu that attracts a young party crowd.

Café Joint   CAFE
(Art District; ☺4pm-late) Art District hang-out for creative types with live acoustic music.

🛍 Shopping

Bacolod has three major malls: **SM City** (Rizal St; ☺10am-9pm), the largest and most centrally located; **Robinsons** (Lacson St; ☺8am-8.30pm) (with a recommended store stocked with regional handicrafts); and Ayala North (Lacson St north of Robinsons). The first two have cinemas.

⭐**Negros Showroom**   ARTS & CRAFTS
(☑034-433 3728; www.anp-philippines.com; Citywalk, Robinsons Pl; ☺10am-8pm Mon-Thu, to 9pm Fri-Sun) 🌿 A one-stop shop for local handicrafts and organic products, including native jewellery, MassKara masks and *piaya* (sugary flat cakes). It's located in Citywalk, behind Robinsons Place.

ℹ Information

All tourism-related queries should be taken to the **Negros Occidental Tourism Center** (☑034-432 3240; http://tourism.negros-occ. gov.ph; Provincial Capitol Bldg, Gatuslao St; ☺8am-5pm), which is passionate about its work.

Office of the Park Superintendent (☑0932 306 7656; www.facebook.com/mount kanlaon; Abad-Santos St; ☺8am-5pm Mon-Fri) Volcano enthusiasts wishing to trek in Mt Kanlaon Natural Park must apply for permits from this office.

Philippine Reef & Rainforest Conservation Foundation (PRRCF; ☑0915 234 7145; in Bacolod 034-441 6010; www.prrcf.org) Arranges trips to Danjugan Island Marine Reserve & Sanctuary (p254).

ℹ Getting There & Away

Bacolod-Silay Airport services Manila hourly on Cebu Pacific (www.cebupacificair.com) and Philippine Airlines (www.philippineairlines. com). Cebu Pacific also flies to Cebu two to three times per day, and to Davao and Cagayan several times per week. The airport is 15km northeast of Bacolod City; a taxi to the city centre is around P500.

Bredco Port is about 1km west of the centre (P15 by tricycle), Banago Wharf is 7km north, Pulupandan is 25km southwest (P15 by jeepney, 25 minutes) and Valladolid 5km further. All ferries have pier-side ticketing offices; **2GO Travel** (☑034-441 1485; https://travel.2go.com.ph; North Arcade, Robinsons Pl) also has an office in Robinsons Place mall.

Ceres has two bus terminals. The large **north terminal** (Lacson St) serves destinations north of Bacolod (including San Carlos), while the **south terminal** (cnr Lopez Jaena & San Sebastian Sts) serves southern destinations, including Sipalay (transport hub for resorts around Sugar Beach and Punta Ballo). Terminals for van lines are scattered around the city.

Jeepneys for Ma-ao (P25, 30 minutes) and Mambukal (P25, 45 minutes) – and hence for the mountain resorts – are stationed behind the market between Libertad St and Lizares Ave.

ℹ Getting Around

Lacson St is the spine of downtown Bacolod. The north bus terminal is on it; to reach it from the south terminal take a 'Shopping' jeepney. Both 'Bata' and 'Mandalagan' jeepneys run north–south along it.

A car with driver is about P1800 per day; you can organise this through the Negros Occidental Tourism Center and many hotels.

Mt Kanlaon Natural Park

Mt Kanlaon Natural Park is 24,388 hectares of cool, dense forest surrounding a towering active volcano with a deep crater. The park is home to wildlife including wild boar, civet cat, leopard cat, spotted deer, hornbill, hawk eagle and bleeding-heart pigeon. However, most of these are rare, endangered or nocturnal, and so spotting them is difficult, even with a guide. For fit hikers after a challenging trek there are trails to the summit. Most visitors focus on the mountain resorts, which offer diverse activities, making this

area an ever-popular and refreshing escape from Bacolod, even if just for a day.

🛏 Sleeping

The cool, refreshing forest and streams on the western foothills of Mt Kanlaon have long been a popular escape from Bacolod. There are several inexpensive mountain resorts here, owned by local municipalities, that are a wonderful complement to the beach. These offer various activities for overnighters and day trippers alike. Trekkers sleep in designated campsites on Mt Kanlaon.

★ **Mambukal** RESORT $
(☏ 034-473 0610; http://mambukal.negros-occ.gov.ph; barangay Minoyan; camping/dm P30/150, r P600-750, villa P1700-2400; ☀ ☎) Negros' most popular mountain resort is a massive property set amid forests, streams and ponds with a historic Japanese-style hot-springs bath. Accommodation runs the gamut from large dorms to two-bathroom family villas that sleep six to 10. There's a lot to do, including a butterfly

BOATS & BUSES FROM BACLOD

Boats

DEPARTS	DESTINATION	FARE (P)	DURATION (HR)	FREQUENCY
Banago Wharf	Manila	1400	20	Wed, Thu & Sun
	Cagayan de Oro	1360	21	Fri
Bredco	Iloilo	235-280	1	every 30min
	Dumangas	120	2	hourly
Pulupandan	Guimaras	85	1	3-4 daily

Buses

DEPARTS	DESTINATION	FARE (P)	DURATION (HR)	FREQUENCY
Ceres North Terminal	Cebu (via Escalante-Tabuelan)	380-420	8	4 daily
Ceres North Terminal	Sagay	90	2½	frequent
Ceres North Terminal	San Carlos (inland route)	165	3	2 daily
Ceres North Terminal	San Carlos (coastal route)	165	4	frequent
Ceres North Terminal	Silay	18	½	frequent
Ceres South Terminal	Dumaguete	275-350	6	hourly
Ceres South Terminal	Sipalay	150-185	5	every 30min

garden, nifty canopy walk (P25), various waterfalls, a climbing wall (P25) and a spa.

Buenos Aires Mountain Resort

RESORT $

(☑ 034-461 0540; tourismbago@yahoo.com; dm P225, cottages from P800, r with air-con from P1100; ❄ ≋) This 1930s resort is famous for having hidden President Quezon from the Japanese during WWII. The large (5 hectare) hacienda-style property is nicely situated by a river in Ma-ao, with a restaurant and classic spring-fed pool. Accommodation, mostly in unattractive concrete buildings, varies in quality. The hostel rooms, which are a walk up the hill, have nice balcony views.

Guintubdan Visitors Center

GUESTHOUSE $

(☑ 034-460 2585; Guintubdan; d P1000) This attractive building ensconced in the forest with fine views offers only basic accommodation. There's a guest kitchen, but availability of food isn't reliable. Guides can take you on excellent day trips (P100) to nearby waterfalls.

❶ Getting There & Away

From Bacolod, catch a jeepney to Ma-ao (P40, 1½ hours) and a tricycle to the resorts (P200 to P300, 30 to 40 minutes) or to La Carlota (P35, one hour); a jeepney from the latter to Guintubdan is P30.

Silay

☑ 034 / POP 127,000

Just 14km north of Bacolod, Silay was once the jewel in the crown of the Negros sugar boom, when plantations connected the island to the world. During its Golden Age (1880–1935) 29 surviving 'ancestral homes' were built here, of which three are now museums. These sugar mansions were bastions of refinement and privilege, forming a culture reminiscent of *Gone with the Wind* (as in Iloilo). But it wasn't to last. WWII and the collapse of the sugar industry left the town in mothballs, making this a fascinating stop for any history or architecture buff.

◉ Sights

★ Hofileña Heritage House

HISTORIC BUILDING

(☑ 034-495 4561; Cinco de Noviembre St; adult/child P50/30; ⊙ 10am-5pm Tue-Sun, otherwise on request) This stately house contains an astonishing private art collection, as well as antiques belonging to one of Silay's principal families. The house is owned by the charismatic and loquacious Ramon Hofileña, a tireless preserver of the region's cultural heritage. If you book ahead, Ramon will proudly show you around his priceless collection of local artworks.

Church of San Diego

CHURCH

(Rizal St) On the main road through town, the silver-domed, Romanesque Church of San Diego (1927) is topped by a crucifix that, when lit at night, is visible far out to sea. Don't miss the garden set in the adjacent ruins of the previous church, which houses an attractive prayer room screened with capiz windows.

Balay Negrense Museum

MUSEUM

(☑ 034-714 7676; Cinco de Noviembre St; adult/child P60/30; ⊙ 10am-6pm Tue-Sun) Also known as the Victor Gaston Ancestral Home (1898), this hardwood home has the most photogenic exterior of any house in Silay. The house has been painstakingly restored and furnished with period pieces donated by locals. The bevelled-glass windows and Chinese carved latticework are all original.

Silay Museum

MUSEUM

(Civic Centre, cnr Zamoa & Gamboa Sts; ⊙ 8am-noon & 1-5pm Mon-Fri) FREE Start your tour with this well-done overview of the town's history, using models, gowns from the sugar era and vintage photos of historic homes.

Bernardino Jalandoni Ancestral House

MUSEUM

(☑ 034-495 5093; Rizal St; adult/child incl tour P60/30; ⊙ 9am-5pm Tue-Sun) Known as the 'Pink House' (1908), this museum looks like the owner left yesterday. In the back room are old photos of beauty-pageant winners from the 1940s and '50s, and a glass case filled with dozens of Ken and Barbie dolls in traditional Filipino costume, including General MacArthur Ken reenacting the (staged) Leyte landing, and Imelda Marcos Barbie surrounded by dozens of shoes.

☞ Tours

Annual Cultural Tour of Negros Occidental

ARCHITECTURE

(tours P1000; ⊙ Dec) For 41 years, Ramon Hofileña has run these annual tours. The three one-day tours are scheduled in December and take in attractions from the nearby region. With a few days' notice, Ramon can arrange architectural tours of Silay as well. Enquire at the Hofileña Heritage House.

CLIMBING MT KANLOAN

The challenging climb to the summit of Mt Kanlaon (2435m), the highest peak in the Visayas, competes with G2 on Sibuyan and Madjaas on Panay for the best in western Visayas.

Route There are four trailheads to the summit: Wasay, Mananawin, Maput and Guintubdan. Most routes take two days, with the exception of Guintubdan, which can be done by fit hikers in one. Whichever one you choose, the best place to camp on the first night is Margaha Valley, the spectacular flat basin of the old (extinct) crater. The most rewarding part of the climb is the home stretch from Pagatpat Ridge to the summit. On a clear day you can see Margaha Valley below, the smoking crater above and Bacolod in the distance. The hardest part of the climb is the long, steep incline leading up to Pagatpat Ridge.

Risk For keen hikers, Mt Kanlaon is not a tricky or demanding climb, but there is some risk involved. Every few years sees some volcanic activity, or 'sneezing' as locals call it. In fact, because of 'activity' it was closed to hikers for three years. There is daily monitoring for any threat of eruption, with no permits issued in such cases. The park superintendent will sometimes evacuate the mountain and enforce a clearance zone of 8km around its base.

Equipment The weather can be unpredictable and the terrain challenging, so bring a light waterproof jacket, climbing shoes and gloves. Prepare for a chilly night: thermals and a woollen hat are recommended.

Permits & Fees Anyone trekking within a 4km radius of the summit (ie climbers) must obtain a permit (P1000) from the Bacolod-based Office of the Park Superintendent (p248). This requires a scanned copy of your passport clearly showing your age.

Guides & Porters A mandatory guide (P500 to P700 per day, maximum 10 trekkers, five per guide) can be arranged through the park superintendent or near any of the trailheads. Otherwise contact **Angelo Bibar** (☑ 0917 301 1410; angelobibar@gmail.com), the ecotourism officer. Porters are recommended and cost an additional P500 per day.

When to Go The primary climbing season is March to May and October to December. The park imposes a limit of 10 trekkers per day per trail, so walk-ins run the risk of the mountain being full.

Tours Volcano-climbing tours are available, but cost significantly more than going it alone. In Bacolod, **Billy Torres** (☑ 0917 887 6476; billytorres369@yahoo.com) arranges trips for P7000 per person, with group discounts and no accommodation; P500 is donated to the Negros Forest Foundation. Advance notice of two months or more is ideal. Or try Cebu-based companies, **Planet Action** (☑ 0917 583 0062; www.action-philippines.com) and **Trail Adventours** (☑ 032-802 3401; www.trailadventours.com) for all-inclusive packages. In Dumaguete, Harold's Mansion (p260) occasionally arranges two-day budget trips (around P2500 plus food).

✦ Festivals & Events

Hugyaw Silay
Kansilay Festival CULTURAL
(☉ Jun) The city's founding is celebrated for nearly a week in early to mid-June, culminating in a raucous parade of elaborately costumed dancers who head down Rizal St before a final performance in the covered central plaza. Locals line the street several deep and others watch from 2nd-floor windows. The whole town shuts down to party.

🛏 Sleeping & Eating

Winbelle
Pension Hauz PENSION $
(☑ 034-495 5898; 2nd fl, Rizal St; d P700; ❄ 🛜)
This family-run hotel just a couple of blocks from the public plaza could use a splash of colour and updating, but offers reasonable

Silay

◎ Top Sights
1 Hofileña Heritage House A2

◎ Sights
2 Balay Negrense Museum A2
3 Bernardino Jalandoni Ancestral
House.. B1
4 Church of San Diego......................... B2
5 Silay Museum.................................... A2

◎ Sleeping
6 Winbelle Pension Hauz B1

◎ Eating
7 El Ideal Bakery.................................... B3
8 Mansion B3

◎ Information
9 Tourist Office A2

◎ Transport
10 Buses & Jeepneys to Bacolod B3
11 Buses & Jeepneys to San Carlos........ B1

value for the night. The lobby is on the 2nd floor, accessible from an entrance down a driveway.

Richmond Inn   HOTEL **$$**
(☏ 0923 521 8618; www.richmondinnsilay.com; J Pitong Ledesma St; r incl breakfast P1500-1800; ❄️ 🛜) Easily the best choice in Silay, the mission-style Richmond has decent rooms. For light, choose the ones facing the street. It's on the edge of town, towards the airport.

★ Mansion   CAFE **$**
(J Pitong Ledesma St; mains P100-140; ⊙ 4pm-late Fri-Sun; 🛜) A terrific place to imagine colonial Silay is this partly renovated regal home, an architectural landmark with colonnades marking the entryway. Enjoy coffee drinks, pastries, sandwiches and a few Filipino dishes surrounded by sugar-era photos and antiques. It's especially popular with Silay's young and artistically inclined.

El Ideal Bakery   BAKERY **$**
(Rizal St; pies & cakes P45-50; ⊙ 6.30am-6.30pm; 🛜) This well-known bakery was set up in 1920, during Silay's heyday, to provide snacks for gamblers who couldn't drag themselves away from the table. Some of its famous creations include *lumpia ubod* (spring rolls filled

with pork, shrimp and the juicy tip of the coconut palm) and *piaya* (flatbread sprinkled with brown sugar and sesame seeds).

Melkens   SEAFOOD **$$**
(☏ 034-495 8835; Bongol Rd; mains P250-330; ⊙ 8am-9pm) This nearly all-bamboo restaurant is out in barangay Balaring among a handful of other seafood restaurants perched over the water. *Kinilaw* (raw seafood cured in vinegar) and the speciality crab (P750 per kg) are recommended.

◎ Information

Tourist Office (☏ 034-495 5553; silaycity_tourism@yahoo.com; cnr Zamora & Gamboa Sts; ⊙ 8am-noon & 1-5pm Mon-Fri) Located inside the civic centre. Can organise tours to nearby sugar plantations and permits to Patag Natural Park.

◎ Getting There & Away

Silay airport is approximately 10 minutes away from the city proper. A van will cost P50.

Both buses and jeepneys travel between Silay and **Bacolod** (P14, 30 minutes). In Silay, all buses and jeepneys heading north and south stop along Rizal St. A taxi will cost between P300 and P400.

From Silay, there are buses all day stopping at the coastal towns towards **San Carlos** (P130, three hours).

Sagay

☑ 034 / POP 43,300

Near the northern tip of Negros is Sagay City, which is actually two cities: New Sagay on the National Hwy and Old Sagay on the coast, 5.5km away. The city is best known as the guardian of the 32,000-hectare **Sagay Marine Reserve**, which has some nice snorkelling spots and white-sand beaches.

For visitors, highlights are the 200-hectare Carbin Reef (P100 entry), about 15km northeast of Old Sagay (20 minutes by bangka), and Suyac Island (P20 entry), where you can walk an elevated 400m bamboo boardwalk and kayak through the mangroves (P300).

To organise a boat, ask at the **tourist office** (☑ 034-454 0696; www.escalantecity.gov.ph; City Hall, New Escalante). Failing that, ask at the pier. A small boat will cost P1200 (maximum 10 people). Snorkelling equipment (P250) can be arranged at the tourist office (it's too shallow to dive). You'll see different species of giant clam, but fish are scarce indeed.

Museo Sang Bata Sa Negros (☑ 034-457 8003; www.museosangbata.org; Old Sagay port; adult/child P40/20; ☺ 8am-5pm) is an interactive marine museum for children at the Old Sagay Port, where on some weekends kids dress up as reef animals and narrate the exhibits, which focus on conservation and protection of the marine environment.

Take any Sagay- or Escalante–bound bus from the Ceres North Terminal in Bacolod (P170, 2½ hours); from there, grab a tricycle to the port at Old Sagay (P30).

San Carlos

☑ 034 / POP 49,300

San Carlos is the main port city connecting Negros to Cebu, with daily ferries heading to Toledo, on Cebu's west coast. It's not overflowing with charm. In contrast, nearby **Sipaway Island** is a nice place to spend a day or two, and is only 15 minutes by bangka from San Carlos port (P15). This pretty, well-kept island has a concrete path that leads through palms and villages from one end to the other, with great views back to Negros. Rent a *habal-habal* (P60) at the pier and take your time exploring. The island is long and thin, so you can't get lost and residents are happy to chat with strangers.

There are also falls, caves and rice terraces in the San Carlos area. Contact the **City Tourism Office** (☑ 034-312 6558; tourism_

sccnegocc@gmail.com; City Hall; ☺ 9am-5pm) for more information.

Pintaflores Festival (☺ 5 Nov) features a parade of revellers dressed in amazing flower costumes, based on a folk tale involving a sick princess and flower tattoos.

🛏 Sleeping

Skyland Hotel & Restaurant   HOTEL **$**
(☑ 0908 774 4388; www.hotelskyland.wixsite.com/skyland; cnr Endrina & Broce Sts; r with fan/air-con P500/750; ❉ 🕸) A two-storey building with Spanish-style roof and clean, if ageing rooms. The restaurant (mains P130) is one of the better ones in town. Conveniently located halfway between the pier and bus terminal.

Whispering Palms Island Resort   RESORT **$$**
(☑ 0929 873 1146; www.whispering-palms.com; Sipaway Island; r P1500-2300; ❉ 🕸 🏊) A large, German–run complex spread out over 4 hectares of beachfront (high-tide swimming only), contains mostly concrete buildings with spacious, spick-and-span rooms, its own minizoo and a dive centre. Book ahead for the private shuttle.

ℹ Getting There & Away

Lite Ferries (www.liteferries.com; San Carlos port) has nine daily boats to Toledo (P145 to P165, two hours), including ones at 7am, 9am, 10am, 1pm and 3.30pm. **EB Aznar** (San Carlos port) has several fastcraft that do the same run in less than an hour (P225) at 6am, 9am, noon and 2.30pm. The schedule changes frequently.

There are regular all-day buses from San Carlos' bus station (1km from the pier; P8 by tricycle) to Dumaguete (P177, four hours) and Bacolod (P180, four hours).

Sugar Beach

With just a handful of eclectic, homespun resorts, a gorgeous stretch of beach and psychedelic sunsets, Sugar Beach remains one of Negros' best-kept secrets, helped along by a tidal river that cuts it off from the road network. It's the simple pleasures, such as quiet lazy days spent combing the beach and peaceful evenings gazing up at the stars, that reward those who journey here. There are some hikes in the area, plus scuba diving and trips to Danjugan Island Marine Reserve & Sanctuary, one of the more intelligently designed protected areas.

◉ Sights

★ Danjugan Island Marine
Reserve & Sanctuary   NATURE RESERVE

(☑ 0915 234 7145; www.danjuganisland.ph) This 42-hectare island is a model of intelligent ecotourism. Well-maintained paths provide access through thick forest to idyllic deserted beaches, sea-eagle nests and a screeching bat cave where pythons feed at the entrance, striking bats during their evening exodus. There are kayaks and a dive centre (P1300 per person, minimum four people). Offshore there are three no-take zones, allowing improved fish-watching. Dorm-style lodging is available in simple open cabanas with mosquito nets or the more comfortable set-up at Typhoon Beach.

The island is managed by the Philippine Reef & Rainforest Conservation Foundation (p248) in Bacolod. Day trips can be arranged through PRRCF or Punta Bulata Resort for P950 to P1950, including boat trip, lunch, kayaking, trekking, snorkelling and all necessary gear. Overnights (P2950 to P3950) include lodging and meals, and are arranged through PRRCF. Three-day advance notice recommended.

🛏 Sleeping & Eating

★ Sulu Sunset   RESORT $

(☑ 0919 716 7182; www.sulusunset.com; r P650-1350) At the far northern end of the beach, Sulu gets the Sugar Beach recipe just right: fan-cooled nipa huts with tile floors, en-suite bathrooms and verandahs with hammocks facing the sea, at affordable prices. The restaurant serves delicious wood-fired pizza and German specialities and the owner and staff are friendly and ready to help.

Big Bam Boo Beach Resort   RESORT $

(☑ 0999 671 6666; www.bigbambooeachresort. com; dm P400; r with fan P600-1400, with air-con P1700; ❄ 🛜) The quality and comfort of the rooms varies, ranging from bare-bones dorm beds to nicer stand-alone cottages. The restaurant dishes out traditional Filipino fare.

Driftwood Village   RESORT $

(☑ 0920 900 3663; www.driftwood-village.com; dm P250-300, d from P450; 🛜) This long-running Swiss-owned place offers a classic mellow beach vibe with hammocks and nipa huts of variable quality scattered about its leafy grounds. The kitchen specialises in Thai food, but European classics are also available (dishes around P200). It also has a mar-

vellous pirate pub hidden under a bushy canopy with billiards and foosball tables.

★ Takatuka Lodge
& Dive Resort   RESORT $$

(☑ 0920 230 9174; www.sipalay.net; d P1275-2400; ❄ 🛜) The amount of love and energy that has gone into this wacky German-owned hotel is in evidence *everywhere,* particularly its nine themed rooms. The Mad Mix room features quirky touches like an upside-down toilet as a showerhead, while the Rockadelic room comes complete with Marshall amps, electric guitars and a gold record mounted on the wall.

★ Punta Bulata Resort & Spa   RESORT $$$

(☑ 034-713 4888, 0917 848 3558; www.punta bulata.com; r P3900-5500, cabana P5700-8200; ❄ 🛜 ⛱) The Danjugan Island Marine Reserve & Sanctuary lies just offshore at this swish resort occupying its own kilometre of golden sand. Designed by its architect-owner, the main complex is an attractive modern-Asian style with local touches. The wide variety of accommodation runs the gamut from enormous rooms in a semi-courtyard to beach cabanas with huge beds and indoor-outdoor bathrooms.

🍷 Drinking & Nightlife

Sugar Rocks Music Bar   BAR

(⊙ 11am-late) This bar perched atop the hill at the northern end of the beach, with its narrow but fabulous view, is good for a drink and the occasional live acoustic music.

❶ Getting There & Away

Sipalay, a sprawling coastal town 21km to the southeast of Sugar Beach, is the area's transport hub. There are 14 daily Ceres buses from Bacolod (regular/air-con P189/289, five hours). Whereas, from Dumaguete, you'll have to first head to Bayawan (P80, two hours) and then transfer to Hinoba-an (P25, 30 minutes) to finally reach Sipalay.

Sugar Beach is isolated by a tidal river, which makes getting there problematic even from Sipalay. If the weather is good, the quickest and easiest way is to take a bangka (P300 to P350, 10 minutes) from Poblacion Beach in Sipalay, 3km to the south. Many resorts pick up clients here.

Otherwise, from barangay Montilla, 3km north of Sipalay, catch a tricycle (P110) to barangay Nauhang, where paddleboats row you across the river (P15 per person; agree on price beforehand). Sugar Beach is a short walk around the point. During high tide, particularly in wet season, you may need to get a motorised boat (P200) from the bridge in Nauhang, or otherwise call your resort to fetch you.

Punta Ballo

Punta Ballo is a promontory with a divine white beach of fine shell sand (high-tide swimming only) and a backdrop of wooded hills. But it's best known for what lies underwater: some of the best diving in Negros with at least 10 marine sanctuaries, and 42 dive sites, including three wrecks.

Easy Diving Beach Resort (🖱 0917 300 0381; www.sipalay.com; r with fan from P1600, with air-con P1950-3900; 🌊🛜) has sunny and pleasant Mediterranean-style rooms, a nice beach and a well-set-up dive centre, with far-ranging multiday trips, including dive safaris to the Cagayan Islands, a string of 30 or so islands 120km west of Sipalay (similar to Tubbataha Reef).

Pioneering owner, Arturo, at **Artistic Diving Beach Resort** (🖱 0919 409 5594; www.artisticdiving.com; r without bathroom P500, with fan/air-con P1350/1770; 🌊@🛜🍽) was the first to establish a diving operation here and the resort has grown over the years. Today, there are 16 fairly dated concrete cottages with cable TV, some with sea-facing private balconies, set in a leafy garden by the beach. It serves tasty Swiss food with home-baked bread, and good vegie curries. Dive and accommodation packages available.

Nataasan Beach Resort & Dive Center (🖱 0999 344 1113; www.nataasan.com; s/d P1200/1400, bungalows P1700-2900; 🌊🛜🍽) is one of the biggest operations here, with a complex of low-slung buildings surrounding a central courtyard and pool area. It's on a bluff overlooking Punta Ballo Beach, so views are nice, however, there's no private resort beach property, rather a long stairway down for public access. Rooms are clean and simply furnished, but service, including at the restaurant, can be slow.

🟢 Getting There & Away

Ceres Liner buses run regularly between Sipalay, 7km north of Punta Ballo, and Dumaguete (P300, five hours) Less comfortable, but quicker minivans (P300) cover the same route in three hours. The turn-off for Punta Ballo is at the Sipalay town plaza, on the left as you come into town. A 7km *habal-habal* (motorcycle taxi; P150 to P200) or tricycle trip leads you to the resorts, which all face the sea.

Apo Island

🖱 035 / POP 920

This tiny 12-hectare volcanic island, with its one beachfront village, is known for having some of the best diving and snorkelling in the Philippines thanks to a vigorously defended community-run protected marine sanctuary established in 1985. There are 400 species of coral (one side of the island's reef was severely damaged by a typhoon) and 650 species of fish, including five types of clownfish and green-sea and hawksbill turtles. You'll also find gorgeous white coral-sand beaches, some fine short walks, a friendly island community and excellent views back to Negros, crowned by Mt Talinis.

🏃 Activities

During high tide in the mornings, just out front on the main beach, you're almost guaranteed to encounter massive green-sea turtles feeding in the shallows, providing a memorable snorkel. All three lodgings offer full-service dive shops.

Apo Island Marine Reserve & Fish Sanctuary   DIVING
(P100, additional snorkelling/diving fee P50/300) This 15,000-sq-metre protected area is one of the most successful marine reserves in the Philippines. The reserve contains a vital marine breeding ground and is a favourite diving and snorkelling site for its excellent visibility and its population of sea turtles that swim close to shore. There are nearly a dozen dive sites, with sloping reefs, walls, coral gardens and drift dives. Most of the bangkas docked here to offload divers are from resorts in Dauin on the Negros mainland.

🛏 Sleeping & Eating

Mario Scuba   GUESTHOUSE $
(🖱 0906 361 7254; www.mariosscubadivinghomestay.com; dm P300, d P500-1000; 🛜) Run by Mario, a former barangay captain of Apo, this small and slightly dishevelled dive centre has sunny rooms. The pricier ones (P1000) are top value: superspacious with polished floorboards and balcony. Meals are available (mains P100 to P180).

★ Apo Island Beach Resort   RESORT $$
(🖱 0917 701 7150, in Dumaguete 035-226 3716; www.apoislandresort.com; dm P800, d P2700-3400) Tucked away in a secluded cove, this refined and peaceful dive resort claims Apo's best white-sand beach. The Spanish Mission

rooms and cottages have fan and cold-water bathroom. The simple menu has good Filipino food (dishes P175 to P210). During high tide, it's accessed via steps leading up past the nearby Liberty's resort – or through the surf and a rocky gorge.

It has the same well-regarded owner and operation as Coco Grove Beach Resort (p268) on Siquijor and Coco Grande Hotel (p260) in Dumaguete.

Liberty's Lodge & Dive
RESORT $$

(☑ 0920 238 5704; www.apoisland.com; dm/s/d incl full board from P900/1650/2100; ❄ 🕾) Perched above the village beach, a bit messy with simply furnished rooms, this is where budget-minded divers tend to stay. Rooms have balconies with outstanding views and the dive shop is professionally run. Room prices include three hearty meals, providing fantastic value. A boat dive including equipment is P1400.

🛈 Getting There & Away

Apo Island is about 25km south of Dumaguete as the crow flies. Departures are from Malatapay Beach (look for the shed where the road ends), where boats (P300, 30 minutes) depart three to four times per day from 7am to 4pm. You can hire your own boat too (four/eight people P2000/3000). Rates are set by the association of pumpboat operators in Malatapay. Otherwise you can try to organise a ride with one of the resorts, share a trip with others or hitch a ride with a dive company.

Dauin

☑ 035 / POP 27,800

Dauin (dow-*in*) is a small coastal town on the Bohol Sea, but diving has put it on the international traveller's radar. It's known for macro diving in the Masaplod Norte marine reserve, and as a base for trips to nearby Apo Island, as well as for good snorkelling over the drop-off about 20m from shore. The beach itself, generated partly by volcanic ash, is not attractive, so you'll probably stick to resort pools. Most resorts – and the number is expanding – offer local excursions, such as popular Twin Lakes (p258) and Lake Balanan trips. The sulphur Baslay hot springs (by donation) are nearby too.

Nearby Malatapay (9km south), the departure point for Apo Island, has a huge and lively market where every Wednesday morning villagers, fishers and Bukidnon tribespeople can be found bartering goods and feasting on *lechón* (spit-roasted whole pig).

🛏 Sleeping & Eating

Bongo Bongo Divers
HUT $

(☑ 0906 202 2152; www.divebongo.com; s/d with shared bathroom P400/700, d with private bathroom & fan/air-con P1000/1500; 🕾) Diving backpackers get bang for the peso at these simple, fan-cooled nipa huts (one has optional air-con) set in a leafy garden. The complimentary drinking water, tea and coffee are nice touches and there's a kitchen for guests' use. There's a friendly and professional dive shop and it's a good place for budget-minded travellers to get PADI certification.

Mike's Dauin Dive Resort
RESORT $$

(☑ 0916 754 8823; www.mikes-beachresort.com; d incl breakfast P3300-4000; ❄ 🕾 🎇) A good midrange choice, Mike's is a compact and perfectly manicured property directly on a wide stretch of beach. Family-run and intimate, with only eight simple and modern rooms in a two-storey building with a nipa roof and surrounded by towering palm trees. Fully outfitted dive operation and good food are added bonuses.

Liquid Dive Resort
RESORT $$

(☑ 035-400 3244, 0917 314 1778; www.liquiddumaguete.com; Km 12.5, Bulak; d with fan/air-con P2000/3500; ❄ 🕾 🎇) One of the best midrange dive resorts in Dauin, Liquid offers simple nipa-hut rooms with sea-facing balconies and more upmarket and stylish common areas. There's a bar and good restaurant with healthy choices and a small central pool. The dive operation is well run and professional and the owners are friendly and committed to the area.

★ Atmosphere
RESORT $$$

(☑ 0917 700 2048, 035-400 6940; www.atmosphereresorts.com; d/ste for 4 incl breakfast P13,000/17,500; ❄ 🕾 🎇) 🌐 The most luxurious resort in Dauin, possibly all of Negros, Atmosphere has a dash of Miami Beach style leavened with Filipino warmth and a dedicated team that knows how to exceed guests' expectations. Large villas with contemporary-minimalist decor line a perfectly landscaped lawn down to the pool, restaurant and beach area. An Edenic outdoor spa is the best in the region.

★ Atlantis Dive Resort
RESORT $$$

(☑ 0917 562 0294, 035-536 0206; www.atlantishotel.com; d incl breakfast P4500-7000; ❄ 🕾 🎇) Combining an attractive property with long years of Philippines diving experience, Atlantis is an excellent choice for high-end divers. There's a lovely pool area, expert masseuses and a laid-back tropical vibe. The charming Spanish-style buildings are cramped, situated along a narrow property down to the beach; rooms are fairly simple with balconies, though they look out on one another.

Azure Dive & Yoga Resort RESORT $$$
(☑ 0917 798 7855; www.azuredive.com; Masaplod Norte; d P4100; ❄ ☎ ⊠) Azure, the only Filipino-owned resort in Dauin, has tastefully minimalist rooms with nice local decorations and wooden touches. The two-storey whitewashed building with nipa roof surrounds a lovely pool area. On-site yoga makes a nice complement to the diving focus. The main market is Asian divers, so the food is Filipino-Chinese.

Thalatta Resort RESORT $$$
(☑ 0939 925 6326, 0920 668 7393; www.thalattaresort.com; Zamboanguita; r P3400; ❄ ☎ ⊠) ✐ Close to Malatapay and Zamboanguita, Thalatta delivers fine food and excellent lodging in mustard-coloured bungalows set around a lovely infinity pool with ocean views. The park-like grounds are a bit faux, but the French owner runs a tight ship, including a dive centre. There's no real beachfront, only a yellow seawall. Most clients are European, roughly half are divers.

★ **Finbar** INTERNATIONAL $
(cnr National Hwy & Washington St; mains P150-300; ⊙ 5pm-late Mon, Tue, Thu & Fri, 11am-10pm Sat, 10am-10pm Sun) This is expatriate central in Dauin for good reason. All the food is homemade, even the halloumi and mozzarella cheese, bread, pizza dough and pasta. Burgers and fries are favourites and specials change daily based on the freshness and seasonality of ingredients. The drinks selection is great, from locally brewed craft beers to its own infused spirits (eg cucumber and jalapeno gin).

❶ Getting There & Away

Jeepneys or tricycles are readily available on the highway to ferry you between resorts and Dumaguete, around 14km north. Many resorts offer transfers from the airport in Dumaguete or town itself. Ceres buses heading south pass along the roadway.

Malatapay, around 9km south of Dauin, is the departure point for Apo Island. It is easily accessible by hopping on one of the many jeepneys or tricycles passing by.

WORTH A TRIP

TAMBOBO BAY

At the southernmost point of Negros, gorgeous Tambobo Bay has the hideaway ambience of a pirate's cove. Popular with yachties who anchor in the safe waters at the mouth of two small rivers, the entrance to the bay has a few stretches of white beach with an evening view of spectacular sunsets (best are from November to January). There's also some real buried treasure here too.

The **Kookoo's Nest** (☑ 0919 695 8085; www.kookoosnest.com.ph; cottage for 3/4 people P1000/1500) is a 1700-step descent from the main road, but you won't mind when you get there. Situated on a lovely white-sand cove, with soothing breezes and breaking waves, this idyllic miniresort of six bamboo cottages could also be called the Love Nest. It has a dive centre and a surprisingly sophisticated restaurant. For variety you can also take a boat to several impromptu eateries on the cove serving local live-aboards. Arrange a pick-up service from Dumaguete with the hotel.

Dumaguete

☑ 035 / POP 131,000

A university town and provincial capital, bustling and relatively urbane, thanks in part to a large and thriving expat community, Dumaguete is also a convenient base for exploring all that southern Negros has to offer.

The small city centre is as cramped, noisy and chaotic as any another city in the Philippines, but Dumaguete's harbour-front promenade, lined with upmarket bars, restaurants and food stalls, and blessed with peaceful sea views, is an undeniable draw. After becoming familiar with the city – one only needs a couple of days – it becomes a comfortable place to return after short stints diving, hiking or swimming nearby.

◉ Sights & Activities

Two landmarks in town are the coral-stone **Bell Tower** (cnr Perdices & Teves Sts) near the public square (1754–76), and the large and lively **public market** on Real St.

Dumaguete

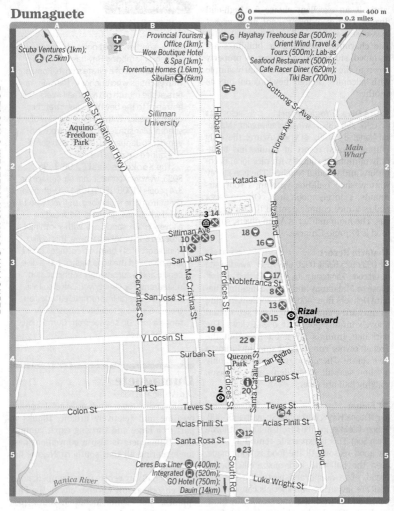

★ **Rizal Boulevard**   STREET

While Filipino cities aren't generally known for their beauty or charm, Dumaguete's waterfront promenade along Rizal Blvd is an exception to the rule. Constructed in 1916, this scenic quarter-mile lined with old-fashioned street lamps is a peaceful spot to stroll, attracting families on picnics, power walkers and those content to sit on benches gazing out to sea.

Nearby is a good selection of restaurants, bars and food stalls.

Twin Lakes
National Park   NATIONAL PARK

(P100) About 20km northwest of Dumaguete, the twin crater lakes of **Balinsasayao** and **Danao** offer some wonderfully scenic hiking. The area is virgin forest and full of wildlife, including monkeys and birds; if you're lucky you might spy a rare Philippine spotted deer or Visayan warty pig.

Entry is payable at the checkpoint office, where guides (P300) are available, but it's better to arrange a guide from the Provincial Tourism Office in Dumaguete.

Dumaguete

Go 900m beyond the entry gate to reach the first lake, where there are kayaks (per hour P100) and paddleboats (per hour P250) available. There's also a pleasant restaurant overlooking shimmering Lake Balinsasayao. Hiking trails include a short trail connecting the lakes; a popular 30-minute trail to some waterfalls; and a longer three-hour trail to the twin falls in Red River Valley. Pack good shoes as this trail can get very slippery.

Arriving from Dumaguete, the entry point for the 13.5km scenic track to Twin Lakes is just before San José on the coastal road at Km 12.4 (you'll see the sign pointing inland). A *habal-habal* from here to the lake is a P400 round trip. To get to the turn-off, catch one of several daily buses from the north bus terminal (P25) or a jeepney from Real St.

Silliman University
Anthropology Museum MUSEUM
(weekday/weekend P50/100; ⊘8.30am-5pm Mon-Fri) Housed in Hibbard Hall on the university campus, this very nice anthropology and ethnobotany collection includes artefacts from the indigenous Negritos and the Islamic period, including a massive ceremonial 10ft-long *kris* (sword).

Orient Wind Travel & Tours TRAVEL AGENCY
(☑035-422 5298; www.orientwind.com.ph; 201 Flores Ave; ⊘9am-5pm) Runs tours including snorkelling Apo (P3400), visiting Casaroro Falls (P1900), Manjuyod Sandbar and dolphin-

watching (P3500) and Oslob whale sharks (P2250). You'll need to be in a big group to make things affordable. Rates are per person for groups of four.

Scuba Ventures DIVING
(☑035-225 7716; www.dumaguetedive.com; Hibbard Ave) This good Filipino-run outfit is the longest-running dive shop in Dumaguete. It's attached to Harold's Mansion and offers diver training and trips to Apo Island, Siquijor and Cebu. Three boat dives to Apo run from P3800 to P5300, depending on the number of people.

☞ Tours

★ **Provincial Tourism Office** TOURS
(☑035-225 1825; www.negrostourism.com; EJ Blanco Dr; ⊘7am-7pm Mon-Fri) This office can help plan trips and can also provide exceptional guides (such as birdwatching expert Jac Señagan; email tourguidejac@yahoo. com). Tours include waterfalls in Valencia, dolphin- and whale-watching in Bais, swimming with whale sharks in Oslob (Cebu), forest hikes in Twin Lakes National Park, caving in Mabinay, trips to Apo and Siquijor islands and birdwatching around Lake Balanan.

Harold's Mansion TOURS
(☑035-522 0144, 0917 302 4455; www.harolds mansion.com; 205 Hibbard Ave) The Harold's empire includes an inexpensive tour

LOCAL KNOWLEDGE

SURFING BAYAWAN

Surfers take note: there's a burgeoning surf scene in Bayawan, midway between Sipalay and Dumaguete, mainly from June to October. The action takes place along the town's 2km seafront boulevard, and is both safe and friendly. Ask around for boardmaker Rex Lamis, a local expert who can provide advice and rental equipment.

operation that ranges far and wide, including trekking to Mt Talinis and Mt Kanlaon, swimming with whale sharks in Oslob (Cebu), visiting Malatapay market, snorkelling in Apo (P1200 per person), plus its own dive shop. It also operates a live-aboard boat in Dauin).

🛌 Sleeping

GO Hotel
HOTEL $

(☑035-522 1100; www.gohotels.ph; South Rd, behind Robinsons Mall; r P1000; ✱🛜) Outpost of nationwide chain with clean and simple rooms. A good budget choice for travellers in transit, if style and character aren't important.

Harold's Mansion
HOSTEL $

(☑0917 302 4455, 035-422 3477; www.harolds mansion.com; 205 Hibbard Ave; dm/s/d incl breakfast P300/400/600; ✱@🛜) This long-running high-rise hostel has seen better days, but luckily you can escape the dysfunctional rooms and grouchy staff by heading up to the the sociable rooftop bar-restaurant, which remains a good place to quaff beers, play pool and meet fellow travellers.

Wow Boutique Hotel & Spa
BOUTIQUE HOTEL $$

(☑0915 349 1132; www.facebook.com/islands leisurehotel; Hibbard Ave; d incl breakfast with/without bathroom from P1600/990; ✱🛜✉) This property combines Zen modernism with indigenous Philippine elements. Think woven lamps, contemporary art, stone love seats and plasma TVs. The courtyard has stylish cabanas and there are spa services on-site.

Coco Grande Hotel
HOTEL $$

(☑035-422-0747; www.cocograndehotel.com; Hibbard Ave; d incl breakfast P1400-1800; @🛜) One of the city's most professionally run hotels with long years of experience helping travellers arrange travel plans. The Spanish Mission decor adds some style to fairly spacious rooms. There's a pleasant alcove for breakfast and the on-site staff will sort out trips to Siquijor and Apo Island – the Australian owner has recommended hotels on both.

Florentina Homes
APARTMENT $$

(☑035-422 0827; www.florentinahomes.com; Rovira Rd; d P1800-2800, apt P4000-5100; ✱🛜✉) Especially good for young families, this complex offers playfully decorated rooms and huge apartments in European themes (these can be hard to discern). An equally eclectically furnished bistro (mains P175 to P395) is full of travel bric-a-brac and there's an ice-cream parlour and nice pool area.

C&L Bayview Inn
HOTEL $$

(☑035-421 0696; www.clhotel.com.ph; Teves St; r incl breakfast P1200-1700; ✱🛜) Boasting a colourful palette of bright yellows, flaming oranges and deep greens and small balconies with good views, this eight-storey hotel is a solid midrange choice just a block off the waterfront boulevard. The breakfast isn't much, but it's served on the rooftop, which offers breathtaking panoramas.

La Residencia Al Mar
HOTEL $$

(☑035-422 0889; www.laresidenciaalmar.com; Rizal Blvd; r P2000-2900; ✱🛜) A faux Spanish hacienda, replete with oil paintings, a wide wooden staircase and pots overflowing with ferns. The rooms have solid wooden floors and colonial-style decor. The pricier, sea-facing rooms with balconies are some of the most appealing in the city, others have some slightly beaten up furniture and dim lighting. Has a good Japanese restaurant.

🍴 Eating

For cheap and tasty options, there's a half-mile of food stalls along Rizal Blvd in the evening. Try a *balut* (duck embryo) if you dare; don't mind the feathers. Several excellent spots with outdoor seating are clustered at the intersection of EJ Bianco Dr and Flores Ave (northern extension of Rizal Blvd). Otherwise, most restaurants are between Perdices and Rizal Blvd.

⭐ Two Story Kitchen
KOREAN $

(☑035-522 0126; Santa Catalina St; Korean meals P189-250; ⊙10am-11pm Sun-Thu, to midnight Fri & Sat) The upstairs teahouse is the draw, with elevated floor seating in semi-private stalls cushioned by floor pillows. The menu is two-sided: standard cafe fare (sandwiches, pasta, pizza etc) on one side and Korean meals on the other. A fun and popular hang-out.

Panda Ice Cream
ICE CREAM $

(☑035-225 9644; Ma Cristina St; ice cream P60; ☺9am-8pm) Known far and wide for its fried ice cream.

Qyosko
FILIPINO $

(cnr Santa Rosa & Perdices Sts; mains P60-120; ☺7am-3am; 🐧) This local legend serves up sticky ribs and hot Filipino dishes, plus delicious shakes and coffee from its air-conditioned adjoining coffee shop.

Scooby's Bean Connection Cafe
CAFE $

(Siliman Ave; mains P85-135; ☺8am-midnight; 🐧) A light and airy spot, especially good for breakfast (waffles, pancakes and French toast) and espresso drinks and pastries. The menu also features burgers, pasta and Filipino dishes and has live music many nights of the week.

★Kri
INTERNATIONAL $$

(☑035-421 2392; 53 Silliman Ave; mains P200-300; ☺11am-9.30pm; 🐧) This chic contemporary restaurant, where the chef works in a glass cube, offers sophisticated dining at affordable prices. The highly international fusion menu defies easy synopsis, but don't worry, there's something creative for all tastes, including Korean and Thai dishes.

★Lab-as Seafood Restaurant
SEAFOOD $$

(☑035-225 3536; Flores Ave; meals around P250; ☺10am-2pm) Loud and lively, this Dumaguete institution has expanded from a small seafood restaurant in 1988 to a diverse culinary, drinking and entertainment complex that includes Hayahay and Taco Surf (you can order from any of three menus). Tanks of fresh seafood are on hand, and there's a steakhouse and sushi bar. It's a one-stop evening, and it's all well done.

Sans Rival Bistro
INTERNATIONAL $$

(☑035-421 0338; cnr Rizal Blvd & San José St; mains P195-375; ☺7am-11pm, to midnight Fri & Sat; 🐧) Much of the menu of burgers, sandwiches, seafood and Filipino standards is ordinary and relatively pricey, however it's worth a visit for the style and ambience of the dining room housed in an attractive colonial-style building facing the waterfront. The all-you-can-eat Sunday breakfast buffet (P285) is a good deal.

Casablanca
EUROPEAN $$

(cnr Rizal Blvd & Noblefranca St; mains P190-575; ☺6.30am-midnight; 🍴🐧) Casablanca is known primarily for its hearty Austrian dishes such as succulent roast pork and Wiener schnitzel, and as an outdoor hang-out spot for old-timer expats. Sit on the patio as the unappealing dining room has heavy furniture and carpeting. Sesame-seared tuna with salsa makes a fine appetiser, and there are lunchtime sandwich options plus delicious eggplant dishes for vegetarians.

Harbour City Dim Sum
CHINESE $$

(Siliman Ave; dim sum P70; ☺10am-10pm) Chain restaurant with waitresses clad in traditional clothing and push carts piled with a variety of buns, rolls and other small dishes. It's a large, two-storey modern and comfortable dining room.

🍷 Drinking & Nightlife

★Hayahay Treehouse Bar
BAR

(201 Flores Ave; ☺4pm-late) Cosy up to the bar or grab a plastic chair at this two-storey pavilion made of driftwood and nipa roof, part of a complex of bars and restaurants on the waterfront 2km north of the town centre. Known for delicious fresh seafood and rockin' reggae Wednesdays. On weekends the live music continues until 4am.

★Coffee & Books
CAFE

(2nd fl, Noblefranca St; ☺9am-midnight; 🐧) You could while away several hours at this student hang-out lined with bookshelves and mini alcoves (inaccessible to anyone over 6ft). Espresso drinks, Filipino snacks and beer help pass the time while playing board games, ping pong or billiards, enjoying a game on the big flat-screen TV or catching up with the latest news.

Tiki Bar
BAR

(☑035-522 0446; www.facebook.com/tikidumaguete; Escaño Beach; ☺4pm-4am) This hopping late-night beach bar offers riotous DJs and live party music, mostly electronic dance music, from its concert stage. Expect a young crowd and weekend tailgates. From 10pm onwards on Friday and Saturday nights there's a P100 cover charge; this includes a free drink so it's basically free.

El Amigo
BAR

(Silliman Ave; ⊙9.30am-1am) Open-air live music makes this a fun and lively bar. Mexican food, not the most authentic, helps wash down the San Miguel.

Bo's Coffee
CAFE

(cnr Rizal Blvd & San Juan St; ⊙7am-midnight; ☎) The Starbucks of Dumaguete, an especially good place to hang out while waiting for a boat or flight.

Cafe Racer Diner
BEER GARDEN

(EJ Blanco Dr; ⊙10am-2am) The American-car-culture theme is obvious from the decor: antique petrol tanks, gas-drum chairs and an old VW van parked inside. Less so from the menu that mixes Filipino dishes such as squid balls and *kwek kwek* (fried quail eggs) with hot dogs and Philly-cheese steaks. Most recommended for drinks – draught beer actually flows from those petrol tanks.

ⓘ Information

The Department of Tourism (DOT) has accredited two travel agencies, **Maganda Travel & Tours**

(☑ 035-225 9090; cnr Santa Catalina & Locsin Sts; ⊙9am-5pm) and Orient Wind (p259).

An excellent resource for anyone planning to hang around Dumaguete for a while is www.dumagueteinfo.com, which includes an active forum.

Bureau of Immigration (BOI; ☑ 035-225 4401; 38 Locsin St; ⊙8am-5pm Mon-Fri) Visa renewals take several days. It's at the end of a long covered alleyway with a fairly obscure entrance.

Dumaguete Tourism Office (☑ 035-225 0549; www.dumaguetecity.gov.ph; Quezon Park; ⊙8am-5pm Mon-Fri) Smaller but more central office focusing on the city proper.

Provincial Tourism Office (p259) Exceptionally helpful staff with great info on Negros Oriental. Can act essentially as its own travel and tour company.

Silliman University Medical Center (☑ 035-225 0841; V Aldecoa Rd; ⊙24hr) Has the best medical facilities in the area, maybe in all of Negros.

ⓘ Getting There & Away

AIR

From Dumaguete Airport Cebu Pacific (www.cebupacificair.com) and Philippine Airlines (www.philippineairlines.com) serve Manila sev-

BOATS FROM DUMAGUETE

DEPARTS	DESTINATION	COMPANY	TYPE	FARE (P)	DURATION	FREQUENCY
Main Wharf	Tagbilaran	Ocean Jet	fastcraft	700	2½hr	1 daily
Main Wharf	Dapitan	Ocean Jet	fastcraft	680	1hr 40min	1 daily
Main Wharf	Dapitan	Montenegro, Aleson, Cokaliong, George & Peter	RORO	295-360	4-6hr	4-5 daily
Main Wharf	Siquijor	GL Shipping	fastcraft	150	1½hr	2 daily
Main Wharf	Siquijor	Ocean Jet	fastcraft	230	40min	1 daily
Main Wharf	Siquijor	Aleson	RORO	120	2hr	4 daily
Main Wharf	Larena, Siquijor	Montenegro	RORO	170	2hr	3 daily
Main Wharf	Zamboanga City	George & Peter, 2GO	RORO	942-1489	10-11hr	Tue & Sun
Main Wharf	Cebu City	George & Peter, Cokaliong	RORO	320-430	6hr	1-2 daily
Main Wharf	Manila	2GO	RORO	1760	15hr	Tue
Sibulan	Lilo-an	various	fastcraft	70	20min	10 daily
Tampi	Bato, Cebu	Maayo	RORO	70	30min	every 90min

eral times per day. Cebu Pacific also serves Cebu every morning. The tiny airport is on the northern edge of town (by tricycle P12); it's a fixed P150/200 for tricycles and taxis from the airport into town. Many hotels offer free airport pick-up.

BOAT

The main wharf is downtown. The Sibulan ferry terminal is 4km beyond the airport. The Tampi port is 22km north of the city; Ceres buses leave for Tampi hourly from 2am to 2.15pm. Boats to Siquijor are generally most relevant to travellers – try to get the **Oceanjet** (☑ 0923 725 3734; www.oceanjet.net; fastcraft to Larena, Siquijor P230-380) fast ferry to Siquijor Town; **GL Shipping** (☑ 0915 891 1426; ☺ Sun-Fri) also has two daily departures. To get to the northern coast of Mindanao, try **Aleson Shipping Lines** (☑ 035-422 8762; www.aleson-shipping.com; ☺ 6am-4am) boats to Dipolog.

After Cebu City, Dumaguete is the best connected port in the Visayas. A number of companies have offices at the pier. Schedules change frequently.

To get to here from Cebu City you can travel by fastcraft to Tagbilaran on Bohol and then transfer to another boat to Dumaguete.

BUS & JEEPNEY

The city's main bus terminal, **Ceres Bus Liner Terminal** (Negros South Rd) is just south of town. A small cafe and grocery is attached and a McDonald's is a block away if you have a long wait. The **Integrated Terminal** (Robinsons Mall) lies 100m further south and handles all north and south jeepneys.

❶ Getting Around

Abundant tricycles charge P8 to P15 for trips around town.

To get to the resorts around Dauin, you have few options. You can board any south-bound Ceres Liner bus, from the terminal or road. Grab any jeepney heading in that direction, get on a tricycle for a shared ride or hire a tricycle yourself. The latter is most expensive but shouldn't run more than P300.

There are several motorcycle rental stalls on the corner of Santa Rosa and Perdices Sts. Expect to pay around P350 per day or P1900 per week. It pays to compare prices and check brakes and headlights.

Valencia & Around

☑ 035 / POP 34,800

Valencia is a clean and leafy town with stately tree-lined avenues and a large, grassed central square. It sits at the foot of **Mt Talinis** (1904m), whose twin peaks are

---

❶ BOATS TO APO ISLAND

Most people visit Apo Island as part of an organised dive or snorkelling trip, or they arrange boat transport directly with one of the three accommodation options on the island. If you want to visit on your own, head to the Malatapay wharf, around 24km south of Dumaguete.

To get there, you can board any south-bound Ceres Liner bus, from the terminal or highway; grab any jeepney heading in that direction; or get on a tricycle for a shared ride or hire a tricycle yourself. The latter is most expensive but shouldn't cost more than P400. Boat prices from Malatapay are set and nonnegotiable.

---

known as los Cuernos de Negros (the Horns of Negros). There are four trails to the summit and guides can be arranged by the Provincial Tourism Office (p259) in Dumaguete and Harold's Mansion (p259). West of town (P15 by tricycle) are ecoparks that make a fun day trip, a very popular choice with local families. And nearly 4km away are the glorious, 30m **Casaroro Falls** (P15), worth the challenging trek to reach them.

The mise en scène of **Forest Camp** (☑ 0917 309 2444; www.forestcampbiz.com; adult/child P100/80, camping P300, d with fan/air-con P1500/1800; ☺ 8am-6pm) is much more naturalistic and low key than its nearby competition, **Tejero Highland Resort & Adventure Park** (☑ 0917 707 0791; www.facebook.com/tejerohighlandresort; adult/child P60/40; ☺ 9am-6pm).

The water flowing away and around the edges of the pool at the base of **Pulang-bato Falls** (P25) is coloured red from the river's rocks. It's a developed site with a thatch cabana and cemented pool area and a bamboo bridge. Nearby is the Red Rock hot springs.

Homespun and eccentric, the **Cata-al War Memorabilia Museum** (☑ 035-423 8078; by donation; ☺ 9am-5pm) is a collection of WWII-era relics housed in a private residence on the outskirts of town. Of the bombs, helmets, bullets etc, most were uncovered by the owner, Felix Cata-an, in the jungle around Mt Talinis, where some estimate up to 10,000 Japanese soldiers died during a month-long bombing campaign.

🛏 Sleeping & Eating

Bambulo Resort
RESORT $

(☑ 0999 797 3318; www.bambulo.com; Valencia-Bacong Rd; r P690, bungalow s/d P1350/1600; ❋ 🞰 🖥 ☲) Recharge your batteries at this peaceful woodland resort. It has a lovely shaded pool on two levels, light and airy bungalows with nice bamboo touches, and rooms with shared bathroom and a nice common area. Its atmospheric outdoor restaurant serves excellent wood-fired pizza. It's around 2km from the coast.

Harold's Ecolodge
CABIN $

(☑ 035-522 0144; www.haroldsmansion.com; dm/r P250/500) Of Harold's Mansion (p259) in Dumaguete fame, this fairly remotely located lodge up a very steep road offers bare-bones dorm rooms (P250) and a handful of attractive cabins (P500) with private porches at the Apolong trailhead to Mt Talinis (P1000, two days). Best to check in advance if food will be available, otherwise bring your own supplies.

ⓘ Getting There & Away

Jeepneys run all day between Dumaguete and Valencia (P15, 20 minutes). A *habal-habal* costs around P200.

Bais City & Around
☑ 035 / POP 76,200

About 45km north of Dumaguete, Bais City is one of the country's top spots for dolphin- and whale-watching. More species of cetaceans (including killer whales), especially leaping spinner dolphins, have been seen in the squid-filled, 3000ft-deep Tañon Strait between Negros and Cebu than anywhere else in the Visayas. Whale sightings are rare, especially outside the March to October migration season. Other Bais highlights include a low-tide visit to the **Manjuyod Sandbar**, as well as the **Bulwang Caves**, a complex of more than 400 caves.

Guides (from P400 for five people) and information are available from the helpful **Bulwang Caves Information Centre** (☑ 0926 973 9386). The most popular and accessible (with lighting and a walkway) is Crystal Cave, an underground fantasy land of sparkling crystal and milky-white stalactites.

In pleasant leafy surrounds, 1910 landmark **La Planta Hotel** (☑ 035-402 8321; www.laplanta.com.ph; Mabini St; d incl breakfast P1450-1650; ❋ 🞰 ☲) has large, simply furnished rooms and an atmospheric restaurant (meals P100 to P180) with high ceilings and black-and-white tile floor. You'll have time to study the photos and memorabilia on the walls while waiting for your food.

Stilt Cottages (cottage P3000-6000) on the Manjuyod Sandbar appear marooned in the middle of the ocean. Bring your own supplies. The rate includes return boat transfer and can be arranged through the Bais City or Manjuyod tourism offices. This is a great opportunity to spot banded sea snakes by day and unlimited stars by night.

There are regular Ceres Liner buses to Dumaguete (one hour, P55).

SIQUIJOR
☑ 035 / POP 96,000

For most Filipinos, Siquijor is a mysterious other-world of witchcraft and the unknown. True, this tiny island province is famous for its mountain-dwelling *mangkukulam* (healers) who brew traditional ointments for modern ailments. But these days Siquijor's most popular healing practice involves a cocktail and a deck chair at any number of its laid-back and wonderfully affordable beach resorts. Attractions include great diving, waterfalls, caves and forest walks in the hilly interior. Just about everywhere on Siquijor is great for snorkelling – find the nearest beach and dive in. Like many beaches in the Visayas, swimming is only possible during high tide, and wearing thongs (flip-flops) is recommended as protection against sea urchins.

ⓘ Getting There & Away

BOAT

Most travellers arrive in Siquijor by boat from Dumaguete. Less frequent ferries from Cebu, Bohol and Mindanao are also an option. The island's two main ports are Siquijor Town and Larena.

Note that the last trip to the island from Dumaguete is the 6pm Montenegro roll-on, roll-off ferry (RORO) to Larena; the first trip off the island is GL Shipping's 6am fastcraft from Siquijor Town; the last trip off the island is Aleson's 5.30pm RORO from Siquijor Town.

Fastcraft to Dumaguete are run by **Oceanjet** (☑ 0923 725 3732; www.oceanjet.net; P230 to P380, one hour, 1.50pm) and GL Shipping (P160, 1¼ hours, several daily). In heavy seas, opt for the more stable, twice-daily RORO run by Aleson Lines (P100, two hours).

Siquijor

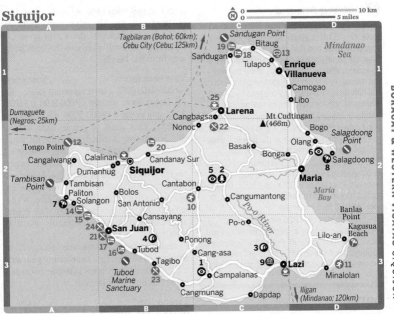

Siquijor

⊙ Sights

1 Balete Tree	C3
2 Bandila-an Mountain View Park	C2
Bandila-an Nature Centre	(see 2)
3 Cambugahay Falls	C3
4 Lugnason Falls	B3
5 Mt Bandila-an	C2
6 Olang Art Park	D2
7 Paliton Beach	A2
8 Salagdoong Beach	D2
San Isidro Convent	(see 9)
San Isidro Labrador Church	(see 9)
9 Siquijor Heritage Museum	C3

⊛ Activities, Courses & Tours

10 Cantabon Cave	B2
11 Kagusua Beach	D3
12 Tongo Point	A2
13 Tulapos Marine Sanctuary	C1

🛏 Sleeping

14 Bruce	A2

🛏 (continued)

15 Charisma Beach Resort	A2
16 Coco Grove Beach Resort	B3
Coral Cay Resort	(see 14)
17 Hambilica Ecolodge	B3
18 Islander's Paradise Beach Resort	C1
JJ's Backpackers Village & Cafe	(see 14)
19 Kiwi Dive Resort	C1
20 Villa Marmarine	B2

⊗ Eating

21 Baha Bar	B3
22 Larena Triad	C2
23 Legend's Sports Bar	B3
24 Marco Polo	B3

ⓘ Transport

Lite Ferries	(see 25)
25 Oceanjet	C1

Note that Seventh-day Adventist GL Shipping does not run trips on Saturdays, while Oceanjet sometimes schedules additional trips; all schedules are fluid.

Oceanjet boats continue on to Tagbilaran (P700, three hours) and Cebu (P1500, six hours).

From Larena, Montenegro Lines has two RORO trips daily to Dumaguete (P136, two hours) in Negros. **Lite Ferries** (☏ Cebu 032-255 1721; www.liteferries.com; Larena Pier) services Cebu (P365, eight hours) via Tagbilaran, Bohol (from P225, 3½ hours) on Tuesdays, Thursdays and Sundays at 7pm; and Plaridel, Mindanao, three times a week (from P350).

ⓘ Getting Around

A great way to explore the island is by motorcycle. The 75km coastal ring road is practically devoid of traffic and distances from Siquijor Town are clearly marked with yellow kilometre signposts. With leisurely stops along the way you can easily circumnavigate the island in a day. The hilly interior is also well covered by sealed roads and ripe for exploring by motorcycle.

Motorcycle hire is available everywhere; the going rate is P300 to P400. A good strategy is to hire a bike when you arrive at the pier in Larena or Siquijor so you can ride to your resort.

Air-con vans, multicabs and three-passenger jeeps are also available for hire through most resorts. Expect to pay P1500 to P2000 for a guided trip around the island by jeep or van, or about P1000 for a multicab.

Public tricycles cost P25 for a 10km trip between major towns; a special trip will set you back about P150 to P250. Public multicabs and jeepneys meet the ferries and circle the island, but are sporadic and stop running around 3pm.

Larena

🌙 035 / POP 14,000

Larena is Siquijor's second port town. It has a laid-back provincial feel, a couple of decent restaurants and a handful of resorts on enticing Sandugan Beach, 6km north of the town centre. Unlike increasingly popular San Juan, Sandugan still feels pretty remote – it's the place for those who want little more than to stare at the sea for hours.

Tulapos Marine Sanctuary is a good spot for snorkelling.

🛏 Sleeping & Eating

Kiwi Dive Resort RESORT $

(🌙 035-424 0534, 0908 889 2283; www.kiwidive resort.com; Km 16.9, Sandugan; d with fan P500-1290, with air-con P800-1600; ✳@ 🛜) It's a lovely walk down a trellis-covered pathway from the simple and clean hillside rooms to this long-running resort's beach and lounge area. It's a hodgepodge of accommodation in a mix of bamboo, nipa and stone; check several before booking. Bathrooms are cramped and beds less than forgiving. There's a dive centre and house reef just offshore.

Islander's Paradise Beach Resort RESORT $

(🌙 035-377 2412; www.islanders-paradise-beach. com; Km 16.9; cottages with fan/air-con P950/1200; ✳@) One of the pioneering Siquijor resorts, Islander's Paradise's day might have come and gone. This loose village of seven faux nipa cottages with little concrete verandahs is showing its age, though sunsets and a relaxed and familial vibe don't ever go out of style. A low seawall separates the leafy property from the beach.

Villa Marmarine BUNGALOW $$

(🌙 035-480 9167; www.marmarine.jp/en; Km 2.5, Siquijor Town; with fan s P800-1600, d P1200-2000, with air-con s P2000-3000, d P2500-4000; ✳@🛜) This oasis of peace, 3km east of Siquijor Town, is run by a cheerful Japanese couple. Some rooms have *furo* baths, wooden ceiling fans and Japanese supertoilets – no two rooms are alike. Many cottages have two levels, some with sprawling sea-facing balconies. It's on a nice whitesand beach, and has an on-site dive centre and excellent restaurant (mains P200 to P300).

Other pluses: wheelchair accessibility, free use of kayaks, free snorkelling gear and a tennis court with open late-afternoon sessions run by owner Daman.

Larena Triad FILIPINO $

(🌙 0906 338 3890; Km 8.5, barangay Nonoc; mains P125-250; ⏲7am-9pm) The weird and wonderful Triad is perched on a hill above Larena like a giant Jesus-themed UFO. The food is nothing special, but you'll hardly notice with such an impressive view. From the highway it's 1km straight up on a rough road; a tricycle one way will cost P30. Admission is P20 if you're not eating here.

San Juan & Around

🌙 035 / POP 15,000

Boasting Siquijor's best dive sites, some of its best beaches and an excellent range of accommodation, San Juan is where most visitors to Siquijor flock these days. The town itself is a typical small Visayan municipality, centred around a plaza and a landscaped enclosure known as Calipay's Spring Park.

Northeast of San Juan is the stunning white-sand **Paliton Beach** (Km 66.6). Keep walking west to discover yet more empty white-sand beaches.

The water is as clear as glass and there are wonderful views of Apo Island. Take the turn-off at the little church in Paliton village, near the island's westernmost point, and head along a sealed track for about 1km to the beach. Keep walking west to discover yet more empty white-sand beaches.

SHAMANS OF SIQUIJOR

Long associated with tales of shamans, witchcraft and black magic, Siquijor is often tagged with the moniker 'the Mystique Island'. This reputation presents the island with a catch 22 from a tourism perspective: while Siquijor's mysteriousness is a draw to foreigners, Filipino tourists can be reluctant to visit the 'spooky' island.

Local authorities and indeed most locals are quick to downplay the existence of black magic or evil spirits on the island, instead promoting Siquijor as a place for 'white magic', in reference to the island's many 'folk healers'. They come in three types: herbal healers, faith healers and *bolo-bolo* (water-and-stone) healers.

Herbal healers, most of whom reside in the mountains around San Antonio, work their magic with potions derived from herbs found in Siquijor's allegedly enchanted forests. Faith healers, who are found throughout the Philippines, use incantation and prayer to perform their magic. Unique to Siquijor, *bolo-bolo* involves a glass of water containing a black stone being blown through a straw, and hovering the glass over the patient's body until it becomes a browny colour, which identifies the ailments.

It takes a bit of pluck to find Siquijor's *mangkukulam* (healers). Villa Marmarine can point you in the direction of lowland *bolo-bolo* healers around Tulapos and Bitaug. San Antonio and Cantabon are where most herbal healers reside, and both towns also have resident faith healers and *bolo-bolo* healers. The tour-guide secretary in Cantabon's Barangay Hall can point you in the right direction.

The Ponces are a well-known family of herbal healers in San Antonio; their estate is out of town on the road to Cantabon (ask around). We've visited them twice over the years and the remedy has been the same: they rub a bit of the smoky mix of herbs and coconut oil on key spots, then induce you to take a sip. Warning: it tastes downright vile. You decide how much to pay; a couple of hundred pesos should do the trick. During the procedure they say nary a word. 'The herbal plants are powerful enough; there's no need for words', one of the taciturn Ponce brothers told us.

The best time to visit healers is during Holy Week, which sees a congregation of folk healers and shamans from all over the Philippines come for the **Lenten Festival of Herbal Preparation** (☉ Black Saturday; day before Easter) in Bandila-an Mountain View Park.

From barangay Tubod, a paved road leads 3km up to **Lugnason Falls** (P50) which cascades into a crisp and clean teal-green swimming hole. You can jump from the rocks or from a rope swing. Comparably little-visited, you might have this beautiful spot to yourself.

Just west of the village of Campalanas is a tremendous **balete tree** (Banyan Tree; Km 51.3; P10) FREE, estimated to be 400 years old and believed by some to be enchanted. In front of the tree is a spring-fed pool filled with flesh-nibbling fish – dangle your feet in for a free 'fish spa'.

🛏 Sleeping & Eating

A backpacker strip of sorts is emerging a couple of kilometres northwest of San Juan in barangay Solangon. Hostels, cheap cafes and even a bar or two have opened. Otherwise, most resorts are clustered between San Juan and Tag-ibo to the south.

Charisma Beach Resort　　RESORT $
(☎ 0908 861 9689; www.charismabeachresort.com; Km 64.8, Solangon; dm P450, d with fan/aircon P1000/1750; ✲ 🛜) This compact place, popular with European families and backpackers, is set on a nice stretch of beach with rooms abutting a concrete pool area. The rooms could use some work and are simply furnished. It's especially good value for backpackers staying in the fan-cooled dorms.

Hambilica Ecolodge　　RESORT $
(☎ 0917 700 0467; www.hambilicasiquijor.com; Km 62.4, Maite; d incl breakfast P1000-1700; ✲ 🛜) 🌿 A quiet spot in a landscaped garden with stand-alone cottages (some have kitchenette) and no-frills rooms in a small concrete building. There's no real beach here, but there are view decks over the rocks and a hammock, and the mangrove location is conducive to the evening firefly-watching tours (P100 admission for outsiders).

JJ's Backpackers Village & Cafe
HOSTEL $

(📱 0918 670 0310; jiesa26@yahoo.com; Km 64.6, Solangon; tent/dm P350/350, d P600-700; @ 🛜) A throwback to when you could camp on a beach, cook your own food and enjoy yourself on a tight budget. Located on a well-maintained patch of beach, it has only a few rooms; if they're booked you're free to pitch a tent. Reception faces the road, sealing off the rest of the property. Service and friendliness can be hit or miss.

★ Coco Grove Beach Resort
RESORT $$

(📱 0939 915 5123, 0917 325 1292; www.cocogrove beachresort.com; Km 60.5, Tubod; d P3500-5500, ste P8000, all incl breakfast; ❄🛜🏊) A well-oiled machine (if you can call a perfectly coiffed Spanish-style beachfront resort a machine), Coco Grove has doubled in size from its original incarnation without losing any of its charm or personality. Two wings of the property are separated by a mini 'fishing village' with accommodation in a variety of buildings, from bungalows to a boutique-hotel-style stucco building.

Bruce
RESORT $$

(📱 0928 601 1856; www.thebruceresort.com; Km 65.3, Solangon; d with fan/air-con P1000/2000, q P2200; 🛜🏊) The huge wooden beachfront cottages, with furnished sunset-facing balconies, are front and centre at the Irish-run Bruce, which sprawls along a prime stretch of Solangon Beach. Cheaper rooms are at the back. There's a quirky fan-cooled tree house (a good deal at P750 if you don't mind cold water and no toilet seat) and a small pool as well.

Coral Cay Resort
RESORT $$

(📱 0919 269 1269; www.coralcayresort.com; Km 65.2, Solangon; d with fan/air-con P1035/2070; ❄🛜🏊) The original and still the best Solangon resort, in large part because of its enviable beach (swimming only at high tide). The charming wood-floored beachfront duplexes are highly recommended, followed by well-appointed garden cottages and merely functional fan rooms out back. The great beach bar has views of the sun setting over Apo Island. Rents kayaks and stand-up paddleboards.

Legend's Sports Bar
INTERNATIONAL

(📱 0926 879 5534; mains P220; ⊘7am-11pm) Come for Tony, the colourful and friendly owner, self-professed American-wrestling fan and repository of stories about luminaries such as Rick Flair and Randy Macho Man Savage. Stay for the excellent burgers, pasta and seafood, and happy-hour drinks. There's not much in the way of a sports bar, except for the photos of wrestlers.

★ Baha Bar
INTERNATIONAL $$

(📱 0998 548 8784; mains P250-350; ⊘8.30am-11pm) One of the island's best stand-alone restaurants, as much for its chill vibe and self-produced craft beer (a pale ale), as for its wide variety of food. The tuna *kinilaw* and beef *bulalo* (soup with corn) are especially good. There's a leafy garden patio, terrace and live music most nights.

Marco Polo
ITALIAN $$

(Maite; mains P145-360; ⊘7am-midnight; 🛜) A wide variety of pastas and thin-crust pizzas at this casual waterfront eatery. Good breakfast as well.

Lazi & Around

📱 035 / POP 20,500

The quiet southeastern town of Lazi is bisected by the island's only major river, the Po-o (po-oh). The town is home to the impressive and stylishly time-worn, pink-coral-stone and timber San Isidro Labrador Church, built in 1884. Over the road, flanked by centuries-old acacia trees, is the oldest Catholic convent in the Philippines, a magnificent timber and stone villa, creaky with age and eerily serene. Upstairs is the small Siquijor Heritage Museum (P20; ⊘10am-4pm Tue-Sun), with historical photographs and a few old *santos*. Downstairs is a working Catholic primary school.

From Lazi, a sealed road leads 2km north to refreshing Cambugahay Falls on the Po-o River. Above the falls, there's a paid parking bay on your left for your motorbike (P20). Steps just across the road will take you down a steep stairway to this series of popular swimming spots. Never leave valuables unattended, as theft isn't uncommon.

A few kilometres past the town of Maria, Salagdoong Beach (Km 29.5; P15) is popular with rowdy day trippers. There's a half-open water park that has seen much better days, and you can jump into the ocean from 6m to 12m concrete platforms built into the rocks.

Between the towns of Lazi and Maria, Kagusua Beach is reached via the pretty village of Minalolan – look for the turn-off to barangay Nabutay and travel past the old limestone mine. A good road leads from the village down to Kagusua, where steep concrete steps take you down to a string of beautiful secluded coves that you might have all to yourself.

Olang Art Park (☑0915 186 5618; anna cornelia@yahoo.com; Km 29.3) is a retreat for Filipino artists set over 3 hectares. There's usually a resident artist or two hanging about, plus a performing-arts stage, a modest collection of modern art, a gallery of antiques and memorabilia and a wall of nude photos by the late American lensman Marlon Despues.

Cantabon

The small mountain village of Cantabon is the site of Siquijor's most thrilling adventure: the 800m spelunk through Cantabon Cave. Also nearby is Siquijor's highest peak, Mt Bandila-an (557m) from where the whole of Siquijor is visible, plus a nature centre and garden.

◉ Sights & Activities

Bandila-an Nature Centre PARK
(adult/child P10/5) The nature centre has been largely neglected but does have walking trails and some impressive trees and other floral life. It's 2km east of Cantabon.

Mt Bandila-an MOUNTAIN
Siquijor's highest peak, Mt Bandila-an (557m), is near Cantabon. Concrete steps lead 10 minutes up to the peak from two clearly marked points on the road between Bandila-an Nature Centre and Bandila-an Mountain View Park. There's a viewing platform at the peak from where the whole of Siquijor is visible.

Bandila-an Mountain View Park PARK
This park is essentially a public garden with lots of flowers, walking paths and little pavilions for picnics. It's great for bird- and butterfly-watching. It's 3km east of Cantabon and is also accessible from Lazi.

Cantabon Cave CAVING
(P20) An exciting adventure, best avoided by the claustrophobic, is the long spelunk through Cantabon Cave. Tours of the cave are arranged through the well-run Barangay Hall in Cantabon and cost P500 for up to three people, including guide (mandatory), helmet and torch (flashlight).

Romblon Province

Tablas Island

☑ 042 / POP 164,000

Tablas, long and shaped like a seahorse, is the largest of Romblon's islands. It has kilometres of white-sand beaches, hidden coves and a handful of marine sanctuaries, plus it's the main entry point to the province and the closest of the three main islands to Boracay – Tablas appears to have tourism potential. However, transport and political challenges have impeded development. Besides a few very out-of-the-way spots, you can head to the area around Ferrol, which has a nice horseshoe-shaped beach between two headlands.

Almost halfway up the west coast of Tablas, Odiongan is an ordinary port town with a grey-sand beach, accommodation options, a few good eateries and sometimes functioning ATMs. Kanidugan, a celebration of the coconut crop, is held on 5 April.

The tiny **Provincial Tree Park & Wildlife Sanctuary** in barangay Rizal (P250, 30 minutes by motorcycle taxi) makes for a pleasant morning walk. For beaches head south to Ferrol. For a longer excursion, take the rugged and scenic road north to San Andres, where there are waterfalls to explore.

Busay Falls, midway between Odiongan and San Andres (about 10km north), offer swimming pools, a picnic area and (forthcoming) rental nipa huts for around P500. There are also some caves nearby that reportedly lead to an underground river.

For snorkelling, head to 48-hectare, coral-reef protected **Looc Bay Marine Refuge & Sanctuary** (☑ 0935 590 2204; P100; ⊙ 8am-4pm), five minutes by bangka from Looc's town pier. The boat ride is included in admission for groups of four or more; for smaller groups the boat is P300. Drop by the sanctuary's office at the Looc Pier, a short walk from town, to make arrangements and rent snorkelling equipment (P50).

🛏 Sleeping & Eating

Beach resorts are scattered around the midsection and northern part of Tablas, including Ferrol. Odiongan and San Augustine, the two port towns relevant for travellers, have a few hotels if you're stuck for the night.

🛏 Odiongan

Sato-Dizon Arcade   HOTEL $
(☑ 042-567 6070; www.facebook.com/satodizonarcade; 039 Quezon St; d with fan/air-con P400/900; ❄ 🛜) Upscale urban accommodation for Odiongan, this bright-yellow hotel and restaurant offers clean rooms with flat-screens and small balconies 50m from the sea.

Wavefront Resort   RESORT $$
(☑ 042-567 5376; doodsendaya@yahoo.com; Circumferential Rd; d P1200-1500; ❄) An attractive modern two-storey building on a grey-sand beach 2km from Poctoy port. Walls are painted in bright colours and rooms simply furnished; waterfront number one is great, with lots of light. The largely Chinese restaurant (mains P120 to P250) serves a good breakfast, and is a nice place to hang out if you're waiting for a ferry.

★ Mouse's Morsels
Beef & Beer   INTERNATIONAL $
(Quezon St; meals P150-275; ⊘ 9am-10pm; 🛜) Fresh off the boat? This Irish-owned sidewalk cafe should be your first stop. The kitchen does excellent thin-crust pizza and the deli has imported meats and wines. There's also good music and you can usually meet a few local expats. Owner Steve is an enthusiastic proponent of tourism in Tablas and can help organise excursions.

Ghetto Plates   PIZZA $$
(☑ 042-567 6169; www.facebook.com/ghetto plates; Gen Luna St; pizza P175-350; ⊘ 9am-10pm Mon-Sat, to 8pm Sun) Don't let the humble entrance fool you: inside lies a real breath of fresh air. This cool cafe and meeting place offers excellent fruit shakes and pizza, live acoustic acts September to April and seating overlooking the jungle. Try the signature Extravaganza pizza (P325).

Star Palace Restaurant   PIZZA $$
(☑ 0918 639 0309; Bonifacio St; pizza P200-295; ⊘ 11am-9pm Mon-Sat) This contemporary-style place, two blocks north of the plaza, is a unique combination of brick-oven pizza joint and tea emporium – try the cookies and cream or watermelon milk tea.

🛏 Ferrol & Around

Binucot Sunset Cove Resort   RESORT $$
(☑ 0929 787 5486; willi.baumeister@gmail.com; near Ferrol; d P1200-2800; 🛜) Fairly remote and certainly quiet, visitors can choose between two interesting types of bungalows, charming Bali-style bamboo huts (P1200) and larger, airy octagonal models (P2800) with nice design features, except surprisingly, no windows. Dorm beds for P300 are also available. The resort can arrange airport pick-up and island-hopping and other tours.

Binucot Beach Resort   RESORT $$
(☑ 0947 207 5504; www.facebook.com/binucot. beach; near Ferrol; r P1500-2200; ❄ ❄) Overlooking a beautiful beach, this expat-owned resort has simply furnished motel-style rooms, a small pool and a restaurant serving a good mix of international fare.

Buenavista Paradise Resort   COTTAGE $$
(☑ 0933 548 3597; buenavistaparadiseresort@ gmail.com; near Looc; d P1200) Italian-owned Buenavista is a perfect place to unplug and dig in for a while. It has a handful of nipa cottages with sea-facing views; there's a bit of an unkempt lawn in between. The chef prepares excellent meals with ingredients from an organic farm.

🛏 Alcantara

★ Aglicay Beach Resort   RESORT $$
(☑ 0915 425 6898; www.aglicaybeachresort.com; Alcantara; s/d P1300/1700; ❄) Some 4km off the highway and with the finest location on the island, the 20-hectare resort sits on a long, private white-sand beach framed by two headlands – the closest has spectacular views down a coastline carved with numerous scalloped bays. It offers a nice outdoor cafe-restaurant, island-hopping, snorkelling and pleasant if conventional rooms. Transfer from Looc by tricycle (P400).

🛏 San Augustin & Calatrava

San Agustin is a picturesque stop on the way to or from the island of Romblon. Although you would never plan on staying the night, you won't have a choice if you miss the last ferry at 1pm. If you get stuck here, there are

BOATS FROM TABLAS

DEPARTS	DESTINATION	COMPANY	TYPE	FARE (P)	DURATION (HR)	FREQUENCY
Looc	Caticlan	various	bangka	200	1½	1 daily
Odiongan (Poctoy)	Batangas	2GO, Montenegro	RORO	760-1000	7-10	2 daily
Odiongan (Poctoy)	Caticlan	2GO	RORO	300	3	Tue-Thu, Sat & Sun
Odiongan (Poctoy)	Culasi, Roxas	2GO	RORO	650	6	Sun & Wed
Odiongan (Poctoy)	Dangay, Roxas (Mindoro)	various	bangka, ferry	350	3½	1 daily, except Tue
Odiongan (Poctoy)	Romblon Town	Montenegro	RORO	320	3	Sun, Tue & Fri
San Agustin	Romblon Town/ Sibuyan (Magdiwang)	Montenegro	RORO	175/375	1/3½	1 daily
San Agustin	Romblon Town/ Sibuyan (Magdiwang)	various	bangka	150/350	1/3½	2 daily
Santa Fe	Carabao	various	bangka	200	1	1 daily
Santa Fe	Caticlan	various	bangka	200	1	1 daily

several streetside barbecues and food stalls around the market.

Accommodation options are clustered on a street running perpendicular to the main road, a one-minute walk from the pier. **Kamilla Lodge** (☑ 0921 375 2288; S Faigao St, San Augin; d with fan/air-con P400/600), a four-storey modern structure with simple motel-style rooms is the pick of the bunch; it also has a rooftop with nice waterfront views.

**Turtle Cove
Island Resort** RESORT $
(Paksi Cove; ☑ 0927 776 9003; Calatrava; d P1500-2500) Has a handful of cottages set on a secluded cove with its own beach at the far northern end of Tablas. It's a great place to get away from it all, with a lush jungle backdrop adding to its romance. Call ahead. Calatrava is about 20 minutes by motorcycle taxi (P35) from San Augustin.

❶ Getting There & Around

Importantly for Tablas and Romblon as a whole, the airport in Tugdan now receives regularly scheduled flights from Manila on Cebu Pacific (www.cebupacificair.com). A jeepney or tricycle from the airport to San Augustin costs around P250 (1½ hours).

Most visitors still arrive by sea, through one of four ports around the island; the Poctoy port serves nearby Odiongan.

Jeepneys connect the main towns throughout the day but run fairly infrequently, the exception being the more popular Looc–Odiongan route (P50, one hour). There are more trips in the morning. Jeepneys between Looc and Odiongan dry up around 3.30pm. The last trips from San Agustin to Looc (P100, two hours) and Odiongan (P100, two hours) are around 2pm, when the last ferries from Romblon arrive. Morning trips in the other direction should get you to the ferries on time.

By far the quickest way around the island is on the back of a motorcycle taxi, known as a 'single'. Looc to Odiongan (35 minutes) is around P150; Looc to San Agustin (1¼ hours) is around P450. Tricycle and single prices double after dark.

Romblon Island

☑ 042 / POP 39,000

Utterly authentic and only lightly touristed, Romblon Island is the charming gem at the heart of its self-named province. A small island, it's even smaller for the visitor, as nearly everything you want to see is within a few kilometres of its main port and only significant settlement, Romblon Town. This includes a handful of excellent resorts, eateries and activities, more than enough for a few relaxing days.

Surrounded by green hills, Romblon Town is like the setting for a Hemingway novel, a languid, somewhat raffish tropical port town filled with bustling tricycles, bangka traffic and a colourful collection of local expats. For those without access to cable, a night walk through the market east of the plaza is better than TV.

◉ Sights & Activities

Fort San Andres
VIEWPOINT

For the best views of Romblon, walk up the stairs to the ruins of this crumbling 17th-century fort overlooking the centre.

★ Anchor Bay Watersports
WATER SPORTS

(📞 0918 247 9942; www.anchorbaywatersports. com; ⏰ 8am-9pm) This jack-of-all-trades on the water 5km west of town primarily rents out water-sports equipment – paddleboards, kayaks, Hobie Cats, windsurfers. However, it also rents rooms (P1500) with excellent views and shared bathrooms, and serves popular sunset meals, including steak and seafood (P200 to P500), plus drinks from the Marlin sports bar (p274). It does cash advances from credit cards too (10% commission).

🛏 Sleeping

★ San Pedro Beach Resort
RESORT $

(📞 0928 273 0515; minamingoa@yahoo.com; Ginablan; d P800) A getaway from the 'big city' (Romblon Town), this resort refuge is set on Talipasak beach in Ginablan, about 10km south of town. From the spotless bamboo cottages you can peer through the jungle canopy to the beach below, where there is good snorkelling at high tide.

Stone Creek House
BOUTIQUE HOTEL $$

(📞 0906 212 8143; www.facebook.com/stone creekhouse; Fetalvero St, Romblon Town; r with fan/air-con from P2000/3000, ste P4000, whole house

P8500; ❄@🖥) This sophisticated stone townhouse is the most fully stocked rental you can imagine, and sleeps six. The design is smart and guests get the run of the common room, with its big flat-screen TV and Playstation. The owner prefers to book out the whole house, which is perfect for families, but may take individual bookings if you email in advance.

Three P Holiday & Dive Resort
HUT $$

(📞 0929 440 7135; www.the-three-p.com; barangay Lonos; d with fan/air-con P2200/2800; ❄) This family-run dive operation (single boat dive P1600, P450 for equipment) has a few well-appointed nipa huts in a leafy compound on the beach about 7.5km southwest of Romblon Town. Meals are available. A tricycle from Romblon port costs P150 (15 minutes).

Dream Paradise Mountain Resort & Spa
HOTEL $$

(📞 0908 748 2272; www.facebook.com/dpmresort; dm P350, d P1275-2000; ❄❄) Like a tropical Potala Palace, this gaily coloured hillside complex soars over the rice paddies below, bursting with balconies, stairways, flags, balustrades, a central pool and a variety of eclectically decorated rooms, no two of which are alike. Dreamy? Gaudy? You choose. Located in Mapula, 9km south of Romblon Town.

🍴 Eating & Drinking

★ Romblon Deli & Coffee Shop
INTERNATIONAL $$

(📞 0939 221 0446; Magallanes Dr; mains P230-325; ⏰ 7am-9pm) The heart of Romblon's lively expat scene is this unassuming venture, smack in the middle of the waterfront near the ferry docks. Part bar, part bistro and part tourist info centre, with especially good pancakes, omelettes, burgers, curries, pizza and sandwiches.

BOATS FROM ROMBLON TOWN

All of these services are roll-on, roll-of car ferries:

DESTINATION	COMPANY	FARE (P)	DURATION (HR)	FREQUENCY
Batangas	2GO	1000	8	Wed & Sat
Batangas	Navios	1000	8	Wed & Sat
Cajidiocan	Navios	300	3½	Wed & Sat
Tablas (Odiongan)	Montenegro	320	3	Tue, Fri & Sun
Tablas (San Agustin)	Montenegro	96	1	1 daily

CANTINGAS RIVER

The rocky Cantingas River, while overstated as an 'eco-adventure zone', does offer a dive tower, a rusty zipline, and some basic rooms (P300) with cooking facilities in a lovely if isolated spot around 3km from San Fernando Town (P40 by tricycle). It can get crowded on weekends.

After its Friday-night happy hour, you may crawl back for the notorious 'Feeling Shitty Breakfast': two smokes, a Coke and a coffee for P70.

★ **JD&G Italian Food** ITALIAN **$$**
(Romblon-Sawang-Sablayan Rd; mains P150-350; ⊙7am-8pm) An Italian-owned hole-in-the-wall doing excellent pizza, pasta and steaks. Grilled tuna, chicken Parmigiana and beef goulash are other favourites. And affogato and gelato for dessert. It doesn't get better than this on the Romblon Islands.

**Republika Bar
& Restaurant** INTERNATIONAL **$$**
(Romblon-Sawang-Sablayan Rd; meals P150-220; ⊙7am-9pm) Waterfront eatery, good for people-watching. Has huge sandwiches and a creative menu.

Marlin Bar Restaurant BAR
(barangay Lonos; ⊙8:30am-9pm) This bar offers beautiful sunset views and sports on a large flat-screen TV. It's part of the highly recommended Anchor Bay Watersports (p273), and will satisfy romantics and sports fanatics. The menu has a wide range of international fare, including excellent steaks.

ⓘ Information

There's a **tourism office** (☑ 0920 629 5838; visitromblon@gmail.com; Capitol Bldg; ⊙8am-5pm) in the capitol building, but the best sources of local information are David and Tess Kershaw, the owners of Romblon Deli (p273), who are happy to provide it.

A PNB bank with a Visa-only ATM is in town, however it's often out of service so be sure to bring cash before arriving.

ⓘ Getting There & Around

The most important boat connection is the daily **Montenegro Shipping Lines** (☑ Batangas 043-740 3206) trip from San Augustin (P96, one hour, 6am), on the northeast tip of Tablas

to Romblon Town and then onwards (P228, two hours, 7.30am) to Magdiwang on Sibuyan. It returns to the same ports in the afternoon beginning with a 10.30am departure from Magdiwang.

Another important connection is the **2GO Travel** (☑ Manila 02-528 7000; www.travel.2go.com.ph) trip between Batangas and Romblon (via Odiongan on Tablas). Boats leave Romblon to Batangas every Wednesday and Saturday evening (eight hours, P1000). **Navios Shipping Lines** (☑ Batangas 0908 146 2243) also has Wednesday and Saturday departures to Batangas.

A circuit of the island by tricycle is difficult because of road conditions on the western side. You're better off hiring a motorcycle (with driver P700 not including petrol, without driver P300 to P500 per day) at the park near the pier. You should be OK driving solo, but be careful in rainy conditions. Jeepneys go around most of the island, but are irregular and thin out the further you go from Romblon Town.

Sibuyan Island

☑ 042 / POP 59,000

At first glance, Sibuyan looks like ecotourism heaven. The island has an impressive peak, an exceptional amount of intact primary forest, loads of waterfalls and a high percentage of endemic species, leading local resorts to cleverly promote it as 'the Galapagos of Asia'.

But in reality there is only one quality resort, hardly any beaches, very little snorkelling (the island is surrounded by a coral plate), no towns of note and no poster animals. The only endemism you're likely to see is tropical plants, and most won't impress you unless you're a botanist. The exception is spectacular Mt Guiting-Guiting (2058m), one of the Philippines' best climbs – if you are careful.

Of the few lethargic towns here, Magdiwang on the northern coast is noteworthy as the gateway to Mt Guiting-Guiting and the main island entry point. Cajidiocan and San Fernando in the south have a few attractions and services.

ⓘ Getting There & Away

Magdiwang's Ambulong port, 2km from town, is the most common port of entry, but the most adventurous (uncomfortable and slightly risky) route is the six-hour bangka ride from Roxas, Panay, to San Fernando. Boats to San Fernando divert to nearby Azagra if weather demands it.

Navios Shipping has Monday and Thursday trips to Batangas (P950).

ⓘ Getting Around

Magdiwang is linked to Cajidiocan (P70, 1½ hours) and San Fernando (P100, two hours) by two daily jeepney trips. Some of these are timed to meet ferries at the pier. San Fernando and Cajidiocan are also linked by jeepneys (P55, one hour, three daily). Most trips are morning trips.

A ring road makes the island easy to navigate, although it is only intermittently paved. You can still hire singles and tricycles to take you between the three main towns. A tricycle from Magdiwang to San Fernando runs P500. Resorts hire out motorbikes (around P600 per day) and mountain bikes.

◉ Sights & Activities

Mt Guiting-Guiting Natural Park   PARK
(P300) This 15,200-hectare natural park (pronounced 'gee-TING gee-TING') is a biological treasure, home to an estimated 700 plant species, 130 bird species and a few rare mammals, including the small, nocturnal tube-nosed fruit bat; many of these are endemic. However, there is hardly any infrastructure. The park is known mainly for its striking peak, G2 (p276), which attracts about 100 climbers per year.

Cataja Falls   WATERFALL
This three-tiered waterfall cascading into a refreshing swimming hole makes for a great half-day excursion. Walk (or ride) east out of Magdiwang past the basketball court (leaving it on your right) and continue about 1km to a fork in the road. Take the right fork, then another quick right up a hill, and continue for another 2km or so to the first sign of civilisation – a cluster of nipa huts along the road.

Lambingan Falls   WATERFALL
(P30) This beautiful waterfall and swimming hole is about 12km east of Magdiwang (4km past the turn-off for the natural park). Tricycles can take you here (P300 round trip, 25 minutes).

🛏 Sleeping & Eating

Magdiwang Nature's View Lodge   HOTEL $
(☑ 0921 463 9422; jedshon@yahoo.com; Rizal St, Magdiwang; dm P250, r with fan/air-con P750/875; ❄) This friendly downtown place offers spotless rooms with a scenic riverfront location and a restaurant with a limited menu. Definitely get the corner triple (P1200) for views.

Rancher's Bed & Breakfast   GUESTHOUSE $
(☑ 0908 786 4006; nonoyradan@yahoo.com; Rizal St, Magdiwang; dm P350, d with fan/air-con from P550/750; ❄) The only place with a hint of style in town, Rancher's offers basic rooms and a rooftop where you can have a drink and wonder how you ever ended up in Magdiwang. Arranges one-hour bangka trips upriver (P250).

BORACAY & WESTERN VISAYAS SIBUYAN ISLAND

BOATS FROM SIBUYAN

DEPARTS	DESTINATION	COMPANY	TYPE	FARE (P)	DURATION (HR)	FREQUENCY
Azagra	Batangas	Navios	RORO	760-1000	17-21	Fri & Sun
Cajidiocan	Romblon	various	bangka	300	2½	Fri
Cajidiocan	Romblon	Navios	RORO	900	4	Wed & Sat
Cajidiocan	Batangas	Navios	RORO	1000	16	Wed & Sat
Cajidiocan	Mandaon, Masbate	various	bangka	450	4	Tue & Fri
Cajidiocan	Culasi, Roxas City	various	bangka	350	5	Tue
Magdiwang (Ambulong)	Romblon	Montenegro	RORO	228	2½	1 daily
Magdiwang (Ambulong)	Tablas (San Agustin)	Montenegro	RORO	324	3½	1 daily
San Fernando	Culasi, Roxas City	various	bangka	350	5-8	daily, except Sat
San Fernando	Romblon	various	bangka	250	3	Thu & Sat

CLIMBING G2

G2, also known as Mt Guiting-Guiting, is one of the best climbs in the Philippines; some in-the-know climbers call it *the* best. The peak is remarkable for its long and dramatic knife edge, which must be walked like a tightrope to reach the summit. Getting there is often a hand-over-hand rock scramble. You don't need rappelling equipment, but you do need a guide, and to be very careful. A dry ascent is one thing, but in wet weather the summit becomes treacherous and is often closed for days.

The traditional route begins near Magdiwang and takes you up and back in two to three days. You reach the first camp on day one, spend the night and reach the summit before noon the next day. At that point you either try to make it all the way back to Magdiwang or overnight en route. There is also a trail from the summit that continues on to Olango, on the other side of the island. This is more for experienced jungle trekkers, particularly near the end, which is a tough slog. However, in all cases it is recommended that the journey begin in Magdiwang, as there is no established, trustworthy guide service from the Olango side of the island – a critical factor in this climb.

You need a permit (P300) to climb the mountain. These are available from the **Protected Area Office** (☑0949 651 6340, 0928 490 1038; mt_guiting2@yahoo.com; barangay Tampayan; ☉8am-5pm Mon-Fri, but staff generally present weekends) at the park entrance, about 8km east of Magdiwang (P100 by tricycle). If you want to arrange the trek yourself, you can hire a guide (P2400 for three days; usually one guide for every three climbers) and porters, which are highly recommended (P1800) here, ideally at least one day prior to setting out. Rain gear, cold-weather gear and good rock-climbing shoes are essential. If you want an established firm to arrange the trek for you, Sanctuary Garden is the only one with the experience necessary to organise a safe and successful journey, and to include all necessary equipment. This is the recommended option.

⭐**Sanctuary Garden** RESORT $
(☑0939 917 1635; www.sanctuarygardenresort.com.ph; barangay Tampayan, Magdiwang; camping/dm P100/250, d P750-1250; ❊) Easily the best resort on the island, Sanctuary Garden does everything well, thanks to its talented owner, Edgar. The 30-hectare property is nestled in the jungle, offering fine views, short walks and a running stream. Accommodation ranges from a nice campsite to a superb dorm to elegant eco-bungalows with marble bathrooms.

Boathouse COTTAGE $$
(☑0917 936 6223; www.isledreams.com; Olango; dm/s/d P350/650/1300) Run by a German expat, this truly off-the-beaten path place has two floors that sleep six; one bed is shaped like a boat. Rooms are priced per person. It's close to a rocky beach and simple Filipino meals are available. Other properties nearby can be viewed on the website.

Cebu & Eastern Visayas

Best Places to Eat

➡ Angelina (p297)
➡ Cafe Laguna (p287)
➡ Mimay's Seafood House (p328)
➡ Canto Fresco (p325)
➡ Anzani (p288)
➡ MJ Square (p299)

Best Places to Stay

➡ La Luna Beach Resort (p341)
➡ Tepanee Beach Resort (p297)
➡ Yellow Doors Hostel (p324)
➡ The Henry (p286)
➡ Sogod Bay Scuba Resort (p330)

Why Go?

Home to dazzling beaches and astonishing coral walls, the world's smallest mammal and its biggest fish, eastern Visayas is the aqua heart of an island nation. This region's natural appeal is utterly compelling – the Chocolate Hills of Bohol and shimmering millions of sardines of Moalboal, waves and caves of Samar and waterfalls and rice terraces of Biliran.

Cebu City has a certain cosmopolitan allure, but elsewhere the region's towns are eminently forgettable. Instead, explore the myriad and varied islands. Start with Bohol, now welcoming visitors to sleek beach resorts via its new airport; beach-blessed Bantayan Island, dive-mecca Malapascua, surf-blessed Calicoan and the pink-sand bays of remote Sila.

Twin disasters (Typhoon Yolanda and the Bohol earthquake) battered eastern Visayas in 2013 but today all areas are very much welcoming travellers again. Even Tacloban in Leyte, which suffered terribly, has transformed into an endearing and relatively urbane provincial capital.

When to Go
Cebu

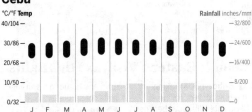

	Jul–Sep	Apr–May	Jan
	Barring a typhoon, Samar and Leyte are dry while most of the country is sopping.	Flat waters for divers in Bohol, Cebu and Southern Leyte.	The coolest month, plus there's the Sinulog Festival in Cebu.

Cebu & Eastern Visayas Highlights

1 Bohol (p308) Taking in teeny tarsiers, rolling Chocolate Hills, cove beaches and reefs teeming with fish.

2 Malapascua Island (p295) Experiencing close encounters of the thresher-shark kind and offshore islets.

3 Moalboal (p300) Enjoying this freediving heaven, party

town and home to a swirling vortex of sardines.

4 Biliran Island (p332) Saddling up and exploring this emerald isle on two wheels before island-hopping.

5 Calicoan Island (p341) Surfing the country's best surf spot not called Siargao.

6 Catbalogan (p338) Swimming, scrambling and slogging through the caves of western Samar.

7 Cebu City (p279) Experiencing Cebu City's quixotic appeal, underground clubs and fine restaurants.

8 Padre Burgos (p329) Searching for whale sharks.

CEBU

POP 4.69 MILLION

Cebu is the hub of the Visayas. It is the most densely populated island in the Philippines and is second only to Luzon in its strategic and economic importance to the country. This is one of the most prosperous regions in the country – the 2016 growth rate was 8.8%, considerably higher than the national average. Cebu draws almost two million foreign travellers a year. The island's prime attractions are its white-sand beaches and spectacular diving, chiefly off the northern tip of Cebu at Malapascua and down on the southwest coast at Moalboal. And don't ignore much-maligned Cebu City, which has lively bars, emerging eateries and burgeoning retail appeal.

ℹ Getting There & Away

Cebu City is the gateway to the Visayas. It has the nation's busiest port and its second-busiest airport. If you happen to be travelling from Asia, it's an attractive alternative to entering the country at Manila, with several direct international flights.

Alternatives to Cebu City for accessing neighbouring islands by boat include Argao for Bohol, Danao for Camotes and Bogo for Leyte. Negros can be accessed from no less than five ports on the west of Cebu island.

Cebu City

📞 032 / POP 936,200

The capital of the Southern Philippines, Cebu City is a bustling metropolis, the hub of a three-million-strong conurbation. Aesthetically, it's gritty and not exactly easy on the eye, but the city is also relatively cosmopolitan thanks to a surging English-language school industry and well-regarded universities. Historic sights are slim on the ground, though there are some colonial-era gems, and the traffic is notorious – but you'll still find plenty to do. Cebu City's energy is infectious: its bar and club scene is justly famous throughout the archipelago and dining out is a delight, with a dizzying choice of restaurants. And with Cebu airport being expanded to accommodate many more domestic and international flights, the city's continuing prosperity seems assured.

History

When Ferdinand Magellan sailed into the Port of Cebu on 7 April 1521, an eyewitness account relates that he was already a late-comer: 'Many sailing vessels from Siam, China and Arabia were docked in the port. The people ate from porcelain wares and used a lot of gold and jewellery...'

He may not have been the first outsider to visit Cebu, but Magellan brought with him something that nobody else had: missionary zeal. Even his death at the hands of warrior-chief Lapu-Lapu on Mactan Island, a few weeks later, would only afford the natives temporary respite from the incursions of the conquistadors. The arrival of avenging Spaniard Miguel López de Legazpi in 1565 delivered Cebu – and eventually the whole of the Philippines – to Spain and Catholicism. The founding in 1575 of Villa del Santisimo Nombre de Jesús (Village of the Most Holy Name of Jesus) marked Cebu City as the first Spanish settlement in the Philippines, predating Manila by seven years.

◉ Sights

Cebu has some colonial and historic sights worth visiting and a few quirky attractions.

★ **Basilica Minore del Santo Niño** CHURCH
(Pres Osmeña Blvd; ⊙5am-9pm; 24hr during Jan pilgrimage season) Cebu's holiest church houses a revered Flemish statuette of the Christ child (Santo Niño) that dates to Magellan's time. The church is no stranger to hardship: established in 1565 (the first church in the Philippines), three earlier structures were destroyed by fire, before the existing baroque structure was built in 1737. Its facade and belfry were badly damaged by the 2013 earthquake but have been restored.

★ **Museo Sugbo** MUSEUM
(MJ Cuenco Ave; adult/child P75/50; ⊙9am-5.30pm Mon-Sat) This excellent museum comprises several galleries in an sturdy old coral-stone building that was Cebu's provincial jail from 1870 to 2004. Rooms are dedicated to eras in Cebu's history. The American-era gallery contains an interesting collection of letters and memorabilia from Thomas Sharpe, one of 1065 teachers known as Thomasites who arrived in the early days of the American period to fulfil President McKinley's pledge to 'educate the Filipinos'.

Casa Gorordo Museum MUSEUM
(35 L Jaena St; P80-180; ⊙10am-6pm Tue-Sun) Downtown, in a quiet residential area, this museum was originally a private home (built in the 1850s). Later it was purchased by the Gorordos, one of Cebu's leading

Cebu

N 0 — 30 km
0 — 15 miles

Roxas (121km)
Cataingan (56km)
Cawayan (45km)
Carnassa Island
Maguino-o (76km);
Catbalogan (88km);
Masbate (130km)

Balasan
Estancia
Batad
Panay
San Dionisio

Visayan Sea

San Isidro

Leyte

Madridejos
Bantayan Island
Bantayan
Sulangan
Santa Fe
Hagnaya
San Remedio

Hilantagaan Island
Bagay
Daanbantayan
Medellin
Malapascua Island
Logon
Maya

Dayhogan Canal

Bogo

Palompon

Cadiz
Old Sagay
New Sagay
New Escalante
Old Escalante
Port Danao

Tabuelan

Tabogon
Tagnucan
Borbon

Isabel

Ormoc (30km)

Doong Islands

Carmelo
Tuburan

Sogod
Catmon

Tulang Island
Camotes Islands
Pacijan Island
Poro Island
Consuelo
Poro

Calatrava

Asturias

Carmen

San Carlos

Balamban
Central Cebu National Park
Mt Manunggal (960m)

Danao

Camotes Sea

Negros

Refugio (Sipaway) Island

Toledo

Lilo-an
Mandaue
Cebu City
Mactan Island
Lapu-Lapu
Olango Island
Cordova

Baybay (44km)

Hilongos (35km)

Basak

Pinamungajan
Aloguinsan
Cebu
Talisay
Naga
San Fernando

Maasin (52km)
Jao Island

Guihulngan

Tangil
Barili
Carcar

Getafe

Talibon

Dumanjug
Ronda
Alcantara
Moalboal
Pescador Island
Sibonga
Talood
Cabilao Island

Tubigon

Bohol

Argao
Talaga
Badian Island
Badian
Montalongon
Balhaan
Kawasan Falls
Dalaguete
Alcoy
Alegria
Moñtaneza
Malabuyoc
Boljoon

Loon

Carmen

Maribojoc Bay

Tagbilaran

Jagna

Samboan
San Sebastian
Tampi
San José
Sibulan
Valencia
Talisay
Mainit
Bato
Lilo-an
Santander
Súmilon Island
Oslob

Panglao Island

Pamilacan Island

BOHOL SEA

Dumaguete
Larena
Siquijor
Siquijor Island

Iligan (117km)
Cagayan de Oro (92km)

families, and served as the residence of the archbishop of Cebu. The lower part of the house has walls of Mactan coral stone and the stunning upper-storey living quarters are pure Philippine hardwood, held together with wooden pegs. Inside the renovated building there's fine antique furniture plus paintings, historic photos and a cafe.

Fort San Pedro FORT
(A Pigafetta St; student/adult P20/30; ⊘ 8am-8pm) Established in 1565 under the command of Miguel López de Legazpi, conqueror of the Philippines, Fort San Pedro has served as an army garrison, a rebel stronghold, prison camp and the city zoo. Today's partly ruined structure, dating from the late 18th century, includes an impressive gateway, a small section of ramparts and a small museum. Its peaceful walled garden is a perfect retreat from the chaos and madness of downtown Cebu, especially at sunset.

Tops Lookout VIEWPOINT
(Cebu Tops Rd; P100; ⊘ 10am-11pm) This viewpoint, high above the city, is best visited at sunset. Cafes (which open from 4pm) sell drinks and snacks. Some taxi drivers may refuse to tackle the steep access road so make your way to JY Square Mall in Lahug, where *habal-habal* (motorcyle taxis) depart for the thrilling 30-minute ride (return P300) up a winding road.

Carbon Market MARKET
(⊘ 6am-7pm) The sprawling Carbon Market is a boisterous, cacophonous frenzy that seemingly never sleeps. It's a local affair: ex-pect mounds of fruit and vegetables, some handicrafts (including basketry) and a large flower section.

Yap-Sandiego Ancestral House HISTORIC BUILDING
(www.facebook.com/yapsandiegoancestralhouse; Mabini St; P50; ⊘ 9am-7pm) The atmospheric Yap-Sandiego Ancestral House is among the country's oldest residential homes, built around 1680 from wood and coral stone, its design combining Spanish and Chinese architectural influences. Inside there's a mass of antiquities, fine furniture, religious art and curios to browse.

University of San Carlos Museum MUSEUM
(Del Rosario St; P30; ⊘ 8am-noon & 1.30-5pm Mon-Fri, 8am-noon Sat) This well-presented museum is best known for its anthropological and archaeological exhibits, including displays depicting the 16th-century practice of artificial skull deformation on infants for aesthetic reasons. We'll let you be the judge of that. There are ancient boat coffins dug up in Anda, Bohol, in the 1970s, and some fascinating limestone burial jars dating from about the 6th century. Note the covers – carved phalluses for men, roofs for women, faces for *datu* (chiefs).

🏃 Activities

Rise Above Foundation VOLUNTEERING
(☑ 032-255 1063; www.riseabove-cebu.org; 252 I Limkakeng St, Happy Valley Subd, V Rama Ave, Cebu City) Housing, education, vocational training projects in Cebu. We've had

CEBU & EASTERN VISAYAS CEBU CITY

THE GENTLE ART OF BUTTERFLIES

Julian Jumalon (1909–2000), a renowned Cebuano artist and avid butterfly collector, set up this **sanctuary** (☑ 032-261 6884; www.jumalonbutterflysanctuary.com; Jumalon St; adult/child P100/50; ⊘ 8.30am-5pm) at his home west of downtown. His knowledge was all acquired through his observations during expeditions into the forests to study butterflies, rather than any formal scientific training (he is credited for discovering many new Philippine butterfly species and won countless awards in the field of biology).

The most interesting reason to visit the sanctuary is for the small art gallery displaying Jumalon's lepido-mosaic works – artworks made entirely from damaged butterfly wings that he collected from lepidopterologists around the world. Jumalon's original watercolour paintings are shown side-by-side with the lepido-mosaic versions, which are superb.

At the outbreak of WWII, Jumalon was commissioned by the Philippine government to design emergency currency notes; these notes are now considered collectors' items and can be seen on display at Museo Sugbo (p279).

The sanctuary itself is a must for butterfly lovers, and is now run by his equally passionate children, who provide an informative tour of the garden, including the living display of the life cycle of the butterfly and Jumalon's exhaustive collection of butterflies and moths in the main room.

Cebu City

La Maison Rose (700m);
La Vie Parisienne (700m)

Arano's
(550m)

Tojong St
Acacia St
Archbishop Reyes Ave

Bataan St

M Velez St

Capitol Building

Villalon Dr

N Escario St

Orchid St

Pres Osmeña Blvd

DG Garcia St

P Rodriguez St

Jasmine St

J Avila St

M Cristina St

M Yap St

J Osmeña St

UPTOWN

F Scotto Dr

Gorordo Ave

San Jose St

V Rama Ave

J Llorente St

M Cui St

Fuente Osmeña Circle

B Rodriguez St

A Pond St

F Ramos St

V Ranudo St

Gen Maxilom Ave (Mango Ave)

J Singson St

D Jakosalem St

R Rahmann St

Sepulveda St

Rise Above Foundation
(700m)

M H Aznar St

A Tormis St

Asuncion St

J Urguello St

Pres Osmeña Blvd

Villanueva St

F Ramos St

R Landon St

Pelaez St

Cui St

Del Rosario St

Junquera St

D Jakosalem St

Sikatuna St

Guadalupe River

P Del Rosario Extn

N Bacalso Ave

Sanciangko St

Borromeo St

Colon St

DOWNTOWN

Cebu Cathedral

Jumalon Butterfly
Sanctuary (5km)

Taoban Market

B Aranas St

C Padilla St

Spolarium St

Santo Niño St

Guadalupe River

Pres Osmeña Blvd

Basilica Minore
del Santo Niño

Magellan's Cross

City Hall

SM Seaside City Cebu
(2.6km)

F Calderon St

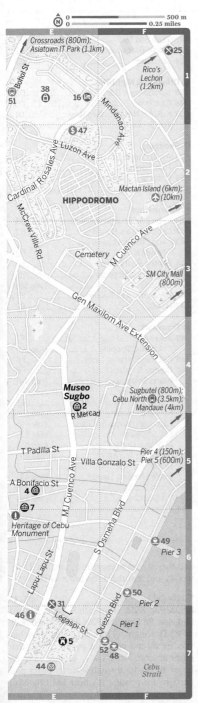

positive feedback from recent volunteers. Medical professionals (including dentists) are also needed. You can also sponsor meal programs.

Sky Experience ADVENTURE SPORTS
(☎032-418 8888; www.skyexperienceadventure. com; Crown Regency Hotel & Tower, Fuente Osmeña Circle; 2 rides incl buffet dinner P900; ⊙2pm-midnight Mon-Fri, 10am-1am Sat, 10am-midnight Sun) Thrill seekers with a head for heights will love this mile-high (well 37th-floor) experience which allows you to 'walk' using a safety harness around the summit of the Crown Plaza hotel, ride an 'Edgecoaster' (tilt-ing rollercoaster) and zipline across the night sky. Phones and cameras aren't allowed, pic-tures and videos must be purchased. Ride packages include a buffet dinner.

Island Buzz Philippines KAYAKING
(☎0917 885 7515; www.islandbuzzphilippines.com; half-day tours for 1/2 people P3500/2500) Island Buzz's tours take you over to Mactan Island, where kayaks and stand-up paddleboards await for guided trips through the sublime mangroves of Olango Island, among other spots. Full day tours include lunch and drinks.

Bugoy Bikers MOUNTAIN BIKING
(☎032-321 6348; www.bugoybikers.com; 5a Wright Brothers, off Upper Fulton St; full-day bike tour 1/2 people P4500/3500) Has a range of exciting half-day to multiday mountain-bike tours, including tours to neighbouring islands such as Bohol and Leyte. It's tucked away in a residential area in Lahug.

☆☆ Festivals & Events

★ **Sinulog Festival** CULTURAL
(http://sinulog.ph; grandstand seats from P1000) Cebu's epic annual Sinulog Festival draws pilgrims from around the Philippines. Cel-ebrated on the third Sunday of January, the Sinulog, or Fiesta Señor, is the Feast of Santo Niño (the Christ Child) and is marked by a colourful procession bearing the basilica's venerated image of Santo Niño.

🛏 Sleeping

Consider carefully where you stay in Cebu. Stay uptown and you'll have cafes and res-taurants on your doorstep. Hotel choices downtown can be very rough; try Junquera St in the youthful University of San Carlos (USC) area for decent budget places. Hostels are scattered around the city.

Cebu City

🛏 Downtown

★ Elicon House
HOTEL **$**

(☏ 032-255 0300; www.elicon-house.com; cnr Del Rosario & Junquera Sts; s/d P600/850; ❈ @ 🛜) 🌿 This inviting, genuinely ecofriendly place has clean, spacious rooms, delightful common spaces loaded with games, a vegie-heavy cafe and slogans on permaculture philosophy plastered on the brightly painted walls. No chemicals are used for cleaning and there's a lot of recycling going on. Daily, weekly and monthly rates are available.

Sugbutel
HOTEL **$$**

(☏ 032-232 8888; www.sugbutel.com; Osmeña Blvd, near Rd East; dm P265-475, r P1450-1850; ❈ 🛜) The Sugbutel has somewhat stark but very clean and compact rooms, plus three *giant* air-con dorms (we're talking 75 to 85 beds). Bunks have small security boxes and curtains for privacy. It's near SM City Mall and is a top choice for hygiene freaks.

🛏 Uptown

Le Village Hostel
HOSTEL $

(☑ 0932 413 3978, 032-416 0038; www.face book.com/levillagehostelcebu; 84 Gorordo Ave; dm with fan/air-con from P300/500, d without bathroom P900-1500; ❄🛜) A long-running hostel with lively, helpful staff and decent dorm rooms – though bathrooms need a deep clean and better maintenance, and facilities need upgrading (more lockers and power points). There's a big, bright common room with pool table and TV/DVDs, kitchen and the location is good, close to Ayala Center (p289).

★ Mayflower Inn
HOTEL $

(☑ 032-255 2800; www.mayflower-inn.com; Villalon Dr; s/d/tr/q P900/1200/1400/1800; ❄🛜) 🍃 The Mayflower's location is excellent, on the north side of uptown, and though they lay on the 'eco' vibe a bit thick, its green credentials are legit. Brightly painted rooms are tidy, and you get a garden cafe and lounge-library with ping pong, foosball, stacks of *National Geographic* mags and board games.

Tr3ats
HOSTEL $

(☑ 032-422 8881; www.tr3ats.com; 785 V Rama Ave; dm/d P350/1600; ❄🛜) Cebu's original hostel has three decent, six-bed, air-con dorms (including a female-only option) and a few tidy en-suite private rooms. Hot showers are available and the communal bathrooms are kept clean. However the location isn't perfect. There's not much of a common area; chill in the rooftop bar.

Pensionne La Florentina
GUESTHOUSE $

(☑ 032-231 3318; www.facebook.com/pensionne laflorentina; 18 Acacia St; r P950-1400; ❄🛜) On a quiet street near the Ayala Center, this elegant, welcoming place is a good uptown budget option. Rooms are quite spacious and well kept, though those downstairs rooms are dark; head up for more light and a balcony. Wi-fi is only strong in the lobby.

Gran Tierra Suites
HOTEL $

(☑ 032-253 3575; www.grantierrasuites.net; 207 M Cui St; s/d/tr P789/989/1189; ❄🛜) Cebu has some terrific-value midrange places and this is a prime example. Bordering on boutique, rooms have canvas prints, small flat-screen TVs and ample desk space. Staff are helpful and there are plenty of eating options close by.

Zen Rooms M Velez Street
HOTEL $$

(☑ 032-231 3338; www.zenrooms.com; M Velez St; r from P1450; ❄🛜) The Zen budget hotel concept is a successful one, with immaculately clean modern rooms, a nod to minimalist design and reliable wi-fi and air-con all at a competitive rate. At this branch the kooky little downstairs cafe only adds to its appeal.

★ Hamersons Hotel
HOTEL $$

(☑ 032-231 3338; www.hamersonshotelcebu.com; Don Mariano Cui St; r from P1400; ❄🛜) A fine no-frills hotel that enjoys a terrific uptown location with cafes, restaurants and shopping options on your doorstep. Rooms are smallish, but perfectly formed with crisp white linen, quiet air-con, laminate flooring, hot-shower en suites, fast wi-fi and flat-screen TV with cable channels.

West Gorordo Hotel
HOTEL $$

(☑ 032-231 4347/8; http://westgorordo.com; 110 Gorordo Ave; s/d/tr incl breakfast from P1350/1620/2370; ❄🛜) 🍃 This environmentally responsible place touts its zero-carbon philosophy, doesn't use plastic and provides free drinking water – however, the structure itself is a lumpish concrete block. Bright, tidy rooms have comfy beds and motivational art, and there's the travel-themed Journeys Cafe downstairs. Bikes are available for hire, there's table tennis and a kids' library. No outside guests allowed in rooms.

Premiere Citi Suites
HOTEL $$

(☑ 032-266 0442; http://premierecitisuites.net; M Yap St; r P1500-1900, ste from P2200; ❄🛜) A modern, centrally located hotel with bright rooms that boast crisp white linen and flat-screen TV – or book a suite for extra space and a contemporary bathroom with tub. There's complimentary filtered water on each floor or, for something stronger, head up to the rooftop bar and take in the mountain views. Some of the cheaper rooms are windowless.

Cebu R Hotel
HOTEL $$

(☑ 032-505 7188; www.ceburhotel.com; 101 M Cui St; s P950-1150, d P1300-1550, ste P1700-2050 incl breakfast; ❄@🛜) The lime-green colour scheme is a tad garish but rooms (there are four price categories) are well presented and kitted out with desks and flat-screen TVs. Deluxe rooms can sleep four.

Casa Rosario
PENSION $$

(☑ 032-253 5134; http://casarosario.net; 101 R Aboitiz St; s/d from P1000/1200; ❄@🛜) A reliable place that's perhaps looking a tad dated but remains a dependable choice, with welcoming staff, a convenient location and tidy, decent-value rooms. Breakfasts and meals are available in the ground-floor cafe.

Red Planet Hotel
HOTEL $$

(☑ 032-232 0888; www.redplanethotels.com; 36 Archbishop Reyes St; d from P1000; ✿ @ 🛜) This chain hotel's rates fluctuate wildly according to demand. If you get in at the low end the small but extremely functional and identical rooms (there are 150) are a great deal. More often, you're looking at P1500 to P2000, which is a bit steep. Location-wise it's just a few steps from the Ayala Center (p289).

Quest Hotel
HOTEL $$

(☑ 032-402 5999; www.questhotels.com; Archbishop Reyes Ave; r/ste from P2350/3710; ✿ 🛜 🏊) This high-rise benefits from a terrific location (a five-minute walk from the Ayala Center and the Terraces). Its rooms have a contemporary look, with luxurious bedding and modish bathrooms. The pool is small-ish, but has a swim-up bar and there's a fitness centre and popular restaurant.

Marriott Hotel
LUXURY HOTEL $$$

(☑ 032-411 5800; www.marriottcebu.com; Cardinal Rosales Ave; d from P7150; ✿ 🛜 🏊) Brushing up against the Ayala Center (p289), and its myriad restaurants and shops, is the ultraplush Marriott. No piped muzak or cheesy white-suited pianist disturbs the peace here. The luxurious rooms are tastefully decorated and bathrooms are fitted with rainfall shower-heads. You'll find the pool big enough for laps and there's a fitness centre.

🏨 Lahug & Banilad

Bugoy Bikers Bed & Breakfast
B&B $

(☑ 0918 908 9594; www.bugoybikers.com; 5a Wright Brothers, off Upper Fulton St; dm P500, d P800-1000; ✿ 🛜) This biking-tour operator (p283) also has a little guesthouse, with cosy bamboo rooms (with air-con or fan, and shared or en-suite bathroom) and a six-bed dorm. The Lahug location, down a quiet lane, is tranquil and there's a kitchen and garden to enjoy. The owners look after guests well and help out with travel plans and renting a bike or scooter.

★ Montebello Villa Hotel
HOTEL $$

(☑ 032-231 3681; www.montebellovillahotel.com; Gov M Cuenco Ave, Banilad; r from P2700; ✿ 🛜 🏊) Built in a Spanish-Colonial style reminiscent of a Mexican hacienda, the Montebello

enjoys a tranquil location 3km north of the Ayala Center in leafy Banilad. The glorious 30m pool and stunning tropical gardens are a delight, and rooms are spacious and well appointed if a little dated in terms of decor.

Harold's Hotel
HOTEL $$$

(☑ 032-505 7777; www.haroldshotel.com; Gordo Ave; r P3400-3600, ste P6000; ✿ 🛜) This efficiently run hotel has a terrific rooftop bar with a 360-degree view of the city – the perfect spot for a sundowner after a long journey, or a busy day sightseeing. Rooms are also great, with splendid beds, plush furnishings and attractive beige and cream colour schemes.

★ The Henry
BOUTIQUE HOTEL $$$

(☑ 032-520 8877; www.thehenryhotel.com; M Cuenco Ave, Banilad; d incl breakfast P4700-8900; ✿ 🛜 🏊) The Henry's marketing says 'like no other' and that's 100% true in Cebu, for this cutting-edge hotel – think industrial-style lobby, artistically designed rooms and hipster-friendly cafe – has no local rival. Expect statement murals and pop art, contemporary furniture and zany colours, while the sumo-sized beds invite entry via flying leap. It's undoubtedly a unique place to stay.

🍴 Eating

Cebu has a wide choice of restaurants and cafes. Lahug is foodie central – in particular Asiatown IT Park and the Crossroads strip mall. There's also a wide selection of cuisines in the Terraces and Ayala Center. For budget food stalls head to Carbon Market (p281). The city is considered the home of *lechón* (spit-roasted pork); meat eaters should try this delicious local speciality.

★ Healthy U
VEGETARIAN $

(☑ 032-401 1386; http://healthyuvg.weebly.com; A Tormis St; meals P60-110; ⏰ 9am-10pm Mon-Sat; ✔) This quirky, inexpensive little place is a haven for vegetarians, with tasty tofu and vegan dishes (most costing P30 to P40). For really cheap eats you can't beat their P59 meal deal which includes soup, rice, a main dish and a drink. It's down a little lane near the University of San Carlos (south campus) and popular with Cebuano yogis.

Yakski Barbecue
BARBECUE $

(☑ 032-254 3977; M Cui St; skewers P20-90; ⏰ 11.30am-2.30pm & 5.30pm-midnight) This casual open-sided place with a happy pig on its sign peddles varieties of meat (pork belly, chorizo, chicken) on a stick to the grateful masses. Show up after 10pm to avoid waiting.

Cora's Lechon
FILIPINO $

(Robinson's Place mall, Fuente Osmeña; portions from P115; ⏰9am-8pm) Delicious *lechón* from a tiny stand in the basement food court of Robinson's. For a true pig-out, a kilo costs P460.

Barbecue Boss
FILIPINO $

(☑0933 722 2677; Pope John Paul 2 Ave; meals P100-170) A lively open-sided place where groups of students and young office workers come to eat, drink and socialise. Grab one of the large wooden tables and tuck into pepper steak, chicken or spicy pork kebabs. Beer is P50 or so a bottle.

Original AA BBQ
BARBECUE $

(☑032-516 9077; Manalili St; dishes P80-130; ⏰10am-9.30pm) Vegetarians have nowhere to hide at this popular open-sided barbecue place where you choose your own meat or seafood and have it charcoal-grilled on the spot. This is a top spot for a chilled beer after an evening stroll by Fort San Pedro.

★Abaca
CAFE $$

(www.theabacagroup.com; Terraces; snacks & meals P130-300; ⏰7am-10pm) Superstylish cafe where you can dine overlooking the Terraces or in the air-con interior. Great for breakfast with healthy and not-so-healthy options – try the eggs Benedict, or a sandwich. Also very popular for coffee and its croissants and pastries are the best in town.

★Cafe Laguna
FILIPINO $$

(☑032-231 0922; mains P195-345; ⏰9.30am-10pm) The cosmopolitan **Ayala Center** (Lahug district; meals P70-120; ⏰10am-9pm) does not have many options for good local food, but highly popular Cafe Laguna is an exception, with excellent, relatively affordable dishes such as chicken cooked in pandan leaves, crispy *pata* (pork leg) and seafood *kare kare* (prepared with peanuts and coconut) really hitting the spot. There's an air-conditioned interior and terrace seating.

★La Vie Parisienne
CAFE $$

(☑032-260 4388; www.lavieparisienne.ph; 371 Gorordo Ave; sandwiches P160-230; ⏰6am-4am; 🖥) This bakery and cafe-bar offers light bites (baguettes start at P160) in a stunning garden setting, with cool sofas, oversized bean bags and hip lighting setting the scene. Order chilled wine by the glass or bottle from the cellar and enjoy the lounge sounds.

★Rico's Lechon
FILIPINO $$

(☑032-344 0119; http://ricoslechon.com; F Cabahug St, Mabolo; portions from P135; ⏰10am-10pm; ❄🖥) Cebu is the place to eat that signature Filipino delicacy, *lechón* (spit-roasted suckling pig), and Rico's has the best in town. It's cooked every morning at its uptown headquarters and shipped off to *lechón* addicts in Manila and abroad, or served at this unassuming eatery east of Ayala Mall.

Tsim Sha Tsui
CHINESE $$

(☑032-238 9209; Terraces; dishes P78-220; ⏰11am-11pm; 🖥) This modish Chinese joint is justifiably popular for its dim-sum deal (P399, all-you-can-eat from the conveyor belt) but there are other tempting choices including Malacca fried rice and hot shrimps with garlic sauce. Eat in the air-conditioned interior or on the slim terrace.

Arano's
SPANISH $$

(☑032-256 1934; 31 Fairlane Village, Gaudalupe; mains P90-350; ⏰6-10pm Mon-Sat) An authentic Basque–Spanish restaurant where the cosy front room is all gingham tablecloths and Spanish memorabilia (check out those pistols on the wall) and leads out to an intimate fairy-lit garden dining area. Seafood highlights include the *gambas al ajillo* (prawns in garlic sauce), squid cooked in its own ink, paella and some excellent steak and pork dishes.

Lunhaw
VEGETARIAN $$

(N Escario St; meals P125-240; ⏰11am-11pm Sun-Thu, 11am-5pm Fri, 7-11pm Sat; 🖊) A smart modern vegan place with a short menu that includes salads, soups, pasta (try the pumpkin spinach lasagna) and Asian fusion dishes such as *sisag* (tofu and mushroom in coconut sauce).

STK ta Bay! Sa Paolito's Seafood House
SEAFOOD $$

(☑032-256 2700; http://stktabay.com; 6 Orchid St; mains P95-400; ⏰9am-3pm & 5-10pm; ❄🖥) Ask a Cebuano where to dine and many will point you to this large ancestral-home-turned-restaurant chock full of family heirlooms. Jerry's crab curry is a favourite and the spicy *calamares* – baby squid fried in spices and topped with green chillies are great. The many Filipino classics include *sinigang* (tamarind-flavoured fish soup). Be prepared – food can take a while to arrive.

Golden Cowie
FILIPINO $$

(☑ 032-505 2121; Salinas Dr, Lahug; mains P85-395; ⊙11am-2pm & 5-10pm) Something of a local institution, Golden Cowie serves authentic Filipino flavours at pretty modest prices. It has mouthwatering fish and seafood – try the fried tuna belly or *imbao* (clam soup); and great meat dishes such as crispy *pata* (deep-fried pork hock or knuckles) and pork *bicol* (pork in coconut and shrimp paste). Vegie highlights include *adobong talong* (eggplant).

Zubuchon
FILIPINO $$

(☑ 032-239 5697; One Mango Pl, Gen Maxilom Ave; meals P170-320; ⊙10am-11pm) A popular pick for a *lechón* fix, with several branches around the city. This place in the heart of town offers a large platter of boneless (or regular) *lechón* for P330. For a side try the *abobong kangkong* (water spinach with pork rind).

Bucket Shrimps
SEAFOOD $$

(☑ 032-260 6520; Orchard St; mains P150-350; ⊙11am-10pm) A fun place where you don goofy cling-wrap gloves and a bib and attack buckets of Cajun-butter shrimp (or ribs, mussels, crab or pork belly) while guzzling buckets of beer.

Persian Palate
MIDDLE EASTERN $$

(☑ 032-412 6795; Mango Sq Mall, Juana Osmeña St; meals P169-395; ⊙10am-10pm; ❇🖥️🥗) Tucked away behind National Bookstore in Mango Sq, this Middle-Eastern-cum-Indian place has mains including baba ganoush (eggplant with yoghurt and tahini), samosas and curries. There's a lot on offer for vegetarians.

Handuraw Pizza
PIZZA $$

(☑ 032-410 7491; www.handurawpizza.com; ground fl, Mango Sq Mall, Juana Osmeña St; mains P129-398; ⊙10am-midnight Mon-Thu, to 2am Fri & Sat, to 10pm Sun; 🖥️) This Cebu institution is famous for its thin-crust pizzas – try the mildly spicy Pizza Cebuana topped with the local chorizo. Pasta, chilli wings, salads and all-day breakfasts are also offered. Local musicians play (mainly acoustic) nightly from 9pm; Wednesday is open-mic night.

★Maya
MEXICAN $$$

(☑ 032-238 9552; www.theabacagroup.com/maya; Crossroads, Gov M Cuenco Ave; mains P300-600; ⊙5-11pm Sun-Thu, to 2am Fri & Sat; ❇🖥️) Enter through heavy wooden doors to this classy, candlelit restaurant with arguably the best Mexican food in the country. Authentic dishes include ceviche (from P525), enchiladas and fajitas, and don't neglect to sample a shot of their 100% agave tequilas (from P210). Watch out for events (salsa on Wednesdays) and promos ('mojito and margarita Mondays').

★Anzani
MEDITERRANEAN $$$

(☑ 032-232 7375; http://anzani.com.ph; Panorama Heights, Nivel Hills, Lahug; meals P1250-2200, set menus from P1050; ⊙5pm-midnight Mon-Sat, 11.30am-2.30pm & 5pm-midnight Sun; 🖥️) One of the best fine-dining restaurants in the Visayas, classy Anzani is the perfect location for a special meal with sweeping views of the city from its terrace. Pasta dishes are around P475, while meat and fish choices such as Norwegian salmon or olive-crusted New Zealand rack of lamb (P1800) really ramp up the pesos. Set menus are good value.

La Maison Rose
FRENCH $$$

(☑ 032-268 5411; www.facebook.com/lamaisonrosecebu; 371 Gorordo Ave; mains P360-1200; ⊙noon-11pm; ❇🖥️) A little slice of France in the middle of Cebu, La Maison offers fine dining in a pale-pink, colonial-style building reminiscent of a French Indochine villa. The tempting menu features sumptuous prix-fixe meals, French classics such as duck confit (P650) and a few lighter options including great salads (try the niçoise or goat's cheese).

🍷 Drinking & Nightlife

Cebu has a well-deserved reputation as a party town. Upmarket clubs and bars are concentrated in central Cebu and in Mandaue, 5km east of the centre. Otherwise Mango Sq (on Gen Maxilom Ave) has unpretentious places, many a tad seedy. Note that a gentrification drive has lead to many Mango Sq joints closing and its future remains uncertain.

★The Social
BAR

(www.thesocial.com.ph; Ayala Center; ⊙11am-midnight, to 2am Fri & Sat; 🖥️) This stylish, buzzing outdoor/indoor bar is a great place to warm up before continuing the night further uptown. Abundant big screens are conducive to sports viewing and the huge terrace is perfect for al fresco quaffing. It draws a mix of locals and expats and there's great food available.

Kukuk's Nest/Turtle's Nest
BAR

(☑ 0933 391 3837; http://kukuksnest.webs.com; 124 Gorordo Ave; ⊙24hr; 🖥️) This bohemian 24-hour restobar is filled with old books and contemporary art and draws a colourful mix of local arty types. Regularly hosts gigs from reggae, ska, acoustic, punk and indie bands.

Bamboozers Bar BAR

(http://bamboozersbar.com; General Maxilom Ave; ⊙7pm-5am; 🐾) A small, sociable Canadian-owned bar that draws a good mix of expats, locals and visitors. Musically things are far better and more up-to-date than most on this strip, with house and electronica, funk and soul, and a dash of hip-hop and R&B.

Sentral CLUB

(Norkis Cyberpark, AS Fortuna Ave, Mandaue; ⊙6pm-2am Mon-Thu, to 3am Fri, to 4am Sat) Rammed most nights with party people, Sentral eschews the EDM and pop hits blueprint favoured by most Cebu clubs for a hip-hop, R&B and funky soundtrack. It's an upmarket venue, with a central bar area that's great for socialising.

Bellini
Champagne Lounge COCKTAIL BAR

(http://anzani.com.ph/bellini; Panorama Heights, Nivel Hills, Lahug; cocktails from P260; ⊙6pm-1am Mon-Thu, to 2am Fri-Sun; 🐾) Upmarket lounge bar with fine city vistas where you rub shoulders with Cebu's beautiful people. Sip on a champagne cocktail (P320), savour a dry martini or enjoy a glass of crisp Sauvignon. Bar snacks are also served and there's live music some nights.

Distillery LOUNGE

(http://thedistillery.com.ph; Crossroads, M Cuenco Ave; ⊙6pm-3am, to 4am Fri & Sat; 🐾) Uptown HQ for Cebu's young and beautiful, who come to socialise and – as the night progresses – dance to some of Cebu's grooviest tunes. There's a wide choice of imported beers, or make good use of their generous happy hour (6pm to 10pm) for discounted cocktails.

Club Holic CLUB

(www.facebook.com/clubholic; Mango Sq, General Maxilom Ave; P100 Fri & Sat; ⊙9pm-3am Tue-Sat) Club Holic keeps the party flag flying high in Mango Sq, with DJs spinning EDM, R&B and house sounds to a young crowd. Yes it's a little seedy around the edges, but cheap drinks (beers P75) and fun vibes means it's always popular.

Linx Lounge Bar BAR

(www.facebook.com/linxloungebar; City Time Sq, Mantawi International Drive, Mandaue; ⊙6am-4pm Tue-Sat; 🐾) Lively, popular lounge with emerging house DJ talent and EDM anthems that draw a cool young crowd. There's also live music some nights. Linx is in Mandaue, around 5km west of central Cebu.

🛍 Shopping

★Ayala Center Cebu MALL

(http://ayalamallcebu.com; Cebu Business Park, Bohol St; ⊙10am-9pm Sun-Thu, to 10pm Fri & Sat) This huge, centrally located mall has it all, from international brands such as Marks & Spencer, Mango and Body Shop to local stores for SIM cards and phone accessories. It fuses with the Terraces complex, which has a terrific selection of restaurants and cafes.

SM Seaside City Cebu MALL

(www.smsupermalls.com; Antuwanga; ⊙10am-9pm) The mother of all malls and the biggest in the Visayas, featuring brands including Levi's and Face Shop, lots of tech shops and also department stores. There's an ice-skating rink, cinema, 'Sky Park' (roof terrace) and tons of cafes and restaurants. Located 3km east of downtown.

SM City Mall SHOPPING CENTRE

(www.smsupermalls.com; North Reclamation Area; ⊙10am-9pm) Huge shopping mall with hundreds of stores (including leading US, European and Asian brands such as Uniqlo), a cinema, IMAX theatre, bowling complex, travel and banking and all other necessities.

National Bookstore BOOKS

(www.nationalbookstore.com; cnr Juana Osmeña St & Gen Maxilom Ave; ⊙9am–8pm) Fiction and nonfiction, and a good map selection. There are additional outlets in other malls.

Fully Booked BOOKS

(www.fullybookedonline.com; Terraces, Ayala Center; 10am-11pm) Has a terrific selection of local and international fiction, nonfiction and magazines as well as maps.

ℹ Information

EMERGENCY

Police Emergency Hotline	☎032-166, ☎032-161
Report Child Sex Tourism National Hotline	in Manila ☎02-524 1660
Tourist Police	☎0939 519 4321, ☎032-412 1838

IMMIGRATION

BOI Office (☎032-345 6441; bimandaue cebu@yahoo.com; 2nd fl, J Center Bldg, AS Fortuna St, Mandaue; ⊙8am-6.30pm Mon-Fri) Generally an efficient office for visa extensions. Best visited in the morning and note they can close before the official time. Located in Mandaue, 5km northeast of central Cebu City.

MEDICAL SERVICES

These city hospitals have a good reputation:

Cebu Doctors Hospital (☑ 032-255 5555; www.cduh.com.ph; Pres Osmeña Blvd; ☺24hr)

Chong Hua Hospital (☑ 032-255 8000; www.chonghua.com.ph; M Cui St; ☺24hr)

MONEY

ATMs are widespread. You'll find plenty around Fuente Osmeña and in the Ayala Center.

Citibank (www.citibank.com.ph; Cebu Business Park, Mindanao Ave; ☺9am-3pm Mon-Fri) Near Ayala Center. Changes US dollars and has an ATM. Has a P15,000 withdrawal limit.

HSBC (Cardinal Rosales Ave; ☺9am-4pm Mon-Fri) Opposite the Ayala Center. Allows large ATM withdrawals.

TOURIST INFORMATION

Airport Tourist Information Desk (☑032-340 8229; Mactan-Cebu International Airport; ☺5am-9pm) At the arrivals terminal.

Cebu City Tourism Commission (☑032-412 4355; www.facebook.com/cebucitytourism; 2nd fl, Rizal Memorial Library & Museum, Pres Osmeña Blvd; ☺8am-5pm Mon-Fri) Centrally located; good for city information.

Department of Tourism (DOT; ☑ 032-254 2811; dotregion7@gmail.com; LDM Bldg, Legazpi St; ☺8am-5pm Mon-Fri) Covers central Visayas.

Travellers' Lounge (☑032-232 0293; ☺6am-8pm; 🛜) Located just outside SM City Mall, this handy lounge has a bag-drop (P30, same-day pick-up only), showers (P50), free wi-fi and sells certain ferry tickets.

❶ Getting There & Away

Cebu City is a vitally important transport hub for the island of Cebu, region of the Visayas and nation of the Philippines. It has excellent air and sea connections. Cebu's seaport and airport are the best connected in the region, sucking in travellers and spitting them out again at destinations throughout the Visayas.

AIR

Mactan-Cebu International Airport (MCIA; ☑ 032-340 2486; www.mactan-cebuairport.com.ph; 🛜) is on Mactan Island, 15km east of Cebu City.

Cebu City has international connections to destinations including Dubai, Singapore, Seoul, Hong Kong, Osaka and Tokyo. Major domestic airlines serve Manila and an ever-growing list of provincial cities, including Bacolod, Butuan, Cagayan de Oro, Caticlan, Davao, Iloilo, Legazpi, Puerto Princesa, Siargao, Surigao and Tacloban.

Several airlines have offices at Mactan-Cebu International Airport (MCIA):

AirAsia Zest (www.airasia.com)

Air Swift (http://air-swift.com)

Cebu Pacific (www.cebupacificair.com)

Philippine Airlines (www.philippineairlines.com)

Scoot (www.flyscoot.com)

BOAT

Cebu's vast, multipiered port is linked with the rest of the country by scores of speedy fastcraft passenger ferries, slower roll-on, roll-off (RORO) car ferries and large multidecked passenger vessels.

All shipping information is vulnerable to change. The *Cebu Daily News* publishes a schedule that is generally reliable, but double-check directly with the shipping companies. Also confirm the pier from which your boat is departing.

Cebu City ferry companies:

2GO Travel (☑ 032-233 7000; http://travel.2go.com.ph; Pier 1, Quezon Blvd)

Cokaliong Shipping (☑ 032-232 7211; www.cokaliongshipping.com; Pier 1, Quezon Blvd)

Gabisan Shipping Lines (☑ 032-255 5335, 0917 791 6618; Pier 3, Quezon Blvd)

George & Peter Lines (☑ 032-255 8695, 032-254 5154; www.facebook.com/gplines; Pier 2, Quezon Blvd)

Island Shipping (☑ 032-422 6329, 032-416 6592; Pier 3, Quezon Blvd)

J & N Shipping (☑ 032-416 6840; http://jnshipping.weebly.com; Pier 2, Quezon Blvd)

Kinswell Shipping Lines (☑ 032-416 6516; Pier 2)

Lapu Lapu Shipping Lines (☑ 032-232 8863; Pier 3)

Lite Shipping (☑ 0977 822 5483, 032-255 1721; www.liteferries.com; Pier 1, Quezon Blvd)

Medallion Transport (☑ 032-412 1121; www.facebook.com/medalliontransportinc; Pier 3, Quezon Blvd)

M/V Star Crafts (☑ 0906 789 6363; www.mvstarcrafts.com; Pier 1, Quezon Blvd)

Oceanjet (☑ 032-255 7560; www.oceanjet.net; Pier 1, Quezon Blvd)

Philippine Span Asia (☑ 032-232 5361-79; Sulpicio Go St, Quezon Blvd)

Roble Shipping Lines (☑ 032-418 6256; www.robleshipping.com; Pier 3, Quezon Blvd)

Super Shuttle Ferry (☑ 032-345 5581; http://supershuttleroro.com; Pier 8, FE Zuellig Ave)

Supercat 2GO (☑ 032-233 7000; www.2go.com.ph; Pier 4, Quezon Blvd)

Trans-Asia Shipping Lines (☑ 032-254 6491; www.transasiashipping.com; Pier 5, Quezon Blvd)

VG Shipping (☑ 032-238 7635; Pier 3, Quezon Blvd)

Weesam Express (☑ 032-231 7737; www.weesam.ph; Pier 1, Quezon Blvd)

BOAT SERVICES FROM CEBU CITY

DESTINATION	TYPE	COMPANY	PRICE (P)	DURATION (HR)	FREQUENCY
Biliran					
Naval	RORO	Roble Shipping	480	9	8.30pm Mon, Sat
Bohol					
Getafe	Fastcraft	MV Star Crafts	200	1	3 daily
Tagbilaran	Fastcraft	Oceanjet, Weesam, Supercat 2GO	400-650	2	frequent
Tagbilaran	RORO	Lite Shipping	210	5	3 daily
Talibon	RORO	VG Shipping	240	4	noon & 10pm
Tubigon	Fastcraft	Kingswell, MV Star Crafts	200	1	11 daily
Tubigon	RORO	Lite Shipping, Island Shipping	100	3	several daily
Ubay	RORO	J & N Shipping	290	6	9pm Mon-Sat, noon Sun
Leyte					
Bato	RORO	Medallion	280	6	8.30pm daily, 9am Sat
BayBay	RORO	Cokaliong, Lapu Lapu Shipping Lines, Roble	250	7	2-3 daily
Hilongos	Fastcraft	Gabisan	280	3½	2.30pm
Hilongos	RORO	Gabisan, Roble	240	5½	daily
Maasin	RORO	Cokaliong	250	5½	7pm Mon, Wed, Fri, noon Sun
Maasin	RORO	George & Peter Lines	240	6	10pm Tue
Ormoc	Fastcraft	Oceanjet, Supercat 2GO, Weesam	625	3	several daily
Ormoc	RORO	Lite Shipping, Roble	400	5	2 daily
Palompon	RORO	Medallion	290	6	9pm daily
Luzon					
Manila	Passenger	2GO, Philippine Span Asia	1310	22	7 weekly
Masbate					
Masbate	Passenger	Trans-Asia, Super Shuttle Ferry	12½	700	6pm Mon, Wed, Fri & noon Sun
Mindanao					
Cagayan de Oro	Passenger & RORO	2GO, Super Shuttle Ferry & Trans-Asia	650-980	8-12	1-2 daily
Dipalog	RORO	Medallion	910	11	8.30pm Mon, Wed, Fri
Surigao	RORO	Cokaliong, Medallion	825-860	7	1-2 daily
Negros					
Dumaguete	RORO	Cokaliong & George & Peter	310	6	daily
Panay					
Iloilo	Passenger	Cokaliong Shipping, Trans-Asia	600	12	5 weekly
Samar					
Calbayog	RORO	Cokaliong	690	11	7pm Mon, Wed, Fri
Siquijor					
Larena	RORO	Lite Shipping	350	8	1pm Mon, Wed, Sat
Siquijor Town	Fastcraft	Oceanjet	1410	6	1-2 daily

BUS

There are two bus stations in Cebu. Most buses are ordinary/standard class but there are a few air-conditioned buses (costing around 20% more) on all the main routes.

Heading south there are buses to Bato (P170, four hours, frequent) either via Moalboal (P118, three hours), or via Argao (P85, two hours) and Oslob (P155, 3½ hours) from the **South Bus Station** (Bacalso Ave; ⊙ 24hr). Quicker air-con vans (V-hires) for southern destinations including Moalboal (P150, 2¼ hours) and Toledo (P100, 1½ hours) leave from the separate **V-hire South Terminal** (Junquera St; ⊙ 5am–11pm). Note the latter terminal has moved several times in the last few years, so check its location before you head here.

All buses and vans heading north use the **North Bus Station** (☑ 032-345 8650/59; M Logarta Ave; ⊙ 24hr) next to SM City Mall. From here there are buses to Hagnaya (P135, 3½ hours, every 30 minutes) for Bantayan Island, and to Maya (P170, 4½ hours, every 30 minutes) for Malapascua Island. Vans also operate from this terminal, and are air-conditioned and quicker, if more cramped. Destinations include Hagnaya (P165, three hours, every 30 minutes) and Maya (P200, 3½ hours, every 30 minutes).

❶ Getting Around

TO/FROM THE AIRPORT

Choose between taxis or bus. For the taxi rank, turn right from the terminal and walk 300m. Yellow airport metered taxis cost P325 to P375 to central Cebu City, regular metered taxis P275.

Air-conditioned **MyBus** (☑ 032-231 0557; www.facebook.com/mybusph; ⊙ 6am–10pm) services (P25) depart every 20 to 30 minutes (between 6am and 10pm) from outside arrivals to the North Bus Station and SM City Mall (p289), near the seaport.

TO/FROM THE PIER

Taxis are plentiful at all the piers and cost about P75 to Fuente Osmeña. To get uptown by public transport, catch one of the jeepneys that pass by the piers to Pres Osmeña Blvd, then transfer to a jeepney going uptown.

Around Cebu City

Mactan Island

☑ 032 / POP 496,000

If you're flying into Cebu City, nearby Mactan (sometimes referred to as Lapu-Lapu) is where you'll actually land. Connected to Cebu City by two bridges, this busy island has some great diving off its southeast coast, and its all-inclusive resorts are popular with weekending visitors from Manila, Hong Kong and Korea. For independent travellers, the main draw is island-hopping trips in the Bohol Strait between Cebu and Bohol.

◉ Sights

Mactan Shrine   HISTORIC SITE

(ML Quezon National Hwy) Mactan is the improbable site of one of the defining moments in the Philippines' history. It was here on 27 April 1521 that Ferdinand Magellan was fatally wounded at the hands of Chief Lapu-Lapu. The event is commemorated at the Mactan Shrine on a stone plinth bearing the date that Magellan was felled. Next to it is a statue of a ripped and pumped Lapu-Lapu, looking like a He-Man action figure.

Alegre Guitar Factory   HANDICRAFTS

(☑ 032-505 0706; alegreguitar@yahoo.com.ph; Old Maribago Rd; ⊙ 7.30am-6.30pm Mon-Sat, 8am-6pm Sun) Mactan is famous for guitar-making, and this factory in Abuno, a short ride from the Maribago resort area, is the best place to observe how they are made – and buy them if you wish. Prices range from the P2500 decoration 'cheapie' to more than P70,000 for 'export quality'. The most expensive model is made from exquisite black ebony imported from Madagascar.

🏃 Activities

Over the years, destructive fishing methods have taken a toll on the coral reefs around heavily populated Mactan. Still, there's surprisingly good marine life in the waters off Mactan and nearby Nalusuan and Hilutungan islands, where coastal reserves have been established. Turtles are regularly spotted, and you may encounter schooling jackfish and lots of reef critters. Many divers fly into Mactan just for the weekend.

Dive rates in Mactan are quite expensive by Philippine standards, averaging P2500 per dive including equipment. It costs more to go to the islands. Reputable scuba schools include **Kontiki Divers** (☑ 0917 323 5776; www.kontikidivers.com; Plantation Bay Resort & Spa, Marigondon), **SK Divers Center** (☑ 0917 625 2313, 0915 568 3722; www.scubacebu.com; Maribago Wharf) and **Free Crew Dive Center** (☑ 032-495 4210; www.freecrew-diving.com; Maribago Wharf) while **Freediving HQ** (☑ 0917 718 5508; http://freedivinghq.com; Mar Beach, Marigondon) offers freediving courses and also has accommodation.

🛏 Sleeping & Eating

Airport hotels are clustered towards the western end of the island. Independent travellers should target the Maribago area near the midpoint of the long southeast coastline. Elsewhere there are lots of exclusive high-rise resorts.

La Place GUESTHOUSE **$**
(📞0922 851 5422; www.facebook.com/laplace lounge; Quezon National Hwy; d with/without bathroom P1100/900; ❋🐱) This is akin to a boutique hostel, with smart rooms (some with garden views) and even smarter shared bathrooms. There's a restobar here too but it was closed when we dropped by.

Amaris Bed & Breakfast B&B **$$**
(📞032-262 1812; www.facebook.com/amarisbed andbreakfast; ML Quezon National Hwy; r incl breakfast P1800-2400; ❋🐱) Offering modern accommodation 2km from the airport, the spacious rooms here show a contemporary touch with clean lines and quality linen. Family rooms sleep up to six.

⭐ **Abacá Boutique Resort** RESORT **$$$**
(📞032-495 3461; www.abacaresort.com; Punta Engano Rd; ste & villas incl breakfast P15,900-28,900; ❋🐱🖬) Abacá boasts a secluded oceanfront position on a narrow peninsula with an infinity pool, fine spa, gourmet restaurant and butler service. As there are only nine accommodation options (furnished in dark woods, warm tones and cooling slate and stone) it's perfect as a tranquil luxury escape. Indeed you half-expect to see James Bond sipping a martini at the poolside bar.

Maribago Grill & Restaurant SEAFOOD **$$**
(Quezon National Hwy, Maribago; mains P125-495; ⊙10am-10pm) Individual nipa-hut tables set among lush fairy-lit gardens attract a mix of locals and tourists to this dining oasis. Seafood choices include meaty garlic crabs and chowder while meatheads will love the *sisig* (sizzling grilled pieces of pork; P225) or *kare kare* (stew with peanut sauce).

Inday Pina's Sutukil SEAFOOD **$$**
(Mactan Shrine; mains P120-600; ⊙7am-10pm) The best of the rustic seafood restaurants hidden behind the market area near the entrance to Mactan Shrine. Pick up your seafood and hand it to the chef: squid, grouper, lobster and crab are available daily at market prices while specials include baked scallops (P550).

⭐ **Abacá Restaurant** INTERNATIONAL **$$$**
(📞032-495 3461; www.abacaresort.com; Punta Engano Rd; mains P795-2250; ⊙7am-10pm; 🐱) The in-house restaurant at this exclusive hotel features California- and Mediterranean-inspired dishes, with oven-roasted meats and fine seafood. Starters include great salt-and-pepper calamari (P475) and the main-course truffle linguini (P925) is superb. Book well ahead for a sea-facing table.

🍷 Drinking & Nightlife

⭐ **Ibiza Beach Club** LOUNGE
(www.facebook.com/ibizabeachclubcebu; Mövenpick Hotel Mactan Island, Punta Engaño Rd; ⊙4pm-midnight Mon-Thu, 3pm-2am Fri-Sun; 🐱) Jutting into the ocean, this is the sleekest beach club in the Visayas, with cool white seating, decking and sail-like canopies drawing Cebu's bright young things. Resident DJs spin electronic sounds and there are hip-hop and Latin parties featuring guest artists. The dining menu won't disappoint either, though pack some pesos as prices are steep.

ℹ Getting There & Away

There are very regular vans and jeepneys to/from Cebu City's **Jeepney Terminal Ayala** (PUJ Ayala; ⊙4am-midnight) and Lapu-Lapu (P13). A taxi from Cebu to the southeastern beaches will cost at least P300. Within the island, jeepneys and tricycles work well for short hops. Taxis are easy to flag down anywhere.

Olango Island & Around

📞032 / POP 32,600

Far less developed than neighbouring Mactan, the low-lying island of Olango is a wildlife reserve and paradise for birders, with extensive mud flats and wetlands. It's a tiny place, stretching just 7km from north to south.

South of Olango is a vast area of shallow water known as the Olongo Reef Flat, and three islets that are frequently visited on island-hopping trips – Nalusuan, Hilutangan and Caohagan. They are all pretty, but certainly don't expect a Robinson Crusoe experience.

👁 Sights & Activities

⭐ **Olango Island Wildlife Sanctuary** BIRD SANCTUARY
(📞0915 386 2314; www.olangowildlifesanctuary. org; P100; ⊙9am-5pm, closed major public holidays) 20 minutes from Mactan by public bangka, Olango Island is home to this

important wildlife reserve. Taking in 1030 hectares of sand flats and mangroves on Olango's southern shores, the sanctuary supports the largest concentration of migratory birds found in the Philippines – 48 species (including the rare Chinese egret, the Asiatic dowitcher and several species of sandpiper and plover).

Timing is everything here. The peak months are October to November for the southward East Asian–Australasian migration, and February to March for the northward leg. Be sure to visit at low tide, when the birds take to the sand flats en masse to fill up on worms, snails and small fish. There aren't many birds here from May to August, but the sanctuary remains an austerely beautiful spot and worth a visit. You can also kayak through mangroves with Island Buzz Philippines (p283).

The sanctuary is 15 minutes from Olango's Santa Rosa pier by tricycle (around P180 round trip with an hour or so waiting time).

Nalusuan Island   ISLAND
(P200) This tiny island, southwest of Olango, encompasses a marine reserve which is managed privately by Nalusuan Island Resort & Marine Sanctuary. The snorkelling on the house reef is good, though expect plenty of company from midmorning to midafternoon, as it's very popular with day trippers (who have to pay a P200 fee to snorkel or dive on the reef and use the resort facilities).

Mokie Dive Center   DIVING
(✆0906 228 0224; http://mokie-dive-center-cebu-olango.webnode.jp; Talima, Olango Island) This locally owned dive centre offers single dives for P1700 including all equipment rental, plus night dives (P250 extra). It also offers boat tours of neighbouring islands. It will pick you up from Mactan.

🛏 Sleeping

Hilutangan Island Homestays   HOMESTAY $
(✆0916 231 3391; P500) Owner Wilson has a basic overwater nipa hut. He can also arrange homestays.

**Talima Beach Villas
& Dive Resort**   RESORT $$
(✆0922 851 3360; http://talimabeach.com; Talima, Olango Island; r P2200-3350, villa P6900; ❄🌐🏊) Talima enjoys a lovely beachside location on the northwest of the island and offers a choice of rooms, some sleeping four, as well as a two-bedroom villa. Staff are

friendly and helpful, the restaurant serves international and local food, including fresh seafood, there's snorkelling directly offshore and it's located next to a dive shop.

Sagastrand Beach Resort   RESORT $$
(✆0929 883 7704, 032-513 1861; www.sagastrand. com; r P2000-2900; ❄🌐🏊) A Norwegian-Filipino-owned shoreside hotel with a choice of clean, attractive rooms, a large pool, restaurant and very good service. It rents bikes and scooters to guests and can arrange island-hopping boat trips.

Nalusuan Island Resort   RESORT $$$
(✆032-505 4595, 032-516 6432; www.nalusuanislandresort.com; r P3500; ❄🌐) These 14 simple yet homely, overwater cottages with private balconies are perfect for those in search of tranquillity, except when the day trippers arrive (usually between noon and 2pm). Electricity and air-con work from 6pm to 8am. Restaurant prices are high but not outrageous. Round-trip boat transfers for resort guests cost P2500.

ℹ Getting There & Away

Maribago Wharf in Mactan is the best place to organise island-hopping trips taking in up to four islands. P2500 is the standard price including snorkelling equipment. The Punta Engaño Port (near the Mövenpick Hotel) and Marigondon Wharf near Plantation Bay Resort are also good places to find boats.

Public bangkas serve Santa Rosa, Olango Island (P15, 20 minutes, every 40 minutes) from the Punta Engaño Port until 6pm. There are also public bangkas every afternoon to Hilutangan (from the Cordova pier) and Caohagan (from Marigondon Wharf), returning to Mactan the next morning.

Tricycles (P50 to P120 per ride) will get you around Olango, and locals also rent motorbikes and bicycles.

Danao
✆032 / POP 119,252
With a scenic mountainous backdrop, the coastal town of Danao, 25km north of Cebu, is where you catch the ferry to the Camotes Islands. Near the pier is gracious, coral-stone **St Tomas de Villanueva Church**, built in 1755 and restored from near ruin in 1981.

Ceres buses from Cebu City's North Terminal run very frequently to Danao port (P50, one hour).

The schedule changes often but you can usually rely on at least six ferry departures per day to Consuelo, Pacijan Island (P180, two hours) with **Jomalia Shipping** (☑ 032-346 0421, 0905 399 8259; www.majesticlegacy.com.ph; P180). The last trip is at 5.30pm, with a 9pm ferry added on Fridays, Saturdays and Sundays.

Super Shuttle Ferry (☑ 0915 646 6857; http://supershuttleroro.com) operates two daily services to Poro at 9am and 5pm (P180, two hours).

Malapascua Island

☑ 032 / POP 4700

This idyllic island off the north coast of Cebu is famous for its world-class diving, above all the chance to dive with thresher sharks, which are present year-round. But even if you've no interest in reefs and marine life, Malapascua makes a beautiful beach destination, the southern part of the island is fringed with gorgeous sandy bays and there's an excellent choice of hotels and guesthouses. Malapascua is justifiably a very popular escape for travellers and Cebuanos.

Malapascua took a direct hit from Typhoon Yolanda, which tore off every roof on the island, but since then locals have been busy repairing the damage. Some displaced villagers now live in tightly packed shanty settlements around the beach hotels in the southern part of the island, where the poverty is all too striking.

☉ Sights & Activities

A good four-hour walk will take you around the entire coast of the island, with plenty of photo opportunities. Attractions include a **cemetery** with sun-bleached graves, the boat-building village of **Pasil** on the east side of the island where locals construct outriggers, a **lighthouse** in Guimbitayan and a 12m-high **lookout** on the island's northwestern tip, which some brave souls treat as a cliff jump. Bring water. You can also tour most of the island by motorcycle, widely available for rent for a hefty P200 or so per hour.

Beaches include **Bounty Beach**, a glorious stretch of pale sand occupying almost the entire southern part of the island, and crescent-shaped **Logon Beach** (Poblacion Beach) on the southwest side of the island.

Diving

Divers head out at 5am to **Monad Shoal**, a seamount, where they park on the seabed at around 15m. Everyone is hoping to glimpse thresher sharks, which congregate here in the early morning to get their beauty scrub courtesy of the cleaner and moon wrasses (reef fish) that peck off parasites. The chances of spotting them are pretty good – about 75%, but be warned that there can be hundreds of divers here on weekends. For more on thresher sharks contact the Thresher Shark Research & Conservation Project (www.threshersharkproject.org), which is studying the behaviour of these magnificent fish. Monad Shoal can also attract manta rays.

Macrophotographers will love the area around **Gato Island**, a marine sanctuary and sea-snake breeding ground (February to September). The **Dona Marilyn ferry**, a passenger ferry that sank during a typhoon in 1988 killing 250 people, is now a site of soft corals and abundant marine life. **Lapus Lapus Island** is a good dive location just off the northwestern tip of the island; bring a picnic to enjoy on the beaches and caves that appear here at low tide.

There are numerous dive centres on the island, most offering standard rates – one dive for US$25 to US$30, equipment rental US$10 and an open-water diving certificate for US$350. There's a P50 marine fee to dive Monad shoal, a P150 marine fee per day to dive the other sites and a P500 marine fee to dive Calangaman Island. The fees pay for guards to patrol the shoals and reefs.

Recommended diving companies on Malapascua include **Divelink Cebu** (☑ 032-231 4633; www.divelinkcebu.com; Logon Beach), **Evolution Diving** (☑ 0917 628 7333; www.evolution.com.ph; Bounty Beach), **Exotic Divers** (☑ 032-516 2990; www.malapascua.net; Bounty Beach) and **Thresher Shark Divers** (☑ 0927 612 3359, 0917 795 9433; www.malapascua-diving.com), plus the more budget-friendly **Fish Buddies** (☑ 0917 576 8632; www.facebook.com/fishbuddiesmalapascua; Bounty Beach), which charges P1400 per dive including equipment.

Island-Hopping

Good snorkelling spots include **Dakit Dakit Island**, a short boat ride off Bounty Beach, and the **Coral Garden** off the east side of the island. A short snorkelling tour by boat costs around P1500 for a small group. Further out, the islands of **Carnassa** (one hour) and **Calangaman** (two hours) both have stunning beaches as well as excellent snorkelling, with prices around P3000 for full-day hire.

Malapascua Island

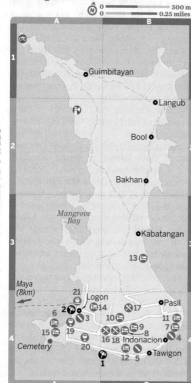

N | 0 —— 500 m
0 —— 0.25 miles

CEBU & EASTERN VISAYAS MALAPASCUA ISLAND

🛏 Sleeping

Malapascua Budget Inn   HOSTEL $
(📱0977 820 3111; www.exploremalapascua.com.
ph; Logon village; dm/r from P400/2000; ❄🛜)
This locally run hostel is well set up, with
a choice of dorms (four, 10 or 14 beds) each
with reading light and privacy curtain –
though bunks are tightly packed together.
There are private rooms too but they're
not great value. It's pretty secure thanks to
CCTV and lockers and there's a great common area for chilling, drinks and meals.

Hiltey's Hideout Home   GUESTHOUSE $
(📱0905 832 5954, 0918 287 0999; www.hilteys
hideout.com; Logon village; r with fan/air-con
P900/1600; ❄🛜) Run by a jovial German,
this backpackers' stronghold has small
rooms grouped around a grassy compound,
each with bright bedspreads and en-suite
bathrooms. Long-term deals are available.

White Sand Bungalows   BUNGALOW $
(📱0927 318 7471; www.whitesand.dk; Logon Beach;
bungalow P500-2500; 🛜) Near the boat landing on Logon Beach, the White Sand has
comfortable and reasonably priced nipa huts
with lofts and roomy balconies. There are
dreamy views of the bay from the property.

**Thresher Cove Resort
& Dive Center**   RESORT $
(📱0908 139 7609; www.threshercove.com; dm
P500 r/villa incl breakfast from P900/3500;
❄🛜🏊) On a private beach a 10-minute
walk north of Bounty Beach, this well-
managed operation is an excellent all-
rounder. Dorms have air-con and are cleaned
daily while the delightful 'native-style' cottages have TV, and either queen or twin
beds. Book the huge Captain's Villa, which

can sleep five, for privacy and luxury. Free motorbike transfer from the boat drop-off.

Mike & Diose's Aabana Beach Resort
RESORT $

(☑ 0905 263 2914; www.aabana.de; east end of Bounty Beach; d P500-2150; ❄ 🤖) This friendly, rambling place fringing the boat-building barangay of Pasil has a range of accommodation, from budget rooms to big air-con options with kitchens. The decor is a little dated, but the German-Filipino family who runs the place looks after guests well. There's a basic beach-facing restaurant for meals (which would really benefit from a fan or two!).

Villa Sandra
HOSTEL $

(☑ 0977 130 0642; jonjonmalapascua@gmail.com; Logon village; dm P360, r with shared bathroom P720; @ 🤖) A backpacker pad next to the elementary school in Logon village, with an eco-rustic vibe, simple shared doubles and dorms, a kitchen, and chill-out and hammock zone. There are four bathrooms and free drinking water, and food in the vegetarian restaurant is well priced and nutritious.

★ Angelina
B&B $$

(☑ 0977 803 4925; www.angelinabeach.com; Logon Beach; r P3000; ❄ 🤖) Above the owners' Italian restaurant (p297), these four units represent a great deal – all are spacious, with polished-wood flooring, exposed stone walls, sofas and modish bathrooms, and decorated with handmade textiles and art. Two have stunning bay views.

★ Malapascua Starlight Resort
HOTEL $$

(☑ 0917 872 1015; www.malapascuastarlightresort. com; Logon village; r P1500-2400; ❄ 🤖) In the heart of the village, this resort has well-presented, immaculately clean and spacious rooms with quality beds and linen, verandahs and efficient air-con. Fine value. It's run by friendly Filipino-American folk who also have a rental house next door with three bedrooms. It's a five-minute walk from Logon or Bounty beach.

★ Tepanee Beach Resort
RESORT $$

(☑ 032-317 0124; www.tepanee.com; Logon Beach; d P3300-4700; ❄ 🤖) The classiest place in Malapascua, this Italian-run hillside resort above Logon Beach is a cut above the competition. Attractive cottages feature soaring Balinese-style thatched roofs, wooden floors and excellent beds. All accommodation has private balconies and vistas, but the ocean-view deluxe rooms, perched over a private

white-sand cove, are sublime. There's a little bar, a small gym, spa and Jacuzzi.

Evolution Resort
RESORT $$

(☑ 0917 628 7333; www.evolution.com.ph; Bounty Beach; r incl breakfast with fan/air-con from P1600/2800; ❄ 🤖) On the southeastern edge of Bounty, this laid-back English/Irish-run dive resort has good-value rooms: garden fan-cooled options for those on a budget and air-conditioned deluxe rooms with minibars and private terraces. It's an environmentally aware place with personable staff, and the Craic House restobar here serves quality food.

Ocean Vida
RESORT $$

(☑ 0917 303 8064; www.ocean-vida.com; Bounty Beach; s/d incl breakfast P3400/3900; ❄ 🤖) This full-service resort smack in the middle of Bounty Beach has some of the nicest rooms on Malapascua behind its popular beachfront restaurant. Plush beds, cosy private balconies, classy prints and a nice array of dark-stained wooden furniture are highlights. Guests also get free yoga sessions and gym access in a neighbouring fitness and spa centre.

🍴 Eating & Drinking

La Isla Bonita
FILIPINO $

(Logon village; meals P70–120; ⊘ 8am-10pm) A great find for budget eats, this courtyard restaurant is run by a jolly family who prepare a selection of fresh local dishes every day, including vegie options. In the evening you may have to wait a while for your meal.

Ging-Ging's Restaurant
FILIPINO $

(Logon village; mains P60-200; ⊘ 7am-10pm) Inland from the beach, Ging-Ging's serves tasty, cheap, filling food including a good breakfast selection, salads and curries. Tables face a large garden filled with flowers and shrubs.

Kiwi Bakhaw
FILIPINO $$

(Logon village; meals P130-220; ⊘ 7am-10pm) This place is well worth sniffing out for its gorgeous cordon bleu and curries. Quality food takes time to prepare: expect to wait up to an hour. Bring bug spray. It's inland from the Malapascua Starlight Resort (p297).

★ Angelina
ITALIAN $$$

(http://angelinabeach.com; Logon Beach; mains P275-695; ⊘ 8am-10pm) Facing a white-sand bay with a pretty terrace, this restaurant offers heavenly creations that will have you craving Italian food for weeks. The home-made *tagliatelle asparagi* is al-dente bliss, or try *fritto misto di pesce* which includes a mix of lightly fried seafood. Many ingredients are imported from Italy and there's an extensive wine list. Don't miss its homemade gelato.

★ **Kocoy's Maldito**   BAR
(http://kokaysmalditodiveresort.com; Logon Beach; ⊘24hr) Kocoy's is the most popular bar on Malapascua, with the action extending well into the night. Bar games such as table football and pool lure punters in; strong cocktails keep them here. There's also a full food menu, featuring local and Western dishes.

Oscar's   LOUNGE
(http://malapascua-diving.com/restaurant.html; Bounty Beach; ⊘7am 'till empty'; 🛜) Named in honour of Oscar Wilde, this stylish bar has fine views over the ocean, smart rattan seating and a devilish drinks menu that includes great cocktails and imported beers. It's located above Thresher Shark Divers (p295).

ⓘ Information

There are a handful of ATMs on Malapascua; note they have a P10,000 limit.

ⓘ Getting There & Away

Bangkas from Maya (P100, 45 minutes) to Malapascua leave roughly every hour until 5.30pm or so (until 4.30pm from Malapascua). The usual drop-off and departure point on Malapascua is Logon Beach, where there's a ticket office and schedule board you can check. However during the *habagat* (southwest monsoon, June to October) you may be dropped off on Bounty Beach or even in Pasil.

Especially late in the day, boaters in Maya are notorious for trying to get tourists to pay extra for a special trip, claiming they don't have any passengers. Relax – there's always a last trip that leaves at 5.30pm or so.

Vans (P200, 3½ hours, every 30 minutes) and buses (ordinary/air-con P170/195, 4½ hours) depart Maya pier for Cebu City until midevening.

Bantayan Island

☎ 032 / POP 129,000

Those looking for the perfect beach destination will love Bantayan Island. Its blinding white-sand beaches are some of Cebu's very best and the island's mellow, easygoing vibe is highly seductive. With little traffic, it's a wonderful place to explore by scooter – circumnavigating the coastline makes a fine day out. Offshore there's a blissful tropical

islet, deservedly popular as a day-trip destination. However, Bantayan does not have any rewarding dive sites and the snorkelling is pretty limited too.

The relaxed, bucolic settlement of Santa Fe on the island's southern coast is where most travellers base themselves. This little town boasts a sublime stretch of sandy beach and a decent selection of hotels and restobars. About 10km west of Santa Fe is Bantayan Town, the island's beautifully preserved administrative heart.

Holy Week sees Bantayan turn into an epic fiesta. People sleep on the beaches and hotel prices double, triple and even quadruple.

⊙ Sights & Activities

Gorgeous **Paradise Beach** (P50) near Santa Fe is aptly named.

Island-hopping trips are possible to nearby **Hilantagaan Island** and **Virgin Island** (2 people P500, each subsequent person P100), which have coral outcrops. Boat hire costs around P1200 for a half-day tour (usually for up to eight people).

Bantayan is perfect for exploring on two wheels; hotels rent out bicycles for P150 per day, scooters are P300.

About 9km east is of Santa Fe is a **mangrove garden** (Maricabon village; P50; ⊘8am-5pm) popular for kayaking.

🛏 Sleeping

Bantayan Cottages   COTTAGE $
(☏032-438 9538; www.bantayancottages.com; F Roska St; d with shared bathroom & fan P400, r with air-con P800-1600; 🕸🛜) A little south of the pier, this family-owned place makes up for its lack of beachfront with friendly service and rustic, verandah-equipped cottages set around a lush garden. 'Backpacker' rooms are basic affairs in the main house while 'deluxe' have two king-sized beds.

★ **Kota Beach**   HOTEL $$
(☏032-438 9042; www.kotabeachresort.com; F Duarte St; r with fan/air-con P900/1400, cottages from P1900; 🕸🛜) This attractive resort hotel sits pretty on one of the best stretches of beach in Bantayan, and its stylish rooms combine a contemporary look with a traditional feel thanks to the bamboo screens and ceilings. Service can be a tad spotty at times, however.

St Bernard
Beach Resort   RESORT $$

(☑ 0917 963 6162, 0908 582 4927; www.bantayan.
dk; cottages incl breakfast with fan P850-1600,
with air-con P1300-3200; 🕸🕾) This attractive
beach resort fronts a wide stretch of sand
and has a wonderfully relaxed island vibe.
Rows of thatched-roofed cottages are set
amid palm trees – all feature polished wood,
throw rugs and lace curtains. It's about 1km
north of Santa Fe pier.

Yooneek Beach Resort   RESORT $$

(☑ 032-438 9124; www.yooneekbeachresort.com;
Saagundo St; r with fan/air-con from P1590/1690;
🕸🕾) An established place on Sugar Beach,
just south of Santa Fe's centre, with spacious
rooms near the water and one of the most
laid-back beach bars on the island. It's managed by friendly folk.

Marlin Beach Resort   RESORT $$

(☑ 032-438 9093; www.marlin-bantayan.com;
Roska St; d P2300-5400; 🕸🕾) Close to the
restaurant and bar action in 'downtown'
Santa Fe, Marlin's large motel-style rooms
may not inspire, but its attractive beachside
location, complete with bar and restaurant,
is appealing. Rates drop around 20% in low
season.

Sunday Flower Beach
Hotel & Resort   RESORT $$

(☑ 032-438 9556; www.bantayan-resort.com; off
C Batiancila St; d/studio P2100/4300; 🕸🕾) On
glorious Sugar Beach on the south edge of
Santa Fe, this Australian-run resort has six
good-value air-con rooms with roomy balconies, plasma TVs, ample wood furniture and
plenty of pizazz. The separate, older 'studio'
accommodation is less attractive.

Coral Blue Oriental   RESORT $$$

(☑ 032-316 8054, 0928 372 3021; http://coral
blueoriental.net; incl breakfast r P2700-5500,
villa P9950; 🕸🕾) Right on the beach, these
bamboo-and-wood rooms and bungalows
are well constructed and equipped with
crisp linen and TV. Villas are huge and well
suited to families. Free pick-ups and drop-
offs to the port are offered.

✖ Eating & Drinking

For such a small island, Santa Fe has an im-
pressive strip of lively restaurants just off
the main road in the centre of town. Head to
the very lively MJ Square open-air court for
a wide choice of places to eat.

★ MJ Square   FOOD COURT $

(A Batobalonos St; meals from P50-250; ⊙ 7am-
1am or later) This open-air food bazaar is
lined with restaurants, mainly serving in-
expensive Filipino food, but there are some
surprises including a fine Mexican joint. The
atmosphere is raucous in the evening with
packed tables of diners and a real buzz in
the air. You'll also find a good bar or two
here.

★ Bantayan Burrito Company   MEXICAN $$

(☑ 0995 366 7452; www.facebook.com/bantayan
burritocompany; MJ Sq; meals from P155-250;
⊙ 10am-11pm Wed-Mon) What's this? A British-
owned Tex-Mex restaurant on a remote
Visayan island? Works for us. Satisfy all
your burrito and taco cravings at this simple place in buzzing MJ Sq. Specials include
tequila-chilli chicken and fish tacos. Wash
it down with a chilled San Mig or a margarita. *Olé!*

Cou Cou's   INTERNATIONAL $$

(☑ 032-438 9055; www.hotelbantayan.com; A Ba-
tobalonos St; mains P150-200; ⊙ 7am-11pm; 🕾)
Popular Belgian-owned restaurant serving
good breakfast, Filipino fare (*adobo*, Bicol
exprés) and Western dishes. There's a good
wine list (or if you're more a Java-head,
there's an espresso machine).

★ Caffe del Mar   ITALIAN $$$

(☑ 0917 514 7279; G Borraska St; mains P280-550;
⊙ 10am-midnight; 🕾) For a taste of the Italian
motherland look no further, Caffe del Mar
serves up fine imported antipasto, gnoc-
chi, seafood and grilled meats, homemade
pasta and the best pizza (from a wood-fired
oven) in Bantayan. Also popular as a bar and
nightspot with live reggae every Friday.

Liquido   BAR

(MJ Sq; ⊙ 4pm-1am) At the far end of MJ
Sq, this friendly little open-air bar is the
perfect place to perch on a stool and enjoy
some banter with locals. Get stuck into the
cocktail list (all are P130), shoot some shots
or just sip a cold beer.

Shake Me   JUICE BAR

(MJ Sq; ⊙ 10am-10pm) A fine juice and shake
bar run by a welcoming Italian. All manor of
tropical flavours are offered, as well as great
ice cream, popsicles, snacks and meals.

ℹ Information

ATMs are thin on the ground in Bantayan.
There's a PNB ATM just off the main plaza in

CEBU & EASTERN VISAYAS BANTAYAN ISLAND

Bantayan town and a **First Agro-Industrial Rural Bank** (C Batiancila St; ☉ 9am-4pm Mon-Fri, to noon Sat) ATM in Santa Fe but it's best to cash up before you arrive.

❶ Getting There & Away

Air Juan (p444) flies twice weekly (P1288, 40 minutes) between Bantayan airstrip (4km north of Santa Fe) and Mactan-Cebu airport.

Hagnaya is the jumping-off seaport to Santa Fe, with roll-on, roll-off ferry (RORO) companies **Super Shuttle Ferry** (☑ 0939 850 6438; http://supershuttleroro.com/en; Santa Fe port) and **Island Shipping** (☑ 0929 678 7930; Santa Fe port) alternating trips every hour until 5.30pm (P170, one hour). The last boat from Santa Fe to Hagnaya departs at 6pm.

Seven daily Ceres buses connect Santa Fe with Cebu City (P200, does not includes ferry ticket, 5½ hours). There are also more regular Ceres buses (ordinary/air-con P140/165, 3½ hours) between Hagnaya and Cebu City, every 30 minutes until evening.

From Bantayan Town, a bangka ferry bound for Cadiz, Negros (P300, two hours) departs daily at 9am. On alternate mornings, a bangka is scheduled to sail for Estancia (P350, four hours) on Panay, but this service is unreliable. There's also a daily 6am ferry from Hagnaya to Cawayan, Masbate (P220, four hours).

Jeepneys (P12) connect Santa Fe with Bantayan town.

Toledo

☑ 032 / POP 174,200

Toledo is a big, bustling and polluted city on the west coast of Cebu. The only travellers here are heading elsewhere.

You can catch boats to Negros from Toledo on Cebu's west coast, as well as from Tabuelan, 65km north of Toledo. Toledo is served by frequent Ceres buses (P82, two hours) from Cebu City's South Bus station and V-hire vans (P100, 1½ hours). Tabuelan is served by less frequent V-hires and local buses from Cebu's north station.

Those headed to Bantayan or Malapascua from Toledo will likely have to make several transfers. Head to Tuburan by slow ordinary bus, then transfer to a jeepney north to Tabuelan, then another jeepney north to Hagnaya for Bantayan, or to Bogo for Malapascua. Those heading to Moalboal from Toledo will need to catch a bus inland to Naga (P50, one hour) and then another bus to Moalboal.

EB Aznar (☑ 032-467 9447; www.facebook.com/aznarshipping), **FastCat** (☑ 032-816 1183; http://fastcat.com.ph; tickets P120-250) and **Lite Shipping** (☑ 032-255 1721, 032-467 9604; www.liteferries.com) are ferry companies in Toledo.

Moalboal

☑ 032 / POP 32,300

Wildly popular with travellers, Moalboal is a small but lively coastal resort around 90km southwest of Cebu City. There's a lot to love about the place, its craggy coastline lined with shoreside bars and restaurants where you can sip a sundowner and gaze over the azure waters of the Tañon Strait to the distant hills of Negros. Directly offshore is a stupendous coral wall, so you can amble out of your hotel room, don snorkelling gear and encounter outstanding marine life (including Moalboal's world-renowned sardine run).

However as there are only a few patches of sand, head to nearby **White Beach** for dreamy days by the sea.

Confusingly, the actual settlement of Moalboal (hard to pronounce – try mo-ahl-bo-ahl) is a humdrum town on the highway, 6km west of the coast. The tourist resort is officially Panagsama Beach. However everyone just calls the area 'Moalboal'.

◉ Sights

★**Kawasan Falls**   WATERFALL

(local/foreigner P20/40) Located 17km south of Moalboal, Kawasan Falls comprise a series of three waterfalls; the largest cascades 15m into a massive, milky-blue swimming hole. Unfortunately this main pool has been a little spoiled by weekend crowds and overdevelopment. The second and third waterfalls are more peaceful, and you can scramble beyond these to more secluded spots. Kawasan may be a popular spot, but its natural beauty is still special.

Mainit Springs   SPRING, WATERFALL

(P20; ☉ 6am-5pm) These natural springs in Montañeza, 32km south of Moalboal make an attractive excursion (particularly on weekdays when it's less busy). The hottest spring tops out at 42°C and, according to the signage, 'cures skin disease and sickness of the body'. Clamber up the pretty canyon behind the springs to a series of 3m to 8m falls dropping into peacock-green swimming holes.

✈ Activities

While diving, freediving and snorkelling are Moalboal's raison d'être, a dizzying array of terrestrial activities are also on offer in the area including canyoning, climbing and mountain biking. For yoga sessions ask at **Freediving Planet** (✆ 0908 608 7864; www. freediving-planet.com) and for cooking classes check out Ven'z (p303).

Diving & Freediving

The big draw in Moalboal is the **sardine run**, a dense concentration of schooling fish that shimmy around en masse to form incredible geometric shapes 5m to 10m under the surface. Pescador Island used to be the place to observe this mesmerising display, but in recent years the sardines have set up shop on the reef wall just 30m off Panagsama Beach. It's a routine shore dive for scuba divers, or just throw on a mask and snorkel and swim out on your own. Thresher sharks occasionally make cameos in pursuit of the sardines, although you have to be awfully lucky to see this.

Moalboal also has some of the Visayas' best reef diving along the coral wall which parallels the coastline just offshore. Further out, tiny **Pescador Island**, accessed via an (often-choppy) 3km boat ride offers stunning coral, an open-top underwater cave known as the **Cathedral** and the chance to see pelagics. The site **Airplane Wreck** is at 23m, the remains of a two-seater airplane, its fuselage now encrusted with coral. White Beach also has fine shore diving and snorkelling.

Dive prices run from P1200 to P1750 per dive, including equipment. PADI open-water certificates cost from P16,000. There is a reef conservation fee of P100 to dive at Savedra Reef and Pescador. Recommended dive operators include **Blue Abyss Dive Shop** (✆ 032-474 3036; www.blueabyssdiving.com), **Nelson's Dive Shop** (Ocean Safari Philippines; ✆ 032-474 3023; www.ibara.ne.jp/~bitoon), **Quo Vadis Divers** (✆ 0917 519 4050; www.quovadisresort.com) and **Neptune Diving** (✆ 032-495 0643; www.neptunediving.com).

Moalboal is also one of Asia's foremost freediving centres, with ideal conditions and two resident schools.

Freediving Planet and **Freediving Philippines** (✆ 0938 263 4646; www.freediving-philippines.com) both offer AIDA freediving courses.

Adventure Sports

★ **Planet Action**   ADVENTURE
(✆ 0917 583 0062; www.action-philippines.com)
Planet Action offers some of the most exhilarating adventure tours in the Visayas. Top of the list are the mountain-biking, canyoning (such as the challenging Tison Falls, P3200 per person) and river-climbing tours, which take place in areas where other operators don't venture. Sea-kayaking, horse-riding and trekking tours in Negros are also available.

Cyan Adventures   ADVENTURE SPORTS
(✆ 0927 426 6886; www.cyan-adventures.com)
This adventure-tour company has a small range of tours, including canyoning at Kawasan Falls and climbing Osmeña Peak (both US$69).

🛏 Sleeping

🛏 Panagsama Beach

Mayas Native Garden   RESORT $
(✆ 0915 480 9610; www.mayasnativegarden.com; cottage with fan/air-con P800/1500, house P2500; ✳ @ 🛜) These five attractive nipa huts vary in size and spec, from simple yet elegant fan-cooled to very spacious double-storey, with all mod cons. The lush surrounding garden has space for kids to play and there's a restaurant here too.

Pacitas   HOTEL $
(✆ 032-474 3017, 0910 858 7222; Panagsama Beach; r with fan/air-con from P800/1200; ✳ 🛜) One of Panagsama's original places to stay, with simple, inexpensive bungalows (some with two bedrooms) and rooms dotted around a shady seaside plot. It's owned by a friendly team and the location is quiet (except on Saturday nights when they host a disco in the grounds).

Le Village
Hostel Moalboal   HOSTEL $
(✆ 0933 153 2719; www.facebook.com/levillage hostelmoalboal; Panagsama Rd; dm/d from P300/600; ✳ 🛜) A basic, inexpensive hostel with choice of air-con (good move) or fan (hot) dorms and three private rooms – all with shared bathrooms. There's a chill-out deck for chatting and restaurant for tasty, cheap local food. It's a kilometre inland from the beach. Cash only.

Panagsama Beach

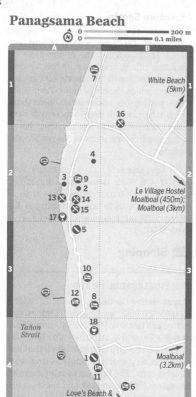

CEBU & EASTERN VISAYAS MOALBOAL

Moalboal Backpacker Lodge HOSTEL $
(☎ 0917 751 8902; www.moalboal-backpacker
lodge.com; dm/s/d/cottage from P300/450/
700/950; 🛜) This hostel's location on the
noisy main drag is not great, but step inside and you'll find airy mixed and wom-
en's dorms and a couple of semiprivate
rooms. The converted VW camper out front
doubles as a kooky coffee shop. There are
discounted weekly rates and, like all good
hostels, there's a sociable vibe.

Il Sogno B&B $$
(☎ 0915 696 5124; prandifranco@yahoo.it; d incl
breakfast P2000; 🌀🛜) This neat bed and
breakfast is run by a very hospitable Italian
and his local wife who look after their guests
very well. Spacious rooms face the ocean
and have king-sized beds and huge bathrooms. Do try the owner's amazing cooking
if he invites you to eat dinner – he'll rustle
up an espresso for you too if you ask.

★ Tipolo Beach Resort RESORT $$
(☎ 0917 583 0062; www.tipoloresort.com; d P1700-
2000; 🌀 @) This small seaside resort has
fine-value, well-constructed accommodation
with clean tiled floors and sturdy bamboo
furniture, along with mod cons such as hot
water, fridge and a safe. But the balconies
are what win us over, amply furnished and
with partial sea views. Staff are well trained,
helpful and chatty and the in-house restaurant is excellent too.

Blue Abyss RESORT $$
(☎ 032-474 3012; www.blueabyssdiving.com; d/tr
P1500/1700; 🌀🛜) With attractive dive-room
packages, the Blue Abyss is ideal for divers
on a budget. The accommodation compound
is attractive, just back from the shore, though
none of the plain, clean rooms enjoy sea
views. Good grub is served in the restaurant
and staff are friendly and accommodating.

Love's Beach & Dive Resort RESORT $$
(☎ 032-474 3086; www.lovesbeachresort.com; d
incl breakfast P1700-3100; 🌀🛜🛖) In a peaceful location on the tranquil southern side

of Moalboal, Love Beach has an attractive bar and pool area, restaurant with excellent sea views, small private beach and well-furnished if slightly dark rooms, each with a balcony and air-con. There's also an apartment with kitchenette ideal for families. Cash only. Check out the hotel's PADI dive shop for scuba action.

Quo Vadis Beach Resort RESORT $$
(032-474 3068; www.quovadisresort.com; d with fan P1880, with air-con P3120-5500;) Quo Vadis boasts a beautiful coastal setting and has extensive gardens around a lovely pool. Staff are sweet, the dive shop is excellent and the restaurant makes the most of the views. Rooms are well kept but somewhat overpriced and a tad dated, with smallish cottages close to the sea and nipa huts at the rear.

Sampaguita Resort RESORT $$$
(032-474 0066; www.sampaguitaresort.com; Tongo Point Rd; s/d incl full board €118/78;) Three kilometres south of Panagsama Beach, this well-managed oceanfront dive resort has 16 traditional bungalows, eight of them suitable for families, set in lush tropical gardens. All but one have dreamy sea views. There's a free shuttle bus to downtown Panagsama and good dive-accommodation packages available.

White Beach

Asian Belgian Resort RESORT $$
(032-358 5428; www.asian-belgian-resort.com; d P2000-4565;) A friendly midranger just south of White Beach, it lacks a sandy coastline but has a good lookout over the house reef, a dive company and free kayak use. Rooms are not fancy but kept tidy. You'll pay more for a sea view.

Blue Orchid Resort RESORT $$$
(0929 273 1128; www.blueorchidresort.com; d with fan P3000, with air-con from P3500;) This resort enjoys a wonderfully secluded location on the rocky coastline just north of White Beach. The snorkelling offshore is the area's best, or just relax by the stunning pool or in one of the ocean-facing gazebos. The spacious rooms have wooden poster beds, exposed stone walls and private balconies, and there's also an excellent restaurant and dive shop.

Club Serena Resort RESORT $$$
(032-516 8118; www.clubserenaresort.com; r P3600-6900;) Someone behind this shoreside place has a strong sense of design,

which is both contemporary and quirky by equal measure. Every structure, from the spacious octagonal bar-restaurant to the sprawling tree-house room, is designed with personal flair. Choose from the modern suites or native-style cottages and casitas.

Badian

★ Badian Island Wellness Resort RESORT $$$
(032-401 3303; www.badianhotel.com; r/villa incl breakfast from P13,800/28,400;) This luxurious island resort boasts some of the most sumptuous rooms in the Philippines, all done up in tasteful native style. The pool villas, which feature their own private salt-water pools, are the ultimate in opulence. There's a fine spa and a floating games room with pool table. Located on Badian Island, 10km south of Moalboal.

Eating & Drinking

Cafe Cebuano CAFE $$
(www.facebook.com/cafe.cebuano; mains P160-320; 9am-midnight;) Boasts a great shoreside deck perfect for quaffing a glass of red or sipping on a cappuccino and soaking up the ocean views. There's a full food menu too, featuring Western and Asian dishes – try the Singapore fried noodles (P250).

★ Last Filling Station INTERNATIONAL $$
(032-474 3016; meals P175-345; 7am-10pm;) An enjoyable little restaurant with efficient service (though with street views rather than ocean vistas). Famous for its energy-boosting breakfasts, replete with yoghurt, muesli and protein shakes. Lunchtime and dinner dishes include baguettes and pita-bread sandwiches (from P195), sizzlers and spicy garlic shrimps (P275).

French Coffee Shop CAFE $$
(snacks from P100, meals from P160-280; 7am-10pm;) It does what it says on the sign – French coffee – well, it serves Italian-style coffee too...plus shakes, crêpes, baguettes, breakfasts and salads. There's often a dish of the day for P280. It's off the water but you can dig your feet in the imported sand.

Ven'z Kitchen FILIPINO $$
(032-4743981; www.facebook.com/venzkitchen; Panagsama Beach; mains P130-260; 10am-10pm;) Everything on the menu is prepared with love and attention at this

simple place run by two friendly local ladies; there's always a daily special and vegans and vegetarians are well catered for. Filipino classics include pork *sisig*, *kare kare* and *adobo*. As the board outside says, 'We don't serve fast food we serve food fast'. It also offers **cooking lessons** (per person P500-1300; ⊘11am & 3pm).

Pleasure Principle
Resto-Bar INTERNATIONAL **$$**
(meals P180-490; ⊘9am-10pm; 🛜) Named after an obscure Gary Numan album, this enjoyable, efficiently run place on the main drag offers an eclectic (too long) menu including French, local, Italian and surprises such as Arab-style pizza (with ground beef and Middle Eastern spices; P330).

Chilli Bar BAR
(⊘9.30am-last customer) A Panagsama institution where the mantra on the wall proclaims, 'The liver is evil and it must be punished'. Yes, this is the liveliest bar in town: expect party tunes and dancing, plenty of banter and competitive games on the pool tables. Draws an incongruous, gregarious mix of local ladyboys, backpackers, dive crews and hard-drinking expats. Also offers pub-grub-style food.

One Eyed Jacks BAR
(www.facebook.com/oneeyedjacksmoalboal; Panagsama; ⊘4pm-2am) A large, two-storey American-owned bar with a keenly priced drinks list and a busy pool table. There's good service and live music some nights.

THE WHALE SHARKS OF OSLOB

In recent years the village of Tan-awan, a barangay of Oslob, has risen to prominence as a site where tourists can interact with whale sharks. It all started in 2011 when internet videos surfaced that showed an Oslob fisherman luring a whale shark away from his catch with small fish. One thing led to another and before long the whale sharks were being fed to entertain tourists.

While the program has been a huge financial boon to Tan-awan, many conservationists worry about possible adverse affects that the hand-feeding might have on a highly migratory endangered species that is just recovering from centuries of exploitation. Scientists studying the program report that about a dozen juvenile whale sharks have stopped migrating and remain in Tan-awan, where they rely at least partially on these 'hand-outs' for sustenance. Reef-World Foundation (www.reef-world.org), Save Philippine Seas (www.savephilippineseas.com) and Green Fins (www.greenfins.net) are among several organisations that have come out against the tourism activities in Oslob, noting that the practice of feeding wildlife is unsustainable.

Proponents of the hand-feeding respond that the project protects the whale sharks by keeping them safely around Oslob and away from the hazards of the open ocean, where they risk being poached. They note that the project supports an alternative livelihood for local fishers who would otherwise put pressure on the local reefs or, worse, kill the whale sharks (although there is little evidence that they were killing whale sharks before).

Regardless of how you feel about the ethics of feeding wild animals, you may or may not be impressed with the Oslob whale-shark interactions. While carefully composed photos may appear to show your friends swimming alone with these leviathans in the big blue, the reality is different. There are hundreds of people in the water at any one time, most of them watching up to a half-dozen or so whale sharks hover near the surface begging for food. You may see people try to touch and 'pet' the sharks (though swimmers are not officially allowed to swim within 5m of them). Efforts have been made to limit the number of boats in the water at any one time, but sharks are still regularly injured by local boats. If you prefer a more natural experience, you'll likely find the whale-shark interaction programs in Donsol and Pintuyan (Southern Leyte) more to your liking.

The NGO Lamave (Large Marine Vertebrates Research Institute Philippines; www.lamave.org) is dedicated to the conservation of marine megafauna in the Philippines. Consult its excellent website for conservation updates, including whale-shark research.

ℹ Information

There are ATMs on the highway in Moalboal and a PNB in the **Gaisano Grand Mall** (Hwy; ◷ 8.30am-9.30pm).

ℹ Getting There & Away

Buses from Moalboal to Cebu City (ordinary/air-con P120/140, 3½ hours) depart every 30 to 45 minutes between 6am and 8pm, plus additional night buses. Cramped air-con vans (P120, 2½ hours) depart every 30 minutes until 5pm. Buses and vans arrive and depart from the highway in Moalboal centre. From here you can take a tricycle (P150) or *habal-habal* (P100) 3km to Panagsama Beach. White Beach costs an extra P50.

A taxi to/from Cebu is around P2500, but if you can find an empty cab on a return trip to Cebu you can negotiate the trip for about half that.

Continuing south from Moalboal, very frequent buses terminate a few kilometres beyond the roll-on, roll-off ferry (RORO) pier in Bato (ordinary/air-con P65/P76, 1½ hours). Ferries from Bato depart every 1½ hours or so to Tampi, Negros (P70, 30 minutes), where you can pick up transport to Dumaguete. To potentially save a couple of hours on this trip, take the bus to its terminus in Bato, then continue south by *habal-habal* from Bato to Lilo-an (10 minutes), where frequent ferries serve Sibulan (25 minutes), which is just 10 minutes from Dumanguete.

Lilo-an & Sumilon Island

☎ 032 / POP 18,200

The gorgeous coastline around the southern tip of Cebu is home to several worthwhile attractions, namely **Sumilon Island**, where there's a marine sanctuary. Lilo-an is also where many tourists arrive to catch boats to Sibulan in Negros. In recent years this area has risen to prominence as the site of a controversial whale-shark interaction program 8km north of Santander in Oslob.

The marine sanctuary off Sumilon Island is a conservation success story in the Philippines. Resorts in Lilo-an run dive trips to the reserve, or you can base yourself in the luxurious **Sumilon Bluewater Island Resort** (☎ 032-318 3129; www.bluewatersumilon.com.ph; Sumilon Island; r from P12,300; ❄ �🛜 ≋). Nonguests can use the resort's facilities for P600 and avail of its free boat transfer from a pier in Banlogan, 1km south of Tan-awan. Visitors to the sanctuary are charged a P10 entrance fee and there is a further fee of P150 for diving.

🛏 Sleeping

⭐ **Farm Resort**　　　　　HOTEL **$$**

(☎ 032-480 9032; www.facebook.com/thefarmresortsantander; 2km east of Lilo-an pier; r P1950; ❄ �🛜) Set back from Cebu's southern shore, this fine place has four attractive, well-constructed rooms with bamboo beds in a large, leafy garden plot. Excellent Filipino food is offered and there's room service. Expect heavy rock on the stereo in the bar area (the owner is a biker).

⭐ **Eden Resort**　　　　　RESORT **$$$**

(☎ 032-480 9321; www.eden.ph; incl breakfast r P2800-4800, ste P7800; ❄ �🛜 ≋) This tranquil Mediterranean-style resort is dramatically perched on a cliff overlooking the Tañon Strait and has a tennis court, infinity pool, mountain bikes and kayaks for hire, and great snorkelling offshore. Its classy accommodation is fine value given the location and facilities but budget rooms have shared bathrooms.

ℹ Getting There & Away

From Lilo-an, fastcraft (P62) and additional bangkas (P38) sail from neighbouring piers to Sibulan near Dumaguete (25 minutes) about every half-hour until 10pm.

There's also a daily ferry to Larena, Siquijor (P155, 2½ hours) at 10am.

Frequent buses run all day from Lilo-an to Cebu City (P155, 3½ hours). For Moalboal, you must change buses in nearby Bato.

CAMOTES ISLANDS

☎ 032 / POP 103,600

Just two hours from mainland Cebu, the Camotes offer an authentic slice of island life. The group's two main islands, Poro and Pacijan, are connected by a mangrove-fringed land bridge that enables visitors to explore the two by motorcycle, the main mode of transport here. The best beaches and most accommodation are on Pacijan. Visitors rarely make it to the third island, Ponson, which looks to Leyte rather than Cebu as its main link to the world.

ℹ Getting There & Away

Be flexible if heading to the Camotes, boat schedules are often changed and cancellations are quite common.

Fastcraft (P500, 1½ hours) operated by Oceanjet (p290) connect Cebu City with Consuelo, Pacijan Island twice daily.

Camotes Islands

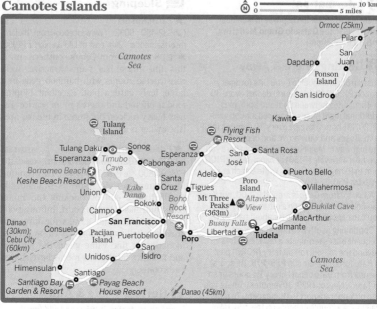

Roll-on, roll-off (RORO) express ferries from Danao, Cebu to Consuelo are run by Jomalia Shipping (p295). There are six daily scheduled departures (P180, two hours) between 5.30am and 5.30pm on this route, with an extra sailing at 9pm on Friday, Saturday and Sunday.

Super Shuttle Ferry (☑ 0915 646 6857; http://supershuttleroro.com) has twice-daily trips (P180, two hours) scheduled from Danao to Poro at 9am and 5pm, returning at 5am and 1pm.

Jomalia Shipping also operates twice-daily connections between Pilar, Ponson Island and Ormoc, Leyte.

🛈 Getting Around

The best way to get around Pacijan and Poro Islands is to rent a motorcycle, as jeepneys are sporadic. *Habal-habal* and tricycle are also useful for trips. Most resorts on Pacijan hire out motorcycles for P400 to P500. An all-day *habal-habal* trip is around P1000, while tricycle drivers charge around P1500.

To get from Poro Island to Ponson Island, charter a bangka from Puertobello to Kawit (P250, 20 minutes). On Ponson, *habal-habal* charge P140 from Kawit to Pilar.

If arriving in Puertobello from Kawit, there is a *habal-habal* stand at the pier with prices posted to San Francisco (P200) and other destinations.

Pacijan Island

☑ 032 / POP 48,900

Pacijan's main attractions are the white-sand beaches around Santiago Bay, which is where the majority of Camotes' resorts are located. The main town is **San Francisco** ('San Fran').

Off the main road south of Esperanza is stunning **Borromeo Beach**, a blinding expanse of white powder.

Tulang Island, off the northern coast of Pacijan, has a stunning sandy beach where you can play Robinson Crusoe for an hour or so. Boaters in Tulang Daku will shuttle you across for P500 return.

Near Esperanza on Pacijan's northwest tip is touristy **Timubo Cave** (P30; ⊙ 7am-5.30pm), where a set of (slippery) stairs leads down to a refreshing cave pool.

🛏 Sleeping & Eating

Payag Beach House Resort   RESORT $
(☑ 0926 144 4461, 032-233 1158; Santiago; r with fan P800, with air-con P1500-1800; ❄ 🐾) This basic crash-pad has eight tiny rooms; bathrooms (which are kept moderately clean) are shared. Service can be spotty. Its location is superb, facing the white sand of Santiago Bay, so it's worth considering.

★**Swiss Lagoon** GUESTHOUSE **$$**
(☑0926 682 4975; http://swisslagoon.com; Santiago Beach; r/nipa hut P2000; ❇🛜) This very welcoming little Swiss-Filipino place has small, neat rooms with air-con, satellite TV and bamboo furniture. A large nipa hut is another option, perfect for groups or families, with a full kitchen. The restaurant serves up great rosti with egg and schnitzel. Andi, the owner is ever helpful and will arrange scooters and advise about transport.

Keshe Beach Resort RESORT **$$**
(☑0929 892 5792; Borromeo Beach; r P1000-1500) This is just a very simple place with a couple of bamboo beachfront cottages on the Camotes' most stunning beach. Food is problematic as there's no restaurant; rent your own two-wheeler if staying.

Santiago Bay Garden & Resort RESORT **$$**
(☑032-345 8599; Santiago Beach; r with fan/air-con from P1200/1600; ❇🛜🏊) This rambling cliffside resort boasts one of the island's finest plots of real estate on Santiago Bay. Expect lots of Woodcrete and tacky art, but the views are terrific and the two infinity-style pools are wonderful. Rooms are not fancy but kept clean; bathrooms could use an update.

Pito's Sukotil FILIPINO **$**
(☑0935 139 3095; Santiago Beach; mains P80-180; ⊙8am-10pm) On Santiago Beach, Pito's Sukotil does inexpensive, excellent seafood including grilled fish and shrimp *guisado* (sautéed with tomato); both P90. Beers are just P30 to P40 a pop. It also has budget rooms.

Nena's Grill FILIPINO **$**
(Santiago Beach; mains P75-120; ⊙8am-10pm) For authentic local flavours, this barbecue place specialises in particularly spicy *kinilaw* (raw seafood cured in vinegar), grilled or chilli shrimp and great sizzling squid – and other delicacies from the sea.

ℹ Information

In San Francisco you'll find the helpful **City Tourism Office** (☑0921 471 1434; opposite the church; ⊙8am-5pm Mon-Fri) which sells island maps (P50).

ℹ Getting There & Away

The main gateway to Pacijan island is the port of Danao on the island of Cebu, from where there are regular ferries. Fastcraft also connect Cebu City with Consuelo, Pacijan. Note that sailings are frequently cancelled during heavy seas.

Poro Island
☑032 / POP 22,800

Poro is the lesser of the two main islands of the Camotes. It lacks the beaches of Pacijan but its mountainous roads are better for bike touring, especially if you have an off-road bike.

Poro is the main town on the island, an unassuming coastal settlement with a hint of Spanish Mediterranean. There's really not much reason to stay here, however.

Boho Rock Resort (P20) is a pleasant swimming spot with a platform for jumping into the turquoise ocean and good snorkelling among the rocks. In the far east of the island, just north of MacArthur, is the remote, well-hidden **Bukilat Cave** (P10).

🛌 Sleeping

My Little Island Hotel HOTEL
(☑032-267 6539; www.mylittleislandhotel.com; Esperanza; r/ste from P1800/2800; ❇🛜) It's looking pretty faded but this hotel does have some pluses including mesmeric sea views and good food in the restaurant. However, when we dropped by the pool looked murky, and the somewhat-dated rooms needed a makeover.

Flying Fish Resort RESORT **$$**
(☑0908 876 5427; www.camotesflyingfishresort. com; r with fan P1000, with air-con P1600-2600; ❇) A dated resort hotel 5km east of Esperanza, Flying Fish is perched above a remote rocky beach, with some cottages enjoying fine sea views. Unfortunately the marine sanctuary out front was damaged by Typhoon Yolanda, though snorkelling can still be rewarding. There's free kayak rental; call for a free pick-up.

ℹ Getting There & Away

Poro is connected by a bridge to Pacijan, which has good ferry connections to ports in Cebu.

There's very little public transport in Poro. Hiring a scooter is the best way to explore the island, or charter a *habal-habal* (P1000 per day).

Ponson Island
☑032 / POP 12,050

The charm in visiting a place as remote as Ponson is the attention you'll get, which varies from warmly effusive to wryly amused. What it tells you is that very, very few travellers make it this far, despite it being relatively easy to get here from Ormoc.

There are two main towns on Ponson: **Pilar** and **Kawit**. Kawit is the more picturesque of the two, with a lovely long, white-sand beach in the town proper: this is a great place to interact with locals in a small-island community.

Halikana Resort (✆0918 349 8349; Kawit Town; d with fan P600-1000, with air-con P1500; ❉) is a delightfully friendly if basic place on Kawit Town's white-sand beach. One of the few upmarket hotels in the Camotes, the new **Moabog Reef Resort** (✆032-239 1941; www.moabogreefresort.com; Moabog; r P3000-3500; ❉ 🛜 ⊠) has 12 smart air-con rooms with refrigerator, safe and a dash of art on the wall. There's a dive school here too.

BOHOL

✆038 / POP 1.33 MILLION

Bohol offers independent travellers a wealth of options both on and off the beaten track. This island province is promoted almost exclusively through images of cute bug-eyed tarsiers and the majestic Chocolate Hills, but there's much more to experience. Offshore there's superb diving, and when you throw in jungle-fringed rivers perfect for kayaking and paddle-boarding and pristine white-sand beaches it's easy to understand the Bohol appeal.

Boholanos still affectionately call their province the 'Republic of Bohol', in reference to the island's short-lived independence at the turn of the 19th century. It's an appropriate appellation – today's successors of the republic are fierce protectors of Bohol's distinctive cultural heritage. The 7.2-magnitude 2013 earthquake killed more than 200 people and destroyed several of the island's majestic Spanish-era churches. Reconstruction is ongoing but otherwise few obvious effects of the quake are visible.

❶ Getting There & Away

There are plenty of flights linking Tagbilaran with Manila, and also connections to Cebu and Caticlan. Tagbilaran is the main port with services to Cebu, Manila, Leyte, Mindanao, Siquijor and Negros. Other Bohol ports include Loon, Tubigon, Jagna, Jetafe, Ubay and Talibon.

The Bohol website (www.bohol.ph) is useful for travel planning and has ferry schedules, plus other cultural and transport info.

Jagna is where you catch the useful RORO ferry to Balbagon, Camiguin run by **Super Shuttle Ferry** (✆in Jagna 0916 568 2236; http://supershuttleroro.com; P425, 3½ hours, 1pm). In addition, **Lite Shipping** (✆0977 822 5483; www.liteferries.com) sends a RORO to Cagayan de Oro on Tuesdays, Thursdays, Saturdays and Sundays at 10pm (from P620, seven hours), and another RORO to Butuan (also in Mindanao) on Mondays, Wednesdays and Fridays at 10pm and 10am on Sundays.

Sailings do sometimes get cancelled, so be sure to confirm departures directly with the ferry companies; many update their Facebook pages more regularly than their websites.

V-hire vans connect Tagbilaran and Jagna (P100, 1½ hours, hourly).

Tagbilaran

✆038 / POP 107,100

Derived from two Visayan words meaning 'hidden shelter' *(tago bilaan)*, the name Tagbilaran is a reference either to its position on a calm, protected strait or its historical role as a sanctuary from Moro invaders. Today the town is overrun by legions of noisy tricycle taxis and there's nothing calming or protected about it. There are no big-ticket sights here, but as the city is surrounded by water it's not unpleasant. That said, there's no real reason to hang around either, and most travellers make a quick getaway to Bohol's beaches or jungle-rich interior.

Just out of Antequera, about 20km from Tagbilaran (bus or jeepney P30), are **Mag-aso Falls** – the largest falls on the island – and **Inambacan Spring & Caves**. Cave guides can be found at the trailhead to Mag-aso Falls, or text Antolin (✆0919 808 6079) if you want to book a guide in advance.

BOHOL HOMESTAYS

For an authentic slice of Boholano life, nonprofit community-run **Process-Bohol** (✆038-510 8255; www.bohol homestay.com; with fan/air-con incl breakfast P600/700, additional meals P200; ❉) 🖉 arranges cheap homestays with families across Bohol. The fee helps struggling communities maintain a sustainable livelihood. Homestays are available in Maribojoc, Cabilao Island, Anda, Balilihan and Ubay. Book at least 24 hours in advance.

Bohol

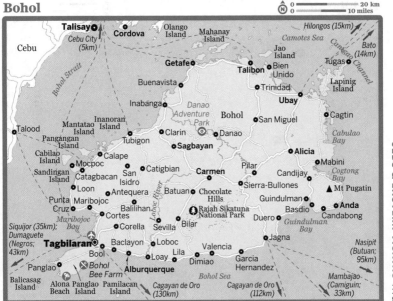

Sights & Activities

St Joseph the Worker Cathedral CHURCH
(JA Clarin St) In the heart of town, this elegant church was built in 1767, burned to the ground in 1798 and rebuilt and enlarged in 1855.

Blood Compact Monument MONUMENT
(National Hwy) This great monument 1km east of Tagbilaran celebrates the March 1565 blood compact, where Spanish conquistador Miguel López de Legazpi and Boholano chieftain Rajah Sikatuna shared a cup of each other's blood as a peace treaty.

National Museum MUSEUM
(JS Torralba St; ⊙8am-5pm) FREE This small museum has a few anthropologically interesting items discovered around Bohol, including five artificially deformed skulls, a 500-year-old Boholana and a display on the cave paintings of Anda.

★ Kayakasia Philippines KAYAKING
(☑ 0933 358 0081, 0932 855 2928; www.facebook.
com/kayakasiaphilippines; Abatan River, Barangay Lincod, Maribojoc; trips per person P1950-2450)
Departing at sunset from Cortes, 10km north of Tagbilaran, Kayakasia Philippine's memorable evening kayak trips set out to see fireflies, which pulsate in the trees like Christmas lights. Grab some beers for the leisurely paddle along the palm-lined Abatan River; prices include dinner and transport to Cortes. The trip climaxes as night descends, revealing branches full of shimmering fireflies.

Festivals & Events

Sandugo Festival CULTURAL
(⊙Jul) This festival celebrates the March 1565 blood compact, and is followed by a string of arts and other festivals that have turned the whole of July into one big party month.

Sleeping & Eating

The city has a moderate selection of places to stay, but most travellers head inland or straight to nearby Alona Beach.

For an authentic slice of Boholano life, consider a homestay in Maribojoc (13km north of Tagbilaran) with Process-Bohol.

Tr3ats HOSTEL $
(☑ 0917 888 2069; www.tr3ats.com; 16 Bagong Lipunan St; dm/d P350/900; ❄ �) Tr3ats is a fine-value hostel with small but tastefully adorned and blissfully air-conditioned five-bed dorm rooms (one female-only) and a few snazzy doubles with flat-screen TVs.

Tagbilaran

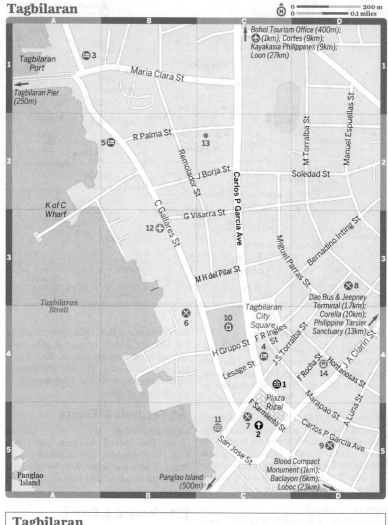

Tagbilaran

◉ Sights
1 National Museum....................................C4
2 St Joseph the Worker Cathedral C5

🛏 Sleeping
3 Belian Hotel...A1
4 Nisa Travellers Hotel C4
5 Sun Avenue B2

🍴 Eating
6 Buzz Cafe B4
7 Garden Cafe C5
8 Gerarda's...D3

9 Payag...D5

🔒 Shopping
10 Bohol Quality Mall C4

ℹ Information
11 Post Office C5
12 Ramiro Community Hospital..................B3

ℹ Transport
13 Boysam Motor Rental C2
14 Bus for Panglao D4

Nisa Travellers Hotel

GUESTHOUSE $

(☎038-411 3731; www.nisatravellershotel.com; CPG Ave; s/d incl breakfast from P500/600; ❇@☎) There's a wide selection of rooms at this hotel with a hostel vibe – welcoming and traveller-friendly, with 24-hour checkout. The cheapest rooms have shared bathrooms and fans. Tours are offered.

Sun Avenue

HOTEL $

(☎038-412 5601; www.sunavenueinn.com; C Gallares St; s/d incl breakfast from P800/950; ❇☎) Fine and modestly priced, this great-value hotel is well located between the pier and town centre. Rooms are clean and have crisp linen, but only those upstairs have windows. Bonus: the attached Sun Cafe has some of the best food in town and good coffee.

★Ocean Suites

BOUTIQUE HOTEL $$

(☎038-411 1031; www.oceansuites.ph; National Hwy; r incl breakfast P2500-5500; ❇☎❇) Overlooking the Tagbilaran Strait and Panglao Island beyond, Ocean Suites enjoys a terrific location and has contemporary rooms, a bright, breezy cafe and an infinity pool. Splurge for the deluxe seafront rooms, which have sunset-facing balconies and are much bigger than the road-facing 'superior' rooms. Also home to a good cafe and restaurant.

Belian Hotel

HOTEL $$

(☎038-411 1507; www.belianhotel.com; Graham Ave; r incl breakfast from P1800; ❇☎) A modern hotel with a contemporary look that's very close to the ferry terminal. The lobby is slick, rooms are a little less impressive – comfortable and modern, but the cheaper choices are small and not all have windows.

Garden Cafe

AMERICAN $$

(JS Torralba St; mains P130-250; ☺6.30am-10pm; ❇☎) A cowboy-themed restaurant that employs deaf waiters and chefs. The menu – which includes a beginner's guide to sign language – is chock-full of good ol' Yankee and Tex Mex fare, as well as some local dishes. Upstairs, dial your order through to the kitchen from tableside phones.

Gerarda's

FILIPINO $$

(☎038-412 3044; www.facebook.com/gerardas resto; JS Torralba St; mains P120-260; ☺10am-10pm; ❇) In a historic family house with antiques, scuffed-wood floors and sparkling cutlery, sophisticated Gerarda's does fabulous Filipino food. Highlights include seafood *kare kare* (fish and crab in peanut sauce) and delicious crispy *pata* (pig trotters with soy-vinegar dip).

Payag

FILIPINO $$

(CPG Ave; mains P100-170; ☺10am-10pm) In a renovated Spanish-era home with a few quirky additions, this restaurant scores for Filipino food including sizzling *gambas* (prawns) and *adobo*. Round off your meal like the locals do with *halo-halo* (shaved ice, evaporated milk and fruit – served in a coconut shell).

Buzz Cafe

INTERNATIONAL $$

(www.boholbeefarm.com; Galleria Luisa, 63 C Gallares St; meals P120-300; ☺7.30am-9pm; ☎) With views of the bay, this family-orientated restaurant has something for everyone including espresso coffee, vegan dishes and plenty of Filipino fare. Specials are chalked up on a board outside. You can also stock up on Boholano products (jams etc) here.

❶ Information

There are ATMs and banks inside the **Bohol Quality Mall** (www.boholquality.com; ☺10am-9pm) and along CPG Ave.

Ramiro Community Hospital (☎038-411 3515; www.ramiromedical.org; 63 C Gallares St) For real emergencies head to Cebu City.

Bohol Tourism Office (☎032-412 3666; www.boholtourismph.com; Governor's Mansion Complex, CPG North Ave; ☺8am-6pm Mon-Fri) Very helpful and professional staff here can provide maps, assist with travel information and book tours and transport. It also has small branches at the airport and pier.

Post Office (☺8am-5pm Mon-Fri) Close to Taytay bridge.

❶ Getting There & Away

AIR

PAL, Cebu Pacific and AirAsia all have daily flights between Manila and Tagbilaran. PAL flies daily from Mactan to Cebu. The airport is 2km north of the centre, a P50 tricycle ride.

BOAT

Ferry ticket offices are at the **pier** (☺24hr).

Cokaliong Shipping Lines (☎038-501 8598; www.cokaliongshipping.com; Tagbilaran Pier)

FJ Palacio Lines (☎038-515 5268)

Lite Shipping (☎038-501 7422; www.lite ferries.com; Tagbilaran Pier)

Oceanjet (☎0932 873 4885; www.oceanjet.net; Tagbilaran Pier)

SuperCat 2GO (☎0925 582 4824; www.supercat.com.ph; Tagbilaran Pier)

Trans-Asia Shipping Lines (☑ 038-411 3234; www.transasiashipping.com; Tagbilaran Pier)

Weesam Express (☑ 0917 301 5749; www. weesam.ph; Tagbilaran Pier)

BUS

Buses (P18) with 'Tawala Alona' signboards head for Panglao Island (and Alona Beach) at least hourly until 6pm from a stop on the corner of Hontanosas and F Rocha Sts.

Most other public transport departs from the Dao Bus & Jeepney Terminal, which is next to Island City Mall, 3km north of the centre. Here you'll find frequent buses to Carmen for the Chocolate Hills (P70, 2½ hours), via Loboc (P28, one hour). Buses also serve Ubay (P120, 3½ hours) via Jagna and Guindulman; transfer in Guindulman for Anda. Buses to Talibon (P110, 3½ hours) go via Tubigon (P52, 1½ hours) and Getafe; buses to Danao go via Sagbayan. All routes are serviced frequently until about 6pm.

V-hire vans also depart from Dao terminal, providing a much quicker option to Jagna (P100, 1½ hours, hourly), Ubay and Tubigon.

ⓘ Getting Around

Consider hiring your own motorcycle in Tagbilaran (P500 per day) to explore the rest of Bohol. This can be done in town at **Boysam Motor Rental** (☑ 0908 936 2866; R Palma St), or at the pier through Mario (☑ 0929 855 6357) – call him in advance and he'll have a bike waiting for you when you walk off the boat.

Both can also find you a car or a van for day trips, or you can use one of the numerous car-hire services at the pier. The going rate is P2000 to P2500 per day for a car, or P2500 to P3000 for a van, depending on destination.

Panglao Island

☑ 038 / POP 83,700

Low-lying sun-baked Panglao Island is generally associated with **Alona Beach**, a busy holiday resort on the southern side of the island. Alona is renowned for its nightlife, and there's a real buzz about the place on weekends when Filipinos cruise into town to join vacationing Koreans and Europeans.

The underwater scene around Alona is exceptional, and divers can score nifty package deals by combining dives with accommodation. Just 15km from Tagbilaran, Alona works just fine as a base for exploring the rest of Bohol – especially when you can return home at the end of the day to two-for-one cocktails in the sand.

Far more mellow than its noisy neighbour Alona, **Danao Beach** consists of patches of fine white sand backed by coconut palms – it's an idyllic tropical setting.

🏃 Activities

Everything is water-related in Panglao. Offshore diving and boat trips are the main draw and there's good swimming around the coast, including the sea cave at **Hinagdanan** (P50, swimming fee P75; ⊙ 7.30am-6pm).

Qi Retreats (☑ 09771366893; www.qiretreats. com; Alona Beach) runs SUP yoga sessions on Alona Beach, and yoga/snorkelling trips to Balicasag Island. SUP yoga sees practitioners go through yoga poses on stand-up paddleboards. Land-based yoga sessions are also available.

BOATS FROM TAGBILARAN

DESTINATION	TYPE	COMPANY	PRICE (P)	DURATION (HR)	FREQUENCY
Argao (Talood), Cebu	RORO	Lite Shipping	200	3	8am, 4pm
Cagayan de Oro	RORO	Trans-Asia	680	9	7pm Mon, Wed, Thu
Cebu City	Fastcraft	Oceanjet; Weesam; Supercat 2GO	500-800	2	frequent
Cebu City	RORO	Cokaliong Shipping Lines; Lite Shipping; FJ Palacio Lines	210-230	4	noon & 10.30pm
Dumaguete	Fastcraft	Oceanjet	700	2	7.30am & 12.10pm
Larena, Siquijor	RORO	Lite Shipping	220	3½	8pm daily except Sun
Larena, Siquijor	Fastcraft	Oceanjet	700	1½	11am

BOHOL BEE FARM

Boholana environmentalist Vicky Wallace dug a small-scale vegetable patch on Panglao 15 years ago and started selling produce. From these fertile beginnings a cafe sprouted, specialising in organic squash muffins, home-baked bread and corn coffee.

Today, Bohol Bee Farm is an epic operation with a huge oceanfront **restaurant** (www.boholbeefarm.com; off Southern Coastal Rd; meals P200-550; ⊙6am-10pm; 🖥🖊) 🍴, lovely on-site **accommodation** (☑038-510 1822; r P3200-6400; ❀🖥🖵) 🍴, a covered swimming pool, a purpose-designed sunbathing deck, Bohol's best gift shop and – naturally – an organic farm. The latest part of the empire is a Bohol Bee Diving. Branches of its heralded **Buzz Cafe** (www.boholbeefarm.com/buzzzalona; mains P180-360; ⊙7.30am-10pm; 🖥🖊) 🍴, where you can nibble on organic munchies and buy a range of environmentally friendly *pasalubong* (small souvenirs), are scattered throughout Alona Beach and Tagbilaran.

Diving

Diving draws many to Panglao, in particular the underwater paradise of Balicasag Island. Pamilacan Island also has reefs but they're less visited as its corals are recovering from years of dynamite fishing.

You can probably score the best deal by combining accommodation with diving. The average price for one shore dive around Alona is P1250 while open-water diving certificates cost around P17,000.

Boat trips to Balicasag Island cost around P3000 with two dives, equipment and lunch.

Snorkellers can swim 75m straight out to sea to enjoy the soft corals of Alona's house reef, but watch out for boat traffic.

There are several recommended dive operators based in Panglao Island; most are close to Alona Beach:

Bohol Bee Diving (☑038-502 2288; www.boholbeefarm.com/diving; Southern Coastal Rd, Km 11)

Genesis Divers (☑032-502 9056; www.genesisdivers.com; Peter's House)

Philippine Fun Divers (☑038-416 2336; www.boholfundivers.com; Lost Horizon Beach Resort)

Sea Explorers (☑in Cebu 032-234 0248; www.sea-explorers.com; Alona Vida Beach Resort)

SeaQuest Divers (☑038-502 9069; www.seaquestdivecenter.net; Oasis Resort)

Tropical Divers (☑038-502 9031; www.tropicaldivers-alona.com; Alona Tropical)

Boat Trips

You can arrange early-morning dolphin-watching tours around Pamilacan Island through most resorts and dive centres, though some of these resemble 'dolphin chasing'. Consider organising a more respectful trip via **Pamilacan Island Dolphin & Whale Watching Tours** (PIDWWT; ☑038-540 9279, 919 730 6108; http://whales.bohol.ph; group of 1-4 P3300, lunch per person P300) out of Baclayon, 6km from Tagbilaran. Figure on paying P1500 for a four-person boat out of Alona – more if you want to extend that into an island-hopping trip taking in Pamilacan, Virgin and Balicasag islands.

🛏 Sleeping

🛏 Alona Beach

Alona Grove Tourist Inn   HUT **$**
(☑038-502 8857; www.facebook.com/alonagrovetouristinn; off Southern Coastal Rd; hut with fan/aircon P750/1300; ❀🖥) This place has some of the cheapest beds near the beach, with 10 nipa huts scattered among its pleasant garden with manicured grass. It's located up a little alley and run by helpful folk.

Peter's House   RESORT **$**
(☑032-502 9056; www.genesisdivers.com; Alona Beach; r P900-1100; 🖥) Exclusively for divers, this nipa-hut complex has a laid-back communal vibe and is perfect for scubaheads on a budget. There are only a few rooms, all sharing cold-water bathrooms, but they are very affordable and prices fall depending on how many dives you do with in-house Genesis Divers (p313).

Chill-Out Guesthouse   GUESTHOUSE **$$**
(☑038-502 4480, 0912 926 5557; www.chilloutpanglao.com; off Southern Coastal Rd; r with fan/air-con from P1200/1275; ❀🖥) A welcoming place with smiley staff and spacious, well-appointed rooms with hardwood floors and private balconies that represent fine value. There's a lovely garden and the location is tranquil, around a 10-minute walk from the beach.

Alona Beach

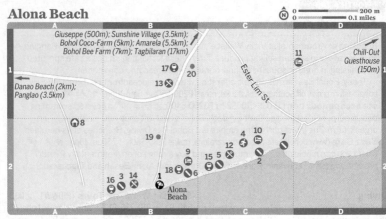

Alona Beach

Sights
1 Alona Beach B2

Activities, Courses & Tours
2 Genesis Divers C2
3 Philippine Fun Divers B2
4 Qi Retreats C2
5 Sea Explorers C2
6 SeaQuest Divers B2
7 Tropical Divers C2

Sleeping
8 Alona Grove Tourist Inn A2
9 Oasis Resort B2
10 Peter's House C2
11 Scent of Green Papaya Resort D1

Eating
12 Buzz Cafe C2
13 Gavroche B1
14 Trudi's Place B2

Drinking & Nightlife
15 Coco Vida Bar C2
16 Panglao Birdwatchers B2
17 Pinarella B1
18 Reggae Bar Aliahailey B2

Transport
19 Parking Lot Car Rental B2
20 Valeroso Travel B1

**Scent of Green
Papaya Resort** HOTEL $$
(☑038-502 8265; http://scentofgreenpapaya.com; Ester Lim Dr; r incl breakfast P2500; ✲🖛🖳) A fine place with eight very smart, well-furnished air-con rooms that enjoy pool views from their balconies and have satellite TV and hip en-suite bathrooms. There's a restobar on-site and a complimentary shuttle to and from Alona Beach for the really lazy (it's only 800m away!), running every half-hour or so.

Oasis Resort RESORT $$$
(☑in Cebu 032-418 1550; http://seaquestdive center.com; Alona Beach; r incl breakfast P3000-6600; ✲🖛🖳) The name is not a misnomer at this mellow resort, with well-appointed thatched cottages set around a central pool and garden behind the busy beating heart of Alona Beach. Standard rooms are twin con-figuration; upgrade to a deluxe if you want

a queen bed. It's popular with divers, with good packages available.

Danao Beach

Calypso Resort RESORT $
(☑038-502 8184; www.philippins.info; Danao Beach; r P890-1500; ✲🖛🖳) Set well back from Danao Beach, this place would be a good deal even without a free motorcycle. If you don't ride, hang out at the pool all day and order cocktails from the cosy bar, equipped with billiards and other games.

Linaw Beach Resort RESORT $$$
(☑038-502 9345; www.linawbeachresort.com; Danao Beach; r P3900-5950; ✲🖛🖳) Smack dab on Danao Beach, rooms at this rambling place are comfortable and well appointed, with flat-screens, fine art and roomy bath-rooms. There's a well-regarded restaurant, oceanfront pool and loads of games to en-

tertain the kids, including foosball, darts and pool.

🛏 Around the Island

⭐ Bohol Coco-Farm   HOSTEL $
(📞 0917 304 9801; www.facebook.com/bohol cfarm; Southern Coastal Rd, Km 13; dm/d incl breakfast P350/800; 🛜) 🍴 The best base for backpackers in Panglao, if you don't mind being inland, with nipa huts that are entirely appropriate for the rustic setting. There's a gregarious vibe, with staff and visitors mixing well. The organic cafe (mains P100 to P190) features produce from its 2.5-hectare grounds. Located 5km east of Alona Beach, it's P60 in a *habal-habal*.

⭐ Sunshine Village   RESORT $$
(📞 0928 552 3431; http://panglaosunshinevillage. com; Barangay Bolod; r P1500-1900) This fine-value resort complex boasts a stupendous pool (around 30m) and attractive gardens, which more than make up for its inland location, 4km east of Alona Beach. Rooms are immaculately clean, with fast wi-fi and modern bathrooms and there's an excellent restaurant on-site. Rent a scooter (available here but cheaper elsewhere) and you're sorted.

⭐ Amarela   RESORT $$$
(📞 038-502 9497; www.amarelaresort.com; Southern Coastal Rd, Km 12.5; d P6600-10700, ste from P12,000; 🅿🛜🏊) 🍴 This elegant and classy beach getaway is run on environmentally sound principles. It's so boutique it has its own art gallery and library. Rooms with polished floorboards get plenty of sun, and most have balconies. Hammocks and deckchairs await at its lovely private beach, or relax in the superb pool surrounded by lush gardens. It's 5.5km east of Alona Beach.

🍴 Eating

⭐ Gavroche   CAFE $$
(http://gavroche.ph; Southern Coastal Rd; meals P130-260; ⊙6.30am-8.30pm) One of the best places in Alona for breakfast, with fresh croissants, Filipino (P150) and French sets (from P130) plus lots of à la carte options. Also great for sandwiches on homemade bread with smoked hams and imported cheeses. Serves smoothies, shakes, juices and espresso coffee and the premises are air-conditioned.

Cafe Lawis   CAFE $$
(Dauis Convent, Dauis; dishes P95-185; ⊙11am-9pm; 🍴) In a rectory, on the southern side of Borja bridge next to Our Lady of the Assumption church, this healthy waterside cafe serves up tasty meals (panini, pasta, *adobo*), snacks, espresso coffee and ice cream.

Sunshine Village   INTERNATIONAL $$
(http://panglaosunshinevillage.com; Bolod; mains P220-400; ⊙8am-10pm; 🛜) This large resort has an unexpectedly good restaurant, with tables overlooking the pool. The German owner is a chef, and it's perfect for hearty Western dishes including farmer's breakfast, pumpkin soup and fish 'n' chips. It's inland, 4km from the coast.

Trudi's Place   FILIPINO $$
(Alona Beach; mains P150-295; ⊙6.30am-11pm; 🛜) Trudi's qualifies as budget eating in pricey Alona Beach. The Filipino food is filling, beers are cheap, tables overlook the sea and there's often a live band.

⭐ Giuseppe   ITALIAN $$$
(📞 038-502 4255; http://giuseppe.panglao.info; Tawala; mains P300-800; ⊙11am-11pm; 🅿🛜) One of the Visayas' best Italians, with choice antipasti, divine pizza (from P300), mouthwatering pasta and a daily specials board. It's cool and classy and has an extensive wine cellar (house wine P120). Round off your meal with a sip of limoncello or grappa. Located around 2km northeast of central Alona.

🍷 Drinking & Nightlife

Reggae Bar Aliahailey   BAR
(Alona Beach; 7am-1am) Shack on the beach with a friendly bar crew. DJs spin dread Jamaican tunes from morning till...morning.

Pinarella   CLUB
(Southern Coastal Rd; ⊙10pm-3.30am) The most credible club in Alona Beach, with visiting DJs from Manila and Cebu on weekends. It's off the beach on the highway.

Panglao Birdwatchers   BAR
(📞 0912 710 8328; www.panglaobirdwatchers. com; Alona Beach; ⊙7am-11pm; 🛜) Aussie-run beach bar that's a good bet for happy hour, drawing a fun crowd for its classic cocktails and ice-cold beers.

Coco Vida Bar   BAR
(www.facebook.com/alonacocovida; Alona Beach; ⊙8am-late) Buzzing bar on the beach, with

live music most nights of the power-ballad or rock-classic persuasion.

① Getting There & Around

Slow buses head from Alona to Tagbilaran roughly every 30 minutes until 7pm (P25, 50 minutes). The quicker and easier option is to hire a tricycle (P300) or taxi (P450).

For day tours, cars and vans can be hired from a **parking lot** (off Southern Coastal Rd; ⊙7.30am-9pm) on the Alona Beach access road, or from **Valeroso Travel** (☑0916 543 1702, 038-502 9126; ralf@valeroso.ralleontour. com; Southern Coastal Rd; ⊙6.30am-9pm). A day tour of Bohol in a car will cost P2000 to P2500. Motorcycle rental is available from most hotels for P400 to P500 per day.

Balicasag Island

☑038 / POP 293

One of the most popular diving spots in the Philippines, tiny Balicasag, about 6km southwest of Panglao, is ringed by a reef that has been declared a **marine sanctuary** (snorkellers/divers P150/300). It drops away to impressive submarine cliffs as deep as 50m. Soft and hard corals can be found around the cliffs, as can trevally, barracuda and wrasse.

There's only one resort here, the **Balicasag Island Dive Resort** (☑0928 217 6810, 0917 309 1417; http://tieza.gov.ph/operating-entities/balicasag-island-dive-resort; dm P500, d incl breakfast P3200-3700; ❄🗑🗃). Its guests get to share this tropical island with a few hundred locals – except when day trippers from Alona swamp the place, but they're usually gone by noon.

Balicasag is a 45-minute boat ride from Alona Beach, visited by dive companies and day trippers. Otherwise ring ahead for the resort to arrange pick-up (one way P1200).

Pamilacan Island

☑038 / POP 1489

The tiny island of Pamilacan, adrift in the Bohol Sea about 23km east of Balicasag, is cetacean central, its rich waters supporting marine megafauna including whales and dolphins, manta rays and sharks. Islanders have always lived off the sea, hunting whales until the ban in 1992, then targeting sharks and rays. In 1993 Sulliman University recorded 30 whale sharks landing in Pamilacan in just 44 days. If you visited the island in the mid-1990s, lanes would be full of shark and manta meat drying in the sun. Finally, in 1998, whale shark and manta hunting were officially banned.

In recent years the descendants of these whalers have found other ways to earn a living, including leading boat tours (though we've heard the odd ray and shark are still caught and eaten here). You'll see bleached whale bones 'decorating' some houses in Pamilacan.

There are no banks or ATMs.

No fewer than three community-based outfits organise whale- and dolphin-watching expeditions. All use old converted whaling boats and local crews. The trip includes a full day on the water and transfers from Baclayon (on Bohol) or Panglao; boats hold four to six people. Whale sightings are relatively rare, but the best time for spotting them is February to July; dolphins are common year-round. Pamilacan Island Dolphin & Whale Watching Tours (p313) is one good operator.

The island is also fun to explore on foot.

🛏 Sleeping

Pamilacan Island Tourist Inn   GUESTHOUSE $
(☑0919 730 6108; d incl full board P1500) These simple huts on the beach are run by an enterprising local (Mary) in conjunction with Pamilacan Island Dolphin & Whale Watching Tours (p313). She prepares good meals and organises squid-fishing and dolphin-watching tours.

Nita's Nipa Huts   HUT $
(☑0921 320 6497; r without bathroom per person incl full board P750) The area's cheapest and most well-established accommodation option. Huts range from double to family – the double with views on the water's edge is best positioned. Nita can organise morning dolphin-watching, daytime fishing trips and night-time squid-fishing trips. A pick-up from Baclayon costs P1000 per small boat; from Panglao it's P1500.

Liwayway Sa Bohol   B&B $$
(☑0927 982 1350; www.liwaywaysabohol.com; r P2500-4000; 🗃) Run by a welcoming, well-informed couple who love the island life, this upmarket B&B has plush rooms that all face the sea and even a spa (which employs local women). They also have a back-up generator.

① Getting There & Away

You can arrange a boat between Pamilacan and Baclayon (one way/return P1500/2000, one hour). Boats from Alona Beach will take you to Pamilacan for a bit more.

Cabilao Island

038 / POP 5345

Legend has it that idyllic Cabilao is inhabited by the dreaded dog-shaped Balikaka monster that sporadically attacks livestock. In reality Cabilao is so chilled out, the only sounds to break the perfect calm are church bells and the odd rooster. There are limited beaches here, so it's a destination that primarily attracts divers, but it can also make a great stop if you want to slow things right down.

Diving is the main draw for visitors; the seas surrounding Cabilao include two community-run marine sanctuaries. You might spot the odd shark and the area is also full of microlife, including the difficult-to-spot pygmy seahorse (Hippocampus bargibanti), which tops out at 8mm and camouflages itself among the surrounding red coral.

The island's top reef is off the northwestern point, near the lighthouse. Highly regarded Sea Explorers (0917 727 8248; www.sea-explorers.com) is based at Pura Vida Cabilao resort.

There's a one-off entrance fee of P100 for diving or snorkelling in the marine sanctuaries, plus a P150 per-day scuba-diving fee.

Sleeping

★Pura Vida Cabilao   RESORT $$$
(0918 943 6057; www.cabilao.com; r P3900-5200, ste P10,000; ❋ ❂) Pura Vida sits alone on the northeastern tip of the island and is managed by a German–Filipino team. Its sophisticated, spotless thatched cottages and rooms are very well furnished. The restaurant has sweeping ocean views, Sea Explorers dive shop is on-site and there's a small spa for massages. It's a five-minute walk from the pier in Cambaquiz.

★Cabilao Sanctuary Beach & Dive Resort   HOTEL $$$
(032-272 3165; http://cabilao-sanctuary.com; r P3500-5200, ste P6000; ❋ ❂ ❂) A new beachside dive resort with modish, spotless A-frame bungalows and rooms; even the cheapest 'superior' options are very well furnished while the suites are palatial. There's a gorgeous decked area for tanning and chilling, and a reef for snorkelling offshore, and the pool area is big enough for laps.

Polaris Resort   RESORT $$$
(0918 903 7187; www.polaris-dive.com; r with air-con P3234-4059, tree house with fan P1859; ❋ ❂ ❂ ❂) A well-run and maintained beach and PADI-dive resort with large rooms in concrete cottages as well as two 'tree houses' on stilts. It gets extra ticks for partially using solar energy and for the restaurant's tasty food. Nearby is a sandbar that at low tide is good for swimming and snorkelling.

Getting There & Away

Most divers organise transport via their resort.

The nearest port is Mocpoc, which is an hour by road from Tagbilaran (around P900 in a taxi). From Mocpoc you can hire a bangka (P250) for the 15-minute transfer to Cabilao, or catch a public bangka (P20) – they leave when full for Cambaquiz pier (for Pura Vida Cabilao) and Talisay (for the northwestern resorts). Weather often disrupts trips to Talisay, in which case head to Cambaquiz.

There is also an (unreliable) twice-weekly boat from Argao, Cebu to Cabilao (P130, 1½ hours) on Tuesday and Saturday at 1pm.

Chocolate Hills Loop

The well-travelled path to the Chocolate Hills can be done as a day trip out of Tagbilaran or Alona Beach. If you have time, it's highly recommended to spend a night or three in Loboc and loop back to Tagbilaran via the scenic road to Sierra Bullones and Jagna, with a short detour to Pilar, which has a scenic lake and rice terraces. It's also easy enough to work the Tarsier Sanctuary in Corella into this loop.

With little traffic and smooth roads, the Chocolate Hills route is tailor-made for a motorcycle. Otherwise, you're looking at around P2200 for a day tour in a car out of Tagbilaran or Alona Beach, or about P3300 for a 10-passenger van.

Baclayon

038 / POP 20,800

About 6km from Tagbilaran, the historic coastal town of Baclayon was the first Spanish settlement in Bohol and is home to several important colonial structures and some wonderful Spanish-era heritage houses. The latter were saved from demolition by the Baclayon Ancestral Homes Association (BAHANDI; 0917 620 1211; Mon-Sat), which

CEBU & EASTERN VISAYAS CHOCOLATE HILLS LOOP

can arrange walking tours and homestays in these houses, which date to 1853.

Baclayon is also a good spot to arrange trips to Pamilacan Island for whale- and dolphin-watching tours; the **tourist office** (☑038-540 9474, 0946 296 4297; www.baclay ontourism.com; Baluarte, off Tagbilaran East Rd; ☺8am-4.30pm Mon-Fri) at the port can book boats.

Facing the Bohol Sea, the huge coral stone **church** (Tagbilaran East Rd), dating from 1727, was severely damaged in the 2013 earthquake. It's connected to an imposing watchtower. The church has been rebuilt.

Loboc

☑038 / POP 16,312

Fast emerging as one of the Visayas' hottest destinations for independent travellers, the tranquil town of Loboc makes an idyllic base for a few days. The settlement's main appeal is its bucolic forest-fringed river, which is perfect for kayak and paddleboarding excursions – search for waterfalls by day and fireflies at night.

For many Filipino families, Loboc is all about its floating restaurants, which line up by the bridge in the town centre and cruise the Loboc river blasting Frank Sinatra tunes and other oldies.

Many travellers base themselves here for day trips up to the Chocolate Hills.

 Activities

SUP Tours
WATER SPORTS

(☑0947 893 3022; www.suptoursphilippines.com; 2hr/half-day tour per person P950/1650) Guided stand-up-paddleboard tours are available through this professional outfit. The nighttime firefly tour (two hours, P950 including all equipment) is highly recommended.

Loboc Eco Adventure Park
ADVENTURE SPORTS

(☑038-537 9292; zipline P350, cable car P250; ☺8am-5.30pm) This adventure park has a thrilling 500m zipline running high (around 120m) over a waterfall and Loboc valley. A tamer cable car plies the same route. Be prepared to wait a while for your ride as it's popular with locals. Avoid weekends if you can. Located 3.5km north of Loboc.

Habitat Bohol Conservation Center
WILDLIFE-WATCHING

(Simply Butterflies Conservation Center; ☑038-535 9400; www.facebook.com/habitatboholwildlife adventure; 1km south of Bilar; P45, night safari P900, s P550, d P850-1000; ☺7.30am-5pm) A popular pit stop for day trippers, this wildlife centre has a smallish collection of butterflies and moths (which highly entertaining guides will explain all about). Night safaris (5.30pm to 7.30pm) offer a (slim) chance to spot tarsiers in the wild close to Rajah Sikatuna National Park. Owls, frogmouths, bats, civet cats and fireflies are sometimes encountered. Book tours a day ahead.

PHILIPPINE TARSIER SANCTUARY

In Canapnapan, a barangay of Corella, you can see saucer-eyed tarsiers in the wild at the **Philippine Tarsier Sanctuary** (☑0927 541 2290; www.tarsierfoundation.org; Canapnapan; P60; ☺9am-4pm). More than 100 of these territorial primates hang out in the immediate vicinity of the centre, though only eight are in the viewing area. The guides will bring you right to them via a short jungle trail; no flash photography is permitted. The visitors centre includes good information boards and the whole forested sanctuary is well managed and a pleasure to visit.

The simultaneously crazy and cuddly looking tarsier can fit in the palm of your hand yet leap 5m, rotate its head almost 360 degrees and move its ears in the direction of sound. It has huge imploring eyes, 150 times bigger than a human's in relation to its body size.

The tarsier is not only one of the world's smallest primates and the oldest surviving member of the primate group at 45 million years old, it is also an endangered species. The main threats to its survival are habitat destruction, introduced species, hunting and the pet trade. While also found in Samar, Leyte and parts of Mindanao, Bohol is the province that is doing the most to promote awareness of the tarsier and attempting to ensure its survival.

Keen hikers can arrange longer guided walks in the surrounding wildlife sanctuary, although you are unlikely to spot tarsiers outside the immediate vicinity of the visitors centre.

From Loboc, take a jeepney (P25, 40 minutes) heading to Tagbilaran.

🛏 Sleeping

⭐**Nuts Huts** HOSTEL $

(☑0920 846 1559; www.nutshuts.org; dm P400, nipa huts P900-1400) This near-legendary place polarises opinion. Ensconced in tropical forest on the Loboc River, it's perfect for those eager to experience and explore the jungle and who don't mind roughing it a bit – the huts are very rustic. If you hate creepy-crawlies and dislike exercise (it's a stiff walk up to the entrance) this isn't the place for you. Book ahead.

⭐**Fox & The Firefly Cottages** HOSTEL $

(☑0947 893 3022; www.facebook.com/foxand thefireflycottages; dm/cottage from P450/1200; 🛜) Virtually on the riverbank, this small, supremely chilled guesthouse has delightful nipa cottages and a well-set-up dorm (with shared bathroom). It's very much a base for paddleboarding on the Loboc with SUP Tours, but birdwatching walks and mountain-biking trips (from P500) are also offered. There's a great cafe-restaurant for delicious meals. It's a little southwest of Loboc's centre.

Loboc River Resort RESORT $$

(☑038-510 4565; www.lobocriverresort.com; cottage incl breakfast P2750-3300; ❄🛜⛱) The only upmarket place in Loboc, this lodge about 1km south of town has a totally sublime riverside setting, good restaurant and a stunning 20m pool by the river. Its bungalows, also perched by the water's edge, are spacious and comfortable enough but dated and need an upgrade for the prices asked.

Water to Forest BUNGALOW $$

(☑0920 619 6957; www.watertoforest.com; bungalow P1700; 🛜) A French– and Filipino–owned place in a superbly tranquil riverside setting. It feels very remote, though it's only 2km from Loboc town. Bamboo-and-thatch cabanas are the best in the Loboc area, well constructed with two levels, quality bedding and private bathroom. SUPs, mountain bikes and scooters are available for rent and meals are offered too.

Chocolate Hills

One of Bohol's premier tourist attractions, and certainly its most hyped, the Chocolate Hills are a series of majestic grassy hillocks that span far into the horizon. The hills get their name from the lawn-like vegetation that roasts to chocolate brown in the driest months (February to July). Their exact origin is still debated, but most scientists believe they were formed over time by the uplift of coral deposits and the effects of rainwater and erosion.

The largest and most visited concentration is 4km south of Carmen, site of the **Chocolate Hills Main Viewpoint** (P50; ⊙6am-6pm). For a less touristy experience, there's another range of Chocolate Hills northeast of Sagbayan on the road to Danao.

The friendly owners of the **Rice Museum** (Balay Sa Humay Batuan; Loay Interior Rd, Batuan; P20; ⊙8am-5.30pm) will explain about rice cultivation (*humay*) in Bohol. It's 4km south of the main Chocolate Hills viewpoint.

Set among mountainous jungle with spectacular gorges, caves and raging rivers, **Danao Adventure Park** (☑047-252 9978; www.danaoadventurepark.com; Danao-Jetafe Rd; P50) is a giant playground for adrenalin junkies. Rappelling, caving (P550), rock climbing (P400), kayaking (P300), tubing and trekking are all highly recommended, but it's the thrill-seeking activities that it's best known for.

🛏 Sleeping

Banlasan Lodge GUESTHOUSE $

(☑038-525 9145; http://banlasanlodge.weebly. com; d with fan/air-con & shared bathroom from P400/600; ❄🛜⛱) If you want to sleep somewhere around the Chocolate Hills, the swimming-pool-equipped Banlasan Lodge is on the highway between the viewpoint and Carmen. Rooms are dated but affordable and there's a decent restaurant (mains P100 to P140).

⭐**Villa del Carmen Bed & Breakfast** B&B $$

(☑0929 831 0115; www.facebook.com/villa.del.car men.2014; Loay Interior Rd, Carmen; r incl breakfast P1200-1800; ❄🛜) Perfectly located for those wanting an early start to catch sunrise over the Chocolate Hills, this chalet-style hotel is run by a charming local family who provide good meals (book ahead for dinner). Rooms are clean, air-conditioned and well furnished, some with fine views. Located just west of Carmen.

ℹ Getting There & Away

From Tagbilaran there are regular buses from the Dao terminal to Carmen (P64, two hours). From Loboc, the Chocolate Hills are a 45-minute motorcycle ride, or you can flag down a Carmen–bound bus. From Carmen there are buses to Talibon (P62, two hours) and Tubigon (P50, 1½ hours).

Anda

📋 038 / POP 1580

Dubbed the 'cradle of Boholano civilisation' for its significant prehistoric sites, the Anda peninsula on the southeast corner of Bohol still seems to belong to a forgotten time. From Anda town, resort hotels are strung along a glorious 3km stretch of coastline to the west which is dotted with white-sand cove beaches. Peace and privacy are the order of the day; if you like to be surrounded by activity, you might find Anda a little *too* chilled.

Anda town's beach is wide and wonderful but can fill up with day trippers. Quieter coves can be found along the coastline at most resorts.

◉ Sights & Activities

There's some good diving on **Basdio Reef**, which can be arranged through **Anda Divers Enjoy** (📋 0929 454 1635; www.facebook.com/pg/andadiversenjoylnc; dive incl equipment €25). A couple of the resort hotels also have dive centres.

The karst-laden Anda peninsula is home to scores of **caves** and there are several **cave pools** in the immediate vicinity of the town – Lamanok Island has some fine examples.

Anda Adventures (📋 0916 509 2643; boholadventurecompany@gmail.com; Coco Loco Cafe; ⊙ 8am-9pm) organises biking, caving and kayaking trips.

Lamanok Island   CAVE
(tour per person P300) This island 7km north of Anda has several anthropologically important cave paintings – made with bare hands – that date back tens of thousands of years. Travel 15 minutes by *habal-habal* or tricycle to the jumping-off point, where small boats bring you out to the island. On the island a small information centre will arrange your tour, which involves walking and canoeing through caves to see these ancient rock paintings as well as old dugout coffins and fossilised giant clams.

🛏 Sleeping & Eating

1PEACE Beach Resort   HOSTEL $
(📋 0928 255 5753; http://boholanda.com; dm P400, r P800-1400; 🛜) European-owned hostel-style place with a social atmosphere on a lovely white-sand cove beach with good snorkelling offshore. It's not exactly a party place but the owners do like mixing with guests, and communal dinners and drinking sessions are not unheard of. Accommodation consists of a 12-bed dorm and private room options.

Dapdap   RESORT $$
(📋 0921 833 2315; www.boholdapdapresort.com; r with fan P900, with air-con incl breakfast P1500-3200; ❇️🛜) Filipino-owned Dapdap is a reasonable budget option located on a lovely, if tiny, cove beach. You'll find a choice of nipa huts and bamboo-walled rooms, all with rather tired decor. There's a high-tide cliff jump here too.

★ **Casa Amihan**   BOUTIQUE HOTEL $$$
(📋 0917 530 7959; https://amihanresortanda.com; r P4100-4500; ❇️🛜❄️) Down a dirt track off the coastal road, this smart boutique beachfront hotel has five cottages with polished floorboards, stucco walls, elegant furniture and top-end linen. The restaurant here is one of the best in the district.

Island View Beachfront Resort   RESORT $$$
(📋 0918 309 7022; http://islandviewbeachfront resort.com; r P3500; ❇️🛜❄️) A fine little beachfront hotel with eight double-level rooms, a lap-sized pool, a great little bar, a bright and breezy restaurant with a view and a stupendous white beach. It's well managed and maintained and staff are superfriendly.

Anda White Beach Resort   RESORT $$$
(📋 0920 946 8127; www.andabeachresort.com; r incl breakfast US$98-135; ❇️🛜❄️) The highlight here is the fantastic beach and infinity pool; the rooms are well appointed but could use a makeover and they are certainly overpriced. There's a pool table, beach volleyball, kayaks for guests and a good restaurant. Located 2km south of central Anda.

Quinale Beach Bar   FILIPINO $
(Anda town beach; mains P70-150; ⊙ 9am-9pm) Enjoying a perfect beach location, this bar-resto serves huge portions of Filipino faves and San Miguels are a steal.

★ **Coco Loco**   CAFE **$$**
(☑0908 508 5847; www.facebook.com/cocoloco
bohol; mains P180-320; ⊘8am-8pm Tue-Sun; 🕾)
A simple, artistically decorated cafe-resto
famous for delicious coco burgers, though
great vegie burgers and couscous are also
available, and homemade ice cream (try the
chilli). Drinks include fresh juices, shakes,
ice tea and Coco Loco cocktails, which pack
a rum punch. It also sells a few local hand-
icrafts (including coco bras made with two
coconut shells!) and snacks.

Casa Amihan   INTERNATIONAL **$$**
(http://amihanresortanda.com; mains P170-320)
This hotel restaurant offers accomplished
cooking right by the waves, with grilled fish,
salads and Filipino dishes presented beautifully on giant white plates.

❶ Information

Tourist Office (☑0912 758 0360, 0908 793
6643; Municipal Plaza; ⊘8am-5pm Mon-Fri) In
Anda town.

❶ Getting There & Away

Guindulman is the gateway to Anda. From Tagbilaran catch a bus (P120, 2½ hours) or a quicker
V-hire (P130, two hours); there are also regular
buses from Ubay (P33, 1½ hours).

From Guindulman public *motorillas* (10-
passenger tricycles) head to Anda (P18, 20
minutes), passing turn-offs to many resort
hotels along the way.

Ubay

☑038 / POP 8840
The remote, scruffy port of Ubay in eastern
Bohol is only frequented by travellers heading somewhere else, chiefly the island of
Leyte. It does have banks and ATMs if you
need to top up your finances. There's a lively
market inland from the pier but no sights.

Schedules change frequently from Ubay,
not least because of tides affecting ports in
Leyte. **Medallion Transport** (☑0923 242
9827; www.facebook.com/medalliontransportinc)
sends a daily roll-on, roll-off (RORO) ferry
to Hilongas at 1pm (P265, three hours).
Additionally, there are usually two morning bangkas to Bato (P280, 2½ hours) and
supplementary bangkas to Hilongos, Leyte
(P250, 2½ hours).

Buses run between Ubay and Tagbilaran
(P135, 3½ hours).

Talibon

☑038 / POP 67,400
The port town of Talibon on Bohol's north
coast is a possible entry point from Cebu for
those heading straight to Anda, Carmen or
Danao. There are no sights but it's a friendly
enough place.

Talibon Pension (☑038-515 5114, 0939
241 0377; CP Garcia Ave; d P300-1000; ❇🕾) is
nothing fancy but this is probably the best
accommodation in Talibon. Tiled rooms
have cable TV and are kept clean and tidy.
It's located on the main road out of town.

VG Shipping (☑038-515 5168; Talibon port)
operates regular roll-on, roll-off (RORO)
ferries to/from Cebu City (from P240, 3½
hours) departing at 10am and 10pm daily.

Buses depart to Tagbilaran (P115, 3½
hours) via Tubigon, and to Carmen (P64, 2½
hours) for the Chocolate Hills. For Guindul-
man/Anda, take a multicab to Ubay (P30, 45
minutes) and transfer to a south-bound bus.
V-hires at the pier are available for special
trips around Bohol.

LEYTE

For students and historians of the Pacific
and WWII, the word 'Leyte' conjures up
images of bloody naval battles and the site
of MacArthur's famous return. For Filipinos
it's equally associated with the rags-to-riches
rise of Imelda Marcos and the nostalgic, ro-
manticised portrait she painted of her birthplace after she made good in the capital. For
travellers, Southern Leyte, wrapped around
the deep-water Sogod Bay, is one of the Philippines' many diving hotspots. The Cebua-
no-speaking Leyteños live in the south, and
their Waray-speaking neighbours live in the
cattle-ranching country of northern Leyte.

It was Leyte's north that endured the
worst of Typhoon Yolanda's tyranny in 2013,
but today the island has bounced back remarkably well. Provincial capital Tacloban
has a vibrant cafe and restaurant scene while
the deep south settlements of Padre Burgos
and Panaon remain as seductive as ever.

❶ Getting There & Away

The most common way into Leyte is by boat, or
overland from Samar. Key ports include Ormoc
in the northwest, with myriad connections to
Cebu City; and Lilo-an and San Ricardo in the far
south, linked by frequent ferries to Mindanao.

Leyte

N

0 — 50 km
0 — 25 miles

Camandag Island
Almagro Island
Santo Niño Island
Libucan Islands
Canahauan Islands
Sambawan Island
Maripipi Island
Parasan Island
◎ **Catbalogan**
Samar
Kawayan ◉
◉ **Culaba**
Daram Island
Buad Island
Almeria ◉
Biliran Island
Caibiran ◉
◉ **Borongan**
Carnassa Island
Jubay ◉
Villalon ◉
◉ **Naval**
Biliran ◉
Cabucgayan ◉
Roxas (158km)
Calubian ◉
San Isidro ◉
Leyte ◉
Babatngon ◉
San Juanico Bridge
Sohoton Caves & Natural Bridge National Park
Malapascua Island
Tabango ◉
Belen ◉
Barugo ◉
San Miguel ◉
Basey ◉
Maya (2km)
Lemon ◉
Carigara ◉
Tunga ◉
◉ **Tacloban**
San Pedro Bay
Villaba ◉
Kananga ◉
Jaro ◉
Libungao ◉
Aguiting ◉
Mt Janagdan ▲
Palo ◉
Tanauan ◉
Bogo (10km)
Lake Danao National Park
Mt Pananguan ▲
Dagami ◉
Tolosa ◉
Palompon ◉
Ormoc ◉
Lake Danao
Leyte ◉
Burauen ◉
Dulag ◉
Leyte Gulf
Isabel ◉
Merida ◉
Albuera ◉
La Paz ◉
Mayorga ◉
Caridad ◉
Lake Mahagnao Volcanic National Park
MacArthur ◉
Pilar ◉
Ponson Island
Gabas ◉
Abuyog ◉
Tulang Island
Camotes Islands
Poro Island
Baybay ◉
Buaya ◉
Danao (7km)
Pacijan Island
Poro Island
Hilosig ◉
Poro ◉
Tudela ◉
Mahaplag ◉
Cebu City (22km)
Plaridel ◉
Silago ◉
Cebu City (20km)
Inopacan ◉
SOUTHERN LEYTE
San Pedro Island
Hindang ◉
San Pablo Island
Camotes Sea
Hilongos ◉
Sogod ◉
Hinunangan ◉
Bato ◉
Bontoc ◉
Libagon ◉
Hinundayan ◉
Talibon ◉
Matalom ◉
Sogod Bay
Anahawan ◉
Canigao Channel
Saint Bernard ◉
San Juan ◉
Ubay ◉
Lapinig Island
Malitbog ◉
Maasin ◎
Hanginan ◉
Lilo-an ◉
Surigao Strait
Bohol
Macrohon ◉
San Francisco ◉
Padre Burgos ◉
Tangkaen Point
Panaon Island
Limasawa Island
Pintuyan ◉
Triana ◉
Magellenes ◉
San Ricardo ◉
Surigao ◎
San Francisco ◉
Mindanao
Bohol Sea

Several other ports on the west coast including Maasin, Bato and Hilongas have services to Cebu City and Bohol.

Tacloban has a useful regional airport while Maasin has connections to Cebu City and Tagbilaran.

Tacloban

📞 053 / POP 248,300

This was Typhoon Yolanda's 'ground zero'. Tacloban took a direct hit on 8 November 2013, when the mother of all tropical storms laid waste to the city. Yet as you walk through Tacloban's streets today, it's impossible to imagine the apocalyptic scenes on that fateful morning. The centre has been fixed up, hotels have been repaired and there's even a degree of cafe culture evident. Tacloban's bars are again filled with local drinkers instead of relief workers. Yes, the city has resumed its role as the commercial heart of both Leyte and Samar.

The psychological wounds will take longer to heal. The images of destruction, the scent of death that permeated the city, the loved ones lost...none of this will ever be forgotten.

For travellers passing through you can expect traditionally warm Visayan hospitality. For this vibrant, somewhat gritty, port city has re-emerged from recovery mode and is once again welcoming visitors.

Huge ships were cast inland during the 7m storm surge caused by Typhoon Yolanda. The bow of one of them, **MV Eva Jocelyn** (barangay Anibong Rd, barangay Anibong), has been kept as a memorial, surrounded by passing traffic and rebuilt shanties. It's around 2km northwest of the centre in barangay Anibong.

☉ Sights & Activities

Be sure to drop by the Hotel Alejandro (p325), which has a brilliant permanent collection of photos on the walls tracing Tacloban's domestic and war history.

Santo Niño Shrine & Heritage Center HISTORIC SITE

(incl guide for up to 3 people P200; ☉8am-5pm) Leyte's most famous daughter is Imelda Romualdez Marcos, whose family is from Tolosa. Her influence in Tacloban is evident in the city's street names and in this prominent mansion built with the Marcos' millions. It was not designed as a home but to showcase regional Filipino arts and culture – each room is dedicated to a province. Some of the furniture, antiques and objets d'art are impressive yet it's incredibly stuffy inside and many treasures are mouldy and decaying.

Zpa SPA

(📞053-321 3888; Hotel XYZ, P Zamora St; 1hr massage from P350) A smart hotel spa with a range of massages and treatments at moderate rates; try a Thai full-body massage or a foot spa.

Bukid Outdoor Shop ADVENTURE SPORTS

(📞053-523 7625; www.facebook.com/bukidoutdoorshop; 206 Burgos St; ☉9am-7.30pm Mon-Sat, climbing wall 1-7pm Mon-Sat) Here you'll find lots of outdoor gear and a group of adventure enthusiasts with information and local

CEBU & EASTERN VISAYAS TACLOBAN

Tacloban

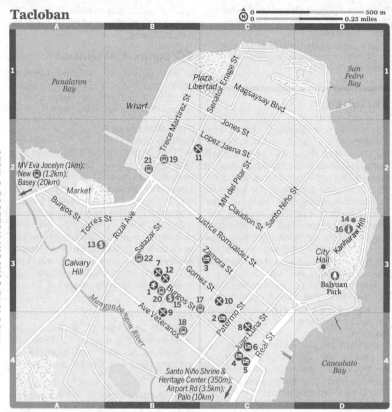

contacts for kayaking, mountain biking and hiking. There's a rock-climbing wall on-site (P150 for two hours).

🎊 Festivals & Events

Tacloban Pride LGBTIQ+
This LGBTIQ+ celebration is held annually for a week in March. There are films and poetry readings; venues including Yellow Doors host events.

Pintados-Kasadyaan CULTURAL
(⊙ 27 Jun) The 'painted' festival celebrates the traditional tattooing practised here before the Spanish arrived; nowadays water-based paints are used for the festival's body decoration.

Sangyaw CULTURAL
(⊙ 29 Jun) Mardi Gras Leyte-style, with colourful floats and dancing troupes through the streets of Tacloban.

🛏 Sleeping

It's highly advisable to stay 'uptown' in the restaurant and bar zone around Burgos St.

★ Yellow Doors Hostel HOSTEL $
(📞 0927 450 0984, 0921 600 0165; www.facebook. com/helloyellowdh; cnr Burgos & Juan Luna Sts; dm/d P490/990; ❄@🛜) A funky hostel run by switched-on locals with quirky recycled decor. Dorms have super beds with privacy-protecting curtains while private rooms have (tiny) en suites. The top deck has a cool restobar for beers and meals. The Filipino owners are travellers and help with transport and sightseeing advice. Located in the thick of things with bars and restaurants on your doorstep.

★ Ironwood Hotel HOTEL $$
(📞 053-321 9999; http://ironwoodhotel.com; cnr Burgos St & Juan Luna St; r from P2200; ❄🛜) The best midranger in town, Ironwood en-

Tacloban

joys a terrific central location with a wide selection of cafes and restaurants within walking distance. Rooms are business smart and well furnished and there's a great downstairs cafe for coffee and meals. It offers a free shuttle-bus service to/from the airport.

Rosvenil Pensione   GUESTHOUSE $$
(☑ 053-321 2676; 302 Burgos St; r P1280-2880; ❄ 🛜) Built around a rambling 1940s wooden house, this is a well-run and conveniently located little hotel. In the old building are clean basic rooms; the newer, more sizeable and comfortable rooms are in a beautiful three-storey building with wrought-iron railings and a balcony.

Hotel Alejandro   HOTEL $$
(☑ 053-321 7033; hotelalejandro360@gmail.com; Patermo St; d P1800-3000; ❄ 🛜 🏊) This three-storey hotel, occupying a handsome 1930s home, looks like a colonial villa. The rooms are comfortable enough, if not as grand as the exterior, but the halls and corridors of the old building, festooned with classic photos of Tacloban, give the hotel a real touch of class. A newer wing houses a small rooftop pool, plus 15 deluxe rooms.

Caluwayan Palm Island   RESORT $$$
(☑ 0977 354 5692; www.caluwayanresort.com; Caluwayan, Marabut; r P3300-4000, beach villa P5000 incl breakfast; ❄ 🛜 🏊) This well-run resort is popular with Tacloban families on weekends but otherwise tranquil. There's a slim sandy private beach with sheltered swimming, huge pool and fine shore-side

restaurant (mains P210 to P445). Rooms have been renovated and are in good shape. Kayaks (P200 per hour) and boats (P400 per hour) are available for exploring the craggy Marabut Islands just offshore.

Hotel XYZ   HOTEL $$$
(☑ 0917 773 8008; www.hotel-xyz.com; P Zamora St; r from P3400-4000; ❄ 🛜 🏊) In the heart of Tacloban's shopping district, this high-rise hotel has more than a touch of boutique about it with its arresting colour schemes and modish decor. Many rooms enjoy fine views of the city and bay (but are perhaps a shade overpriced). It's also home to a superb sky restobar and spa.

🍴 Eating & Drinking

Libro   CAFE $
(cnr Santo Niño & Gomez Sts; sandwiches from P50; ⊙ noon-8pm Mon-Sat; 🛜) A fantastic **secondhand bookstore** that serves fine coffee (P38), sandwiches on ciabatta bread (from P50) and a great selection of cakes – try the *calamansi* (Filipino lime) cheesecake.

★ Canto Fresco   MEDITERRANEAN $$
(☑ 053-523 9085; Burgos St; mains P140-330; ⊙ noon-midnight; ❄ 🛜) There's an authentic flavour to this boho, Italian-influenced place. On the menu you'll find rustic hand-rolled pizza, pasta, sandwiches, fine salads and a few Asian tastes. Sit on the streetside tables or in the air-conditioned interior, which vaguely resembles a beach shack. It also offers good wine by the glass or bottle.

★ Cocina Juan Luna
FILIPINO $$

([☎]053-321 6397; www.facebook.com/cocinajuan
luna; meals P120-220; [⊗]8am-9pm) Offering
a rustic feel in the city, this delightful res-
taurant is set in an open-sided, traditional
wooden structure in a garden with bench
seating. Choose a dish or three from the
earthenware pots on display; all have a
home-cooked Filipino flavour. Between 5pm
and 10pm get 50% off all meat items.

Ochó Seafood & Grill
SEAFOOD $$

([☎]053-832 8808; Senator Enage St; mains P200-
500; [⊗]10am-10pm; [❄][?]) A local favourite,
Ochó is a bustling, authentic place where
you select your fish or seafood from the display and get them to cook it however you
like it. Try shrimp with chilli and garlic
sauce. Vegos are catered for and can choose
the cooking style for tofu and greens. Be prepared to wait for a table, it's very popular.

Giuseppe's
ITALIAN $$

([☎]053-321 4910; www.giuseppesresto.net; 173 Ave
Veteranos; mains P100-575; [⊗]10.30am-10.30pm;
[❄][?]) A longstanding Tacloban eatery, brick-
walled Giuseppe's is decorated like an Italian
bistro and serves pastas (try the fettuccine
puttanesca, P220), pizza (from P320) and
meat dishes such as osso bucco or seafood.

Sunzibar
MEXICAN $$

(Burgos St; mains P170-400; [⊗]11.30am-9.45pm
Mon-Sat; [?]) An atmospheric place on Ta-
cloban's Street of Restaurants (aka Burgos
St) where you can count on tasty Filipino-
Mexican grub such as beef nachos and finger-
licking rum ribs.

Fyzz
LOUNGE

(Zamora St; [⊗]4pm-midnight; [?]) On the top
floor of Hotel XYZ (p325), this sleek lounge
bar has a terrific cocktail selection (P150 to
P220), wine by the glass, imported beers and
killer views. Also serves Greek and Japanese
food (meals about P320), which sounds a bit
odd but actually works well.

❶ Information

Metrobank (Burgos St; [⊗]9am-4pm Mon-Fri)
and **BDO** (Rizal Ave; [⊗]8.30am-5pm Mon-Fri)
are among the many ATMs.

Bureau of Immigration ([☎]053-325 6004;
Kanhuraw Hill; [⊗]8am-5pm Mon-Fri) Next to
the Regional Tourist Office.

Regional Tourist Office ([☎]053-832 0901,
053-321 2048; dotreg8@yahoo.com; Kanhuraw
Hill; [⊗]8am-5.45pm) Very helpful. It can provide you with an abundance of information for
Leyte and Samar.

❶ Getting There & Away

AIR
Tacloban is well connected to Manila, with many
daily connections via Cebu Pacific, PAL and Air
Asia. Cebu Pacific has flights to Cebu and Davao.

The airport is 7km from the centre of town.
Jeepneys (P13) run to/from the airport from Real
St on the southern edge of the centre. Otherwise
it'll cost P120 in a tricycle or P160 in a taxi.

Note that drivers at the airport are notorious for
overcharging passengers on arrival. Bargain hard.

BUS, VAN & JEEPNEY
Throughout Samar and Leyte, 13-passenger air-
con vans take precedence over buses. They are
quicker, more frequent and cost negligibly more
than the bus. There are many private companies, each operating from its own terminal, most
of which are in the city centre.

The two main operators are **Duptours** ([☎]0939
937 7002; Santo Niño St) and **Van Vans** ([☎]0939
416 1060, 053-523 1274; Salazar St), which
have vans servicing most destinations every
30 minutes or so until around 5pm, sometimes
later. **Grand Tours** ([☎]053-325 4640; www.
vsgrandtours.com; cnr Trece Martirez & A Mabini
Sts) does trips to Ormoc and Catbalogan, **City
Tours** ([☎]031-534 1770, 0942 463 3622; www.
facebook.com/citytourscatbalogan; Burgos St)
serves Catbalogan and there are other smaller
operators including **Guiuan Express** ([☎]055-271
2454; 279 Burgos St) and **East Visayan Tour**
([☎]0997 311 1104; Tabuan National Hwy). For
Calbayog it's often quicker to take the first van
to Catbalogan. Getting to Allen usually requires a
change in Catbalogan or Calbayog.

You'll find slow local buses and additional vans
to many destinations at the **New Bus Terminal**
(Tinta-Patik Rd; [⊗]24hr) at Abucay, about 2km
west of the city centre. To get to Padre Burgos,
transfer in Sogod or Maasin. Also at the bus station are jeepneys to Basey (P30, one hour).

Long-distance buses from the bus station to
Manila do not typically provide passage to destinations in Leyte or Samar unless you pay full fare.

Ormoc
[☎]053 / POP 221,600

The hillsides surrounding Ormoc Bay make
a scenic backdrop for those arriving by boat
from Cebu. Strolling the breezy waterfront
promenade, which has some decent restaurants and bars, is a pleasure but otherwise
this a typically busy port city. Some of the
bloodiest WWII battles in the Philippines

Ormoc

took place in Ormoc Bay in 1944. The bay is literally littered with shipwrecks, but you'll need your own gear and some serious technical diving experience to explore them.

⊙ Sights & Activities

Lake Danao Natural Park   PARK
(permit P45) Lake Danao is beautifully situated in Leyte's inland hills 18km east of town, making it a good day trip from Ormoc. There's some great hiking around the guitar-shaped lake, 650m above sea level and fringed by forest, as well as on and around the undermaintained **Leyte Mountain Trail**. Hikers can get in touch with Kim of Eastern Visayas Adventure Team.

Formerly called Lake Imelda (as in Marcos) it's a popular picnic spot with locals.

**Eastern Visayas
Adventure Team**   TREKKING
(☏ 0923 744 9954, 0956 432 0972; k.lumogdang@ yahoo.com) Kim leads treks and ascents of peaks throughout Leyte and Biliran Island.

🛏 Sleeping

★ **David's Inn**   HOTEL $
(☏ 053-255 7618; davids_inn88@yahoo.com; Carlos Tan St; r P800-1050; ❄ 🛜) A fine budget hotel with good-value, well-appointed

Ormoc

🛏 Sleeping

⊗ Eating

ⓘ Information

ⓘ Transport

rooms (some with balconies) all with aircon, hot water, attractive furniture and cable TV. There's switched-on service and a great little cafe. It's 700m inland from the pier.

Ormoc Villa Hotel   HOTEL $$

(☑ 053-255 5006; http://ormocvillahotel.com.ph; Obrero St; r P2500, ste P3900-7300; ❋ 🐾 ⛱ ☰) In the middle of the city this upmarket, neo-colonial hotel is set in palm-studded land-scaped gardens with a lovely heat-busting pool. Rooms are spacious and those on the 3rd floor enjoy sea views. In the restaurant you'll find a good selection of local and international dishes.

✕ Eating & Drinking

Barbecue Stalls   BARBECUE $

(Burgos St; meals P50-150; ⊘ 5.30-11pm) Just west of the Superdome is a cluster of barbecue stalls that come to life from sunset onwards. Try the fresh, juicy pineapple sold by vendors, which the region is known for.

Lorenzo's Cafe   CAFE $

(I Lazzarabal St; meals P100-260; ⊘ 7.30am-11.30pm; ❋ 🐾) This large, popular cafe with wraparound windows has a terrace facing the promenade and air-conditioned interior. The menu has great breakfast choices and plenty of Western and Asian dishes, plus espresso coffee and pastries.

★ Mimay's Seafood House   SEAFOOD $$

(☑ 053-561 6037; Bonifacio St; mains P130-400; ⊘ 10.30am-2pm & 5.30-9.30pm; 🐾) This buzzing place has seafood and fish so fresh it's actually alive – just make a selection from the bubbling display tanks and choose how you want it cooked. It's three blocks in from the promenade.

Roma Cafe   PUB FOOD $$

(Aviles St; mains P150-250; ⊘ 9am-midnight; ❋ 🐾) American-owned Roma Cafe has healthy salads and Thai and Mexican tastes to accompany the speciality noodle dishes. It's also a popular drinking venue in the evening, with a busy terrace and live music some weekends.

ℹ Information

Ormoc City Tourism Office (☑ 053-255 8356; www.ormoc.gov.ph/tourism; Ebony St; ⊘ 8am-5pm) Right next to the port.

ℹ Getting There & Away

BOAT

Oceanjet (☑ 053-834 5066; www.oceanjet.net), **SuperCat 2GO** (☑ 053-561 9818; www.supercat.com.ph) and **Weesam Express** (☑ 053-561 0080; www.weesam.ph) each have daily fastcraft that ply the Ormoc–Cebu

City route (P550 to P1000, 2½ to three hours). Slower **boats to Cebu** (P390 to P410, five to six hours) include Lite Shipping (p290) at 10pm daily and **Roble Shipping** (☑ 053-255 7613; www.robleshipping.com) at 11am daily.

For Camotes, there are two or three daily bangkas to Pilar on Ponson Island (P150, 1½ hours), departing between 9am and noon. Usually one continues on to Kawit. There are sometimes boats to Poro Island, but not daily.

The City Tourism Office has schedules.

BUS & JEEPNEY

Duptours (☑ 053-321 1370) and **Van Vans** (☑ 053-523 1274; Osmeña St) both have air-con vans to Tacloban (P130, 2½ hours) about every 30 minutes until 7pm, with plenty more vans and slower buses leaving from the **bus station** (⊘ 24hr). Also at the bus station you'll find vans to Naval (P130, two hours) until 5pm, and to Palompan (P70, 1¼ hours) and Maasin (for Padre Burgos, P170, three hours). Buses are slower, less frequent and not much cheaper to all of these places.

Maasin

☑ 053 / POP 87,100

Maasin (mah-*ah*-sin) is a sprawling, bustling port city with boat connections to Cebu and Bohol. It's the capital of Southern Leyte, a laid-back, picturesque province that offers a wealth of natural attractions and great diving. Maasin is a potential base for some hikes and also has a beautiful early-18th-century church, but for travellers it's mainly a transport hub.

Few people explore the area around Maasin, even though there are several good hikes, and caves and waterfalls to investigate. Among the more accessible options is the hike to **Guinsohoton Cave** and **Cagnituan Falls**, an easy jaunt out of Maasin; look for the turn-off in barangay Maria Clara 4.5km east of town. The cave has a neat subterranean river where you can swim.

Contact the **Provincial Tourism Office** (☑ 0915 879 4923, 053-570 8300; www.southernleyte.gov.ph; ⊘ 8am-4.30pm Mon-Fri) for more hikes in the region.

Ampil Pensionne (☑ 053-570 8084; www.maasincity.com/ampilpensione; T Oppus St; r P400-950; ❋ 🐾) is a decent budget option with air-con and some rooms with hot water.

Caimito Beach Hotel (www.caimitobeachhotel.com; s/d from P1300/2380; ❋ 🐾 ⛱) is 6km out of town on the road to Padre Burgos, with nine smart tiled rooms, eight with fine sea and pool views. There's a decent restaurant plus kayaks and snorkelling gear for rent.

❶ Getting There & Away

AIR

Air Juan connects Maasin and Cebu (via Tagbilaran) with four weekly flights. Maasin airstrip is 13km northwest of the city.

BOAT

Boat connections from all ports in Southern Leyte are subject to very frequent change due to local tides. Always check schedules in advance directly with ferry companies.

For Cebu City there are several options from Maasin: **Weesam Express** (☑ in Cebu 032-231 7737; www.weesamexpress.net; Port) operates one daily fastcraft (P550, 3½ hours); Cokaliong Shipping (p290) has four weekly ferries and George & Peter Lines (p290) has one weekly ferry (P250, 5½ to six hours).

Cokaliong Shipping also connects Maasin with Surigao (P325, four hours) on Wednesdays and Fridays at 8.30am.

Other ferries and fastcraft dock a bit further north of Maasin in Bato or Hilongos.

From Hilongos, Gabisan Shipping Lines (p290) has a daily fastcraft to Cebu (P280, 3½ hours) at 8.30am while Roble Shipping has a daily RORO (P240, 5½ hours) to Cebu. **Medallion Transport** (☑ 0923 242 9827; www.facebook.com/medalliontransportinc) has a daily ferry to Ubay, Bohol (P265, three hours) and there are usually supplementary bangkas on this route to Ubay too.

From Bato, Medallion Transport sails daily to Cebu (P280, six hours) at 9pm, with an extra service on Saturdays at 9am. Medallion also has a daily 9am RORO to Ubay (P270, three hours) on Bohol, and there are two daily bangkas to Ubay.

BUS

Jeepneys and multicabs head east from the **bus terminal** (Captain Iyano St; ⊙ 24hr) to Padre Burgos every 20 minutes or so until around 6.30pm (P30, one hour).

Duptours and Van Vans send vans from the main bus terminal to Tacloban every hour until 5pm (P220, 3½ hours). You can also find vans to Ormoc at the bus station (P170, three hours) and occasional vans and buses to Sogod.

Padre Burgos

☑ 053 / POP 11,600

Laid-back Padre Burgos (just 'Burgos' to locals) straggles for about 3km in a lazy green line along the edge of the lovely **Sogod Bay**.

It's considered one of the premier diving spots in the Philippines for its pristine hard and soft coral reefs, deep wall, caves and current dives.

Offshore from Burgos, the lovely island of Limasawa, which has deep religious significance for Filipinos, is well worth a day trip or even an overnighter.

◎ Sights & Activities

Scuba diving is the reason most people come here, and there are three established dive resorts. Dive trips to Limasawa Island are rewarding, but possibly the best sites are in the marine sanctuaries off Panaon Island.

There's decent **snorkelling** directly offshore from Sogod Bay Scuba Resort (p330), though there's a constant battle against invasive crown-of-thorns starfish, which can decimate the coral in no time.

Trips to swim with **whale sharks** around Pintuyan are also offered in season.

★**Limasawa Island**   ISLAND
(rems_0418@yahoo.com) Tranquil Limasawa Island, a place of historical and religious significance, is well worth a visit. The island has around 6000 inhabitants and five tiny villages. This is where the Spanish first celebrated Mass on 31 March 1521, thereby starting the Christianisation of the country.

A five-minute walk to the left from the pier leads to the original **Mass site**. Next to it, a set of 450 steps leads up to the commemorative **Magellan's cross**. From here you can gaze at gorgeous views out across the ocean to Mindanao, Bohol and mainland Leyte. The island also has beautiful small coves that are ideal for swimming and snorkelling, and a few guesthouses.

Between Monday and Saturday four big bangkas make the journey to and from Burgos (P50, 45 minutes); the last trip from Burgos is at 3pm, while the last trip off the island is at 12.30pm. On Sundays there's only one boat, leaving Limasawa at 12.30pm and returning from Burgos at 3pm. Chartering a bangka will cost around P1500 return.

Cambaro Caves   CAVING
The turn-off to these spectacular caves is 10km west of Burgos in Molopolo, a barangay of Macrohon. From here a partially paved road leads 7km to Cambaro, where you can secure guides and flashlights at the barangay hall.

HINUNANGAN

The town of Hinunangan on the eastern frontier of Southern Leyte Province is a place to escape civilisation entirely. It's home to sublime, honey-brown **Tahusan Beach**, one of the finest in the Visayas, with great swimming and occasional surf.

Lounge here, or walk or horseback ride to nearby caves and waterfalls – get advice from the helpful **municipal tourist office** (☑ 0910 238 9734, 0909 354 6023; Municipal Hall). Or hire a bangka (P1200 return) and head out to the nearby offshore islands of **San Pedro** and **San Pablo**, both with white coral sand, snorkelling and swimming.

There's very little in Hinunangan. Simple huts can be rented from locals on San Pedro island or you can camp; be sure to bring supplies and snorkelling gear. **Doña Marta Boutique Hotel** (☑ 0915 670 5900, 0929 773 7407; www.facebook.com/malinawon; Tahusan Beach; incl breakfast r P2700-3000, ste P3500; ❄ 🛜) is the best place to stay in Hinunangan, or there are a couple of other budget-friendly places to stay both on and off the beach.

From Tacloban's New Bus Terminal (p326) catch a van or bus (P140, 2½ to three hours) heading to St Bernard (via Silago *not* Sogod). For San Pedro or San Pablo ask to be dropped at Brgy, Canipaan, from where local boaters will shuttle you over to the islands (public one way P20, private charter return P1500, 20 minutes).

🛏 Sleeping & Eating

Limasawa Guesthouse
GUESTHOUSE $

(☑ 0917 633 8215; rems_0418@yahoo.com; r P450; ❄) This guesthouse (run by the local government) is near the municipal hall in the island's main barangay, Cabulihan. The two rooms have air-con, but not at night (when the island's power cuts off). The Limasawa tourism officer, Remigilda, is the contact.

Dak Dak Beach Resort
GUESTHOUSE $

(☑ 0915 520 3660; Lugsongan, Limasawa; hut with fan P700, r with air-con P1000; ❄) On the east coast of idyllic Limasawa Island, this is the perfect place to really get off the grid, write a novel, meditate or spend days snorkelling the offshore reef. Two rooms and seven tiny nipa huts face a slim white-sand beach. Meals are available by arrangement.

Peter's Dive Resort
RESORT $

(☑ 0917 791 0993; www.whaleofadive.com; Lungsodaan; dm P400, r with shared bathroom P880-980, r with private bathroom P1300-3300; ❄ 🛜 🏊) Peter's is just off the road on a pebble beach with a great variety of rooms catering to all budgets. The dorms and budget rooms are in the main building over the restaurant, while the larger, more comfortable private cottages are right on the water. There's a bar area for hanging out. Rooms are slightly more expensive for nondivers.

★ Sogod Bay Scuba Resort
RESORT $$

(☑ 0915 520 7274; www.sogodbayscubaresort.com; Lungsodaan; r P1100-2400; ❄ @ 🛜) Run by a welcoming Australian, this fine place has a prime waterfront location, with simply but elegantly furnished rooms with terraces. Cheaper options are in a concrete building 200m up the road, away from the water. The restobar serves excellent, though slightly pricey meals (P200 to P240).

JD Beachfront Hotel
GUESTHOUSE $$

(☑ 0921 576 1155, 0905 320 9137; Pook Beach; d with fan/air-con P1400/1600; ❄ 🛜) This welcoming place has five spacious, spiffy rooms and a great shoreside location on Tangkaan Peninsula, 500m south of Burgos centre. There's good snorkelling directly offshore and great meals are prepared by the hospitable owners (who offer discounts if you stay for more than two nights).

Southern Leyte Dive Resort
RESORT $$

(☑ 053-572 4011; www.leyte-divers.com; San Roque; d P1600-2350, tr P2250-3900; ❄ 🛜) The oldest and prettiest of the dive resorts, the spacious cottages here – bamboo with fans, or comfortable modern air-con – are off the main road and front a lovely sandy beach. Excellent food in the garden bar-restaurant includes pasta and German sausages (and German beer).

Alma & Jerry's Kitchen
FILIPINO $$

(Lungsodaan; mains P120-290; ⊙ 8am-9pm) On the waterfront a kilometre northwest of the centre, this friendly locally owned restaurant serves tasty Asian food including Filipino-style curries, seafood and vegetarian dishes. Order in advance for crispy *pata,* sashimi or roasted suckling pig. It also rents out motorbikes here.

ⓘ Getting There & Away

Regular jeepneys and multicabs to Maasin leave from the pier (P30, one hour). Connect in Maasin for Ormoc and Tacloban.

Jeepneys heading towards Malitbog and Sogod pass every 30 minutes or so. You can connect to Tacloban in Sogod, but you may have to wait awhile.

Panaon Island

☏ 053

This beautiful island, connected to mainland Leyte by a bridge at Lilo-an, is home to a highly seasonal whale-shark interaction program out of the town of Pintuyan.

This is also where you go to catch the ferry to Lipata, near Surigao City on Mindanao, from either the port at Lilo-an or Benit, San Ricardo, on the island's southern tip.

🏃 Activities

Whale-shark watching is the big draw, but there is also great diving all along the west coast of Panaon Island. **Napantao Reef**, off the Coral Cay Conservation (www.coralcay.org) group's base in San Francisco, is a highly regarded and popular site where reef sharks and turtles are regularly spotted. Dive trips originating out of Padre Burgos head across the bay to Panaon, or you can dive with Pintuyan Beach Resort.

★ Whale Sharks   WILDLIFE-WATCHING
(☏ 0917 301 4047; per 1/2/3 people P1600/1850/2100) Few tourists make the scenic journey down to Pintuyan, where the local tourist office organises community-based snorkelling trips to see whale sharks (locally known as *tiki-tiki*) in three-passenger bangkas owned by the local fisher's association. Tours are run out of barangay Son-ok, 3km north of Pintuyan, and the fee includes boat, guide and spotters. Snorkelling equipment costs P150.

Dive shops in the Sogod Bay area also run trips here, but guests are not allowed to dive at the main site in Son-ok. You may get lucky and spot *tiki-tiki* while diving elsewhere, however. Whale sharks are not hand-fed in Son-ok and the visibility is usually good. The season for whale-shark spotting is roughly November to May.

Keep in mind that Pintuyan's *tiki-tiki* are fickle – some years they show up only briefly, or not at all. Before setting out, contact Moncher Bardos of the local **Ecotourism Office** (☏ 0917 301 4047; moncher64bardos@yahoo.com; Municipal Development Office, barangay Poblacion, Pintuyan) to see if they are around.

🛏 Sleeping & Eating

La Guerta Lodge   LODGE $
(☏ 0908 170 9724, 0926 142 6986; www.facebook.com/laguertalodginghouseunoanddos; 42 F Castanares St, Pintuyan; s P300-500, d P350-650; ✳🔊) This family-owned lodge has simple, clean rooms in a row off the water near the centre of Pintuyan. Fan or air-con options are available, though no meals are offered.

Leyte South MPC   HOTEL $
(☏ 0917 302 7971; off Lilo-an–San Ricardo Hwy, Lilo-an; ◔ r from P490-1250; ✳🔊) The garishly painted new place has a selection of rooms, including family-sized units, all with cable TV and air-con. It's 1km west of the port.

★ Pintuyan Beach Resort   RESORT $$
(☏ 0921 736 8860; www.pintuyan.com; Pintuyan; r/bungalow incl half-board P2060/2850; ✳🔊🏊) This is the best place to stay on Panaon Island and a fine base for diving excursions in Sogod Bay. There are five spacious bungalows, four with ocean views, and three rooms; the restaurant serves good Asian and Western cuisine. Dives cost P1100 excluding equipment and boat hire, excursions to Limasawa Island are possible and whale-shark-spotting trips are offered.

ⓘ Getting There & Away

Southern Leyte has good boat connections to Mindanao.

From Lilo-an, **FastCat** (☏ in Cebu 032-816 1183; http://fastcat.com.ph; port, Lilo-an) operates three daily fastcraft to Lipata at 4am, midday and 8pm (P300, two hours). A **Southwest Ferries** (☏ 0917 650 2462; www.facebook.com/southwestferries; port, Lilo-an) RORO sails twice-daily at 6am and 6pm to Surigao, Mindanao (P300, four hours) and other companies offer additional services on this route.

From Benit port near San Ricardo, **Montenegro Shipping** (☏ in Batangas 043-740 3206; www.facebook.com/montenegroinc) has five daily scheduled RORO ferries for Surigao at 4am, 8am, midday, 4pm and 8pm (P140, 1¼ hours) and there are sometimes additional bangkas.

Local buses from Sogod serve Lilo-an, Pintuyan and San Ricardo.

BILIRAN ISLAND

📞 053 / POP 178,400

Tourism is slowly taking off on this quiet island province, which has the potential to be an adventure wonderland. Verdant Biliran has a long and beautiful coastline and mountainous interior, plus several sandy white beaches on offshore islands. A mostly sealed ring road runs around the island, offering stunning vistas of volcanoes and vivid green rice terraces. It's a great spot to escape the crowds for a few days and do some DIY exploring.

Biliran became a province separate from Leyte in 1992; a short bridge connects the two. The island is lush and it can rain any time, with the most rainfall in December and the least in April. Most people are subsistence farmers or fishers who generally speak Cebuano on the west coast and Waray-Waray on the east.

ℹ️ Getting There & Away

The vast majority of travellers arrive by land from Leyte. Handiest are the air-con vans run by Duptours and **Van Vans** (📞 0927 270 2975; P Inocintes St). These run every 30 minutes until 4.30pm to Tacloban (P150, 2¾ hours) and Ormoc (P130, two hours). A few local buses make trips to both places in double the time for about the same price.

Direct flights now connect the island with Cebu. Air Juan (www.airjuan.com) operates two direct weekly flights between Biliran airfield (8km south of Naval) and Cebu.

From Naval, Roble Shipping (p290) sends a roll-on, roll-off ferry (RORO; P480, nine hours) to Cebu City at 8.30pm on Sundays and Tuesdays.

ℹ️ Getting Around

Public transport is sporadic so you're best off exploring the island by motorcycle. *Habal-habal* cost about P1000 for an all-day trip around the island. Hotels can arrange scooters or try **Norkis** (Vicentillo St; per day P400; ⊙ 8am-6pm Mon-Sat).

Biliran Island

The **bus terminal** (P Inocintes St) in Naval is at the public market next to the pier. From here buses and jeepneys make regular daily trips from Naval north to Kawayan (P25, 45 minutes) via Almeria until 5pm. Rickety buses head across the island to Caibiran roughly hourly until 4pm (P50, one hour), and there are a few morning trips to Bunga via Cabucgayan along the southern route (P40, 1½ hours).

Pedicabs are the way around the towns. Local trips cost P5 to P10.

Naval

☑ 053 / POP 56,500

Naval (nah-*vahl*), the provincial capital, is stretched along a road from a handful of government buildings to the low-rise harbour area. There's little to do here but it makes a handy base for day trips. The **Provincial Tourism Information Office** (☑ 053-500 9571; http://tourism.biliranisland.com; Naval-Caibiran Cross Country Rd; ⊘ 8am-5pm Mon-Fri) can help with ideas. There are several ATMs in town.

🛏 Sleeping & Eating

D'Mei Residence Inn Naval   HOTEL **$$**

(☑ 053-500 9796; www.facebook.com/dmeiresidenceinn; 213 P Inocentes St; r P900-1600; 🕸 🛜) This smart little hotel has modern, clean rooms with hot-water en suites. It's the best of the two D'Mei hotels in Biliran. Some rooms enjoy mountain views and there's a handy minimart on the ground floor and a restobar for drinks and meals. It's 1km east of the port.

Chamorita Resort   RESORT **$$**

(☑ 0918 608 3499; www.chamoritarp.com; Km 1018; r with fan P500, with air-con P950-1500; 🕸 🛜) This waterfront resort in Catmon, 7km south of Naval, has fine-value, very comfortable rooms, plus a great bar loaded with booze and bar games. Rooms have great big beds and flat-screens. There's no real beach but several hang-out pavilions provide prime sea views. American owner Leo is a fountain of information on Biliran.

★ **Jelo's Place**   CAFE **$$**

(☑ 053-500 3032; P Inocentes St; snacks & meals P60-240; ⊘ 8am-9pm; 🛜) Popular cafe-restaurant serving filling breakfasts, Filipino dishes, sandwiches and burgers and pasta. There's one of the best cake selections in all the Visayas – try Jelo's signature mousse cake or the green-tea cake. It's air-conditioned and there's a small store selling international foods.

D'Adaone   INTERNATIONAL **$$**

(☑ 053-500 9796; www.facebook.com/dadaonebarandrestaurant; 213 P Inocentes St; mains P110-220; ⊘ 11am-midnight, to 9pm Sun; 🕸 🛜) One of Naval's best places to eat or drink, on the 2nd floor of D'Mei Residence Inn Naval, offering tasty Western and Asian dishes. Doubles as a lounge bar with live acoustic music on Saturdays.

North of Naval

The pretty stretch of coast from Naval to Kawayan is the only part of the island that is easy to explore by public transport. Beyond Kawayan, the road is mostly sealed all the way around the northeastern part of the island to Caibiran, but public transport along this stretch is rare.

Sights here include several impressive waterfalls, the **Sampao Rice Terraces**, **Agta Beach** (from where boat trips can be organised) and **Masagongsong**, known for its natural springs.

The 25m-high **Ulan-Ulan Falls** are some of the most spectacular in Biliran. A short scramble above Ulan-Ulan are a second set, Recoletos Falls, with a wonderful natural swimming pool. *Habal-habal* drivers from Almeria or Naval charge about P500 return including an hour waiting time. The closest village is Sampao, from where it's a 15-minute walk to the falls.

Agta Beach Resort (☑ 0906 225 6265; http://agtabeachresort.com; Km 1038; d P1500-3500; 🕸 🛜 ⊠) is a popular hotel with several pools, Biliran's only dive centre (P1800 per dive including all gear) and a multitude of tours and excursions to offshore islands and around Biliran.

East & South of Naval

To the south of the cross-country road you'll see several peaks, including **Biliran Volcano**, which last erupted in 1939; it can be climbed in a steady 1½ hours. Check with the provincial tourism office in Naval for directions. You will need to hire a guide, which can be arranged in Caibiran at barangay Pulang Yuta.

There are several waterfalls in the area including **Tomalistis Falls**, **Casiawan Falls** (P50) and **Kasabangan Falls** (P20).

Higatangan Island

Due west of Naval is Higatangan Island, where a shifting white sandbar is good for swimming and snorkelling. On the western side of the island, accessible by boat only, is a series of interesting rock formations with small sandy bays between them. Former President Marcos, along with fellow resistance members, reportedly took refuge on the island in WWII, and Marcos Hill is named in his memory.

There's accommodation on the island in the form of the simple and welcoming **Higatangan Island Beach Resort** (☎0910 573 5963; www.higatanganislandresort.com; hut P500, r P800-1800; ❄📶); its owners can arrange bike and boat hire.

There are daily bangkas (noon and 1pm) from Naval (P60, 45 minutes), and the boats leave in the other direction at 7.30am, so overnighting is a must if you're using public transport. A one-way charter costs around P1600.

Maripipi Island

☎053 / POP 7300

Off the northwest tip of Biliran, this dramatic island is dominated by dormant Maripipi Volcano (924m). On the north side of Maripipi is delightful **Napo Beach Resort** (☎0921 212 5164; www.napobeachresort.com; r P1000-2500; ❄📶🏊), which offers scuba diving and real isolation.

From Kawayan you can arrange an all-day island-hopping trip (P2500) taking in Maripipi and the tiny neighbouring **Sambawan Island**, which has fine snorkelling and diving around Biliran.

Sambawan Dive Camp & Beach Resort (☎0918 910 2141; www.facebook.com/sambawandivecampbeachresort; bungalows P2500) is the only accommodation on Sambawan Island, with simple beach bungalows.

One or two daily passenger boats leave from Naval to Maripipi (P70, 1½ hours) midmorning, returning the following day. Or hire a bangka (one way P2000, 45 minutes) at the pier in Kawayan, 18km north of Naval.

A *habal-habal* (P300) can take you around the 27km circumference of Maripipi in an hour or so.

SAMAR

The word most often associated with Samar is 'rugged'. It has a heavily forested, virtually impenetrable interior, around which runs a beautiful coastline of turquoise bays, secret surf breaks, towering cliffs and sandy beaches. Not surprisingly, Samar tends to draw a more adventurous tourist – the spelunker; the canyoner; the diehard surfer looking for an undiscovered break. Transport connections are quite good between the main towns, but to really explore Samar, a motorbike and lack of time pressure are ideal. The main language of Samar is Waray-Waray.

Parts of northern Samar have long been a refuge for small groups of the New People's Army (NPA). The conflict has died down in recent years, and any action tends to occur in the remote hinterlands and does not affect tourists.

History

Magellan first set foot in the Philippines here in 1521, on the tiny island of Homonhon (off the deep south of Samar). During the Philippine-American war, Samar was the scene of some of the bloodiest battles. Tales of brutal combat wove their way into US Marine Corps folklore, and for years after the war American veterans of the campaign were toasted in mess halls by their fellow marines with, 'Stand, gentlemen, he served on Samar'.

ℹ Getting There & Away

There's a daily PAL flight from Manila to Calbayog and a few weekly PAL flights to Manila from Catarman. Regular roll-on, roll-off (RORO) ferries sail from Matnog, Sorsogon, in Luzon to Allen.

Tacloban (in Leyte) is the main gateway to southern Samar. There are very regular vans and buses from this city to many towns in Samar.

The road that runs (most of the way) around Samar is sealed, but not always in very good shape. Be ready to be jarred by a few potholes.

Catarman

☎055 / POP 96,600

Catarman, the somewhat dilapidated capital of seldom-visited northern Samar region is not a destination to hang around long – it's a port city with no sights for travellers and

Samar

perennially sultry air. That said, there are some pretty beaches nearby that occasionally get surf and Catarman airport is a useful gateway to northern Samar.

Sleeping & Eating

⭐ SaSa Pension House   GUESTHOUSE $
(☎ 055-251 8415; sasapensionhouse@yahoo.com; Jacinto St; r P500-1200; ✳🛜) Offering fine value and a convenient location, Sasa has 15 smart, modern rooms with air-con and private hot-water bathrooms; the 'executive' options have bath-tubs. Wi-fi is speedy and staff is friendly.

North Hill Pension   HOTEL $
(☎ 055-500 9085; F Marcos St; s P450-600, d P650-900; ✳🛜) A clean, attractively designed budget hotel in a great central location. Staff are helpful and the air-con singles in particular are great value.

⭐ Café Eusebio Bed & Breakfast   B&B $$
(☎ 055-500 9245; www.facebook.com/cafe-eusebio-bed-and-breakfast; cnr Annunciacion & Marcos Sts; d incl breakfast P2000-3000; ✳🛜) Offering real character in the centre of town, this classy, artistically designed B&B has rooms with magnificent dark-wood floors, designer sinks, hip lighting, lush beds and huge flat-screens. Also home to a great cafe, with the best cakes in town.

Binang & Cadio Resort   RESORT $$
(☎ 0906 213 1611; www.binang-and-cadio.com; Bobon Beach; d P1850; ✳🛜🏊) A well-run, family-owned resort on an enticing sweep of Bobon Beach. Spacious rooms with terraces are grouped around a pool area.

Miko Miko Resort   RESORT $$$
(☎ 0917 856 3124; www.mikomiko.com.ph; cottage incl breakfast P5000; ✳🛜🏊) The first higher-end accommodation to open on northern

Samar's stunning coastline, Miko Miko features five smart cottages and an infinity pool set above a wind-swept beach. Its remote feeling makes for a great romantic getaway. However, service is spotty and at these rates should be better. It's 10km east of Catarman.

Isla Cafe   CAFE $
(GH del Pilar St; meals P100-250; ⊘8am-7.30pm; ❋🛜) A fine cafe with air-con, functional wi-fi, Western and Pinoy food, various coffee drinks and delicious cakes in busy downtown Catarman.

★**Our Nest Restaurant**   FILIPINO $$
(🗹055-500 9659; F Marcos St; mains P85-300; ⊘10am-midnight; 🛜) This stylish restaurant is the best in town, serving great seafood, chicken, beef, pork and pasta and some Chinese dishes. Order the 'sexy ribs' (P300), sizzling squid (P280) or canton noodles (P200).

🍷 **Drinking & Nightlife**

Lucas Place   BAR
(Catarman Diversion Rd 2; ⊘6pm-1am) 2km southwest of the centre, this barn of a place hosts the best live acts in town.

ℹ️ **Getting There & Away**

PAL connects Catarman with Manila with four early-morning flights a week. The airport is 3km from town (P120 for a private tricycle, P20 for a public one).

Jeepneys to Allen depart from the bus terminal every 30 minutes until 6.30pm (P60, 1¼ hours), while vans (roughly half-hourly) by **Grand Tours** (🗹0917 510 9240; www.vsgrandtours.com; JP Rizal Ave) and **D'Turbanada Transport** (🗹055-500 9724; Balite St) take the cross-country road via Lope de Vega to Calbayog (P110, two hours); some continue on to Tacloban (P345, five hours), departing until 5pm. Mostly morning buses serve Manila (ordinary/air-con P880/1200, 16 hours).

Biri Island

🗹055 / POP 11,850

At the centre of the marine-protected Balicuatro group of islands, Biri is known for its marvellously bizarre rock formations, tidal pools and sea waterfalls. There's great surf on occasion near the rock formations, especially from October to January.

Biri Island can be done as a day trip or you can sleep here; just be aware that electricity is erratic and cut off at midnight.

Some of the most renowned **rock formations** are 2km to 3km from Biri town. Head to the northeast edge of the island, where two boardwalks take you halfway out to the offshore formations. Many Filipino film directors have used this location for location shoots. Continue to the rocks via a vast tidal area where some prime swimming holes have formed; a few are deep enough to snorkel in.

The cliff-like Magasang and Magsapad formations are our favourites. If the tide allows, walk behind them and observe the incredible power of the open ocean as it meets the land here. If it's calm you can jump in and snorkel off the west side of Magasang. Many reef fish, moray eels and even banded sea snakes are spotted here.

The best waves for **surfing** are at Sitio Cogon on Talisay Island. You can go scuba diving through **Biri Resort & Dive Centre** (🗹0915 509 0604; http://biri-resort.com; Biri town; r P1500-2500; ❋🛜), which heads to 15 different sites around the islands and is working to restore the island's damaged coral reefs through the BIRI Initiative (http://biri-initiative.org).

Homey **Glenda's B&B** (🗹0926 743 5479; johnryan55599@yahoo.com; barangay Sto Niño; r P1100-1400; ❋🛜) has attractive, spacious rooms, good food, a nice waterfront location, and – importantly – battery-operated fans. It's near the boat landing in barangay Sto Niño, 2km south of Biri town proper.

Villa Amor (🗹0935 366 1415; www.facebook.com/biriislandsvillaamor; Biri town; d with fan/air-con P900/1400; ❋🛜) is a three-storey shorefront hotel with well-kept, spacious rooms and a lush sea-facing garden partly shaded by palms. It's run by helpful folk who offer free paddle- and surfboards for guests, and there's a rooftop terrace perfect for sundowners (or as a yoga deck).

ℹ️ **Getting There & Away**

Boats from Lavezares (P50, one hour), 8km from Allen, leave for Biri when full until 5.30pm or so, or you can take a special trip for P500. Most mornings there is a cargo and passenger boat to Matnog (P150, 1½ hours). *Habal-habal* charge P70 for one-way rides to rock formations, or around P300 for an excursion around the island.

Allen

🗹055 / POP 26,800

This port town services the ferry route between northern Samar and southern Luzon. A word of advice: if it's getting late, stay the night in Allen and catch a morning boat. You do not want to be benighted in Matnog (over in Luzon), where the ferries arrive.

Located incongruously next to a meat shop, just north of Dap Dap pier, **Kinabranan Lodge** (☑ 0917 324 6328; d P900; ❋ 🛜) has modern, well-designed rooms with plush beds and plasma TV. **AllenYon Silogan** (www.facebook.com/allenyonsilog; Rizal St; meals P39-80; ☺ 6am-8pm) is a bright, popular and very inexpensive little cafe for Pinoy comfort grub including tasty breakfasts and meat and fish dishes

ⓘ Getting There & Away

Roll-on, roll-off (RORO) ferries from Allen to Matnog (P120, 1½ to two hours) are operated by several companies at the main **Balwharteco Pier** (☑ 055-300 2041; terminal fee P20). There are no set schedules, but expect a departure at least every two hours round the clock. Call the pier for weather and schedule updates. Some Matnog–bound ferries use the much mellower Dap Dap pier, 2km south of town. **FastCat** (☑ 0998 845 3321; http://fastcat.com.ph; San Isidro port) fastcraft sail from San Isidro port, 16km south of Allen, to Matnog (P144, 1½ hours) four times daily.

Vans depart Allen for Calbayog (P100, 1¾ hours), then Catbalogan, then Tacloban through **Grand Tours** (☑ 0917 700 8071; www.vsgrandtours.com) roughly every hour. There'll usually be one waiting by the pier. Jeepneys run to Catarman (P60, 1¼ hours) up until 6pm.

Dalupiri Island

More commonly called San Antonio after its only municipality, Dalupiri has good beaches and clear water, and is close to the mainland. Such is its appeal, this is the kind of place where you can expect to get stranded longer than you planned.

There is a growing range of chilled-out accommodation options on the beachfront. Electricity is off from 6am to noon each day, so rooms can be hot if there is no breeze.

The neighbouring forested island of **Capul**, to the west, has an even slower pace of life and is definitely worth a day trip, or an extended stay. Or head to the remote but idyllic **Seven Islands** for pink-sand beaches and total isolation.

🛏 Sleeping

Haven of Fun   RESORT $
(☑ 0917 303 1656; www.havenoffunbeachresort.com; San Antonio; r with fan P700-1000, with air-con P1400-2000; ❋ 🛜) Well-established and pret-

tily landscaped Haven of Fun is just a short walk from the pier. There's a good selection of rooms including cute little thatched cottages and a good restaurant. Cash only.

Capul Island Beach Resort   RESORT $
(☑ 0919 680 1454; www.facebook.com/capulislandbeachresort; Capul Island; r with fan/air-con P600/1200; ❋) This chilled out Capul resort has four rooms in a guesthouse on the beach and a large villa with two additional bedrooms.

7 Islands Resort   RESORT $$
(☑ in Dalupiri 0917 336 9740; www.7islandsresort.com; Sila Island; r from P1500) Large thatched bungalows with private bathrooms directly on a crescent-shaped pinkish-sand beach on remote Sila Island. To book rooms and boat transfers, contact the Swedish-Filipino owners of Crystal Sand Beach Resort in nearby Dalupiri, who manage the resort, well in advance.

**Birmingham Allen
Beach Resort**   RESORT $$
(☑ in Cebu 032-911 2696; http://birminghamallen.com; r P2000-3200; ❋ 🛜 ⛶) This new shoreside place (there's no real beach) has four elegant modern rooms with all mod cons (some with four-poster beds) in a compound that enjoys fine sea views. There's good food available too.

Crystal Sand Beach Resort   RESORT $$
(☑ 0917 336 9740; www.crystalsandbeachresort.weebly.com; San Antonio; d with fan P500-1400, with air-con P1300-1500; ❋ 🛜) This long-running Swedish-owned beach resort is up from the village centre with a great location 500m off a marine sanctuary. Accommodation is a little old-fashioned, with rooms in a dusty-pink concrete structure and simple bungalows better suited to the beach location. Snorkelling trips to Seven Islands are offered.

ⓘ Getting There & Away

Public boats to San Antonio (P30, 25 minutes) leave when full from Victoria, 8km southeast of Allen. To avoid waiting awhile, spill out P400 for a special trip. Additionally there are three or four daily bangkas to San Antonio from the Dap Dap pier in Allen (P40, 45 minutes).

Public bangkas leave Capul in the early morning bound for Allen's Balwharteco Pier and Matnog, Sorsogon (both P100, about one hour); return trips are around 11am from Allen, and around 10am from Matnog.

Calbayog

☑ 055 / POP 188,600

This large city lies on both banks of the broad Calbayog river and is a useful transport hub, with an airport and ferry connections. If not exactly scenic or cosmopolitan, it's a pleasant enough place for a stopover if you're heading south or north.

Ciriaco Hotel (☑ 055-533 9300; www.ciriaco hotel.com; National Rd, Km 735; r incl breakfast P2700-3100; ❋ ☎ ☀) is the highest-end hotel in Calbayog, located 2km southeast of the centre. It boasts business-class rooms with quality furnishings, plus has a pool big enough for laps and sea views. It also runs tours to waterfalls and other natural attractions in the area.

If you're on a budget **Eduardo's Hotel** (☑ 055-553 9996; Pajarito St; d with fan/air-con from P650/800; ❋ ☎) is walking distance from many cafes and restaurants.

At **S&R Bed & Breakfast** (☑ 055-533 9026; http://srbedbreakfast.blogspot.co.uk; National Hwy; d incl breakfast P1300-1650; ❋ ☎) five immaculate rooms come with a huge flat-screen and great bed with reading light. Located 2.5km west of town, close to the airport.

The most authentic Filipino food in the area, served in an open-sided nipa hall, is at **Kamayan Sa Carayman** (☑ 055-301 1258, 0906 532 0327; Carayman; mains P120-495; ☉ 10am-10pm). Feast on chilli crab or grilled fish, butter chicken and crispy *pata* (deep-fried pork hock or knuckles). Portions are huge. Located 4km east of the centre in barangay Carayman, 100m off the highway.

Carlos & Carmelo's (Nijaga St; mains P150-200; ☉ 8am-9pm, to midnight or later Fri & Sat; ☎) serves tasty burgers, pasta, bar food and perhaps the best ribs in eastern Visayas, plus live music on Fridays and Saturdays.

❶ Getting There & Away

PAL fly between Calbayog and Manila three times a week. Cebu Pacific connects Cebu City with Calbayog with four weekly flights. The airport is 6km west of town, just off the coastal highway.

Grand Tours (☑ 055-209 6177; www.vsgrand tours.com; Marharlika Hwy, 700m east of centre) has the most van services to and from Calbayog, with vans every 30 minutes to Catbalogan (P100, 1½ hours), and at least hourly to Allen (P110, 1¾ hours) and Catarman (P110, two hours). Change in Catbalogan for points further south; vans stop running at 5pm. There are other van companies (all on the coastal highway east of town) including

Duptours (☑ 055-534 3020; Marharlika Hwy) which has vans to Catbalogan (P100, 1½ hours) and Tacloban (P220, 4½ hours) and **D'Turbanada** (☑ 055-533 9822; Marharlika Hwy) for Catarman (P110, two hours).

Local buses and jeepneys can take double the time of the vans and don't save you much money. They depart from the new **bus terminal** (Magsaysay Ext; ☉ 24hr) 2km southeast of town, or flag them down on the highway.

Cokaliong Shipping (p290) has ferries to Cebu City (from P850, 12 hours) on Tuesday, Thursday and Saturday at 7pm, departing from the pier in Maguino-o, 20km north of Calbayog. From the city pier, there is a bangka to Masbate (P600, six hours) departing Fridays and Sundays at 8am.

Catbalogan

☑ 055 / POP 106,100

Catbalogan, the capital of Samar Province, was founded in 1596 by Spanish missionaries. This port city has a long history, though apart from the odd colonial-era church its sights are few. Nevertheless it's a possible base for exploring the interior of Samar, with its spelunking, climbing, birdwatching and canyoning opportunities. From Catbalogan's piers you can spot about 30 different islands offshore, plus some giant peaks on Biliran Island off Leyte.

In Pieta Park, the **Doña Paz Memorial** is for the victims of the 1987 Doña Paz ferry disaster; most of the 4300 or so victims were from Catbalogan and elsewhere on Samar. Just 24 people survived.

Trexplore   CAVING
(☑ 0919 294 3865, 055-251 2301; www.trexplore. weebly.com; Allen Ave; tours from P2500) Run by Joni Bonifacio, Trexplore is the one-stop shop for Samar adventure tours. Caving, canyoning, trekking and mountain-biking trips are offered. The **Jiabong caves** tour, near Catbalogan, is one of the Visayas' top one-day adventures. One-third of the six-hour tour, which ends with a pleasant 45-minute paddle in a dugout canoe, is spent swimming underground in full spelunking kit.

🛏 Sleeping & Eating

Rolet Hotel   HOTEL $
(☑ 055 251 5512; Mabini Ave; d P950; ❋ ☎) A convenient location in the thick of it, a few blocks from the port. Rooms have been renovated (though some are windowless) with efficient air-con and hot showers. Great value.

Summers Garden
Pension House GUESTHOUSE $

(☑055-251 5135; Del Rosario St; r incl breakfast P700-1300; ❄ 🛜) This creaky old house with a patio and garden out front will suit those looking for homey accommodation. The rooms are simple, clean and well kept (though some are very small); you pay extra for air-con.

★M Grand Royale Resort HOTEL $$
(☑055-251 5555; https://mgrandroyale.com; Executive Heights, Guinsorongan; r incl breakfast P2450-3950; ❄ 🏊) This hilltop hotel enjoys wonderful views of the Catbalogan bay and its islets, particularly at sunset. Rooms are smart and well equipped, the pool is huge and there's a free shuttle service to the city centre.

San Francisco Hotel HOTEL $$
(☑055-543 8384; hotelsanfranciscocatbalogan@yahoo.com.ph; San Francisco St; d incl breakfast P1450-1700, tr from P2500; ❄ 🛜) Modish hotel with a contemporary design and modern art hanging about. The rooms aren't quite as snazzy as the lobby might indicate, and are on the small side, but still inviting and competitively priced. There's a rooftop terrace for drinks.

Green Hub Diner FILIPINO $
(City Plaza; mains P50-180; ⊙9am-8pm; 🛜🍴) A funky, hip little cafe serving lots of vegetarian dishes including delicious, nutritious salads, *lumpia* (spring rolls) and juices using locally sourced ingredients. Chicken burgers and seafood are also available.

103 Bar & Grill PUB
(cnr Callejon St & Allen Ave; ⊙4pm-1am) Popular bar with happy hour (4pm to 7.30pm) and live music at weekends. Try its sizzling Filipino dishes (meals P60 to P200) too.

❶ Getting There & Away

Duptours (☑0907 276 4342; Allen Ave) and **Grand Tours** (☑055-251 5243; www.vsgrandtours.com; San Bartolomew St) vans head to Tacloban (P130, two hours) and Calbayog (P100, 1½ hours) until 6pm or so. Duptours has two to three daily trips to Borongan (P200, four hours) while Grand Tours has services directly to Catarman (P160, three hours). For Allen transfer in Calbayog. **D'Turbanada** (100 Mabini Ave) also has vans to points north and south in Samar.

Much slower buses run on all the above routes. There are also two daily buses to Guiuan (P210, 5½ hours, last trip noon) and three daily services to Borongan (P140, five hours, last trip 1pm). Buray, a 30-minute ride southeast of

Catbalogan, has additional services to Taft and Borongan. The **bus station** (Rizal Av) is next to the port.

Buses to Manila (ordinary P1150, air-con from P1300, 18 hours) leave fairly regularly around the clock. These buses do not accept passengers for local trips, you have to pay the full fare to Manila.

Roble Shipping Lines (p290) runs to and from Cebu City (P625, 12 hours) on Fridays at 7pm from Catbalogan wharf.

Borongan
☑053 / POP 70,900
Borongan is a genuine beach town. The spiritual centre is honey-brown Baybay Beach, where barbecue shacks and vendors of all stripes line a long boulevard. Head here to catch the sunrise, jog, bodysurf or, in the late afternoon, imbibe cheap beer with the locals. Baybay Beach has five 'stations' – Baybay 1 is to the south, Baybay 5 to the north.

The capital of Eastern Samar Province, Borongan is a good base for travellers or surfers who want to explore Samar's largely untouched Pacific coastline. While the southern bits of the province took a direct hit from Typhoon Yolanda in 2013, Borongan and points north were spared heavy damage.

☉ Sights & Activities

Borongan is a surf town. When the waves are up (October to March, with December and January prime months), the local surfing cabal emerges to take advantage on Baybay or on the next beach south, **Bato Beach**. There's no organised board rental in Borongan, but resident surfers can scare up a board if you ask, or head south to Maydolong, where Surf Omawas (p340) rents boards.

The dense jungle around Borongan has waterfalls and caves to explore. **Huplag Speleo** (☑0928 995 0449; http://huplagspeleo.weebly.com) is a local group of spelunkers who run caving and other adventure tours.

Just offshore from Borongan, pretty little **Divinubo Island** is ringed by white-sand beaches and has a few secret surf breaks. There's a lighthouse built by the Americans in 1906. It's a good spot to take a picnic. To get here, take a tricycle to barangay Lalawigan south of town (P50, 15 minutes), where you can wait for a boat to fill up (P20 per person) or charter a special trip (P300, 15 minutes).

🛏 Sleeping & Eating

GV Hotel
HOTEL $

(☑ 055-560 9791; www.gvhotels.com.ph; Circumferential Rd; r with fan/air-con from P550/750; ✲🕾) Yes it's a rather bland budget chain hotel, but the GV is actually one of Borongan's better budget options with neat small rooms and efficient air-conditioning. Located inland, 1km north of the centre.

Surf Omawas
B&B $

(☑ 0932 934 3164; www.surfomawas.com; Maydolong; r incl surfboard rental P700; 🕾) This surf camp is on the beach in Omawas, a barangay of Maydolong, 17km south of Borongan. It's run by a Californian and his local wife and has clean, well-presented rooms with en suites. There are ample surf mags to browse and, of course, a choice of boards.

★ Primea Hotel
HOTEL $$

(☑ 055-560 9618; www.primeahotel.com.ph; G Abogado St; r P1650-2650, ste P2775 incl breakfast; ✲🕾☒) With a strong contemporary feel throughout, Primea has a wide choice of rooms, all presented in soothing shades of beige and cream, with good quality mattresses and bed linen; the more expensive options have balconies. The pool is for dipping in and out rather than swimming lengths. In the centre of town, just north of the bridge.

Boro Bay Hotel
HOTEL $$

(☑ 0936 604 2336, 0917 533 5618; www.facebook.com/borobayhotel; Baybay 5; d incl breakfast P1200-3500; ✲🕾) Enjoying a quiet location towards the northern end of Baybay Beach, this is Borongan's fanciest hotel. Rooms are spacious and nicely designed, with flat-screen TV. Wi-fi coverage is poor and service is friendly, though a little spotty.

Starbeach Cafe
CAFE $

(☑ 055-560 9362; www.facebook.com/starbeach cafeborongan; Baybay Blvd; mains P50-140; ◷7am-9pm; 🕾) Smart beach-facing cafe offering burgers, noodle dishes, pastries (try the empanadas) and Filipino snacks. Good fruit shakes too. It also offers a delivery service.

Domsowir Restaurant
FILIPINO $

(☑ 055-560 9093; off Cinco St; mains P60-180; ◷7am-9pm; ✲🕾) The long-running Domsowir has a great location on the riverbank, a good range of Filipino food and some Chinese-style dishes.

510 Shots & Grill
BAR

(Baybay Blvd; ◷9am-midnight) On the boulevard, this restobar has popular acoustic sessions and reggae nights. There's a lively vibe on weekends and a full food menu.

ℹ Information

The **tourist office** (☑ 0917 426 9167; muntour@ yahoo.com; Baybay Beach 2; ◷8am-5pm Mon-Fri) has a city map and brochures and can help you get to the nearby islands.

ℹ Getting There & Away

Vans are your best bet to or from Tacloban, with **Duptours** (Real St; ◷hourly until 5pm) and Guiuan Express (less frequently from the bus terminal) doing trips (P230, four hours) via Basey. Duptours has three daily vans to Catbalogan (P100, four hours).

From the **bus terminal** (off Cinco St), hourly jeepneys serve Guiuan until 2pm (P125, 3½ hours), and local buses serve Catbalogan three times daily (P140, five hours). A better way to get to Catbalogan is on a morning Manila–bound bus; there are several offices in town.

Guiuan

☑ 053 / POP 54,600

The literal and metaphorical end of the bumpy road to the southeastern tip of Samar, Guiuan (ghee-won) is recovering well after being flattened by Typhoon Yolanda, which made its first landfall here. Protected by Calicoan Island, Guiuan was fortunately spared the type of storm surge that killed so many people elsewhere – miraculously fewer than 200 people died here as record 400km/h winds pummelled the town. But the storm nonetheless destroyed or heavily damaged most buildings.

Today reconstruction is ongoing, but the town is very much up and running again and its people are welcoming.

⊙ Sights

Weather Station
VIEWPOINT

During WWII, the US military transformed the area into a launching pad for attacks on Japan, and it was once the largest PT (patrol boat) base in the world, with as many as 300 boats and 150,000 troops stationed here, including a young future–President Kennedy. You can walk up to the weather station, 4km east of Guiuan, for sweeping views across the Pacific Ocean and Leyte Gulf. The 2km,

US-built runway below was instrumental in getting in relief supplies post-Yolanda.

🛏 Sleeping & Eating

★ Tanghay View Lodge
RESORT $

(☑0936 531 9495; susan_guiuan@yahoo.com.ph; Luboc; r with fan & shared bathroom P400-500, with air-con P700-1500; ❄️🛜) Managed for many years by gregarious Susan Tan, Tanghay is a three-storey structure with tidy rooms (in many categories) and a waterfront restaurant opposite Tubabao Island. Susan is a great source of information on southern Samar and can arrange tours to the islands.

Marcelo's Restotel
HOTEL $

(☑0905 372 3637; Luboc; r P900; ❄️🛜) Teal-green Marcelo's has no-nonsense air-con rooms that are fine value for Samar. Most rooms sleep three. It's around 1km west of the centre, just off the sea.

Addison Pension House
GUESTHOUSE $

(☑055-271 2682; Lugay St; r P1150; ❄️🛜) This centrally located minihotel is perhaps a little soulless but certainly doable for a night or two. Its functional rooms have en suites and bright bedspreads and there's a little cafe on the 1st floor for drinks and meals.

Amy's BBQ
BARBECUE $$

(☑0997 230 7225; www.facebook.com/amysbbqplace; Luboc; mains P100-280; ⏱6am-midnight; 🛜) Norwegian Klaus and Amy run this friendly place in Luboc. They serve giant pork chops (marinated for 24 hours) or concoct a mean salad if you want some greens. There's live acoustic on weekends and a convivial crowd most nights.

Tanghay View Lodge
FILIPINO $$

(Luboc; meals P70-180; ⏱7am-9.30pm; 🛜) Dine by the river on the huge deck at this very popular hotel restaurant. The menu includes Filipino and Chinese dishes; try the speciality: stir-fried conch with ginger.

ℹ️ Information

The very helpful **tourist office** (TIPC; ☑0927 458 1175; jetanairsel@yahoo.com; City Plaza; ⏱9am-noon & 1-7pm) can provide information on the surrounding region, and doubles as a souvenir store.

ℹ️ Getting There & Away

Vans are the best way to Tacloban; there are departures about every half-hour with Duptours, Van Vans and Guiuan Express until 5pm (P180,

3½ hours). From the bus station behind the market, slow local buses serve Tacloban until 3.30pm (P140, six hours), and jeepneys serve Borongan until 1pm (P200, 3¾ hours).

Calicoan Island

☑053 / POP 7400

Easily accessible by bridge from Guiuan, Calicoan Island took a direct hit from Typhoon Yolanda. However, the island has now made a fine recovery: its beaches remain beautiful and its famous waves still delight surfers.

Continuing south, the fishing village of **Sulangan** on neighbouring Sulangan Island is linked by bridge to Calicoan's southeastern tip. You'll find some amazing white-sand beaches and swimming around here.

The best surfing is two-thirds of the way down the island at **ABCD Beach**, named after the four reef breaks along this coast, and also after 'Advance Base Construction Depot', which is one for the WWII buffs. It has great left- and right-handed reef breaks between June and October. The ABCD Surf Community, led by local surf guru **Jun Jun** (☑0917 765 6797; lesson per hour incl board rental P500), is based in a nipa hut here.

Rustic **White Sand Beach Resort** (☑0927 214 7386; www.facebook.com/whitesandbeachresortsulangan; hut P700) enjoys a wonderful beach setting and has cute little nipa huts (with fans) for affordable prices. It is isolated, but that's the point.

Near the bridge at the far southern end of Calicoan, **La Luna Beach Resort** (☑0917 324 3129; www.resortlaluna.com; d with fan/air-con incl breakfast P2200/2500; ❄️🛜🏊) is one of Samar's best. Spacious rooms are elegant, with high ceilings, lofts and wood furniture; two have direct sea views. It's best known for owner Giampo's home-cooking (meals P220 to P350); drop by for lunch or dinner.

Calicoan Villa (☑0917 206 9602; www.calicoanvilla.com; ABCD Beach; huts P1200, d P2000-3000, cottage P1500-2500; ❄️🛜🏊) has a pool and restaurant right opposite the surf break. There are four smart rooms in a villa by the ocean, three (large, fan-cooled) surf huts and eight new cottages across the road.

Multicabs and jeepneys run roughly hourly between Guiuan and Sulangan via ABCD Beach (P20), or you can hire a tricycle (P180). The last transport back to Guiuan is around 4.30pm.

Mindanao

Best Places to Eat

➡ Claude's le Cafe de Ville (p370)

➡ Guerrera (p354)

➡ Kawayan (p364)

➡ Panagatan (p348)

Best Places to Stay

➡ Harana (p363)

➡ Balai sa Baibai (p354)

➡ Siargao Island Emerald House (p363)

➡ Ponce Suites Art Hotel (p368)

➡ Kalinaw Resort (p363)

Why Go?

Despite jaw-dropping beaches, surf, rugged mountains and indigenous cultures living much as they have for centuries, Mindanao, with the exception of Siargao and to an extent Camiguin, remains off the tourism industry's radar. Of course, the conflict that has simmered for several generations bears much of the responsibility for this. That's not to say, however, that there isn't development and the woes that go with it – the southern city of Davao is, for example, fairly cosmopolitan.

Though big and bulky, Mindanao's varied ethnographic make-up, competing land claims and highly prized natural resources can make it seem undersized. Since the 1950s Muslims have been outnumbered and currently muster a majority in only five of Mindanao's 21 provinces. Of these five, 14,000 sq km are given over to the Bangsamoro Autonomous Region in Muslim Mindanao (BARMM), an area that includes islands stretching towards Malaysia and Indonesia.

When to Go
Cagayan De Oro

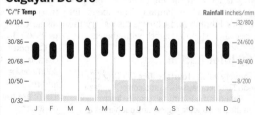

Jun–Sep	Sep–Dec	Nov–Apr
Driest season on the northern and eastern seaboard, but Davao can see heavy rain.	Prime waves at Cloud 9.	Dry season, aside from the northern and eastern seaboard, where it's wet to March.

History & Security

Mindanao's history diverged early on from that of the rest of the Philippines because of geography, and more specifically its proximity to centres of Arab influence. Islam was introduced in the Sulu archipelago in the early 1300s, and was soon after brought to Cotabato and the Lanao area. Afterwards, the region was united by the sultanate and most of the population converted to Islam. When the Spaniards arrived in 1527, they were only able to establish outposts in northern Mindanao and Zamboanga.

It was only in the middle of the 19th century that the Spaniards were able to make substantial inroads in Mindanao and assert their sovereignty. The US became the next colonial power in 1898, but its presence in Mindanao wasn't felt for years, and it wasn't until a decade or so later that the province was formally incorporated as an administrative region under the rule of in Manila.

From the beginning, the rights of tribal minority groups and traditional property rights were violated. The peoples of Mindanao were economically and demographically threatened by the influx of Christian Filipinos from the north, who were encouraged by the government to settle in less populated Mindanao. Some argue that the policy simply opened up a sparsely populated region to immigration and created a more diverse ethnic mix. Others claimed it was the occupation and annexation of their homeland, and armed resistance developed in the late 1960s.

Soon after, large multinational agricultural companies entered the region en masse, impacting small-scale farming and traditional ways of life regardless of ethnicity or religion. Less militant groups, as well as the communist New People's Army (NPA), active in Mindanao, argue that the crux of the conflict is not simply the result of Muslim and Christian populations living together, but the consequence of the exploitation of the island's resources without ensuring that the people see the benefits of development.

In 1976 an agreement was struck with one of the rebel groups, the Moro Islamic National Liberation Front (MNLF), establishing the Autonomous Region of Muslim Mindanao (ARMM); in 1996 the MNLF was legitimised as a political group by Manila. Other groups didn't agree that limited autonomy within a federalised system was adequate (of course, some objected because they weren't considered when divvying up the spoils); as a result a breakaway group, the Moro Islamic

Liberation Front (MILF), was established in 1978. The most radical of the groups was Abu Sayyaf, a small group of former MILF members affiliated with Al Qaeda and Jemaah Islamiyah, an Indonesia–based organisation.

Successive government regimes have tried to assert their control through different means; Marcos tried through a combination of military action and amnesty offers, but it was talks between Cory Aquino and Nur Misuari, the founder of the MNLF, that finally led to a reduction in violence in the late 1980s. Unfortunately, most of the outstanding issues were never resolved, and in the late 1990s and early 2000s the violence resumed.

When Benigno Aquino III came to power in 2010, his government immediately began to engage in peace talks in Malaysia with the leader of the MILF. However, once again, breakaway groups dissatisfied with negotiations brought more violence from both sides. Aquino resisted calls for war, but thousands of civilians were again displaced as a result of air and ground assaults.

In the summer of 2014 a transitional commission of MILF and Aquino administration members finished drafting the Basic Bangsamoro Law (BBL), which granted some of the autonomy sought for decades by Muslim leaders. Observers responded with cautious optimism; however, Congress failed to ratify it. The Mamasapano Massacre in January 2015, in which 44 Philippine special forces soldiers were killed in a raid to capture a Malaysian bomb maker from a MILF stronghold, buried hopes for a peaceful resolution.

When Rodrigo Duterte, the former mayor of Davao, became president in 2016, he vowed to transform the Philippines into a federalised system. When ISIS–affiliated groups including the Maute, as well as foreign fighters, began operating, a negotiated solution seemed even more distant. In late May 2017 Philippine security forces went to Marawi City to arrest Isnilon Hapilon, the ISIS–designated emir of Southeast Asia. Two months later, much of the city was destroyed, with hundreds killed and thousands evacuated, and parts of the city remained in the control of the militants. Hapilon was not captured. The strength and sophistication of the resistance, including an enormous cache of weapons and money, surprised the Philippine security forces. Duterte declared martial law throughout Mindanao, the first time since the rule of Marcos. It was only lifted – after two-and-a-half years – in late 2019. For more on the security situation in the region, see p355.

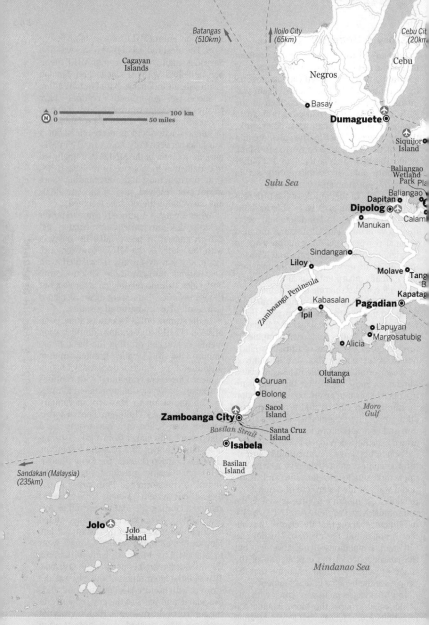

Mindanao Highlights

1 Cloud Nine (p362)
Catching a wave at Siargao's best-known surf break or watching others from its picturesque pavilion.

2 Camiguin (p350)
Hopping from natural springs to waterfalls to underwater coral reefs around this lush island.

3 Sugba Lagoon (p364) Snorkelling around emerald-green waters at this dramatically beautiful spot on Siargao.

Bohol

Jagna

agbilaran

Dinagat
Island

San Ricardo

Surigao

Placer

Pacifico

Sugba
Lagoon ③

Cloud
Nine ①

Siargao
Island

Cantilan

Madrid

Lanuza

Mambajao

Camiguin
Island ②

Camiguin

Guinsiliban

Cabadbaran

Tandag

Bohol
Sea

Kinogitan

Balingoan

Nasipit

Butuan

Cagwait

Gingoog

Bayugan

PHILIPPINE
SEA

Balingasag

Prosperidad

San
Francisco

Jasaan

El Salvador

Bugo

Talacogon

roqueta

Initao

Na-Awan

Cagayan de Oro

Agusan Marsh
Wildlife Sanctuary

Manticao

nenez

Cagayan de Oro
River ④

Iligan

Mt Kitanglad
(2899m)

Malaybalay

Bunawan

Bislig

amiz

Kolambugan

bod

Marawi City

Lake
Lanao

Mt Kalatungan
(2880m)

Valencia

Agusan River

Mindanao

Malabang

Kibawe

Cateel

Nabunturan

Bongo
Island

Sultan
Kudarat

Tagum

Maco

Mabini

Maragusan

Cotabato City

Philippine
Eagle Center ⑦

Calinan

ian

Talayan

Kidapawan ⑥

Mt Apo
(2954m)

Davao ⑤

Samal
Island

Talikud
Island

Mati

Tacurong

Mt Apo
National Park

Mayo Bay

Isulam

oak

Alah
Valley

Lake
Buluan

Digos

Davao
Gulf

Koronadal City
(Marbel)

Surallah

Malita

Lake
Sebu

T'boli

General Santos
(Dadiangas)

Maitum

Alabel

Glan

④ **Cagayan de Oro River**
(p348) Rolling through white
water on a rafting trip through
the countryside.

⑤ **Matina Town Square**
(p370) Bar-hopping and

catching some live music at
this buzzing Davao compound.

⑥ **Mt Apo** (p373) Breathing
in the fresh air and views on
the highest mountain in the
Philippines.

⑦ **Philippine Eagle Center**
(p368) Viewing the world's
largest eagles in this lush
forest sanctuary.

❶ Getting There & Away

AIR

Between **Philippine Airlines** (www.philippineair lines.com) and **Cebu Pacific** (www.cebupacific air.com) there are regular daily flights from Manila to Butuan, Cagayan de Oro, Cotabato, Davao, Dipolog, General Santos, Ozamiz, Surigao and Zamboanga City; from Cebu to Camiguin, Davao, General Santos, Siargao and Zamboanga City; and Cebu Pacific has daily flights between Iloilo City on Panay and Cagayan de Oro and Davao.

Most noteworthy is the new direct service between Manila and Siargao on **Skyjet** (☑ Manila 02-863 1333, mobile 0997 503 5654; www.flyskyjetair.com).

Internationally, Cebu Pacific and **Silk Air** (☑ 082-232 8021; www.silkair.com) have several weekly flights between Davao and Singapore, and Air Asia (www.airasia.com) has flights between Davao and Kuala Lumpur, Malaysia.

BOAT

You can get to Mindanao by boat – **Super Shuttle Ferry** (☑ Cebu 032-412 7688; www.supershuttle roro.com) covers many of these routes – from Bohol, Cebu, Leyte, Luzon, Manila, Negros, Palawan, Panay and Siquijor in the Philippines, and directly from Indonesia (to Zamboanga City).

❶ Getting Around

Most of Mindanao is easily traversed by a mix of buses and minivans. Quality and comfort vary widely within companies and routes. Jeepneys might be required for out-of-the-way locations.

These days it's possible to fly between Camiguin and Siargao, two of the most popular northern Mindanao destinations, with a stop in Cebu (admittedly a long day). Most people choose not to travel overland on the Zamboanga Peninsula and fly from Davao – or less commonly take a **2GO** (☑ Manila 02-528 7000; http://travel.2go.com.ph) ferry from General Santos – to Zamboanga City. Cebu Pacific connects Cagayan de Oro and Zamboanga City with Davao.

NORTHERN MINDANAO

The coastline from Cagayan de Oro to Surigao and the offshore islands off the far northeastern tip is a region apart from the rest of Mindanao. Though largely spared from the violence experienced by other parts of the island, it's often inaccurately stigmatised simply by dint of association. Siargao is one of the best places in the Philippines to hang ten or simply hang. Volcanic Camiguin is seventh heaven for outdoor-lovers, and the university town of Cagayan is both a gate-

way to the region and a base for adventures in the surrounding Bukidnon Province.

Cagayan de Oro

☑ 088 / POP 676,000

Walking the crowded, student-laden downtown streets of Cagayan de Oro (the 'Oro' refers to the gold discovered by the Spanish in the river here), not only do you move faster than traffic, but you also pick up on the energy of youth. Otherwise, it's a mostly ordinary expanding and developing Filipino city with a strong culinary scene. Much of Cagayan's relatively robust economy centres on the Del Monte pineapple-processing plant north of town. Nestlé and Pepsi also make their corporate homes in the Philippines here. Popular with Korean tourists who come for English lessons, the comparatively cool climate and golf, the city is also the base for outdoor adventures such as rafting, hiking, rock climbing and caving.

◉ Sights & Activities

Museum of Three Cultures   MUSEUM
(www.cu.edu.ph; Corrales Ext, Capitol University; P100; ⊙9am-noon & 1.30-5.30pm Mon-Fri, to noon Sat) The three galleries here have an interesting mix of photos, ceramics, art and artefacts, including several huge ceremonial M'rano swords and a full-scale *pangao,* a four-poster bed meant to accommodate the sultan's entire family. It's housed in a building of classrooms on the grounds of Capitol University.

Viajero Outdoor Centre   OUTDOORS
(☑ 0917 708 1568; viajerocdo@yahoo.com; 137 Hayes St) One of the hubs of Cagayan de Oro's outdoor-adventuring community is this one-stop shop run by husband and wife Eric and Reina Bontuyan. They can arrange and guide mountain treks, rock climbing and spelunking in the area, and teach as well.

🛏 Sleeping

GC Suites   HOTEL $
(☑ 088-858 1234; www.gcsuitescdo.com; 4th fl, Hayes St; s/d incl 1 meal P850/1000; ❀ ⃰) Occupying the 4th and 5th floors of a mini-mall with several restaurants, GC Suites is a welcome low-cost addition to this part of town. All rooms have Ikea–level furnishings and 'theme' drawings and quotes on the wall,

Cagayan de Oro

and guests are given a voucher for a meal at one of the six small eateries on the floors below.

Nature's Pensionne   HOTEL **$**
(☎ 088-857 2274; T Chavez St; r P750-1250; ❋ 🛜) This is a professionally run operation, and the all blonde-wood rooms in the 'business class' wing come with modern bathrooms; the older building's rooms have flimsy wooden walls. Just outside is one of the city's most chaotic, tangled bundles of street wiring – in itself, a sight to behold.

VIP Hotel   HOTEL **$$**
(☎ 088-856 2505; www.theviphotel.com.ph; cnr Apolinar Velez & JR Borja Sts; r incl breakfast P1950-2800; ❋ 🛜) Somewhat barren rooms and mismatched furniture in need of an upgrade; however, the centrally located six-storey VIP does have professional staff and a welcoming lobby and restaurant.

MINDANAO CAGAYAN DE ORO

New Dawn Pensionne HOTEL **$$**
(☎ 088-857 1900; www.grandcityhotelscdo.com/
newdawnpensionne; cnr Apolinar Velez & Macaham-
bus Sts; r P1500; ❉ 🛜) This seven-storey hotel
has compact, efficiently designed rooms and
professional and responsive service.

Seda Centrio HOTEL **$$$**
(☎ 088-323 8888; www.sedahotels.com; cnr CM
Recto Hwy & Corrales Ave; d 4200-6500; ❉ 🛜 🏊)
There's no more convenient top-end address than this high-rise attached to one
of Cagayan's premier malls and above the
fray of one of the city's busiest intersections.
Plush bedding and boutique-style bathrooms are the rooms' best features, and the
pool lounge area is relaxed and the nicest
in the city.

🍴 Eating & Drinking

The **Rosario Arcade** (Rosario Cres) in front
of the Limketkai Center is one of Cagayan's
culinary and entertainment centres; the
other primary one is the **Ayala Centrio
Mall** (CM Recto Ave), which is loaded with
restaurants and cafes and a variety of international cuisines. The freshest seafood is
served at **Panagatan** (Opol; mains P125-275;
⊙ 6.30am-10.30pm).

On streets around the **Cogon Market**
(near the intersection of Osmeña and JR
Borja Sts) vendors hawk *isaw* (chicken intestines) for P5 a skewer and the question-
ably appetising *proven* (or *proben*, a fried
mix of parts from the chicken's digestive
system). Also look out for the region's speciality *kinilaw,* raw seafood cured in vinegar
and spiced with *tabon tabon,* a fruit native
to northern Mindanao. Cagayan foodies

claim their city's *lechón baboy* (roasted pig),
stuffed with herbs and spices, is the tastiest in Mindanao. Most grilling gets started
around 6pm.

Mai Cafe CAFE **$**
(Apolinar Velez St; mains P140-170; ⊙ 7am-10pm)
True to its old-school decor of antique plates
and doilies that would make grandma happy,
there's no wi-fi on offer at this postage-
stamp-sized cafe. However, you can enjoy
espresso drinks, cake, pastries, all-day breakfast like eggs and French toast, and lasagne
for later in the day.

**Redtail
Shrimps & More** SEAFOOD **$$**
(☎ 088-855 0004; Apolinar Velez St; mains P155-
345; ⊙ 11am-10pm) No plates and utensils – a
bit of a gimmick – does prompt table photos
of everyone in their bibs and plastic gloves.
No matter how the crabs, prawns, mussels,
tuna and *kinilaw* (raw seafood cured in vin-
egar) make their way into your gullet, you'll
probably be satisfied.

4Daboys Tavern FILIPINO **$$**
(GC Mall, Hayes St; mains P175; ⊙ 11am-midnight)
Filipino comfort food, especially *lechón*
(roast suckling pig) and *kambing* (goat)
dishes, and imported beers like Stella Artois
and Asahi are on offer at this small, dark and
contemporary spot. Two other locations in
the city.

Lokal Grill FILIPINO, SEAFOOD **$$**
(Corrales Ave; mains P120-300; ⊙ noon-2am, to
3am Fri & Sat) In addition to standard Fili-
pino meat and noodle dishes, Lokal does its
own version of *pinakbét* (an Ilocano dish
of mixed vegetables steamed in fish sauce),

WHITEWATER RAFTING IN CAGAYAN DE ORO

The standard three-hour rafting trip (P1200) takes you through 14 Class II to III rapids;
several Class IV rapids are part of an alternative longer trip (P1800, six hours); plus P200
for a grilled lunch. Much of the trip is spent floating past bucolic scenery, and enthusias-
tic guides and excited first-timers add to the fun. Six companies are officially registered,
including the recommended **CDO Bugsay River Rafting** (☎ 088-850 1580; www.
cdorafting.com; Everlasting St; per person P1200-1800).

Rafting is good year-round – during the dry season, from January to May, the water
is clearer and the runs more technical, while in June and July the water is faster, if
murky.

Makahambus Adventure Park (☎ 088-310 8226; barangay Bayanga; sky bridge, zipline
& rappelling P500; ⊙ 8am-5pm) is a common stop for rafters (and often offered as a pack-
age), since it's on the way to the river. It has a 120ft-long sky bridge tethered more than
40m above the jungle, and also offers a zipline and rappelling.

which is mixed with deep-fried squid. Other specialities are grilled tuna belly, crocodile *sisig* and seafood by weight cooked to your preference.

★ **Circa Eatery** INTERNATIONAL $$$
(☑ 088-852 1850; CM Recto Ave; mains P295-700; ⊙ 7am-2.30pm & 5.30-10pm) The ground floor of the Red Planet Hotel, on the city's primary traffic-jammed road, is an unusual spot for a restaurant espousing slow-food movement bona fides and organic, locally grown ingredients. From croque madames for breakfast to grass-fed beef burgers and sesame-crust salmon, Circa is one of the city's best restaurants any time of the day.

Oak Room BAR
(Corrales Ave; ⊙ 5pm-1am Mon-Thu, to 2am Fri & Sat) A few touches, including a ceiling arched like a wine barrel and an old red British phone booth stocked with liquor, give this dimly lit spot a cool vibe. Good for conversation, imported beers and a decent selection of single malt Scotch.

ℹ Information

Bureau of Immigration (BOI; ☑ 088-880 1824; YMCA Bldg, Julio Pacana St; ⊙ 8am-5pm Mon-Fri) Provides visa extensions.

City Tourism Office (☑ 088-857 3165; cnr Divisoria Park & Apolinar Velez St; ⊙ 8am-5pm Mon-Fri) Flyers for hotels and transport; not much English spoken.

Department of Tourism (DOT; ☑ 088-880 0172; dotr10_nmy@ahoo.com; Gregorio Pelaez Sports Center, Apolinar Velez St; ⊙ 8.30am-5.30pm Mon-Fri) A large office with enthusiastic staff; can make calls to verify transport schedules.

ℹ Getting There & Away

AIR

There are several daily flights from Manila (1½ hours) with **Cebu Pacific** (☑ Cebu 032-230 8888, Manila 02-702 0888; www.cebupacificair. com; cnr Hayes & Rizal Sts, Cagayan de Oro) and **Philippine Airlines** (PAL; ☑ Cebu 032-340 0191, Manila 02-855 8888; www.philippineair lines.com; Tirso Neri St, Cagayan de Oro); Cebu Pacific also flies daily to Cebu (45 minutes), Iloilo City (one hour) and Davao (one hour). All flights operate out of Laguindingan International Airport, 32km west of the city and 55km east of Iligan.

A taxi between the airport and town is around P500 (45 minutes). Several companies, including **LAX Shuttle** (☑ 0917 710 1529) and **Magnum**

WORTH A TRIP

BALANGAY SHRINE MUSEUM

Towards the Butuan airport, at barangay Libertad, is the **Balangay Shrine Museum** (6th St, barangay Libertad, Butuan; ⊙ 8.30am-4.30pm Mon-Sat) **FREE**, home to the remains of a balangay (seagoing outrigger boat) dating from 321, one of the oldest-known artefacts in the Philippines (the word 'barangay' in fact derives from balangay, as the boats were big enough to move whole communities of settlers in one journey.) Unearthed a few metres away are several coffins dating back to the 13th and 14th centuries. A tricycle (P50) will take you to the site.

Express (☑ 0917 771 2255) run minivans hourly to the airport (P199) from several locations (Ayala Centrio Mall, Limketkai Center and others). Upon exiting the airport terminal, touts will rush you, steering you to their ticket booth. All are next to one another and offer the same price and service.

BOAT

You can get to Macabalan pier by jeepney; a taxi will cost about P70.

2GO (p346) services the following destinations: six weekly trips to Manila (P2100 to P3400, 35 hours); Cebu City (P925, 10 hours, Tuesday, Wednesday and Friday); Iloilo on Panay (P1200, 14 hours, 11pm Saturday); and Bacolod on Negros (P1470, nine hours, 11pm Saturday).

Trans Asia Shipping (☑ Cebu 032-254 6491; www.transasiashipping.com) services Tagbilaran on Bohol (P775, 10 hours, 7pm Monday, Wednesday and Thursday).

Lite Ferries (☑ Cebu 032-255 1721; www. liteferries.com) has four weekly trips between Cagayan de Oro and Jagna on Bohol (from P680, seven hours).

BUS

East-bound and south-bound buses leave from the **Integrated Bus Terminal** (Gabucayan St) at the Agora fruit and vegetable wholesale market. Air-con buses stop running in the early evening. To catch a boat to Camiguin, take any east-bound bus to Balingoan. For Surigao (departure point for boats to Siargao), you must transfer to another bus in Butuan. West-bound buses depart from the **terminal** (cnr Saarenas Ave & West Coastal Rd) a few kilometres northwest of the city centre in barangay Bulua. In general, buses leave every 30 minutes to an hour.

WORTH A TRIP

MALASAG ECO-TOURISM VILLAGE

Set in acres of botanical gardens with a small wildlife collection of butterflies, birds and deer, the **Malasag Eco-Tourism Village** (☑ 088-309 3752; P50; ⊙ 7am-5pm) is a theme park of sorts, featuring tribal houses, a museum and an education centre. There are camping, cottages (from P500), a swimming pool (P50) and a pleasant restaurant. Take a jeepney to Cugman and get off at Malasag, then take a motorcycle (P25) up the hill to the village. A taxi from Cagayan de Oro will cost about P150 one way.

Rural Transit, Bachelor Express and Super 5 bus companies dominate the scene. However, Pabama Tours, a smaller company that services destinations south in Bukidnon Province, recently started using brand-new buses with mini-trays, cup-holders, and even seat-back computer tablets that play music, games and movies!

DESTINATION	FARE (P)	DURATION (HR)
Balingoan	200	1¾
Butuan	350	4¼
Davao	600	6
Iligan	145	2
Malaybalay	130	2½

❶ Getting Around

Jeepneys to many points – including the pier, Cugman (for Malasag Eco-Tourism Village) and Limketkai Center – pass by in front of Nature's Pensionne on T Chavez St.

Camiguin

☑ 088 / POP 88,000

Relatively unspoiled and an ideal size for exploration, Camiguin (cah-mee-*geen*) is notable for its imposing silhouette – drop it down next to Hawaii or Maui and it wouldn't look out of place. With more than 20 cinder cones 100m-plus high, Camiguin has more volcanoes per square kilometre than any other island on earth. And because it's untouched by large-scale tourism and one of the more tranquil islands around – the 10km of Gingoog Bay separating the island from the mainland is partly responsible – those who do come feel proprietorial

about this little jewel and guard news of its treasures like a secret. Besides the usual diving, snorkelling and sandy beaches (except for offshore ones, beaches have brown sand), Camiguin offers a chance to climb a volcano and a seeming endless supply of jungle waterfalls and hot and cold springs.

◉ Sights & Activities

The waters surrounding Camiguin are good for diving, especially for beginner divers, and there is a well-regarded free-diving centre. Customised climbing, trekking, mountain biking, fishing can be arranged through your accommodation.

Diving

There are more than 10 sites of note, some with steep slopes where rays, sea turtles and thresher sharks can be found. Muck-dive enthusiasts can search for cuttlefish, frogfish, nudis, seahorses and octopus on the sea floor. Some of the best diving is probably off **Jigdup Reef**, **White Island** and **Mantigue Island**; **Old Volcano** has interesting rock formations, a result of lava flow from Hibok-Hibok's eruptions; **Black Forest**, with its gentle, gradual slope and the fairly healthy reef of **Sunken Cemetery** make them other favourites. Expect to pay about P3000 for two boat dives including equipment (the municipal government charges an additional P150 per diver per dive in marine-protected areas). Snorkelling equipment is rented out for P200 (mask and snorkel), plus another P200 for fins and booties.

Reconnect Discover   DIVING

(☑ 0908 430 8444; www.reconnectdiscover.com; Yumbing; 1 week from $1000) Kaisa and Arno, a friendly and well-informed Finnish–Dutch couple, run weeklong retreats (only in April–May and October-November) combining yoga, meditation and diving. Arno also runs dives year-round (2-/3-tank dives P3000/P4250, including equipment, excluding sanctuary fees). Operations are on temporary hiatus, though – check the website for the latest.

Kurma Freedive & Yoga   DIVING

(www.kurmafreedive.com; Yumbing) Run out of the hotel of the same name by Diggi and Valerie, the first female Filipino free-dive instructor. Well-regarded and professional courses run from very basic one-day introductory how-to-breathe-better underwater (P7000) to advanced three- to four-day free-diver courses (P16,500).

Benoni to Mambajao

Katibawasan Falls
WATERFALL

(P30) A beautiful clear stream of water dropping more than 70m to a plunge pool where you can swim and picnic. The few souvenir kiosks and concrete walkway mean it doesn't feel like a natural refuge. A special trip by jeepney or multicab from Mambajao will cost about P300 return; from the resorts around Agoho it's about P350 return.

Hibok-Hibok Volcano
HIKING

Hibok-Hibok volcano (1320m), which last erupted in 1951, provides a dramatic spark – no pun intended – to the island's interior. Housed in a building about 525m off the main road is the **Philippine Institute of Volcanology & Seismology (Philvolcs) Station** FREE, which monitors the volcano's activity.

In dry weather, it's possible to climb the volcano, but it's a demanding three- to four-hour steep, rocky climb (nearly the same time for the descent) and you need to be reasonably fit. From the peak you can see Bohol, Cebu and Negros on a clear day. Most resorts can provide guides (per group of four or fewer P1200, plus admission P500 and environmental fee P200); aim to leave around daybreak.

Ardent Hot Springs
HOT SPRINGS

(P30; ⊙ 6am-10pm) Head out late in the afternoon when the air temperature has cooled down for the lukewarm-to-hot waters. The big pool is emptied for cleaning on Wednesday and takes the best part of the day to refill. The springs are in a lush but developed setting and get very busy on weekends.

Saai Springs
SPRING

FREE Around 4km inland from the church in Mambajao is this concrete pool fed with cold spring water.

North Coast to Guinsiliban

Kuguita, **Bug-ong**, **Agoho** and **Yumbing** are the most developed of the northern beaches, and where much of the accommodation is located. However, because of erosion, a great deal of the actual beach between Agoho and Yumbing continues to disappear into the sea. In fact, a number of sea walls have been erected to protect seafront properties. Where the beach does still exist, it's of the dark and coarse variety, a result of the island's volcanic activity.

White Island
BEACH

(P20) Uninhabited White Island (Medano Island), a pure white-sand bar a few hundred metres offshore, is accessible by boats (P500, up to six people) that leave from a spot next to Paras Beach Resort in Yumbing. At any time but the early morning, the sun can be brutally intense. The shape of the island is constantly evolving, fighting a constant battle against the tide, erosion and occasional sand theft. Aside from sunbathing, there are some nice snorkelling spots and a few resident turtles.

Binangawan Falls
WATERFALL

At 15m or so this is the shortest of the falls on Camiguin and one of the most difficult to reach. You can go on your own or with a guide arranged through your accommodation. Do not try this hike during or soon after rain: the road and path can get extremely slippery and treacherous, and landslides up here aren't uncommon.

Stations of the Cross
VIEWPOINT

Heading west from Mambajao, just before Bonbon, you'll pass the Old Camiguin Volcano, whose slopes have been turned into a steep and beautiful Stations of the Cross. There are great views from the top and a few souvenir stalls clustered at the bottom of the steps.

Spanish Watchtower
HISTORIC SITE

In Guinsiliban, behind the elementary school by the pier, are the remains of this centuries-old sight, which used to guard against possible Moro attacks from the mainland. A pretty shrine is maintained here.

Tangub Hot Spring
HOT SPRINGS

Water temperatures here fluctuate with the tides, from cold to warm to hot, depending on the source; a volcanic spring below the sea bed provides the hot water at this completely undeveloped site 12km west of Mambajao. There's good diving offshore from here.

Cantaan Kabila White Beach Giant Clam Sanctuary
SWIMMING

(⊙ 7.30am-5pm) Some of the best-preserved coral around Camiguin, as well as giant clams, can be found in the waters just off this small white-sand beach halfway between Benoni and Guinsiliban in barangay Cantaan. The population is only now rebounding from typhoons in 2011 and 2012. The family that owns the property charges for a guide (P150), entrance (P25) and environmental fee

Camiguin

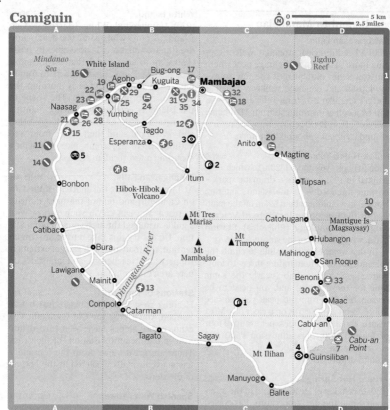

(P25), and rents masks and snorkels for P100 and fins for an additional P100.

Santo Niño Cold Spring   SPRING
(P30; ⊙ 10.30am-8pm Mon & Thu, from 8am other days; 🚻) This developed cold-water pool close to Catarman is good for a dip on a hot day. It's around 2½ km off the highway along a paved road.

🎊 Festivals & Events

Panaad   RELIGIOUS
During Holy Week, the Panaad involves a 64km walk around the island, an expression of devotees' penitence. Stations of the Cross are placed on the route, ending with 'Tabo' on Easter Sunday in Mambajao.

Lanzones Festival   CULTURAL
(⊙ Oct) The annual paean to this delicacy, a small yellow fruit that tastes like a mix of lemons and lychees, takes place around the third week of October. Gluttony is encour-

aged during a week of parades, pageants and dancing.

🛏 Sleeping & Eating

Most of the resorts are clustered along a stretch from Agoho to Naasag. Reservations are recommended from March through May. It's hot, but reliable weather means boat and flight cancellations are rare and visibility is excellent for diving. January and February, though they are rainy months, are also busy with Europeans escaping their winter. Locals celebrate family homecomings during Christmas and the semester break from late October to early November.

🛏 Mambajao & Around

Camiguin Souldivers   HOSTEL $
(📞 0947 411 1189; www.camiguinsouldivers.com; Tupsan; dm/s/d/cottage P200/300/350/600; 🛜) The simple, fan-cooled, cave-like dorms

Camiguin

MINDANAO CAMIGUIN

and rooms here cater to shoestring divers. It abuts the highway where the road divides about 6km southeast of Mambajao.

Ba'ay by VjANDEP Hotel HOTEL $
(formerly Sector 9 Hotel; ☎0917 329 5500; cnr Neriz & Rizal Sts, Mambajao; dm P350, d incl breakfast P2500; ❋☎) Each of the four light-filled, wood-floor rooms on the 3rd floor, even the dormitory with four bunk beds, has high ceilings and homey touches.

Nypa Style Resort COTTAGE $$
(☎0921 638 3709; www.nypastyleresort.jimdo.com; Bug-ong; d incl breakfast P1800-2900; ☎) If sea views aren't a priority, the tranquil garden ones at this meticulously maintained property 500m inland from the highway are an alternative. Each of the four bamboo cottages is uniquely designed, and in lieu of the ocean there's a small plunge pool. The Italian owners brew some of the best espresso around and change up their set menu daily (nonguests can make reservations).

★Casa Roca Inn GUESTHOUSE $$
(☎088-387 9500; www.casarocacamiguin.com; Naasag; r with shared bathroom P1000-1500; ☎) Gnarly tree branches hold up this two-storey home with just three rooms, perched

on a headland with waves breaking below. The gorgeous sea-facing room, with its sprawling mahogany balcony, is the best on the island. The rooms at the back are more modest but terrific value. The restaurant (mains P200) is highly recommended.

**Bahay-Bakasyunan
sa Camiguin** RESORT $$$
(☎088-387 1057; www.bahaybakasyunan.com; Balbagon; r incl breakfast P3600-P5100; ❋☎☀) No longer the classiest of Camiguin's resorts, this property stretching from the highway to the water could use some attention. More modern A-frame cottages face older bamboo bungalows across a manicured lawn shaded by a towering grove of coconut trees. On closer inspection, the furnishings in both are showing their age. The seaside pool and restaurant are the best features.

Vjandeap Bakery BAKERY $
(57 Plaridel St; pastries P5-25; ⊗6am-8pm) Stop by Vjandeap Bakery for the island's speciality pastries.

Samuel by VjANDEP FILIPINO $$
(cnr Neriz & Rizal Sts; mains P130-285; ⊗6am-10.30pm) Despite the clunky name, this is Mambajao's best restaurant. The menu

ranges widely, from typical Filipino dishes to burgers and fried chicken, and the service is attentive.

J&A Fishpen SEAFOOD $$
(mains P100-450; ⊙ 6am-8pm) Seafood (such as bangus P60 per 100g) comes straight from the pens on the Benoni lagoon, which this restaurant overlooks; popular with large groups on weekends. You can pay an additional P150 for the little shelters perched over the water or rent a fishing rod to reel in your own catch for the kitchen to prepare. Pizza, meat and noodle dishes are also served.

La Dolce Vita ITALIAN $$
(National Hwy, Mambajao; mains P210-400; ⊙ 6am-10pm; 🛜) Allesandro, the Italian owner-chef at this open-air place across from the airport, fires up delicious thin-crust brick-oven pies using only high-quality ingredients. Locals say the quality isn't up to snuff when he's not in the kitchen. Homemade pastas and cappuccinos (P110) are also standouts.

🛏 Northern Beaches

**Volcan Beach Eco Retreat
& Dive Resort** COTTAGE $$
(☎ 088-387 9551; www.camiguinvolcanbeach.com; Naasag; r with fan/air-con P1500/2500; ❄🛜) A line of well-constructed thatch-roofed cottages face one another across a palm-tree-filled garden (with several hammocks) that ends on a rocky shore battered by waves – there's a neat bamboo platform for sunbathing. Each has its own small private balcony, high ceilings and mosquito nets. German-owned Volcan has its own full-service dive shop. Service can be inconsistent.

Kurma Freedive & Yoga INN $$
(www.kurmafreedive.com; Yumbing; d with fan/air-con P12300/2700; @🛜) Small, cramped waterfront spot with brightly painted rooms, each with its own porch. Warm and friendly, with a familial vibe created by the German–Filipino owners (both free-dive instructors). Yoga classes and retreats offered.

⭐**Balai sa Baibai** VILLA $$$
(☎ 088-387 9594, mobile 0918 962 2808; www.balaisabaibai.com; Agoho; d P4800-5500, villa P6900; ❄🛜♨) ✏ Meticulously manicured oasis of style and sophistication, created by a Filipino–British couple whose finely calibrated taste is evident in every feature, especially the luxuriously appointed

Balinese-style villas with kitchenettes, outdoor showers and their own plunge pools – surely the nicest rooms on the island. The beachfront bar (5pm to 10pm) has an elevated platform with two plunge pools and is the best place for a sundowner on the island.

⭐**SomeWhere Else
Boutique Resort** VILLA $$$
(☎ mobile 0939 8090 928; www.facebook.com/privateluxuriousvilla; Agoho; villa for 3 P5500; ❄🛜) European modernism with a tropical twist describes these two large villas set back from the beach on a lush lawn. Each is stylishly furnished with whimsical flourishes and open floor plans. Both have outdoor showers, and one has a small plunge pool and roof deck. Not clearly signposted from the highway and not open to walk-ins.

**Guerrera Rice
Paddy Villas** BUNGALOW $$$
(☎ 0917 311 9859; www.guerrera.ph; Pearl St, Yumbing; villa P3500-4000) The three rooms here overlook a picturesque rice paddy. They're tastefully decorated with hardwood furniture and Vietnamese-style antique lamps. Each has memory-foam mattresses, and the two 'paddy villas' have outdoor bathtubs on their private porches (the beach villa will have one soon). Very personal service; has its own restaurant.

⭐**Beehive** CAFE $
(☎ 0939 932 0334; Catibac; mains P95-215; ⊙ 8am-7pm) ✏ Made from recycled wood, shells, rocks and a hotchpotch of other materials a la Robinson Crusoe, this eccentrically designed oceanfront cafe is a good place for a pit stop on a round-the-island motorbike tour. Healthy items such as vegie burgers, salads, pizzas with crusts made from whole-wheat, dragonfruit juice and herbs are on the menu.

Hayahay Cafe INTERNATIONAL $
(Bug-ong; mains P150-200; ⊙ 9am-9pm) Charming little cafe with seating indoors and out, serving healthy fare like granola bowls and smoothies, excellent shakshouka (Tunisian egg dish) and mains like chicken stew with vegetables.

⭐**Guerrera** SOUTHEAST ASIAN $$
(☎ mobile 0917 311 9859; www.guerrera.ph; Pearl St, Yumbing; mains P250-325; ⊙ noon-2pm & 4-9pm; 🛜) Camiguin's culinary profile is

ⓘ TRAVEL ADVISORY

In late 2017 the political and security situation in Mindanao was at a crisis point, yet again. ISIS–affiliated fighters from the Maute and Abu Sayyaf groups, among others, occupied and laid siege to Marawi City beginning in late May. Several hundred residents were held hostage, and 45 civilians, 122 soldiers and more than 500 militants were killed. Tens of thousands of residents were evacuated once the military created a safe corridor, and President Duterte declared martial law on the island.

Martial law was finally lifted in late 2019, however, Mindanao continues to face the threat of violence from extremist groups.

Aside from the no-go zone around Marawi, and periodic clashes between the military and rebels (primarily confined to the Sulu Archipelago, Maguindanao, Lanao del Sur, Sultan Kudarat and North and South Cotabato), there have been a number of deadly bombings elsewhere – most notably, a September 2016 bombing of a central night market in Davao that killed 15 and wounded dozens more. Members of the Maute group are said to be responsible. Kidnappings for ransom carried out by rogue elements of rebel groups and armed gangs are of concern. The New People's Army (NPA) is active and there are clashes with government troops; however, the NPA has not targeted ordinary Filipinos and tourists.

Embassies of many nations, including Australia, Britain, France and the US, advise against any travel in central and western Mindanao, and advise against all but essential travel elsewhere (with the exception of Camiguin and Siargao). Attacks against transport and commercial targets (buses, ferries, shopping malls etc) have resulted in significant loss of life. Check the latest advisories, and check with Filipinos who know specific parts of Mindanao well, before venturing into any potentially dangerous areas.

All these caveats aside, certainly most who do visit the region return home without incident. Ensure you stay away from specific hotspots, rely on local knowledge and err on the side of caution when choosing where and how to travel.

given a big boost by this restaurant housed in a large yellow villa on an isolated bit of waterfront. The culinary-school-trained Filipino owner-chef focuses mostly on versions of Thai and Vietnamese street food but also does daily specials like Indonesian–style chicken, Bangkok pork and Indian *dal tadka* (smoked yellow lentil and chickpea soup).

Luna Ristorante   ITALIAN $$
(National Hwy, Yumbing; mains P190-420; ⊙7.30am-11pm; 🛜) Luna does excellent thin-crust brick-oven pizza, a mean mixed-seafood grill and good-value breakfasts. Pasta dishes are of uneven quality. Tables are spread out on a lawn, some with shade from the elements, on the main road in Yumbing.

Checkpoint   FILIPINO $$
(National Hwy, Yumbing; mains P200-350; ⊙6.30am-10pm; 🛜) The open-air 2nd-floor space of the Checkpoint mini-mall at the 'major' intersection in Yumbing. Choices run the gamut from simple sandwiches to garlic shrimp; the P150 buffet breakfast is

good value. It's a pleasant spot with mountain views.

ⓘ Information

Philippine National Bank (PNB) and Landbank in Mambajao have unreliable ATMs; the PNB accepts MasterCard. PNB changes US dollars but only accepts extremely crisp bills of US$5 and above (Swiss francs accepted but travellers report difficulty changing euro). Best to get cash elsewhere before arriving.

Tourist Office (☑ 088-387 1097; www.camiguin. gov.ph; Mambajao Municipal Hall; ⊙8am-5pm Mon-Fri) Ask for Pacita Romualdo, who, if available, can be helpful with transport questions.

ⓘ Getting There & Away

AIR
Cebu Pacific (p349) flies a 60-plus passenger single-prop twice daily (sometimes only one daily flight in low season) between Camiguin Airport (Mambajao) and Cebu (from P700 to P3500, 30 minutes, 6.30am). The ticketing office is across the street from the old Landbank near the PNB. There's a 15kg limit on checked-in baggage, and weather delays aren't uncommon. Terminal fee is P50.

BOAT

Camiguin has two ports relevant to travellers: **Benoni**, 18km south of Mambajao, where ferries connect to Balingoan on the mainland; and **Balbagon**, only 2km southeast of Mambajao, with connections to Cebu and Jagna on Bohol.

Eight to 10 boats ply the channel between Benoni and Balingoan roughly hourly from 4.30am until 5.30pm (P170, 1¼ hours). If white caps are visible, the crossing can be unpleasant in the smaller and less-seaworthy-looking ferry. Before leaving, local kids climb up the outside of the boats and leap into the water soliciting tips.

Heading to Camiguin from the mainland, you purchase ferry tickets at the bus terminal in Balingoan (and then pay a nominal terminal fee at the port entrance itself 200m away).

Additionally, from Balbagon port, 2km southeast of Mambajao, Super Shuttle Ferry (p346) has an on again, off again roll-on, roll-off ferry (RORO; P470, 3½ hours, Monday, Wednesday and Friday at 8am) to Jagna on Bohol. The price includes an additional terminal and 'environmental fee'.

There's talk of bringing back the Oceanjet fastcraft service between Cagayan de Oro and Benoni and then from Benoni to Jagna on Bohol. Both legs cost around P600 and take two hours. Email reports (don't rely on websites, which often contain outdated information) for the latest.

From the Balbagon pier, Lite Ferries (p349) has a daily RORO ferry to Cebu (P880, 11 hours, 7pm); unfortunately, its ferry (P425, 3½ hours, 8am) to Jagna is unreliable, especially during the low season.

ℹ Getting Around

The road around the island is 64km long and paved, so it's possible to make the circuit in a few hours. For ease of travel and access to places that jeepneys and *motorillas* (the local term for a motorised tricycle) don't go, the best option is to rent a motorcycle (P300 to P500); be sure to wear a helmet and carry your licence. Alternatively, hire a multicab that can comfortably seat six (P1500).

Jeepneys and multicabs (air-con minivans usually as well) meet arriving boats in Benoni to transport passengers to Mambajao (P30 to P50, 30 minutes). A special ride to Mambajao costs P150; to the resorts north of Mambajao you'll pay P250 to P500.

From Mambajao, it's easy to hop on a 'westbound' *motorilla* (these are red; 'east-bound' *motorillas* are green) for the majority of resorts. Getting around on these is convenient, cheap and cramped (P9).

Surigao

☑ 086 / POP 88,000

For those heading to Siargao Island, this fairly nondescript, gridlocked city, the capital of Surigao del Norte Province, is usually a necessary overnight stop (unless flying directly). The town plaza is the centre of activity, hosting everything from impromptu chess matches and cheap massages to first dates, while a portion of the long waterfront boulevard is lined with makeshift alfresco KTV (karaoke) bars and night-time second-hand clothing stalls.

Attractions in the area include **Silop Cave**, 7km away, with its 12 entrances leading to a big central chamber; **Day-asin**, a floating village, 5km from the city; and **Mati**, to the south, where the Mamanwa people have created a 'village' to showcase their culture. There are also several beaches nearby, including **Mabua Pebble Beach**, where you can spend a few hours waiting for your outbound flight.

🛏 Sleeping

EY Miner Suites (Borromeo St)   HOTEL $

(☑ 086-826 6480; Borromeo St; d P1100; ❄ 🛜) Centrally located with comfortable if cramped rooms. Has a shiny, slightly kitschy lobby and no elevator – so best to request a lower-floor room.

Bohol Traveller's Inn   HOTEL $

(☑ 086-826 8884; San Nicolas St; d P600-900; ❄ 🛜) A clean and basic cheapie close to the market. Don't be discouraged by the 'reception' area, which looks like someone's basement storage space.

★ Hotel Tavern   HOTEL $$

(☑ 086-826 8566, 0918 963 6184; www.hoteltavern.com; Borromeo St; d incl breakfast P1900-3600; ❄ @ 🛜) The most upscale place in Surigao, and the only hotel to take advantage of the city's waterfront location. More sophisticated sea-view rooms are worth the price. In addition, there's an outdoor bar and a restaurant called EJ's Garden by the Bay, with live music most nights of the week, and EJ's Cafe. Free airport transfers are a bonus.

Annex Hotel Tavern   HOTEL $$

(☑ 086-826 9732; www.annexhotelsurigao.com; Borromeo St; d P1250-2500; ❄ 🛜) Nondescript, simply furnished rooms a short walk from the main pier. Professionally managed with a convenience store at street level.

Surigao & Around

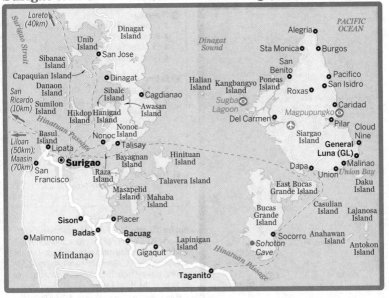

✗ Eating

Fast-food restaurants are clustered on the southwest side of the plaza on Rizal St, and a few are in the **Gaisano Mall** (Figaro Cafe is a good place to wait for a bus) next to the bus terminal. An appetising row of **fruit stalls** lines the east side of the plaza (Magallanes St). **Barbecue stalls** (open at night) can be found on Borromeo St around the pier.

EJ's Cafe   INTERNATIONAL **$**
(Borromeo St; mains P130-200; ⊙10am-11.30pm; 🛜) Part of the Hotel Tavern complex, this contemporary cafe qualifies as hip, for Surigao. Sandwiches, burgers, plus pastries, cookies and excellent coffee are available, or you can order off the fuller menu of the attached restaurant.

★ Calda's Pizzeria   PIZZA **$$**
(Boulevard; pizza P200-280; ⊙2-11pm) Excellent and massive thin-crust pizzas with a few tables and waterfront boulevard seating. 'Extra super-size' pies are a ridiculous 36in with 50 slices.

EJ's Garden by the Bay   FILIPINO **$$**
(Borromeo St; mains P250-370; ⊙10am-11.30pm) Surigao's most dependably lively spot is an open-air pavilion within the Hotel Tavern's grounds. Fresh seafood is the speciality (you can select from the display and pay by weight), but the usual meat and noodle dishes are also on the menu. Live acoustic music is on tap most nights.

**357 Steakhouse
& Sushi Bar**   JAPANESE **$$**
(☑086-310 1338; Borromeo St; mains P200-400; ⊙11am-10pm) Not much curb appeal to this utilitarian-looking restaurant next to the Surigao Coast Guard office. However, it's pleasant enough inside and serves especially good ramen, sashimi, *okonomiyaki* and *kani* (crab) or spicy, crunchy tuna salads.

ℹ Information

There are several banks with ATMs (get cash before heading to Siargao) around the plaza; the main port terminal also has two ATMs.
Surigao City Tourism Office (☑086-826 8064; www.surigaocity.gov.ph; Luneta Pavilion; ⊙8am-5pm) Conveniently located in the central plaza, but don't expect more than maps and brochures here.
Surigao del Norte Provincial Tourism Office (☑086-826 9017; surigaodelnortetourism@ yahoo.com; Capitol Rd; ⊙9am-5pm Mon-Fri) For information about travel elsewhere in the region; located by the city grandstand (basketball courts and soccer fields).

Surigao

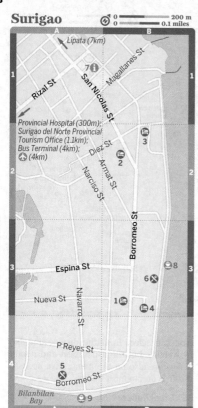

Surigao

🛏 Sleeping
1 Annex Hotel Tavern B3
2 Bohol Traveller's Inn......................... B2
3 EY Miner Suites (Borromeo St) B2
4 Hotel Tavern....................................... B3

🍴 Eating
5 357 Steakhouse & Sushi Bar A4
6 Calda's Pizzeria.................................. B3
EJ's Cafe .... (see 4)
EJ's Garden by the Bay .... (see 4)

ℹ Information
7 Surigao City Tourism Office............... A1

ℹ Transport
8 Boulevard Docking Area B3
9 Main Pier... A4

opt for the daily *M/V Reina Magdalena* roll-on, roll-off (RORO) ferry (P250, four hours, noon), which also uses the main pier. Less comfortable options are the 5.30am and 6am bangkas (2½ hours) leaving from the boulevard docking area in front of the Hotel Tavern.

If your destination on Siargao Island is Del Carmen, near the airport in the northwest of the island, there are two daily bangka departures from the boulevard docking area: the *M/V Donilyn/ Kinmet* at 5am and *M/VPilar Tuna* at 11am.

Medallion Transport Inc has boats to Cebu Tuesday, Thursday and Sunday at 8pm (P1000).

Bangkas (P100) for San José on the island of Dinagat leave at approximately 7am, 9am and noon from the boulevard docking area in front of the Hotel Tavern. *M/V Cab-ilan* goes to San José from the main pier at 3.30pm daily (P120), except Sunday. And the *M/V Yohan Blue* fast ferry travels daily from the main pier to Albor and Loreto (P300), further north on Dinagat; check departure times.

ROROs serving the Southern Leyte towns of San Ricardo (P140, 1¼ hours, noon, 3am and 2pm) and Liloan (P300, four hours, 6.30am, 11am, 1pm, 6pm and midnight) leave from the pier in Lipata, 8km west of Surigao. Also, a daily 8am fast ferry departs Lipata for San Ricardo (two hours).

Tickets for all boats leaving from the main pier are purchased at the respective company's ticket window at the terminal. For other boats, especially the bangkas, you buy tickets on board.

ℹ Getting There & Away

AIR
Philippine Airlines (www.philippineairlines.com) and Cebu Pacific (www.cebupacificair.com) have daily flights to Manila; the latter also has several weekly flights to Cebu. Pay attention to arrival and departure times in order to connect with boat transfers to and from Siargao Island. Airline announcements are piped in to **Basti's** (Airport; mains P75-200; ☺7am-10pm; ☎), a coffee shop just inside the airport entrance. Catch a tricycle (P40) or jeepney (P10) to the airport, 5km west of the town centre.

BOAT
The most important boat connection for travellers is Dapa on Siargao Island. And the best boat for relative comfort (opt for air-con and take a sweater and earplugs) and a reasonable departure time is the 11.30am *Fortune Angel* (P220 to P250, 2½ hours), leaving from the **main pier** (Eva Macapagal Terminal; Borromeo St), 2km south of the plaza on Borromeo St. In bad weather,

BUS
The bus terminal is next to the Gaisano Mall about 4½km west of town and around 50m before the airport; a jeepney to or from the pier costs P10 and a tricycle around P30. For Cagayan de Oro or Balingoan (for boats to Camiguin), you must change buses in Butuan.

Minivans also service the destinations listed here. The following fares are for air-con buses:

DESTINATION	FARE (P)	DURATION (HR)	FREQUENCY
Butuan	215	3	every half-hour or so
Davao	720	8	hourly
Tandag	315	5	when full

Siargao

Initially drawn to Siargao (shar-*gow*) by good year-round waves and a tranquillity and beauty lost in other Philippine islands, a small group of passionate Aussie, American, European and now Filipino surfers are still living the good life. Even with a marked surge in development over the last several years, more hotels and flights and better roads, the island's laid-back resorts are still the norm. Besides surfers looking for the next challenge on their international *wanderjahr,* low-key do-it-yourself types do well here and prolong their stay by weeks. There are rock pools, mangrove swamps, twisty rivers, offshore islands with strange rock formations and wildlife, waterfalls and forests, with hammock sitting the usual coda to any day.

The port is in the main township of **Dapa**. On arrival you'll probably make for one of the resorts located along the road between General Luna (known locally as GL) and 'Cloud Nine'.

 Activities

Surfing

Surfing is what has put Siargao on the map, but there are plenty of other things on tap. Island-hopping – searching for beaches or out out-of-the-way lagoons for snorkelling – is more and more popular. **Anahawan Island** to the south has a guesthouse with dormitory rooms and excellent surf. These days, **Daku Island** can get so crowded it recalls Manila traffic. Usually, people combine Daku with visits to **Naked** and **Guyam** islands.

Surfing is year-round, but generally it's considered best from August to November, when there are some big swells as a result of typhoon winds. The period from December to April has some strong crosswinds, while from May to July the surf tends to be lighter. Surfboard rental and lessons can be arranged at resort. Booties are highly recommended to protect your feet, since some of the breaks are along reefs, albeit 'soft' ones. Cloud Nine is the most famous break, but there's no shortage of others along Siargao's shoreline or around offshore islands.

★ **My Siargao Guide**   OUTDOORS
(☑ 0921 797 2791; www.facebook.com/mysiargao guide) This one-stop tour company, run by a couple based at Bravo Surf Resort (p361) in General Luna, runs a variety of tours on the island. Most popular are Sugba Lagoon (P2000) and island-hopping (P1000); others are Magpupungko (P1000) and Sohoton (P2000). All include lunch, drinks, snorkel gear and, for Sugba, stand-up paddleboards.

Diving & Snorkelling

Deep caves, such as the Blue Cathedral, mean that some of the more interesting dives in the area are for the experienced only. However, in general there's excellent visibility and a large number of sites, making it a good place to learn. **Palaka Siargao Dive Center** (☑ 0918 626 2303; www.palaka divecenter.com), owned and operated by an enthusiastic and professional Frenchman, is located on the beachfront behind the public market in General Luna (it has a cool little cafe). Palaka also runs **free-diving** clinics, an increasingly popular course for surfers.

Sohoton Cove, maze of inlets on the island of Bucas Grande, is a sometimes-rough two-hour boat ride from southern Siargao. The scenery from the boat in itself justifies the trip for some. Non-stinging jellyfish float in the emerald waters, and you can jump from a platform near the cave entrance.

Other Activities

Siargao is also one of the few places in the country with organised deep-sea fishing (day trip for up to three people P5000); by all accounts, it's top-notch. Reeling in a 130kg sailfish isn't uncommon – mahi-mahi and Spanish mackerel are also on the menu. The fishing is good year-round, although seas can be rough December to February. Contact Junior Gonzalez (☑ 0920 772 8875), who also offers accommodation at his home in Pilar. Best to give several days' advance notice.

Viento Kite School   KITESURFING
(☑ 0919 242 8089; www.vientodelmar.com/kite surfing-siargao) The shallow, wide lagoon with a sandy bottom out front of the Viento del Mar Resort, where this school is based, is the best place on Siargao to learn this challenging sport. Instructors speak English, Russian, Tagalog and Visayan.

MINDANAO SIARGAO

Lotus Shores
YOGA

([phone] 0917 838 5743; www.lotusshores.com) As many as four yoga classes a day are held in a Balinese–style yoga pavilion located around 150m from the beach road.

★★ Festivals & Events

Siargao Cup
SPORTS

This surfing competition, one of the largest international sporting events in the country, is held at Cloud Nine in late September or early October. The **Filipino National Cup**, another competitive surfing event, is usually the week before.

ℹ Information

Unlike other parts of Mindanao, and Manila for that matter, the wet season on Siargao coincides with the *amihan* (northeast monsoon), roughly from December to March. The dry season, when the *habagat* winds blow from the southwest, is from June to September.

The two banks in Dapa – Green Bank and Cantilan Bank – should not be relied upon for cash withdrawals (some report Green Bank accepting foreign Visa cards). They're often out of money or not functioning. Jabinas, a store in GL, gives cash advances – the fee is 5% of the amount.

Wild Siargao (www.wildsiargao.com) An authoritative website run by long-time American expat Greg of Greg's Place Pizza & Beer (p364) in San Isidro, covering flora, fauna and the environment of Siargao.

ℹ Getting There & Away

AIR

Cebu Pacific flies daily to Siargao from Manila while Cebu Pacific and PAL both have several daily flights to/from Cebu. Siargao's airport is in Del Carmen, 15km north of Dapa and about 29km northwest of General Luna.

Group shuttle vans run out to the airport (P300, 30 minutes) with pick-ups at your resort in Cloud 9 or GL with prior notice. Just ask at your accommodation.

A few habal-habal (motorcycle taxis) and minivans wait outside the airport's gates for arrivals; however, it might be convenient to arrange transport in advance with your accommodation.

The airport is being expanded to accommodate international flights.

BOAT

All boats to Siargao arrive in Dapa, 15km west of General Luna. A habal-habal/tricycle between Dapa and GL costs P200/300.

Several 'fastcraft' (P350, 1½ hours) and 'RORO' (car ferry; P100, three hours) ferries serve Dapa daily from the port in Surigao. There are about nine morning departures (from 4am to noon) in either direction. From Surigao the last trip is the M/V Sean fastcraft at 3pm. From Dapa the last trip is at 1pm.

You can purchase tickets (P270) the morning of departure. The early-morning boats from Dapa allow you to connect to flights in Surigao or travel by bus to Cagayan de Oro or Davao in a single day (these would be long, tiring days); however, it means leaving Cloud Nine extremely early. Arrange a motorcycle to Dapa through your accommodation.

Bangkas to Socorro on Bucas Grande leave from the municipal wharf next to the main one.

ℹ Getting Around

Jeepneys run from Dapa to GL (one hour); a better option is to hop on a *habal-habal* (motorcycles large enough to seat more than one passenger with bags) to GL (P200, 30 minutes) or Cloud Nine (P300, 35 minutes). Price depends on your negotiating skills and time of day (early-morning trips are more expensive). Tricycles cost a bit more and are much slower. A great way to spend the day is to tour the island on your own (most of the 'circumferential road' is paved); the going rate for motorcycle hire is around P500 per day.

A new venture, **Binggo** ([phone] 0977 642 3765; www.binggoride.com), offers Indian-made tuk-tuks available for self-drive (P1200 per day) or with a driver (P1500 per day).

General Luna
[phone] 086 / POP 16,800

Several blocks of dirt roads, dilapidated buildings and a few eateries ending in a public beach lined with a row of *sari-sari* (neighbourhood) stores and barbecue shacks: that's General Luna. And to foreign visitors who stay at one of the resorts, it might as well be the big city – albeit one where the dress code is flip-flops and shirts are optional. Somehow, it adds up to a fairly charming small town. There are several surfing breaks south of GL reached by bangka, including a few around offshore islands. A river perfect for swimming in during high tide is near the village of Union, between GL and Cloud Nine.

🛌 Sleeping

Some of the places are on a narrow sandy beach that's unfortunately not well suited for swimming. The area is undergoing a construction boom, including a few large condo and hotel developments. Malinao, 3½km south, has a few resorts.

★ Kermit Surf Resort
HOTEL $

(📱 0917 655 0648; www.kermitsiargao.com; d with fan/air-con P950/1200, bungalow P1800; ❄️ 🛜) Located down a quiet road just northeast and inland from the centre of GL, Swiss–Italian-owned Kermit is a deservedly popular choice for budget-minded surfers closed out of Cloud Nine. The 10 rooms include several large stand-alone thatch-roofed cottages with tile floors and large, modern bathrooms. The restaurant has candlelit tables in a sandy garden, and pizza, pasta and fish (mains P230 to P300) are the specialities.

Paglaom Hostel
HOSTEL $

(www.paglaomhostel.com; dm P350; 🛜) At this price, it's the vibe not the creature comforts that matters. And Paglaom gets it right. It is laid-back but socially inclined, with an open lounge area where bunkmates get to know another. The open-air dorms with bunk beds draped in mosquito nets are cooled by a few fans. There are cold showers and a separate kitchen area for guests to use.

Hangout Siargao
HOSTEL $

(📱 0995 011 7805; camillebanzon@gmail.com; Purok 5; dm P250; 🛜) At this tiny hostel with a warm and relaxed vibe, you bunk down in hammock-like mesh beds suspended 3m above the floor, a unique sleeping arrangement. There are a few other sleeping options, including an attic and tents. Has a kitchen for self-caterers.

Malijon Siargao
BUNGALOW $

(📱 0928 854 8874; www.facebook.com/malijon siargao; d P1200) The three stand-alone huts at Swedish–run Malijon, just off the main road about halfway between GL and Cloud Nine, are justifiably coveted. They are spacious and attractively designed, with thick mattresses, big bathrooms and glorious balconies.

★ Buddha's Surf Resort
HOTEL $$

(📱 0919 945 6789; www.siargaosurf.com; r incl breakfast P2500-3800; ❄️ 🛜) On the inland-side of the road, this spacious property has a sophisticated and contemporary island vibe. The five rooms are sparely furnished with flat-screen TVs and nice bathrooms, and the large open-air pavilion restaurant has a Thai–influenced menu and is vegan-friendly (though a traditional pig roast is available upon request). Towering palm trees shade the manicured lawn and its volleyball net.

★ Bravo Surf Resort
BUNGALOW $$

(📱 0999 877 8518; www.bravosiargao.com; dm/d incl breakfast P1200/P3400; ❄️ 🛜 🏊) Young, Spanish–owned Bravo has become one of GL's happening spots. This is thanks in part to its attractive, closely spaced nipa-roofed cottages with brushed concrete floors and tasteful furniture, and in part to its open-air restaurant (mains P180 to P320), which is run by a Basque chef. The four-person surfer bunk is a luxurious version of a dorm.

Turtle Surf Camp
HOTEL $$

(📱 0908 517 3805; www.surfcampsiargao.com; s/d P2400/2600; ❄️ 🛜 🏊) Intimate and cool, this small spot with only four rooms is especially good for groups of surfing friends. Minimally designed concrete rooms have modern features, and you can cool off in the small pool or watch movies in the little lounge. A family room (with fan/air-con P3900/4200) with its own lounge sleeps four.

Siargao Inn Beach Resort
BUNGALOW $$

(📱 0999 889 9988; www.siargao-inn.com; d/q P2200/3500; ❄️ 🛜) Owned and operated by a friendly young couple, one of whom is a top surfer and can school you on the basics, this laid-back place has a number of simple cottages with nipa roofs and mahogany floors and walls. The bathrooms are especially nice, and there's a pleasant beachside restaurant-bar. Most of the rooms are best suited to three or four people.

Isla Cabana
RESORT $$$

(📱 0928 559 5244; www.islacabanaresort.com; r incl breakfast P7100-8400, ste P14,000; ❄️ 🛜 🏊) High marks go to the design of these large hardwood-floored cabanas at this meticulously cared for upscale development. Several suites face the water with their own hot tubs; the rest open inward onto a sandy landscaped path that ends at the pool and a white-sand beach.

✖️ Eating & Drinking

All of the resorts have restaurants, some highly recommended, and welcome non-guests. Barbecue shacks line the town's beachfront, and there are a few basic eateries, really just informal places with an array of dishes lined up buffet-style on the street.

Italian Food Specialist
MARKET $

(🕐 8am-noon & 1-5pm Mon-Sat) The place to go for imported wines, pasta, cheese and olive oil, plus dried meats.

MINDANAO SIARGAO

Mama's Grill
BARBECUE $

(skewers P50-70; ⊘6-9pm) Every evening the surfing herd converges to feed on skewered pork chops, chicken and beef at this modest BBQ shack about 1.5km north of GL. And then, just like that, they're gone...until the next evening.

Ronaldo's
FILIPINO $

(mains P75-125; ⊘7am-10pm; 🛜) Cheap juices, shakes and noodles, including more than a dozen varieties of *pansit,* are the speciality at this fan-cooled open-air place. Service can be sloooooow.

Miguel's Taqueria
MEXICAN $

(tacos P100; ⊘noon-8pm) Literally a hole-in-the-wall with a couple of stools, doling out good tacos and burritos. Also serves frozen beer.

Lunares Cafe
CAFE $$

(mains P160-200; ⊘7.30am-5.30pm Thu-Tue; 🛜) Small Italian–owned spot with excellent drinks, including iced coffee, *calamansi* juice, cheesecake and focaccia sandwiches.

Warung
INDONESIAN $$

(mains P220; ⊘11am-10pm) Warung's Indonesian chef serves up good-value specialities like *nasi rames* (dish with small portions of rice, meat and vegies), *laksa* (spicy noodle soup) and *bakwan* (fried vegies), to a soundtrack of rhythmic Indonesian music.

Palaka Restaurant
INTERNATIONAL $$

(mains P220-280; ⊘8am-7pm; 🛜) Part of the dive centre of the same name, this pleasant spot along the GL waterfront does a good mix of salads, burgers and paninis. Waffles and crepes are good choices for breakfast.

Rum Bar
BAR

(⊘2pm-late) The roving party scene heads here late on Monday, Wednesday and Saturday nights. Located around 1km west of GL.

☆ Entertainment

Island Life
CINEMA

For Siargao's only cinema, and a unique and sweaty experience (air-con was supposedly in the works), head to this converted shack just outside GL. Popcorn: check. Stadium seating (cushioned benches): check. Screenings run the gamut from all-day *Game of Thrones,* Hollywood blockbusters and 10pm weekend screenings of 'erotica'.

🛍 Shopping

Kudo Surf Shop
SURF

(⊘8am-5pm) Australian–owned shop selling high-performance quality beachwear and surf gear; every article is made from recycled materials. An active collaborator in the Siargao Environmental Awareness Movement (www.facebook.com/seamovementph).

Fat Lips Surf Shop
SURF

(📲0930 876 6757; www.surfsiargao.com; ⊘8am-9pm) Big shop that sells good beachwear and surf gear and also rents boards and offers instruction. Canadian–owned, with friendly and helpful staff.

Cloud Nine
📲086

Solidly ensconced in the international surfing circuit, the surf break at Cloud Nine is unmistakably marked by the raised walkway and three-storey wood pavilion offering front-row seats to the action. It's a friendly and open surfing community, with up-and-coming local Filipinos welcoming foreigners and beginners. For the experienced, there are several other breaks that are accessible by bangka, including **Rock Island**, visible from the Cloud Nine beach, and at least a dozen good beaches are within an hour by boat or road.

All the resorts here can help organise island-hopping and lagoon day tours, as well as arrange surf lessons (P500 per hour, including equipment) and board rental (P300 per half-day). Or stop by **Hippie's Surf Shop** (⊘6am-6pm); Hippie also teaches yoga classes on many mornings.

A few minutes' boat ride from Cloud Nine is **Rock Island**, with its long right-hander. Any accommodation can arrange a boat, or try Jonrel Noguera (0948 659 3770). Most charge around P200 per person for several hours. Nearby, **Stimpy's** is one of the longest lefts around Siargao.

Book island-hopping or Sugba and Sohoton lagoon tours with My Siargao (p359).

🛏 Sleeping & Eating

Ocean 101 Beach Resort
HOTEL $

(📲0910 848 0893; www.ocean101cloud9.com; d with fan P900-1500, with air-con P1700-2500; ❄🛜) No longer the backpacking surfer's HQ, Ocean 101, spread over a manicured lawn facing a sea wall just north of the Cloud Nine break, has evolved over the years. Basic budget rooms are part of the older 101 and the pricier beachfront quarters with high ceilings and big bathrooms part of the new. A two-storey waterfront pavilion provides scenic lounging space.

Villa Solaria   HOSTEL $
(☑0920 407 7730; dm P300, d P1600-2000; ❄🛜) Just south of Cloud Nine, Solaria has ordinary private rooms in nipa-style cottages in a cramped garden setting, and one large outdoor dormitory on the second floor of an open-air pavilion that fills up fast with shoestring surfers.

★Siargao Island

Emerald House   COTTAGE $$
(☑0949 161 9165, 0909 423 5236; www.emerald housevillage.com; cottage P2000-6000; 🛜) This large, leafy property on the inland side of the road, with a mix of attractively designed and stylishly furnished cottages, is great value. From a small loft apartment to a large house with full kitchen, there are a variety of layouts ideal for groups and families. Dalvina, the Swiss owner, ensures things run smoothly. Discounts for weekly and monthly stays.

★Harana   BUNGALOW $$
(☑0998 849 5461; www.haranasurf.com; dm P800, d P3200; ❄🛜) Boasting typical Filipino uses of wood with contemporary architectural flourishes, Harana's aesthetic is a sophisticated combination of the traditional and modern. The coed dorm villa is beautiful and the open-air restaurant, which serves innovative Filipino dishes like shwarma *sisig* (mains P150 to P300), and lounge area is one of the area's best hang-outs. Beach and Tuason surf break are directly out front.

★Kalinaw Resort   BEACH RESORT $$$
(☑0921 320 0442; www.kalinawresort.com; villas for 2 incl breakfast from P9900; ❄🛜🏊) The five villas of this French–owned resort could make the centrefold of any contemporary design magazine. Massive and whimsical bathrooms are the highlight, but minimalism reigns throughout. A refreshing breeze often blows through the sophisticated open-air restaurant (mains P440 to P600), which does the best pizza (only after 7pm) on the island. It's about 800m south of the Cloud Nine break.

Kawayan Resort   COTTAGE $$$
(☑0920 364 0663; www.kawayansiargaoresort. com; d incl breakfast P5500; ❄🛜) Just behind the highly recommended restaurant of the same name are a few beautifully crafted, sophisticated wood cottages, with stone-lined outdoor showers and toilets with palm fronds and trees poking through. The resort is situated in a leafy garden on the other side of the road from the beach.

Villa Maya Resort   GUESTHOUSE $$$
(☑0908 875 3292; www.siargaovilla.com; r incl breakfast from P3500; ❄🛜🏊) Perched on a hill overlooking the **golf course** (www.siargao villa.com; 18 holes per person incl clubs, balls & tees P650) is this large villa, which resembles a suburban McMansion. The three large rooms, more like apartments, are tastefully furnished and feel quite homey. Nonguests can eat and drink at the bar and lounge area situated over the pool – the friendly Israeli owner is known for his shwarma and falafel.

Sagana Beach Resort   RESORT $$$
(☑0919 809 5769; www.cloud9surf.com; per person incl 3 meals P3500; ❄🛜🏊) 🖉 This low-key, high-end resort occupies prime beachfront steps away from the Cloud Nine pavilion. Each of the Balinese–inspired cottages features dark-wood floors, porches with hammocks and large bathrooms. Owners Jerry and Susan Deegan are warm and knowledgeable about virtually everything happening on the island. Meals – dinners especially – are worth the price alone.

Kawayan Gourmand   CAFE $
(pastries P80-200; ⊙6am-6pm; 🛜) For the island's best croissants, pastries and espresso drinks, head to this comfortable oasis of cool, both in terms of temperature and style.

Catangnan Fried Chicken   INTERNATIONAL $
(CFC; mains P150; ⊙10am-10pm) The clever play on words aside, CFC's speciality rivals KFC's. Sandwiches and other basic grilled-meat dishes round out the menu.

Cafe Loka   CAFE $$
(sandwiches P120; ⊙6am-6pm; 🛜) Associated with neighbouring Sagana Beach Resort, this place sits under palm trees on a rare (for Cloud Nine) patch of sand, offering sandwiches, brownies, healthy juices, shakes and Aussie–style coffee.

Shaka Siargao   HEALTH FOOD $$
(mains P250; ⊙6.30am-5pm; 🛜) To maintain the healthy vibe after hours out in the surf, try one of the delicious bowls and smoothies at this postage-stamp-sized spot. The super bowl (quinoa, yoghurt, fruit, granola and honey) is especially good.

★ **Kawayan**   INTERNATIONAL $$$
(mains P350-650; ⊙7am-9.30pm Wed-Mon)
Kawayan's restaurant does food inspired
by French, Basque, Moroccan and Filipino
cuisines (tagine is the speciality), served in
a sumptuously furnished all-wood dining
area; the bar area with billiard table stays
open late. The truffles risotto is a favourite.

Northern Siargao

Tourism is still a minor blip for most of
Siargao. Fishing and farming determine
daily rhythms, so exploring this region is an
opportunity to experience everyday coastal
and rural life. On the road north to the
eastern side of the island you pass through
barangay **Pilar**, which is largely built on
stilts over mangrove flats. Not far north
are the white-sand beach and swimming
holes at **Magpupungko** (P50). The lovely
little town of **Burgos** has a crescent-shaped
beach and light-blue waters, and the waves
here and in nearby Pacifico are excellent.
Locals might be willing to let you tag along
on fishing trips.

On the western side of Siargao, around
10km from the airport, **Del Carmen** is the
gateway for highly recommended boat trips
through the mangrove swamps of Caob and
to picturesque **Sugba Lagoon** (these days,
you might have to share the lagoon with
boatloads of other tourists).

Hope for the Island (🗹0917 717 4390;
www.hopeorganicfarm.org; Burgos; ⊙8am-5pm
Mon-Sat) FREE is an 8-hectare organic farm
that grows vegetables and raises goats and
ducks (it supplies some resorts in GL and
Cloud 9). Arrange a visit in advance directly
or through Pacifico resort. The related or-
ganisation runs a malnourishment and
scholarship program for Siargao children.
Volunteers are welcome every Tuesday
morning.

Unique and lovely **stand-up paddle-
boarding tours** (P1800 per person) of the
San Isidro River are run out of the Pacifico
Beach Resort. You begin or end your tour
where the mouth of the river empties into
the ocean very close to the resort. It's around
three hours one way (return by truck).

Another equally interesting but less phys-
ically taxing way to see the river is on a **ca-
noe tour** (P600 per person, includes beer
and food) run out of Greg's Place Pizza &
Beer in San Isidro. You put into the river di-
rectly behind the restaurant and are paddled
6km through the mangroves to the village of

San Miguel. If craving a little exercise, you
have the option of trekking back through
rice paddies or along the road, though the
latter is obviously less scenic.

🍽 Sleeping & Eating

Pacifico Beach Resort   HOTEL $
(🗹0917 127 5450; www.pacificbeachresort.com;
d P950-1300; 🗟) If the bright lights and big
barangay of southern Siargao are too much,
head to this peaceful resort just south of
the village of Pacifico. Good surf and a nice
white-sand beach are out front. Some rooms
are above the restaurant and there's a rus-
tic hut; furnishings are basic. Some rooms
have private bathrooms and some only cold
water.

Jafe Surf & Sail Camp Resort   RESORT $
(🗹0919 991 2685; www.jaferesortsiargao.com;
Pacifico; camping P100, s/d with fan P300/650, s/d
with air-con P800/1000; ✳) A few kilometres
south of barangay Pacifico is the Surf & Sail
Camp Resort, a large, eclectically decorated
octagonal-shaped house with a restaurant,
beachfront property and some nearby surf
breaks.

Greg's Place Pizza & Beer   INTERNATIONAL $$
(San Isidro; mains P290; ⊙7am-7pm) American-
Filipina–owned roadside spot in sleepy San
Isidro dishing out a variety of pizzas, including Hawaiian, vegie and seafood (squid,
mussels and shrimp). Spicy Korean chicken
and fresh crab is also on the menu. If no one
is around, walk towards the house at the
back and shout a few times.

Barrel Spot   PIZZA $$
(Pacifico; mains P270; ⊙hr vary) Newly opened
Spanish–owned spot serving up thin-crust
pizza and homemade pasta in a small open-
air space. Jam sessions with neighbours and
friends most Saturday nights.

SOUTHERN MINDANAO

The area around Davao is ripe for adven-
tures, from climbing Mt Apo and hiking
opportunities in the Compostela Valley to
exploring the long coastline, both north and
south of the city, plus several offshore is-
lands. It sees few foreign travellers, but does
get more than its fair share of weekending
Davaoeños. Lake Sebu is an out-of-the-way
spot to experience tribal cultures and savour
the beauty of the countryside. Wherever

you travel in the region, roadside stands are piled high with distinctive fruits such as *marang, mangosteen, rhambutan, lanzones, doco* (a variety of the latter) and, of course, durian (there are more than eight varieties available), not to mention more ordinary fruits (bananas, pineapples and papayas are farmed on an industrial scale).

Check the latest travel advisories regarding safety in this region. There have been several incidents of violence and high-profile kidnappings in recent years.

Davao

082 / POP 1,325,200

This sprawling city – the culinary, cultural, economic and commercial capital of the south and home town of the country's president – is, for better or worse, becoming more like Manila. More traffic, more malls, more multinationals, more subdivisions hidden behind security gates. However, Mt Apo looms majestically in the distance, symbolising the typical Davaoeño's dual citizenship as both an urbanite and someone deeply rooted to the land outside the city. Locals know that Davao (dah-*bow*, and sometimes spelt 'Dabaw') has more than enough action to keep them satisfied, and yet it's only a short drive or boat ride from forested slopes and white-sand beaches.

Able to hold out against the invading Spaniards until the mid-19th century, Davao is an interesting mix of Muslim, Chinese, tribal and even Japanese influences – the latter because of early abaca-processing warehouses in the area and less happily because of WWII. Predominantly Christian, the city has seen its share of hard times, especially in the 1980s when there was guerrilla fighting in the streets. Rodrigo Duterte, the country's current president, was mayor of Davao for more than two decades. Many of the same tactics and rhetoric he's now practising on the national stage will be familiar to residents and observers. His daughter Sara is now in her second term as mayor and his son Paolo was previously the vice-mayor.

A September 2016 bombing at the Roxas Ave night market in the city centre killed 15 and wounded dozens of others. Members of the Abu Sayyaf and ISIS–affiliated Maute group claimed responsibility. Prior to this, Davao had mostly avoided any major violent incidents in the past decade.

◉ Sights & Activities

For information on outdoor activities, especially hiking and climbing Mt Apo, visit **Edge Outdoor Shop** (0919 817 2298; 4th fl, Gaisano Mall, JP Laurel Ave; 5-9pm).

★**Kublai's Gallery** GALLERY
(Yahu Plaza, cnr Magsaysay Ave & Bangoy St; 9am-6pm) **FREE** An unconventional setting for a fine-art gallery, paintings by artist Kublai Millan fill the walls of this large space. Take an elevator to the 4th or 5th floor of the ordinary Chinatown shopping plaza.

★**Museo Dabawenyo** MUSEUM
(082-222 6011; cnr A Pichon St & CM Recto Ave; 9am-6pm Mon-Fri) **FREE** An excellent museum with two floors of well-designed galleries exploring the complex patchwork of indigenous tribal groups, religions and ethnicities of Davao and Mindanao as a whole. Especially interesting are the photographic exhibitions documenting the Japanese and American occupations of the city.

Bankerohan Public Market MARKET
(cnr A Pichon St & E Quirino Ave; 7am-noon & 4-6pm) Vibrant, chaotic, claustrophobic, smelly and resembling a sprawling shanty town, Bankerohan provides a taste of local flavour. Everything that appears in Filipino kitchens is sold here. Mornings are the best time to visit.

Dabaw Museum MUSEUM
(082-233 1734; davaomuseum@yahoo.com; Insular Village, Phase 1, Agusan Circle, Lanang; P20; 9am-5pm Mon-Sat) This museum, next to the Waterfront Insular Hotel northeast of downtown, has a good collection of tribal weaving and artefacts from most of the Mindanao tribes.

Davao Crocodile Park ZOO
(082-221 7749; www.crocodilepark.ph; Riverfront Dr, Ma-a; adult/child P250/150; 8am-6pm) Around 5km north of the city centre is this large complex spread out along the Davao River. A combination conservation centre and zoo, there are croc 'shows', including feeding sessions, tightrope walking, a cultural show and an excellent riverfront restaurant serving up crocodile four ways – sizzling, pasta, omelette and plain old steak – as well as other meats (including ostrich) and seafood. Also runs a zipline (P300) in the hills nearby with panoramic views.

MINDANAO DAVAO

Davao

MINDANAO DAVAO

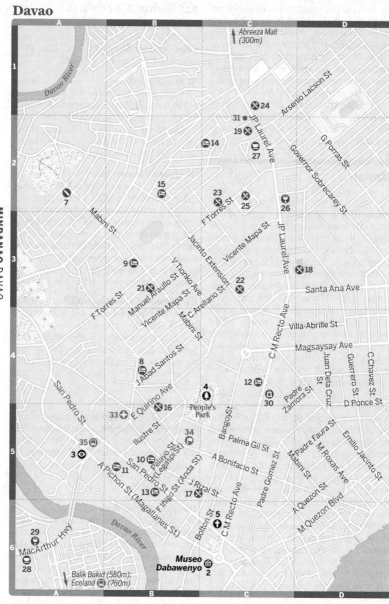

People's Park
PARK

(cnr J Camus & Illustre Sts; ⊙ 5.30-10am & 3-11pm) **FREE** A family-friendly expanse of more concrete than green space with larger-than-life-sized sculptures of native peoples of Mindanao, all designed by artist Kublai Millan.

San Pedro Cathedral
CATHEDRAL

(San Pedro St) This centrally located cathedral on the site of the city's oldest church has an interesting design meant to resemble an ark. Daily mass in English at 6am and noon.

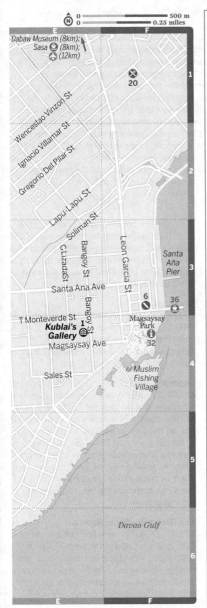

Davao

◎ Top Sights
1	Kublai's Gallery	E4
2	Museo Dabawenyo	C6

◎ Sights
3	Bankerohan Public Market	A5
4	People's Park	C4
5	San Pedro Cathedral	C6

✦ Activities, Courses & Tours
6	Carabao Dive Center	F3
	Edge Outdoor Shop	(see 18)
7	South Shore Divers	A2

⊨ Sleeping
8	Green Windows Dormitel	B4
9	LA Interline Hotel	B3
10	Legaspi Suites	B5
11	Manor Hotel	B5
12	Marco Polo Hotel	C4
13	My Hotel	B5
14	Ponce Suites Art Hotel	C2
15	Sea Green Boutique Rooms	B2

✕ Eating
16	Bulca Chong	B5
17	Claude's Le Cafe De Ville	B5
18	Gaisano Mall	D3
19	Gomone	C2
	Lachis	(see 7)
20	Malagos Farmhouse	F1
21	Original Conching's Native Chicken	B3
22	Tadakuna	C3
23	Tiny Kitchen	C2
24	Victoria Plaza Compound	C1
25	Yellow Fin	C2

◉ Drinking & Nightlife
26	Alcatraz Penal Bar	C2
27	Bluegré Coffee	C2
28	Coffee for Peace	A6
29	Matina Town Square	A6

ⓐ Shopping
30	Aldevinco Shopping Centre	C4
	Got Heart Community Shop	(see 18)

ⓘ Information
31	Bureau of Immigration	C2
32	City Tourism Office	F4
33	Davao Doctors' Hospital	B5
	Department of Tourism	(see 27)
34	Malaysian Consulate	B5

ⓘ Transport
35	Buses to Calinan	A5
36	Santa Aña Pier	F3

★ **Davao Wildwater Adventures**

RAFTING

(📞 0920 954 6898; www.facebook.com/davao wildwater; Riverfront Dr, Ma-a; per person P1700) If you're planning on rafting the Davao River west of the city, expect to spend some time

PHILIPPINE EAGLE CENTER

To view the largest eagles in the world (in terms of their 7ft wingspan), head to the **Philippine Eagle Center** (PEC; ☎ 082-224 3021; www.philippineeagle.org; adult/child P150/100; ⏱ 8am-5pm), which is dedicated to conserving this endangered species. Also known as monkey-eating eagles, these birds, with an average lifespan of 20 years in the wild (longer at the centre), are threatened by deforestation and hunting. About 400 pairs remain in the wild in the Philippines, and around 20 of the 35 here were bred through artificial insemination. The complex is set in a lush pocket of native forest near Malagos, 36km north of Davao. There are other wild birds flitting around and other animals, including the Philippine brown deer and Philippine warty pig. Volunteer guides are around to answer questions. Or check out the Philippine Eagle Foundation (www.philippineeaglefoundation.org).

To stay overnight in the area, try the collection of cottages at Malagos Garden Resort, set in a large landscaped property with gardens, walking paths, a bird park and a butterfly sanctuary.

in the water, especially in rapids that resemble washing machines after heavy rains. The best time to go for thrills is June or any time in the wet season. This highly recommended professional outfit can be found on the same premises as the Crocodile Park.

South Shore Divers　DIVING
(☎ 0917 700 3590; www.southshorediversdavao.com; Ruby St, Marfori Heights) Stop by this small shop to arrange Samal and Talikud snorkelling and diving trips. Two-/three-tank dives with equipment run P2800/P4000.

✯✯ Festivals & Events

Kadayawan sa Dabaw Festival　CULTURAL
(⏱ 3rd week Aug) Much more than a simple harvest celebration, this festival showcases tribal cultures, agriculture and crafts with street parades, performances and fantastic displays of fruit and flowers.

🛏 Sleeping

★ **Ponce Suites Art Hotel**　HOTEL $
(☎ 082-224 7207; www.poncesuiteshotel.com; cnr 3 & 4 Rds, Doña Vicenta Village, Bajada; d P975-1395; ❄🔁) Practically every inch of this mother-and-son-run hotel, inside and out, is covered with art – sculptures, poetry, photographs and paintings – all of it by the incredibly prolific Kublai Millan, who has transformed an otherwise ordinary building into a funky vision of hospitality. Rooms are ordinary motel quality, but the Gaudí-esque rooftop is the highlight.

Manor Hotel　HOTEL $
(☎ 082-221 2511; www.manorhoteldavao.com; A Pichon St; s/d P850/1200; ❄🔁) The pleasant ground-floor coffee shop and in-room

massage are bonuses at this small, professionally run downtown place. Some of the cosy – read, small – and efficient rooms with modern bathrooms and TVs have more light than others. Offers van rentals for trips to spots outside the city.

My Hotel　HOTEL $
(☎ 082-222 2021; www.myhoteldavao.com; San Pedro St; d with fan/air-con P280/1200; ❄🔁) A colourfully painted high-rise with sparkling floors and large, leanly furnished rooms; street-facing ones get good light.

Legaspi Suites　HOTEL $$
(☎ 082-227 8613; www.legaspisuitesdavao.com; 115 Pelayo St; d incl breakfast P1500; ❄🔁) One of downtown's best midrange options and one of the few in the city to be housed in a building with colonial-era architectural features. The red-tile Spanish–style roof and white clapboard exterior are a nice counterpoint to comfortable, modern rooms. A coffee shop, a spa and a travel agency are in the complex.

Sea Green Boutique Rooms　B&B $$
(☎ 082-327 4572; www.facebook.com/seagreencafe; 15 Jacinto Ext; d incl breakfast P1800; ❄🔁) Essentially, a boutique homestay on a quiet residential street attached to a pleasant cafe. Three stylish rooms (Rosemary is the nicest) with a black-and-white colour scheme.

LA Interline Hotel　HOTEL $$
(☎ 082-222 5389; lainterline.hotel@yahoo.com.ph; cnr Mabini & Voyager Sts; r incl breakfast from P1800; ❄🔁) This gleaming multistorey hotel has a large lobby and a nice cafe. F Torres St restaurants are within walking distance.

Green Windows Dormitel   HOTEL $$
(☑082-300 3893; www.greenwindowsdormitel.
com; 5th fl, FTC Tower, 1034 Mt Apo St; dm/d
P188/1450; ❈ ☎) A centrally located large
high-rise with a wide range of accommo-
dation options, including good-value dorm
rooms – many have flat-screen TVs and all
have lockers.

Malagos Garden Resort   RESORT $$
(☑082-221 1545, 0917 625 2467; www.malagos.
com; Calinan-Baguio-Cadalian Rd, Malagos; dm per
person P350, q from P3400; ❈ ☎) The Malagos
Garden Resort has a collection of cottages
set in a beautifully landscaped property with
gardens, walking paths, a bird park, a butterfly sanctuary etc. Tents are provided for
those interested in camping.

⭐**Marco Polo Hotel**   HOTEL $$$
(☑082-221 0888; www.davao.marcopolohotels.
com; CM Recto Ave; r from P4800; ❈ @ ☎ ☒)
The city's most luxurious hotel couldn't be
more centrally located. Has several recom-
mended restaurants.

✕ Eating

⭐**Victoria Plaza Compound**   INTERNATIONAL
(JP Laurel Ave) An unassuming sun-baked
collection of low-slung buildings behind the
mall of the same name. More than a dozen
quality restaurants, including several large
seafood (Sen Ton Whan Seafood, Grand Em-
erald Seafood and Ahfat Seafood), Chinese,
Korean and Filipino eateries, are found
here.

Abreeza Mall   INTERNATIONAL
(JP Laurel Ave; ⊙ store hr 10am-9pm) An upscale
mall not far north of downtown with a wide
range of cuisine for varying budgets.

Gaisano Mall   INTERNATIONAL
(JP Laurel Ave; mains P175-450; ⊙10am-10pm)
Centrally located. 'The Peak', a 5th- and 6th-
floor addition, has an outdoor plaza lined
with cafes and restaurants, including Kub-
lai Khan's, an all-you-can-eat Mongolian
place. A crowd of students watch pick-up
basketball games on the two half-courts
there.

Lachis   FILIPINO $
(☑082-224 5552; Ruby St, Marfori Heights; mains
P90-150; ⊙11am-8pm Mon-Sat) Especially busy
at lunch, this brightly coloured and casual
restaurant is best known for its home-style
cooking: barbecue pork ribs, pies, cakes and
a wide variety of pastries.

**Original Conching's
Native Chicken**   BARBECUE $
(☑0925 620 8004; Araullo St; mains P150;
⊙10am-10pm) A whole chicken and a bucket
of beers. What's not to like? Celebrities ap-
parently are on board. Their photos are plas-
tered on one wall of this otherwise open-air
casual eatery, an institution in the city. Pork
belly and grilled squid also on the menu.

⭐**Balik Bukid**   FILIPINO $$
(☑0917 972 8540; Quimpo Blvd, Sandawa Park;
mains P200; ⊙11am-2pm & 5-10pm Mon-Sat,
5-10pm Sun) 🌿 Three siblings – a chef, a deco-
rator and a farmer – have opened up this 'barn
to table' restaurant in which they've vowed to
get back to the basics. Almost everything on
the plate – except the fresh fish – comes from
their chemical-free organic farm. The airy
dining room has a high ceiling and handicrafts decorating the bamboo walls.

⭐**Malagos Farmhouse**   CAFE $$
(☑082-300 4541; www.malagosfarmhouse.com;
Bolcan St, Agdao; tastings per person P300, mini-
mum 6) 🌿 The base for the growing artisanal
cheese-making business of Olive Puent-
espina and her husband. Tastings accom-
panied by wine and Olive, a passionate and
interesting fount of information on organic
farming in the Philippines, are available in
the afternoons. She chooses from more than
20 varieties of organic cheese, and you can
snack on cornichons, meats and bread.

Tadakuna   JAPANESE $$
(☑0927 960 5507; Jacinto Extension, near Arel-
lano; mains P220-400; ⊙11am-10pm) Tadakuna
doesn't look like much: a handful of tables
in a modest dining room. However, the
owner, a passionate fisherman, knows how
to turn out some of the best sushi, sashimi
and Tokyo–style ramen in town. Several new
franchises elsewhere in the city.

Tiny Kitchen   SPANISH $$
(☑082-305 9232; F Torres St; mains P175-375;
⊙10am-8.30pm Mon-Sat) Paellas and other
Iberian–style meat dishes dominate most
of the chalkboard menu at this bustling and
homey place, where the owner roves the
tables greeting regulars. Also known for its
artisanal bread, cakes, pastries and other
desserts displayed up front.

Yellow Fin   SEAFOOD $$
(☑082-222 0338; F Torres St; mains P200; ⊙10am-
2pm & 5.30-10pm) One of three locations in
the city, this informal and popular eatery

specialises in seafood by the kilo (eg lapu lapu and tuna). When it's busy here, most dishes take close to half an hour to arrive.

Bulca Chong FILIPINO $$
(☑ 082-225 8665; General Luna St; mains P175; ☺24hr) Late-night cravings meet their match at this modest eatery serving this restaurant's eponymous dish made of stewed carabao with ginger root, onion, chilli, *calamansi* and an unidentified sauce.

Gomone KOREAN $$
(Doña Vicenta Dr; mains P200; ☺10.30am-2.30pm & 5.30-10pm) A modest place serving authentic Korean dishes across the street from Victoria Plaza Mall. More leafy greens than other places, so a good choice for vegetarians.

★**Claude's Le Cafe**
De Ville EUROPEAN, FRENCH $$$
(☑ 082-222 4287; www.claudescafedavao.com; 143 J Rizal St; mains P320-1500; ☺10am-10.30pm Mon-Sat) The polished wood floors, carved trellis work and white clapboard exterior make this beautifully restored colonial-era home one of Davao's treasures. Easily the most elegant and romantic restaurant in the city, Claude's cuisine rivals its atmosphere. Steaks by weight are the speciality – from T-bones to wild boar and deer – but fish and pasta dishes are equally good.

🍷 Drinking & Nightlife

★**Matina Town Square** BEER GARDEN, BAR
(MTS; MacArthur Hwy) A collection of outdoor bars and food joints, and a handful of more upscale restaurants and clubs, MTS is a lively and fun spot. On Tuesday nights there's a free outdoor show of indigenous music and dance; other nights there's also live music, usually of the pop variety. The stage fronts dozens of tables and several barbecue restaurant stalls.

Coffee for Peace CAFE
(www.coffeeforpeace.com; G/F Frederic Bldg, MacArthur Hwy, Matina; ☺7am-midnight Mon-Sat; 🛜) 🍴 This small cafe is the retail outpost of a fair-trade community-oriented organisation, one of the first in the Philippines to export arabica coffee. A quarter of the net profits go towards projects with its partner Peace Builders, an NGO working with indigenous communities in the Philippines.

Alcatraz Penal Bar CLUB
(Palma Gil St; ☺5pm-1am Wed-Sun) Named for the American prison, as well as a defunct '90s Davao bar, but there's little nostalgia. DJs spin the latest club dance tracks, and strobes and laser lights pierce the air. The questionable theme only really materialises in the VIP areas, which resemble detention cells.

Bluegré Coffee CAFE
(☑ 082-222 7675; LANDCO-PDCP Corporate Center, JP Laurel Ave; ☺7am-midnight) One of the city's coffee culture pioneers and purveyor of durian-flavoured coffee drinks. Cosy and good food and pastry selection. A few other cafes are located in this small complex of office buildings.

🛍 Shopping

★**Got Heart**
Community Shop ART
(☑ 0906 496 2153; Gaisano Mall, JP Laurel Ave; ☺1-9pm) 🍴 Head up to the 5th floor, part of an outdoor plaza called the Peak, for this shop selling locally produced products such as organic cacao, coconut oil and ginger candy, as well as the work of local artists.

Aldevinco Shopping Centre ARTS & CRAFTS
(CM Recto Ave; ☺10am-7pm) If you're looking for handicrafts, shop around this rabbit warren of stalls with textiles, batik, weavings, carvings and jewellery. You can also pick up a *malong,* a traditional Mindanao tribal cloth used as a skirt, turban, blanket or baby carrier; handwoven ones run P1500, while cheap machine-made ones from China cost P300. Take your time and bargain – almost every day is a slow day. The stallholders are also keen to change euro and US dollars.

ℹ Information

Bureau of Immigration (BOI; ☑ 082-228 6477; bidavao@gmail.com; JP Laurel Ave; ☺8am-5pm Mon-Fri) Directly across the street from Victoria Plaza Mall.

City Tourism Office (☑ 082-222 1956; www.davaocity.gov.ph; Room 8, Magsaysay Park Complex; ☺8am-5pm Mon-Fri) General information and contact details for people and agencies handling hiking, diving and other activities.

Department of Tourism (☑ 082-221 6955; dotrdavao@gmail.com; Room 512, LANDCO Corporate Center, JP Laurel Ave; ☺9am-4:30pm Mon-Fri) Good source of information if travelling elsewhere in the province.

Davao Doctors' Hospital (📞 082-222 8000; www.ddh.com.ph; cnr E Quirino Ave & Gen Malvar St) The largest and possibly most modern hospital in Mindanao.

ℹ️ Getting There & Away

AIR

The **Francisco Bangoy International Airport** (Davao International Airport; barangay Buhangin) is 12km north of the city centre; a metered taxi is around P150. From the city, jeepneys heading for Sasa go towards the airport; you'll then need to take a tricycle to the airport terminal.

Philippine Airlines (www.philippineairlines.com) and Cebu Pacific (www.cebupacificair.com) fly to Manila, Cebu, Zamboanga City and Iloilo City. Silk Air (p346) and Cebu Pacific fly to Singapore several days a week.

BOAT

Big inter-island boats use the terminal at **Sasa**, by the Caltex tanks 8km north of town. This is also where boats to Paradise Island Beach Resort on Samal Island leave from. Jeepneys run here, or take a taxi for about P85.

Other boats to Samal and Talikud Islands go from Santa Aña Pier in town.

BUS

All long-distance bus transport is based at the **Ecoland** (Candelaria Ave) terminal, 2km south of the city centre. Buses generally leave every 30 minutes to an hour. Minivans service many of the same destinations, including General Santos and Mati; there's a north-bound terminal near the Victoria Plaza entrance and another outside the Gaisano Mall (vans for Kidapawan leave from here). Decrepit buses to Calinan (for the Philippine Eagle Centre and Malagos Garden Resort) leave from a shed next to the Bankerohan Public Market. The following prices are for aircon buses:

DESTINATION	FARE (P)	DURATION (HR)
Butuan	500	7¼
Cagayan de Oro	535	6
General Santos	300	3½
Mati	280	4
Surigao	720	7

General Santos

📞 083 / POP 474,500

Known to locals as 'Gensan', to fishmongers as the 'Tuna Capital of the Philippines' and to sports fans as the home town of Manny Pacquiao (aka Pacman), General Santos is the southernmost city in the Philippines.

Formerly Dadiangas, the city was renamed in 1965 in honour of General Paulino Santos who, with accompanying Christian Visayans and Tagalogs, established a settlement here in 1939.

These days it's a typically congested city, notable mostly for the huge ships that dock at the port here on Sarangani Bay, loading up freshly caught tuna for the journey to dinner tables all over Asia. Gensan is really only worth a detour during the Tuna Festival, held in the first week of September, and the Kalilangan Festival, celebrated in the last week of February and commemorating the founding of Gensan in 1939 with traditional dance, cooking and handicrafts.

🛏️ Sleeping & Eating

Driggs Pension House   HOTEL $
(📞 083-553 0088; driggspensionhouse@yahoo.com; Eve St, Paradise Subdivision; d incl breakfast P800-1000; ❄️🛜) Located in the City Heights neighbourhood a few kilometres north of the centre is this well-cared-for two-storey building with clean rooms and professional service.

Dolores Tropicana Resort Hotel   RESORT $
(📞 083-553 9350; www.doloreshotels.ph/dolores-tropicana-resort; Tambler; r incl breakfast P875-1500; ❄️🛜🏊) A better choice than staying in the city, the beachside cottages at this large complex, though nothing spectacular, have views of Sarangani Bay right out their front doors. It has a pleasant open-air restaurant.

Hotel San Marco   HOTEL $$
(📞 0947 893 2237, 083-301 1818; www.hotelsanmarco.com.ph; Laurel East Ave; s/d incl breakfast P1680/3000; ❄️🛜) The faux Italianate facade and Three Tenors lobby soundtrack signal San Marco's striving for sophistication. Many rooms lack natural light but all are modern, comfortable and have coffee makers and large flat-screen TVs. Front-desk staff can help with transport plans, and it's within walking distance of several restaurants and Gaisano mall.

Kambingan sa Depot   FILIPINO $
(KSD; Acharon Blvd; mains from P50) Directly across the street from several large oil depots, this spot serves goat meat in a variety of ways, including goat testicle soup – which some consider to be the Filipino Viagra. Many of the dishes sell out before early afternoon.

Tiongson Arcade
SEAFOOD $$

(Tiongson St; mains P150; ⏱6-10pm) An outdoor night market and culinary adventure where pointing at your choice of freshly caught seafood results in a delicious meal minutes later.

ℹ Getting There & Away

AIR

Tambler airport is 12km west of the city centre; a taxi costs P170. Cebu Pacific (www.cebupacificair.com) and Philippine Airlines (www.philippine airlines.com) fly daily from Manila (two hours). Cebu Pacific has flights to Cebu (1½ hours).

BOAT

Makar Pier is 2km west of town. 2GO (http://travel.2go.com.ph) has boats bound for Manila (54 hours) via Zamboanga and Iloilo (30 hours), on Panay, several days a week; it also runs weekly trips to Zamboanga City (12 hours).

BUS

Yellow Bus, Rural Bus, Mindanao Star, Husky and Holiday run regular buses between General Santos and Davao (P195 to P265, 3½ hours); executive-class buses with wi-fi and air-con leave a quarter past every hour until 7pm. For Cagayan de Oro, only two Rural Transit buses go direct (P800, 10 hours, 3am and 10am).

For the first leg of the trip to Lake Sebu, hop on a bus or van to Marbel (Koronadal City; P120, one hour, every 20 minutes).

The integrated bus and jeepney terminal is at Bula-ong on the western edge of town, about 1km from the town centre (tricycle P15).

Lake Sebu

POP 87,400 / ELEV 300M

The watery bottom of a beautiful bowl, Lake Sebu is surrounded on all sides by hills and forests. Occasionally, dugout canoes slowly skim its placid surface; however, the picturesque scene is marred by the ring of bamboo fish traps spreading inward from the shore. A large church sits on top of a hill, and several other modern concrete buildings interrupt otherwise pristine views. Several beautiful waterfalls are in the surrounding countryside, and expert craftspeople ply their traditional arts in rural and remote barangays.

◉ Sights & Activities

Hire a **boat** (P500, 30 minutes) from any of the resorts for a swing around the lake (the light before sunset can be beautiful); if alone, ask to join a group. Saturdays are the best time to visit, when tribespeople from surrounding communities descend on the town for the **weekly market**.

Seven Falls
WATERFALL

A motorcycle (half-day with driver P300) can take you to **Hikong Alu** and **Hikong Bente** (also known as falls #1 and #2), two of the nearby Seven Falls (P20). Hikong Bente is an impressive sight and at 70ft the highest of the bunch. It's a short walk from where you park to both falls. A sometimes-operating Superman–style **zipline** (P300) takes you over three of the falls – views are magnificent.

School for Indigenous Knowledge & Traditions
CULTURAL CENTRE

(School for Living Traditions; SIKAT; ☑0935 456 9359; www.facebook.com/LakeSebuSLT) 🖉 The School for Indigenous Knowledge & Traditions' mission is to educate, advocate, lobby and promote cultural tourism. Maria Todi, an accomplished chanter, dancer and musician (*hegalong*, the two-string lute of the T'boli), founded and runs SIKAT. You're introduced to artists and elders and have the chance to learn about T'boli customs, history and stories. Music and dance classes for area children are on Saturdays. You can sleep on a mattress (P250) in the *gono bong* (longhouse) on the main road through town.

SIKAT also offers homestays, and Maria can arrange visits to villages deeper into the surrounding countryside. If you go, consider bringing something simple like noodles to share. Closer by is T'bong village where you can visit a bamboo hut in which weavers produce textiles in the traditional colours of white, red and black in T'nalak patterns. In general, weavers apprentice for six years, and the average piece made from *abaka* material takes four months to complete. If you can, check out *Dreamweavers* (2000), a documentary about T'boli artists and their practices and challenges in a rapidly modernising culture. Besides T'boli, other tribes in the area are Ubo, Tasaday and Manobos.

T'boli Museum
MUSEUM

(⏱7am-5pm) You can buy locally made handicrafts here – it's a small native-style house selling the same weavings and brassware items found at roadside souvenir stalls.

🛏 Sleeping

Punta Isla
RESORT $

(☑083-236 1053; Sitio Tokufol; r incl breakfast P950; 🛜) This resort offers lovely views from its restaurant (try the tilapia *kinilaw*, but avoid the dry and rock-hard fried chicken) and the balconies of its simply furnished rooms. Groups of locals occupy the wood pavilions lining the lake at lunchtime, and the resort puts on T'boli dance and music performances when enough guests are present.

ⓘ Getting There & Away

Reaching Lake Sebu via public transport involves several transfers. From General Santos (or Cotabato) catch a bus or van to Marbel (Koronadal City; P120, one hour), then transfer to a bus or van to Surallah (P37, 30 minutes) and finally hop in a van (P50, 45 minutes) for the final leg. Waits for departures aren't long.

If staying by the lake, don't get off at the first stop at a terminal in Lake Sebu despite the pleas of motorcycle 'taxi' drivers. The final stop is further along and in walking distance of lakeside resorts.

Mt Apo

☑ 082

Literally the 'grandfather' of all mountains, Mt Apo is a volcano that has never blown its top and, at 2954m, is the highest peak in the Philippines. Most mornings it is clearly visible towering above Davao. However, by 8am a mass of clouds resembling a fluffy snake usually conceals the peak. Local tribes believe deities reside near the summit and worship it as a sacred mountain, but it's the environmental stress caused by human traffic that makes permission to climb it difficult to obtain. The situation is fluid and should be sussed out at the tourist office (p370) in Davao, which can provide a list of reputable guides, or in Kidapawan, 110km from Davao

and the closest municipality to the starting point for hikes to the summit – the office of the **Kidapawan Tourism Council** (☑ 064-278 3361; pipayging@yahoo.com; Kidapawan) is in the City Hall. Coffee is grown on the mountain's slopes, which sit at the same latitude as Ethiopia.

For one of the longest **ziplines** (P350) in Southeast Asia, stop at Camp Sabros near Kapatagan, on the southern slopes of Mt Apo – it's long enough to feel like you are flying over pine trees below. **Tudaya Falls**, one of the highest in the Philippines at 300ft, is nearby.

🛏 Sleeping

Mt Apo Highland Resort   RESORT **$$**
(☑ 0918 959 1641; booking@dvaocrocodilepark. com; Kapatagan; tent per person P300, d cottage P1800-2000; ❄) This resort incorporates a handful of small cottages on concrete stilts around Lake Mirror and the mountain slope area, referred to as Hillside. Camping is a good option at both, and air mattresses and tents are available for rent. The restaurant at Hillside has a great view of Mt Apo.

Eden Nature Park Resort   RESORT **$$**
(☑ 082-286 0385; www.edennaturepark.com.ph; cottage/cabin P1400-4000; ❄❄) This once denuded slope – a victim of overzealous logging – at the foot of Mt Talomo has been transformed into a lush forest with hiking trails, sports fields, playgrounds and a 20-second-long zipline. A wide variety of cottages are scattered throughout the property. Shuttle service is available from the park's main office in Matina Town Sq in Davao.

MINDANAO MT APO

CLIMBING MT APO

The climb takes in primeval forests, rushing waterfalls and the possibility of spotting endangered plant and animal species, such as the carnivorous pitcher plants and the Philippine eagle. Vanda Sandariana, more commonly known as *waling-waling* and to be considered the mother of all commercial orchid plants, is endemic.

The ascent is strenuous (extremely steep in parts) and the path almost impossible to follow on your own. You'll have to visit one of the tourist offices to hire a guide. Experienced climbers recommend allowing a minimum of four days, and you'll need warm clothes and sleeping gear, since temperatures drop at night near the peak. Hiking permits cost P500, guides and porters around P500 and P300 per day respectively; food and equipment aren't included. A so-called 'VIP trail' spirals to the peak through property of the Philippine National Oil Company (PNOC; exploring geothermal projects in the area) and takes four to five hours one way. Few take this route since both the mayor and governor need to grant permission. The best time to go is from March to August when there's less chance of rain.

Most people actually begin their climb after a jeepney ride to Ilomavis and Lake Agko (1193m), where they stay overnight and arrange porters before heading for Lake Venado (2182m) and the summit.

ⓘ Getting There & Away

From Davao, take a bus from the Ecoland bus terminal to Kidapawan (P95, two hours, every 30 minutes). To jump-off points for the trek, take a jeepney from Kidapawan to Ilomavis (P55, one hour), 17km away.

Samal Island

☎ 082 / POP 104,000

Ignore the official name, the Island Garden City of Samal (Igacos): this island just across the bay from Davao is simply referred to as Samal. Much like New Yorkers heading to the Hamptons or the Jersey Shore on weekends, Davaoeños make the quick commute to this island's 116km of beaches. Of course, not all of this beachfront is picture perfect – in fact, the majority of the resorts on the west coast face unsightly refineries and shipping terminals just across the busy channel. The east side of the island is quieter and more unspoiled.

The island's idyll and reputation were rocked by the 2015 kidnapping of four tourists from a resort by Abu Sayyaf militants. The two Canadians were later killed, a Norwegian man freed after a large ransom was paid, and the Filipino woman released. Security has since been tightened, but foreign tourist numbers have yet to rebound.

◉ Sights & Activities

If you just want to escape the city for a day, all of the resorts charge day fees (P50 to P400) for use of their beach and pool (if they've got one) – even if you eat at their restaurants. There are **snorkelling** and dozens of **diving** opportunities around the island, including two Japanese wrecks just off Pearl Farm Beach, Big and Little Liguid islands off the northeast coast, and several good wall dives with healthy coral. Try **Carabao Dive Center** (☎ 082-300 1092; www.divedavao.com; Monteverde St, St Ana Pier, Davao) or South Shore Divers (p368); two-/three-tank dives with equipment run around P2800/4000.

The road around the island is paved; a day on a motorbike can cost around P600.

In barangay Tambo, around 11km north of Babak, is the largest colony of Geoffroy's Rousette fruit bats in the world at **Monfort Bat Cave** (☎ 082-286 6958; www.monfortbatsanctuary.org; Sitio Dunggas; adult/child P100/40; ☺ 8am-5pm). A knowledgeable guide will walk you around the five openings where an estimated 2.5 million of these nocturnal and smelly creatures flutter and hang (no smok-

ing, since the guano is like gunpowder). Visit at dusk just before they wake and search for food – mostly overripe bananas and mangoes.

Near San Jose in barangay Cawag, **Hagimit Falls** (P50; ☺ 6am-6pm) has a seemingly endless number of small cascades and pools you can navigate in your own private slip 'n' slide tour. This is a very developed site with concrete paths and picnic huts.

🛏 Sleeping

Bluewaters Resort RESORT $$
(☎ 0915 568 4446; www.bluewatersvillageandresort.com; d with fan/air-con P1200/1500; ❄ ✿) This resort has a handful of cottages and nondescript 'apartment' rooms, plus a nice infinity pool (day guests pay P100).

★ **Chema's by the Sea Resort** RESORT $$$
(☎ 082-303 0235, 0917 814 0814; www.chemasbythesea.com; d/q cottage P5500/8000; ❄ ✿) The relatively intimate Chema's has large, beautifully furnished upscale native-style cottages with Balinese influences. The property is on a leafy hillside leading down to an infinity pool and beach with a wonderful patio and lounge area.

Paradise Island Park & Beach Resort RESORT $$$
(☎ 082-233 0251; www.paradiseislanddavao.com; cottages P3700; ❄ @ 🛜) This Samal stalwart is its own mini–Boracay. It's a huge, immaculately landscaped complex with its own zoo and a sandy beachfront strip lined with shops, eating and activity areas; every water sport is available, only a pool is missing. Most of the 76 rooms are nicely furnished cottages with porches and their very own private fenced-in garden.

ⓘ Getting There & Away

Bangkas go regularly to Samal (P20, 10 minutes, frequent from 5am to 11pm) from the big Caltex tanks near Davao's Sasa pier; walk through the market to reach the departure point. Most of the resorts organise transfers for their guests from different piers around Davao. The Island City Express (P45, every 15 minutes) runs from the Ecoland terminal in Davao to the Sasa pier and then continues dropping passengers off on Samal.

Talikud Island

☎ 082

This little island to the southwest of Samal offers a real refuge for those looking to escape. Developers are eyeing its long white-sand beaches; however, for now, there's not much here other than a few low-key resorts and pellucid waters. A handful of good dive sites are off the west coast and there's a chance of spotting dugongs. Some beaches get crowded with day trippers on weekends.

🛏 Sleeping

Babu Santa COTTAGE **$**

(☑ 0918 726 1466; tid@yahoo.com; camping P75, r P400) For off-the-grid, do-it-yourself accommodation in basic cottages on a beautiful white-sand beach, head to this place on Talikud's northwestern tip. Worth bringing your own food supplies.

Isla Reta COTTAGE **$**

(☑ 0998 991 6690; camping P400, cottages P900) On a beautiful beach on the eastern side of Talikud Island facing Samal, Isla Reta has basic bamboo cottages and tents for campers. Simple meals (P180) can be provided, and it's the closest accommodation to the pier in Santa Cruz; some boats will drop you here. Book in advance. It can feel overcrowded at times.

★ Leticia's by the Sea COTTAGE **$$$**

(☑ 082-224 0501, mobile 0917 702 5427; www.leticiabythesearesort.com; r with 3 meals P4800-11,000; ❄️ 🛜) This exquisite property on the eastern side of the island combines rustic, native-style touches with contemporary features. Cottages are set in meticulously landscaped gardens with hardwood balconies – less expensive are the charming 'Bali Houses', essentially luxury versions of sleeping outdoors in a picnic hut.

ℹ️ Getting There & Away

Boats run to the tiny township and jetty at Santa Cruz on Talikud (P80, one hour) hourly from 6am to early afternoon from Santa Aña Pier in Davao.

WESTERN MINDANAO & ZAMBOANGA PENINSULA

Stretching nearly to Malaysia and encompassing the Bangsamoro Autonomous Region in Muslim Mindanao (BARMM), which includes the Philippines' Islamic heartland, this region, while large, receives few foreign visitors. Islam, the oldest religion here, was introduced in 1475, with Christianity a comparatively recent arrival, brought by Jesuits in 1871. Under different circumstances, the jungle-clad mountains, waterfalls and lakes

and rural areas inhabited by tribal groups would be worth exploration.

In recent years the city of Marawi has been under siege by ISIS–affiliated fighters but martial law was lifted in 2019. The security situation (p355) was especially heightened in the provinces of Lanao del Sur and Maguindanao. These areas were considered no-go zones.

👁 Sights & Activities

Hidden deep in a mountain, **Tinago Falls** (Iligan; P10) is the most spectacular of Iligan's waterfalls; you can drive to the start of the very steep stairway (365 steps) down. The super-cold **Timoga Springs** (Iligan; P50) are refreshing on a hot day

President Gloria Macapagal-Arroyo's Childhood Summer Home NOTABLE BUILDING

(Iligan) Directly in front of Timoga Springs, along the main highway, this is only really interesting to political buffs. Perhaps most curious are the family photos documenting Macapagal-Arroyo from child to adult.

🛏 Sleeping & Eating

Rene's Diner & Pension House HOTEL **$**

(☑ 063-223 8441; Roxas Ave Extension, Iligan; r with fan/air-con P350/480; ❄️ 🛜) A convenient option if you want to spend the night, Rene's sits on the main road, a few minutes west of the centre. Rooms are spacious if poorly maintained.

Corporate Inn Boutique Hotel HOTEL **$**

(☑ 063-221 4456; corpor8inn@yahoo.com; 5 Sparrow St, Isabel Village, Iligan; s/d incl breakfast from P750/1200; ❄️ 🛜) Quiet but out of the way, this place is more personable than its unfortunate name implies, especially the outdoor sitting area. A handful of restaurants are within walking distance.

Cheradel Suites HOTEL **$$**

(☑ mobile 063-221 4926; Jeffrey St, Iligan; r incl breakfast P1100-2200; ❄️ 🛜 🏊) The somewhat kitschy top-end choice in Iligan is about five minutes east of town near the post office and Landbank.

Gloria's Ihaw Ihaw FILIPINO **$**

(Iligan; mains P100; ⏱ 6am-6pm) Across the street from Timoga Springs and along the waterfront is Gloria's Ihaw Ihaw, serving delicious *kinilaw* (raw seafood cured in vinegar), grilled fish and chicken.

Zamboanga City

📞 062 / POP 695,000

When the sun sets in the Philippines, this city, whose otherwise banal skyline is punctuated by several minarets, is one of the last places to see it go. Besides an edge-of-the-map frisson, other attractions are an excellent museum and some offshore islands. While geographically the end of the line, historically Zamboanga City has been a first step, from Islam's arrival to the islands in the 1400s to waves of migrants from the Sulu Archipelago. Even though the city is 70% Muslim, most women don't wear headscarves, and modern fashions are as strong here as elsewhere.

Zamboanga City has seen conflict over the years. Most significantly, a large contingent of MNLF forces laid siege to the city for three weeks in September 2013. There have been several other serious incidents, as well as foiled attacks, and caution is advised; check the latest advisories before arrival.

At the southeastern end of town near the waterfront is **Fort Pilar Museum** (NS Valderosa St; ⏰ 9am-4pm Mon-Fri) FREE, partially restored to maintain its historic character. Inside is a museum with several impressive and recently renovated galleries.

🛏 Sleeping & Eating

Grand Astoria Hotel HOTEL $
(📞 062-991 2510; Mayor Jaldon St; s/d from P850/1200; ❄ @ 🛜) This efficiently run Zamboanga City institution is often booked by groups attending seminars, conventions, weddings and the like. Ask for one of the renovated rooms. Airline ticketing offices and a restaurant are on the ground floor.

Marcian Business Hotel HOTEL $$
(MBH; 📞 062-991 0005; www.marcianhotels.com; Mayor Cesar Climaco Ave; s/d P1520/1800; ❄ 🛜) Gleaming tile floors, spacious bathrooms with top-of-the-line shower heads, and tastefully designed boutique-style rooms make this the best midrange choice in the city. Located at a busy intersection, the Marcian is a refuge from the noise and smog.

Mano-Mano na Greenfield FILIPINO $
(📞 062 992 4717; Governor Ramos St, barangay Santa Maria; mains P70-275) About 1km north of the Edwin Andrews Air Base, and housed in a large, flashy version of the native-style pavilion, Mano-Mano specialises in grilled pork spareribs and baby back ribs. Its Paseo del Mar location gets extremely crowded.

⭐ **Alavar Seafood House** SEAFOOD $$
(📞 062-992 4533; barangay Tetuan; mains P200) Seafood, of course, is the speciality here – choose the species, size and cooking method from a menu of delicacies. What sets Alavar apart is the beautiful trellis-covered backyard. Enjoy a lantern-lit dinner serenaded by the loud squawking from an aviary of exotic birds.

ℹ Information

Department of Tourism (DOT; 📞 062-993 0030; cnr Alvarez & Claveria Sts; ⏰ 8am-noon & 1-5pm Mon-Sat) Helpful provincial tourism office.

ℹ Getting There & Away

Few travellers venture to Zamboanga overland and most arrive by plane. However, for the intrepid who want to travel throughout northern Mindanao before visiting the city, it's possible to get either a fast ferry (four hours) or bus (eight hours) in the town of Pagadian in Zamboanga del Sur. If you go by road, only travel during the daytime.

AIR

Philippine Airlines (www.philippineairlines.com) and Cebu Pacific (www.cebupacificair.com) fly between Manila and Zamboanga City (1½ hours) several times daily; the latter also flies to Cebu (one hour) and Davao several times a week (one hour), and to Jolo and Tawi-Tawi in the Sulu Archipelago. Plans for a new international airport have been in the works for many years; it appears to be moving forward. International links might include Kota Kinabalu or Sandakan, both in Malaysia.

BOAT

George & Peter has a weekly trip to Cebu (P1000, 29 hours); and **2GO** (p346) goes once weekly to Dumaguete (P550, 12 hours) and Manila (P1800, 48 hours)

Weesam Express (📞 062-992 3986; www.weesam.ph) goes to Isabela (P190, 45 minutes, four daily) on nearby Basilan Island and Jolo (P800, 3½ hours, 8.30am); the ticketing office is at the ferry terminal. **Aleson Shipping Lines** (📞 062-991 2687; www.aleson-shipping.com; 172 Veterans Ave, Zamboanga) and **Ever Lines Shipping Inc** (📞 062-991 0293; Mutual Bldg, 47 Valderosa St) have trips to Jolo and Tawi-Tawi.

Aleson Shipping Lines has a boat to Sandakan in Malaysia (economy/air-con/cabin P7620/8020/8240, 20 hours) every Monday and Thursday at 2pm. It departs Sandakan on Tuesday and Friday at 5pm.

Palawan

Why Go?

Drifting on the Philippines' western edge, Palawan is one of the country's last ecological frontiers. The main attraction is the west coast, which comprises one breathtaking bay after another leading up to the limestone cliffs of El Nido in the north. Four hours north of mainland Palawan by boat, the Calamian group of islands offers incredible island-hopping and wreck diving. Around the province, waterfalls thunder out of the jungle, remote tribes spearfish for supper and sand-swept islands beckon travellers looking to leave the civilised world behind.

Despite becoming something of a travel-media darling during the 2010s, Thailand-style tourist hordes never arrived, and the province bottled up tight during the pandemic. Many resorts shuttered up and bangka captains returned to their villages to live off the land and sea. Palawan could have a new, considerably more upscale look when things finally return to normal.

Best Places to Eat

➡ Kalui (p383)

➡ La Plage (p401)

➡ Trattoria Altrove (p411)

➡ Gorgonzola (p392)

➡ Bulalo Plaza (p401)

Best Places to Stay

➡ Sangat Island Dive Resort (p411)

➡ Flower Island Beach Resort (p395)

➡ Daluyon Resort (p387)

➡ Pangalusian Island Resort (p405)

➡ Coconut Garden Island Resort (p390)

When to Go
Puerto Princesa

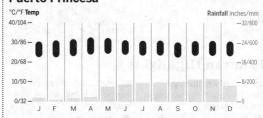

Apr–early Jun The best time for sea travel.	**Jul–Sep** The southwest monsoon peaks, bringing heavy rains (but cheap prices).	**Dec–Feb** Cooler and drier, but high winds can foul up boat schedules.

Map labels:

South China Sea

Manila (125km)
Mamburao
Santa Cruz
Sablayan
Mindoro
Apo Reef National Park
Concepcion
San José
Mindoro Strait
Semirara Islands
Buluang
Basuanga Island
Coron Bay Wrecks ❺
Coron ❷
Coron Island
Culion Island
Calamian Islands
Linapacan Strait
Linapacan Islands
Agutaya Island
Cuyo West Passage
Cuyo Islands
Cuyo
Cuyo East Passage
El Nido ❸
Bacuit Archipelago ❶
Liminangcong
Taytay
Taytay Bay
Imuran Bay
San Vicente
Araceli
Dumaran Island
Iloilo City (117km)
Palawan Passage
Mayday Bay
Port Barton ❹
Roxas
St Paul Bay
Sabang ❻
Caramay
Iloilo City (115km)
Bahile
Bacungan
San Rafael
Honda Bay
Long Point
Tagburos ❼
Puerto Princesa
Malanut Bay
Palawan
Cagayan Islands
Tabon Caves
Aborlan
Village Bay
Narra
Rasa Island
Quezon
Island Bay
Malapackun Island
Iraan Bay
Rizal
Mt Mantalinghan (2086m)
Brooke's Point
Sulu Sea
Tubbataha Reefs
Bataraza
Rio Tuba
Welcome Point
Buliluyan
Ursula Island
Basterra Reef
Sulu Sea
Sebaring
Bugsuk Island
Balabac
Bancorn Island
Balabac Island
San Miguel Islands

Scale: 0 — 100 km / 0 — 50 miles

Palawan Highlights

❶ **Bacuit Archipelago** (p403) Snorkelling your way in and out of lagoons.

❷ **Calamian Islands** (p405) Island-hopping till you drop in these paradisiacal islands: hidden lakes and empty white-sand beaches.

❸ **El Nido** (p395) Exploring the stunning beaches, waterfalls, cliffs and islands around north Palawan's main tourist town.

❹ **Port Barton** (p389) Moving in the slow village pace, from hammock to beach and back again.

❺ **Coron Bay Wrecks** (p406) Wriggling through the portholes of WWII–era wrecks is the experience of a lifetime for scuba divers.

❻ **Sabang** (p386) Staying at the home of the Underground River to enjoy its luscious beach and raw jungle scenery.

❼ **Puerto Princesa** (p379) Breezing through the countryside outside Palawan's capital on a motorcycle.

ℹ️ Getting There & Away

AIR

Palawan's two main airports are **Puerto Princesa International Airport** (National Hwy), which serves all of mainland Palawan; and Busuanga Island's **Franciso B Reyes Airport** (USU; www. franciscoreyesairport.com; Santa Cruz), which serves the Calamian Islands. Both airports are served by most of the major domestic carriers.

El Nido and the Bacuit Archipelago are served by the small, privately owned Lio Airport, which is used by just one airline, Air Swift. Travellers heading this way tend to fly into Puerto Princesa and take a public van to El Nido instead. The new **San Vicente Airport** (Poblacion Rd) could become a new hub for El Nido–bound travellers.

Lastly, Air Juan (www.airjuan.com) and its fleet of six-seat sea and land planes have been expanding into Palawan, connecting Busuanga and Puerto Princesa with popular tourist destinations like Caticlan (Boracay).

Boat

There are sturdy passenger ferries connecting Puerto Princesa and Coron with Manila, and a less sturdy ferry connecting Manila and El Nido. There is also a route between Puerto Princesa and Iloilo (Visayas) via the remote Cuyo Islands. Trips on all of the above routes are irregular (usually just a couple of trips per week).

In the north, bangka ferries connect Coron with San José, Mindoro.

Puerto Princesa

📞 048 / POP 255,116

Palawan's bustling capital is mainly a gateway to El Nido and the beaches of the west coast, but 'Puerto' does have enough diversions to warrant a day or two if you're passing through. A decent food scene, some nightlife along main drag Rizal Ave, and a growing number of boutique hotels increase the appeal.

The city is immense. The underground river in Sabang, some 60km away to the northwest, technically lies within municipality limits (hence the official name: Puerto Princesa Subterranean River). Filipinos arrive in droves to book overpriced day trips to the underground river out of Puerto. You're better off staying in idyllic Sabang and launching your trip there.

👁️ Sights & Activities

Several sights within the vicinity of Puerto are often visited as part of a day-long 'city tour' (P600), which caters primarily to Filipinos from Manila. We would advise against

these. Instead, hire a tricycle or rent a motorbike and create your own tour.

Plaza Cuartel   HISTORIC SITE

(Taft St; P50; ⏰7am-7pm) Behind the Immaculate Concepcion Cathedral (c 1872), this restored WWII garrison is the site of an open-air war museum and shrine to American prisoners of war burned alive here by the Japanese on 14 December 1944 – an incident known as the Palawan Massacre. Only 11 of the 154 survived.

World War II Museum   MUSEUM

(Rizal Ave; ⏰8am-5pm Mon-Sat) This is an interesting, privately owned museum set up by Eugenio Mendoza, whose father was a member of the Fighting 1000, a group of local guerrillas who fought the Japanese (his father was ultimately beheaded). The museum is chock-full of war memorabilia and has tributes to the Fighting 1000 and to the 143 Americans who died in the notorious Palawan Massacre at Plaza Cuarte.

Palawan Museum   MUSEUM

(Mendoza Park, Rizal Ave; adult/student P50/20; ⏰8.30am-noon & 1.30-5pm Mon-Sat) Housed in the old City Hall building adjacent to Mendoza Park, this newly modernised museum has two floors of exhibits about the ethnological and archaeological significance of Palawan, most with interesting accompanying explanations in English.

👁️ Out of Town

Iwahig Prison & Penal Farm   PLANTATION

FREE About 15km from Puerto, this penal colony invites visitors to drop in and mingle with the prisoners. In the gymnasium of the central compound, inmates sell souvenirs and perform dance routines for tour groups; these are definitely worth seeing if you can time it right. From the central compound, make your way 3km through agricultural fields to pleasant **Balasahan Natural Pools**, a swimming hole fed by a small waterfall.

The prison entrance is just off the National Hwy; register here and proceed about 3km to the central compound. You'll need private transport to get here (tricycle about P700 round trip from Puerto).

Nagtabon Beach   BEACH

This beach, on the northern side of the isthmus, has several hundred metres of white sand and shallow water good for swimming. Jeepneys from San Jose terminal (they leave around noon) aren't a convenient option, so best to go by motorbike or rental car or van. The road is rough once it leaves the highway.

Irawan Eco-Park ADVENTURE
(☑ 048-434 1132; irawan_ecopark@yahoo.com; zipline P800; ⊙8am-5pm) The main attraction is a three-stage zipline totalling 1.3km, but it also has a canopy walk and offers a four-hour jungle-survival course. It's in a protected area in Irawan, 10km north of Puerto Princesa (P200 by tricycle or P28 by multicab from the corner of Rizal St and the National Hwy).

☞ Tours

★**Pasyar Travel & Tours** OUTDOORS
(☑ 048-433 5525; http://pasyarpalawantravel. weebly.com; Gabinete Rd) 🌿 Genuinely dedicated to conservation and community-based tourism, Pasyar runs a unique, multiday old growth forest-trekking tour that involves tagging along with enforcement officers on the look-out for illegal loggers around Palawan. It also runs the important **Environmental Enforcement Museum** (Gabinete Rd; P20; ⊙8am-6pm) 🌿 out of its headquarters,

---

TUBBATAHA REEFS

A 10- to 15-hour boat ride from Puerto Princesa is the **Tubbataha Reefs Natural Park** (conservation fee US$100) 🌿, a marine protected reserve often compared to the Galapagos Islands. It was declared a Unesco World Heritage Site in 1993 and is home to hundreds of species of seabirds and fish, including mantas, whale sharks and the full gamut of pelagic marine life. The season for visiting Tubbataha runs from mid-March through to mid-June.

The only way to visit is on one of 14 or so live-aboard vessels, jumping off from Puerto Princesa. The cost for a six-day live-aboard trip runs from US$1300 including gear if you go by bangka with a discount operator like **M/Y Sakura** (www.sakuracharter.com), to US$3810 aboard a yacht operated by luxury provider **Siren Fleet** (http://sirenfleet. com). Most trips are in the US$2200 to US$2600 range. Contact the **Tubbataha Management Office** (☑ 048-434 5759; www.tubbatahareef.org; Manalo St Ext) in Puerto Princesa for more information.

---

which displays confiscated chainsaws, boats, dynamite and (sometimes) animals such as civets.

Dolphins & Whale Sharks WILDLIFE WATCHING
(☑ 0915 263 2105; www.dolphinandwhales.com; Rizal Ave; whale-shark tours per person P1800, dolphin tours per person P1000; ⊙Apr-Oct only; whale sharks 7am-2pm, dolphins 6.20-10.30am) The effusive Toto Kayabo runs separate tours to spot these creatures in Honda Bay. This is your best chance to spot wild whale-sharks during the country's southwest monsoon (May to October). Weather permitting, the whale shark tours (minimum six people) usually only take place in the 10 days before and the two days after a full moon, while the dolphin tours (minimum 14 people) are daily.

🎊 Festivals & Events

Baragatan Festival CULTURAL
(⊙3rd week Jun) Palaweños from all over come together on the grounds of the Provincial Capitol Building for dancing, singing, eating and drinking; vendors sell traditional handicrafts and culinary specialities.

🛏 Sleeping

Puerto has plenty of excellent budget options and a growing array of top-end boutique hotels, but there's a dearth of mid-range quality.

★**Casa Linda Inn** INN $
(☑ 0917 749 6956, 048-433 2606; casalindainn@ gmail.com; Trinidad Rd; s/d with fan P650/750, with air-con P850/1000; ❄🛜) The meticulously maintained garden courtyard make centrally located Casa Linda feel like a country refuge. The surrounding wood-floored rooms are clean and simply furnished, though they lack hot water and have thin walls. Yet noise isn't really a problem, as it's set 100m back from Rizal Ave. Easily the best-value hotel in town.

★**Sheebang Hostel** HOSTEL $
(☑ 0915 370 0647, 048-433 0592; judy.sheebang@ gmail.com; 118 Libis Rd; dm P350, d P850; ❄🛜) In a gorgeous wooden house, Sheebang Hostel has three air-con dorms with sturdy bunk beds and big lockers, plus some basic ensuite private rooms with air-con. An open-air bar, sprawling garden and competent travel desk make up for the out-of-the-way location.

Central Palawan

Pagdayon
Traveler's Inn
INN $

(☑ 048-434 9102; off Rizal Ave; d P950-1100; ❈ 🛜) Central but quiet, native-style Pagdayon has six well-kept rooms, each with individual verandahs, set around a thatched open-air common-dining area. It's just off Rizal Ave next to the giant new Best Western.

★ Puerto Pension
HOTEL $$

(☑ 048-433 2969; www.puertopension.com; 35 Malvar St; s P1280-2080, d P1380-2180; ❈ 🛜)
🖉 An impressive-looking four-storey wood-and-bamboo building, located close to the Baywalk, with sweeping views of the bay from the top-floor restaurant. Rooms are masterpieces of tasteful native-style design. Swathed in rattan, with wood floors, they practically define 'cosy'. The standard rooms are tiny, so spend just a few hundred pesos extra on a plush 'superior' double.

★ Palo Alto Bed & Breakfast
B&B $$

(☑ 048-434 2159; www.paloalto.ph; A Cabanag St; d/q incl breakfast from P2800/3500; ❈ 🛜 🏊) 🖉
Surrounded by tall trees in a rambling complex 3km north of the airport, Palo Alto is a refuge from the city's noise. The 19 rooms are set amid beautiful gardens and some front a shady pool. The disabled-friendly rooms have flat-screen TVs, nice bathrooms and traditional art, but could use more furniture.

Hibiscus Garden Inn
INN $$

(☑ 048-434 1273; www.puertoprincesahotel.com; Manalo St Ext; r incl breakfast P1950-2800; ❈ 🛜) For those seeking a sanctuary, well-managed Hibiscus will do the job. Large orange-toned rooms are in a low-slung building surrounding an attractive garden. All rooms have hammocks out front under a wide, shaded verandah, and four of the 14 rooms have their own small backyard sitting areas.

Puerto Princesa

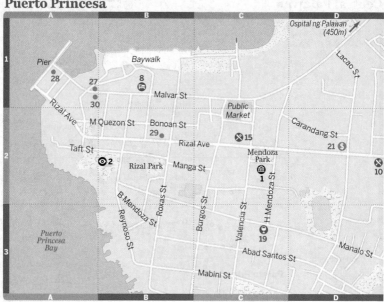

Puerto Princesa

★ **Canvas Boutique Hotel** BOUTIQUE HOTEL **$$$**
(National Hwy; r incl breakfast from P5500;
❄@🛜🏊) A refreshing lobby equipped
with public iMacs heralds that you are in
one of Palawan's most sleek and stylish
refuges. The bright, buoyant rooms are all
polished concrete, contemporary lighting
and open storage spaces. Each features a

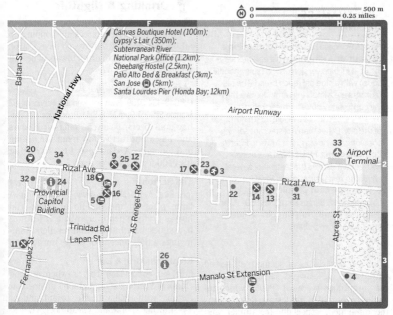

Canvas Boutique Hotel (100m);
Gypsy's Lair (350m);
Subterranean River
National Park Office (1.2km);
Sheebang Hostel (2.5km);
Palo Alto Bed & Breakfast (3km);
San Jose (5km);
Santa Lourdes Pier (Honda Bay; 12km)

Airport Runway

Airport Terminal

Rizal Ave

Rizal Ave

Provincial Capitol Building

Trinidad Rd
Lapan St

Manalo St Extension

wonderful, individually designed mural. A playful pool area with blow-up furniture and a good buffet breakfast (walk-ins: P300) rounds it out.

Aziza Paradise   BOUTIQUE HOTEL $$$

(☎ 048-434 2405; www.azizaparadisehotel.ph; BM Rd; r incl breakfast P5000-8500; ❋ ⏚ ☎ ⋸) Best described as an urban – and urbane – resort, Aziza wows right away with a soaring open-air reception area that reflects the hotel's leaf theme. It's flanked by two restaurants and a nice-looking pool that inexplicably lacked pool furniture on our visit. All rooms are well appointed; shoot for one with a balcony overlooking the pool and lush gardens.

✗ Eating

Puerto has a surprisingly good variety of restaurants, most of them conveniently located in the centre along Rizal Ave. Along the waterfront near the port is **Baywalk,** a mostly concrete expanse with sunset views and more than half a dozen informal **barbecue tents** (meals P200 to P500) specialising in grilled seafood – a quintessential Puerto experience. **Robinson's Place** (National Hwy; ⏰ 10am-9pm Mon-Thu, to 10pm Fri-Sun) has the usual assortment of fast food and a grocery.

Scribbles & Snacks   CAFE $

(off Rizal Ave; dishes P50-100; ⏰ noon-9pm) This mural-splashed, open-air *kubo* (native-style shelter) hidden behind a Best Western hotel is a hang-out for the local 'Art on the Move' group. Creative types lap up the budget pizza breads (P35), pasta and other light meals while sipping San Miguel or iced tea.

Cafe Itoy's   CAFE $

(Rizal Ave; mains P115-230; ⏰ 7am-11pm; ☎) Long-running coffee joint on the main drag with functional wi-fi, an agreeable Spotify soundtrack and an extensive menu of sandwiches and Filipino faves.

Ima's Vegetarian   VEGETARIAN $

(Fernandez St; dishes P85-140; ⏰ 11am-9pm Sun-Thu, to 3pm Fri, 6.30-9pm Sat; ⋔) ✿ A decidedly healthy and delicious option run by Seventh-Day Adventists. Try the spicy bean burrito or vegan-cheese pizza for *meryenda* (a daytime snack).

★ Kalui   FILIPINO $$

(☎ 048-433 2580; 369 Rizal Ave; mains P245-265; ⏰ 11am-noon & 6-10.30pm Mon-Sat; ⋔) An institution, this shoes-off eatery has a lovely Balinese ambience – colourful paintings, sculptures and masks adorn the walls, and there's a general air of conviviality. Choose

A VIETNAMESE CULINARY LEGACY

Puerto Princesa has dozens of **chaolong restaurants**, small informal eateries serving up a Filipino version of *pho* (spicy noodle soup) with a side of French bread. The restaurants are a lingering reminder of a thriving community of Vietnamese refugees who mostly settled in 'Viet Village' 13km north of the city. Other than a restaurant serving *chaolong*, it's now a ghost town. In Puerto, **Lou Chaolong Hauz** (Rizal Ave; mains P50; ⊗8am-4am) is the tastiest of several *chaolong* restaurants along Rizal Ave. Other options are **Pham Chaolong** (Rizal Ave, btwn Valencia & Burgos Sts; dishes P50; ⊗7am-9pm) and **Thant-Tam Chaolong** (Rizal Ave; mains P50-60; ⊗5-11pm).

from a few varieties of seafood, all served with vegies, a seaweed salad, or opt for the sumptuous set meal (P695), which includes coconut flan for dessert. Reservations recommended, especially for dinner and groups.

★**Artisans** INTERNATIONAL **$$**
(Rizal Ave; mains P150-250; ⊗11.30am-10pm) The Scottish owner calls the style here 'obscurity'; it basically consists of anything he fancies. The menu is a best-of-the-world affair, where *tikka masala* mingles with Mexican, Indonesian *rendang*, sloppy joes, giant salad bowls and – for drinkers – margaritas. An unorthodox approach; somehow he pulls it off.

Gypsy's Lair FILIPINO, MEXICAN **$$**
(Mercado de San Miguel, Km 1 National Hwy; mains P120-200; ⊗9am-midnight Mon-Sat; ❋🔊) This bohemian-style complex consists of a postage-stamp, air-conditioned cafe and an open-air restobar with nightly live acoustic music and palm readings on Friday and Saturday evenings. It has excellent desserts like ice *biko*, basically sweet sticky rice with home-made ice cream.

★**La Terrasse** FRENCH, FUSION **$$$**
(Rizal Ave; mains P200-400; ⊗11am-11pm Tue-Sun; 🔊) This is a sophisticated open-air dining room with a small menu of pasta, seafood and grilled or stewed meats (including duck *rendang*). Attention is paid to organic and locally sourced ingredients. Palawan oysters are available by the dozen.

🍷 Drinking & Nightlife

There's a whole lot of drinking going on in Puerto by night. New places are popping up all the time along Rizal Ave, so have a stroll around. Locals love to drink towers of beer at Baywalk or at food parks.

★**Palaweño Brewery** BREWERY
(📞048-434 0709; www.palawenobrewery.com; 82 Manalo St; ⊗1-9pm Mon-Sat) Producer of Ayahay craft beers, Palaweño offers free tours and has an attractive tap room for tasting and lounging. A glass costs P150 to P170 or it's P400 for a five-beer flight.

Tiki Restobar BAR
(cnr Rizal Ave & National Hwy; ⊗7pm-2am) A large place in the middle of town, Tiki heaves pretty much every night. It features bar games, beer buckets and revellers shimmying on the dance floor to live music.

Kinabuchs Grill & Bar BAR
(Rizal Ave; ⊗5pm-1am) This is where a good chunk of Puerto goes at night. It's an open-air restobar with a billiard table, a giant outdoor TV showing sports and cheap beer. The extensive menu (mains P200 to P400) features many exotic offerings, including *tamilok* (woodworm), which is said to taste like oyster.

ℹ️ Information

INTERNET ACCESS
Several internet cafes are located along Rizal Ave, between the National Hwy and Jollibee restaurant. Although all hotels and many cafes advertise wi-fi, connections and 4G services are notoriously slow in Puerto.

MONEY
Note that in all of Palawan only Puerto, El Nido and Coron have ATMs. In Puerto, moneychangers and ATMs line Rizal Ave west of the National Hwy junction, including **BDO** (Rizal Ave).

TOURIST INFORMATION
Palawan Provincial Tourism Office (📞048-433 2968; www.palawan.gov.ph; ground fl, Provincial Capital Bldg, Rizal Ave; ⊗8am-5pm Mon-Fri) This helpful office is a good first stop for all things Palawan. Ask for Rosalyn or Maribel.
Subterranean River National Park Office (📞048-434 2509; City Coliseum, National Hwy; ⊗8am-4pm Mon-Fri, to noon & 1-4pm Sat & Sun) Underground River permits issued here or in the **satellite office** (2nd fl, Robinson's Place; ⊗10am-6pm Mon-Fri).
Tubbataha Management Office (p380) Provides information on trips to Tubbataha Reefs Natural Park.

MEDICAL SERVICES

Ospital ng Palawan (☑ 048-433 2621; Malvar St) Central hospital has a decompression chamber and can handle any malaria concerns.

TRAVEL AGENCIES

Inland Tours & Travel (☑ 048-434 1508; 399 Rizal Ave; ⏲ 7.30am-7pm) Can book Underground River trips and minivans to El Nido.

Sanctuary Tours & Travel (☑ 048-434 7673; sanctuarytours@yahoo.com; Rizal Ave) Underground River tours, city tours and all kinds of tickets.

VISAS

BOI Palawan Office (☑ 048-433 2248; Servando Bldg, Rizal Ave; ⏲ 8am-noon & 1-5pm Mon-Fri) Provides visa extensions in 15 minutes.

ⓘ Getting There & Away

AIR

The entrance to Puerto Princesa's **international airport** (p379) terminal is on the National Hwy about 1km north of the centre. A tricycle from the airport to anywhere in the centre costs P50; to the bus station it costs P120.

Cebu Pacific (www.cebupacificair.com) and PAL (www.philippineairlines.com) both fly to Puerto Princesa from Manila and Cebu, while AirAsia (www.airasia.com) serves Manila. Cebu Pacific also has thrice weekly flights to Iloilo on Panay.

Air Juan (www.airjuan.com) flies little six-seaters to Coron (Busuanga) on Thursdays and Sundays, and to the Cuyo Islands on Wednesdays and Fridays.

BOAT

2GO (☑ 043-433 0039; Malvar St) has trips from Puerto Princesa to Manila (P2000 to P2800, 31 hours) on Wednesdays and Saturdays at 11.59pm. They go via Coron (P1450 to P2280, 15 hours).

Milagrosa Shipping (☑ 048-433 4806; Rizal Ave) serves Iloilo via the Cuyo Islands with departure at 3pm Thursday (P870 to P1450, 36 hours), as does sturdier **Montenegro Lines** (☑ 048-434 9344; Malvar St) at 6pm Monday (P1220 to P1590, 26 hours). All departures are from the **Ferry Port** (Malvar St).

BUS, JEEPNEY & MINIVAN

Buses, jeepneys and most minivans leave from the **San Jose Bus Terminal** (New Public Market; barangay San Jose) – otherwise known as the 'New Public Market' – 5km north of Puerto city centre, off the National Hwy. To get there, grab a tricycle (P120) or multicab (mini-jeepney; P13) from the corner of Rizal Ave and the National Hwy.

The station is also the best place to secure a private van at affordable rates. The following are fares for private van hire, but you'll need to negotiate: Narra (P3000), Sabang (P2500), Port Barton (P3500) and El Nido (P7,000).

CAR & MOTORCYCLE

Hiring a self-drive motorbike or car is a great way to get around not just Puerto but all of Palawan. One-way rentals to El Nido or anywhere else are available, but usually incur a pick-up fee of P4000 to P5000 for short-term rentals (less or even free for rentals of at least a week). Companies that rent out both cars and motor-

PALAWAN PUERTO PRINCESA

HONDA BAY

Popular **island-hopping tours** (P1300 to P1500 for up to six people) in scenic Honda Bay are run out of Sta Lourdes, 12km north of Puerto proper. Booking these through tour agencies in Puerto costs an exorbitant P1500 or so per person including lunch and various entrance fees. Instead, put your own group together or show up at the pier and try to join one.

Compared with the islands in the Bacuit Archipelago, Honda Bay may be a poor stepchild; however, this is a bit of an unfair comparison and a day spent **snorkelling** and **island-hopping** is worth doing if you're in the area for more than a night.

Tours generally take in three islands; the most popular are **Cowrie Island** and **Luli Island**, and during the windiest months (December to February) these are often the only ones you can get to. When it's calmer, **Pandan Island**, **Starfish Island** and the aptly named **Snake Island**, a winding strip of white sand that changes shape with the tides, are less-crowded alternatives.

Most islands charge nominal entrance fees and you'll have to pay a P150 environmental fee through the boat dispatcher at the pier in Sta Lourdes. Snack shacks are available on most islands and there's a restaurant on Cowrie Island.

The luxurious **Dos Palmas Island Resort & Spa** (☑ in Puerto 048-434 3118; www.dospalmas.com.ph; d weekday/weekend incl breakfast from P6500/7250; ❄ 🌐 ☲) on Arreceffi Island offers a day package for P1800/900 per adult/child, including round-trip boat transfer, lunch, use of kayaks and snorkelling.

A multicab from the corner of Rizal Ave and the National Hwy to Sta Lourdes costs P30, or take a tricycle (P200).

bikes include **Plong Car Rental** (📞 0917 553 0889; www.palawanselfdrivecarrental.com; cnr Fernandez St & Rizal Ave), **San Francisco DV's** (📞 0920 604 4840; mariodiego60@yahoo.com; Rizal Ave) and **Peter Motorcycle & Car Rental** (📞 0921 788 5506; Rizal Ave).

❶ Getting Around

Multicabs ('multis') clog the city's arteries; it's P10 to P13 for short hops, including from the centre of town to Robinson's Place or Santa Monica; grab multis to either location at the corner of National Hwy and Rizal Ave.

Sabang & the Underground River

📞 048

Tiny Sabang has a beautiful, wind-lashed beach, huge tracts of pristine jungle and a famous underground river that draws van loads of day-tripping tourists from Puerto Princesa. While the underground river is certainly worth doing, Sabang's main appeal lies in its wild setting. The surrounding rainforest is part of the Puerto Princesa Subterranean River National Park, and offers world-class hiking and birdwatching.

Unfortunately, the authorities close Sabang Beach at the slightest hint of surf. They close the underground river too during periods of heavy rain, although this is entirely understandable as downpours can flood the cave. There's basically one road in Sabang – the National Hwy leading into town and terminating at the wharf. Everything is either on this road or on the beach.

◎ Sights

Puerto Princesa Subterranean River National Park   CAVE

(Underground River; park permit incl paddle boat adult/child P500/150, plus environmental fee P150; ⊗8am-3.30pm) At 8km in length, Sabang's famous underground river is one of the longest navigable river-traversed caves in the world and draws scores of tourists. Trips aboard unmotorised paddle boats proceed about 1.5km upstream into the cave (45 minutes return) and now include audioguide headsets. Book a bangka through the Sabang Information Office (p388; P1120 for up to six people, 15 minutes) to get you from the wharf to the cave entrance, or walk 5km via the Jungle Trail (P200 incl guide).

Crab-eating monkeys and monitor lizards roam the area around the cave entrance.

When looking up, keep your mouth shut: bats and swiftlets flutter above and are responsible for the guano that 'perfumes' the cave.

Important note: if travelling independently, you must secure your park permit in advance from a tour operator or the Subterranean National Park Office (p384) or its satellite office (p384) in Puerto Princesa. However, if you are sleeping in Sabang, or if you are coming direct from El Nido or points north, you can purchase your permit on the spot at the Sabang Information Office provided you can show an environmental fee receipt from El Nido or Port Barton; an accommodation receipt may also work.

Of course, you can do what most people do and visit the park on an all-inclusive tour out of Puerto Princesa (P2350 including transport, lunch and all fees). Unless you are pressed for time, we don't recommend these as they herd you in and out of the park and preclude you from exploring Sabang's rich coastal rainforest.

It's possible to proceed 4.3km into the underground river with a permit from the Subterranean National Park Office in Puerto Princesa (P1000, four hours return), secured at least two days in advance.

Officials often close the park due to excessive rain or rough seas, so when there's inclement weather, we suggest contacting the Sabang Information Office in advance to save you a disappointing trip.

🏃 Activities

After all of that activity, dial it down a notch with a massage – a half-dozen massage huts line the pathway along the Sabang beach.

Poyuy-Poyuy River   BOATING

(P150; ⊗8am-4pm) This community-driven project involves paddling with a guide a few kilometres up the mangrove-lined, brackish Poyuy-Poyuy River. The trip takes less than an hour and is best done in the early morning when the bird life (parrots, hornbills, herons etc) is more active. Otherwise, you might spot a few baby pythons and mangrove snakes.

Sabang Zipline   ADVENTURE SPORTS

(📞in Puerto Princesa 048-434 2341; P550; ⊗8am-5pm) This 800m long zipline starts on the other side of Poyuy-Poyuy River at the far eastern end of Sabang. The ticket office is at the wharf.

Hiking
Based in the village of Kabayungan, local guides **Jungle Jorz** (📞 0935 533 3541) and **RJ** (📞 0905 485 6591) lead a variety of walks, including the day hike up **Mt Bloomfield** (780m), which offers gorgeous views of the coastline extending all the way up to Mt Capoas in Taytay. **Kabayungan**, 7km south of Sabang, makes a great base for hikes, including the challenging half-day walk to **Daylight Hole**, a cave with a natural skylight, and walks to indigenous Batak villages.

Birdwatching
There are some 165 bird species in the national park, many of them endemic to Palawan. Birding is possible through the Sabang Information Office (p388), although it does not provide telescopes or even binoculars. For serious birders, **Birding Adventures Philippines** (www.birdingphilippines.com) offers multiday tours that include Sabang.

Snorkelling
Sabang Beach is rough most of the year and not conducive to snorkelling, but more sheltered **Ulugan Bay** in Buenavista barangay, 20km south of Sabang on the road to Puerto, has a few good spots, including **Rita Island**. **Lyanin Tour Office**, near the Sabang Beach footbridge, can arrange a day trip. It costs plus P2500/3500 for a four-/eight-person boat; overland transfer to Buenavista is extra.

🛏 Sleeping
There are two high-end resorts, some exceedingly simple budget places and very little in between. Other than at the two high-end resorts, there is no hot water in Sabang, although Sabang now has 24-hour electricity.

⭐ Cafe Sabang   GUESTHOUSE $
(📞 0905 592 8947; dm/s/d P250/350/700) Budget travellers finally have a go-to place to congregate in Sabang thanks to this warm and welcoming place in a wooden house. Nothing pretentious at all here, just rustic little private rooms with shared facilities, a cosy five-bed dorm and an earthy cafe. It's about a five-minute walk south of the beach on the road to Puerto.

Dab Dab Resort   BUNGALOW $
(📞 0949 469 9421; cottage with/without bathroom P800/500, with air-con P1800; 🛜) This place, 200m northwest of Sabang pier, is an appealing haven. There's no beach here, only a rocky shoreline, but the seven hardwood cottages, equipped with ceiling fans, private porches and hammocks, are much nicer than those on the beach.

Bambua Nature Cottages   LODGE $
(📞 0927 420 9686; www.bambua-palawan.com; s/d without bathroom P300/500, cottage s/d from P800/1250) Get up close and personal with Sabang's magnificent rainforest in this garden lodge about a 15-minute walk south of town along the main road. There's a variety of rooms to choose from, many with stunning views, although they are fairly basic.

⭐ Daluyon Resort   RESORT $$$
(📞 048-723 0889; www.daluyonbeachandmountainresort.com; r incl breakfast from P5500; ❄🛜♨) 🍃 The Daluyon goes to show that luxury doesn't have to damage the aesthetic vibe of a beautiful locale. Inside the thatched-roof, split-level cottages, the rooms are all contemporary high end, from the flat-screen TVs to the bathroom fixtures. The Daluyon has the best restaurant (mains P300 to P600) in Sabang and has won several awards for being ecofriendly.

Sheridan Beach Resort   RESORT $$$
(📞 048-434 1449; www.sheridanbeachresort.com; r incl breakfast from P6500; ❄@🛜♨) This contemporary, somewhat generic resort wouldn't be out of place in Boracay. While it feels a tad orphaned here, we have to admit the 100m (or so) pool is impressive and the swim-up bar certainly has its merits. The tastefully designed rooms are set back and face the pool rather than the beach.

🍴 Eating
There's not a whole lot to choose from, though the situation is improving. The two high-end resorts are definitely worth a splurge for a meal.

Smoky Place   CAFE $
(Sabang Beach; dishes P150-300; ⏱4-10pm; 🌱) A charming little beachfront eatery associated with Cafe Sabang guesthouse. Pasta, sandwiches and wood-fired pizza are the specialities.

Why Not   BARBECUE $$
(Sabang Beach; mains P150-500; ⏱8am-9pm; 🌱) If you're looking for a square meal, this is the best of the dedicated eateries on the beachfront. Lots of grilled seafood, fresh sashimi, a nice vegetarian selection and some Thai and North African flavours.

ℹ️ Information

Sabang Information Office (☎ 048-723 0904; ⊙ 8am-4pm) Your first stop for visits to the underground river. If you're not on a group tour, this is where you pay all fees and arrange your boat.

ℹ️ Getting There & Away

Coming from Puerto, the turn-off to Sabang along the main highway is in Salvacion, from where it's a scenic 35km drive over a winding, sealed road.

Lexus Shuttle (☎ 0915 347 9593) vans connect Sabang and Puerto Princesa five or six times daily in either direction (P200, 1½ hours, last trip 6pm). Jumbo jeepneys (with/without baggage P150/120, 2½ hours) make four daily trips as well (last trip: 2pm). Lexus also offers five daily trips to El Nido, with a transfer in Salvacion (P800, 5½ hours).

For Port Barton, pre-arrange a pick-up in Salvacion through one of the Puerto–Port Barton van operators (p393), or flag down the twice-daily Puerto–Port Barton buses from the National Hwy in Salvacion. Alternatively, an El Nido–bound bus can get you to the highway junction at San Jose, from where a tricycle or motorbike (P400, one hour) can take you to Port Barton.

It's easy enough to get a private van to Port Barton (from P4000, three hours) or El Nido (from P5500, five hours); if you're having trouble, ask Lexus Shuttle, which is based at the wharf area.

There are no more public boats heading north to Port Barton and El Nido.

Southern Palawan

As central and northern Palawan become more inundated, adventurous travellers are starting to look toward southern Palawan to stay ahead of the pack. The main towns of Narra, Quezon and Brooke's Point are easily accessible via sealed roads and offer jungle- and marine-based diversions: rare birds, ancient-man caves, waterfalls and beautiful islands. The going gets rougher as you travel further south, which is populated by indigenous tribal groups and Muslim communities. Few people make it down to the Balabac islands off Palawan's far southern tip; those that do are rewarded with a Maldives–like paradise, minus the five-star resorts (or any resorts, for that matter).

Narra

This town is generally considered the rice granary of Palawan, a boast not often made on tourist brochures. The daily market is worth a stop, and there are a few beaches in the area, the finest offshore on private

Arena Island, home to dreamy **Arena Island Resort** (☎ 0917 580 0446; www.arenaisland.com; d incl all meals & transfers P18,000; ❄ 🛜).

Rasa Island is home to a colony of endangered Philippine cockatoos. Arrange visits through the **Katala Foundation** (☎ 0946 963 9550, 0907 653 8003; a.argullo14@gmail.com; City Hall Compound); ask for Anna Argullo. Fees are P180 per person for admission plus boat (P1000) and guide (P250), both good for six people. The island is off-limits during the January-to-June breeding season.

Northwest of town, **Estrella Falls** are fed by **Mt Victoria** (1726m), the third-highest mountain in Palawan. These consist of some 64 falls along the Estrella River. Jehson in the **tourism office** (☎ 0999 992 8464, 0939 882 6987; cjehson@yahoo.com; City Hall Compound; ⊙ 8am-5pm Mon-Fri) guides hikes to the falls and Mt Victoria (permit P150).

Regular buses and vans link Narra with Puerto (two hours), Brooke's Point (one hour) and Quezon (1¼ hours).

Quezon

This is the nearest town to the **Tabon Caves** (☎ 0921 763 3824) complex, where the remains of some of the earliest Philippine humans have been discovered. Fronted by turquoise waters and surrounded by primary-growth jungle, the caves on **Lipuun Point** are in a strikingly beautiful setting and can be accessed only by boat.

Drop by the **Tabon Caves Museum** (☎ 0921 763 3824; barangay Alfonso Trece; ⊙ 8am-5pm) 𝗙𝗥𝗘𝗘 to arrange a boat (P800, 35 minutes) and pick up a free permit. Boats leave from the Coast Guard station at the town pier, just a few minutes north of the town centre. A guard stationed at the cave site will collect your permit and guide you through the seven accessible caves, some of which are reached by steep stairs carved into the limestone.

You can have a picnic on the beach near the entrance to the caves and swim and snorkel offshore. Ask Mabel at the **Quezon Tourism Office** (☎ 0947 951 4047; City Hall Complex; ⊙ 8am-5pm Mon-Fri) about islands in the vicinity of the caves.

Fontera Garden Suites (☎ 0921 577 4940; www.fonteragardensuite.wixsite.com/mysite; National Hwy; r P900-1800), about five minutes south of town, is the nicest place to stay. For low-budget digs, try **Zambrano Pension House** (☎ 0921 612 1767, 0910 380 1819; Pagayona St; r P500) in the centre.

There are six daily buses to Puerto via Narra. Jeepneys tackle the rough road south to Rizal.

Rizal

Rizal is the jumping-off point for climbing Palawan's highest mountain and visiting one of the most primitive tribes in Asia, the nomadic Tau't Bato.

Climbs up 2086m **Mt Mantalingahan** are best done out of barangay Ransang. This is no climb for the faint-hearted. You'll need a minimum of four days to conquer it, and it's both rigorous and technical. The rewards include encounters with the Tau't Bato, rare flora and incredible bird life.

Long-time guide Anthony Lorenzo heads the **Rizal Tourism Office** (☎0999 993 8869; bojielorenzo@gmail.com; City Hall Complex; ⊙8am-5pm Mon-Fri) and is the authority on climbing Mt Mantalingahan and visiting the Tau't Bato. He can supply camping equipment. Hikes to local waterfalls are also possible.

In Rizal, you can stay at the simple **Castelar Store & Lodging Inn** (☎0921 504 4108; r with fan per person from P150, with air-con P1000). From Puerto there are van and bus services to Rizal until 2pm (P300, five hours), and two or three jeepneys per day to/from Quezon.

Brooke's Point, Bataraza & Balabac

South of Narra the highway continues for almost 200km to the village of Buliluyan on mainland Palawan's southern tip. Beyond this is Balabac, an indescribably beautiful archipelago at the confluence of the Sulu and South China Seas. Few tourists make it down here, partly because of safety concerns – the area is home to smugglers and modern-day pirates. However, the area has become safer in recent years and is ripe for DIY travel.

Brooke's Point is a large commercial centre that can be used as a base to hike up Mt Mantalingahan – though it's easier to do it from Rizal – and numerous waterfalls and beaches in the area; ask for Arlene Piramide (☎0905 919 0134), the tourism officer in town, to help arrange guides and supplies.

Further south, Rio Tuba, a barangay of Bataraza, is the jumping-off point for public boats to Balabac. Two daily boats depart around 11am or noon for the four- to five-hour trip to Balabac Island, which is the largest of the archipelago's 31 islands. Charter a boat from local fishermen in Bal-

MALARIA WARNING!

Malaria (chloroquine resistant) is considered endemic in rural areas of southern Palawan. Antimalarial medication is recommended for anyone planning on spending any time in the bush, especially if visiting remote indigenous tribes. There is little risk in the main population centres. Several types of antimalarial drugs are available at Mercury Drug outlets in Puerto, but you are better off bringing your own (malarone is the best). To reduce your chances of contracting the disease, wear insect repellent, long trousers and long sleeves at night and use a mosquito net. Malarial mosquitoes are most active at night, especially from 10pm to 2am.

abac port to explore other islands. There is a new port being built in Buliluyan that will replace the one in Rio Tuba and will eventually offer international services to Malaysia.

AJ Peria (☎0917 774 7787), the tourism officer in Bataraza, can help with boat schedules and charters and can arrange other excursions in the area. For an organised tour of Balabac, **KilometerZero** (www.kilometer zeroph.com) offers multiday trips. Regular buses from Puerto Princesa go as far south as Rio Tuba (four to five hours).

Port Barton

POP 5000

Essentially a two-road town where the jungle drops precipitously into the bay, Port Barton offers simple pleasures. It's the kind of place where, after just a few strolls down the beach, you don't want to share the tranquillity with outsiders. Several islands with good beaches and snorkelling lurk offshore surrounded by rows and rows of buoys, the sign of working pearl farms.

Chilled out as it is, Port Barton is quickly becoming a drawcard on the backpacker trail, complete with funky hostels, hipster cafes and reggae bars staffed by hunky island boys. In the high season you'll want to book ahead. Port Barton is a barangay of San Vicente, but they aren't particularly close to each other – two hours by road or 45 minutes by boat. Be aware of this when booking online, and know where you're going, to avoid a costly backtrack.

◉ Sights & Activities

Pamuayan Falls WATERFALL
(suggested donation P50) These refreshing 8m falls are a 4km walk or motorbike ride north of town on the rough new road to San Vicente. The falls slow to a trickle at the height of the dry season (March to mid-May).

Island-Hopping

Tours A, B, C and D (P700 per head) take in a mix of islands, beaches, reefs and **Bigaho Falls** (suggested donation P50), with lunch and snorkel stops along the way. Friendly local boatman Gensen Gabco (☑0921 626 9191) can be recommended. You can arrange visits to nearby **mangroves** (P700 for two, three hours) through the Tourist Assistance Center (p392).

Diving

Dives are best done in the morning for the nice sunlight. **Easy Dive** (☑0918 402 7041; www.palawaneasydive.com), at the southern end of the beach, offers three boat dives including equipment and lunch for P3500 to P4000.

🛏 Sleeping

At almost all places electricity runs only from 6pm to 11pm, although you can usually pay extra for extended generator hours.

★Dragon House HOSTEL $
(☑0919 322 3054; dm P400-450) Easily the coolest and most creative hostel in Port Barton. Practical adds include personal battery fans for every bed to combat Port Barton's power issues; and huge, clutter-eliminating storage drawers under the bunks. Showers have pressure, and hammocks are inverted and turned into chairs on the common balcony. It's at the back of Deep Moon Resort: book through Deep Moon.

Harmony Haven Hostel HOSTEL $
(☑0917 711 0069; Pamuayan sitio; dm incl breakfast P500, d/q P1200/2400; 🛜) If Port Barton is too buzzing for you, then this somewhat isolated hostel 2km north of the centre might suit. It consists of a large concrete house and a few cottages, all set back from a narrow beach. You can kayak fairly easily to absurdly idyllic beaches and islands just offshore; kayak hire is P300 per day.

Besaga Beachfront Cottages BUNGALOW $
(☑0918 570 4665; besagabeachresort@gmail.com; r P1200-2500) With the best resort food in Port Barton, solar-powered fans (usually available all night) and a quiet location at the north end of the beach, Besaga is a cut above most of the beachfront places. The seven cottages are concrete but tasteful, adorned with bamboo and Filipino rattan.

★Sunset Colors RESORT $$
(☑0936 966 2657; http://sunsetcolors.strikingly.com; Nao Nao sitio; r P2700-3700; 🛜) It's on the mainland but feels like a fantasy private island. It consists of five homey cottages, all swathed in rattan, and one larger, pricier room above the restaurant. Free use of kayaks, stand-up paddleboards (SUPs) and bikes. Arrive by boat (20 minutes, free pick-up) or on your own via the rough Port Barton–San Vicente road (11km, dry season only). The generator is switched off at 9pm; solar lights are available, but fans are not.

Deep Moon Resort RESORT $$
(☑0919 322 3054; www.deepgoldresorts.com; fan cottages P1000-1600, f with air-con P2000-2500; ❄🛜) This resort at the southern end of the village boasts a couple of A-frames – with clean tile floors and modern bathrooms – that are the only places in Port Barton where your front door opens directly onto the beach. Otherwise, there are several more cottages and rooms set further back.

Ausan RESORT $$
(☑0929 444 0582; www.ausanbeachfront.com; d/family cottage P1250/2850; ❄🛜) Port Barton's best all-around midrange option, centrally located Ausan is one of the few places with all-day (7am to midnight) electricity. There is a huge range of rooms on offer; the best are the 'treehouse' bungalows and the beachfront fan cottages with attractive wood floors and panelling. The breezy restaurant has reasonably tasty Filipino food.

🛏 Offshore

There are a handful of resorts on private islands or secluded mainland coves near Port Barton. These are exclusively generator- and/or solar-powered, with electricity typically running from 6pm to 10pm plus two hours in the morning. Arrange boat transfers (often free) through your resort.

★Coconut Garden Island Resort BUNGALOW $
(☑0918 370 2395; www.coconutgardenisland resort.com; Cacnipa Island; basic s/d P860/995, cottages P1700-2200; 🛜) Occupying a white-

Port Barton

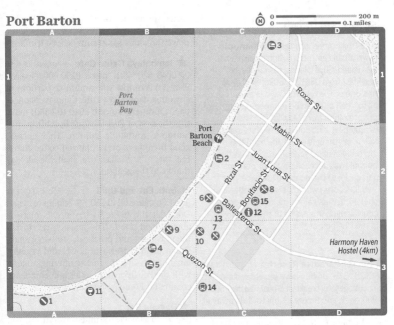

Port Barton

Activities, Courses & Tours
1 Easy Dive A3

Sleeping
2 Ausan C2
3 Besaga Beachfront Cottages C1
4 Deep Moon Resort B3
5 Dragon House B3

Eating
6 Ayette's Bamboo House
   Restaurant..C2
7 Gacayan.. C3
8 Gorgonzola C2

9 Jambalaya Cajun Cafe B3
10 Mabuti. Eat and Chill C3

Drinking & Nightlife
11 Reggae Bar A3

Information
12 Tourist Assistance Center C2

Transport
13 Nature Island Transport C2
14 Recaro Transport C3
15 SBE C2

sand beach on Cacnipa Island, 45 minutes by boat from Port Barton, this is affordable private-island living at its finest. It has a nice restaurant, a dozen or so cottages and a row of basic rooms, all with ocean views and outdoor sitting areas. Owner Henry keeps the grounds immaculate, and all but the basic rooms have 24-hour solar power.

★**Thelma & Toby's Island Camping Adventure** TENTED CAMP $
(Palawan Camping; ☑ 0998 983 3328, 0999 486 3348; www.palawancamping.com; per person incl full board P2500) Offers upscale camping in canopy-covered, fan-cooled tents on a divine

mainland beach 20 minutes north by boat from Port Barton. This hidden gem is also accessible overland via the rugged Port Barton–San Vicente road.

Blue Cove Island Resort BUNGALOW $
(☑ 0908 562 0879; www.bluecoveresort.com; Albaguen Island; cottages P1200-1800; ❄️🛜) On Albaguen Island, a half-hour bangka ride from Port Barton, Blue Cove's handful of cottages, basic in design and tucked underneath palms set back from the beach, are a miniretreat from the world. Some rooms have an air-con option, but you'll pay P200 an hour to keep the generator running after 11pm.

SUPER SPLURGE!

The Philippines' top resort **Amanpulo** (www.aman.com/resorts/amanpulo; Pamalican Island, Cuyo Islands; casita/villa incl breakfast from US$1210/3025; ✳ @ 🛜 ⊠) has one of the remote Cuyo Islands all to itself and can be reached only by private plane from Manila. The island is ringed by a ribbon of fine white sand, and everything is exquisite, from the incredible island scenery to the luxurious bungalows (accessed by your personal golf cart), to the nonpareil service.

Villas come with a personal butler and chef. Activities galore, including a tennis court, sailing and some of the best diving in the Philippines.

⭐**Secret Paradise Resort**　　　RESORT $$$
(🖂 0928 339 9446; www.secretparadiseresort. com; cottages incl breakfast & boat transfer P5600-14,900; ✳ 🛜) 🍴 Stress seems to slide away at this hideaway, on a pretty mainland bay one hour by boat from Port Barton. The British owners, dedicated to conservation, have created a mini protected marine area and turtle sanctuary in front of several impeccably manicured white-sand beaches. It offers 24-hour electricity and free use of kayaks. The new top-whack villas are truly luxurious.

🍴 Eating & Drinking

Port Barton's nightlife scene is concentrated at the southern half of the beach, where you'll find live acoustic music emanating from up to a half-dozen beach bars on any given evening.

Gacayan　　　FILIPINO, EUROPEAN $
(Bonafacio St; meals P50-250; ⊙ 6.30am-midnight; 🛜) Backpackers flock here, and it's no wonder: Gacayan is as reliable as it gets for cheap, tasty meals. It offers backpacker staples like banana pancakes mixed with local specialities like grilled stuffed squid. A free drink is thrown in with most meals – even the popular budget rice meals (P50).

⭐**Gorgonzola**　　　ITALIAN $$
(Bonafacio St; mains P150-350; ⊙ 7.30am-11pm Nov-May) With a big open-plan kitchen filling the street with divine garlicky scents, Gorgonzola will inevitably draw you in at some point. Don't hesitate to sit down. The famously large brick-oven pizzas feed three.

Other specialities on the chalkboard menu include focaccia sandwiches, bruschetta, power breakfasts and sinful choco truffles.

⭐**Jambalaya Cajun Cafe**　　　INTERNATIONAL $$
(🖂 0948 520 4811; mains P200-400; ⊙ 8am-9pm; 🛜) A quirky vibe and huge portions of steaming jambalaya (the Cajun version of paella, properly spiced, P240 to P350) make this the best of Port Barton's beachfront restaurants. Authentic gumbo, Thai curries, good breakfasts and imported coffee round out the mix. Shakes are available all day thanks to the generator.

Mabuti. Eat and Chill　　　CAFE $$
(Rizal St; mains P140-250; ⊙ 7am-11pm; 🛜🍴) Don't let the name fool you: this place is about good food. The mostly vegetarian menu is tight and practical. Multi-egg shakshuka breakfasts, pasta bowls and vegetarian burgers are the main offerings, along with the Polish owner's killer homemade ice cream and French–pressed coffee.

⭐**Reggae Bar**　　　BAR
(⊙ 5pm to late) Pretty much everything you need in a backpacker beach bar: prime beachfront location, cheap drinks and an absolutely rocking house reggae band fronted by one of the owners. It often parties until the wee hours, and just about anything can and will happen here. Goes by several other names, but everybody calls it Reggae Bar.

ℹ Information

Tourist Assistance Center (🖂 0949 770 9597, 0909 151 1769; Ballesteros St; ⊙ 8am-5pm) This helpful place is two blocks back from the beach, next to the town basketball court. Call ahead if you're unsure where your accommodation is (ie, in San Vicente or Port Barton). The centre collects an environmental fee from all incoming travellers (P100) and posts van schedules and rates for island-hopping tours and private boat charters.

There's no bank, but you can wire yourself money through a local pawnshop; ask at the Tourist Assistance Center how to do this. A few resorts accept Visa and MasterCard.

ℹ Getting There & Away

BOAT
Most travellers heading to Sabang or El Nido travel overland these days, but chartering a boat is still an option to save a little time and/or do some island-hopping en route. Posted rates for a four-passenger boat are P5000 to both Sabang (3½ hours) and El Nido (four hours). San Vicente

North Palawan

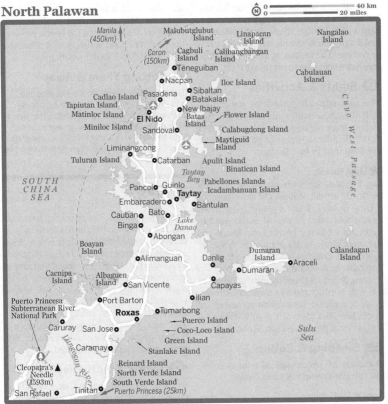

costs P1500 (45 minutes). Figure on 30% more for an eight-passenger boat.

JEEPNEY & MINIVAN

There are seven or eight daily van trips to Puerto Princesa (P350, 2½ hours, last trip 5pm) and six direct trips to El Nido (P500, four hours, last trip 1pm). **Recaro Transport** (☑ 0905 405 8597; Bonafacio St), **Santolis** (☑ in El Nido 0995 238 9142) and **Nature Island** (☑ 0915 649 3007; Rizal St) are the companies for El Nido, while Recaro and **SBE** (☑ in Puerto 0928 765 2181; Bonafacio St) serve Puerto. A private van to El Nido/Sabang/Puerto costs P4500/4000/3500 (negotiate hard).

Additionally, a daily jumbo jeepney lumbers to Puerto, departing around 2pm (P250, four hours) from the waiting shed near **Ayette's Bamboo House Restaurant** (cnr Ballesteros & Rizal Sts; mains P100-200; ⊙7am-10pm). The departure from Puerto is at 8am. There's an 8am jumbo jeepney to Roxas (P150, one hour); the reverse trip is at noon. Change in Roxas for a bus to El Nido or a jeepney to San Vicente.

Another option for going north or south is to take a motorcycle taxi or tricycle out to the National Hwy at San Jose (P300, 45 minutes, 23km) and flag down a bus there.

For Sabang, take a Puerto-bound vehicle and hop off in Salvacion; arrange a pick-up in Salvacion through **Lexus Shuttle** (☑ 0917 585 9613; www. lexusshuttle.com; San Jose Bus Terminal), or flag down the thrice-daily Puerto-Sabang jeepney.

San Vicente

☑ 048 / POP 10,000

This sleepy fishing village on Palawan's west coast is home to a famously long beach, but has long been off the tourist trail due to poor road connections and an almost complete lack of services. But that changed when an ambitious international airport (p379) opened in 2017, and resorts started to spring up on aptly named Long Beach north of the centre.

Port Barton is a barangay of San Vicente, but the two towns are not well connected to each other. Double check your booking to make sure you're staying in the right town, or you could be looking at a long drive or an expensive boat ride to set things right.

☉ Sights & Activities

The same island-hopping trips you can get in Port Barton (p390) are available in San Vicente from the town pier. It's a bit further to the islands, so expect to pay P100 more per head than in Port Barton.

★ Long Beach   BEACH
San Vicente's signature attraction is a real beauty. It actually consists of three beaches – Long Beach 1, 2 and 3 – which combined yield about 14km of almost empty golden-hued, sunset-facing beach. Long Beach 2 is the most glorious; it's 50m wide, faces the sunset and stretches uninterrupted for 7km, navigable by foot or motorbike.

Long Beach 1 is closer to town; Long Beach 3 is well north of town in barangay Aliman-guan. Speculators have driven up real-estate prices here, but for now the only serious resort on Long Beach 2 is Club Agutaya.

🛏 Sleeping & Eating

There are no restaurants of note in town, but the main resorts all serve food.

April's Tourist Inn   INN $
(☑ 0949 151 8111; barangay New Agutaya; r with fan/air-con P900/1500; ❄ 🤖) This is a pleasant and quiet in-town option run by a friendly family. The five rooms are clean and spacious enough, if somewhat tacky and lacking hot water. There's an open-air restaurant in the delightfully leafy courtyard.

Sunset Beach Resort   HOTEL $$
(☑ 0919 974 3997; www.sunsetbeach-palawan.com; sitio Macatumbalen; r P3000; ❄ 🤖 ♨) A very simple and agreeable German–owned resort on a narrow beach near the airport, about 2km south of San Vicente proper. The six well-appointed rooms are set around a small pool. The swim-up and beachfront restaurant bars work equally well for sunset cocktails.

Club Agutaya   RESORT $$$
(☑ 048-723 1050; www.clubagutaya.net; Long Beach 2; r P6600-15,400; ❄ @ 🤖 ♨) Occupying the central portion of Long Beach all by its lonesome, this full-service resort is a statement of confidence that San Vicente

has what it takes to become an upscale resort town. Most of the comfortable, modern rooms are set back from the beach, closer to the pool. The food is decent and affordable (mains P200 to P400) for walk-ins.

❶ Getting There & Away

There are three rickety local buses (five hours), and several vans (P300, three hours) per day to Puerto via Roxas. For Port Barton, transfer in Roxas to the noon jeepney or save oodles of time by chartering a boat (P1500, 45 minutes). There is no public transport along the rough new coastal road to Port Barton.

Taytay
☑ 048 / POP 19,966

Formerly the capital of Palawan, Taytay today is a port town that most travellers pass through unknowingly on their way to/from El Nido. Its appeal lies in being everything El Nido is not: sleepy, provincial and almost completely devoid of tourists. Diversions include island-hopping in Taytay Bay, several waterfalls and an old Spanish fort. North of town on the west coast, extinct volcano Mt Capoas (1000m) looms over Malampaya Sound, where dugongs and Irrawaddy dolphins can sometimes be spotted.

☉ Sights & Activities

You can spot endangered Irrawaddy dolphins in Malampaya Sound; early morning and late afternoon are the best times. Arrange a boat (P1500) at the pier in barangay Pancol, 15km north of Taytay.

★ Kuyawyaw Falls   WATERFALL
(Cataban Falls; Km 236, National Hwy, barangay Cataban; entrance & environmental fee P200) This is a series of three falls cascading into fresh pools 27km north of Taytay. There's a fun little 4m cliff jump at the second falls, which are less than a 15-minute walk from the entrance. These are also the highest falls at close to 10m. To access the peaceful third falls (7m) – which are a steep, rope-assisted, 10-minute climb from the second falls – requires a guide (P200). It's worth it, especially if there are crowds at the second falls.

Fort Santa Isabel   FORT
(P50) With thick walls and a strategic position on the waterfront overlooking Taytay Bay, Fort Santa Isabel guarded against attacks from Moro pirates during the Spanish era. Erected by the Augustinian Recollects (an order of Catholic priests) in 1667, the

fort today is a pleasant retreat with a well-maintained garden, a small museum and sweeping views of the bay.

🛌 Sleeping

Taytay's simple and affordable guesthouses make great bases for launching island-hopping excursions in Taytay Bay. Taytay is also the jumping-off point for several luxury resorts based on private islands in the bay.

Casa Rosa   HOTEL $
(☑0920 895 0092; casarosataytay@gmail.com; d P700, cottage P1100-1460; 🐾) Casa Rosa offers a choice between simple rooms with pleasing terracotta floors and more spacious cottages with hammock-strewn balconies. There are outstanding views of Fort Santa Isabel and Taytay Bay from the restaurant, and island-hopping trips and terrestrial tours are offered.

Pem's Pension & Restaurant   PENSION $
(☑0977 681 5549; pemspensionandresto@gmail. com; Rizal St; r with fan/air-con P700/1500; ❉🐾) On the main road in town near Fort Santa Isabel, Pem's is a friendly place with good-value stand-alone cottages arranged around a quiet courtyard. The staff can arrange tours in the area.

★Flower Island Beach Resort   RESORT $$$
(☑0917 504 5567; www.flowerisland-resort.com; cottages incl all meals per person with fan/air-con from P7000/8500; ❉🐾) 🌿 Warning: leaving this idyllic low-key resort can induce severe depression. The staff are warm and friendly, the native-style cottages are a perfect mix of modern comforts and rustic charm, and the small beach is of the whitest sand. Full moons induce skinny-dipping with a rum and Coke in hand.

ℹ Getting There & Away

Plans are to expand Taytay's Sandoval Airport in the hopes of turning it into a gateway to El Nido, but this is a long-term project. At the time of research, there were no flights.

Boats still serve some remote towns and islands on Palawan's east coast north of Taytay, departing from the Embarcadero Pier, 8km north of town, but as roads improve these are going out of style.

Frequent south-bound buses from El Nido serve Roxas (for Port Barton and San Vicente) and Puerto Princesa (P220, five to six hours). It's usually easy to get a seat on these or on passing north-bound buses going to El Nido (P150, 1½ hours). Vans plying the route between Puerto and El Nido are usually full, so don't count on finding a seat on these. The bus station is out on the National Hwy, 2.5km west of the town pier; a tricycle from the bus station to the pier costs P50.

El Nido

☎048 / POP 41,606

El Nido is the primary base for exploring Palawan's star attraction, the stunning Bacuit Archipelago (p403). Tiny swiftlets build edible nests out of saliva in the immense limestone cliffs that surround the ramshackle town proper – hence the name, El Nido (nest in Spanish). The town proper has an ordinary beach, but is home to an emerging restaurant and bar scene. Brooding Cadlao Island looms just offshore.

Many visitors prefer to stay in communities outside the town proper. Nearby options include Corong Corong, a long, narrow beach to the south that faces Bacuit Bay; or Caalan, a rocky strip of quiet resorts immediately to the north. Further afield, more and more resorts are sprouting along El Nido's beautiful north coastline, in places like Nacpan Beach and the east coast villages of San Fernando and Sibaltan.

👁 Sights

While the Bacuit Archipelago are the main draw, the El Nido area is also blessed with arguably the best beaches (p398) in the country, both onshore and on islands offshore. Some places have all the luck. Despite the tourism boom, many of the best beaches, including those on the east coast around Sibaltan, remain virtually empty.

Taytay's Kuyawyaw Falls are easily reachable from El Nido.

Balay Cuyonon   MUSEUM
(Sibaltan Museum; ☑0915 967 2743; Sibaltan; admission by donation) You can take a guided tour of this complex of well-preserved traditional Cuyonon houses to learn about ordinary village life. Consider a night in a native-style room (P600 to P800) to experience this community's daily rhythms. It's right on the Sibaltan town beach and you'll find a bar and a restaurant.

Nagkalit-kalit Waterfalls   WATERFALL
(Km 285, National Hwy) From a signpost on the National Hwy 3km south of the Nacpan Beach turn-off, it's a 40-minute walk through several

PALAWAN EL NIDO

PALAWAN EL NIDO

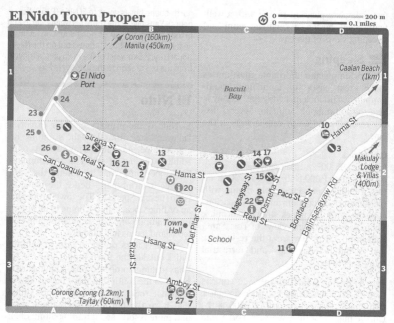

El Nido Town Proper

rivers to these gentle falls, with a refreshing pool. Hire a guide (P300) at the trailhead to avoid getting lost.

Activities

All visitors to El Nido must pay a one-time 'ecotourism development fee' of P200, payable to your tour operator or the City Tourism

Office (p402) and good for 10 days, if they plan to do activities.

Island-Hopping & Kayaking

The 'alphabet' group tours (A, B, C, D) of Bacuit Bay are universally available and cost P1200 to P1400 per person including lunch, mask and snorkel. Unfortunately these tend to follow identical itineraries, creating boat traffic and crowds at popular sights like Big/Small Lagoon and Snake Island. To dodge the crowds, consider shelling out for a private tour by bangka (P8000 give or take) or speedboat (from P15,000) and departing well before the group tours head out at 9am.

Better yet, DIY to some of the closer attractions, like Seven Commandos Beach and Cadlao Island, by **sea kayak**, which are available for rent (P600 to P800 per day) all along El Nido Beach and Corong Corong Beach. El Nido Boutique & Art Café (p401) has been encouraging more kayaking and stand-up paddleboarding (SUP) to limit the environmental impact of tourism, and has a fleet of SUPs and kayaks, including a clear-bottomed variety. It also offers a kayak option on its Miniloc Island bangka trips. **Waz SUP** (www.wazsupelnido.com) is another good option for SUP tours.

For the ultimate island-hopping adventure, consider a multiday expedition (p410) to Coron.

Diving

El Nido has outstanding diving, and more than a dozen dive shops are ready to take you there. Dives range from shallow reefs to deep wall and drift dives, and it's a popular destination for PADI certification courses.

A few highlights are South Miniloc's cabbage coral and school of yellow snapper; North Rock's barracuda, spade fish and interesting rock formations; Twin Rocks for turtles and stingrays; and for advanced divers, Helicopter Island's 50m-long natural tunnel.

Figure on about P4000 for a three-dive day including gear, and P19,000 to P22,000 for an open-water course.

Palawan Divers DIVING
(☑ 048-244 0381; www.palawan-divers.org; Hama St) Efficient and friendly dive shop. Instructors speak many languages, and they do speedboat sunrise dives that offer a chance to see some bigger fish.

Submariner Diving Center DIVING
(☑ 0905 484 1764; www.submariner-diving.com; Hama St) A good dive shop that also does multiday trips over to Culion Island in the Calamianes to dive the wrecks. The Culion trips require advanced open-water certification (P10,000 to get certified on the trip).

Deep Blue Seafari DIVING
(☑ 0917 803 0543; www.deepblueseafari.com; Hama St) In addition to the standard fun dives around El Nido, this operator offers

highly recommended four-day, three-night diving safaris between El Nido and Coron from mid-October to May (P36,000 per person including dive gear and 14 dives).

Turtle Divers DIVING
(☑ 0920 601 7532〔; Sirena St) This is one of the few Filipino owned and managed dive shops in El Nido. The rates are some of the best in town.

Other Activities

There's a growing **surfing** scene in the El Nido area, with the action focused on Duli Beach (p398) between November and March. **Kitesurfing** is becoming popular on the east coast. Gear rental and courses are available at Qi Palawan (p401) in San Fernando and on **Tapik Beach** in Sibaltan.

Although often overlooked, the inland area around El Nido offers several interesting trips for the active and adventurous. Climbing the local **taraw** (cliffs) is an option, albeit not one for the faint of heart. Expect marvellous views from the top.

El Nido Boutique & Art Café (p401) is a one-stop-shop for **hiking, mountain-biking** and **cliff-climbing** (P350, one hour) trips; half-day treks on Cadlao Island are popular.

🛌 Sleeping

In a nutshell, stay in El Nido proper if you want to be close to the action; Caalan is central yet has a secluded feel; Corong Corong has variety, beach bars and the sunset; offshore is for private-island opulence; and the north peninsula or east coast is where to escape the tourist scene. Low-season discounts average 30% wherever you stay.

🛌 El Nido Proper

The town proper and Corong Corong have 24-hour electricity nowadays, notwithstanding the more than occasional 'brownout'. To be safe, do not brush your teeth with tap water, as there have been many reports of contaminated water causing illnesses.

★Bulskamp Inn GUESTHOUSE **$**
(☑ 0956 648 2901; www.bulskampinn.com; Osmeña St; r P1400-2200; ❄ 🛜) Under new management, this old-timer has spruced up its outdoor area and restaurant while supplying the same friendly service and good value that it has long been known for. The compact rooms, fan-cooled or air-conditioned, have small beds but are spotless.

EL NIDO'S TOP 5 MAINLAND BEACHES

Nacpan Beach This incredible, golden-hued, 3km beach somehow remains undeveloped save for a few snack shacks and some basic lodging. Change seems imminent – a Mad Monkey hostel was going up when we were there – so enjoy the mellow atmosphere while it lasts. Nacpan already gets quite crowded during the high season; walk north to find solitude. Nacpan is 20km north of El Nido proper, the last 4km over a rugged access road. A **shuttle van** (Discover El Nido, Amboy St) does the journey (round-trip P600, eight daily).

Duli Beach This incredibly beautiful, jungle-backed stretch of golden sand toward the north tip of mainland Palawan is the centre of El Nido's surfing community. The season is November to March and board rental is available (P500 per hour) through a couple of places, including idyllic **Duli Beach Resort** (p400). To get here, turn off the National Hwy around the Km 294 marker and continue 3.5km on a very rough road that ends in a slippery single track to the beach proper.

Maremegmeg Beach Often called Las Cabanas Beach after a local resort, this is the closest nice beach to El Nido town proper and has a rockin' sunset bar scene. A zipline (one way/return P500/900) flies over the water between the mainland and an offshore island. Every tricycle driver in town wants to take you here. The 6km trip from the town proper should cost P150 one way.

Dagmay Beach Another 2km north of Duli Beach the way the crow flies (4km on a rough road if you're not a crow), this lonely beach is the site of **Villa Verde Safari & Pagi Dive Center** (☏ 0929 481 5928; https://villaverdesafari.com; barangay Teneguiban; tent/d/f incl breakfast P1500/2500/9000), with comfortable fan cottages, kayaks and a dive centre.

Lio Beach (Airport Beach) The wealthy Ayala conglomerate, in conjunction with **Ten Knots Travel** (p404), are developing this wide white-sand beach 7km north of El Nido proper into a swanky world-class resort area. For now it remains almost empty save for a few early-adopting restaurants and half-built hotels, so finding your own private patch of sand shouldn't be a problem.

Pawikan Hostel HOSTEL $
(☏ 0943 438 5397; www.pawikanhostel.com; San Joaquin St; incl breakfast dm P700, r P1500-2000; ❋ 🖥) A super-friendly, locally run hostel with a generous breakfast (for a hostel) in a three-storey high-rise a five-minute walk from Hama St. The private rooms are a tad small for the price, but the dorms are great – they are tidy four-bed affairs with personal charging stations and nice lighting.

Spin Hostel HOSTEL $$
(www.spinhostel.com; Balinsasayaw Rd; dm/d incl breakfast P1000/3000; ❋ @ 🖥) The eye-popping design of this luxury hostel draws its inspiration from the nests of the local swiftlets. The prices are eye-popping as well, but you can expect quality. The four-bed dorms are en suite and fully accessorised, and all rooms are integrated seamlessly into the central nest. Regular fun events and a sociable vibe round out the package.

Amakan Bed, Bunk & Breakfast HOTEL $$
(☏ 0918 933 9072; www.amakan.ph; Amboy St; d incl breakfast P2500-3500; ❋ 🖥) Inviting stone paths show the way into this central hideaway a short walk from El Nido's beach. The common areas make the place. They consist of a lush garden outside and a lovely living room and dining area strewn with tasteful furniture inside. These areas are particularly welcome because the rooms, while attractive, are positively Lilliputian.

Bill Tourist Inn HOTEL $$
(☏ 0915 092 4508; www.billtouristinnelnido.com; Amboy St; d P1900-2500, q P3100) There's nothing fancy about the Bill (much like its name). It's just a clean, modern, business hotel that's quieter than most places in town – a classic 'safe bet'. If the Bill can't billet you, try its even quieter new sister hotel, Den'gi Inn, around the corner.

Rosanna's Beach Cottages
HOTEL $$

(☑ 0920 605 4631; www.rosannaspension.com; Hama St; d incl breakfast P2500-3500; ❄ 🛜) Rosanna's has a modern beachfront building containing small but in-demand sea-facing rooms with balconies. There's an older wing across the street with six large, fairly nondescript rooms that are good for groups. Solar-powered hot-water showers.

🛏 Caalan Beach

Peaceful Caalan faces the sunset and has stunning views of Cadlao Island. However, its beach lacks sand, and swimming is really only feasible around high tide. It's accessible via a walkway around the headland from El Nido (navigable by tricycle, so you don't have to walk with your bags).

★ Garden Bay Beach Resort
RESORT $$

(☑ 0918 310 9683; www.gardenbaybeachresort. com; Caalan Beach; d incl breakfast with fan/air-con P2000/3800; ❄ 🛜) A small hidden paradise at the very end of Caalan Beach, Garden Bay takes some work to get to, but that's part of its appeal. The seven pleasingly rustic cottages, nestled at the foot of the jungle, have quality beds and private verandahs facing a sandy beach strewn with palm trees and hammocks. Great food too, especially the pancakes.

Caalan Beach Resort
RESORT $$

(☑ 0977 844 4032; www.elnidocottages.com; Caalan Beach; r P2000-4000; ❄ 🛜) A nice mix of rooms and a knowledgeable and helpful owner make this family-run place towards the quiet far end of rocky Caalan Beach an excellent option. Accommodation ranges from beachfront cottages to modern air-con rooms to spacious family quarters. All rooms were being upgraded when we dropped in, and a swimming pool is planned.

Makulay Lodge & Villas
GUESTHOUSE $$

(☑ 0916 401 9590; www.makulaylodgeelnido.com; Caalan Point; r P2400-3500, apt P4000-4900; ❄ 🛜) On the headland between El Nido Beach and Caalan Beach, French-run Makulay offers convenience, privacy and wonderful views from the hilltop apartments. There's a small sandy area with lounge chairs down below, and an urbane beach bar with regular film nights and other events up above. All just a five-minute walk from El Nido.

The food is excellent – come for the all-you-can-eat-mussels Mondays.

🛏 Corong Corong & Maremegmeg

Corong Corong extends south from El Nido proper for about 3km (P50 to P100 by tricycle). There's a narrow sandy beach with prime views of Bacuit Bay, but shallow water makes swimming a high-tide affair.

Cavern Pod Hotel & Specialty Cafe
HOSTEL $

(☑ 0915 102 3272; National Hwy, Corong Corong; dm P675; ❄ 🛜) Simply the nicest dorm beds in El Nido. The Japanese–inspired design of the 'pods' features a colour scheme of slate grey and black, beautiful linens, reading lights and a staircase to the top bunk. There are just four beds to a room, and each room has its own beautiful bathroom with rain shower and designer-shampoo dispensers.

Blue Mango
BOUTIQUE HOTEL $$

(☑ 0939 590 6825; bluemangoelnido@gmail.com; sitio Lugadia, Corong Corong; r incl breakfast P3500-6500; ❄ 🛜) This fantastically conceived complex on a ridge overlooking Bacuit Bay makes generous use of native materials and is built around a huge mango tree in the central courtyard. It's all leafy goodness and exquisitely carved wood. The pricier rooms have sea-facing terraces and are preferred to the standard rooms, which, while spacious and tasteful, are closer to the road.

Outpost Beach Hostel
HOSTEL $$

(☑ 0977 373 5229; www.outpostbeachhostel. com; sitio Lugadia, Corong Corong; 4-/9-bed dm P1200/900, r P4000-5500; ❄ 🛜) Outpost ticks all the boxes for hedonistic backpackers, provided they can afford the lofty prices. Beautiful young crowd mingling gleefully in contemporary dorm rooms? Check. Rockin' beach bar with shooter specials and regular beer pong tourneys? Check. Social island tours by day? Of course.

Pukka Beach Hotel
BOUTIQUE HOTEL $$

(☑ 0908 488 8832; sitio Lugadia, Corong Corong; r P3500-4800; ❄ 🛜) Part of the growing Pukka Bar (p402) empire, this whitewashed, compact Miami Beach–style hotel on emerging Lugadia Beach is aimed at flashpacker couples. Rooms are small, but beds are huge, and the best rooms have huge glass windows framing Bacuit Bay – quite a scene to wake up to. A beachfront plunge pool flanks the bar in the courtyard.

Birdhouse TENTED CAMP $$$
(✆ 0998 318 8918; www.thebirdhouseelnido.com; Maremegmeg Beach; incl breakfast d P6500, extra person P825; ◈) ✐ The Birdhouse brings true glamping to El Nido. Emerge from your luxurious 'nest' perched high over Maremeg-meg Beach and take in the astonishing view of Bacuit Bay from your private pavilion – they don't call it Birdhouse for nothin'. Friendly, knowledgeable owner-couple, and a great new restaurant, the Nesting Table, is open to walk-ins. The spacious tents sleep four.

Last Frontier RESORT $$$
(✆ 0917 204 4612; www.lastfrontierbeachresort. com; Corong Corong; r incl breakfast P4150-7350; ❋◈❋) On a particularly desirable slice of Corong Corong's beach, Last Frontier is flanked by casual beach bars and has out-standing views of Bacuit Bay. Rooms are great value for El Nido. Choose from luxurious thatched-roof cottages or attractive standard rooms in the main building with sliding glass doors opening to private porches. Delightful pool area with beanbag seating.

Las Cabanas Beach Resort COTTAGE $$$
(✆ 0930 369 2741; www.lascabanasresort.com; Maremegmeg Beach; d/tr incl breakfast P5000-6500; ❋◈) A clutch of large cottages, spread out in a large, nicely landscaped garden, front the beach with great views of south Bacuit Bay. You'll need to walk about 10 minutes along the beach to get here from the entrance to Maremegmeg Beach.

🛏 North Peninsula (Nacpan to Sibaltan)

Nacpan has a small but growing colony of backpacker-focused retreats. The resorts in and around Sibaltan, 42km from El Nido proper, can arrange island-hopping in the Linapacan group of islands just offshore. Some resorts on Sibaltan's Tapik Beach have a tent option. There's no electricity in these parts so guesthouses rely on generators, which they tend to run only for a few hours in the evening.

★ Where 2 Next HOSTEL $
(✆ 0917 804 0434; www.where2nexthostel.com; Nacpan Beach; dm P550, r P1200-1700, d in tent Mar-May only P800; ◈) Enviably placed just off Nacpan Beach, peaceful Where 2 Next is well positioned to ride Nacpan's surging popularity. The dorm rooms are charmingly rustic, or you can opt for a snug private. So-

lar power, great food, friendly management and the most beautiful common bathroom in Palawan round out the package.

★ Eda Beach Campsite BUNGALOW $
(✆ 0905 572 0646; edabeach@gmail.com; Km 316, National Hwy, Sibaltan; cottages P500-1500; ◈) This delightfully rustic collection of bunga-lows has a real castaway feel. It's south of, and isolated from, the other Sibaltan resorts. Despite the name, it's a significant step up on camping. Owner Randy is, simply, the man. He cooks well and leads superb boat trips to the many remote islands off El Ni-do's east coast.

★ Duli Beach Resort COTTAGE $$
(✆ 0947 969 8210; www.dulibeach.com; Duli Beach; bungalow P2500) Duli features six thoughtfully conceived bungalows mixing European (the owners are Dutch) and local styles on what is essentially a private beach. The bungalows are enclosed by thin screens that bring you closer to the raw nature that surrounds you. A generator provides elec-tricity for a few hours at night. Great food and surfing from November to March.

Board rental is P350 an hour or you can negotiate a daily rate. It takes about an hour to get here from El Nido. Take the Duli Beach access road followed by a 10-minute walk.

Ursula Beach Club BUNGALOW $$
(✆ 0917 580 0040; www.ursulabeachclub.com; Sibaltan; cottages P2400-4000, tent P500) Just a few cottages here, but they are delightful, and the food is the best in Sibaltan. The pric-ier rooms are up the hill at the back with views and private balconies. It's a good spot for kiteboarders; owner Dennis kitesurfs and the Palawan Kite Club (www.kiteclub palawan.com) sets up shop right next door in season (November to March).

Jack's Place BUNGALOW $$
(✆ 0995 237 4811; Nacpan Beach; d/q cottage incl breakfast P1600/1800; ◈) Walk toward the north end of Nacpan Beach and you'll encounter this castaway-style gem. It con-sists of five basic en suite cottages on stilts, all fashioned of wood and equipped with beach-facing balconies. Kayak rental availa-ble (per hour/day P150/500).

Tapik Beach Park Guesthouse COTTAGE $$
(✆ 0915 768 0688, 0935 537 2106; www.tapik beach.com; Sibaltan; cottages P1200-2500, tents P500) This funky complex has some beauti-

ful A-frame cottages with private balconies and sea views. More rudimentary bungalows and tents are down by the beach (make sure you know what you're getting). There's an eclectic restaurant, and motorbike rental and island-hopping are available, but service can be indifferent. Electricity runs from 6pm to 6am.

★**Qi Palawan** BUNGALOW $$$
(☑0939 925 9433; www.qipalawan.com; Km 308, National Hwy, San Fernando; d/q cottage incl breakfast from P9250/13,500; ❋ ☎ ☎) The husband-and-wife-run Qi Palawan is a beautiful top-end option on El Nido's remote east coast. Eight stand-alone bungalows dot the lush grounds; the two-storey beachfront family villas with massive open-air bathroom stand out. It has a fully equipped kiteboarding centre (season: November to April), a dive centre, and yoga, kayaking and mountain biking on offer. A generator provides 24-hour electricity.

✖ **Eating**

The dining scene is really starting to emerge thanks to a host of new international eateries and bars in the town proper and in Corong Corong. Fresh seafood eateries line central El Nido Beach near where Rizal St dead-ends. There's not much difference between them: just pick out something that looks fresh, and staff will grill it up good for you.

★**El Nido Boutique & Art Café** INTERNATIONAL $$
(☑0920 902 6317; www.elnidoboutiqueandartcafe.com; Sirena St; mains P220; ☉7am-11pm; ☎) Everyone ends up here at some point. Rightfully so. The large 2nd-storey dining room is a warm and relaxed place to eat, drink and get your bearings. Especially good are the salads (using lettuce and arugula from its own organic farm), homemade bread, seafood curry, pizza, pineapple upside-down cake, and chocolate and mango tarts. It has a bar and live music four nights a week.

★**La Plage** FRENCH $$
(☑0947 068 5272; Corong Corong; mains P350-450; ☉noon-10pm) Besides having the best food in El Nido and sterling sunset views, this beachfront French restaurant has its own plunge pool open for guests. It's known for exciting specials and the heavenly fish steamed in banana leaf.

★**Bulalo Plaza** FILIPINO $$
(mains P150-200; ☉24hr) ✈ In-the-know travellers flock to this nondescript open-air eatery on the road to Corong Corong for the best fresh-cooked Pinoy eats in town. It's all *sarap* (delicious), but the black squid *adobo,* sizzling pork *bulgogi* and seafood curry stick out. Cheap breakfasts and lots of vegetarian choices.

★**Trattoria Altrove** ITALIAN $$
(☑0947 775 8653; Hama St; mains P240-450; ☉5-10pm) This upstairs Slovenian–owned place does the best pizza in El Nido, made with imported mozzarella in the street-level brick oven. There are a dozen types of pasta from Italy, plus T-bone steak and other meat dishes on the menu. It's very popular, so get here early (or late) during the high season to avoid a long wait.

Boodle Fight Restaurant FILIPINO $$
(☑0907 767 1901; National Hwy, Corong Corong; mains P150-250; ☉7am-2pm & 5-11pm) What's a Boodle Fight, you ask? It's a Filipino feast served on a huge banana leaf and eaten communally by hand. A four-person feast here costs P650 (meat) to P850 (surf and turf). Advance bookings recommended.

Taverna Agape GREEK $$
(El Nido Beach; mains P270-350; ☉11am-10.30pm) With a blue-and-white Mediterranean motif, this beachfront eatery scores points for authentic *saganaki* (fried cheese), moussaka, and souvlaki over orzo (short-cut wheat pasta), among other delights.

Odessa Mama UKRAINIAN $$
(Hama St; mains P190-250; ☉7am-11pm) This counter-top Ukrainian–food bar on El Nido's main drag is a surprise. Run by actual Odessans, it serves up authentic motherland faves like *varenyky* (dumplings) and *nalysnyky* (crepes), plus original meat-stuffed 'patty pockets'.

🍷 **Drinking & Nightlife**

El Nido beach lacks a sunset view so the happening happy-hour bars are all along Corong Corong and Maremegmeg beaches. The backpacker bar at Outpost (p399) on Lugadia Beach (Corong Corong) is always lively, but by 11pm all the action shifts back to El Nido proper.

Party Boats such as **Mellow Yellow** (Tour Z; ☑0917 835 6969; ladiha.matevz@gmail.

com; Sirena St; P1500) are a fun option for all-day drinking and island-hopping.

★ **Bella Vita**   BEACH BAR
(Corong Corong) Quite simply our favourite sunset bar. It has dangerous mojitos, groovy tunes and two-for-one San Miguel during happy hour (3pm to 5pm), plus superb pizza and fresh-baked bread. But most importantly it has that elusive sunset view, unlike many places in El Nido.

★ **Beach Shack**   BAR
(Maremegmeg Beach) The ubercool beach bar that makes Maremegmeg Beach (aka Las Cabanas Beach) tick. In the high season it assumes a Miami Beach vibe around sunset as it turns up the tunes and the pretty people flock to it.

★ **Happiness Bar**   COCKTAIL BAR
(Sirena St; ⊙6am-midnight; 🖻) The cool kid on El Nido's main drag, diminutive Happiness features contemporary beats, top-class cocktails and hipster swings at the streetside bar. By day its vegan-friendly Middle Eastern menu (mains P200 to P350), with delicious hummus and other small plates as well as pita sandwiches, draws healthy eaters.

SAVA   COCKTAIL BAR
(Hama St; ⊙8am-2am) Finally, a contemporary cocktail bar/club worthy of El Nido's status as a rising international starlet. Cocktails are expertly made with top-notch booze, and the bar menu features some of the best food in town. Try the *chimichanga* or baked mussels. Top DJs set the beachfront dance floor alight as the evening wears on.

Pukka Bar   BAR
(Hama St; ⊙4pm-4am; 🖻) Long the most happening place in El Nido, this reggae bar suddenly has a lot more competition and has responded by expanding. It now has two entrances – one on Hama St, one on the beach. Live reggae music and buckets of beer are what make it tick.

Republica Sunset Bar   COCKTAIL BAR
(sitio Lugadia, Corong Corong; ⊙2pm-midnight) Perched up on the highway over Lugadia Beach 4km south of El Nido proper, Spanish-owned Republica has arguably the best sunset views around. Belly up to the long wooden countertop staring right at Bacuit Bay and order a craft cocktail and tapas like *huevos rotos*.

ⓘ Information

TRAVEL AGENCIES

Hama St is chock-a-block with streetfront booking and travel agencies.

El Nido Boutique & Art Café (p401) Run like clockwork by the Swiss owner, this longstanding cafe is a repository for information about El Nido.

Philippines à la Carte (🗷0917 596 6903; Real St; ⊙8am-9pm) Can book all airlines and boats, plus car rental, speedboat hire, sunset cruises and camping trips in the Bacuit Archipelago.

TOURIST INFORMATION

City Tourism Office (🗷0917 775 6036; www.elnidotourism.com; Real St; ⊙8am-8pm Mon-Fri, to 5pm Sat & Sun) Hit and miss. The better staffers can answer all of your transport and infrastructure questions. You can pay your environmental fee (good for 10 days) here to avoid doing it while on a tour.

MONEY

Credit cards are accepted at some of the fancier resorts and at one restaurant (SAVA), but they incur at least a 4% surcharge.

BPI (Real St) El Nido's only reliable ATM is here.

ⓘ Getting There & Away

AIR

Air Swift (http://air-swift.com) has at least daily flights to Manila, Caticlan (for Boracay), Cebu and Clark. One-way fares range from P4500 to P7000, depending on the season. All flights are into Lio Airport, 7km north of town (P200 by tricycle). Air Swift and the airport are both owned by El Nido Resorts, and guests of that company's resorts have priority on the flights, although there is usually plenty of room for outsiders.

Many people heading to El Nido take a cheaper flight to Puerto Princesa, then drive north five hours by van. The airport in San Vicente (p379) cut that van trip in half. Sandoval Airport in Taytay, just an hour from El Nido, is in the process of upgrading in the hope of landing commercial flights.

BOAT

All public boats use El Nido Port at the west end of Sirena St in the town proper.

The most important boat service for visitors to northern Palawan is the El Nido–Coron connection. **Montenegro Lines** (🗷0905 371 0787; Real St) runs a daily fastcraft at 6am (adult/student P1760/1500; 4½ to 5½ hours). Book this ahead in the high season via a travel agent or www.biyaheroes.com). **M/Bca Bunso** (🗷0910 720 8443; Real St) runs a slower bangka ferry that's a better option if you want to take in the scenery (P1200 including lunch, eight hours, 8am).

Atienza Shipping (☑ 0998 881 7226; El Nido Port) has a Tuesday 2am departure to Manila (P1700 to P1850, 25 hours) via Linapacan (P500, five hours). It's a big cargo boat with rudimentary bunk beds for passengers – a real experience. Additional departures to Linapacan (a few weekly) are via bangka ferry from barangay San Fernando on the east coast.

BUS, JEEPNEY & VAN

All ground transport leaves from the **Bus Station** (Km 270, National Hwy), 1km south of town in Corong Corong (P50 by tricycle).

The vast majority of visitors to El Nido arrive on cramped minivans from Puerto Princesa (P500, five hours, frequent), but buses are more comfortable and there is no need to book them ahead. Cherry Bus and Roro Bus alternate trips every hour until 10pm, with a mix of air-con and ordinary buses (P350 to P450, 6½ hours).

Nature Island (☑ 0915 644 1630), **Recaro Transport** (☑ 0920 502 5797) and Santolis run direct vans to Port Barton, each with at least a morning and an early-afternoon departure (P700, four hours). Alternatively, take a 7am or earlier bus to Roxas (P250, four hours) and catch the noon jumbo jeepney to Port Barton. For San Vicente, you must also transfer to a jeepney in Roxas.

Lexus Shuttle (☑ 0917 686 1110) vans head to Sabang with a change in Salvacion (P700, six hours, 4am, 8am & 11am).

Minivans can be booked everywhere, and a few, such as pricier VIP carrier **Daytripper** (☑ 0917 848 8755, 048-723 0533; www.daytripperpalawan.com), offer hotel pick-ups. El Nido Boutique & Art Café (p401) has a useful booking service for select van companies on its website; you can pay via PayPal or direct bank deposit.

Privately hired vans to Puerto Princesa cost P7000 to P10,000, depending on your negotiations skills. For Port Barton/Sabang, they start at P4500/5500.

🛈 Getting Around

The town of El Nido encompasses the entire northern peninsula of mainland Palawan. Heading north (clockwise) out of the town proper, the ring road is sealed all the way to Sibaltan on the east coast. South of Sibaltan the highway deteriorates, although it's gradually being upgraded.

Three or four vans serve Sibaltan daily from the bus station (these originate in Puerto Princesa). Contact Tapik Beach Park Guesthouse (p400) to reserve. There's also a noon jeepney to Sibaltan (P150, 2½ hours).

Hiring a motorbike is a great way to get around the northern peninsula, and bike hire is ubiquitously available in El Nido town proper for P400 to P500 per day. Do note that the access roads to Nacpan and Duli beaches are very rough and require some off-road experience in the wet season.

Bacuit Archipelago

The crystalline waters of Bacuit Bay are a fantasy-scape of limestone islands, mesmerising from any vantage point, whether under the water, in the air or lying on a beach. Easily the rival of southern Thailand or Halong Bay in Vietnam, the islands hide so many white-sand beaches, lagoons and coves, not to mention hundreds of species of fish and coral, that you'll be overwhelmed.

👁 Sights

Miniloc Island   ISLAND
Miniloc Island is perhaps the most interesting of the archipelago's islands. The main attractions are **Big Lagoon, Small Lagoon** and **Secret Lagoon**, three of the more photographed sights in all of Palawan. Big Lagoon is entered by an extremely shallow channel (you may have to swim into the lagoon and leave the boat outside). Inside, surrounded by jungle-clad karst walls, is an enormous natural swimming hole.

To enter Small Lagoon, you can swim through a hole in a rock wall or paddle through in a kayak at low tide – be sure to leave before the tide changes; otherwise you may not be able to squeeze back through. Inside is a wonderful hidden world, complete with a small cave to explore. To reach diminutive Secret Lagoon, you must scramble or swim through, depending on the tide.

Kayak rental is available at both Big Lagoon and Small Lagoon.

Cadlao Island   ISLAND
Cadlao Island is like a mini–Tahiti miraculously relocated to the Bacuit Archipelago. In addition to being a wonderful piece of eye candy for those staying on the beach in El Nido, it's also home to lovely Cadlao Lagoon (also known as Ubugun Cove). This lagoon offers some good snorkelling in the shallow coral gardens that lie off the beach at the head of the bay. More and more people are kayaking out here on their own from El Nido.

Matinloc Island   ISLAND
Like the back of a half-submerged stegosaurus, Matinloc Island snakes some 8km along the western edge of the Bacuit Archipelago. Along with neighbouring Tapiutan

Bacuit Archipelago

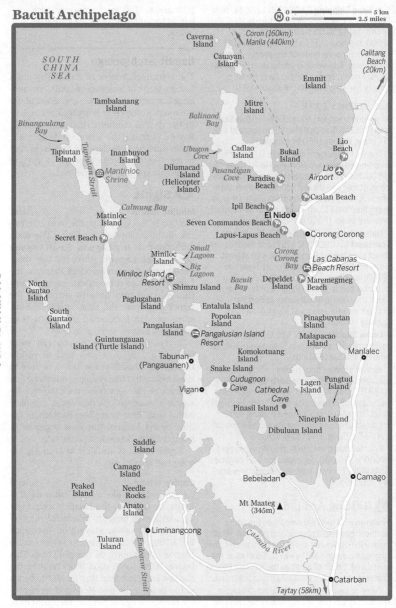

SOUTH
CHINA
SEA

Caverna Island

Coron (160km);
Manila (440km)

Cauayan Island

Calitang Beach (20km)

Emmit Island

Tambalanang Island

Mitre Island

Balinaod Bay

Binangculang Bay

Tapiutan Island

Inambuyod Island

Ubugon Cove

Cadlao Island

Bukal Island

Lio Beach

Tapiutan Strait

Mantinloc Shrine

Dilumacad Island (Helicopter Island)

Pasandigan Cove

Lio Airport

Calmung Bay

Matinloc Island

Paradise Beach

Caalan Beach

Ipil Beach

El Nido

Seven Commandos Beach

Secret Beach

Lapus-Lapus Beach

Corong Corong

Miniloc Island

Small Lagoon

Corong Corong Bay

Las Cabanas Beach Resort

North Guntao Island

Miniloc Island Resort

Big Lagoon

Bacuit Bay

Depeldet Island

Maremegmeg Beach

Shimzu Island

Paglugaban Island

Entalula Island

South Guntao Island

Popolcan Island

Pangalusian Island

Pinagbuyutan Island

Guintungauan Island (Turtle Island)

Pangalusian Island Resort

Malapacao Island

Manlalec

Tabunan (Pangauanen)

Komokotuang Island

Snake Island

Vigan

Cudugnon Cave

Cathedral Cave

Lagen Island

Pungtud Island

Pinasil Island

Ninepin Island

Dibuluan Island

Saddle Island

Camago Island

Bebeladan

Camago

Peaked Island

Needle Rocks

Anato Island

Mt Maateg (345m)

Tuluran Island

Endeavour Strait

Liminangcong

Cataaba River

Catarban

Taytay (58km)

Island, it forms narrow Tapiutan Strait, the walls of which offer some of the best snorkelling in the archipelago. Likewise, there is some excellent snorkelling plus some good beaches on the eastern side of Matinloc.

Sleeping

Bacuit Bay is well-known for several luxury private-island resorts, several of them owned and operated by El Nido Resorts out of the **Ten Knots Travel Office** (☎ 0917 553 7986; www.elnidoresorts.com; Real St) in El Nido.

Overnight island-hopping trips offer a far more affordable option for sleeping in the Bacuit Archipelago. These usually involve camping in tents on Seven Commandos Beach or the beaches of Cadlao Island.

★ Pangalusian
Island Resort
LUXURY $$$

(☎ 0917 843 7819; www.elnidoresorts.com/pangulasian-island/; d villa incl breakfast P36,800-168,000) The newest and fanciest of El Nido Resorts' Palawan properties, this is luxury living at its finest. The villas are honeymoon-ready, the horseshoe-shaped beach is a beauty and the private island setting is divine.

Matinloc Resort
RESORT $$$

(☎ 0905 274 8046; www.matinloc.com; Matinloc Island; r incl breakfast P18,000-35,000; ❋ 🛜 ❄) If you're looking for a private-island luxury resort that isn't *quite* as expensive as the competition, Matinloc Resort has you covered. It's in a downright paradisiacal location. The rooms are sumptuous, although they lack an over-water option. One major fuss is that it doesn't serve alcohol (you can bring your own), and the food is just average.

Miniloc Island Resort
RESORT $$$

(☎ 0917 843 7819; www.elnidoresorts.com/miniloc-island; d cottage with full board P27,300-35,300; ❋ 🛜) This is the least swanky of El Nido Resorts' four Palawan properties, although you'll hardly be slumming it. The cottages, many of them over-water, are native style with thatched roofs. In the early morning you can kayak in Big Lagoon and Small Lagoon before the tourist hordes arrive. Pure bliss.

Busuanga
& the Calamian Islands

This group of islands in the far north of Palawan, also known simply as the Calamianes, is a bona fide adventurer's paradise, with wreck diving, kayaking, island-hopping and motorbiking leading the way. It's a bountiful region filled with white-sand beaches, coral reefs, dense rainforests, mangrove swamps and the crystal-clear lakes of Coron Island.

Busuanga is the largest and most developed island. It comprises just two municipalities: Busuanga town covers the northwestern half, while more touristy Coron town covers the southeastern half. Most of Busuanga Island is extremely rural, but newly sealed roads are bringing development even to more remote bits.

OTHER BACUIT GEMS

Every island in the archipelago has secret spots that await the adventurous explorer. Tiny **Pinasil Island** holds **Cathedral Cave**, an aptly named cavern with soaring limestone columns and wall-climbing monitor lizards, which call to mind the gargoyles of an actual cathedral. A ceiling lets in a shaft of light.

Dilumacad Island (Helicopter Island) has a fine beach on its eastern shore, which is topped only by the wonderful **Seven Commandos Beach** on the Palawan mainland. **Snake Island**, connected to the mainland by a narrow, winding strip of sand at low tide, offers striking panoramic views from the top.

Heading south from Busuanga by boat, you'll pass brooding Coron Island, laid-back Culion Island and, lastly, the Linapacan islands, which are closer to El Nido than to the rest of the group. In between are countless small islands where clusters of huts hug the foreshore of beautiful beaches.

Coron Town
☎ 048 / POP 51,803

Approaching Coron Town proper from the water, it's not uncommon to wonder whether the journey was worth it. There's no beach and the waterfront is a mishmash of buildings and ramshackle houses. But Busuanga's commercial centre shouldn't be judged by appearances alone, for it is but a gateway to other adventures in and around Coron Bay and the heavenly Calamian Islands.

From the town proper, Coron sprawls northeastward and also includes the airport in barangay Santa Cruz, 20km north of Coron proper, as well as up-and-coming barangays Decalachao and San Jose on the north-central coast of Busuanga Island.

👁 Sights & Activities

Mt Tapyas
VIEWPOINT

FREE Grunt your way up 700+ steps to Mt Tapyas for astounding views of Coron Bay. It's a quintessential Coron experience.

Mt Tundalara
HIKING

(Map p406; Mt Dalara) Hiking to the top of 640m Mt Tundalara, the highest point in northern Palawan, is an endurance test,

Busuanga Island/Calamian Islands

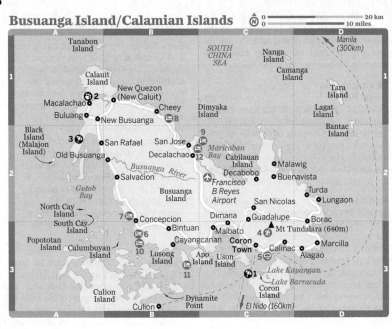

N 0 _____ 20 km
   0 _____ 10 miles

Busuanga Island/Calamian Islands

◉ Sights
1 Banol Beach C3
2 Calauit Safari Park A1
3 Ocam Ocam Beach A2

◯ Activities, Courses & Tours
D'Divers ....(see 6)
Jack's Place ....(see 6)
4 Mt Tundalara C3
Pirate Divers ....(see 7)
5 Siete Pecados C3
Tribal Adventures ....(see 8)

◯ Sleeping
6 Al Faro Cosmio Hotel B3
7 Ann & Mike's Guesthouse...................... B2
Busuanga Backpackers .... (see 6)
Busuanga Bay Lodge .... (see 6)
8 Cashew Grove... B1
9 El Rio y Mar C2
10 Elsie's Bungalow B3
11 Sangat Island Dive Resort B3
12 Vicky's Place B2

◯ Eating
Laura's Garden Tropical
Restaurant .... (see 6)

especially in the midday heat. It takes around 2½ hours each way. To get to the trailhead, take a tricycle to Mabingtungan, 3km north of Coron proper.

Wreck Diving

Coron Bay is a world-class **wreck-diving** destination, and Coron town proper is the main base for dive trips. More than two dozen Japanese navy and merchant ships can be found in the waters off Busuanga, sunk by US Navy aircraft on 24 September 1944. Ten of these are accessible to divers. You'll need at least advanced open-water certification to dive most of the wrecks, although a few are open to intermediate divers, and one – the *Lusong* gunboat – can even be snorkelled.

You're looking at a minimum 1½ hours to reach most of the wrecks from Coron town proper (unless you pay up for a speedboat). To be much closer to the wrecks, consider an island stay in Coron Bay, or in Concepcion or Salvacion (Busuanga town).

The closest wrecks to Coron proper are the Tangat Wreck (*Olympia Maru*) and the *Tere Kaze Maru,* both near Sangat Island; the

Kogyo Maru; and the deeper-water *Irako.* The seaplane tender *Akitsushima* and the *Okikawa Maru* are just outside Dipuyai Bay in Concepcion. The Black Island Wreck *(Nanshin Maru)* is off **Ocam Ocam Beach** (Map p406; www New Busuanga) in northwest Busuanga. One wreck, the *Kyokuzan Maru,* is on the north coast, accessible from barangay San Jose on Maricaban Bay.

Sadly the visibility at most wrecks, which was around 18m to 20m several decades ago, is down to 3m to 5m at some sites, largely because of polluted run-off.

Coron Bay and the Busuanga Island perimeter also have scores of excellent **reef-diving** sites. Barracuda Lake (p409) on Coron Island is another popular dive site, less for what's visible than for the sensation of shifting temperatures underwater. Several companies offer multiday dive safaris to nearby Apo Reef off Mindoro.

Cashew Grove (p414) and Vicky's Place (p411) are good options for the east coast and Maricaban Bay. The following are based in Coron proper:

Freediving Coron (Map p408; ☑0915 172 6809; http://freediving-coron.com; GMG Hotel, National Hwy)

Neptune Dive Center (Map p408; ☑0927 418 4118; www.neptunedivecenter.com; National Hwy)

Reggae Dive Center (☑0928 835 5657; www.rocksteadydivecenter.de; National Hwy)

Sea Dive (Map p408; ☑0917 808 6697; www.seadiveresort.com)

Island-Hopping

As in El Nido, full-day island-hopping tours are all the rage in Coron, with scores of bangkas departing the **town pier** (Map p408; Lualhati Park) every morning on set tours of the main islands and snorkelling sites. Most of them follow one of four set routes – Tour A, B, C and D – resulting in big crowds at marquee sites like Twin Lagoon (p409) on Coron Island, **CYC Beach** and **Sunset Beach** (a popular overnight camping spot).

Can't-miss sites around Coron include Coron Island (p409), **Siete Pecados** (Map p406; P100), **Banana Island** and **Malcapuya Island** near Culion. More northern sites, such as **Calumbuyan Island**, Pass Island and Black Island, are best accessed from Busuanga town. Tour operators still advertise boat trips to Calauit Safari Park (p413), but you'll save a lot of money and time going overland.

Kayaking

Coron Bay and the islands around Busuanga offer world-class sea kayaking. Several places in the town proper offer day rentals for P500 to P1000. Coron Island is a reasonable target only for strong kayakers; others should stick to the bay.

You'll find even better kayaking in Dipuyai Bay off Concepcion, or in Maricaban Bay on the northeast coast, with kayak rental locally available.

To really experience the Calamianes, consider a multiday trip run by Calamianes Expeditions Eco Tour (p409) or Tribal Adventures (p413).

CULION ISLAND

Culion Island (pop 20,139), the second largest island in the Calamianes after Busuanga, has waterfalls, pristine reefs and a fascinating history: in 1906 the Americans established one of the world's largest leper colonies here.

The **Culion Information & Tourism Center** (☑0920 454 5676; Balala; ☺8am-5pm) hands out an excellent brochure with a heritage walking tour of the centre and descriptions of all there is to do on the island, including instructions on how to get to eight waterfalls and possible tour routes. You can hire motorbikes for P500 per day to explore the island's unsealed roads. Ask the tourist office for assistance.

Most people visit Culion on a boat tour from Coron (P3000 to P3500), but it's well worth staying a night or two and soaking up the relaxed provincial island vibe. Accommodation options include the excellent **Hotel Maya** (☑0920 627 6467; hotelmaya@gmail.com; Libis; s with fan P800, d with air-con P1300-1500; ❄🛜) 🍴, owned and operated by enthusiastic students of Ateneo-Loyola College; and, for shoestringers, **Safari Lodge & Restaurant** (☑0947 309 4852; Balala; s/d from P350/550; ❄🛜).

There's a daily boat to Culion from Coron Port at 1pm, and an additional departure most days at 7.30am (P200, 1½ hours). Departures from Culion are at 7.30am and 3pm.

PALAWAN BUSUANGA & THE CALAMIAN ISLANDS

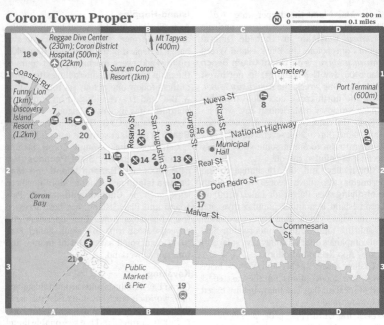

Coron Town Proper

Coron Town Proper

🌀 Activities, Courses & Tours
1 Calamian Tourist Boat
   Association...A3
2 Calamianes
   Expeditions Eco
   Tour...B2
   Freediving Coron ....(see 11)
3 Neptune Dive Center............................B2
4 Red Carabao Travel
   Hub..A1
5 Sea Dive...B2
6 Tao Philippines......................................B2

🛏 Sleeping
7 Coron Backpacker
   Guesthouse...A1
8 Coron Bluewave Resort.........................C1
9 Happy Camper Hostel............................D2
10 Island's View Inn B2
11 Seahorse Guest House...........................B2

🍽 Eating
12 Blue Moon Restobar B2
13 Get Real Cafe B2
14 Trattoria Altrove....................................B2

🍷 Drinking & Nightlife
15 Coffee Kong A1

ℹ Information
16 BPI C2
17 Metrobank..C2

🚍 Transport
18 Boyet Motorcycle
   Rental...A1
19 Bus Lot..B3
20 Coron Motorcycle
   Rental...A2
21 Coron Town Pier.....................................A3

Tours

Red Carabao
Travel Hub   OUTDOORS
(Map p408; ☎ 0905 338 1314; www.redcarabao
philippines.com; National Hwy; ⊗ 8am-8pm) The
culturally immersive Manila hostel (p70) has
created a space in Coron for travellers to find
alternatives to the area's predominant but
almost inescapable 'alphabet tours' (A, B,
C, etc). It offers its own tours and provides
a venue for others with unique tour ideas to
see and be seen. For independent travellers
looking to hook up with a group for a great
tour, it's the perfect spot. Upstairs is a common area for games and mingling. Great stuff
all around.

★**Calamianes**
Expeditions Eco Tour OUTDOORS
(Map p408; ☑0920 254 6553; www.corongaleri.
com.ph; San Augustin St) A highly competent
tour company that runs all the standard island-hopping tours plus a long list of adren-
alin-based alternative activities. Highlights
include six-day/five-night tailored 'seafaris'
around the Calamianes, mountain-bike tours
on state-of-the-art bikes, multiday sea-kayaking trips, and river kayaking on the De-
calachao River in northeastern Coron (ask
about the new farmstay there). It also hires
out camping gear and a speedboat.

**Calamian Tourist
Boat Association** BOATING
(Map p408; ☑0920 403 7965; town pier) An
alternative to joining the ubiquitous island-hopping group tours is to tailor your
own trip through the Calamian Tourist Boat
Association. Round-trip rates for four- and
eight-person bangkas are clearly posted and
reasonable: P2200 for a four-person boat to
Coron Island, P3850 to Culion, P4400 to Calumbuyan. Add P500 for a tour guide. Bring
your own food.

★**Tao Philippines** BOATING
(Map p408; www.taophilippines.com; Don Pedro St)
Multiday Coron–El Nido expeditions run by
Tao Philippines are highly recommended.
Tao's headquarters is in El Nido (p410).

🛏 **Sleeping**

🛏 **Coron Town**

Happy Camper Hostel HOSTEL $
(Map p408; ☑0926 503 9616; happycamper.
hostel@gmail.com; dm P350) This hidden place is
like a wealthy uncle's living room converted
into a spacious en-suite dorm room. Just
seven single beds, each with its own night-
stand, electrical socket and fan. Lovely wood
floor, a few antique chairs for kicking back in,
and a long wooden desk. The downside is no
service whatsoever.

Seahorse Guest House HOSTEL $$
(Map p408; ☑0927 497 7559; www.seahorse
coron.com; Don Pedro St; dm/d incl breakfast
P600/2000; ❄🛜) This tidy, narrow high-rise
houses six cool, crisp, four-bed mixed dorms
and just two private rooms. The dorm beds,
with personal plugs, lights and cabinets,
are the nicest in town. The complimentary
breakfast is on the 4th-floor rooftop, which
looks out to Coron Bay and Coron Island be-
yond. Noise is the only concern – it's right in
the centre of town.

PALAWAN BUSUANGA & THE CALAMIAN ISLANDS

CORON ISLAND

This island, only a 20-minute bangka ride from Coron, has an imposing, mysterious skyline that wouldn't be out of place in a King Kong film. Flying over Coron, you see that the fortresslike, jungle-clad interior is largely inaccessible terrain pockmarked with lakes, two of which, **Kayangan Lake** (P300) and **Barracuda Lake** (P200), can be visited. The entire island is the ancestral domain of the Tagbanua indigenous group, who are primarily fishermen and gatherers of the very lucrative *balinsasayaw* (birds' nests).

Concerned about the impact of tourism, the Tagbanua have limited access to a hand-ful of sights. Accessible by a steep 10-minute climb, the crystal-clear waters of Kayangan Lake are nestled into the mountain walls. Underwater is like a moonscape; there's a wooden walkway and platform to stash your things if you go for a swim. Don't expect privacy or quiet, though, as the lagoon where bangkas unload passengers looks like a mall parking lot at noon.

Scenic **Barracuda Lake** is of interest to divers for its unique layers of fresh, salt and brackish water and dramatic temperature shifts underwater (it can get as hot as 38°C). It's accessible by a short climb over a jagged, rocky wall that ends directly at the water's edge.

Other stops that are open to visitors include **Banol Beach** (Map p406; P100), a small sandy area with shelter from the sun, and photogenic **Twin Lagoon** (P200), one half of which is accessed by swimming through a narrow crevice.

All of the above are popular stops on island-hopping trips out of Coron town, although standard group tours A and B take in at most two of the above at a time because of the relatively stiff admission fees at each site. To visit all sites, you should book a private trip through the Calamian Tourist Boat Association, which costs P2200 for up to four people, not including admission fees or snorkelling gear.

ISLAND EXPEDITIONS: EL NIDO TO CORON

Zigzagging through the islands of Bacuit Bay, Linapacan and the Calamianes on a multi-day island-to-island bangka expedition is the highlight of any trip to northern Palawan and perhaps all of the Philippines. These trips bring you up close and personal with remote islands of breathtaking beauty, and offer a rare opportunity to experience and interact with island communities and people, unmediated by the mass tourism industry.

Close to half a dozen companies run these trips, but the pioneer – and the company that does it best – is **Tao Philippines** (www.taophilippines.com; National Hwy, Corong Corong). Tao has established island bases throughout northern Palawan, complete with beautifully designed beachfront 'tuka' huts and soaring bamboo common areas. The food, often consisting of freshly caught fish, is superb.

A socially conscious company that runs education and nutrition program in northern Palawan, Tao operates its classic five-day, four-night open-group trips between El Nido and Coron year-round except for September. The all-inclusive trips cost P25,000 per person. You can also opt for a *paraw* trip on a uniquely constructed traditional outrigger sail boat (P28,500 for five days, October to June only). The minimum age for both trips is 14.

Tao also runs three-day/two-night open group or private trips around El Nido and Linapacan, and it continues to introduce new products. It has offices in El Nido and **Coron** (p409), a huge fleet of boats and numerous bases; the high season might see half a dozen Tao bangkas on the water at one time.

Despite that, it can be hard to find a spot on these enormously popular trips. Several other companies run trips from Coron to El Nido, ranging from three days to five days; some do accept younger kids; others have a dive component. **Calamianes Expeditions Eco-Tour** (p409) runs a six-day trip that sticks to the Calamianes. For real adventurers, Coron–based **Tribal Adventures** (p413) runs an 11-day sea kayak expedition from Coron to El Nido.

Coron Backpacker Guesthouse HOSTEL **$**
(Map p408; ☑0916 400 4871; http://palawan-coron-backpacker.com; off National Hwy; d/q without bathroom P550/750; 🗟) This place has nine basic rooms in a shack over the water near the centre of town. The shoes-off common area is pleasantly rustic, with a kitchen and lots of reading material.

Fat Monkey Hostel HOSTEL **$**
(☑0998 271 4111; www.fatmonkeyhostel.com; Km 5, National Hwy; dm P380) This simple, sociable hostel 2km north of town has some of the cheapest dorms on Busuanga, and guests are eligible to take the 'Fat Monkey Tour' of the islands, which focuses on drinking and aims to avoid the notorious crowds at hotspots like Kayangan Lake.

Sunz en Coron Resort HOTEL **$$**
(☑0999 659 1891; www.sunzencoron.com; d P2400-2950, f 3600-5200; 🌼🗟🏊) Coron has a dearth of quality at the midrange, but Sunz en Coron fills that void with its collection of compact but efficient rooms set around an elegant pool, and with a restaurant serving the best Korean food in town. The drawback

is the location – it's on a dark backstreet about 1.5km north of the centre.

Island's View Inn HOTEL **$$**
(Map p408; ☑0999 993 0361; www.islandsviewinn.com; Don Pedro St; r incl breakfast P1500-2200; 🌼🗟) Rooms here are sparkling clean, with flat-screen TVs, hot water and a 3rd-floor outdoor restaurant and lounge area.

★**Funny Lion** HOTEL **$$$**
(☑0905 395 5445; www.thefunnylion.com; Coastal Rd; d incl breakfast P6400-7400; 🌼🗟🏊) Funny Lion has the nicest rooms in town and incredible views from its 5th-floor walk-up bar area, where duelling cold-water whirlpools, sunset views and yummy bar snacks make for a delightful happy hour. There's a bigger pool down below, overlooked by rooms done up in a tasteful island style, with boutique sinks, flat-screen TVs and plenty of handsome dark wood.

Coron Bluewave Resort HOTEL **$$$**
(Map p408; ☑0905 570 5978; coronbluewave@gmail.com; Nueva St; d P3600-3900, q P6600-7000; 🌼🗟🏊) The 13 whitewashed rooms are snug to the pool – indeed, you could

dive right in from the ground-floor rooms. The pool-access rooms are tiny and lack furniture, but make up for it with lovely beds and cleanliness. Stay upstairs if you want a desk or space to put your luggage. It's a short walk downhill to the centre.

Offshore

Discovery Island Resort
RESORT $$
(☎ 0977 839 9147; www.discoverydiversresort.com; r with fan/air-con P3400/3800; ✴ 🛜 ⊠) This dive-focused resort is on a small island just a five-minute boat ride from town (free transfers). A nice mix of native-style fan rooms with huge beds and roomy if somewhat musty air-con rooms. Rooms slink up a hill and have furnished sea-facing balconies. The restaurant, with sunset views through the mangroves, is a delight, as is the swimming pool.

★ Sangat Island Dive Resort
RESORT $$$
(Map p406; ☎ 0917 650 9191; www.sangat.com.ph; cottages per person incl transfers & 3 meals US$131-156; 🛜) 🏊 Pulling up at the beach here feels like discovering the cool kids' secret hideout. Less than 40 minutes by speedboat from Coron proper, and perfect for R&R or action, Sangat has a full-service dive centre, kayaks and jet skis. Several raised native-style bungalows front a nice white-sand beach, and two others are perched atop small hills tucked into the encroaching jungle.

San Jose

★ Vicky's Place
GUESTHOUSE $
(Map p406; ☎ 0946 433 5257, 0935 105 7428; www.facebook.com/Guesthouse.Vickys; Maricaban Bay, San Jose; r with/without bathroom P800/600; 🛜) This quiet budget option on luscious Maricaban Bay, run by eco-conscious local dive instructor Brenda, is a wonderful place to chill out. She maintains a small dive shop and leads boat excursions around the bay, including dugong-spotting trips (per person P2500 including lunch). It has no beach per se, but you can easily kayak to a few good ones.

★ El Rio y Mar
RESORT $$$
(Map p406; ☎ 0928 500 6015; www.elrioymar.com; Maricaban Bay, San Jose; r P4560-7200; ✴ 🛜 ⊠) This hidden beach resort on luscious Maricaban Bay (northeast Busuanga) represents excellent value at the upper midrange. It's on the mainland, but access is by boat from San

Jose (free transfer, 10 minutes) and it feels like a private island. It boasts a nice range of accommodation, from rustic to modern, plus a spa, dive centre and activities galore.

✕ Eating & Drinking

Coron is still waiting for an El Nido–style restaurant boom, but there are a few decent places to eat. Worthy resort eateries in town include Sunz en Coron and Funny Lion. Cashews, especially especially in the form of *bandi*, a sugary treat made from the nuts, are sold everywhere.

Get Real Cafe
CAFE $$
(Map p408; Real St; mains 175-280; ⊙ 9am-2pm & 5pm-midnight) Works equally well for drinks or a meal. It's sort of a TexMex menu with more emphasis on the Tex (marbled Angus rib-eye steak) than the Mex (ellotos callejeros, or street corn). Sausages are another speciality. Pretty cheap beer on offer(P55).

Blue Moon Restobar
INTERNATIONAL $$
(Map p408; National Hwy; mains P200-300; ⊙ 8am-1am; 🛜) Offers up fresh Thai–style food, pizzas and Mexican faves, and will cook Indian food on request. Stay late and enjoy mean cocktails and buckets of San Miguel for P125.

Trattoria Altrove
ITALIAN $$$
(Map p408; Rosario St; mains P300-500; ⊙ 11.30am-2.30pm & 5-11pm) The Slovenian behind Altrove in El Nido now works his magic in Coron, with a similar formula of delicious antipasti (try the carpaccio), pasta and Palawan's best pizzas. It's in a lovely elevated open-air space awash with dark wood and overhung by whirring ceiling fans on what has become Coron's mini Pub St.

Coffee Kong
CAFE
(Map p408; National Hwy; ⊙ 7am-10.30pm; 🛜) There are a couple of air-conditioned coffee shops in Coron nowadays. Coffee Kong is the original and the best. Espresso drinks, tea, muffins and waffles for breakfast.

ⓘ Getting There & Away

AIR
Francisco B Reyes Airport (p379) is 20km north of Coron town proper. PAL, Cebu Pacific, and SkyJet fly to/from Manila, while small Air Juan planes fly to/from Caticlan (for Boracay). Vans to Coron town (P150, 30 minutes) meet the flights.

BOAT

All boat departures are from Coron Port, 1.5km east of the town proper (P50 by tricycle).

2GO (☑ 0977 849 5305) has ferry services from Coron to Manila on Thursday and Sunday at 4.30pm (from P1900, 14 hours). Trips from Manila are on Tuesday and Friday at 1.30pm. 2GO also serves Puerto Princesa on Wednesday and Saturday at 6am (from P1160, 15 hours). All 2GO trips include meals.

Atienza Shipping Lines (☑ 0939 912 6840) serves Manila on rickety cargo boats with dorm-style beds. Departures are Monday, Thursday and Saturday at 2.30pm from Coron, and Tuesday, Thursday and Saturday evening (times vary) from Manila (ordinary/air-con P1000/1150, 18 hours).

The fastest way to El Nido is on the **Montenegro Lines** (☑ 0915 176 9095) fastcraft, which departs daily at noon (adult/student P1760/1500; 4½ to 5½ hours). Montenegro alternates a small, 70-seat, completely enclosed boat with a larger 120-seat vessel with an open deck. The boats can sell out in the high season, so reserve ahead through your hotel or via www.biyaheroes.com.

M/Bca Bunso (☑ 0910 371 0621) runs a slower bangka ferry to El Nido, departing in either direction at 8am (P1200 including lunch, eight hours). Many prefer this not only because it's cheaper, but also because the more deliberate pace and open-air seating allows one to better appreciate the gorgeous island scenery.

Bunso bangkas also serve San Jose (Mindoro) on Monday, Wednesday and Friday at 8.30am (P800, six hours).

BUS

From the bus lot near the public market in Coron town proper, buses depart roughly hourly for Salvacion (P80, 2¼ hours) via Concepcion, with some continuing to Buluang (for Calauit Island).

ⓘ Getting Around

Motorbike hire is widely available in town, with rates starting at P400 to P500 per day. Try **Coron Motorcycle Rental** (Map p408; ☑ 0926 420 5391; National Hwy) or **Boyet Motorcycle Rental** (Map p408; ☑ 0928 292 9884; National Hwy). Minivan hire is widely available through any hotel or travel agent.

Busuanga Town

☑ 048 / POP 22,046

Encompassing roughly the northern half of Busuanga Island, Busuanga Town makes a fine alternative base for those looking to escape the crowds of Coron town proper. The administrative centre is in Salvacion, but most accommodation is 15km south of Salvacion in barangay Concepcion. North of Salvacion the highway brings you to remote beaches and Calauit Island and Calauit Safari Park.

From barangay New Busuanga, 15km north of Salvacion, a rough road rings around to barangay Cheey in northeast Busuanga, where rarely explored islands await. A few beach resorts have set up along the coastline south of Cheey for people seeking complete escape. The road around here

ISLAND-HOPPING OUT OF BUSUANGA TOWN

Several attractions advertised as island-hopping stops out Coron town proper are much easier (and cheaper) to access from Concepcion and Salvacion. These include **Pass Island** and **Calumbuyan Island**. Both have superb snorkelling and white-sand beaches and are also great overnight camping locations. Staying the night at either costs P400 and includes the P200 admission fee and sleeping in a basic hut, a hammock or tents you bring on your own; pay the caretaker.

A good snorkelling and diving spot is the coral garden off the southwestern tip of **Lusong Island**; the shallowest wreck, the Lusong gunboat, found off the southern edge, is also prime snorkelling territory. More good snorkelling is near the *Okikawa Maru* wreck at the mouth of Dipuyai Bay.

A white sandy beach and magnificent sunsets make a trip out to **North Cay Island** (admission P100) from Salvacion worthwhile. The reef on the north side is well preserved. You can camp here too or stay in basic huts. Brooding, karst- and cave-studded **Black Island** (Malajon Island; admission P150) is best accessed from Ocam Ocam Beach (p407) near New Busuanga. Both islands have stunning beaches.

You can book a boat through the boatman associations in Concepcion or Salvacion. Day trips to the above islands cost P1500 to P3000, depending on where you're jumping off from and where you're going.

is being gradually sealed, so expect Cheey to join the mainstream in the near future.

⊙ Sights & Activities

Calauit Safari Park WILDLIFE RESERVE
(Map p406; foreigner/Filipino incl tour guide P400/200) Just off the northwestern tip of Busuanga, African megafauna roam on Calauit Island. Species include 25 or so giraffes and about 35 zebras. Both species are easy to spot. Antelope species are here too, but sightings are less reliable. You'll also see lots of Calamian deer, repatriated to Calauit from mainland Busuanga to prevent poaching. Private boats to Calauit (five minutes) leave from Macalachao, 7km north of Buluang, and cost P400 round-trip.

Kayaking
The **kayaking** in and around protected Dipuyai Bay (Concepcion) is superb, with mangroves and islands to explore. **Jack's Place** (Map p406; 0917 988 1849; Km 37, National Hwy, Concepcion) and Anne & Mike's Guesthouse offer kayak rental.

Tribal Adventures ADVENTURE
(Map p406; in Boracay 0920 558 7188; www.tribaladventures.com; Palawan Sandcastles Resort, barangay Lakdayan, Cheey) A sea-kayak specialist that organises multiday or multiweek kayak expeditions around the Calamianes (launch point at Coron town pier), plus mountain biking, 4x4s, kayaking, bangka trips and dugong interaction out of its base in Cheey.

Diving
The wreck dives offered in Coron are generally much easier to access from Concepcion.

Pirate Divers DIVING
(Map p406; 0905 237 3758; www.piratedivers.org; Concepcion; 2/3 dives incl gear P3000/4000) English Simon has lovely little dive shop right at the pier in Concepcion. The main wrecks are just a short boat ride away in his large dive bangka.

D'Divers DIVING
(Map p406; 0935 403 1816; www.ddivers.com; Km 37, National Hwy, Concepcion) Diving, kayaking and a range of land-based pursuits, including horseback riding, are on offer at this dive shop attached to Puerto del Sol Resort on Dipuyai Bay. German owner and old Busuanga hand Gunter is an area legend.

🛏 Sleeping & Eating

Most accommodation is in Concepcion. There are budget lodges around the town pier and various options around Dipuyai Bay, a couple of kilometres south.

Ann & Mike's Guesthouse GUESTHOUSE $
(Map p406; 0929 582 4020; mcbare13@gmail.com; town pier, Concepcion; r with fan P800-1000, with air-con P1500) This friendly little place near the pier in Concepcion has a simple nipa hut with shared bathroom, and a newer duplex with two mural-splashed air-con rooms. It has the best food in town, including delicious curries, and is a good source of information on the area.

Busuanga Backpackers LODGE $
(Map p406; 0916 401 8703; Km 36, National Hwy, Concepcion; d P500) This rustic place just off the highway has four simple fan-cooled rooms with shared bathrooms and a kitchen for self-caterers. Walk up a small hill to a hut with sea views – a good spot for a sunset drink. The food is good and it has an ecofriendly tour arm (http://tourbusuanga.com) for island-hopping and other fun excursions.

Renting a motorbike (P500) is advisable to explore the area.

Elsie's Bungalow GUESTHOUSE $$
(Map p406; 0927 542 6740; www.elsiesbungalow.ph; house P2500) This three-room native-style house on Dipuyai Bay, accessible only by boat, works best for a group, although it would also suit a couple seeking full escape. The proprietress cooks great Bicol–inspired cuisine using organic vegetables and herbs from her garden and seafood delivered fresh. Electricity runs from 6pm to 11pm; pay P100 an hour to keep the generator running later.

★ Al Faro Cosmio Hotel HOTEL $$$
(Map p406; 0917 532 0401; www.alfaropalawan.com; Dipuyai Bay, Concepcion; r incl breakfast P3600-4150; ⊗ closed Jul-Sep; 🖥🏖) A touch of Mediterranean and a dash of Disney–like fairy-tale architecture, this place is perched on a hilltop overlooking Dipuyai Bay. There's no air-con, but plenty of fresh air filters through the unique honeycomb windows of the tower rooms and massages the spacious terraces of the bungalows. Excellent food and views from the restaurant. Accessible by boat only.

PALAWAN BUSUANGA & THE CALAMIAN ISLANDS

DUGONG SPOTTING

The waters off Calauit Island in the extreme northwest are home to a resident dugong (sea cow), an endangered species and the only marine herbivorous mammal. Resorts in northern Busuanga advertise dugong-spotting trips. These usually involve a two-hour bangka or shorter speedboat ride to the Calauit area, where you stand a great chance of seeing this dugong and, very occasionally, others as well.

There are other dugongs around Busuanga Island, especially off the northeast coast, but sighting them is a matter of chance. Vicky's Place (p411) in San Jose does dugong-spotting trips in Maricaban Bay, while Tribal Adventures (p413) has a spot about 4km south of its base in Cheey. Your chances of seeing them in this area are less than at Calauit, but you won't have to go as far and it's arguably a greater thrill when you do spot one.

Cashew Grove   RESORT $$$
(Map p406; ☑ 0908 264 0909; www.cashewgrove. com; barangay Lakdayan, Cheey; d incl breakfast P3800-4800; ❄ 🛜 ❄) This beach resort is brilliantly situated on Busuanga's northeast flank, with a private golden-hued beach and in a group of islands not covered on hopping tours out of Coron. Large rooms around the pool are in split-level duplexes, with tile floors and a more modern look, while the beachfront cottages have wood floors, open-air bathrooms and a native motif.

Busuanga Bay Lodge   RESORT $$$
(Map p406; ☑ 0927 418 3126; www.busuangabay lodge.com; Km 38, National Hwy, Concepcion; r incl breakfast from P16,500; ❄ @ 🛜 ❄) A luxurious whitewashed Caribbean–style resort whose centrepiece is large restaurant pavilion and infinity pool overlooking stunning Dupuyai Bay. Cottages are furnished in a low-key, stylish fashion, and every activity imaginable is on offer: kayaking, diving, hiking, mountain biking, spa, gym, and excursions to its private beach club up the coast.

Laura's Garden
Tropical Restaurant   FILIPINO $
(Map p406; Km 36, National Hwy, Concepcion; mains P100-165; ⊙ 7am-7pm) This simple eatery adjoins a beautiful garden near the resorts of Dipuyai Bay. Just a few items on the menu, including pesto pasta, sweet and sour, seaweed salad and *kinilaw* (raw fish cured in vinegar).

There's a single bungalow out back you can ask about renting (P300).

❶ Getting There & Away
Hourly buses from Coron town proper to Salvacion (P80, 2¼ hours) pass through Concepcion.

There is no public transport from the airport to Salvacion or Concepcion, so the only option is to bus from Coron town, or hire a private van direct from the airport (P2000 to P3000).

Understand
the Philippines

History

Ancient Filipinos stuck to their own islands until the 16th century, when Ferdinand Magellan claimed the islands for Spain and began the bloody process of Christianisation. Filipinos revolted and won their independence in 1898, only to have the Americans take over, whereupon they revolted again and lost. Out of the bloody ashes of WWII rose an independent republic. However, the defining moment of modern Filipino history is the overthrow of elected hardliner President Ferdinand Marcos in the 1986 'People Power' revolution.

A History of Being 'Different'

The islands' first colonisers arrived by boat from the north, south and west, establishing a loose network of settlements that had little contact with each other. Thus, from early on the idea of a Philippine 'identity' was a tenuous one. If you were to arrive in North Luzon 1000 years ago, you would have confronted the Ifugao tending to their spectacular rice terraces, which still wow tourists today around Banaue. It is thought the ancestors of the Ifugao arrived some 15,000 years ago from China and Vietnam.

If you arrived 1000 years ago in southern Luzon or the Visayan lowlands, you would have encountered mostly animists of Malay origin, while in the southern regions of Mindanao and Sulu, Islam would already be spreading by way of immigrants from Brunei. Meanwhile, the archipelago's original inhabitants, the Negritos (also called Aeta, Dumagat or Ati), were sprinkled all over the place, much as they are today.

Rarely sedentary, the disparate communities of the Philippines roamed around hunting, gathering, fishing and growing a few basic crops such as rice. They formed small 'barangays' – named after the *balangay* boats in which the Malays arrived – under the leadership of a *datu* (chief). These simple barangays represented the highest form of political unit. The 'country', if you could call it that, possessed neither a centralised government nor a common culture or religion.

Into this diverse jumble strode the Spanish, with the singular mission to unite the Philippine islands around Christianity. Remarkably, they would largely succeed, and over the next several centuries a semblance of a unified Filipino identity, bearing traces of both Spanish and traditional culture, began to emerge.

History of the Philippines: From Indios Bravos to Filipinos by Luis H Francia and *Under the Stacks* by Saul Hofileña Jr are impressionistic accounts of Filipino history from the 'beginning'.

TIMELINE	45,000 BCE	CE 100–200	100–1000
	'Tabon Man', the oldest discovered inhabitant of the 7000 islands, leaves a bit of his skull in a cave on Palawan, shedding light on the Philippines' deep, dark prehistory.	The Chinese become the first foreigners to trade with the islands, which they call Mai. Thus begins a long history of Chinese economic and cultural influence in the Philippines.	Malays in outrigger *balangay* boats arrive in several waves, becoming the islands' dominant ethnic group. The archipelago's eight main languages derive from various Malay tongues spoken by these immigrants.

Catholicism Arrives

In the early 16th century, Islam was beginning to spread throughout the region. Barangays as far north as Manila had been converted, and all signs pointed to the archipelago adopting Islam on a wide scale. But on 16 March 1521 Portuguese explorer Ferdinand Magellan changed the course of Filipino history by landing at Samar and claiming the islands for Spain. Magellan set about giving the islanders a crash course in Catholicism and winning over various tribal chiefs. Having nearly accomplished his goal, Magellan was killed in battle against one of the last holdouts, Chief Lapu-Lapu of Mactan Island off Cebu.

Determined to press its claim after conceding the more strategically important Moluccas (Spice Islands) to Portugal, Spain sent four more expeditions to the Philippines: Ruy Lopez de Villalobos, commander of the fourth expedition, renamed the islands after the heir to the Spanish throne, Philip, Charles I's son. Philip, as King Philip II, ordered a fresh fleet led by Miguel Lopez de Legazpi to sail from Mexico to the islands in 1564 with strict orders to colonise and Catholicise. In 1565 Legazpi returned to the scene of Magellan's death at Cebu and overran the local tribe. An agreement was signed by Legazpi and Tupas, the defeated *datu*, which made every Filipino answerable to Spanish law.

Legazpi, his soldiers and a band of Augustinian monks wasted no time in establishing a settlement where Cebu City now stands; Fort San Pedro is a surviving relic of the era. Legazpi soon discovered that his pact with Tupas was meaningless because the chief had no authority over the islands' myriad other tribes. So Legazpi went about conquering them one by one.

After beating the local people into submission, Legazpi established a vital stronghold on Panay (near present-day Roxas) in 1569. The dominoes fell easily after that, the big prize being Manila, which he wrested from Muslim chief Rajah Sulayman in 1571. Legazpi hastily proclaimed Manila the capital of Las Islas Filipinas and built what was eventually to become Fort Santiago on Sulayman's former *kuta* (fort).

The new colony was run by a Spanish governor who reported to Mexico. But outside of Manila real power rested with the Catholic friars – the *friarocracia* (friarocracy). The friars attempted to move people from barangays into larger, more centralised *pueblos* (towns). They built imposing stone churches in the centre of each *pueblo* (dozens of these still stand) and acted as sole rulers over what were essentially rural fiefdoms.

The Philippine Revolution

Spain grew weaker as the friars grew more repressive and the natives started to resist. Several peasant revolts, easily quashed, marked the end of the 18th century. But in the 19th century the face of the resistance would change as a wealthy class of European-educated mestizos (Filipinos of mixed Spanish or Chinese blood) with nationalist tendencies

A Country of Our Own (2004) takes the controversial view that the Philippines will never be a strong nation because it has never had a unified soul, but author David C Martinez offers some possible solutions.

The Spanish documentary *Returning to the Siege of Baler* (2008) recounts how 50 Spaniards holed up in Baler's church and held out for 11 months against 800 Filipinos during the Philippine Revolution.

1100	1521	1565	1700
Traders from China, India, Japan, Vietnam, Cambodia, Thailand and other countries are regularly trading with Philippine islands. The Chinese establish trading posts along the Luzon coast.	Ferdinand Magellan lands at Samar and claims the country for the Spanish, but soon after is murdered by Chief Lapu-Lapu on Mactan Island off Cebu.	Legazpi lands in Cebu and forces the local chieftain to sign an agreement making every Filipino answerable to Spanish law. Within 10 years Spain controls most of the Philippines.	The galleon trade shuttling Chinese goods between the Philippines and Acapulco, Mexico, is in full swing, enriching Manila and earning it the moniker Pearl of the Orient.

The following four baroque churches are Unesco World Heritage sites: Church of Santo Tomas de Villanueva in Miag-ao; Church of San Agustín at Paoay; Church of the Immaculate Conception of San Agustín in Itramuros (Manila); and Church of Nuestra Señora de la Asuncion in Santa Maria.

began to emerge. Known as *ilustrados,* the greatest and best known was Dr José Rizal, doctor of medicine, poet, novelist, sculptor, painter, linguist, naturalist and fencing enthusiast. Executed by the Spanish in 1896, Rizal epitomised the Filipinos' dignified struggle for freedom.

By killing such figures, the Spanish were creating martyrs. Andres Bonifacio led an aggressive movement known as the Katipunan, or KKK, which secretly built a revolutionary government in Manila, with a network of equally clandestine provincial councils. Complete with passwords, masks and coloured sashes denoting rank, the Katipunan's membership (both men and women) peaked at an estimated 30,000 in mid-1896. In August, the Spanish got wind of the coming revolution and the Katipunan leaders were forced to flee the capital.

Depleted, frustrated and poorly armed, the Katipuneros took stock in nearby Balintawak, a barangay of Caloocan, and voted to launch the revolution regardless. With the cry 'Mabuhay ang Pilipinas!' (Long live the Philippines!), the Philippine Revolution lurched into life following the incident that is now known as the Cry of Balintawak.

After 18 months of bloodshed, a Spanish-Filipino peace pact was signed and the revolutionary leader General Emilio Aguinaldo agreed to go into exile in Hong Kong in December 1897. Predictably, the pact's demands satisfied nobody. Promises of reform by the Spanish were broken, as were promises by the Filipinos to stop their revolutionary plotting.

Meanwhile, another of Spain's colonial trouble spots – Cuba – was playing host to an ominous dispute between Spain and the USA over sugar. To save face, Spain declared war on the USA; as a colony of Spain, the Philippines was drawn into the conflict. Soon after, an American fleet under Commodore George Dewey sailed into Manila Bay and routed the Spanish ships. Keen to gain Filipino support, Dewey welcomed the return of exiled revolutionary General Aguinaldo and oversaw the Philippine Revolution phase two, which installed Aguinaldo as president of the first Philippine republic. The Philippine flag was flown for the first time during Aguinaldo's proclamation of Philippine Independence in Cavite on 12 June 1898.

The 1904 World's Fair: The Filipino Experience (2005) is a page-turning account by Jose D Fermin of the 1100 Filipinos who were taken to the St Louis World's Fair in the US and displayed under zoolike conditions as examples of colonial triumph.

The Philippine-American War

With the signing of the Treaty of Paris in 1898, the Spanish-American War ended and the USA effectively bought the Philippines, along with Guam and Puerto Rico, for US$20 million. A fierce debate raged in the US over what to do with its newly acquired territory. Hawks on the right clamoured to hold onto the islands for strategic and 'humanitarian' reasons, while 'anti-imperialist' liberals attacked the subjugation of a foreign peoples as morally wrong and warned that the battle to occupy the Philippines would drag on for years (about which they were correct).

US President William J McKinley opposed colonisation before caving in to hawks in his Republican party and agreeing to take over the islands.

1762	1815	1850	1871
Great Britain occupies Manila for two years before being chased out. The incident demonstrates the weakness of the Spanish regime and marks the start of a united, nationalist Filipino spirit.	The last Spanish galleon sails between Manila and Acapulco, marking the end of Manila's lucrative monopoly on global trade with Mexico, and hence much of South America.	The sugar and tobacco industries thrive, creating a class of wealthy mestizos. The *ilustrados,* who studied abroad and brought ideas about independence back to the Philippines, emerge from this class.	Spanish King Amadeo I appoints hardliner General Rafael de Izquierdo as governor of the Philippines in an effort to stamp out rising nationalist sentiment in the archipelago.

Echoing the imperialists, McKinley opined that, because Filipinos 'were unfit for self-government', he had no choice but to take over the islands and 'civilise' them. Filipinos led by Aguinaldo had other ideas. They set up a capital in Malolos, outside Manila, in open defiance. The Americans, in turn, antagonised the Filipinos and war broke out in February 1899.

The guerrilla campaign launched by Aguinaldo and rebels who included Gregorio del Pilar and Apolinario Mabini proved remarkably effective at neutralising American military superiority. Aguinaldo was captured in March 1901, but still the war dragged on. As it did, and as casualties on both sides mounted, the American public's opposition to the war grew. Resentment peaked in September 1901 in the aftermath of the Balangiga Massacre. It was only on 4 July 1902 that the US finally declared victory in the campaign, although pockets of guerrilla resistance continued to dog the Americans for several more years. Some 200,000 Filipino civilians, 20,000 Filipino soldiers and more than 4000 American soldiers died in the war from combat or disease.

The American Era
The Americans quickly set about healing the significant wounds their victory had wrought. Even before they had officially won the war, they began instituting reforms aimed at improving the Filipinos' lot, the most important of which was a complete overhaul of the education system. Whereas the Spanish had attempted to keep Filipinos illiterate and ignorant of Spanish, the Americans imported hundreds of teachers to the country to teach reading, writing, arithmetic – and English. Within 35 years the literacy rate among Filipinos had risen from a miniscule percentage to almost 50%, and 27% of the population could speak English.

READING LIST

There has been a treasure trove of books published about the unique relationship between the US and the Philippines.

➡ *In Our Image: America's Empire in the Philippines,* by Stanley Karnow. Definitive work on America's role in the Philippines.

➡ *Waltzing with a Dictator: the Marcoses and the Making of American Policy,* by Raymond Bonner. An investigation into how and why the US helped prop up a dictatorial regime.

➡ *Benevolent Assimilation: The American Conquest of the Philippines 1899–1903,* by Stuart Creighton Miller. Eye-opening account of the Philippine-American War and how the US media treated that war.

➡ *America's Boy: A Century of United States Colonialism in the Philippines,* by James Paterson-Hamilton. Absorbing look at Marcos' symbiotic relationship with the US.

1872	1892	1899	1901
Izquierdo's execution of Padre José Burgos and two other popular Filipino priests on suspicion of harbouring mutinous intentions reawakens the nationalist spirit spawned during the British occupation 100 years earlier.	José Rizal returns home one year after his *El Filibusterismo*, which skewered the Spanish, is published. He forms La Liga Filipina, a social reform movement, and is banished to Mindanao.	William Grayson, an American army private from Nebraska on night patrol near Manila, fires the first shot in the Philippine-American War. The shot kills a drunk Filipino noncombatant.	The Americans capture revolutionary leader General Emilio Aguinaldo, who later urges his countrymen to accept US rule. They don't listen, and the war drags on another 1½ years.

Besides schools, the Americans built bridges, roads and sewage systems. They brought the recalcitrant Moros in Mindanao to heel and Christianised the Cordillera tribes of the north – two groups the Spanish had tried and failed to influence. And they instituted an American-style political system that gradually gave more power to Filipinos. The Americans also made a gesture considered unprecedented in the history of imperialism: they openly promised the Filipinos eventual independence.

Critics describe American benevolence during this period as a thinly veiled carrot disguising America's true goal of establishing economic hegemony over the islands. Whatever the motive, the US endorsed the Commonwealth of the Philippines in 1935, along with the drafting of a US-style constitution and the first national election. On paper at least, democracy and freedom had at last come to the Philippines. Unfortunately, WWII would ensure that they would be short-lived.

Terror in Manila: February 1945 (2005) by Antonio Pérez de Olaguer is an unflinching account of Japanese atrocities during the battle for Manila. It's based on oral histories by Spanish survivors.

The Destruction of Manila

When Japan bombed Hawaii's Pearl Harbor in 1941, other forces attacked Clark Field, where General Douglas MacArthur was caught napping, despite many hours' warning, setting off a string of events that would lead to the Japanese occupying the Philippines from 1942 to 1945.

In 1944 MacArthur honoured his now-famous pledge to return, landing at Leyte, determined to dislodge the Japanese. The main battleground in this onslaught was Manila, where defenceless residents suffered horrifically in the ensuing crossfire during February 1945. By the time MacArthur marched into the city, the combination of Japanese atrocities and American shelling had killed at least 150,000 civilians, and a city that had been one of the finest in Asia was destroyed.

A fierce debate rages to this day about who was to blame for the destruction of Manila. The vast majority of civilian casualties resulted from US artillery fire. But many argue that, by failing to abandon Manila and declare it an open city, the Japanese gave MacArthur little choice. Whatever the truth, Manila belongs in a category with Warsaw, Hiroshima and Hamburg as cities that suffered the most damage in WWII.

The American military practised for the Vietnam War in the Philippines in the 1950s under the command of General Edward Landsdale, the model for Graham Greene's The Quiet American.

The Marcos Era

In 1965 Ferdinand Marcos, a dashing former lawyer from a prominent Ilocos political family, was elected the Philippines' fourth post-WWII president under the seductive slogan 'This nation can be great again'. At first it indeed was a new era, and Marcos and his even more charismatic wife Imelda went about trying to bring back some of Manila's pre-war energy. By 1970 widespread poverty, rising inflation, pitiful public funding and blatant corruption triggered a wave of protests in Manila. When several demonstrators were killed by police outside the presidential Malacañang Palace, Marcos' image as a political saviour died with them.

1935	1942	1969	1972
Manuel L Quezon, a wealthy mestizo, wins the first national presidential election, marking the establishment of the Philippine Commonwealth. True Philippine independence would have to wait until after the war.	75,000 American and Filipino troops surrender to Japan at Bataan – the largest surrender of troops in US history. The Bataan Death March ensues, and one month later Corregidor falls.	Ferdinand Marcos becomes the first Philippine president to win two terms in office, even as resentment over Marcos' increasingly heavy-handed rule and the Philippines' involvement in Vietnam simmers.	As resentment of Marcos rises, the embattled president imposes martial law and jails thousands of teachers, journalists, union leaders and opposition leaders, including Benigno 'Ninoy' Aquino Jr.

Citing the rise of leftist student groups and the communist New People's Army (NPA), Marcos imposed martial law on the country in 1972. Normally a constitutional last resort designed to protect the masses, martial law was declared by Marcos to keep himself in power (the constitution prevented him from running for a third term) and to protect his foreign business interests. Under martial law, a curfew was imposed, the media was silenced or taken over by the military, international travel was banned and thousands of anti-government suspects were rounded up and put into military camps. An estimated 50,000 of Marcos' opponents were jailed, exiled or killed. Marcos would not lift martial law until 1981.

Ferdinand Marcos died in exile in 1989 and his shoe-happy wife, Imelda, soon returned to the Philippines. Despite evidence that she and her husband helped themselves to billions of dollars from the treasury, Imelda lives freely in Manila and was elected to her fourth term in Congress in 2016 (once for Leyte and thrice for Ilocos Norte).

Imelda Marcos ran unsuccessfully for president in both 1992 and 1998 while still under investigation for some 900 counts of corruption and other crimes. She ran successfully for Congress in 1995, 2010, 2013 and again in 2016 at the age of 87.

The Birth of People Power

People Power was born in the streets of Manila in February 1986. As the whole world watched, millions of Filipinos, armed only with courage and religious faith, poured out onto the streets to defy the military might of the Marcos regime. Despite Marcos' unpopularity in the mid-1980s, People Power might never have happened were it not for the assassination of immensely popular opposition figure Ninoy Aquino. With his death, Filipinos felt they had lost their hope for a peaceful return to democracy.

The decline and fall of the Marcos dictatorship came swiftly after that. By 1986 even the USA, which had backed Marcos against communism in Southeast Asia, began to withdraw its support. In the face of criticism abroad and rising unrest at home, Marcos called for snap elections on 7 February 1986. Corazon 'Cory' Aquino, Ninoy's widow, became the (reluctant at first) standard bearer of the opposition at the instigation of the Roman Catholic Church. Marcos won the election, but the people knew Cory had been cheated, and they were no longer to be silenced.

On 26 February a massive sea of humanity gathered around Camp Aguinaldo and Camp Crame, along Epifanio de los Santos Ave, better known as EDSA, where two of Marcos' former ministers, Juan Ponce Enrile and Fidel Ramos, had taken refuge after defecting to the side of the people. They sang, chanted, prayed and shared food and drink, both among themselves and with government troops, who refused to fire into crowds and eventually went over to the side of the people. By nightfall the restless crowds were threatening to storm the palace. At this point the US stepped in and advised Marcos to 'let go'. Hurriedly the Marcoses boarded a US aircraft and flew to Hawaii and into exile.

The Filipino people had staged the world's first successful bloodless revolution, inspiring others to do the same across the world.

Inside the Palace (1987) by Beth Day Romulo documents the rise and fall of the Marcoses – a couple made for drama.

1980	1981	1983	1986
Ninoy Aquino is released from custody to undergo a triple-bypass operation in the United States. He remains in exile for more than three years.	Martial law is lifted on the eve of a visit by Pope John Paul II, who criticises Marcos' human-rights record. Shortly after, a rigged election hands Marcos another six-year term.	Aquino is shot dead at Manila's airport as he disembarks from a flight returning him from exile in the USA. Two million mourners pour onto the streets to accompany Aquino's funeral cortège.	The bloodless EDSA I Revolution, popularly known as People Power, chases Marcos from the Philippines. Ninoy's widow, Corazon, who had lost the presidential election to Marcos days earlier, becomes president.

Same Old, Same Old

The first decade of the 21st century was a tumultuous one in Philippine politics. It began with an impeachment trial that saw millions of Filipinos take to the streets to oust President Joseph Estrada over corruption allegations – the country's second 'People Power' revolution in 15 years. Estrada gave way to his vice president, Gloria Macapagal Arroyo, whose nearly 10 years in office were also dogged by scandals, including alleged improprieties in her 2004 re-election.

In the 2010 presidential elections, the country found the fresh face it was looking for in the form of Benigno 'Noynoy' Aquino III, the squeaky-clean son of Corazon Aquino, hero of the first People Power revolution in 1986. Riding a wave of national grief after his mother's death in 2009, Aquino won a landslide victory with 42% of votes, emerging from a pack of candidates which included former president Estrada. Alas, the party would not last as even Aquino would flirt with scandal and see

THE MORO PROBLEM

Muslim dissent emanating out of Mindanao has been the one constant in the Philippines' roughly 450 years of history as a loosely united territory. After Legazpi landed in Cebu in 1565, he discovered that Muslim missionaries from Malacca had been living in the islands for decades. Legazpi managed to dislodge Muslim chiefs from Maynilad (now Manila) and the Visayas, but the southern territories would prove more difficult to conquer.

Over the next 400 years a religious war would smoulder in Mindanao between the government and rebel groups seeking an autonomous Muslim homeland. The country's largest separatist Muslim group, the 12,500-strong Moro Islamic Liberation Front (MILF), signed a ceasefire with the government in 2001, but periodic violence and bombings continued in Mindanao's predominantly Muslim Autonomous Region in Muslim Mindanao (ARMM), culminating a three-week siege of Zamboanga City by separatist rebels in 2013, which displaced 100,000.

In 2014, the government and the MILF agreed to the basic framework for a new Bangsamoro Autonomous Region in Muslim Mindanao (BARMM) to replace the ARMM. Other groups objected and periodic violence continued apace until 2017 when nearly 600 ISIS–affiliated militants seized the Islamic City of Marawi. It took the Philippine military five months to take it back, during which time scores died and the city was reduced to rubble. The siege of Marawi led President Rodrigo Duterte, who had come into office in 2016 promising to grant more autonomy to Muslim Mindanao, to place all of Mindanao under martial law.

Since then some progress has been made. The BARMM was officially established in early 2019, and martial law in Mindanao was lifted – after two-and-a-half years – in late 2019. However, Mindanao continues to face the threat of violence from extremist groups and those opposed to the BARMM.

1989	1991	1999	2007
A coup attempt against Cory Aquino sees hundreds of foreigners taken hostage in rebel-seized condos and hotels in Makati. Alleged US involvement in suppressing the siege stokes rising anti-American sentiment.	Mt Pinatubo erupts, rendering the American military base at Clark unusable. The Philippine Senate votes to end the US military presence at Philippine bases permanently.	As all-out war rages with the Moro Islamic Liberation Front (MILF), President Estrada signs the controversial Visiting Forces Agreement, which allows American troops back to train Filipino forces.	Renegade soldiers on trial for plotting a coup in 2003 escape their courtroom and take over Manila's Peninsula Hotel in another attempted coup against Arroyo.

his popularity erode, despite overseeing a period of unprecedented economic growth and making some headway towards ending the conflict
in Mindanao.

The Rise of Duterte

Leading up to the presidential election of 2016, confidence in Aquino and
traditional politics was diminishing and relations with China were deteriorating over disputed territories in the West Philippine Sea. Promising
to end corruption and crime and reset relations with China, Rodrigo
Duterte, a tough-talking, foul-mouthed former mayor of the southern
city of Davao, beat out Aquino's preferred pick in a landslide in the 2016
presidential elections.

Duterte, who was often referred to as the 'Death Squad Mayor' during
his more than two-decade reign in Davao, ran a populist campaign based
on fighting crime, drugs and corruption. Upon taking office, Duterte un-
leashed a torrent of extrajudicial killings targeting mainly drug dealers.

Human rights groups estimate that more than 30,000 people were
killed in the so-called war on drugs in the first four years of Duterte's
term. Many of those murdered were suspected dealers and users of
shabu (methamphetamine), killed by police or by vigilantes who essentially operated with impunity under the strong-armed president. Scores
of others were innocent victims caught in the cross-fire or, some say,
human rights and environmental activists targeted for political reasons.

Despite the carnage, both Duterte and his war on drugs, backed by a
fawning mainstream media and a relentless social media campaign, remained popular into 2020 before the COVID-19 crisis gripped the country. Missteps in managing the virus, which saw the Philippines register
Southeast Asia's second-highest infection rate despite imposing one of
the longest and strictest lockdowns in the world, put a dent in the popularity of the president, who simultaneously began to draw fire for his
pro-China policies.

Despite these setbacks for Duterte, all signs pointed to the president
being able to hand-pick a successor in the 2022 presidential election.

'Jihadists in
Paradise' is a
riveting *Atlantic
Monthly* article
by Mark Bowden
about Abu Sayyaf
rebels' seizure of
a Palawan resort
and subsequent
18-month
detainment of
two American
missionaries.

2013	2016	2017	2020
Typhoon Haiyan (known locally as Typhoon Yolanda) sweeps through the Central Visayas in November, killing an estimated 15,000 to 25,000 people and destroying coastal communities.	An international tribunal rejects China's claim over Philippine islands and resources in the West Philippine Sea. Newly elected president Rodrigo Duterte largely ignores the decision as part of his pivot to China.	Nearly 600 militants affiliated with Islamic State, including many foreign fighters, lay siege to the Mindanaoan city of Marawi from late May until a ceasefire in October.	Duterte places the country under tight quarantine amid coronavirus fears in what would become one of the world's longest and strictest lockdowns.

People & Culture

It's impossible to deny it: Filipinos have a zest for life that may be unrivalled on our planet. The national symbol, the jeepney, is an apt metaphor for the nation. Splashed with colour, laden with religious icons and festooned with sanguine scribblings, the jeepney flaunts the fact that, at heart, it's a dilapidated pile of scrap metal. No matter their prospects in life, Filipinos face them with a laugh and a wink. Whatever happens...'so be it'.

The National Psyche

The fatalism of the Filipino people has a name: *bahala na,* a phrase that expresses the idea that all things shall pass and in the meantime life is to be lived. *Bahala na* helps shape the carefree, welcoming nature of the Filipino people – and their tolerance. Travellers of any race, creed or sexual orientation are uniformly received with the utmost warmth and courtesy.

Eye of the Fish is an interesting collection of essays by Manila-born, New York–raised journalist Luis H Francia that is a good introduction to the various issues facing the Philippines and its people today.

Family and religion are the two most important forces in Filipino society. The close-knit Filipino family unit extends to distant cousins, multiple godparents, and one's *barkada* (gang of friends). Almost without exception, all members of one's kinship group are afforded the utmost loyalty; respect for elders is paramount.

Filipino families, especially poor ones, tend to be large. It's not uncommon for a dozen family members to live together in a tiny apartment, shanty or nipa hut. Because of this, personal space is not the issue for Filipinos that it is for Westerners. Visitors to Philippine resorts are often amazed – or appalled – when a family of 10 takes up residence in the room next door, complete with pets, videoke machine and cooking equipment.

The most basic political unit, the barangay, is merely an extension of the family-based community unit that defined the social structure in pre-Hispanic times. The idea of working together for the common good, virtually nonexistent at the national level, is alive and well at the barangay level, where it's known as *bayanihan*. Originally a rural entity, the barangay today is no less relevant in urban shanty towns, where a healthy cooperative spirit is essential for survival.

Another thread in the fabric of Filipino society is the overseas worker. At any given time more than a million Filipinos are working abroad, and combined they send home tens of billions of dollars. The Overseas Filipino Worker (OFW) – the nurse in Canada, the construction worker in Qatar, the entertainer in Japan, the cleaner in Singapore – has become a national hero.

Altar of Secrets: Sex, Politics, and Money in the Philippine Catholic Church (2013) is journalist Aries Rufo's damning account of the leadership of the country's predominant religion.

Faith & Superstition

More than 80% of Filipinos are Roman Catholic. While the separation of church and state is formalised in the Filipino constitution, the Catholic Church deeply influences national and local politics. A subtle hint from the church can swing a mayoral race and mean millions of votes for presidential or congressional candidates.

To the chagrin of the Catholic Church, Filipinos are also a superstitious lot. In urban areas, faith healers, psychics, fortune-tellers, tribal shamans, self-help books and evangelical crusaders can all help cast away ill-fortune. In the hinterland, caves and forests are inhabited by spirits, ghosts and *aswang* (vampirelike figures who eat unborn children).

Ethnic Groups

Ethnologically, the vast majority of Filipinos are related to Malaysians and Indonesians, with substantial Chinese influence as well as a smattering of colonial American and Spanish blood thrown into the mix. There are also close to 100 cultural minority groups in the Philippines, depending on your definition, and 170 or so different languages and dialects are spoken in the archipelago. In general, ethnic minorities can be divided into three main, blurred groups: Negrito, Igorot and Manobo.

PEOPLE & CULTURE ETHNIC GROUPS

Aswang – mythical vampirelike figures who eat unborn children – have been the subject of at least one American cult horror flick. Any rural Filipino will tell you in a matter-of-fact manner about the many *aswang* living in their local forests.

The Negrito

Often referred to as the aborigines of the Philippines, the Negrito are represented by the Aeta, Ati, Eta, Ita and Dumagat peoples. Now thought to number as few as 30,000 to 35,000, Negrito people are generally the most racially victimised of the Filipinos. The Negrito mainly live in extremely poor conditions on the coastal fringes of North Luzon and in the highlands of Mindoro, Negros, Samar, Leyte and Panay, where the famously festive Ati are said to have initiated the present-day Ati-Atihan festivals in Kalibo and surrounding towns.

The Igorot

The Cordillera region of Luzon is home to the mountain-dwelling tribes collectively known as the Igorot. They include the Apayao (or Isneg), Kalinga, Ifugao, Benguet, Bontoc and Tingguian (or Itneg). While generally considered unbowed by outside pressures, many Igorot traditions were suppressed first by the Spanish and then by the Americans. However, most Igorot rituals, fashions and beliefs remain in some form and some rural villagers continue to live much as their ancestors did, tending rice terraces and living off the land.

PROSTITUTION IN THE PHILIPPINES

The sex business in the Philippines grew up around the American military bases at Clark and Subic Bay, reaching its heyday during the late Marcos era. The Americans were booted out in 1991, but prostitution remains rampant around their former bases and in most major cities. Various estimates put the number of sex workers in the country at about 400,000, with up to 20% of those underage. Although prostitution is officially illegal, the police tend to turn a blind eye.

The Asia-Pacific office of the **Coalition Against Trafficking in Women** (☏02-426 9873; www.catwinternational.org) is in Quezon City, Manila. Its website has information about prostitution in the Philippines, and several useful links. In Angeles, the **Renew Foundation** (www.renew-foundation.org) works to keep former sex workers and trafficked women off the streets by teaching them alternative work skills and providing safe shelter.

Of particular concern is the problem of child prostitution. A culture of silence surrounds child sex abuse in the Philippines. While *hiya* (shame) plays a big role in the silence, for the most part this silence is bought. There's big money in paedophilia, both for ringleaders who arrange meetings between paedophiles and children, and for law enforcers who get paid to ignore it.

ECPAT Philippines (☏02-920 8151; www.ecpatphilippines.org) in Quezon City works to promote child-safe tourism and to end the commercial sexual exploitation of children through child prostitution, child pornography and the trafficking of children for sexual purposes. To report an incident, contact ECPAT, the **Philippine National Police Women & Children's Division** (☏0919 777 7377) or the **Human Trafficking Action Line** (☏02-1343).

The Manobo

The term Manobo is used to describe the major indigenous groups of Mindanao. Of these groups, five regard themselves as Muslim – the Badjao, Maguindanao, Maranao (or Maranaw), Tausag (or Tausug) and Samal. Regarded as the least Islamic of the Muslim groups, the animist Badjao are the 'sea gypsies' of the Sulu sea. Maguindanao people are the largest of all the Muslim groups, famed for their skills as musicians and weavers. Maranao people are the traditional owners of Lake Lanao, and are among the Philippines' most ingenious craftspeople. Tausag people were the earliest Filipino Islamic converts back in the 15th century and as such were the ruling class of the Jolo Sultanate. Samal people are the poorest of the Muslim groups, having long been the loyal subjects of the Tausag dynasties. The main non-Muslim indigenous groups of Mindanao are the Bukidnon, Bagobo, Mandaya and Mansaka peoples.

Ghosts of Manila (1994) by James Hamilton-Paterson is a chilling yet entertaining 'docufiction' of life, death and the corrupt chains binding Filipinos in the city's slums.

Arts

Music

Filipinos are best known for their ubiquitous cover bands and their love of karaoke, J-pop, K-pop and American pop, but they need not be in imitation mode to show off their innate musical talent.

Dating from the late 19th century, the *kundiman* genre, with its bittersweet themes of love, fate and death, remains one of the best-loved modes of musical expression in the Philippines. Traditional musical instruments used in *kundiman* include the *kudyapi*, a hauntingly melodic lute, and the *kulintang*, a row of small gongs mounted on a *langkungan*, a resonating platform.

Filipino rock, known as 'OPM' (Original Pinoy Music), had its heyday in the '70s, when blues-rock outfits such as the Juan de la Cruz Band, Anakbayan and Maria Cafra ruled the roost. They looked and sounded the part, with big hair, bandannas and endless, soulful electric-guitar riffs. The Juan de la Cruz Band is credited with inventing Pinoy rock by busting out lyrics in Tagalog – the first big act to do so. From those

ARNEL PINEDA'S JOURNEY

He was just a small-town boy, as his favourite band once put it, working on the not-so-lonely cover-band circuit in Quezon City, Manila, as lead singer for a band called Zoo. Arnel Pineda didn't reckon on achieving more or less fame than any of the zillion other Filipino cover-band singers that keep the crowds entertained in the bars and lounges of hotels from Bahrain to Beijing. One thing was for sure, though: Arnel Pineda could imitate the throaty wail of Journey's erstwhile lead singer Steve Perry like nobody's business.

In 2006 something happened that made few waves in the international rock scene, but would change Pineda's life forever. The ageing rockers of Journey were forced to drop lead singer Steve Augeri, who was losing his voice but had never *really* sounded like Perry anyway. The next year, after another lead singer didn't work out, the band stumbled across some clips of Pineda on YouTube. Incredulous, they invited him to LA for an audition.

When Pineda applied for his visa, the story goes, nobody at the US embassy believed his ostensible 'purpose for travel' – auditioning to be lead singer of Journey. So they asked him to sing a few bars of 'Wheels in the Sky.' He nailed it, they issued the visa, and he was on his way to rock 'n' roll infamy.

The band introduced Pineda as their new lead singer in early 2008, turning 90 million Filipinos into Journey fans overnight. In February 2017 Pineda and Journey returned to Manila for a concert at the Mall of Asia in Manila. Filipinos love a good rags-to-riches story to affirm their hope that things can always get better. Pineda, a one-time homeless kid on the streets of Manila, has done more than give Filipinos a good story – he has given them something to be proud of.

humble origins evolved Eraserheads, the country's first modest international success. This four-man band, known as the Philippines' Beatles, rose to prominence in the early '90s with catchy guitar-heavy alternative rock songs with lyrics about ordinary Filipinos' struggles.

Other styles evolved from this. *Tunog kalye (*street music), featuring slang lyrics about everyday experiences like drinking, drugs, corruption, and unrequited love, is uniquely Filipino. In the 2000s, three bands dominated the OPM scene, singing in both English and Filipino. This trio was led by the sometimes sweet, sometimes surly diva Kitchie Nadal, who continues to tour internationally. The eponymous band fronted by the singer Bamboo rose to prominence with a heady mixture of political invective and ballads laden with angst-ridden garage rock. Rounding out the big three, the agreeable Rivermaya, formerly fronted by Bamboo, made minor waves internationally with its 2005 hit 'You'll Be Safe Here'.

Established and up-and-coming OPM artists can be seen playing at Ortigas' 12 Monkeys Music Hall & Pub; look out for Mumford & Sons–esque folk rockers Ransom Collective, and jazzy vocalist Jireh Calo. Seasoned artists such as Joey Generoso, formerly of Side A, and Southborder also perform there.

Karaoke

Many people would sooner have their wisdom teeth removed without anaesthetic than spend an evening listening to inebriated amateurs pay homage to Celine Dion and Julio Iglesias. But when Filipinos want to unwind, they often do it with karaoke – or 'videoke' as it's known throughout the Philippines.

Filipinos are unabashed about belting out a tune, whenever and wherever, alone or in company. They pursue the craft without a hint of irony, which means that criticising or making fun of someone's performance is decidedly taboo, and may even provoke violence.

Architecture

Long before the Spanish arrived, the simple, utilitarian nipa hut defined Filipino architecture. The most basic nipa hut is made of wood and bamboo, with a roof of palm thatch – cool and breezy in hot weather and easily repaired if damaged by typhoons.

The Spanish brought new forms of architecture, such as the *bahay na bato* (stone house) and squat, fortresslike 'earthquake-baroque' churches. But the basic design of the nipa hut endured. By the 19th century, Filipinos of means were building hybrid residences that mixed Spanish and Asian styles with elements of the nipa hut. These composite structures, distinguishable by their capiz-shell windows and huge upstairs *sala* (living room), remain the most elegant and distinctive architectural specimens the Philippines has to offer.

Maria Virginia Yap Morales' *Balay Ukit: Tropical Architecture in Pre-WWII Filipino Houses* explores late-19th- and early-20th-century buildings that exhibit this hybrid style, the vast majority of which have been destroyed or abandoned, overwhelmed by quicker, cheaper and generic concrete structures. The Spanish colonial city of Vigan (Luzon) and Silay (Negros) are the best places to view these houses, although you will sometimes stumble across fine examples in the most remote barangays.

Imelda Marcos, in the 1970s, helped introduce another hybrid style that utilised indigenous materials in grand and opulent ways; the Coconut Palace in Manila is a lasting legacy. These days, most notably in Manila's ever-expanding micro-cities, the anonymous aesthetics of the international high-rise dominate.

PEOPLE & CULTURE ARTS

Sari-Sari Storybooks (www.sarisaristorybooks.com), a publishing venture run by a Brooklyn, NY-based Filipino-American woman, produces bilingual (English and another Filipino language) illustrated children's books inspired by local, regional and Filipino themes, beliefs and traditions. For example, *Kalipay and the Tiniest Tiktik*, written in Cebuana, is based on a popular mythical creature.

Filipino-American writer Laurel Fantauzzo's *The First Impulse: Notes on Love, Film and Death in the Philippines* tells the true story of two young film critics murdered in Quezon City in 2009.

Theatre

Filipino theatre evolved from marathon chants and epic legends, such as the Unesco-recognised Ifugao *hudhud,* sung in the rice fields around Kiangan in North Luzon to alleviate boredom while planting and harvesting. In the 17th century the Spaniards introduced *sinakulos* – passion plays depicting the life and death of Christ – to convert the locals to Christianity. Other early forms of theatre were the *moro-moro,* which glorified the Christian struggle against Muslims in the 19th century, and a light, localised musical form known as *zarzuela,* which was used to protest American occupation at the outset of the 20th century.

When the Americans arrived, English became the language of the national theatrical scene. The journalist, novelist and playwright Nick Joaquin wrote his signature work, *Portrait of a Young Artist as a Filipino,* in 1951. Other important playwrights of the 20th century were Rolando Tinio, whose Filipino adaptations of English-language classics such as Shakespeare's tragedies remain unparalleled in their field; and Rene Villanueva, best known for his children's books but also highly regarded as a playwright.

Contemporary playwrights blend tradition with the issues of the day. The Philippine Educational Theater Association (PETA; www.peta theater.com) in particular, which celebrated its 50th anniversary in 2017, produces works that blend social satire with cutting-edge style and has an excellent development program for up-and-coming playwrights.

Painting & Sculpture

The most recognisable form of artwork in the Philippines is centuries old and, in fact, wasn't conceived as artwork: the *bulol,* sacred wood figures carved by the Ifugao, have for centuries been used to guard rice fields. The names of the sculptors were rarely recorded, but elder Ifugao can often identify the sculptor of original *bulol* based on the statue's style. Reproductions of these powerful statues flood souvenir shops across the country.

Modern Filipino sculpture is epitomised by Guillermo Tolentino's neoclassical masterpiece in Caloocan City, the resplendent *Monumento,* honouring the revolutionary hero Andres Bonifacio. Davao-based Kublai Millan, prolific in nearly every medium, has installed massive sculptures depicting various Mindanao ethnic and religious groups in a number of cities on the island. Most easily visible are the giant durian at the Davao International Airport and the massive eagle and Bagobo children in People's Park, also in Davao. Another name visitors may notice is Jose Mendoza, whose sculptures adorn the streets of Makati.

The contemporary Filipino art scene is ever abuzz. Conceptual artist David Cortez Medalla, based in Britain, has pioneered avant-garde art movements such as minimalism and performance art. In addition to being well received internationally, artist-with-a-conscience Benedicto Cabrera ('Bencab') has dedicated considerable effort to the development of contemporary Cordillera art, and created Tam-awan village, an artists retreat in Baguio. Other Filipino artists are experimenting with alternative mediums, including using *tuba* (coconut wine), coffee grounds and even the sun (the process is called pyrography).

Dance

Filipino dance is as rich and varied as the islands themselves. The national folk dance is the *tinikling,* which involves a boy and a girl hopping between bamboo poles, held just above the ground and struck together in time to music or hand-clapping. Some say this dance was inspired by the flitting of birds between grass stems or a heron hopping through the rice paddies. A version of the *tinikling* is the breathtaking *singkil,*

David Byrne and Fatboy Slim's *Here Lies Love,* a rock musical about Imelda Marcos, did a run at the Public Theater in New York City in 2013 and 2014.

Po-on is an easy introduction to Filipino author F Sionil Jose, with all the tropes of Filipino literature: evil Spanish priests, heroic *ilustrados,* passive resistance and armed struggle. It's the first in a five-part series.

Mindanao artist Kublai Ponce-Millan's nine statues of indigenous Filipinos playing musical instruments in St Peter's Sq, Vatican City, was the first time a non-Italian artist was allowed to participate in the Vatican's annual nativity scene display.

in which two dancers representing a Muslim princess and her lady-in-waiting weave through four poles struck together at increasing speed.

Two of the best known and most successful Filipino folk-dance troupes are the Bayanihan National Folk Dance Company, which first wowed the world in 1958 at the Brussels Universal Exposition, and the Ramon Obusan Folkloric Group, founded in 1972. Both are resident companies of the Cultural Center of the Philippines.

Many Filipino ballet talents have won international recognition abroad, among them Maniya Barredo, former prima ballerina of the Atlanta Ballet, and Lisa Macuja, who played Giselle with the Kirov Ballet in Russia. Macuja now runs her own ballet company, Ballet Manila.

In 1942 Filipino statesman Carlos P Romulo became the first Asian to win a Pulitzer Prize, for a series of articles on pre-WWII Asia.

PEOPLE & CULTURE SPORT

Sport

Sport in the Philippines is dominated by one man: boxer Manny Pacquiao (aka 'Pacman'), widely considered the best pound-for-pound prizefighter in the world. Pacquiao, who emerged from poverty in Mindanao to win title belts in five different weight classes, is a tremendous source of national pride for Filipinos. While his hall-of-fame boxing career may be nearing its end – he lost a controversial decision for the world welterweight title to Australian Jeff Horn in July 2017 – other pursuits beckon. He ran successfully for Philippine congress in 2010 and 2013 and was elected to the Senate in 2016, tallying more than 16 million votes. He was the oldest rookie drafted in the Philippine Basketball Association in 2014 – notably, by the team he coaches; he's released several albums of Tagalog songs and acted in a handful of films.

An even quirkier national hero takes the form of stocky, bespectacled Efren 'Bata' ('The Kid') Reyes, one of the world's best nine-ball billiards players. The other big sport, besides cockfighting, is basketball. Most midsized towns have at least one concrete court with a corrugated-iron roof, and you'll find at least a crude interpretation of a court in even the poorest, most remote barangays. The overwhelmingly popular Philippine Basketball Association (PBA) draws many former US college stars and the leagues' games are televised nationally. To learn about the ubiquity and cultural significance of the game in the Philippines, check out *Pacific Rims: Beermen Ballin' in Flip-Flops and the Philippines' Unlikely Love Affair with Basketball* (Rafe Bartholomew; 2010), a book as riotous as the title implies.

Football (soccer) is growing rapidly in popularity as the national team, Azkals, has improved markedly in recent years and now competes with the best teams in Asia.

Tong-its, a three-player card game like rummy, is played for big pesos in backyard contests all over the country. Don't be fooled by the humble setting: players can be cutthroat and square off for the entire day, tossing jewellery and phones into the pot when cash is low.

Cockfighting

Cockfighting is to the Philippines what baseball is to the USA or rugby is to New Zealand. A couple of times a week, mostly male crowds pack their local cockpit (usually dubbed a 'sporting arena') and watch prized roosters fight to the death. Important matches and championships are shown on national television.

Expensive fighting birds are fitted with 7.5cm ankle blades and let loose on one another. Fights are short and brutal. The winner is whisked away to a team of waiting surgeons, who stitch up any gaping wounds and dose the bird with antibiotics. The loser usually makes his way into the cooking pot.

The practice has its critics, both in the Philippines and abroad, including a range of organisations like People for the Ethical Treatment of Animals (PETA) and the Philippines Animal Welfare Society. But as yet animal-rights groups have made little progress stemming a pastime that is so deeply ingrained in the country's culture.

The yo-yo, which means 'come back' in Tagalog, was invented by a Filipino-American. The original yo-yo was a studded weapon attached to 6m ropes.

Environment

The environment of the Philippines has two very different faces: one is a spectacular tropical-island-topia, home to a global treasure of endemic species; the other is one of the world's top conservation priorities, due to the many grave threats to its health. The visitor might begin by understanding both, then focus on finding the diamonds in the rough, safe in the knowledge that selective ecotourism can not only be tremendously rewarding here, but also do an enormous amount of good.

The Land

The Philippines is the world's second-largest archipelago, with 7107 islands – although when asked how many, locals commonly joke 'at what tide?' This vast network, stretching some 1810km from the tip of Batanes to the Sulu archipelago, is the defining characteristic of the country, shaping it socially, politically and economically. Only its next-door neighbour, Indonesia, offers a larger string of pearls. In fact, combine the two and you could hop to a different island every day for over 50 years!

While the Philippine islands range from tiny coral islets to the sprawling, amoeba-like giants of Luzon and Mindanao, they are all tropical. On a map, the archipelago looks like a puzzle that has broken apart, but it actually congealed over tens of millions of years from the complex interactions of various sea plates along the Ring of Fire, the extraordinary volcanic fault line that circles the Pacific Basin. This explains why the wildlife in Palawan, which has drifted eastward over millions of years, is more like Borneo's than the rest of the Philippines'. And why volcanoes are plentiful. At least 17 are active, the femme fatale being highly active Mt Mayon (2462m), with its classic, perfectly symmetrical cone.

Wildlife

When you think of wildlife in the Philippines, one quasi-technical term rises to the top: 'endemic'. Millenniums of isolation from the rest of Southeast Asia resulted in the evolution of thousands of species found nowhere else on earth, leading biologists to dub the archipelago 'Galápagos times 10'. In fact, species are still being discovered at a remarkable rate.

Some statistics tell the tale: the Philippines has 191 species of mammals, of which 16 were only discovered in the last 15 years. Over 100 of these are endemic – even more than in Madagascar. Some 600 species of bird also call the Philippines home, nearly 200 of which are endemic. Reptiles are represented by about 235 species, some 160 (68%) of which are endemic. The country is also home to approximately 13,500 species of plant; only four countries can boast more. Scientists estimate that 30% to 40% of those species are unique to the Philippines.

The Philippines is also part of the 'Coral Triangle', the global centre for marine biodiversity. It has a higher concentration of species per unit area than anywhere else in this region, making it the 'centre of the centre'.

However, while the Philippines is renowned for its underwater life, it's not well known for terrestrial wildlife-spotting. This is because the ecotourism infrastructure doesn't exist and the animals themselves are elusive, particularly in the face of ongoing development.

The Mindanao Trench in the Philippine Sea, at 10,497m, is the second-deepest spot in the world's oceans.

BEST WILDLIFE-SPOTTING

Pythons (Danjugan Island, off Negros) Yes, monster pythons do eat bats in mid-air.

Green turtles (Apo Island) You can swim alongside these creatures while snorkelling or scuba diving.

Whale sharks (Donsol, Pintuyan) Spot these giants in their natural habitat in southern Leyte (also around Puerto Princesa).

Tarsiers (Bohol) See these adorable creatures at the sanctuary in Corella, not far from Tagbilaran.

Fruit bats (Monfort Bat Cave, Samal Island, off Mindanao) Just you and 2.5 million of them.

Dugong (off Busuanga Island, Palawan) Is it a whale, or a seal? This strange hybrid is worth the search.

Philippine eagles (Mt Apo, Mindanao) What better place to spy this majestic bird than the tallest peak in the Philippines?

Animals

As you would expect from such a hotspot of biodiversity, the Philippines contains some extraordinary animals. The poster mammal is the lovable, palm-sized tarsier, a primate found mainly on the island of Bohol, and easiest seen at the Tarsier Sanctuary (p318) there. Contrary to popular belief, they are not the world's smallest primate – this is a distinction belonging to the pygmy mouse lemur of Madagascar. However, the Philippines can still proudly lay claim to the world's smallest hoofed mammal – the rare Philippine mouse deer of Palawan – one of four deer species on the islands. Other furry favourites include the Palawan bearcat, or binturong, and the small but charming Visayan leopard.

The most impressive land mammal and the only wild-cattle species in the Philippines is the *tamaraw*, a dwarf water buffalo whose only remaining refuge is Mindoro's Mt Iglit-Baco National Park. A century ago their population numbered 10,000; today around 400 remain. However, their survival is a minor success story since it's double the number from 2014. More common are the eight species of fruit bat (flying fox) that dwell in caves across the country, at least by day. Those visiting Boracay need only look up at dusk to spot the nightly bat migration, including that of the giant golden-crowned flying fox, which has a 1.7m wingspan.

There are a few places where you might spot whales if your timing is right, such as the channel between Negros and Cebu, and the Bohol Sea, between Bohol and Mindanao. However, you're more likely to spot dolphins; the acrobatic spinner dolphin is a perennial favourite. Less well known are dugong (known locally as *duyong*), a type of sea cow found in great numbers in Philippine waters but now relatively rare. Two places where you can spot them (if you're lucky) are in Malita, Mindanao, and around Calauit, off Busuanga Island, in northern Palawan.

The national bird is the enormous Philippine eagle. A few hundred survive in the wild, mostly in the rainforests of Mindanao, Samar, and the Sierra Madre Mountains of North Luzon. They are more easily seen at the Philippine Eagle Center (p368) in Calinan, outside of Davao. Further south, the Sulu hornbill is one of several extraordinary hornbills on the islands, part of a genus known for its blazing beaks. The Palawan peacock pheasant is also a remarkable bird: the males of this species have a metallic blue crest, long white eyebrows and large metallic blue or purple 'eyes' on the tail. Now nearing endangered status, these ground-dwellers are found only in the deepest forests of Palawan.

Among the reptiles, geckos are ubiquitous. There are also 10 species of flying lizard, which glide from tree to tree using a flap of skin on either

The world's biggest pearl was found by a Filipino diver in the waters off Palawan in 1934. It weighed over 6kg and was valued at US$42 million.

side of their body. More elusive is the rare sailfin dragon, which is just as advertised, with a sail-like fin standing atop its back. Rarest of all is the endangered, and enormous, Philippine crocodile, which can be seen in Sierra Madre Natural Park. There's also a wide variety of snakes, including pythons, sea snakes (which can be seen when snorkelling), and the Philippine cobra, which can spit its venom 3m; pack an umbrella.

Of course, divers and snorkellers also flock to the Philippines to see any of the islands' 2500-plus species of fish. Some of the larger denizens include whale sharks, which are typically seen in Donsol, southern Leyte or around Puerto Princesa (whale-shark 'tours' around Oslob, Cebu, have been criticised by animal-welfare groups); and thresher sharks, which use their enormous tails to herd their prey. Sea turtles are often a common sight while snorkelling, with a resident tribe lying off the beach at Apo Island.

A 6.5m-long crocodile, one of the largest in the world, was captured in 2011 near Bunawan, Mindanao.

Plants

While the pretty yellow-flowered *nara* is the national tree of the Philippines, the unofficial national plant must surely be the nipa palm, whose leaves form the walls and roofs of nipa huts all over the country. The national flower is the highly aromatic *sampaguita*, a variety of jasmine. For both quality and quantity, you can't beat the some 900 endemic species of orchid, including the waling-waling *(Vanda sanderiana)* of Mindanao and the red-spotted star orchid *(Rananthera mautiana)*. Another favourite is pitcher plants; climbers exploring at remote elevations may stumble upon rare examples of these.

Ecotourism

With so many natural wonders, you might think that the Philippines would have a highly developed ecotourism industry. And below the water, you might be right. In southern Negros alone, new dive resorts are sprouting like hotels in Boracay. Even remote resorts have dive centres now. Along with this upsurge has come the ongoing creation of dozens of marine reserves. Palawan has more than 60; southern Negros over a dozen. This has led to a marked increase in marine life in places such as Hundred Islands National Park and Apo Reef Natural Park. However, there is still an ongoing battle to protect marine reserves from local fisherman, who frequently invade them at night.

In 2014 Unesco de-listed several World Heritage sites in the Philippines, including Panglao Island, Mt Apo and Taal Volcano, for environmental violations.

While ecotourism on land is no less challenged, it is far less advanced, due primarily to a lack of basic infrastructure. At first glance the Philippines would appear to have a robust national park system. Hundreds of land and marine areas are designated as protected and in May 2017 the Philippine Senate voted to bring an additional 92 sites under the protected areas system. However, few actually meet the international definition of a national park and funds for enforcement and protection are generally lacking. According to Conservation International, two-thirds have human settlements, and one-quarter of their lands have already been disturbed or converted to agriculture.

This lack of infrastructure extends to local tour companies. Only a handful of enterprises offer the spelunking, jungle-trekking, rappelling, kayaking, wildlife and mountain-bike tours for which the Philippines is tailor-made. Consequently, one has to be downright careful when trying to find a trekking company or guide, or when planning an outdoor expedition of any kind. The necessary accreditation, training, emergency procedures, accountability and professional organisation are scarce. When assessing key factors such as local weather conditions, remember that your guide's opinion may be driven more by economics than safety, given that a guide's wage is less than $2 a day. If you're not sure where to turn, visit local tourism offices, which are generally excellent.

One rule of thumb is that group van tours generally don't operate with environmental principles in mind. Some operators are attempting to combine ecotourism with adventure sports.

Environmental Issues

Given its extraordinary geography of 7107 tropical islands and population of 100 million people, many of whom live well below the poverty line, it seems inevitable that environmental issues will arise. Deforestation, soil erosion, waste disposal, air and water pollution, overfishing, destructive fishing and coral-reef loss are all of a concern. Not all the damage is self-inflicted, however. The Philippine environment is also suffering from some well-known external pressures, from plastic bottles floating ashore from the rest of Southeast Asia to the many impacts of climate change.

There is an ongoing battle between the many sources of these problems, and the many conservation organisations, both governmental and non-governmental, arrayed against them. The environment of the Philippines today is basically the product of this conflict, whose shifting frontline is everywhere to be seen.

Land

Over the course of the last century the forest cover of the Philippines has dropped from 70% to under 20%, with only about 7% of its original old-growth, closed-canopy forest left. At current levels of deforestation, the country's forests will be extinct by 2100. Nevertheless, an astonishing 75% of Philippine forest is still classified as production forest. In addition to severe soil erosion, this trend is particularly concerning because Philippine forests are the last home for so many endemic species.

Unregulated logging, mining, massive farming expansion and urbanisation have all taken their toll. Indigenous people's claims on upland regions have been ignored by urban elites. The government has regularly granted logging concessions of less than 10 years, with loggers having no incentive to replant. From 2011 to 2015 the mining sector is said to have reforested 47,000 hectares. Much of what's left of Philippine forests is only safeguarded by high altitudes, as they're difficult to reach.

Environmentalists, in an effort to draw attention to the estimated 640 threatened species in the Philippines, have begun to use creative monikers to highlight the issues. On Panay, the Visayan writhed-hornbill, the flowering plany Raflessia, the Visayan warty pig, the Visayan spotted deer and the Panay monitor lizard are known as the 'Big Five'.

ENVIRONMENT ENVIRONMENTAL ISSUES

CONSERVATION ORGANISATIONS

The following websites contain information related to the environmental concerns facing the Philippines. Some organisations are Philippines-specific, others work elsewhere as well.

Biodiversity Management Bureau (www.bmb.gov.ph) Links to the various conservation projects of the Philippine government.

Conservation International (www.conservation.org) Partners with the government and local communities to protect threatened ecosystems.

Coral Cay Conservation (www.coralcay.org) Works to protect coral reefs.

Haribon Foundation (www.haribon.org.ph) Active in preserving habitats of endangered species and other areas.

Negros Forests & Ecological Foundation Inc (www.negrosforests.org) Works to protect various Philippine habitats, focusing on Negros.

Oceana Philippines (www.ph.oceana.org) Dedicated to the preservation of marine environemnts.

Pasyar Travel & Tours (www.pasyarpalawantravel.weebly.com) Monitors illegal logging, mining, fishing and other prohibited activities in forests and waters of Palawan.

Rare (www.rare.org) Works with local governments to responsibly manage fishing zones and promote sustainable practices.

Sea

With a coastal ecosystem that stretches for almost 20,000km, the Philippines has become one of the earliest victims of climate change. Indeed, according to the UN, it is the country third most at risk from its effects. The combination of high sea temperatures, acidification and unseasonable storms has done enormous damage to the country's reefs. Centuries-old coral is dying almost overnight. The World Bank estimates that only about 1% of Philippine coral reefs remains pristine, while more than 50% is unhealthy. Snorkellers around Puerto Galera and Boracay now face a coral graveyard; pearl farms are increasingly unproductive.

Coastal development has further damaged the marine environment, including mangroves and seagrasses. Population growth has driven increasing need for construction materials and living space; excavation, dredging and land reclamation have followed. Mangroves have further suffered at the hands of the aquaculture industry, which has reduced mangrove stands by over 60% in the past century.

As the population of fishing villages has expanded, overfishing has depleted fish stocks. Meanwhile, local fishing communities continue to employ destructive methods such as homemade bombs (called '*bong bong*'), cyanide and chlorine. The result is a completely unsustainable fishing industry. According to the Asian Development Bank, certain areas in the Philippines have seen a 90% drop in trawler hauls, in what should otherwise be one of the world's most productive fisheries.

The Bohol Sea, the body of water between Bohol and Mindanao, hosts 19 cetacean species including sperm whales, pilot whales, Bryde's whales, melon-headed whales and even a blue whale, whose presence was only first officially recorded in 2010.

Pollution

According to the World Wildlife Fund (WWF) only about 10% of waste in the Philippines is treated or disposed of in an environmentally sound manner. Not surprisingly, water pollution is a growing problem for the country's groundwater, rivers, lakes and coastal areas. Only a third of Philippine river systems are considered suitable for the public water supply. Poor management, including bad planning and a lack of regulatory enforcement, is largely to blame.

Mining

There are an estimated 500,000 small-scale mines operating in the Philippines, many of them illegal, and, according to Human Rights Watch reports, many also using toxic mercury and child labour. At the other end of the scale are the huge mining conglomerates, which continue to lobby the government for more access. The Philippines is the world's leading exporter of nickel ore (gold, copper and chromite are also in abundance) and there are an estimated 236,000 Filipinos employed in the industry.

The 24sq km of Mt Hamiguitan Range Wildlife Sanctuary was declared a Unesco World Heritage site in 2014 (Mindanao's first) and an Asean Heritage Park in 2016. The reserve is home to Philippine eagles, tarsiers and cockatoos, as well as an immense number of other fauna and flora species.

The government claims that adequate safeguards are in place to prevent the social and environmental damage that has dogged past mining projects, such as the Marcopper disaster in 1996, which poisoned an entire river system. However, a number of environmental activists were killed during the Aquino administration by forces under military control. In 2007 Sibuyan Island councillor Armin Marin was shot dead on camera, surrounded by scores of witnesses, while leading a picket of anti-mining advocates. After five years of investigations and court hearings, the accused, a plain-clothed mining security officer, was given a three-year sentence for 'criminal negligence', then released early.

More recently, environmental activist turned Acting Environment Secretary Gina Lopez was denied confirmation to her post by Congress after moving aggressively against illegal mining practices. She ordered the closure of 28 operations and the cancellation of 75 government-mineral sharing agreements. President Duterte, to the chagrin of the companies, appointed Lopez and has spoken out against the environmental devastation caused by the mining (and logging) industry.

Survival Guide

Directory A–Z

Accessible Travel

Steps up to hotels, tiny cramped toilets, narrow doors and dysfunctional lifts are the norm outside of three-star-and-up hotels in Manila, Cebu and a handful of larger provincial cities. The same goes for restaurants, although mall restaurants tend to be more accessible.

Boarding any form of public or rural transport is likely to be fraught with difficulty.

On the other hand, most Filipinos are more than willing to lend a helping hand, and the cost of hiring a taxi for a day, and possibly an assistant as well, is not excessive.

Some resources for disabled persons travelling to the Philippines:

Disability Rights UK (http://disabilityrightsuk.org)

Mobility International USA (www.miusa.org)

National Council on Disability Affairs (http://www.ncda.gov.ph)

Society for Accessible Travel & Hospitality (SATH; www.sath.org)

Download Lonely Planet's free Accessible Travel guide from https://shop.lonely planet.com/categories/accessible-travel.com.

Accommodation

From homestays in basic nipa huts to modern boutique hotels in big cities, there's something for everyone in the Philippines.

The top end includes big-city Shangri-Las (including the actual one in Manila) to extravagant private island resorts where guests arrive by helicopter or float plane. The very bottom end includes cold water, windowless cells with paper-thin walls and neither fan nor air-con. Of course the vast majority of accommodation options are somewhere in between.

It's worth noting the very real divide between accommodation that caters to Filipino tourists and those that target foreigners. The former tend to be concrete with air-con, family-sized rooms and little attention to aesthetics, whereas the latter, or at least those owned by foreigners (most often Europeans), are usually more sophisticated

and tastefully done and utilise native-style features such as thatched roofs.

During the high season, reservations are recommended in popular tourist areas such as Boracay or El Nido. At other times, you should do fine walking in.

Resorts These range from ultraluxurious, the rival of any in Southeast Asia, to basic fan-cooled bungalows.

Hotels Many cater to the domestic market, which means generic concrete construction and air-con. Five-star hotels in Manila are truly sumptuous affairs.

Pensionnes Sort of a catch-all term referring to less expensive, independently owned hotels.

Hostels Those that target foreign travellers tend to be more comfortable and stylish, but also more expensive, than ones for primarily young Filipinos.

Costs & Seasons

Within the budget category, rooms for less than P500 are generally dorms or private fan-cooled rooms with a shared cold-water bathroom. Rooms between P700 and P1000 usually have a fan and private bathroom. Anything higher (and some within this range) should have both air-conditioning and a private bathroom.

High-season rates are from November to April or May. While prices in resort areas go down around 20% to 50% in the low season, they may double, triple or

---

PLAN YOUR STAY ONLINE

For more accommodation reviews by Lonely Planet authors, check out www.lonelyplanet.com. You'll find independent reviews, as well as recommendations on the best places to stay.

even quadruple during the 'superpeak' periods of Holy Week (Easter) and around New Year.

Chinese New Year (usually in February) and the Japanese holiday period of Golden Week (29 April to 5 May) are additional times of heavy travel that may cause price spikes in resort areas.

Booking Ahead

As more and more Filipinos travel it's becoming more difficult to just walk in and find a room in the most popular resort areas and touristy towns. Booking ahead is not a bad idea in the high season and is essential in 'superpeak' periods. That said, if you don't book ahead, even in the high season, you'll find something eventually.

Deposits

Many resorts, especially at the top end, require a deposit, often 100% but usually closer to 50%. This is usually nonrefundable if you cancel less than two weeks prior to your arrival. Annoyingly, a few still ask you to wire or direct-deposit the money into a Manila bank account, although fancier resorts will allow credit-card deposits.

Circumvent this by choosing another resort. Or consider just showing up without a reservation. Call the resort a day or two ahead to make sure there are vacancies (if you try this, have a backup resort in mind just in case).

Discounts & Promo Rates

A few potential money-saving tips for booking hotels in the Philippines:

Promo rates Especially during off-peak periods, hotels often offer 'promo rates' that they won't tell you about unless you ask. So always ask.

Walking in In many resort areas, the 'walk-in' (ie no reservation) rate is substantially cheaper than the reservation rate. Conversely, in some hotels the reservation rate is actually cheaper than the walk-in rate. It always helps to ask.

Websites Direct booking on a hotel's website is often, but not always, cheaper than booking through online travel agencies. At any rate it helps to check.

Fan v air-con Some midrange places have two-tiered pricing for the same room. Even if not formally offered, you can say no to the air-con and request a fan for cheaper rates.

Children

Filipinos are simply crazy about kids, and are rather fond of parents, too – you and your offspring will be the focus of many conversations, and your children won't lack playful company. See Lonely Planet's *Travel with Children* for useful advice about travel with kids.

➜ You can buy disposable nappies (diapers) and infant formula in most towns and all cities, but be sure to stock up on such things before heading off the beaten track.

➜ Many hotels and resorts offer family rooms (this is how Filipinos travel), and can provide cots on request.

➜ Discreet breastfeeding in public is acceptable in all areas except some conservative Muslim areas in the south.

➜ It is almost impossible to arrange a taxi with a child seat.

➜ Many restaurants can provide a high chair upon request.

Customs Regulations

➜ Firearms and pornography are forbidden.

➜ You can bring up to 2L of alcohol and up to 400 cigarettes (or two tins of tobacco) into the country without paying duty.

➜ Foreign currency of more than US$10,000 and local currency of more than P10,000 must be declared upon entry or exit.

Electricity

Type A
120V/60Hz

Embassies & Consulates

The **Philippines Department of Foreign Affairs** (DFA; www.dfa.gov.ph) website lists all Philippine embassies and consulates abroad, and all foreign embassies and consulates in the Philippines.

Some countries that require Western visitors to

have visas for entry maintain embassies in Manila, including China, India, Myanmar and Vietnam.

Australian Embassy (Map p62; ✆02-757 8100; www.philippines.embassy.gov.au; 23rd fl, Tower 2, RCBC Plaza, 6819 Ayala Ave, Makati) Manila

Canadian Embassy (Map p62; ✆02-857 9000; www.manila.gc.ca; Levels 6-8, Tower 2, RCBC Plaza, 6819 Ayala Ave, Makati) Manila

Canadian Consulate (✆032-254 4749; cebu@international.gc.ca; RD Corporate Center, 96 Governor MC Cuenco Ave, Banilad; ☺9-11am Mon-Fri) Cebu

Dutch Embassy (Map p62; ✆02-786 6666; www.netherlandsworldwide.nl; 26th fl, BDO Equitable Tower, 8751 Paseo de Roxas, Makati) Manila

Dutch Consulate (✆032-346 1823; zeny.monterola@aboitiz.com; Metaphil Bldg, Tipolo, Mandaue; ☺9am-noon Mon-Fri) Cebu

French Embassy (Map p62; ✆02-857 6900; www.ambafrance-ph.org; 16th fl, Pacific Star Bldg, cnr Gil Puyat & Makati Aves, Makati) Manila

German Embassy (Map p62; ✆02-702 3000; www.manila.diplo.de; 25/F Tower 2, RCBC Plaza, 6819 Ayala Ave, Makati) Manila

German Consulate (✆032-236 1318, 0929 667 6386; www.honorarkonsul-cebu.com; Ford's Inn Hotel, AS Fortuna St; ☺9am-noon Tue-Thu) Cebu City

---

EATING PRICE RANGES

The following price ranges refer to the cost of a main course. Prices in Manila, Boracay and El Nido tend to be higher.

$ less than P150

$$ P150–P300

$$$ more than P300

Indonesian Consulate (✆082-297 2930; www.kemlu.go.id/davaocity/id/default.aspx; General Ecoland Subdivision, Matina; ☺8:30am-4:30pm Mon-Fri) Davao

Malaysian Consulate (Map p366; ✆082-221 4050; www.kln.gov.my/web/phl_davaocity; 3rd fl, Florentine Bldg, A Bonifacio St; ☺8am-4pm Mon-Fri) Davao

New Zealand Embassy (Map p62; ✆02-234 3800; www.nzembassy.com; 35th fl, Zuellig Bldg, Makati Ave, Makati City) Manila

UK Embassy (Map p50; ✆02-858 2200; www.gov.uk; 120 Upper McKinley Rd, McKinley Hill, Taguig)

US Embassy (Map p68; ✆02-301 2000; http://manila.usembassy.gov; 1201 Roxas Blvd, Ermita) Manila

---

Insurance

A travel-insurance policy to cover theft, loss and medical problems is a good idea. Note that some policies specifically exclude 'dangerous activities', which can include scuba diving, motorcycling and even trekking.

Internet Access

Theoretically, wi-fi and 4G internet access is available in much of the Philippines. However, the reality is a different story. It's frequently not working, intermittent or very slow, especially in the provinces (Palawan being the poster child for dysfunctional wi-fi).

That huge caveat aside, most hotels, cafes and restaurants in touristy areas and provincial centres provide free wi-fi.

For smartphone users, local SIM cards with data (4G) are easy to purchase, and data is cheap at less than P50 per day.

Not travelling with a computer? You can still find internet cafes in most decent-sized cities. Business

hotels and an increasing number of boutique hotels and hostels have computers for guests to use.

Legal Matters

➡ Drugs are illegal and very risky, especially in the era of President Duterte's 'drug war'. Be smart and avoid any and all drugs, including marijuana.

➡ Filipinos litter like it's going out of style but that doesn't mean you should join them, and you can be fined for littering in some cities.

➡ Small bribes remain a common way of getting out of traffic infractions, although Duterte has promised to eliminate the practice.

➡ Should you find yourself in trouble, your first recourse is your embassy.

LGBTIQ+ Travellers

Bakla (gay men) and *binalaki* or *tomboy* (lesbians) are almost universally accepted in the Philippines. Harrassment is rare and you can usually be as 'out' as you want to be.

The traditional nexus of gay life is the Malate district of Manila, specifically around the intersection of J Nakpil St and M Orosa St. While there is still a scene there, the more popular clubs and bars have moved uptown to the Fort ('BGC') district. Other major cities such as Cebu also have well-established gay centres.

There's a roving pride march every year in Manila in late June.

Online gay and lesbian resources for the Philippines include:

Outrage Magazine (www.outragemag.com)

Utopia Asian Gay & Lesbian Resources (www.utopia-asia.com)

Travel Gay Asia (www.travelgayasia.com)

B-Change (ww.b-change.org) is a social enterprise group that works to promote LGBTI rights.

For Manila-related events, the best site is www.thegay passport.com/gay-manila.

Maps

➡ For a map of the entire country, the best of the lot is probably Nelles Verlag's 1:1,500,000-scale *Philippines* (US$20), which is available internationally.

➡ For local travel, E-Z Maps and Accu-Map produce excellent maps covering most major islands, large cities and tourist areas. They are widely available at hotels, airports, bookshops and petrol stations.

➡ To buy (or see online) highly detailed topographical maps of virtually any region, contact the government's mapping agency, **Namria** (Map p50; ☎02-887 5466; www.namria.gov.ph; Lawton Ave, Fort Bonifacio, Makati, Manila).

Money

ATMs dispensing pesos are widely available. Credit cards are accepted at hotels, restaurants and some shops in all but remote areas.

ATMs

➡ Prevalent in any decent-sized provincial city; dispense pesos.

➡ More remote towns do not have ATMs.

➡ The most prevalent ATMs that accept most Western bank cards belong to Banco de Oro (BDO), Bank of the Philippine Islands (BPI) and Metrobank.

➡ Standard ATM charge is P200 per withdrawal.

➡ Most ATMs have a P10,000 to P15,000 per-transaction withdrawal limit. Exception: HSBC ATMs in Manila and Cebu let

you take out P40,000 per transaction.

Cash

➡ Cash in US dollars is a good thing to have in case you get stuck in an area with no working ATM. Other currencies, such as the euro or UK pound, are more difficult to change outside of the bigger cities.

➡ 'Sorry, no change' becomes a very familiar line in the provinces. Stock up on coins and P20, P50 and P100 notes at every opportunity.

Credit Cards

➡ Major credit cards are accepted by most hotels, high-end restaurants and businesses in Manila, Cebu City and other large cities.

➡ Outside of large cities, you may be charged an extra 3% to 5% for credit-card transactions.

➡ Most Philippine banks will let you take a cash advance on your card.

Tipping

Restaurants 10% service charge added to bill in cities and tourist hotspots. Otherwise leave 5% to 10%.

Taxis Round up taxi fares, but consider tipping more (P50 to P70) for honest taxi drivers who turn on the meter.

Hotels Not expected, but slide P50 to porters or leave a few

hundred pesos in the staff tip box at resorts.

Guides Always tip your guides, as they can really use it.

Bargaining

A modest amount of negotiating is expected in many outdoor markets, especially where tourist handicrafts are sold. However, prices for food commodities are usually set.

Bargaining is the rule when hiring motorbikes, or hiring tricycles, bangkas or taxis for the day. Bargaining may also bear fruit when you're walking into hotels, especially in resort areas in the low season.

Opening Hours

Offices and banks are closed on public holidays, although shops and malls stay open (exception: Maundy Thursday and Good Friday, when virtually the entire country closes down).

Banks 9am to 4.30pm Monday to Friday (most ATMs 24 hours)

Bars 6pm to late

Embassies and consulates 9am to 5pm Monday to Friday

Post offices 8am to 5pm Monday to Friday, to 1pm Saturday

Public offices 8am to 5pm Monday to Friday

Restaurants 7am or 8am to 10pm or 11pm

Shopping Malls 10am to 9.30pm

Supermarkets 9am to 7pm or 8pm

Post

On average, it takes two weeks or so for mail sent from the Philippines to reach the US or Europe. Mail sent from abroad to the Philippines is slower and less reliable and you're better off sending via FedEx or UPS.

Public Holidays

New Year's Day 1 January

People Power Day 25 February

Maundy Thursday Varies; around March or April

Good Friday Varies; the day after Maundy Thursday

Araw ng Kagitingan (Bataan Day) 9 April

Labour Day 1 May

Independence Day 12 June

Ninoy Aquino Day 21 August

National Heroes Day Last Sunday in August

All Saints' Day 1 November

End of Ramadan Varies; depends on Islamic calendar

Bonifacio Day 30 November

Christmas Day 25 December

Rizal Day 30 December

New Year's Eve 31 December

Safe Travel

The Philippines certainly has more than its share of dangers. Typhoons, earthquakes, volcano eruptions, landslides and other natural disasters can wreak havoc with your travel plans – or worse if you happen to be in the wrong place at the wrong time.

➡ Keep an eye on the news and be prepared to alter travel plans to avoid trouble spots.

➡ Mindanao (the central and southwest regions in particular) and the Sulu Archipelago are sometimes the scenes of clashes between the army and Muslim separatist groups.

➡ Manila in particular is known for scams targeting tourists.

Government Travel Advice

The following government websites offer travel advisories and information on current hot spots.

Australian Department of Foreign Affairs (www.smarttraveller.gov.au)

Canadian Department of Foreign Affairs (www.voyage.gc.ca)

German Foreign Office (www.auswaertiges-amt.de)

New Zealand Ministry of Foreign Affairs (www.safetravel.govt.nz)

UK Foreign Office (www.gov.uk/foreign-travel-advice)

US State Department (http://travel.state.gov)

Telephone

The Philippine Long-Distance Telephone Company (PLDT) operates the Philippines' fixed-line network. International calls can be made from any PLDT office for US$0.40 per minute. Local calls cost almost nothing, and long-distance domestic calls are also very reasonable.

PRACTICALITIES

Newspapers The best of the broadsheets are the *Philippine Daily Inquirer* (www.inquirer.net), *Business World* (www.bworldonline.com) and *Business Mirror* (www.businessmirror.com.ph). Other big national dailies include the *Philippine Star* (www.philstar.com) and *Manila Bulletin* (www.mb.com.ph). Online, Rappler (www.rappler.com) is an excellent source for breaking news as well as feature stories. The Philippine Center for Investigative Journalism (www.pcij.org) publishes hard-hitting investigative pieces.

Radio Manila radio stations worth listening to: Monster Radio RX 93.1 for contemporary popular music and Jam 88.3 for more indie and alternative.

TV About seven major channels broadcast from Manila (including ABS-CBN and GMA), sometimes in English, sometimes in Tagalog. Most midrange hotels have cable TV with access to between 20 and 120 channels, including some obscure regional channels, a couple of Filipino and international movie channels, and the big global news and sports channels such as BBC and ESPN.

Smoking Filipinos like to smoke and until recently they could do it just about anywhere. President Rodrigo Duterte has put an end to that, enacting legislation in 2017 that bans smoking and vaping in all public places and spaces – including many outdoor parks. However, in practice it may take time for establishments to adapt to the new law.

Weights and measures The Philippines generally uses the metric system. Inches, feet and yards (for textiles) are common in everyday use for measuring things.

Mobile Phones

Mobile (cell) phones are ubiquitous, and half the country spends much of its time furiously texting the other half. Local SIM cards are widely available and can be loaded up cheaply with data and phone credit. Roaming is possible but expensive.

➡ Prepaid SIM cards cost as little as P40 and come preloaded with about the same amount of text credits.

➡ The two companies with the best national coverage are **Globe** (www.globe.com.ph) and **Smart** (www.smart.com.ph).

➡ Text messages on all mobile networks cost P1 to P2 per message; local calls cost P7.50 per minute (less if calling within a mobile network).

➡ International text messages cost P15, and international calls cost US$0.40 per minute.

➡ To dial a landline or mobile number from a mobile phone dial ☎0 or +63 followed by the three-digit prefix and the seven-digit number.

➡ Mobile prefixes always begin with a 9 (eg 917, 906).

➡ Roaming with your home phone is another, though likely very expensive, option.

Phonecards

PLDT cards such as 'Budget' (for international calls), 'Pwede' and 'Touch' cards can be used to make calls from any PLDT landline or from card-operated PLDT phones located in hotel foyers, commercial centres and shopping malls. Calls to the US using the Budget card cost only P3 per minute; other international destinations cost slightly more. Pwede and Touch cards allow dirt-cheap domestic calls from any PLDT landline or payphone.

Important Numbers

For domestic long-distance calls or calls to mobile numbers dial 0 followed by the city code (or mobile prefix) and then the seven-digit number.

Useful dialling codes from land lines:

Philippines country code ☎63
International dialling code ☎00
PLDT directory ☎101171
International operator ☎108
Domestic operator ☎109

Time

The Philippines is eight hours ahead of GMT/UTC. Thus, noon in Manila is 1am in New York, 7am in London, noon in Hong Kong and 2pm in Sydney.

Toilets

➡ Toilets are commonly called a 'CR', an abbreviation of the delightfully euphemistic 'comfort room'.

➡ Other than at some bus terminals and ports, public toilets are virtually non-existent, so aim for one of the ubiquitous fast-food restaurants should you need a room of comfort.

➡ Most toilets are sit-down affairs, but in remote areas some might not have toilet seats.

➡ In Filipino, men are *lalake* and women are *babae*.

➡ Filipino men will often avail themselves of the nearest outdoor wall – hence the signs scrawled in many places: *'Bawal Ang Umihi Dito!'* ('No Pissing Here!').

Tourist Information

The official organ of Philippine tourism is the **Philippine Department of Tourism** (www.visitmyphilippines.com), with headquarters in **Makati** (DOT; Map p62; ☎02-459 5200; www.visitmyphilippines.com; JB Bldg, 351 Sen Gil Puyat Ave, Makati; ⊗7am-6pm Mon-Sat) and regional offices in provincial centres. Additional DOT booths can be found at airport arrivals in Manila and Cebu City.

Visas

A free 30-day visa is issued on arrival for most nationalities. You can extend, for a fee, in major provincial centres, or extend upon arrival at the airport.

Visa Extensions

Visa rules and fees remain fluid, so check the latest rules and regulations on the website of the Bureau of Immigration, whose head office is in **Manila** (BOI; Map p54; ☎02-465 2400; www.immigration.gov.ph; Magallanes Dr, Intramuros; ⊗8am-5.30pm Mon-Fri).

In a nutshell, the situation is as follows:

➡ It is easy to extend your initial 30-day visa (technically a visa 'waiver') for an additional 29 days. This costs about P2200 for most nationalities.

➡ Thereafter, you may apply for additional one-month, two-month or six-month extensions. The cost for the first month is about P4000 and includes purchase of an 'ACR I-Card' identity card valid for one year; subsequent extensions cost P1000 to P2000 per month.

➡ You can apply for visa extensions at the head office in Manila or at any BOI provincial office. Most regional hubs and touristy areas such as Boracay have BOI offices; a full list of the regional offices can be found on the BOI website.

➡ You can apply for your initial 29-day extension at the airport upon arrival in the Philippines; just request this service once you reach the immigration control booth.

This may only work at the Manila and Cebu airports.

➡ It may or may not be possible to extend retroactively (and pay at least a P1010 fine in addition to retroactive visa-extension fees) upon your departure from the Philippines – we wouldn't chance it.

➡ The maximum stay for most nationalities that qualify for the visa waiver is 36 months.

➡ Dress respectably when applying; shorts and flip-flops are definite no-no's.

➡ The visa process is generally painless, especially in provincial offices, but you can also pay a travel agent to handle everything for you.

Onward Tickets

Be prepared to show the airline at your point of departure to the Philippines a ticket for onward travel. If you don't have one, most airlines make you buy one on the spot.

Volunteering

Coral Cay Conservation (www.coralcay.org) Works to protect coral reefs in Southern Leyte.

Gawad Kalinga (✍in Manila 02-533 2217; www.gk1world.com/ph) GK's mission is building not just homes but entire communities for the poor and homeless. Volunteers can build houses or get involved in a host of other activities. Contact the volunteer coordinator, Fatima Amamo (maamano@gawadkalinga.com).

Habitat for Humanity (✍02-846 2177; www.habitat.org) Builds houses for the poor all over the country, concentrating on disaster-affected areas.

Hands On Manila (✍02-843 7044; www.handsonmanila.org) Always looking for volunteers to help with disaster assistance and other projects throughout the Philippines.

Haribon Foundation (✍02-911 6088; http://haribon.org.ph) A longstanding conservation organisation focused on scientific research and community empowerment programs.

Rise Above Foundation (✍032-255 1063; www.rise above-cebu.org; 252 I Limkak-eng St, Happy Valley Subd, V Rama Ave, Cebu City) Housing, education and vocational training projects in Cebu. We've had positive feedback from recent volunteers.

Save Palawan Seas (✍0917 824 1488; www.savepalawan seasfoundation.org) NGO owned by one of largest pearl producers in Philippines and supported by **Flower Island Beach Resort** (✍0917 504 5567; www.flowerisland-resort.com; cottages incl all meals per person with fan/air-con from P7000/8500; ❄🐾🛜) 🐾, dedicated to educating local fishermen in Palawan about the dangers of destructive fishing and agricultural practices.

Springboard Foundation (✍02-821 5440; www.spring board-foundation.org) Not a volunteer organisation, per se, but has ties to many charity organisations doing volunteer work in the Philippines.

Stairway Foundation (www.stairwayfoundation.org) Qualified volunteers can apply for long-term assignments (at least six months) to work with formerly homeless children out of a base in Puerto Galera, Mindoro. Most kids were rescued from the streets of Manila. In Puerto Galera they learn life skills, with the long-term goal of being reunited with their families. One program involves teaching the kids about marine conservation through PG-based NGO EACY Dive.

Volunteer for the Visayas (✍0917 846 6967; www.visayans.org) Runs various volunteer programs around Tacloban, Leyte.

World Wide Opportunities on Organic Farms (✍0905 643 4069; www.wwoof.ph) There are several WWOOF sites in the Philippines, including the **Julia Campbell Agroforest Memorial Park** (✍+1 512-305-3367, in US +1 210-859-4342; www.bantaicivetcoffee.com) and the **ENCA Farm** (✍0919 834 4542, in the US +1 425 698 5808; www.encaorganicfarm.com), both in North Luzon.

WWF Philippines (www.wwf.org.ph) Contact the organisation to get involved with biodiversity and species-conservation projects.

Women Travellers

Foreign women travellers will generally have few problems in most of the Philippines, although they might get more attention than they're used to, particularly if travelling solo outside major tourist areas. This isn't necessarily particular to the Philippines, but it's probably a good idea to check on the reputation of guides if booking overnight trips.

Work

There are scores of expats in the Philippines, but the vast majority work for multinational organisations and are sent by their jobs. It's not really the place to show up without a job and expect that you'll find something. There's a fair amount of labour-protection legislation in place and obtaining a work visa can be difficult.

On the other hand, the Philippines is fertile ground for retirees, with an accommodating climate and several methods for obtaining a retiree's visa.

Transport

GETTING THERE & AWAY

Most people enter the Philippines via one of the three main international airports:

Manila Ninoy Aquino International Airport (NAIA), by far the most popular and best connected to the rest of the country.

Cebu A good option if you are heading to the Visayas.

Clark Budget-flight hub north of Manila, expanding and becoming more popular.

A handful of international flights also go straight to Kalibo, near Boracay; Bohol's new airport on Panglao Island; Iloilo City on the island of Panay; and Davao in southern Mindanao.

Flights, cars and tours can be booked online at lonely planet.com/bookings.

Air

Book well in advance if you plan to arrive in the Philippines from mid- to late December – expat Filipinos flood the islands to visit their families during Christmas and New Year. The lead-up to Chinese New Year in late January or early February can also get congested.

Airports & Airlines

Ninoy Aquino International Airport (www.miaa.gov.ph) The busiest international airport in the country and the one you're most likely to fly into and out of. Even after recent upgrades to the main international terminal, Terminal 1, the airport receives negative reviews from travellers.

Mactan-Cebu International Airport (www.mactan-cebuairport. com.ph) Cebu's airport is second only to Manila in terms of air traffic, but way ahead in terms of user-friendliness. Note that the airport is actually on Mactan Island, 15km east of Cebu City.

Clark International Airport (http://crk.clarkairport.com) Near Angeles, a two-hour bus ride north of Metro Manila. It's traditionally a hub for low-cost airlines but an increasing number of legacy Asian and Middle Eastern carriers are flying here. There's talk of a high-speed railway to Manila but that's still some way off. Airlines serving Clark with international flights include Cebu Pacific, Air Asia and Qatar Airways.

Davao International Airport (www.davaointernational.com) For now, only SilkAir has flights to Singapore; routes to Malaysia might begin operating.

Kalibo International Airport (www.kalibointernational.com) Useful direct flights to Kalibo, near Boracay, from Beijing, Kunming, Hong Kong, Seoul, Shanghai, Singapore and other Asian hubs.

Besides the international airlines that come up on any

TERMINAL DIFFICULTIES

Navigating Manila's convoluted **Ninoy Aquino International Airport** (NAIA; Map p50; www.miaa.gov.ph) is a nightmare. NAIA's four terminals are linked only by busy public roads, and shuttle vans linking them are unreliable, so take a taxi between terminals if you're in a hurry.

Pay close attention to which terminal your airline uses and allow plenty of time between connecting flights if you have to switch terminals. Most international flights use recently upgraded but still dismal Terminal 1. However, international flights run by Cebu Pacific, ANA, Cathay Pacific, Delta, Emirates Air, KLM and Singapore Airlines use newer Terminal 3.

Some domestic flights run by Philippine Airlines (PAL), and all domestic flights run by Cebu Pacific, also use T3. Meanwhile, all PAL international and some PAL domestic flights use yet another terminal, the Centennial Terminal 2.

Lastly, all AirAsia and Skyjet flights, and 'Cebgo'-branded Cebu Pacific flights, use the ancient Manila Domestic Terminal (Terminal 4), located near Terminal 3.

internet flight search, the following regional budget and Philippine carriers are worth checking out for flights into and out of the country:

AirAsia (☏02-722 2742; www. airasia.com; NAIA Terminal 4)

Cebu Pacific (☏02-702 0888; www.cebupacificair.com)

Jetstar (☏02-810 4744; www. jetstar.com)

Philippine Airlines (PAL;☏02-855 8888; www.philippine airlines.com; NAIA Terminal 2)

Sea

The only international route open to foreigners is Zamboanga to Sandakan in the Malaysian state of Sabah. **Aleson Shipping Lines** (☏062-991 2687; www. aleson-shipping.com; 172 Veterans Ave, Zamboanga) leaves Zamboanga on Monday and (sometimes) Thursday, and departs Sandakan on Tuesday and (sometimes) Friday (economy/cabin P2900/3300, 23 hours).

Cruise ships frequently dock in Manila and elsewhere.

GETTING AROUND

Air

AirAsia (☏02-722 2742; www. airasia.com; NAIA Terminal 4), **Philippine Airlines** (PAL; ☏02-855 8888; www.philippine airlines.com; NAIA Terminal 2) and **Cebu Pacific** (☏02-702 0888; www.cebupacificair. com) are the main domestic carriers. **Skyjet** (☏in Manila 02-863 1333; www.skyjetair. com; NAIA Terminal 4) is a newer carrier with good deals on some key routes

such as Manila–Caticlan and Manla–Busuanga.

Other carriers:

Air Juan (Map p72;☏02-718 8111; www.airjuan.com; CCP Complex Jetty, Pasay) Runs small sea planes (usually six-seaters) out of its terminal in Manila, and is easing regional travel by opening direct routes between key provincial tourist towns (such as Busuanga–Caticlan, Puerto Galera–Caticlan and Cebu City–Bantayan).

Air Swift (Map p50;☏02-318 5942; http://air-swift.com; Andrews Ave, Pasay) Serves El Nido from Manila, Caticlan and Cebu City; owned by luxury resort operator El Nido Resorts, but these days has plenty of space for nonguests.

Northsky Air (in Tuguegarao ☏078-304 6148; www.north skyair.com) Scheduled flights connect Tuguegarao (North Luzon) with Batanes and the remote Sierra Madre towns of Maconacon and Palanan in Isabela Province, North Luzon. Also available for charter.

Sky Pasada (☏in Cebu 032-912 3333; www.skypasada.com) Links several cities in North Luzon from its hub in Binalonan, Pangasinan (2½ hours north of Manila), including Vigan, Tuguegarao, Basco (Batanes), Palanan and Maconacon, using 15- to 19-seat turboprop planes. Planes available for charter.

Booking Tips

➡ Pay attention to baggage allowances – some routes and airlines are more restrictive than others.

➡ Pre-pay for your baggage online or you'll pay triple at the check-in counter.

➡ If you book a month or so in advance, you'll rarely pay more than P1500 (about US$30) for a one-way ticket on the main carriers (ex-

ceptions on touristy routes such as Manila–Caticlan and Manila–Siargao, and during peak domestic-travel periods).

➡ On most airlines you will not pay a premium for one-way tickets nor save money by purchasing a round-trip ticket.

➡ Flight routes are skewed towards Manila and (to a lesser extent) Cebu. If you want to fly between any other cities you'll likely have to purchase two tickets and transfer through one of those hubs. Air Juan's inter-regional flights are improving the situation somewhat.

➡ Don't plan too tight a schedule for connecting flights – flight delays are a fact of life in the Philippines.

➡ Typhoons and other adverse weather often ground planes from July to December – some routes are more susceptible than others.

➡ A good way to avoid delays is to depart painfully early in the morning, before runway congestion disrupts schedules.

Bicycle

If you're away from the traffic and exhaust fumes of major cities, cycling can be a great way to get around quieter, less-visited islands.

➡ You can take bicycles on domestic flights (you may have to partially disassemble the bicycle), but take heed of the baggage allowance on small planes.

➡ If there's room, you can stow your bike on a bus or jeepney, usually for a small charge.

➡ Depending on where you are, mountain bikes can be hired for P300 to P700 per day, with price very much linked to quality.

➡ In the big cities you will find bicycle shops where you can purchase brand-new bikes of varying quality. Outdoor-gear shops (most malls have at least one) are good places to enquire about local cycling clubs and events.

Boat

The islands of the Philippines are linked by an incredible network of ferry routes, and prices are generally affordable. Ferries usually take the form of motorised outriggers (known locally as bangkas), speedy 'fast-craft' vessels, roll-on, roll-off ferries (ROROs; car ferries) and, for long-haul journeys, vast multidecked passenger ferries. It's worth highlighting the mega company **2GO Travel** (www.travel.2go.com.ph), which serves the majority of major destinations in the Philippines.

Most ferry terminals have a small fee (P20 on average); Manila's is P95.

You can check out the real-time locations of the various larger ferries plying the waters at www.marine traffic.com. The website www.schedule.ph is not entirely comprehensive but it's a good place to start for ferry schedules.

Bangkas The jeepneys of the sea, also known as pumpboats. They are small wooden boats with two wooden or bamboo outriggers. Bangka ferries ply

regular routes between islands and are also available for hire per day for diving, snorkelling, sightseeing or just getting around. The engines on these boats can be deafeningly loud, so bring earplugs if you're sensitive to noise. They also aren't the most stable in rough seas, but on some islands they're preferable to travelling overland. Time schedules should be taken with a grain of salt.

'Fastcraft' These are passenger only, and are mainly used on popular short-haul routes; they cut travel times by half but usually cost twice as much as slower RORO ferries. One modern convenience used to excess on these spiffy ships is air-conditioning, which is permanently set to 'arctic' – take a sweater or fleece.

ROROs Popular on medium-haul routes, especially along the so-called 'Nautical Highway' running from Manila to Davao in southern Mindanao. ROROs are slow but, in good weather, are the most enjoyable form of ocean transport, as (unlike most fastcraft) they allow you to sit outside in the open air and watch the ocean drift by.

Passenger Liners Multidecked long-haul liners, which carry up to 4000 passengers as well as cars. They are pretty reliable but you'll need to be prepared for changes in itineraries due to adverse weather conditions or maintenance.

Tickets

➡ Booking ahead is essential for long-haul liners and can be done at ticket offices or travel agencies in most cities.

➡ For fastcraft and bangka ferries, tickets can usually be bought at the pier before departure (exception: book El Nido–Coron ferries ahead in the high season).

➡ Passenger ferries offer several levels of comfort and cost. Bunks on or below deck in 3rd or 'economy' class should be fine, as long as the ship isn't overcrowded. First class nets you a two-person stateroom.

➡ Before purchasing your ticket, it pays to ask about 'promo rates' (discounts). Student and senior-citizen discounts usually only apply to Filipino citizens.

Bus & Van

➡ Philippine buses come in all shapes and sizes. Bus depots are dotted throughout towns and the countryside, and most buses will stop if you wave them down.

➡ Bus 'terminals' also run the gamut. Some are well-secured large garagelike structures with destinations clearly signposted and even ticket booths, whereas

---

FERRY SAFETY

For the most part, ferries are an easy, enjoyable way to hop between islands in the Philippines, but ferry accidents are not unknown.

In May 2008 a Sulpicio Lines ferry went down off Romblon in Typhoon Frank; fewer than 60 passengers survived and more than 800 perished. A large 2GO Ferry vessel collided with a cargo ship off Cebu in August 2013, resulting in more than 115 deaths. And in 2015 more than 60 people were killed when an overloaded bangka ferry bound for Pilar, Camotes Islands, from Ormoc, Leyte, tipped over in relatively calm seas.

Sulpicio Lines was also responsible for the sinking of the *Doña Paz* in 1987, in which almost 4500 people are believed to have perished. It's still the largest peacetime maritime disaster in history.

Bad weather, lax regulations and maintenance, equipment breakdowns, overcrowding and a general culture of fatalism are to blame for most accidents. It's best to follow your instincts – if the boat looks crowded, it is, and if the sailing conditions seem wrong, they are. Bangkas during stormy weather are especially scary. It's always worth checking that life jackets are on board.

CLIMATE CHANGE & TRAVEL

Every form of transport that relies on carbon-based fuel generates CO_2, the main cause of human-induced climate change. Modern travel is dependent on aeroplanes, which might use less fuel per kilometre per person than most cars but travel much greater distances. The altitude at which aircraft emit gases (including CO_2) and particles also contributes to their climate change impact. Many websites offer 'carbon calculators' that allow people to estimate the carbon emissions generated by their journey and, for those who wish to do so, to offset the impact of the greenhouse gases emitted with contributions to portfolios of climate-friendly initiatives throughout the world. Lonely Planet offsets the carbon footprint of all staff and author travel.

others are nothing more than a few run-down outdoor sheds with drivers clamouring for your business.

→ More services run in the morning – buses on unsealed roads may *only* run in the morning, especially in remote areas. Night services, including deluxe 27-seaters, are common between Manila and major provincial hubs in Luzon, and in Mindanao.

→ Air-con minivans (along with jeepneys) shadow bus routes in many parts of the Philippines (especially Bicol, Leyte, Cebu, Palawan and Mindanao) and in some cases have replaced buses altogether. However, you may have to play a waiting game until the vehicles are full.

→ Minivans are a lot quicker than buses, but also more expensive and cramped.

→ As in most countries, it pays to mind your baggage while buses load and unload.

→ Reservations aren't usually necessary; however, they're essential on the deluxe night buses heading to/from Manila (book these at least two days in advance, if possible, at the bus terminal).

→ Bus and van tickets on some popular routes – such as Manila–Banaue (North Luzon), Manila–Bicol (Southeast Luzon) and Puerto Princesa–El Nido (Palawan) – can be reserved online through booking sites such as www.pinoytravel.com.ph or www.biyaheroes.com.

Car & Motorcycle

If time is short, driving yourself is a quicker option than relying on jeepneys and other public transport, but it's not for the faint of heart. The manic Filipino driving style is on full display in Manila, and driving on the congested streets of the capital definitely takes some getting used to.

International car-hire companies are in the larger cities; however, these are exactly the places where you probably don't want to drive. But if you want to get out of the city you have to begin somewhere – rates start at around P3000 per day. Fuel costs P40 to P50 per litre.

Defensive driving is the order of the day: even relatively quiet provincial roads are packed with myriad obstacles. Right of way can be confusing to determine and obedience to stop signals is selective. Most drivers roll into intersections before or without checking for oncoming traffic.

It's best to avoid driving at night if you can, not least because tricycles, jeepneys and even large trucks are often without lights (many drivers believe that driving without lights saves petrol), not to mention the issue of potential robberies in political trouble spots.

Motorcycle

Small and midsized islands such as Camiguin, Siquijor and Bohol beg to be explored by motorcycle. You can even ride down to the Visayas via the 'Nautical Highway' – the system of car ferries that links many islands – and enjoy pleasant riding on larger islands such as Cebu and Negros.

Most touristy areas have a few easy-to-find shops or guesthouses renting out motorcyles – usually in the form of Chinese- or Japanese-made motorcycles (75cc to 125cc). The typical rate is P400 to P500 per day, but you'll likely be asked for more in particularly popular resort areas. Ask for a helmet; these aren't always automatically included.

In more remote areas, just ask around – even if there's no rental shop, you can always find somebody willing to part with their motorcycle for the day for a fee.

Driving Licence

Your home country's driving licence, which you should carry, is legally valid for 90 days in the Philippines. Technically, you are supposed to have an International Driving Permit for any period longer than this, and some car-hire companies may require you to have this permit when hiring vehicles from them.

Insurance

Philippine law requires that when hiring a car you have third-party car insurance with a Philippines car-insurance company. This can be arranged with the car-hire company. You are required to have a minimum of P750,000 of insurance.

Road Rules

Driving is on the right-hand side of the road. With the exception of the expressways out of Manila, most roads in the Philippines are single lane, which necessitates a lot of overtaking. Local drivers do not always overtake safely. If an overtaker coming the other way refuses to get out of your lane, they're expecting you to give way by moving onto the shoulder. It's always wise to do so.

Local Transport

Jeepney

The first jeepneys were modified army jeeps left behind by the Americans after WWII. They have been customised with Filipino touches such as chrome horses, banks of coloured headlights, radio antennae, paintings of the Virgin Mary and neon-coloured scenes from action comic books.

➜ Jeepneys form the main urban transport in most cities and complement the bus services between regional centres.

➜ Within towns, the starting fare is usually P8, rising modestly for trips outside of town. Routes are clearly written on the side of the jeepney.

➜ Jeepneys have a certain quirky cultural appeal, but from a tourist's perspective they have one humongous flaw: you can barely see anything through the narrow open slats that pass as windows. The best seats are up the front next to the driver.

Light Rail

Some parts of Manila are served by an elevated railway system, akin to rapid transit metro.

Taxi

Metered taxis are common in Manila and most major provincial hubs. Flagfall is P40, and a 15-minute trip rarely costs more than P150. Airport taxi flagfall is usually P70.

Most taxi drivers will turn on the meter; if they don't, politely request that they do. If the meter is 'broken' or your taxi driver says the fare is 'up to you', the best strategy is to get out and find another cab (or offer a low-ball price). Rigged taxi meters are also becoming more common, although it must be said that most taxi drivers are honest.

An alternative is to arrange a taxi and driver for the day – from P2000 to P4000 – through your hotel or another trustworthy source.

Though it's not common, there have been cases of taxi passengers being robbed at gun- or knifepoint, sometimes with the driver in cahoots with the culprits or the driver himself holding up the passengers.

Get out of a cab straight away (in a secure populated area, of course, not in the middle of nowhere or in a slum area) if you suspect you're being taken for a ride in more ways than one.

Tricycles, Kalesa & Habal-Habal

Tricycles Found in most cities and towns, the tricycle is the Philippine rickshaw – a little, roofed sidecar bolted to a motorcycle. The standard fare for local trips in most provincial towns is P10. Tricycles that wait around in front of malls, restaurants and hotels will attempt to charge five to 10 times that for a 'special trip'. Avoid these by standing on the roadside and flagging down a passing P10 tricycle. You can also charter tricycles for about P300 per hour or P150 per 10km if you're heading out of town.

Pedicabs Many towns also have nonmotorised push tricycles, alternatively known as pedicabs, *put-put* or *padyak*, for shorter trips.

Kalesa Two-wheeled horse carriages found in Manila's Chinatown and Intramuros, Vigan (North Luzon) and Cebu City (where they're also known as tartanillas).

Habal-habal These are essentially motorcycle taxis with extended seats (literally translated as 'pigs copulating', after the level of intimacy attained when sharing a seat with four people). Also known as 'singles' in some regions, they function like tricycles, only cheaper. They are most commonly found in the Visayas and northern Mindanao.

Train

The *Bicol Express* train route south from Manila to Naga in southeast Luzon – the only functioning railway line in the country – is suspended indefinitely; the southbound train out of Manila goes only as far as Laguna Province.

Health

Health issues and the quality of medical facilities vary enormously depending on where and how you travel in the Philippines. Many of the major cities are very well developed – indeed Manila and Cebu are 'medical tourism' destinations where foreigners flock for affordable yet competent health care. Travel in rural areas is a different story and carries a variety of health risks.

Treat our advice as a general guide only; it does not replace the advice of a doctor trained in travel medicine.

BEFORE YOU GO

Health Insurance

➡ Even if you are fit and healthy, don't travel without health insurance.

➡ Declare any existing medical conditions you have (if you make a claim, the insurance company will check if your problem is pre-existing and will not cover you if it is undeclared).

➡ You may require extra cover for adventure activities such as rock climbing or scuba diving.

➡ The Philippines has a few excellent hospitals in Manila and Cebu, and you can get affordable care there if your insurance won't cover your medical or medevac costs.

➡ Ensure you keep all documentation related to any medical expenses you incur.

Vaccinations

Specialised travel-medicine clinics are your best source of information; they stock all available vaccines and will be able to give specific recommendations. The doctors will take into account factors such as your vaccination history, the length of your trip, planned activities and underlying medical conditions.

Medical Checklist

Recommended items for a personal medical kit:

➡ antibacterial cream, eg Mupirocin

➡ antibiotics for diarrhoea, eg Norfloxacin, Ciprofloxacin and Azithromycin for bacterial diarrhoea; Tinidazole for giardiasis or amoebic dysentery

➡ antibiotics for skin infections, eg Amoxicillin/Clavulanate or Cephalexin

➡ antifungal cream, eg clotrimazole

➡ antihistamine for allergies, eg Cetirizine for daytime and Promethazine for night

➡ anti-inflammatories, eg Ibuprofen

➡ iodine-based antiseptic, eg Betadine

➡ antispasmodic for stomach cramps, eg Buscopan

➡ contraceptives

➡ a decongestant, eg pseudoephedrine

➡ DEET-based insect repellent

➡ diarrhoea treatment – consider an oral rehydration solution, eg Gastrolyte; diarrhoea 'stopper', eg Loperamide; and anti-nausea medication, eg Prochlorperazine

➡ first-aid items such as scissors, safety pins, sticking plasters, bandages, gauze, thermometer (electronic, not mercury), tweezers, and sterile needles and syringes

➡ indigestion medication, eg Quick-Eze or Mylanta

➡ iodine tablets (unless you are pregnant or have a thyroid problem) to purify water

➡ laxative, eg Coloxyl

➡ migraine medication, if a migraine sufferer

➡ paracetamol for pain

➡ permethrin (to impregnate clothing and mosquito nets) for repelling insects

➡ steroid cream for allergic/itchy rashes, eg 1% to 2% hydrocortisone

➡ sunscreen

➡ thrush (vaginal yeast infection) treatment, eg clotrimazole pessaries or Diflucan tablet

➡ Ural or equivalent if you're prone to urinary tract infections

Websites

World Health Organization (WHO; www.who.int/ith) Publishes a superb book called *International Travel & Health*,

RECOMMENDED VACCINATIONS

The World Health Organization (WHO) recommends the following vaccinations for travellers to Southeast Asia:

Adult diphtheria and tetanus Single booster recommended if none has been given in the previous 10 years. Side effects include a sore arm and fever.

Hepatitis A Provides almost 100% protection for up to a year; a booster after 12 months provides at least another 20 years' protection. Mild side effects such as headache and a sore arm occur in 5% to 10% of people.

Hepatitis B Now considered routine for most travellers. Given as three shots over six months. A rapid schedule is also available, as is a combined vaccination with hepatitis A. Side effects are mild and uncommon, usually headache and a sore arm. Lifetime protection occurs in 95% of people.

Measles, mumps and rubella Two doses of MMR are required unless you have had the diseases. Occasionally a rash and flulike illness can develop a week after receiving the vaccine. Many young adults require a booster.

Polio Only one booster is required as an adult for lifetime protection.

Typhoid Recommended unless your trip is less than a week. The vaccine offers around 70% protection, lasts for two to three years and comes as a single shot. Tablets are also available; however, the injection is usually recommended as it has fewer side effects. A sore arm and fever may occur.

Varicella If you haven't had chickenpox, discuss this vaccination with your doctor.

The following are recommended only for long-term travellers (more than one month):

Japanese B encephalitis Three injections in all. Booster recommended after two years. A sore arm and headache are the most common side effects.

Meningitis Single injection. There are two types of vaccination: the quadrivalent vaccine gives two to three years' protection; meningitis group C vaccine gives around 10 years' protection. Recommended for long-term travellers aged under 25.

Rabies Three injections in all. A booster after one year will then provide 10 years' protection. Side effects are rare – occasionally a headache and sore arm.

Tuberculosis A complex issue. Adult long-term travellers are usually advised to have a TB skin test before and after travel, rather than vaccination. Only one vaccine is given in a lifetime.

---

which is revised annually and is available free online.

MD Travel Health (https://redplanet.travel/mdtravelhealth) Provides complete travel-health recommendations for every country and is updated daily.

Centers for Disease Control and Prevention (CDC; www.cdc.gov) Good general information and country-specific warnings.

IN THE PHILIPPINES

Availability of Health Care

Good medical care is available in most major cities in the Philippines. It is difficult to find reliable medical care in rural areas, although there will usually be some sort of clinic not too far away. Your embassy and insurance company are also good contacts.

If you think you may have a serious disease, especially malaria, do not waste time – travel to the nearest quality facility to receive attention. It is always better to be assessed by a doctor than to rely on self-treatment.

Philippine pharmacies are usually well stocked with sterilised disposable syringes, bandages and antibiotics, but it doesn't hurt to bring your own sterilised first-aid kit, especially if you're going to be travelling off the beaten track. Contact-lens solution and spare contacts are readily available in cities.

Infectious Diseases

Chikungunya Fever

This less common viral infection poses only a small risk to travellers in the Philippines, mainly in the Visayas. Sudden pain in one or more joints, fever, headache, nausea and rash are the main symptoms.

Cutaneous Larva Migrans

This disease is caused by dog hookworm; the rash starts as a small lump, then slowly spreads in a linear fashion. It is intensely itchy, especially at night. It is easily treated with medications and should not be cut out or frozen.

Dengue Fever

This mosquito-borne disease is by far the most prevalent of the diseases you have a chance of contracting in the Philippines. It's especially common in cities, especially in metro Manila, and it's the leading cause of hospitalisations of children in the country.

While not usually fatal, dengue can kill; of more than 213,000 cases diagnosed in 2016, 1019 resulted in death, according to the Department of Health (DOH).

There is no vaccine available so it can only be prevented by avoiding mosquito bites. The mosquito that carries dengue can bite day and night. Symptoms include high fever, severe headache and body ache. Some people develop a rash and experience diarrhoea. There is no specific treatment, just rest and paracetamol – do not take aspirin as it increases the likelihood of haemorrhaging. See a doctor to be diagnosed and monitored.

Filariasis

This is a mosquito-borne disease that is very common in the local population, yet very rare in travellers. Mosquito-avoidance measures are the best way to prevent this disease.

Hepatitis A

A problem found throughout the region, this food- and water-borne virus infects the liver, causing jaundice, nausea and lethargy. There is no specific treatment for hepatitis A; you just need to allow time for the liver to heal. All travellers to Southeast Asia should be vaccinated against hepatitis A.

Hepatitis B

The only sexually transmitted disease that can be prevented by vaccination, hepatitis B is spread by body fluids. In some parts of Southeast Asia up to 20% of the population are carriers of hepatitis B, and usually are unaware of this. The long-term consequences can include liver cancer and cirrhosis.

Hepatitis E

Hepatitis E is transmitted through contaminated food and water and has similar symptoms to hepatitis A, but is far less common. It is a severe problem in pregnant women and can result in the death of both mother and baby. There is currently no vaccine, and prevention is by following safe eating and drinking guidelines.

Japanese B Encephalitis

While a rare disease in travellers, at least 50,000 locals are infected each year. This viral disease is transmitted by mosquitoes. Most cases occur in rural areas and vaccination is recommended for travellers spending more than one month outside of cities. There is no treatment, and a third of infected people will die while another third will suffer permanent brain damage.

Malaria

For such a serious and potentially deadly disease, there is an enormous amount of misinformation concerning malaria. Malaria is caused by a parasite transmitted by the bite of an infected mosquito. The most important symptom of malaria is fever, but general symptoms such as headache, diarrhoea, cough or chills may also occur. Diagnosis can only be made by taking a blood sample.

According to the Centers for Disease Control and Prevention (CDC), in the Philippines there is no malaria risk in Bohol, Boracay, Catanduanes, Cebu, Manila or other urban areas. The risk of side effects from anti-malarial tablets probably outweighs the risk of getting the disease in these areas.

In general, malaria is only a concern if you plan to travel below 600m in extremely remote areas such as southern Palawan. Before you travel, seek medical advice on the right medication and dosage for you. Note that, according to the CDC, chloroquine is not an effective antimalarial drug in the Philippines.

Measles

Measles remains a problem in some parts of Southeast Asia. This highly contagious bacterial infection is spread via coughing and sneezing. Most people born before 1966 are immune as they had the disease in childhood. Measles starts with a high fever and rash and can be complicated by pneumonia and brain disease. There is no specific treatment.

Rabies

This often fatal disease is spread by the bite or lick of an infected animal – most commonly a dog or monkey. You should seek medical advice immediately after any animal bite and commence post-exposure treatment. Having pre-travel vaccination means the post-bite treatment is greatly simplified. If an animal bites you, wash the wound with soap and water, and apply iodine-based antiseptic. If you are not pre-vaccinated you will need to

---

TAP WATER

Drinking tap water should be avoided in the Philippines. It is rarely purified and may lead to stomach illness.

That said, it's generally OK to have a few ice cubes in your drink or brush your teeth with tap water. One notable exception is El Nido, which occasionally experiences more acute water-quality problems.

Bottled water isn't cheap so carry your own bottle around and refill it at the many water-refilling stations.

receive rabies immunoglobulin as soon as possible.

Schistosomiasis

Schistosomiasis is a tiny parasite that enters your skin after you've been swimming in contaminated water. Travellers usually only get a light infection and hence have no symptoms. Schistosomiasis exists in the Philippines but it's not common and is confined to a few areas well off the tourist trail. On rare occasions, travellers may develop 'Katayama fever'. This occurs some weeks after exposure, as the parasite passes through the lungs and causes an allergic reaction – symptoms are coughing and fever. Schistosomiasis is easily treated with medications.

Tuberculosis

Tuberculosis (TB) is rare in short-term travellers. Medical and aid workers, and long-term travellers who have significant contact with the local population, should take precautions. Vaccination is usually only given to children under the age of five, but for adults at risk, pre- and post-travel TB testing is recommended. The main symptoms are fever, cough, weight loss, night sweats and tiredness.

Typhoid

This serious bacterial infection is spread via food and water. It causes a high and slowly progressive fever and headache, and may be accompanied by a dry cough and stomach pain. It is diagnosed by blood tests and treated with antibiotics. Vaccination is recommended for urban areas, not just smaller cities, villages or rural areas.

Typhus

Murine typhus is spread by the bite of a flea; scrub typhus is spread via a mite. These diseases are rare in travellers. Symptoms include fever, muscle pains and a rash. You can avoid these diseases with general insect-avoidance measures. Doxycycline will also prevent them.

Traveller's Diarrhoea

Traveller's diarrhoea is by far the most common problem affecting travellers. In over 80% of cases, it is caused by bacteria (there are numerous potential culprits), and therefore responds promptly to treatment with antibiotics. Treatment with antibiotics will depend on your situation – how sick you are, how quickly you need to get better, where you are etc.

Traveller's diarrhoea is defined as the passage of more than three watery bowel actions within 24 hours, plus at least one other symptom such as fever, cramps, nausea, vomiting or feeling unwell.

Treatment consists of staying well hydrated; rehydration solutions like Gastrolyte are the best for this. Antibiotics such as Norfloxacin, Ciprofloxacin or Azithromycin will kill the bacteria quickly.

Loperamide is just a 'stopper' and doesn't get to the cause of the problem. It can be helpful, for example if you have to go on a long bus ride. Don't take Loperamide if you have a fever, or blood in your stools.

Amoebic Dysentery

Amoebic dysentery is very rare in travellers but is often misdiagnosed by poor-quality labs in Southeast Asia. Symptoms are similar to bacterial diarrhoea, ie fever, bloody diarrhoea and generally feeling unwell. You should always seek reliable medical care. Treatment involves two drugs: Tinidazole or Metronidazole to kill the parasite in your gut and then a second drug to kill the cysts. If left untreated, complications such as liver or gut abscesses can occur.

Giardiasis

Giardia lamblia is a parasite that is relatively common in travellers. Symptoms include nausea, bloating, excess gas, fatigue and intermittent diarrhoea. The parasite will eventually go away if left untreated but this can take months. The treatment of choice is Tinidazole, with Metronidazole being a second-line option.

Environmental Hazards

Diving

Divers and surfers should seek specialised advice before they travel, to ensure their medical kit contains treatment for coral cuts and tropical ear infections. Divers should ensure their insurance covers them for decompression illness – get specialised dive insurance through an organisation such as **Divers Alert Network** (DAN; www.diversalertnetwork.org). Have a dive medical before you leave your home country – there are certain medical conditions that are incompatible with diving, and economic considerations may override health considerations for some dive operators.

Heat

For most people from colder climates it takes at least two weeks to adapt to the hot climate. Swelling of the feet and ankles is common, as are muscle cramps caused by sweating. Prevent these by avoiding dehydration and excessive activity. Take it easy when you first arrive. Don't eat salt tablets (they aggravate the gut), although drinking rehydration solution or eating salty food helps. Treat cramps by stopping activity, resting, rehydrating with rehydration solution and gently stretching.

Heatstroke is a serious medical emergency. Symptoms come on suddenly and include weakness, nausea, a hot dry body with a body temperature of over 41°C, dizziness, confusion, loss of coordination, fits and eventually collapse and loss of consciousness. Seek medical help and commence cooling by getting the person out of the heat, removing their clothes, fanning them and applying cool wet cloths or ice to their body, especially to the groin and armpits.

Prickly heat is a common skin rash in the tropics, caused by sweat being

DIVING EMERGENCIES

There are five stationary recompression chambers in the Philippines. The Philippine Commission on Sports Scuba Diving has new chambers being built in Puerto Princesa (Palawan) and Tagbilaran (Bohol).

Advance Hyperbaric Life Support (Map p50; ☑02-957 1340; www.hbotphilippines.com; 11 Tagdalit St, Brgy Manresa, Quezon City) Private recompression facility in Metro Manila with a modern chamber.

Batangas Hyperbaric Medicine & Wound Healing Center (☑ext 1911 043-723 7089–92; www.divemed.com.ph; St Patrick's Hospital Medical Center, Lopez Jaena St, Batangas) Privately owned facility is the nearest recompression chamber to dive centres Puerto Galera and Anilao.

Cebu Doctor's University Hospital (Map p282; ☑0918 807 3837; Osmena Blvd) Contact Memerto Ortega.

PCSSD Hyperbaric Chamber Manila (Map p76; ☑0928 242 6237, 02-524 2242; www.dive philippines.com.ph; Lung Center of the Phiippines, Quezon Ave, Quezon City) The main chamber of the Philippines Commission on Sports Scuba Diving.

PCSSD Hyperbaric Chamber Cebu (PCSSD; ☑032-349 3179; www.divephilippines.com. ph; TIEZA Building, P Burgos St, Mandaue, Cebu City) Chamber in Cebu run by the Philppines Commission on Sports Scuba Diving.

trapped under the skin. The result is an itchy rash of tiny lumps. Treat by moving out of the heat and into an air-conditioned area for a few hours and by having cool showers. Creams and ointments clog the skin so they should be avoided. Locally bought prickly-heat powder can be helpful.

Insect Bites & Stings

Bedbugs don't carry disease but their bites are very itchy. They live in the cracks of furniture and walls and then migrate to the bed at night to feed on you. You can treat the itch with an antihistamine. Lice can inhabit various parts of your body but most commonly your head and pubic area. Transmission is via close contact with an infected person. Lice can be difficult to treat and may require numerous applications of a lice shampoo such as Permethrin. Pubic lice are usually contracted from sexual contact.

Ticks are contracted after walking in rural areas. If you have had a tick bite and experience symptoms such as fever or muscle aches and/or a rash at the site of the bite or elsewhere, you should see a doctor. Doxycycline prevents tick-borne diseases.

Leeches are found in humid rainforest areas and are very common in the Philippines. They do not transmit disease but their bites are often intensely itchy for weeks and can become infected. Apply an iodine-based antiseptic to any leech bite to help prevent infection.

Bee and wasp stings mainly cause problems for people who are allergic to them. Anyone with a serious bee or wasp allergy should carry an injection of adrenalin (eg EpiPen) for emergency treatment. For others, pain is the main problem – apply ice and take painkillers.

Most jellyfish in Southeast Asian waters are not dangerous, just irritating. An exception is the box jellyfish, whose sting is extremely dangerous and can be fatal. They are not common in Philippine waters but they do exist, so ask around to make sure there have been no recent sightings in areas where you'll be swimming.

First aid for jellyfish stings involves pouring vinegar onto the affected area to neutralise the poison. Do not rub sand or water onto the stings. Take painkillers, and anyone who feels ill in any way after being stung should seek medical advice.

Skin Problems

Cuts and scratches become easily infected in humid climates. Take meticulous care of any cuts and scratches to prevent complications such as abscesses. Immediately wash all wounds in clean water and apply antiseptic. If you develop signs of infection (increasing pain and redness) see a doctor. Be particularly careful with coral cuts as they can easily become infected.

Snakes

Southeast Asia is home to many species of both venomous and harmless snakes. Assume all snakes are venomous and never try to catch one. Always wear boots and long pants if walking in an area that may have snakes. First aid in the event of a snakebite involves pressure immobilisation via an elastic bandage firmly wrapped around the affected limb, starting at the bite site and working up towards the chest. The bandage should not cut off circulation, and the fingers or toes should be kept free so the circulation can be checked. Immobilise the limb with a splint and carry the victim to medical attention. Do not use tourniquets or try to suck the venom out. Antivenene is available for most species.

Language

Tagalog, Pilipino, Filipino – the various language names might cause confusion, but they reflect the political history of the lingua franca across the 7000-island archipelago of the Philippines. Although not the mother tongue of every Philippine citizen, Filipino is spoken as a second language throughout the country (with over 165 other languages), and is an official language used for university instruction and in most legal, business and governmental transactions (the other official language being English). It belongs to the Malayo-Polynesian language family and has around 45 million speakers worldwide.

Filipino is easy to pronounce and most sounds are familiar to English speakers. In addition, the relationship between Filipino sounds and their spelling is straightforward and consistent, meaning that each letter is always pronounced the same way. If you read our coloured pronunciation guides as if they were English, you'll be understood just fine. Note that ai is pronounced as in 'aisle', ay as in 'say', ew like ee with rounded lips, oh as the 'o' in 'go', ow as in 'how' and ooy as the 'wea' in 'tweak'. The r sound is stronger than in English and rolled, and the ng combination – which is found in English words such as 'sing' or 'ringing' – can appear at the beginning of words. Filipino also has a glottal stop, which is pronounced like the pause between the two syllables in 'uh-oh'. It's indicated in our pronunciation guides by an apostrophe ('), and in written Filipino by a circumflex (ˆ), grave (`) or acute (´) accent over the vowel that's followed by a glottal stop.

In our pronunciation guides the stressed syllables are indicated with italics. The markers 'pol' and 'inf' indicate polite and informal forms respectively.

BASICS

Good day.	*Magandáng araw pô.* (pol)	ma·gan·*dang* a·row po'
	Magandáng araw. (inf)	ma·gan·*dang* a·row
Goodbye.	*Paalam na pô.* (pol)	pa·a·lam na po'
	Babay. (inf)	ba·bai
Yes.	*Opò.* (pol)	o·po'
	Oo. (inf)	o·o
No.	*Hindí pô.* (pol)	heen·*dee'* po'
	Hindî. (inf)	heen·*dee'*
Thank you.	*Salamat pô.* (pol)	sa·*la*·mat po'
	Salamat. (inf)	sa·*la*·mat
You're welcome.	*Walá pong anumán.* (pol)	wa·*la* pong a·noo·*man*
	Waláng anumán. (inf)	wa·*lang* a·noo·*man*

How are you?
Kumustá po kayó? (pol) koo·moos·*ta* po ka·*yo*
Kumustá? (inf) koo·moos·*ta*

Fine. And you?
Mabuti pô. Kayó pô? (pol) ma·*boo*·tee po' ka·*yo* po'
Mabuti. Ikáw? (inf) ma·*boo*·tee ee·*kow*

What's your name?
Anó pô ang pangalan ninyó? (pol) a·*no* po' ang pa·*nga*·lan neen·*yo*
Anó ang pangalan mo? (inf) a·*no* ang pa·*nga*·lan mo

My name is ...
Ang pangalan ko pô ay ... (pol) ang pa·*nga*·lan ko po' ai ...
Ang pangalan ko ay ... (inf) ang pa·*nga*·lan ko ai ...

WANT MORE?

For in-depth language information and handy phrases, check out Lonely Planet's *Filipino Phrasebook*. You'll find it at **shop.lonelyplanet.com**, or you can buy Lonely Planet's iPhone phrasebooks at the Apple App Store.

| person | katao | ka·ta·o |
| week | linggó | leeng·go |

air-con	erkon	er·kon
bathroom	banyo	ba·nyo
toilet	kubeta	koo·be·ta
window	bintanà	been·ta·na'

NUMBERS

1	isá	ee·sa
2	dalawá	da·la·wa
3	tatló	tat·lo
4	apat	a·pat
5	limá	lee·ma
6	anim	a·neem
7	pitó	pee·to
8	waló	wa·lo
9	siyám	see·yam
10	sampû	sam·poo'
20	dalawampû	da·la·wam·poo'
30	tatlumpû	tat·loom·poo'
40	apatnapû	a·pat·na·poo'
50	limampû	lee·mam·poo'
60	animnapû	a·neem·na·poo'
70	pitumpû	pee·toom·poo'
80	walumpû	wa·loom·poo'
90	siyamnapû	see·yam·na·poo'
100	sandaán	san·da·an
1000	isáng libo	ee·sang lee·bo

Do you speak English?
Marunong ka ba / ma·roo·nong ka ba
ng Inglés? / nang eeng·gles

I don't understand.
Hindí ko / heen·dee ko
náiintindihán. / na·ee·een·teen·dee·han

ACCOMMODATION

Where's a ...? Násaán ang ...? na·sa·an ang ...

campsite	kampingan	kam·pee·ngan
guesthouse	bahay-bisita	ba·hai·bee·see·ta
hotel	otél	o·tel
youth hostel	hostel para sa kabataan	hos·tel pa·ra sa ka·ba·ta·an

Do you have a ... room? Mayroón ba kayóng kuwartong ...? mai·ro·on ba ka·yong koo·war·tong ...

single	pang-isahan	pang·ee·sa·han
double	pandala-waha	pan·da·la·wa·han
twin	may kambál na kama	mai kam·bal na ka·ma

How much is it per ...? Magkano ba para sa isáng ...? mag·ka·no ba pa·ra sa ee·sang ...

| night | gabí | ga·bee |

DIRECTIONS

Where's the (market)?
Násaán ang (palengke)? / na·sa·an ang (pa·leng·ke)

How far is it?
Gaano kalayo? / ga·a·no ka·la·yo

What's the address?
Anó ang adrés? / a·no ang a·dres

Could you please write it down?
Pakísulat mo? / pa·kee·soo·lat mo

Can you show me (on the map)?
Maáari bang ipakita mo sa akin (sa mapa)? / ma·a·a·ree bang ee·pa·kee·ta mo sa a·keen (sa ma·pa)

It's ... Iyón ay ... ee·yon ai ...

behind ...	nasa likurán ng ...	na·sa lee·koo·ran nang ...
in front of ...	sa harapán ng ...	sa ha·ra·pan nang ...
near (...)	malapit (sa ...)	ma·la·peet (sa ...)
next to ...	katabí ng ...	ka·ta·bee nang ...
on the corner	nasa kanto	na·sa kan·to
opposite ...	katapát ng ...	ka·ta·pat nang ...
straight ahead	diretso	dee·ret·so

Turn ... Lumikó sa ... loo·mee·ko sa ...

at the traffic lights	ilaw-trápiko	ee·low·tra·pee·ko
left	kaliwâ	ka·lee·wa'
right	kanan	ka·nan

EATING & DRINKING

I'd like to reserve a table for ... Gustó kong mag-reserba ng mesa para sa ... goos·to kong mag·re·ser·ba nang me·sa pa·ra sa ...

| (eight) o'clock | (alás-otso) | (a·las·ot·so) |
| (two) people | (dalawáng) tao | (da·la·wang) ta·o |

I'd like the menu.
Gustó ko ng menú. goos·*to* ko nang me·*noo*

What would you recommend?
Anó ang mairere- a·*no* ang ma·ee·re·re·
komendá mo? ko·men·*da* mo

What's in that dish?
Anó iyán? a·*no* ee·*yan*

I don't eat (red meat).
Hindî akó heen·*dee'* a·ko
kumakain ng (karné). koo·ma·*ka*·een nang
(kar·*ne*)

Cheers!
Tagayan tayo! ta·*ga*·yan *ta*·yo

That was delicious!
Masaráp! ma·sa·*rap*

Please bring the bill.
Pakidalá ang tsit. pa·kee·da·*la* ang tseet

Key Words

bottle	*bote*	*bo*·te
breakfast	*almusál*	al·moo·*sal*
cafe	*kapiteryá*	ka·pee·ter·ya
cold	*malamíg*	ma·la·*meeg*
dinner	*hapunan*	ha·*poo*·nan
drink	*inumin*	ee·*noo*·meen
fork	*tinidór*	tee·nee·*dor*
glass	*baso*	*ba*·so
grocery	*groseryá*	gro·ser·ya
hot	*mainit*	ma·ee·neet
knife	*kutsilyo*	koot·*seel*·yo
lunch	*tanghalian*	tang·ha·*lee*·an
market	*palengke*	pa·*leng*·ke
plate	*pinggán*	peeng·*gan*
restaurant	*restoran*	res·*to*·ran
spoon	*kutsara*	koot·*sa*·ra
vegetarian	*bedyetaryan*	bed·ye·*tar*·yan
with ...	*may ...*	mai ...
without ...	*walâ ...*	wa·*la'* ...

Meat & Fish

beef	*karné*	kar·*ne*
chicken	*manók*	ma·*nok*
duck	*bibi*	*bee*·bee
fish	*isdâ*	ees·*da'*
lamb	*tupa*	*too*·pa
meat	*karné*	kar·*ne*
mussel	*paros*	*pa*·ros
oysters	*talabá*	ta·la·*ba*
pork	*karnéng baboy*	kar·*neng* ba·boy
prawn	*sugpô*	soog·*po'*
tuna	*tulingán*	too·lee·*ngan*
turkey	*pabo*	*pa*·bo
veal	*karnéng bulô*	kar·*neng* boo·*lo'*

Fruit & Vegetables

apple	*mansanas*	man·*sa*·nas
bean	*bin*	been
cabbage	*repolyo*	re·*pol*·yo
capsicum	*bel peper*	bel *pe*·per
cauliflower	*koliplawer*	ko·lee·*pla*·wer
cucumber	*pipino*	pee·*pee*·no
fruit	*prutas*	*proo*·tas
grapes	*ubas*	*oo*·bas
lemon	*limón*	lee·*mon*
mushroom	*kabuté*	ka·boo·*te*
nuts	*manê*	ma·*ne'*
onion	*sibuyas*	see·*boo*·yas
orange	*kahél*	ka·*hel*
pea	*gisantes*	gee·*san*·tes
peach	*pits*	peets
pineapple	*pinyá*	peen·ya
potatoes	*patatas*	pa·*ta*·tas
spinach	*kulitis*	koo·lee·tees
tomato	*kamatis*	ka·*ma*·tees
vegetable	*gulay*	*goo*·lai

Other

bread	*tinapay*	tee·*na*·pai
butter	*mantekilya*	man·te·*keel*·ya
cheese	*keso*	*ke*·so
egg	*itlóg*	eet·*log*
garlic	*bawang*	*ba*·wang
honey	*pulót-pukyutan*	poo·*lot*-pook·*yoo*·tan
ice	*yelo*	*ye*·lo
oil	*mantikà*	man·*tee*·ka
pepper	*pamintá*	pa·meen·*ta*
rice (cooked)	*kanin*	*ka*·neen
salt	*asín*	a·*seen*
soup	*sopas*	*so*·pas
sour cream	*kremang maasim*	*kre*·mang ma·a·*seem*
sugar	*asukal*	a·*soo*·kal
vinegar	*sukà*	*soo*·ka'

Drinks

beer	serbesa	ser·be·sa
coffee	kapé	ka·pe
juice	katás	ka·tas
milk	gatas	ga·tas
tea	tsaá	tsa·a
water	tubig	too·beeg
wine	alak	a·lak

EMERGENCIES

Help!	Saklolo!	sak·lo·lo
Go away!	Umalís ka!	oo·ma·lees ka
Call ...!	Tumawag ka ng ...!	too·ma·wag ka nang ...
a doctor	doktór	dok·tor
the police	pulís	poo·lees

There's been an accident.
May aksidente.   mai ak·see·den·te

I'm sick.
May sakít akó.   mai sa·keet a·ko

It hurts here.
Masakít dito.   ma·sa·keet dee·to

I'm allergic to (antibiotics).
Allergic akó sa   a·ler·jeek a·ko sa
(antibayótikó).   (an·tee·ba·yo·tee·ko)

I'm lost.
Nawawalâ akó.   na·wa·wa·la' a·ko

Where are the toilets?
Násaán ang kubeta?   na·sa·an ang koo·be·ta

SHOPPING & SERVICES

I'd like to buy ...
Gustó kong bumilí   goos·to kong boo·mee·lee
ng ...   nang ...

I'm just looking.
Tumitingín lang   too·mee·tee·ngeen lang
akó.   a·ko

Can I look at it?
Puwede ko bang   poo·we·de ko bang
tingnán?   teeng·nan

How much is it?
Magkano?   mag·ka·no

That's too expensive.
Masyadong mahál.   mas·ya·dong ma·hal

Can you lower the price?
Puwede mo bang   poo·we·de mo bang
ibabâ ang presyo?   ee·ba·ba' ang pres·yo

There's a mistake in the bill.
May malí sa kuwenta.   mai ma·lee sa koo·wen·ta

bank	bangko	bang·ko
internet cafe	ínternet kapé	een·ter·net ka·pe
post office	pos opis	pos o·pees
public telephone	teléponong pampúbliko	te·le·po·nong pam·poob·lee·ko
tourist office	upisina ng turismo	oo·pee·see·na nang too·rees·mo

TIME & DATES

What time is it?
Anóng oras na?   a·nong o·ras na

It's (10) o'clock.
Alás-(diyés).   a·las·(dee·yes)

Half past (10).
Kalahating oras   ka·la·ha·teeng o·ras
makalampás ang   ma·ka·lam·pas ang
(alás-diyés).   (a·las·dee·yes)

am	ng umaga	nang oo·ma·ga
pm (12–2pm)	ng tanghalì	nang tang·ha·lee'
pm (2–6pm)	ng hapon	nang ha·pon
yesterday	kahapon ng	ka·ha·pon nang
today	sa araw na itó	sa a·row na ee·to
tomorrow	bukas ng	boo·kas nang

Monday	Lunes	loo·nes
Tuesday	Martés	mar·tes
Wednesday	Miyérkoles	mee·yer·ko·les
Thursday	Huwebes	hoo·we·bes
Friday	Biyernes	bee·yer·nes
Saturday	Sábado	sa·ba·do
Sunday	Linggó	leeng·go
January	Enero	e·ne·ro
February	Pebrero	peb·re·ro
March	Marso	mar·so
April	Abríl	ab·reel
May	Mayo	ma·yo
June	Hunyo	hoon·yo
July	Hulyo	hool·yo
August	Agosto	a·gos·to
September	Setyembre	set·yem·bre
October	Oktubre	ok·too·bre
November	Nobyembre	nob·yem·bre
December	Disyembre	dees·yem·bre

TRANSPORT

Public Transport

Which ... goes to (Bataan)?	Alíng ... ang papuntá sa (Bataan)?	a·leeng ... ang pa·poon·ta sa (ba·ta·an)
boat	bapór	ba·por
catamaran	catamaran	ka·ta·ma·ran
ferry	ferry	pe·ree

Is this the ... to (Baguío)?	Itó ba ang ... na papuntá sa (Baguío)?	ee·to ba ang ... na pa·poon·ta sa (ba·gee·o)
bus	bus	boos
jeepney	dyipni	jeep·nee
megataxi	mega-taksi	me·ga·tak·see
train	tren	tren

When's the ... (bus)?	Kailán ang ... (bus)?	ka·ee·lan ang ... (boos)
first	unang	oo·nang
last	hulíng	hoo·leeng
next	súsunód na	soo·soo·nod na

A ... ticket (to Liliw).	Isáng tiket ... na (papuntá sa Liliw).	ee·sang tee·ket ... na (pa·poon·ta sa lee·lew)
1st-class	1st class	pers klas
2nd-class	2nd class	se·kan klas
one-way	one way	wan way
return	balikan	ba·lee·kan

What time does the (bus) leave?
Anóng oras áalís ang (bus)? a·nong o·ras a·a·lees ang (boos)

What time does the (boat) get to (Samal)?
Anóng oras daratíng ang (bapór) sa (Samal)? a·nong o·ras da·ra·teeng ang (ba·por) sa (sa·mal)

Does it stop at (Porac)?
Humihintó ba itó sa (Porac)? hoo·mee·heen·to ba ee·to sa (po·rak)

Please tell me when we get to (Tagaytay).
Pakisabi lang sa akin pagdatíng natin sa (Tagaytay). pa·kee·sa·bee lang sa a·keen pag·da·teeng na·teen sa (ta·gai·tai)

I'd like to get off at (Rizal).
Gustó kong bumabá sa (Rizal). goos·to kong boo·ma·ba sa (ree·sal)

Please take me to (this address).
Pakihatíd mo akó sa (adrés na itó). pa·kee·ha·teed mo a·ko sa (a·dres na ee·to)

SIGNS

Pasukán	Entrance
Labásan	Exit
Bukás	Open
Sará	Closed
Bawal	Prohibited
CR	Toilets
Lalaki	Men
Babae	Women

bus stop	hintuan ng bus	heen·too·an nang boos
ticket office	bilihan ng tiket	bee·lee·han nang tee·ket
train station	istasyón ng tren	ees·tas·yon nang tren

Driving & Cycling

I'd like to hire a ...	Gustó kong umarkilá ng ...	goos·to kong oo·mar·kee·la nang ...
4WD	4WD	por·weel·draib
bicycle	bisikleta	bee·seek·le·ta
car	kotse	kot·se
motorbike	motorsiklo	mo·tor·seek·lo

Is this the road to (Macabebe)?
Itó ba ang daán patungo sa (Macabebe)? ee·to ba ang da·an pa·too·ngo sa (ma·ka·be·be)

Can I park here?
Puwede ba akóng pumarada dito? poo·we·de ba a·kong poo·ma·ra·da dee·to

The (car) has broken down at (San Miguel).
Nasiraan ang (kotse) sa (San Miguel). na·see·ra·an ang (kot·se) sa (san mee·gel)

I have a flat tyre.
Plat ang gulóng ko. plat ang goo·long ko

I've run out of petrol.
Naubusan akó ng gasolina. na·oo·boo·san a·ko nang ga·so·lee·na

bike shop	tindahan ng bisikleta	teen·da·han nang bee·seek·le·ta
mechanic	mekániko	me·ka·nee·ko
petrol/gas	gasolina	ga·so·lee·na
service station	serbis istesyon	ser·bees ees·tes·yon

GLOSSARY

arnis de mano – pre-Hispanic style of stick-fighting (more commonly known simply as *arnis*)

bagyo – typhoon

bahala na – you could almost call this the 'national philosophy'; before the advent of Christianity, god was called bathala by ancient Filipinos; the expression *bahala na* expresses faith (God will provide) as well as a kind of fatalism (come what may); it's somewhere between an Australian 'no worries' and Kurt Vonnegut's 'so it goes', but less individualistic: all things shall pass and in the meantime life is to be lived, preferably in the company of one's friends and – most importantly – family

bahay na bato – stone house

balangay – artfully crafted seagoing outrigger boat

balikbayan – an overseas Filipino returning or paying a visit to the Philippines

balisong – fan or butterfly knife

bangka – a wooden boat, usually with outriggers and powered by a cannibalised automotive engine; a pumpboat

barangay – village, neighbourhood or community, the basic sociopolitical unit of Filipino society

barkada – gang of friends

barong – a generic term to describe the Filipino local shirt (for men) that is the 'national costume'; it usually has a heavily embroidered or patterned front

Barong Tagalog – traditional Filipino formal shirt (the barong was originally for men only; it refers only to the shirt), with elaborate embroidery or patterning down the front; made of jusi or pinya

baryo – Filipiniation of the Spanish word barrio (neighbourhood). Now known as a barangay.

bayanihan – tradition wherein neighbours would help a relocating family by carrying their house to its new location. The word has come to mean a communal spirit that makes seemingly impossible feats possible through the power of unity and cooperation

BPI – Bank of the Philippine Islands

butanding – whale shark

carabao – water buffalo, sometimes called a kalabaw

CBST – Community-Based Sustainable Tourism

CR – Comfort Room (toilet)

fronton – *jai alai* court

GROs – 'Guest Relation Officers' are officially glorified waitresses; unofficially they are sex workers

haribon – the Philippine eagle, an endangered species; haribon literally means 'king of birds'

ilustrado – a 19th-century Filipino of the educated middle class

jai alai – a fast-paced ball game, and one of the more popular sports in the Philippines

jeepney – a brightly painted vehicle that looks like an extended jeep, fitted with benches, adorned with everything but a kitchen sink and crammed with passengers

jusi – fabric woven from ramie fibres; used to make a *barong*

kalesa – horse-drawn carriage

kundiman – a melancholy genre of song originating in Manila (and the Tagalog region); one of the country's most loved musical idioms

lahar – rain-induced landslide of volcanic debris or mud from volcanic ash, common around Mt Pinatubo

mestizo – Filipino of mixed (usually Chinese or Spanish) descent. A Filipino of mixed Asian ancestry other than Chinese is not called a mestizo.

MILF – Moro Islamic Liberation Front

MNLF – Moro National Liberation Front

Moro – Spanish colonial term for Muslim Filipinos, once derogatory but now worn with some pride

nara – a hardwood tree, the Philippine national tree

nipa – a type of palm tree, the leaves of which are used for making nipa huts, the typical house in rural areas

NPA – New People's Army

paraw – traditional outrigger with jib and mainsail

pasyon – Christ's Passion, sung or re-enacted every Holy Week

Philvolcs – Philippine Institute of Volcanology & Seismology

Pinoy – a term Filipinos call themselves

pinya – fabric woven from pineapple fibres; commonly used to make a *barong*

PNP – Philippine National Police

poblasyon – town centre

sabong – cockfighting

sala – living room

santo – religious statue

sari-sari – small neighbourhood store stocked with all kinds of daily necessities; *sari-sari* literally means 'assortment'

swidden farming – the cultivation of an area of land that has been cleared through the use of slash-and-burn agricultural practices.

Tagalog – the dominant dialect of Manila and surrounding provinces, now the basis of the national language, Filipino

tamaraw – an endangered species of native buffalo, found only in Mindoro

tinikling – Philippine national folk dance

tricycle – a Philippine rickshaw, formerly pedal-powered but now predominantly motorised

v-hire – local van/minibus

Behind the Scenes

SEND US YOUR FEEDBACK

We love to hear from travellers – your comments keep us on our toes and help make our books better. Our well-travelled team reads every word on what you loved or loathed about this book. Although we cannot reply individually to your submissions, we always guarantee that your feedback goes straight to the appropriate authors, in time for the next edition. Each person who sends us information is thanked in the next edition – the most useful submissions are rewarded with a selection of digital PDF chapters.

Visit **lonelyplanet.com/contact** to submit your updates and suggestions or to ask for help. Our award-winning website also features inspirational travel stories, news and discussions.

Note: We may edit, reproduce and incorporate your comments in Lonely Planet products such as guidebooks, websites and digital products, so let us know if you don't want your comments reproduced or your name acknowledged. For a copy of our privacy policy visit lonelyplanet.com/privacy.

WRITER THANKS

Paul Harding

Thanks firstly to Laura Crawford at Lonely Planet and to fellow writer Greg Bloom for help and support. In the Philippines, thanks to Jay, Elvie and friends, Meann and Martine in Legazpi and Harvey in Caramoan. This trip was tinged with more than a little sadness so, as always, thanks and love to Hannah and Layla and family for putting up with my absence and welcoming me home.

Greg Bloom

A giant thanks to my crack research assistants in Manila: Windi (fountain of knowledge on all things drinking and dining), Anna ('Manila for Kids' guinea pig) and Callie (baby-related stress relief and laughs). Couldn't have done it without you guys. Also to Will and LT for the (costly) casino research. To Bart for accommodating Lonely Planet writers when needed. To Pia for Palawan tips. And to Luc for doing yeoman's work post-hockey on QC nightlife.

Celeste Brash

Thanks to Andrea, Raf and Rafael. To Mon in Pagudpud; Francis and Archie Baccoy and his family in Kalinga; Grail in Batad; Siegrid and Ryan in Sagada; Ryan Baldino and his uncle in Kabayan; policeman Peter in Abatan; a huge thanks to Tuvyan Savoy in Baguio. Mostly thanks to my coauthor Greg and DE Laura for dedication and know-how, to my family for understanding and the people of North Luzon for unfaltering friendliness.

Michael Grosberg

Thanks to all the kind people I met on the road. Especially to folks at the Iloilo provincial tourism office; Jac Señagan in Dumaguete; Ulrika, Julia and Fiona in Dauin; Mike of Coco Grove on Siquijor; Arno and Kaisa on Camiguin; Gerry and Susan for their warmth and friendship in Siargao; Princess Villarama, Sarah Sapo, Angelo Balao and Joaquin de Jesus on Boracay for their insight on Filipino music. To Carly, Rosie and Boone for making me never feel far from home.

Iain Stewart

Thanks to Laura for the commission, to Greg Bloom for help and contacts in the region, to Jamie Marshall for sharing some of the hard yards on the road, to Gino and Nikki in Bantayan and Cebu, Jacques and Lucia in Tacloban for expert advice and to the good folk of Calicoan Island, particularly Luna Beach resort. Many tourist information staff helped me on the way across the region – I am grateful to you all.

ACKNOWLEDGEMENTS

Climate map data adapted from Peel MC, Finlayson BL & McMahon TA (2007) 'Updated World Map of the Köppen-Geiger Climate Classification', *Hydrology and Earth System Sciences*, 11, 1633–44.

Cover photograph: Secret Lagoon, Miniloc Island, Palawan, R.M. Nunes/Shutterstock ©

BEHIND THE SCENES

THIS BOOK

This 14th edition of Lonely Planet's *Philippines* guidebook was curated by Paul Harding and Greg Bloom and researched and written by Paul and Greg along with Celeste Brash, Michael Grosberg and Iain Stewart. The previous edition was written by Michael, Greg, Trent Holden, Anna Kaminski and Paul Stiles.

This guidebook was produced by the following:

Destination Editor
Laura Crawford

Senior Product Editor
Daniel Bolger

Product Editors
Katie Connolly, Kate Chapman, Vicky Smith

Senior Cartographers
Corey Hutchison, Julie Sheridan

Book Designers
Ania Bartoszek, Katherine Marsh

Assisting Editors
Imogen Bannister, Janice Bird, Andrea Dobbin, Shona Gray, Kate Kiely, Helen Koehne, Kellie Langdon, Kathryn Rowan, Gabrielle Stefanos,
Ross Taylor, Sam Wheeler, Amanda Williamson, Simon Williamson

Assisting Cartographer
Rachel Imeson

Cover Researcher
Naomi Parker

Thanks to
Ronan Abayawickrema, Nicolas Combremont, Daniel Corbett, Grace Dobell, Judith Garrett, Chris Georgi, Paul Harding, Karen Henderson, Martin Heng, Nigel Hutton, Sonia Kapoor, Amy Lysen, Genna Patterson, Monique Perrin, Rachel Rawling, Jessica Ryan, Maureen Wheeler

Index

Map Legend

Sights

- Beach
- Bird Sanctuary
- Buddhist
- Castle/Palace
- Christian
- Confucian
- Hindu
- Islamic
- Jain
- Jewish
- Monument
- Museum/Gallery/Historic Building
- Ruin
- Shinto
- Sikh
- Taoist
- Winery/Vineyard
- Zoo/Wildlife Sanctuary
- Other Sight

Activities, Courses & Tours

- Bodysurfing
- Diving
- Canoeing/Kayaking
- Course/Tour
- Sento Hot Baths/Onsen
- Skiing
- Snorkelling
- Surfing
- Swimming/Pool
- Walking
- Windsurfing
- Other Activity

Sleeping

- Sleeping
- Camping
- Hut/Shelter

Eating

- Eating

Drinking & Nightlife

- Drinking & Nightlife
- Cafe

Entertainment

- Entertainment

Shopping

- Shopping

Information

- Bank
- Embassy/Consulate
- Hospital/Medical
- Internet
- Police
- Post Office
- Telephone
- Toilet
- Tourist Information
- Other Information

Geographic

- Beach
- Gate
- Hut/Shelter
- Lighthouse
- Lookout
- Mountain/Volcano
- Oasis
- Park
- Pass
- Picnic Area
- Waterfall

Population

- Capital (National)
- Capital (State/Province)
- City/Large Town
- Town/Village

Transport

- Airport
- Border crossing
- Bus
- Cable car/Funicular
- Cycling
- Ferry
- Metro/MRT/MTR station
- Monorail
- Parking
- Petrol station
- Skytrain/Subway station
- Taxi
- Train station/Railway
- Tram
- Underground station
- Other Transport

Routes

- Tollway
- Freeway
- Primary
- Secondary
- Tertiary
- Lane
- Unsealed road
- Road under construction
- Plaza/Mall
- Steps
- Tunnel
- Pedestrian overpass
- Walking Tour
- Walking Tour detour
- Path/Walking Trail

Boundaries

- International
- State/Province
- Disputed
- Regional/Suburb
- Marine Park
- Cliff
- Wall

Hydrography

- River, Creek
- Intermittent River
- Canal
- Water
- Dry/Salt/Intermittent Lake
- Reef

Areas

- Airport/Runway
- Beach/Desert
- Cemetery (Christian)
- Cemetery (Other)
- Glacier
- Mudflat
- Park/Forest
- Sight (Building)
- Sportsground
- Swamp/Mangrove

Note: Not all symbols displayed above appear on the maps in this book

Michael Grosberg

Boracay & Western Visayas, Mindanao, Michael has worked on more than 45 Lonely Planet guidebooks. Whether covering Myanmar or New Jersey, each project has added to his rich and complicated psyche and taken years from his (still?) relatively young life. Prior to his freelance writing career, other international work included development on the island of Rota in the western Pacific; time in South Africa where he investigated and wrote about political violence and helped train newly elected government representatives; and a stint teaching in Quito, Ecuador. He received a Masters in Comparative Literature and taught literature and writing as an adjunct professor at several New York City area colleges. Michael also researched the Understand the Philippines section.

Iain Stewart

Cebu & Eastern Visayas Iain trained as journalist in the 1990s and then worked as a news reporter and a restaurant critic in London. He started writing travel guides in 1997 and has since penned more than 60 books for destinations as diverse as Ibiza and Cambodia. Iain has contributed to Lonely Planet titles including *Mexico*, *Indonesia*, *Central America*, *Croatia*, *Vietnam* and *Bali & Lombok*. He also writes regularly for the *Independent*, *Observer* and *Daily Telegraph* and tweets at @iaintravel. He'll consider working anywhere there's a palm tree or two and a beach of a generally sandy persuasion. Iain lives in Brighton (UK) within firing range of the city's wonderful south-facing horizon.

...et and a sense of ...n Wheeler needed ...d Asia overland to Australia. It took several months, and at the end – broke but inspired – they sat at their kitchen table writing and stapling together their first travel guide, *Across Asia on the Cheap*. Within a week they'd sold 1500 copies. Lonely Planet was born.

Today, Lonely Planet has offices in the US, Ireland and China, with a network of more than 2000 contributors in every corner of the globe. We share Tony's belief that 'a great guidebook should do three things: inform, educate and amuse'.

OUR WRITERS

Paul Harding
Curator, Around Manila, Southeast Luzon As a writer and photographer, Paul has been travelling the globe for the best part of two decades, with an interest in remote and offbeat places, islands and cultures. He's an author and contributor to more than 50 Lonely Planet guides to countries and regions as diverse as India, Iceland, Belize, Vanuatu, Iran, Indonesia, New Zealand, Finland, Philippines and – his home patch – Australia.

Greg Bloom
Manila, Mindoro, Palawan Greg is a freelance writer, tour operator and travel planner based out of Siem Reap, Cambodia, and Manila, Philippines. Greg began his writing career in the late '90s in Ukraine, working as a journalist and later editor-in-chief of the *Kyiv Post*, an English-language weekly. As a freelance travel writer, he has contributed to some 35 Lonely Planet titles, mostly in Eastern Europe and Asia. In addition to writing, he now organises adventure trips in Cambodia and Palawan (Philippines) through his tour company, Bearcat Travel. Greg also researched the Plan Your Trip section and the Survival Guide section.

Celeste Brash
North Luzon Like many California natives, Celeste now lives in Portland, Oregon. She arrived, however, after 15 years in French Polynesia, a year and a half in Southeast Asia and a stint teaching English as a second language (in an American accent) in Brighton, England – among other things. She's been writing guidebooks for Lonely Planet since 2005 and her travel articles have appeared in publications from *BBC Travel* to *National Geographic*. She's currently writing a book about her five years on a remote pearl farm in the Tuamotu Atolls and is represented by the Donald Maass Agency, New York.

OVER PAGE | MORE WRITERS

Published by Lonely Planet Global Limited
CRN 554153
14th edition – Dec 2021
ISBN 978 1 78701 612 5
© Lonely Planet 2021   Photographs © as indicated 2021
10 9 8 7 6 5 4 3 2 1
Printed in Singapore

Although the authors and Lonely Planet have taken all reasonable care in preparing this book, we make no warranty about the accuracy or completeness of its content and, to the maximum extent permitted, disclaim all liability arising from its use.